The structure of phonological representations

Linguistic Models

The publications in this series tackle crucial problems, both empirical and conceptual, within the context of progressive research programs. In particular *Linguistic Models* will address the development of formal methods in the study of language with special reference to the interaction of grammatical components.

Series Editors:
Teun Hoekstra
Harry van der Hulst
Michael Moortgat

Other books in this series:

1. M. Moortgat, H. van der Hulst, T. Hoekstra
   The scope of lexical rules

2. Harry van der Hulst and Norval Smith
   The structure of phonological representations. Part I.

4. Gerald Gazdar, Ewan Klein, Geoffrey K. Pullum
   Order, Concord and Constituency

The structure of phonological representations
(Part II)

Edited by
Harry van der Hulst
INL, *Dutch Lexicological Institute, Leyden*
Norval Smith
Institute for General Linguistics, *University of Amsterdam*

1982
FORIS PUBLICATIONS
Dordrecht - Holland/Cinnaminson - U.S.A.

Published by:
Foris Publications Holland
P.O. Box 509
3300 AM Dordrecht, The Netherlands

Sole distributor for the U.S.A. and Canada:
Foris Publications U.S.A.
P.O. Box C-50
Cinnaminson N.J. 08077
U.S.A.

ISBN 90 70176 59 9 (Bound)
ISBN 90 70176 58 0 (Paper)

© 1982 by the authors.
No part of this publication may be reproduced or transmitted in any form or by any means, electronic or mechanical, including photocopy, recording, or any information storage and retrieval system, without permission from the copyright owner.

Printed in the Netherlands by ICG Printing, Dordrecht.

Table of Contents

Stephen R. Anderson
Differences in Rule Type and their Structural Basis 1

Colin J. Ewen
The Internal Structure of Complex Segments 27

Steven G. Lapointe and Mark H. Feinstein
The Role of Vowel Deletion and Epenthesis in the Assignment of
Syllable Structure 69

William J. Poser
Phonological Representations and Action-at-a-Distance 121

Maria L. Zubizarreta
The Formal Interaction of Harmony and Accent: The Tone Pattern
of Japanese 159

George N. Clements and Engin Sezer
Vowel and Consonant Disharmony in Turkish 213

Roland Noske
Syllabification and Syllable Changing Rules in French 257

Harry van der Hulst and Norval Smith
Prosodic Domains and Opaque Segments in Autosegmental Theory . 311

Elisabeth O. Selkirk
The Syllable 337

Jonathan D. Kaye
Harmony Processes in Vata 385

References 453

Index of Names 465

Index of Languages 469

Subject Index 471

Preface and acknowledgements

Like its predecessor, *The Structure of Phonological Representations. Part I*, this volume contains ten articles, all addressing important questions in the field of *Three-dimensional Phonology*.

In the Introductory article in Part I an outline is given of the two major lines of research that have led to the adoption of the three dimensional model, viz. *Autosegmental Phonology* and *Metrical Phonology*. We refer the reader to this article for background information. Let us briefly sketch here the questions that are at issue.

In the standard theory (as formulated in Chomsky and Halle's *The Sound Pattern of English*) phonological representations consist, at every level, of a linear arrangement of *segments* and *boundaries*. Segments are conceived of as unordered sets of features. Harmonic features that eventually show up on several segments (in some domain) are attributed to one of the segments and "spread out" by a rule. The boundaries interspersed between the segments, motivated on morphological or syntactic grounds, partition the string of segments into substrings that constitute possible domains for phonological generalizations. The *hierarchical* morpho-syntactic structure that determines the location and type of the boundaries is not relevant for the application of phonological rules, with the exception of stress rules, which apply cyclically. Segments then have no *internal structure* nor are they themselves grouped into larger constituents such as *syllables* or *feet*. Both these aspects of the standard theory have been called into question, once the principles of rule formulation and interaction proposed in the *Sound Pattern* were confronted with a wider array of data.

Both *sub*segmental and *supra*segmental phenomena have led to the rejection of the segment as an unstructured set of features. In the theory of Autosegmental Phonology it is proposed that the standard *one-tiered* representation be split up into several tiers, each constituting a linear arrangement of segments. Segments of different tiers, linked to each other by *association lines* that indicate how they are coarticulated, can be referred to by rules independently. The autosegmental theory was originally designed to handle tonal phenomena, but its domain was rapidly extended to other areas such as *complex segments, vowel and consonant* *harmony, pitch accent, syllable structure* and morphological operations that involve various kinds of 'copying'.

The second major modification of the standard paradigm concerns the organization of segments into larger constituents. In the theory of Metrical Phonology hypotheses are advanced concerning hierarchical relations that hold between segments and larger units. The resulting hierarchical organization, which is distinct from but related to the morphosyntactic hierarchy, provides the basis for a new theory of syllable structure and stress.

We hope that the present collection, like its predecessor, gives a faithful representation of ongoing research in the newly emerging phonological framework.

Differences in Rule Type and their Structural Basis

Stephen R. Anderson
U.C.L.A.

Much of the recent history of phonological theory has consisted in the development of richer notions of phonetic (and by implication, phonological) structure. The development of "Autosegmental" theory and related notions (see, e.g., Goldsmith 1976a, 1979, as well as Anderson 1976) has made it clear that feature specifications should not be regarded as uniformly synchronized by a single temporal function, as required by a uniformly segmental model. On the other hand, the development of "Metrical" theory has shown that units larger than (but hierarchically related to) the segment are relevant both as the domain of specification of some properties and as the environment of some phonological processes.

Along with richer notions of structure, of course, has come an enrichment of our notion of the character of phonological rules themselves: new types of structure require new devices to create and manipulate them. Autosegmental representations require that there be rules inserting, deleting or changing elements on one autosegmental "tier" without necessarily affecting the elements on other tiers. While this is fundamentally similar to the operation of classical phonological rules, autosegmental theory also requires us to posit rules which manipulate not the features themselves, but rather the associations between one tier and another. Such an alteration in the internal organization of a representation is of course unimaginable in a theory (such as that of classical generative phonology) in which such organization is completely uniform.

Similarly, the recognition of hierarchically organized units with significant internal structure (syllables with their internal onsets, rhymes, etc.; feet, and perhaps larger elements as well) only becomes significant when we also admit rules which alter such structure, or which refer to it in ways that cannot be simulated by reference simply to its segmental com-

---

* This paper has benefited considerably from discussions with Will Leben, whose own work is obviously the primary stimulus which has led to its being written. For other assistance with this work, the contribution of our mutual friend George Dickel is gratefully acknowledged.

position. Rules of resyllabification make little sense in a framework with no overt recognition of syllables, and of course the suggestion that some features (typically, stress) can only be coherently defined as relations between elements of higher order than the segment necessarily entails a different view of the rules affecting these features than that prevailing under the picture of all features as properties of segments.

As these new formalisms in phonology have been explored, it has been noted that a great many traditional rules can be reformulated in such terms, often with considerable increase in insight and in the perspicuity of the rule's expression. A particularly clear case of this sort is the range of processes that are sensitive to position in syllable structure. A rule such as "shorten vowels in closed syllables" or "lengthen them in open syllables" can usually be given a formulation in terms of strings of segments alone (depending on the complexity of the language's principles of syllabification), and it can be regarded as part of the theoretical program of Chomsky and Halle (1968) to see whether such formulations are always available (without significant loss of generalisation, of course). Once we admit the metrical structure of syllables into representations, however, a great many unenlightening (and frequently baroque) disjunctions such as "___ C {C,#}" can be replaced with more meaningful expressions. The point here is that the replacement of segmental by metrical (or autosegmental) formalisms may lead to a gain in insight even in cases where it is not, strictly speaking, necessitated by the surface form of the facts themselves.

Naturally, the observation that autosegmental and metrical formalisms can be profitably extended to some examples in the traditional domain of "segmental" phenomena raises the question of whether or not all "segmental" rules can be so replaced. Allowing three distinct formalisms for phonological processes (segmental, autosegmental, and metrical), where these have significantly different properties, would have the effect of loosening and consequently weakening our notion of phonological structure insofar as all three possibilities are simultaneously available. If we could completely subsume one of these types (e.g., segmental rules) under the others, we could mitigate this consequence without abandoning the gains achieved by the new formalisms.

A recent paper by Halle & Vergnaud (1981) dealing with the typology of vowel harmony processes typifies this research strategy. Halle & Vergnaud argue that among the harmony processes traditionally formulated in segmental terms, some (which they call "dominant" harmony) are suitably described by the formalism of autosegmental phonology; while others (called "directional" harmony) are better described by metrical formalisms. If their conclusions extend to all "harmony processes" in all languages[1] (including, on their account, such things as obstruent voicing assimilation in Russian), they would thus succeed in reducing the scope of segmental rules considerably, and one might hope to pursue the same program into other areas of phonology as well. In fact, the recent rash of activity in extending metrical and autosegmental description to a variety of areas beyond those of tone, nasality, and stress where they were first motivated (cf., for example, the papers in *MIT Working Papers in Linguistics*, Vol. 1, or many of the papers in the present volume and its predecessor) can be seen in just this light.

In a paper in Part I of the present collection, Leben raises an important additional question. He notes that, in their extensions into traditionally segmental domains, autosegmental and metrical formalisms actually share a number of properties, and that the ways in which they (potentially) differ from one another are not in fact relevant to such descriptions. On this basis, he suggests that instead of allowing both metrical and autosegmental descriptions of "segmental" phenomena, a single unified formalization can be provided which expresses the relevant properties of both, but which is more restrictive than either taken alone. If this is indeed possible, the result would be a further gain in explanatory power: instead of three possible forms for any given process, we would now be back to the condition of a narrower and more explanatory theory which allowed only one.

The present paper is intended to further extend Leben's crucial observation that the full power of metrical and autosegmental formalisms can be replaced in the relevant domains by a single, more limited rule type. We will suggest, however, that instead of being a sort of hybrid of autosegmental and metrical formalisms, the relevant rule type is essentially the traditional segmental one. It will be argued that the ways in which the two formalisms fall together are such as to exclude just those properties which originally motivated them; and that the modifications which are necessary to extend them to properly "segmental" domains are such as to rob them of their original explanatory power. We will thus contend that the proper way to constrain the possibilities of formalization in phonology is to seek a more careful delimitation of the domains studied in phonology so that, while all three possibilities remain, only one is available (in principle) for the formulation of any given rule.

The arguments presented by Leben make a substantial case for a high degree of homomorphism between autosegmental and metrical solutions in the traditional segmental domain. As we will detail below, however, the same homomorphism extends also to the solutions available within classical segmental formalisms. The nonsegmental descriptions, though, typically require modifications of the relevant theoretical principles. Insofar as these involve a weakening of the theory in question with respect to its original empirical support, one must require strong justification for such a change. The literature is not, however, replete with such justification: indeed, it can be argued that much of the current enthusiasm for non-segmental solutions in traditionally segmental domains is based more on their novelty than on their appositeness with respect to individual problems.

An example of the sort of reasoning involved is found in Leben's discussion of various analyses of vowel harmony in Khalkha Mongolian. An analysis involving standard segmental rules, applied iteratively, was presented by Anderson (1980); a metrical analysis is provided by Halle & Vergnaud (1981). Disregarding for the moment the comparison of these analyses on internal grounds, Leben contends that their empirical coverage is substantially the same. Leben feels, however, that there is a basis for preferring the metrical account, "because the constraints it posits are needed independently *for the description of stress systems*" (emphasis mine: sra).

This appears, however, to mis-state the issue. The origins of metrical phonology, which are to be found in the work of Liberman (cf. Liberman & Prince 1977), were based on the argument that stress could only be defined in a rational way if it were treated as a relational notion within hierarchically organized structures not limited to concatenated strings of segments. As this notion was explored (by e.g. Hayes 1980, where a typology of stress systems is proposed and defended in detail), it became clear that manipulations of stress were thus *ipso facto* manipulations of metrical structure. The same conclusion can hardly be drawn, however, for manipulations of such properties as vowel quality, for which a strictly segmental definition seems at least coherent, if not self-evidently correct.

There is an interesting historical parallel to be drawn here between the development of metrical theory and the notion of the transformational cycle in phonology. Like metrical theory, the cycle was initially motivated by a consideration of the facts of (English) stress. Given its apparent success in accounting for complex patterns and alternations of stress, attempts were then made to extend the cycle to handle strictly segmental alternations (in particular, to deal with recalcitrant ordering problems in segmental systems). Most of these attempts must be judged in retrospect, however, to have been misguided, and the cycle remained a mechanism with its only essential support in the area of stress. It was exactly by considering why there should be this specific dependence between stress in particular and a structure-dependent principle such as the cycle that the basic insights of metrical phonology were achieved: an insistence on the universality of cyclic application would only have obscured them. The empirical content of a linguistic theory is often to be evaluated by the specificity of its principles, rather than by their generality (a point made in a syntactic context by Chomsky 1972).

Furthermore, as we will attempt to show below, the level of generality at which the "same" constraints are motivated for (canonical) metrical and segmental phenomena is one which is perfectly accessible to "garden-variety" segmental rules. Rather than extending metrical (and autosegmental) formalisms to new domains, the most interesting move available to phonological theory would appear to be an attempt to restrict (and thereby enrich) the three available ways of formulating phonological descriptions so that they no longer overlap in empirical coverage. It would appear that the level of generality at which the three fall together is so abstract that we have little if any motivation for abandoning strictly segmental accounts, at least in a number of domains.

Of course, the question would not be moot if we had reason to believe that in general segmental mechanisms of the classical sort (which we will henceforth refer to as "GV" or "Garden Variety" rules) were inferior to metrical or autosegmental formulations. If there were no domain whatsoever in which GV rules appeared to be motivated, the question of how to account for areas of potential overlap would hardly even be at issue. It would seem, however, that the status of rules manipulating only strings of segments (whose internal structure, if any, beyond a collection of features is irrelevant) is fairly well assured. For a somewhat trivial example, consider the rule that devoices obstruents in English before the ending -*ive* (as in intrusive, from intrude). It is quite clear that this rule does not involve the transfer of a phonological property from one segment to another, as is involved in autosegmental re-associations. It is also fairly clear that hierarchical structure is essentially irrelevant to its operation: all that is involved is a voiced obstruent, followed in linear sequence by the particular formative -*ive*. There is thus no motivation for calling this a manipulation of metrical structure, and even if one were to impose a (trivial) metrical structure on the form, the essential content of the rule would remain to be stated segmentally.

A great many morphologically conditioned processes are like the English rule just noted, but the domain of GV rules is not limited to this area. Consider processes of dis-similation, for example. The rule of Woleaian (cf. Sohn 1975) by which /a/ is replaced by /e/ when the next vowel is low, producing alternations such as [meramę] "moon" vs. [maremali] "moon-of" from the stem /marama/^{2} provides an instance. Again, the change involved cannot apparently be treated as a reassociation of some autosegmental property. While one can, of course, construct a metrical "tree" consisting of exactly the vowels of the word, and then perform the operation of dissimilation on the elements of this tree, the fact remains that the rule in question in no way involves a manipulation of metrical structure *per se*: the change still remains to be stated after the tree is constructed, and it is not obvious that one gains very much by saying first "disregard the consonants" (i.e., construct a tree containing only the vowel-projection[3]) and then "/a/ ⟶ [e] /___/a/" rather than simply saying "/a/ ⟶ [e] /___C_o/a/".

Even some processes that would appear to be natural candidates for metrical or autosegmental formulation turn out, on further examination, to be based directly on segmental structure. In Icelandic, for example, there is a comparatively "low-level" phonetic rule by which vowels are specified as long before, roughly, at most one consonant; but short before two or more. Thus we have *súpa* "to sip"([su:pa]), with a long vowel, but *súptu* "sip!" ([suftu]) with a short vowel. If this were the whole story, it would of course simply illustrate the rather common state of affairs in which "vowels are long in open syllables, but short in closed syllables". Since such a rule makes essential reference to syllabic structure, it might be assumed to be uncontroversially "metrical" in character.

This impression of the relevance of metrical (specifically, syllabic) structure to the Icelandic length rule is reinforced when we note that some clusters of two consonants are preceded by long, rather than short vowels: specifically, clusters of /p/, /t/, /k/, or /s/ followed by /j/, /r/, or /v/. Thus, one has *völlur* "field" ([vödlür]) "field" with a short vowel before [dl] (phonologically /ll/), but *uppgötva* "discover" ([üpgö:tva]) with a long vowel before [tv]. Of course, the clusters involved are just those which one might plausibly claim are syllabified together into the following syllable, thus yielding open (rather than closed) syllables and strengthening the apparent relevance of syllabic organization to the rule.

Unfortunately, the appearance of such a neat open/closed syllable basis for the Icelandic length rule is illusory. This is shown rather directly by the fact that monosyllables in which a vowel is followed by a single consonant nonetheless show long vowels; and the long vowel of e.g. *bak* "back" ([ba:k]) cannot reasonably be claimed to be produced in an open syllable. One might attempt to argue that in fact, Icelandic has a different principle of syllabification than many other languages, and syllabifies consonants with a preceding (stressed) vowel. The length rule might then be stated as something like "vowels are long before at most one consonant in the same syllable".

In this case, however, the set of obstruent plus semivowel or /r/ clusters noted above becomes an embarrassment to the analysis. There is a (somewhat unusual) class of Icelandic monosyllables ending in clusters of obstruent plus /r/, typified by *sötr, pukr, snupr*, etc. (which are semi-productively derived by deleting the *-a* ending of infinitives, as observed by Orešnik and Pétursson 1977). In these words, we still find long vowels: [sö:tr], [pü:kr], [snü:pr]. We must conclude that the vowel length rule in Icelandic yields long vowels when followed by at most one consonant, or by a cluster of voiceless obstruent plus /j/, /v/, or /r/, followed either by another vowel or by the end of the word. For whatever reason, the me-

Differences in Rule Type

trical structure of the word is not relevant, and the rule in question can (indeed, must) be stated in terms of a string of segments rather than the internal composition of syllables.

SIMILARITIES AMONG TYPES OF RULES

We begin, then, from the premise that three types of rules can be shown to be necessary in phonology: Classical segmental (or GV) rules; autosegmental rules (as motivated by the facts of tone and nasality, at a minimum); and metrical rules (as motivated by facts of stress on the one hand, and of syllable and foot structure, on the other). In the ensuing sections we will review Leben's arguments for identifying autosegmental with metrical formulations, insofar as these fall within the traditional domain of segmental processes.

1. Projection type

Leben notes first that autosegmental and metrical processes in these areas operate on "the same sorts of projections of phonological units". In order to make clear what the issue is here, we must first briefly summarize the notion of a "projection". This construct comes from (so far unpublished) work by Vergnaud & Halle (1978), who suggest that the usual sort of variables employed in segmental rules are too powerful and need to be replaced by some more constrained device. They propose that instead of employing expressions such as "C_0" (representing any number of consonants), "$[+seg]_0$" (representing any number of segments), etc., or direct variables such as "Q (where Q contains no [+syllabic] segment)", etc., phonological representations should rather make use of a different device. They suggest that, corresponding to a well-formed phonological expression such as "[+syllabic]" there is, for any given form, a *projection* of that form consisting of exactly the elements within it which satisfy the expression. Thus, the "[+syllabic] projection" of a word will consist (exactly) of a string containing all of the vowels in the word, in the same order. If rules are then stated as applying to such projections of forms (rather than directly to the forms themselves), it may be that their formulation can dispense entirely with (explicit) variable terms.

Some further discussion is necessary to clarify the ways in which this view could be taken to impose an empirical limitation on possible rules. For example, if only one expression is allowed to define the projection which a given rule operates on, this would correspond to the claim that at most one type of variable can appear in a single (traditionally formulated) rule. Furthermore, this variable must be interpreted as implicitly appearing between any two terms of the rule. In this respect, the idea is quite similar to Wilkins' (1980) "Variable Interpretation Convention" in syntax, though Wilkins goes further and contends that not only the place of the variable, but also the form of the expression defining it is derivable from the form of the nonvariable terms in the rule.

In fact, such a stronger proposal has also been made in phonology, in the work of Palacas (1971), Howard (1972), and Jensen (1974), as well as other references. This work was devoted to defining a notion of "adjacency" in phonology, which can be characterized approximately as follows. Let us identify the element of a form which may undergo a given rule as the *focus* of the rule, and the element of the rule which is the primary "trigger" of its operation (e.g., the stop to which a nasal assimilates, the vowel with which other vowels harmonize, etc.) as its *determinant* (employing terminology first introduced by Howard). We might then be able to say that the focus and the determinant of a given rule must be strictly adjacent, except for the optional presence of material whose type is predictable from the expressions which define them.

The goal of the works referred to above was largely to formulate this relation between the definition of the focus and determinant of a rule and the implicit variable separating its terms. While Vergnaud & Halle's notion of a projection corresponds to the claim that for any given rule, a single expression defines (the only) material which can appear freely between the specified terms of the rule, the proposals of Palacas, Howard, and Jensen can be seen as bearing on the stronger claim that the relevant projection for any given rule can be predicted from the form of its specified terms.

For the concept of a projection to have empirical content beyond the claim that only one (type of) variable can appear in a given rule, it is clearly important to specify what is and what is not a possible projection for a particular rule. If a claim along the lines of those made by earlier writers could be sustained, this would be a highly useful result. In general, however, that literature must be regarded as inconclusive: various proposals concerning the relation between (what we here interpret as) the relevant projection and the definitions of the focus and the determinant have been shown to be inadequate, and none can be regarded as sufficient to cover all known cases.

For example, in the Takelma Umlaut rule (cf. Sapir 1922), (suffixal) /a/ becomes /i/ before a following /i/, provided no voiceless consonant intervenes (a condition not stated by Sapir, but inferrable from the range of forms given in his grammar that do and do not undergo umlaut). There is no obvious sense in which voiceless consonants are a function of either the focus (/a/) or the determinant (/i/) of the rule, and it seems unlikely that this condition can be predicted from any other factor in its formulation.

Differences in Rule Type

Even if it is impossible to predict the form of the relevant projection from the remainder of a rule, however, it may well be the case that only a limited number of expressions are available to define projections. Clearly we need to be able to project "vowels", "coronal consonants" (for rules such as Sanskrit retroflexion), "sibilants" (for Navajo sibilant harmony), "syllable rhymes" (typically relevant to stress rules, to the exclusion of onsets), etc., but perhaps there are some fairly narrow limitations on just what material is available to define a projection. There is little reason to anticipate a rule which operates on the projection of a form's syllable-final voiced non-coronals, for example (including vowels as well as labial and velar consonants).

Leben's observation thus reduces to the claim that, once we specify the class of possible projections relevant to autosegmental rules, and the class relevant to metrical rules, these classes will turn out to be the same (or at least non-distinct). Notice, however, that it still remains to be shown that the projections relevant to GV rules are in some way distinct from this class. There is clearly no incompatibility between GV rules and the basic notion of a projection (indeed, in the strong form of an "adjacency constraint", the issue was first raised exactly in connection with such rules). Furthermore, when metrical and autosegmental formalisms are extended into the domain of such processes as vowel harmony, voicing assimilation, and the like, it stands to reason that whatever projections are available to the corresponding segmental rules will also have to be in the class of projections available to metrical and autosegmental rules. This would certainly appear to be the case from the examples treated in the literature thus far. It would seem, then, that we arrive at the conclusion that, whatever the class of projections available to rules, the defining conditions of this class do not distinguish among our three rule types. Once an adequate set of criteria for defining the notion of "possible projection relative to a given rule" is found, there is no reason to believe that it cannot be directly incorporated into the theory of GV rules (as well as others), and thus this theoretical issue does not (so far as we have reason to believe) distinguish metrical and autosegmental facts from others.

When we examine this conclusion, we may feel that it is an unfortunate one. Indeed, the rules that manipulate "canonically metrical" facts such as stress and syllable structure typically refer to a rather limited range of properties as their "characteristic class". Stress rules refer to syllable structure (including syllable "weight", vowel length, etc.), but not to properties that do not have a metrical representation. That is, we do not find stress rules which require us to assign, e.g., alternating stress before a [-Back] vowel. Rules adjusting syllable structure may well require access to the composition of individual segments, and also to stress (represented as a relation between syllable nodes), but not (arguably) to structure above this level. Similarly, strictly segmental rules may hinge on facts of syllable structure (e.g., in French the vowels schwa and /e/ are replaced by [ɛ] in closed syllables). There appear to be limits, however, on the extent to which rules manipulating one kind of structure (intra-segmental, intra-syllabic, inter-syllabic, intra-foot, etc.) can "see into" other types of structure. Some concrete suggestions for such a constraint of "metrical locality" are made in work of Hammond (1982).

Once the issues in this domain, concerning the sorts of structure which may be accessible to rules of a given type, are clarified sufficiently we may find that it is possible to assimilate the relevant constraints into a uniform notion of a "projection", applicable to rules of all types. On the other hand, we may not, and it may turn out that different constraints apply to the projections on which metrical, autosegmental, and GV rules are based. The point to be made here is that, at minimum, the class of relevant projections in the traditionally segmental domain does not appear in any way to raise issues which would exclude "GV rule" accounts of such facts, and indeed the only way such issues could bear on the problem would be if we found it necessary to *exclude* certain strictly segmental projection types from the class of those available to metrical or autosegmental rules.

2. Well-formedness constraints

Another similarity noted by Leben between autosegmental and metrical accounts is that both "obey identical well-formedness constraints": specifically, the constraints suggested by Goldsmith (op. cit.). Leben argues, for example, that metrical structures do not skip over and thus ignore elements of their projection, just as co-ordinate autosegmental tiers are associated in a mutually exhaustive fashion. This is potentially a very significant similarity between the two domains, and one which does not appear to have any substantial analog in the theory of GV rules; but we must note that, in order to maintain it, it is apparently necessary to exclude the analysis of phenomena such as vowel harmony from the scope of metrical or autosegmental treatments.

Leben observes, indeed, that the analysis provided by Halle and Vergnaud (1981) for Khalkha Mongolian rounding harmony constitutes a *prima facie* counter-example to the claim that metrical structures exhaust their projections. Their rule constructs a metrical structure starting with a vowel, and incorporating subsequent vowels so long as these are not both [+high] and [+round][4]. After this tree is constructed, however, it is necessary to "prune" it, by removing all nodes dominating [+high] vowels[5]. The result is a metrical structure which is defined on the vowel-projection of a word, but which does not incorporate all vowels (specifically, it omits [+high] vowels)[6].

On Leben's view, this difference between Halle & Vergnaud's account of Khalkha (and certain other processes discussed in their paper) and other metrical and autosegmental rules is simply a matter of mechanics: the projections that are relevant are merely harder to specify here than usual, since they involve a complex, two step algorithm with a notion of "tree-pruning". Alternatively, however, since this sort of additional complexity appears to arise precisely when metrical and autosegmental accounts are extended into areas other than those in which they are structurally necessitated, we might take it as an argument against such extensions.

Vowel harmony in a language like Khalkha Mongolian propagates from one non-high vowel to another; it ignores intervening /i/'s, but is stopped by other high vowels (/u/ or /ü/). We must note that all of /i/, /u/ and /ü/ are distinctively specified for the feature [±Round], which is manipulated by the rule; it is thus impossible to claim (as various proposed adjacency constraints would require) that both the foci and the determinants of the rule are (the exclusive) parts of a single unit specified by the harmonizing feature. It is quite clear, indeed, that material which neither conditons nor undergoes the rule is nonetheless relevant, and it is precisely this possibility which is excluded by the requirement that a metrical tree exhaust its projection (or that autosegmental tiers be exhaustively co-associated).

The Khalkha rounding harmony rule appears to furnish a counterexample to such a requirement, but we can nonetheless preserve the associated claim about metrical and autosegmental analysis if we exclude examples of this sort from their scope. This is easy enough to do on a principled basis, of course, if we simply limit metrical and autosegmental accounts to the manipulation of (independently motivated) metrical and autosegmental structure. GV rules are quite adept at describing such discontinuous (even in terms of a projection) dependencies as that arising in Khalkha rounding harmony; it is only if we insist that there are no non-metrical (or non-autosegmental) facts at all that this example forces us to such a radical weakening of the notion of metrical structure as that entailed by Halle & Vergnaud's two step tree-pruning analysis. Such algorithms vastly increase the range of possible metrical structures and relations between such structures and the projections of rules, since there is no possible *empirical* difference between allowing them and allowing metrical structures to ignore part of a relevant projection. They should thus be limited as narrowly as possible, and confining them to the domain of GV rule analyses is at least a step in the direction of limiting the power of phonological descriptions.

In addition to the requirement of exhaustive association, autosegmental representations are also subject to a constraint that association lines do not "cross" (in a geometrically obvious sense). Leben suggests that the same constraint, in essence, extends to metrical structures in the requirement that metrical trees do not overlap.

We must note first of all that if this is true, it must be relativized to the structure associated with a particular rule. Metrical trees that appear in segmental analyses, at least as far as these have been presented in the literature, are constructed *ad hoc* for each particular rule; after the rule has applied, they are not relevant (or accessible) to other rules. For example, the trees constructed for describing rounding harmony in a language like Turkish are not the same as those necessary for describing backness harmony in the same language. Trees constructed for distinct rules, thus, can and must overlap.

It might be proposed that this sort of overlap does indeed have an analog in the autosegmental domain: the associations between one pair of tiers are constructed independently of those between other pairs of tiers (e.g., associations between the "segmental core" of a form and its tonal representation are in principle independent of those between this core and its associated nasality tier). As a result, one set of associations may in fact "cross" or overlap with another set.

This apparent parallel, however, is so severely limited as to suggest that it is illusory. In fact, the relativization of the non-crossing requirement for autosegmental structures is to *tiers*, or structurally motivated aspects of forms, and not to *rules*. All of the rules manipulating tone-segment associations, that is, must respect the same set of non-crossing associations, while there is no such requirement that could apparently be imposed on metrical analyses of segmental phenomena that trees for different rules do not overlap insofar as they are defined by the same features.

We would, nonetheless, like to maintain the important constraint indicated by Leben, and prohibit overlap between metrical structures insofar as possible. In this regard, there is an important difference between the metrical trees constructed by rules designed to account for fundamentally segmental phenomena, and those constructed for essentially metrical facts (stress, syllabification, etc.). In the former case, there is in fact no way (even in principle) to verify the nature of the metrical structure assigned, since that assigned for one rule is by its very nature irrelevant to that assigned for another. Such structures, as we have noted, tend to show a significant degree of overlap from rule to rule.

By contrast, metrical structure which is motivated by the structural nature of the facts (rather than by the necessities of rule formulation) does not have such a character at all. The stress tree which is relevant for one rule, that is, is not allowed to be arbitrarily different from the stress tree which another rule requires for the same form. If the stress trees assigned to a given form must differ from one rule to another, this can only be by virtue of the existence of an independently motivated rule specifying the difference (a stress shifting rule, or the like). Similarly, the syllabification which is relevant to one rule can only differ from that relevant to another insofar as the grammar contains a rule of resyllabification.

It would seem, then, that an assimilation of segmental phenomena to metrical facts, through the attribution of rule-particular metrical trees to processes of the former sort, involves a conceptual confusion which would prevent the imposition of a useful constraint on the notion "metrical tree". The notion of "non-overlapping structure" which is relevant for (metrical formulations of) segmental processes would appear to be distinct in character from that which is relevant for genuinely metrical phenomena.

We might ask, however, just what analog of a "non-overlap" constraint there is in the segmental domain. If it is indeed true (as it appears to be) that the ad hoc metrical structures assigned by an individual segmental rule do not overlap with one another, we can nonetheless formulate this constraint purely in terms of the properties of GV rules. What this constraint involves, that is, is roughly the following: when a given form contains multiple "determinants" (in the terminology used above) that could each influence the same "focus", only the determinant nearest to a given focus is allowed to be taken into account. Similarly, perhaps, when multiple foci are potentially subject to the influence of a single determinant, only the nearest is allowed to be affected[7], though this is somewhat more controversial.

This constraint, requiring that the action of phonological rules be essentially local in character, is one which it could be argued has generally been taken for granted, though it has only been explicitly addressed in the literature referred to above on possible "adjacency conditions" and the like. Indeed, Leben also makes use of a similar constraint later in his paper, in a rather revealing way. In discussing the rule of *t*-flapping in English, he notes that, in cases where more than one *t* is found in a given foot, one which is distant from the conditioning factor (here, the location of main stress within the foot) can only be flapped if those closer to the determinant are also flapped. Given the rest of the analysis[8], this appears to be a constraint which does not follow directly from the metrical formalism itself, and which must be stated separately in some way. Of course, we may hope that such constraints can, when fully understood, be formulated in a general fashion rather than on a language-particular basis. Since they appear to be applicable precisely to GV rules (or the pseudo-trees involved in metrical re-formulations of these), this would seem to furnish another potential argument for separating GV rules from metrical (and autosegmental) processes.

3. *Prominence*

Leben next notes that metrical and autosegmental formalisms are similar in that both contrast "prominent vs. less prominent elements". That is, in an autosegmental representation some elements on one tier may be directly associated with designated (or "starred") elements on another, while other elements are not so associated. General principles of re-association may reorganize the lines connecting previously unassociated elements, but designated and pre-associated elements are not altered by convention. In metrical phonology, similarly, trees are constructed on the basis of some designated terminal element, and the device by which e.g. assimilation is performed is by the assignment of some feature from the designated terminal element of a (sub-)tree to a higher level node, from which it "percolates down" to other, less prominent nodes.

It is probably accurate to suggest that the designated elements of metrical and autosegmental structures are analogous, since both serve as the locus from which derived properties are spread. This similarity hardly excludes the class of GV rules, however. Its content seems precisely the same as that of the contrast between an element that conditions a rule (the determinant, in the terminology employed above) and that which undergoes it (the focus). The focus is "non-prominent" with respect to the determinant. Insofar as this distinction is an appropriate one to make, then, it can be made in the segmental realm independently of the utilization of metrical or autosegmental formalisms.

4. Preservation of ancillary structure

Another similarity noted by Leben between metrical and autosegmental formalisms is that both leave unchanged the structure to which rules do not explicitly refer. An autosegmental rule affecting the tonal tier, for example, does not alter the segments associated with the tones unless explicitly formulated so as to do so, and vice versa. The result is the well-known phenomenon of tone preservation (when a segment, but not its tone, is deleted), as well as the spreading of (remaining) tones when a tone, but not its associated segment, is deleted. In the metrical domain, this corresponds to the fact that a rule only operates on the tree built on its projection: unprojected elements are not affected.

A natural interpretation of the preservation of unprojected elements in metrical processes leads to an interesting account of vowel reduction. In a language like English, vowels are reduced to schwa under lack of stress (with certain additional conditions); and it has always been somewhat problematic to formulate this process in a way which reveals its real effect on vowel quality. This is because a positive specification of the quality of schwa is rather complex, and there is no evident reason why such a vowel (often described as a higher-mid back unrounded quality) should be produced as the result of what is, evidently, a simplificatory process. An attempt to specify the quality of schwa directly also runs into the problem that this vowel shows substantially more contextual variation than others.

These difficulties are resolvable if we treat schwa not as some particular (partly context dependent) set of quality features, but rather as a vowel position which is not specified at all for (at least some) quality features. If we thus regard schwa as simply a "vocalic transition" from a preceding to a following consonant, rather than as a determinate set of articulatory (or auditory) position features, this naturally suggests treating it formally as a segmental slot occupying the position of nucleus within a syllable. but with no segmental features assigned to that slot (a phonological analog of an "unfilled node" in syntax). Such an analysis is proposed and defended at some length for French by Anderson (1982), where it appears to have a number of advantages.

If we apply this treatment to English schwa, we can then formulate the vowel reduction rule not as a change in quality, but rather as the deletion of the segmental quality features associated with certain unstressed nuclei. This description properly captures the fact that we are dealing with a rule of vowel reduction, but it is crucially dependent on the assumption that, when we delete the quality features, this change does not by itself entail the deletion of the vowel's segmental slot. The latter, as an aspect of the metrical structure of the syllable, is of quite a distinct type from the quality features, and it seems natural to apply the principle (that ancillary structure is preserved unchanged) in such a way that it is not affected.

As the other side of this coin, there are also some instances in which the deletion of a segmental position does not result in the complete loss of its associated features. A fascinating example is found in the Panoan language Capanahua, discussed by Halle & Vergnaud (1981 - ultimately on the basis of the description by Loos 1969). In this language, nasality is found basically on consonants only, but spreads in regular ways to adjacent (arbitrarily long) sequences of vowels and glides. We will not repeat the facts cited by previous authors in detail here, but simply summarize the principles involved. When a nasal consonant appears in (the surface form of) a word, its nasality spreads to a sequence of non-consonantal segments to its left only. We assume this can be adequately described by a rule of regressive nasalization, applying iteratively:

(1)   [-Cons] $\longrightarrow$ [+Nasal] / ____ [+Nasal]

Alternatively, the process could be formulated as one of autosegmental reassociation:

(2)   [+Nasal]
       ╱╲
   [−Cons]   X

Under certain circumstances[9], however, nasal consonants may be deleted. When this happens, their nasality is nonetheless preserved, and spreads not only to the left of their original position, but rightward as well.

We could accomodate these facts by the assumptions that a) all and only [+consonantal] segments are associated with a value of nasality in underlying structure; and b) the deletion rule deletes the segmental position of the nasal, and its other features, but not the associated nasality value. As a result, when the segment is deleted, the remaining [+nasal] autosegment will be re-associated by convention with those non-consonants which are accessible to it (i.e., not separated from it by a segment linked to a nasality value). Such re-association is by its nature non-directional, accounting for its spread both to the right and to the left.

It thus appears that the proper perspective to adopt with regard to deletion rules is an autosegmental one. Assuming that a segmental position (in the metrical structure of a syllable) can be associated with autosegmental material on several tiers (i.e., nasality, tone, oral articulation, etc.) we can allow rules to delete any or all of these associated elements, potentially independent of one another. If we recognize that, from an autosegmental perspective, rules must thus specify[10] the parts of a "segment" to which they apply, we can thus maintain the generalization that material unreferenced by a rule is not changed by it.

In any event, this property of "structure conservation" which is shared (in some form) by metrical and autosegmental formalisms is also a characteristic of GV rules. It has always been assumed, of course, that features not mentioned in a given rule are conserved unchanged[11]. The principal exception to this (disregarding the observations of footnote 11) is found in the domain of deletion rules: when a rule deletes a segment (to simplify a consonant cluster, for example), we normally assume that the segment's features are lost as well, whether they are explicitly mentioned in the rule or not. As we have just seen above, however, such deletions are probably to be regarded as based on the autosegmental structure of the form, and thus do not form a real exception. There is no reason, therefore, to suggest that the property of conserving unreferenced structure separates GV rules from autosegmental and metrical ones.

5. Idiosyncratic specification

Leben next observes that both autosegmental and metrical structure, while generally assigned by rule, may also be specified exceptionally. Thus, some autosegments are lexically associated with elements on other tiers; and some metrical structure may have to be assumed present in underlying representations. It is of course hardly remarkable that this similarity also carries over to the GV rules: it has often been noted that a property which is generally assigned by rule may (exceptionally) be lexically listed instead.

Indeed, we can make the parallel more precise. Both autosegmental and metrical structure, when specified idiosyncratically, preclude the assignment of comparable structure by a general rule. Lexical associations, that is, are not subject to reorganization by the principles of the well-formedness condition; and a form which has been given an idiosyncratic stress pattern or syllabic structure does not have this annihilated by the language's general principles. Similarly, we can note that exceptional segmental specification overrides a general rule. In the domain of vowel harmony, for example, a word with an exceptional internally non-harmonic pattern does not have this replaced with regular harmony by the rules applying to non-exceptional forms. Similarly, if a language normally admits only clusters of a certain form, exceptional clusters found in borrowings and other unusual words are not thereby converted into regular, non-anomalous clusters. Morphological exceptions (e.g., irregular plurals or past tense forms in English) are not also supplied with regular endings, etc. Again, GV rules appear to share all of the relevant properties of autosegmental and metrical formulations in the segmental domain.

6. Scope of Application

Finally, Leben notes that both metrical and autosegmental analyses distinguish between two sorts of structure. One of these is strictly local and bounded: in metrical terms, this is the type of a binary tree, while in autosegmental terms, it is the notion of a limited, language-particular reassociation. The other sort of structure is a global, unlimited one: metrically, an unbounded tree, and autosegmentally the kind of unbounded association identified with the operation of the well-formedness conditions.

This is, in a way, the area in which we can find the most substantive parallel between metrical/autosegmental analyses and those provided by GV rules. Anderson (1974), among others, argues for a distinction in phonological rules between those that do and those that do not re-apply to their own output (i.e., between iterative and non-iterative rules). For instance, some languages have rules which delete a final short vowel, but reduce a final long vowel to short. This can be formulated as a simple rule which deletes a final vowel position, and which does not re-apply to its own output. Other languages, however, have rules which delete a final consonant if this is preceded by another consonant; and such a rule often re-applies until an original final cluster of arbitrary length is reduced to a single consonant. The distinction between iterative and non-iterative rules is well motivated for GV rules, and corresponds quite directly to the difference between local and unbounded structure in autosegmental and metrical analyses.

DIFFERENCES BETWEEN AUTOSEGMENTAL AND METRICAL ACCOUNTS

After arguing that there are important similarities between autosegmental and metrical analyses, Leben then goes on to consider the areas in which the two theories appear to make rather different claims. He argues that the differences are actually illusory, and that a single formalism can accurately represent the essential properties of both.

1. Internal structure

The first area in which the formalisms of autosegmental and metrical theory differ concerns the internal structure of units. Metrical trees, that is, contain a considerable amount of internal structure (based on the fact that they organize potentially arbitrary amounts of material by an operation of binary branching), while autosegmental structures are essentially "flat". Leben suggests that the structure imposed by metrical analyses, however, is unnecessary and unmotivated by anything other than the requirements of the theory. If true, this would suggest that flat structures such as those characteristic of autosegmental analyses would suffice in both cases.

A consideration of instances in which metrical formalisms have been employed to handle essentially segmental phenomena (such as those discussed in Halle & Vergnaud 1981) confirms the claim that, where such internal structure is assigned, it plays no subsequent role in the analysis. Leben also argues at length that structure internal to the foot is never necessary. On the other hand, there are some areas in which the internal structure of metrical trees clearly *does* play a role. For instance, it is only in terms of the internal organization of word trees that the complex array of stress distinctions in a language like English can be represented adequately. Similarly, the internal constituent structure of syllables provides us with a representation of crucial differences between syllable onsets and rhymes, nuclei and margins (or codas). Arguably, it is the internal structure of the syllable which represents the property treated in somewhat *ad hoc* fashion by Chomsky & Halle (1968) as the feature [±Syllabic] (cf. Anderson 1982 for some discussion).

We must thus conclude that the internal structure of metrical representations cannot in general be dispensed with; but on the other hand, it is equally true that there are substantial domains in which it cannot be motivated. The answer to this dilemma, of course, is to constrain metrical theory in such a way that it does not apply (with the concomitant necessity of imposing unmotivated internal structure) in such areas. In particular, it seems clear that it is the extension of metrical analyses to facts of straightforwardly segmental character that is largely responsible for the problem. We leave the issue of internal structure for feet unresolved: in the general development of metrical theory the foot is evidently the least well understood of the various structural entities that have been posited. With this possible exception, we should recall that it is precisely the assumption of internal hierarchical structure that constitutes the important central point of metrical analyses. It would thus be a considerable loss to abandon this, as Leben proposes. We can avoid his conclusion, however, by confining metrical analyses to facts of a metrical nature, and describing segmental changes within some theory such as that of GV rules.

2. Directionality

Another apparent difference between analyses within the framework of metrical phonology and those carried out in autosegmental terms rests on the fact that the construction of metrical trees is performed on a directional basis, while the spreading of autosegmental associations is inherently directionless. Indeed, Halle & Vergnaud (1981) make use of exactly this difference in their characterization of harmony systems. Some of these, they suggest, are bidirectional ("dominant" harmony), while others are directional, and they propose that this difference should be represented as the distinction between autosegmental and metrical treatments.

Leben suggests that this, like other differences between the two frameworks, is largely illusory. He argues that autosegmental analyses sometimes need to make use of directional determinations (to determine the location of "anchoring" of floating tones), and that metrical analyses sometimes have bidirectional aspects. On this basis, Leben proposes to unify the two formalisms; his suggestion is a system in which (internally unstructured) trees are constructed in a directional fashion, presumably with an option as to whether binary or unbounded structures are the result. Bidirectional processes are, on this view, to be treated as the simple conjunction of two symmetric directional sub-cases.

Without questioning all of the parts of this claim, we can note that Leben's proposed instance of a bidirectional metrical rule does not really establish the point it is intended to make. In the analysis of Garawa stress given by Hayes (1980), it is observed that *main* stress is determined by a principle that operates from left to right, while *secondary* (and tertiary) stress are determined by a rule that operates from right to left. Since these are two quite separate rules, however, this fails to establish the point that *individual* metrical processes may be bidirectional.

In fact, while the two formalisms may not be mutually exclusive (because of the possibility of directionally restricted autosegmental associations), it is apparent that they differ from one another in this respect. Metrical structures (taken individually) seem quite resolutely directional in character, while autosegmental processes at least admit the possibility of bidirectional application (indeed, this is clearly the most common case). Since in some domains (e.g., vowel harmony and similar assimilations) the directional/bidirectional distinction seems to have a typological significance, we might feel that it is appropriate to capture it by the metrical/autosegmental difference.

The conclusion that metrical and autosegmental formalisms must be extended into the area of harmony processes in order to capture the difference between directional and bidirectional rules is not at all a necessary one, however. In fact, the theory of GV rules already contains a device which represents this parameter in an simple and direct fashion. Discussion within this framework, orginating with the work of Bach (1968) and continuing in Anderson (1974) and other references, has argued that a class of *mirror-image* rules must be recognized in phonology, as well as the class of ordinary directionally unique rules. A mirror-image rule, of course, is exactly a (systematically recognised) pair of symmetrically related directional rules, similar to Leben's analog of bidirectional processes, but without the assumption of any crucial structure beyond that of the sequence of segments.

We can completely accept Halle & Vergnaud's proposed distinction between "dominant" and "directional" harmony rules, then, but without moving outside of the domain expressible by GV rules: directional harmony corresponds to the simple case of an ordinary assimilation rule, while dominant harmony corresponds to the mirror-image version of essentially the same rule. Again, the decisive facts in the area for which Leben argues for similarity between autosegmental and metrical accounts turn out to be completely expressible without loss of generality in the more traditional theory. Indeed, in this case, the issue has already been addressed quite explicitly in the literature of that theory.

CONCLUSIONS

In the above discussion we have found (on the basis of Leben's previous discussion) a number of areas in which metrical and autosegmental formalisms have similar properties; and we have seen that these similarities extend, by and large, to descriptions in terms of traditional ("GV") segmental rules. Among these properties, which evidently constitute general characteristics of phonological systems, we can cite the distinction between prominent elements ("determinants") and less prominent, or subordinated elements ("foci"); the principle that unreferenced structure is conserved unchanged under the operation of a rule; and the principle that the (lexicalised) specification of a property in a way idiosyncratic to a form over-rides a competing but incompatible specification of the same property by general rule.

In other areas, however, we find that differences between these formalisms can only be eliminated at the cost of depriving them of some of their (potential) theoretical significance. For instance, we have argued above that the imposition of significant limitations on the range of possible projections on which a given rule may be based will only be possible if we base the theory of projections on a maximally articulated typology of rules. We also saw above that the distinction between strictly local and unbounded processes is one which has already been discussed in the traditional literature, as the difference between rules that do not iterate and those that do. Indeed, it is argued by Anderson (1974) that the use of iteration to express processes extending across unbounded segmental domains is an interestingly restrictive one[12]. Until it can be shown that comparable constraints fall out in other formalisms, it would seem to be undesirable to replace the device of iterative application with a less restrictive mechanism. Finally, metrical and autosegmental processes (at least in their central motivating cases) seem to differ significantly in their degree of symmetry (or directionality), and the attempt to eliminate this difference again reduces the conceptual content of both theories.

The principal thrust of the discussion in this paper, however, has not been to question Leben's conclusion that metrical and autosegmental mechanisms have significant similarities. Rather, it is to point out that some of these apparent similarities arise precisely when the formalisms in question are extended beyond the areas in which they were originally motivated to accomodate phenomena of a "segmental" sort. If we admit these proposed extensions, the result is a major weakening of the empirical content of the two theories; but we need not do so, since the domains in question are already accomodated within the traditional theory of segmental rules.

For example, we saw above that there is a significant amount of overlap between the well-formedness constraints applicable to autosegmental representations and the character of metrical trees. In order to extract a set of conditions generally applicable to phonological principles, however, there are certain cases which must be excluded. We would like to claim that metrical trees, like autosegmental representations, are subject to a condition of exhaustiveness which requires that all of the elements of their projection be incorporated. Analyses of segmental phenomena such as vowel harmony, however, violate this condition since some elements of their projections must be systematically pruned from the metrical tree. Again, metrical trees for well-motivated properties such as stress and syllable structure are subject to conditions of non-overlap quite similar to the requirement that autosegmental association lines do not cross; but the trees constructed *ad hoc* for particular segmental rules may well overlap, regardless of the features that define the elements on which they are constructed. In both of these instances, the general condition suggested by Leben as a similarity between metrical and autosegmental formalisms can only be maintained if we limit the class of processes which these describe.

The most important reason to restrict the application of non-segmental mechanisms to segmental processes is that the failure to do so has direct consequences for their underlying empirical content. The essence of metrical representations, for example, is the imposition of an articulated hierarchical structure on a string of segments; but precisely in the extension of the metrical tree device to segmental phenomena, we encounter the objection that the internal structure assigned is unmotivated by any but theoretical considerations. By contrast, the internal structure of genuinely metrical representations such as those for stress and syllable structure is abundantly motivated by the facts themselves.

A similar point can be made with respect to autosegmental structure. The important insight of this theory is that the phonetic properties of speech, while generally coordinated and synchronized in a unitary way as expressed by the notion of the segment, may also display a certain amount of independence from one another in this regard. The formal reflection of this fact is the representation of distinct phonetic properties as distinct tiers of autosegmental structure, with the coordination among them represented by lines of association between the units on different tiers. When autosegmental analysis is extended beyond domains such as tone and nasality, however, and made to accomodate vowel harmony and the like, this conceptual content must evidently be greatly reduced. Analyses of vowel harmony must evidently allow the *same* phonetic property to be simultaneously and independently represented on two or more autosegmental tiers. This move vastly reduces the extent to which autosegmental theory is a claim about phonetic structure, and converts it into a mere mechanism for stating certain processes algorithmically.

Such moves might well be justified if they were unavoidable, in that only metrical or autosegmental accounts could properly express the properties of rules such as those of vowel harmony. This is far from being the case, however. As argued in Anderson (1980), segmental rules of assimilation formulated within a theory of GV rules, applied iteratively where appropriate and either unidirectionally or in mirror-image fashion, are quite capable of expressing the properties of harmony systems in a constrained fashion. As a result, we should prefer to retain a maximal degree of empirical content for non-segmental formalisms by excluding them from such areas.

This does not at all entail the conclusion that the insights of metrical and autosegmental phonology should be abandoned, or that segmental formulations of all rules traditionally treated in such terms are appropriate. For example, it is quite clear that many rules usually written in terms of strings of segments are more appropriately formulated by reference to syllabic structure. We must distinguish here, however, between the use a rule makes of metrical (or autosegmental) structure in its structural description, and the utilisation of the associated formalism in stating its change (e.g., as a matter of tree construction, with properties assigned to higher level nodes then percolating down; or as a matter of redrawing association lines). If the claims of recent work in phonology are generally correct, then they must result in the conclusion that speech has an essentially metrical and autosegmental structure. If this is the case, and the forms to which rules apply necessarily have these aspects, there is no reason to prevent analyses which refer to them.

However, we should not allow the insights achieved in recent years to blind us to the fact that speech also has a segmental aspect, apparently; and that the theory of segmental rules is actually quite successful in accomodating many phonological properties. This is not to say that there is a complete, fully determined theory of "GV-rules": far from it, since there clearly remain many open questions to be resolved in that area. It is not obvious, however, that non-segmental alternatives have been notably more successful to date in dealing with these issues, and that there is therefore warrant for a wholesale replacement of the traditional theory. Rather, we should recognize that work in autosegmental and metrical theory has taught us *new* things about phonology, ways of looking at domains that had previously been recalcitrant to analysis. The best way to consolidate the gains of this work is to attempt to delimit as carefully as possible the aspects of structure for which each of the mechanisms currently available to us is appropriate. A richly articulated theory, with substantial internal structure, is much more likely to provide an adequate overall view of the nature of language than one which displays complete internal homogeneity.

NOTES

1. A comparison between autosegmental and segmental treatments of vowel harmony was made in Anderson (1980), where it was concluded that autosegmental analyses offered no serious advantages over traditional accounts (once these are adequately formulated), and in fact seem inferior to these on some counts. Although Halle & Vergnaud deal with some of the same examples, they do not in fact address the arguments presented for this conclusion, and their own paper does not furnish (at least in my opinion) grounds for reversing this earlier judgement.
2. In the isolation form of this word, the final vowel is devoiced and raised to [e̥]; the penultimate /a/ is thus preserved (since it does not precede /a/), but the antepenultimate /a/ is dissimilated. In the "possessed" form, on the other hand, no change takes place in the final vowel, and it is thus the penult (of the stem) which dissimilates. After this change, of course, the initial vowel is no longer followed by /a/, and is thus preserved.
3. The notion of a "projection" will be further discussed below.
4. When a [+high, +round] vowel is encountered, it initiates a new tree of which it serves as the leftmost branch.
5. This is because [+high, +round] vowels do not trigger harmony, and [+high, -round] ones are transparent (or "neutral") with respect to the propagation of harmony from a preceding vowel.
6. Notice that it would not suffice simply to define the rule on the projection of [-high] vowels in a word, since rounded high vowels, while they do not initiate or undergo harmony, block its propagation to their right.
7. We can note that this latter portion of the proposed constraint is quite close to the issue discussed by Anderson (1974) in connection with the prohibition of the "(X)*" notation of Chomsky and Halle (1968), and its replacement by iterative re-application of a single, simple rule. The spirit of the constraint, that is, is to prohibit phonological action at a distance except where intermediate elements exist which themselves are changed by the rule in question into potentially "local" determinants.
8. A somewhat different analysis of t-flapping, not based on a rule sensitive to foot structure, is argued for by Hammond (1982).
9. According to Loos (1969: 178f), this happens when the nasal is a) final; b) followed by a continuant consonant or a glide (including [ʔ]); or c) medial in a three consonant cluster.
10. It may well be that this specification is partly a global property of languages, rather than simply a local property of rules. It has often been suggested, that is, that languages differ to some extent in the amount to which they are "autosegmentalized". In some languages, properties such as tone, nasality, etc. behave exactly as any segmental feature, and apparently appear on the same tier with other features. Other languages, in contrast, allow considerable autonomy in such properties. It might be suggested that the amount of specification necessary for particular rules is a function of the amount of autosegmental independence displayed by the language as a whole.
11. The theory of markedness proposed by Chomsky and Halle (1968) constitutes a possible exception to this observation, since the notion of "linking rules" which forms a part of this theory is an explicit provision for changes (by convention) in features not mentioned explicitly in the rule. It must be said, however, that this theory has been little discussed since its initial presentation, and few phonologists would probably feel that the notion of "linking rules" forms a substantive part of phonological theory. One exception, perhaps, is to be found in the case of features which are incompatible by their logical nature, and for which we must assume some adjustments by convention; thus, when a rule makes a segment [+low], it must also

become [-high] by virtue of the definition of the feature system. Such cases, we assume, are comparatively limited in their import for the principles under discussion here.

12. This follows from the fact that, in order to apply across an unbounded domain, an iterative rule must create outputs that also satisfy the structural description of its primary determinant. No comparable constraint appears to exist on the relation between focus and determinant in unbounded metrical processes.

The Internal Structure of Complex Segments

Colin J. Ewen
University of Leyden

1. THE STRUCTURE OF SEQUENCES

The notational framework of METRICAL PHONOLOGY, developed by Liberman and Prince

> employs two basic ideas about the representation of traditional prosodic concepts: first, we represent the notion *relative prominence* in terms of a relation defined on constituent structure; and second, we represent certain aspects of the notion *linguistic rhythm* in terms of the alignment of linguistic material with a 'metrical grid'. (1977:249).

Thus, prominence relations are defined in terms of a constituency-based system of representation, in which, for example, "it accords quite directly with the intuition behind metrical comparison to regard the stressed syllable as *strong*, its unstressed compeers as *weak*" (Liberman and Prince 1977:264). Notice that because 'relative prominence' is a relational notion (in Liberman and Prince's terms, "a relation defined on sister nodes"), the labels *s* ('strong') and *w* ('weak') are only meaningful with respect to each other; i.e. a node can only be strong in comparison with a sister node which is (relatively) weaker. Notice further that all branching is binary: the relative prominence relation holds only between the two sisters of a binary branching structure.

The aspect of metrical phonology which is most relevant to the discussion which follows in this paper is its treatment of the internal structure of the syllable. Kiparsky (1979: 432) argues that

> syllabification is governed by a universal rule which assigns a metrical structure to strings of segments, and which may be augmented by language-particular rules. The universal core rule requires an optimal matching of the *syllabic template* [(1a)] to the well-known *sonority hierarchy* [(1b)]:

---

* An earlier version of this paper (Ewen 1980c) appeared in Anderson and Ewen (1980) (*Ludwigsburg Studies in Language and Linguistics* 4). I am very grateful to the editor of the series, Reinhard Strauch, for permission to publish the paper in this volume. My thanks are also due to John Anderson, Frits Beukema and Marc Dupuis for their comments on a draft version of this paper.

28   Colin J. Ewen

(1) a.

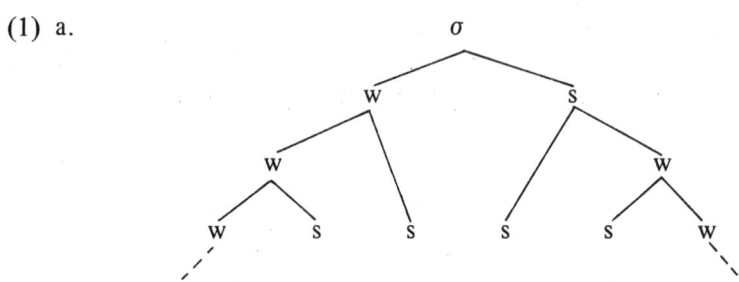

   b. *Sonority Hierarchy:* stops, fricatives, nasals, l, r, w, y, u, i, o, e, a

(where the label σ denotes a syllable). Within any "pair of adjacent segments in a σ", the one marked *s* is the more sonorous in terms of the sonority hierarchy. Thus, the more sonorous element is interpreted as being relatively more prominent than its less sonorous counterpart.

Notice that the metrical tree in (1)a., as well as utilising labels which identify the various constituents as being *s* or *w*, also contains a label σ, which identifies the syllable constituent. This approach to prosodic structure is developed further by Selkirk (1980:2), who observes:

> it is necessary to posit *prosodic categories,* i.e. specific differentiated sub-units of prosodic structure, which 'label' the nodes of the tree. These prosodic categories are the syllable, the foot, the prosodic word, the phonological phrase, the intonational phrase and the utterance.

On the basis of this, she sets up three "prosodic units at the level of the syntactic word or lower": the syllable (σ), the foot (Σ), and the prosodic word (ω), each of which has its own hierarchically arranged internal structure, as in (2), her tree for English *irrespective*:

(2)

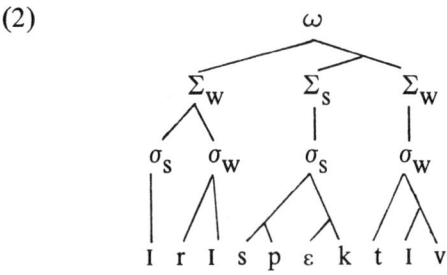

In this conception of phonological structure, then, the prosodic word is viewed as being made up of a number of foot-constituents (in this case 3), which in turn consist of a number of syllables (2 for the first foot and 1 for each of the others), which have an internal structure of the type represented in (1)a. Each of the prosodic categories has a constituent-label, and one of each pair of nodes is marked as *s*, the other as *w*, with the whole constitute being labelled ω.

Complex Segments

The notational framework of DEPENDENCY PHONOLOGY shares one of metrical phonology's most important insights, that the characterisation of the notion relative prominence is crucial to a successful account of phonological structure, but offers a rather different approach to the representation of this property. The framework was first presented in Anderson and Jones (1974), and has since been developed in a number of publications, in particular Anderson and Jones (1977), Anderson (1980), Anderson and Ewen (1980, to appear), and Ewen (1977, 1980a).

Whereas prosodic structures in metrical phonology are assigned a constituency-based system of representation, in dependency phonology they are characterised in terms of dependency structures. Each construction, such as the syllable or the foot, is assigned a HEAD, which is obligatory for that construction, and which may GOVERN a MODIFIER (or modifiers), which are then DEPENDENT on the head. Thus, a foot such as English *modest,* which Selkirk characterises as (3), will be given the dependency representation in (4) (in which governing nodes are placed higher on the graph than the nodes they govern; thus the dependency relation is represented on the vertical axis, and linear order on the horizontal axis):

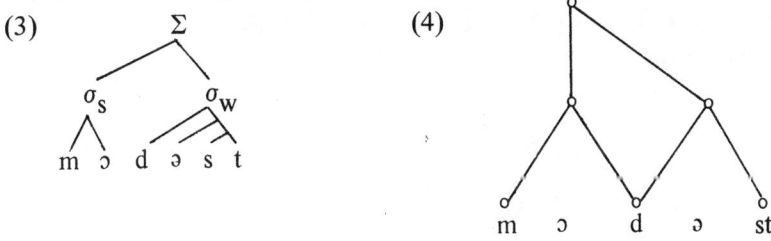

/ɔ/, as the obligatory element of the first syllable, is therefore its head and governor, while the non-syllabic elements (/m/ and /d/) of the first syllable are dependent on the syllabic. I assume here an analysis in which intervocalic /d/ is assigned to both syllables, and hence is dependent on both syllabics (i.e. /d/ terminates two dependency arcs); for discussion, see Anderson and Jones (1974), Anderson and Ewen (to appear). /ə/, as governor of the second syllable, has /d/ and /st/ dependent on it (I ignore for the moment the internal structure of the /st/ cluster). /ɔ/ is not only head of its syllable, but also head of the foot, as it is the stressed syllabic. Hence, as head of the construction, /ɔ/ has /ə/, the other syllabic, dependent on it. Thus /ɔ/ is simultaneously head of a more inclusive construction, the foot, and of a less inclusive construction, the syllable. This dual status is characterised by the fact that /ɔ/, as head of the foot, governs itself, as head of the syllable. /ɔ/ is, in other words, SUBJOINED to itself (i.e. dependent, but not distinct in precedence), while /m/ and /d/ are also dependent on /ɔ/, as head of the syllable, but are ADJOINED dependent, and distinct in precedence).

30   Colin J. Ewen

Consider now a dependency representation of *irrespective* (in which I assume a rather more traditional analysis, involving two bisyllabic feet):

(5)
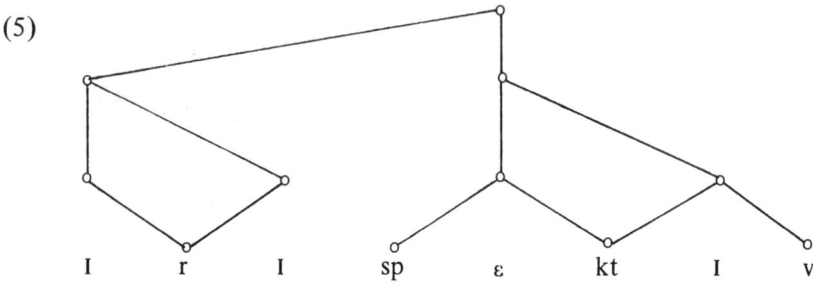

In (5), /ε/, as head of its syllable, governs /sp/ and /kt/; as head of its foot, it governs the last /I/; and as head of the TONE GROUP (or phonological word), it governs the first /I/, which is in turn the governor of its foot. Notice that the /sp/ cluster is not ambisyllabic, as it is foot-initial (for discussion, see Anderson and Ewen to appear).

In addition to prosodic units above the syllable, we can also represent units of smaller than syllable size. Thus constructions such as RHYME, ONSET, and CODA may be distinguished in (6), the structure for Dutch *krant* 'newspaper':

(6)
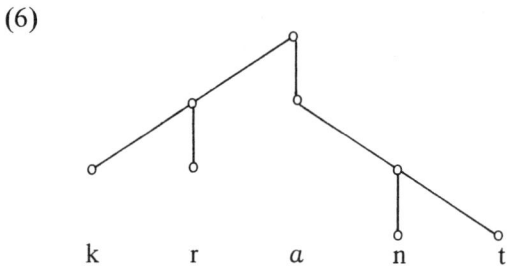

In (6), /a/ is head of the syllable, and also head of a lower prosodic unit, the rhyme. /r/ is head of the cluster forming the onset, while /n/ is head of the cluster forming the coda.

It is clear that, as is argued in Anderson and Ewen (to appear), a dependency representation incorporating both sub- and suprasyllabic information, such as that in (7) for Dutch *koop een krant* 'buy a newspaper', makes the use of the prosodic category labels σ, Σ, and ω redundant:

(7)

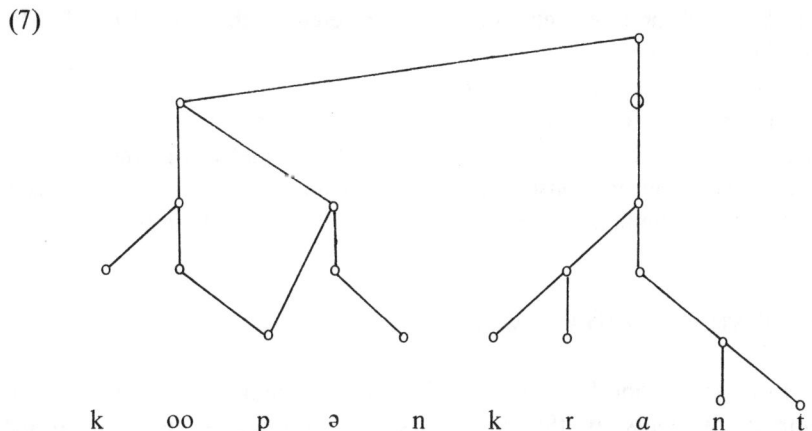

k　　oo　　p　ə　n　k　r　a　n　t

(I ignore the internal structure of the complex nucleus of the first syllable.) In those constructions which are obligatory (i.e. the tone group, the foot, the syllable, and the rhyme), and in which, therefore, the head is obligatorily present, we can observe a recurrent pattern. The head of the tone group takes a stressed syllabic (i.e. the head of a foot) as its modifier, and takes this modifier to its left. The head of the foot takes an unstressed syllabic as its modifier, to its right. The head of the syllable (i.e. the syllabic) takes a consonant as its modifier, to the left, while the head of the rhyme (again the syllabic element) takes the coda as its modifier, to the right. Thus, for each more, or less, inclusive construction-type, the direction of modification is reversed. The identity of each (obligatory) construction-type can be determined from its place in the fixed hierarchy of types, together with the direction of modification, and hence category-labels are redundant. Even if the modifier is absent, as in the case of the head of the second foot in (7), the status of /a/ as head of this foot can still be established from its place in the hierarchy of nodes in the subjunction path characterising /a/.

Although we can characterise the head in these constructions as being that element which is obligatorily present, it is clear that the notion of relative prominence is also relevant here – the head of any construction-type is more prominent than its modifier. Because relative stress correlates with relative prominence, the heads of the tone group and the foot are more prominent than their modifiers, and within the syllable the syllabic element is more prominent than the non-syllabics, and hence the heads of the syllable and the rhyme are more prominent than their modifiers. For other (non-obligatory) construction-types, relative prominence is the only criterion for the head-modifier relationship: in the clusters forming the onset and coda in *krant*, for example, neither element can be said to be obligatory. Thus the notion of relative prominence is always the source of the head-modifier relationship, interpreted in this model by the dependency relation.

The use of dependency representations, of course, also eliminates the need for the auxiliary symbols *s* and *w* used in metrical phonology. The use of these symbols in the constituency-based metrical phonology, like the $\bar{X}$ notation in constituency-based syntax (Jackendoff 1977), is a reflection of the failure to model prominence relations directly.

2. THE STRUCTURE OF SEGMENTS

I turn now to another aspect of dependency phonology, the representation of segments. In this framework, segments are assigned an internal structure utilising the dependency relation. Recall that in the representation of prosodic categories, the head of a construction might take itself as a modifier, i.e. might have itself subjoined. Such subjunctions are unlabelled, in that the subjoined node is not categorially distinct from the governor. In the internal structure of certain segments, we again find subjunction structures, in which, however, the subjoined node differs from the governing node.

For the purposes of this paper, I will only consider the representation in dependency phonology of the 'categorial' properties of segments, i.e. those properties denoting the 'major class' membership of segment-types (cf. Chomsky and Halle 1968), which in the dependency model form the CATEGORIAL GESTURE (Ewen 1980a, Anderson and Ewen to appear). In particular, I will confine the discussion to voiced and voiceless plosives, voiced and voiceless fricatives, nasals, liquids, and vowels.

Two components have been proposed for the characterisation of the categorial gesture. These are |V|, a component which can be defined as 'relatively periodic', and |C|, a component with a definition similar to the Jakobsonian consonantal feature, i.e. one whose presence in the representation of a segment correlates with the presence of zeros in the acoustic record of that segment. Components such as |V| and |C| may be absent or present in the representation of a particular segment. When more than one is present in the representation of a segment, they may either simply combine, or enter into a non-symmetric relation, in which one element is more preponderant than the other(s). Just as prominence in sequences is associated with the head-modifier relation, so within the segment one component may govern another, where relative preponderance is again modelled by dependency. In the case of the categorial gesture, we have the following representations (cf. Anderson and Jones 1974, Ewen 1977):

Complex Segments 33

(8) V   V   V   V,C   V,C   C   C
     | | | | |
     V,C   C   V   V

     vowels liquids nasals voiced   voiceless voiced   voiceless
                             fricatives fricatives plosives plosives

The vowels and the voiceless plosives, respectively the most '|V|-like' and most '|C|-like' segment-types, are represented as {|V|} and {|C|} (notice that segmental representations are enclosed within { }). In comparison to voiceless plosives, voiced plosives involve an extra periodic sound source, and hence involve an extra |V| component. Similarly, nasals, in comparison to vowels, show an acoustic structure more like that of consonants, and hence show an extra |C|. Thus, both nasals and voiced plosives show a ¡V¡ and a |C| in their representations. However, in the case of the voiced plosives |C| is relatively more preponderant than |V| (i.e. voiced plosives are more |C|-like than |V|-like), while for the nasals the reverse holds. For segmental representations, relative preponderance has the same status as relative prominence for suprasegmental representations; it is the source of the dependency relation. In the representation of the voiced plosives, then, ¡V¡ is subjoined to ¡C¡; for the nasals, |V| governs ¡C¡. In the representation of the voiceless fricatives, where we again find both |V| and |C|, the two components are mutually preponderant, and have a representation in which |V| and |C| are MUTUALLY DEPENDENT, i.e. |V| and |C| have the same hierarchical status. As voiced fricatives involve the addition of voicing, they differ in the same way from voiceless fricatives as voiced stops do from voiceless stops, i.e. by the addition of a subjoined |V|. Notice, then, that voiced fricatives have two occurrences of |V|. This appropriately represents the fact that, in comparison to voiceless stops, voiced fricatives are more |V¡-like (and hence less ¡C¡-like) in two respects – the addition of voicing, and the change from stopness to close approximation. Liquids, the remaining category, differ from nasals in being closer to the vowel end of the sonority scale, and in having a more complex articulation, and therefore have an extra |V| in their representation. (For a full discussion of these representations, see Ewen 1980a: ch. 6.)

The adoption of this system of representation permits the characterisation of a number of categorial natural classes. For example, all sonorants show governing |V| alone, while sonorant consonants show |V| alone governing (at least) |C|. Obstruents have (at least) governing |C|, with voiced obstruents showing an additional subjoined |V|. Continuant consonants (fricatives and liquids) all have a |V,C| node, while non-continuant consonants all have a |C| node. Further, notice that there is a natural relationship between phonological complexity (in the sense of Jakobson

1968) and complexity of representation: phonologically simple segments (vowels and voiceless plosives) have simple representations, involving only a single component, while the most complex segments (liquids and voiced fricatives) have the most complex representations.

One of the most important properties of this system of representation is that it allows the syllabic template of Kiparsky (1)a, and the associated sonority hierarchy (1)b, to be directly determinable from the segmental representations. The following simple statement serves to predict the order of elements in the canonical syllable: more |V|-like elements are closer to the syllabic than less |V|-like elements. The place of any segment-type in the sonority hierarchy, and hence its behaviour in the syllable (and in other phonological processes determined by the sonority hierarchy, such as lenition) is a function of its representation. This, then, is the equivalent within dependency phonology of Kiparsky's 'universal core rule', but in dependency phonology we require neither a syllabic template nor a sonority hierarchy as distinct elements in the phonological theory; rather, their character follows from the segmental representations.

We can now give an alternative representation of *krant*, as in (9):

(9)

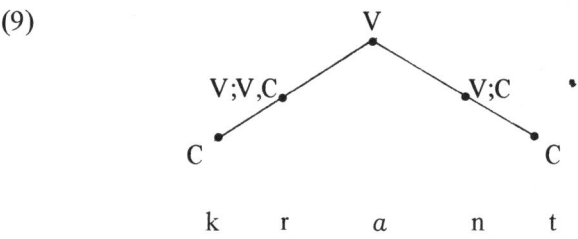

(In (9), I ignore the representation of any sub-syllabic structure (such as the rhyme). Further, each node is labelled directly with the categorial representation of the segment-type in question, and each segmental representation is given, not in its graph form, but in a form in which unilateral dependency is represented as ';', and mutual dependency as ','. Thus, liquids are { |V;V,C| }, while voiced fricatives, for example, are { |V,C;V| }. In what follows, I will use whichever type of representation is most appropriate for the issue under discussion.)

In (9), then, we see that the syllabic structure is a function of the segmental representations. /k/ is less |V|-like than /r/, and so is dependent on it (i.e., as is apparent from (6), /r/ is the head of the onset), and /r/ is less |V|-like than /a/, and so /a/ is the head of the syllable. The same relations hold for the elements of the rhyme.

3. COMPLEX SEGMENTS

In the rest of this paper, I will be concerned with a number of consonantal phenomena whose phonological representation has given rise to controversy. This controversy is due to disagreement as to whether they should be characterised as single segments, as sequences of segments, or as something 'in between'. Certain of these phenomena appear to involve, among other things, a violation of the principle that relative dependency and relative precedence are linked in such a way that, within the syllable, relatively more dependent segments are, in terms of linear order, further from the syllabic than less dependent ones. In other words, the principle that syllabic structure is determined by the sonority hierarchy does not appear to hold in these cases.

Much of the discussion with respect to the 'one segment or two' issue has centred around the status of affricates, which, at least phonetically, appear to involve two distinct phases - a closure phase, and some kind of friction phase; but various other phenomena which also appear to involve some kind of change in the course of the production of a consonant are relevant here. For example, prenasalised and postnasalised consonants involve phonetically a change from velic opening to velic closure (or vice versa) in the course of the production of something which appears to be of normal segment length, while preaspiration has a similar status. We shall also see that there is another area relevant to this discussion, which is, however, traditionally interpreted as involving simply two successive segments. This is the representation of clusters of [s] followed by a stop, which, I shall argue, show certain of the properties of the items mentioned above.

There have been various proposals to characterise such items as 'compound phonological segments' (Hoard 1967, 1975, 1978, St Clair 1972, 1973, Campbell 1974). Hoard claims that the (segmental) feature [delayed release] (which distinguish plosives from affricates)

> covers up the difference between a simple and a complex segment. By a complex segment I mean one with intrinsic sequential properties. . . Affricates are complex segments by this definition; it is reasonably clear that the first part of affricates is [-continuant], the second part [+continuant].

Thus, the English affricate /t͡ʃ/ is represented as (10), while the (bisegmental) sequence /ts/ has the representation in (11):

(10) $\begin{bmatrix} C \\ +\text{coronal} \\ +\text{anterior} \\ -\text{continuant} \quad +\text{continuant} \\ -\text{voice} \\ \text{etc.} \end{bmatrix}$ (11) $\begin{bmatrix} C \\ +\text{coronal} \\ +\text{anterior} \\ -\text{continuant} \\ -\text{voice} \\ \text{etc.} \end{bmatrix} \begin{bmatrix} C \\ +\text{coronal} \\ +\text{anterior} \\ +\text{continuant} \\ -\text{voice} \\ \text{etc.} \end{bmatrix}$

We find similar approaches in phonemic analyses, in which, however, no internal structure is assigned to the segment. Bloomfield (1933), for example, proposed that the voiceless alveopalatal affricate [č] in Polish *czy* 'whether' (but not in English) acts as a single unit, but is composed of two phonemes — a voiceless alveolar stop, and a voiceless palatal sibilant. It is in Bloomfield's terms a 'compound phoneme', i.e. one in which two simple phonemes act as a unit.

S. Anderson (1974, 1976) is concerned with the characterisation of prenasalised stops:

> In a variety of languages of Africa, South America, South Asia, New Guinea, and various areas of the Pacific, elements transcribed as [m͡b n͡d ŋ͡g] etc. clearly behave as single units. (1976: 331).

In addition, he notes the existence in various languages of another type, referred to as 'postnasalised stops' or 'pre-stopped nasals', transcribed [p͡m t͡n k͡ŋ] etc. Like the prenasalised stops, they have the distributional and phonological properties of single segments. He observes that these two types, and ordinary nasals, differ from each other only in relative timing, and for this reason "any feature which purports to characterise the entire segment uniformly, like [continuant] or [sonorant], is apparently destined to fail". It is this that leads him to propose that pre- and post-nasalised stops are complex segments, characterised as in (12), or, alternatively, as in (13) (1976: 338):

(12) [...o b͡m   n ...]   (13) [...o b͡m   n ...]

		b͡m					b͡m	
syll	+	−	−	syll	+	−	−
cons	−	+	+	cons	−	+	+
nasal	−	−	+	+	nasal	−	+
high	−	−	−	high	−	−	−

(13), he claims, is more appropriate, in that it reflects the fact that nasality may have as its domain more than just a single segment, and may 'spread' into adjacent segments. Thus [nasal] is treated in (13) as a feature whose domain is not coterminous with the segment.

Complex Segments

This account is not dissimilar to various autosegmental approaches to prenasalisation (Goldsmith 1976, Hart 1981; see also van der Hulst 1981). Hart offers an account of nasality in Guarani, in which the nasality feature is assigned to a separate autosegmental tier. Thus [m͡b] is assigned the representation in (14):

(14)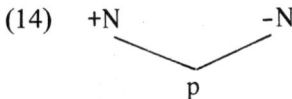

where the obstruent on the 'segment level' (p) is associated first with a +N specification and then with a -N specification on the 'span level' (so called because Guarani words can be broken down into oral and nasal spans; thus prenasalised stops occur at the border between a nasal span (or prosody) and a non-nasal span).

S. Anderson (1978) and Hoard (1978) offer complex segment analyses with respect to other phenomena. Anderson (1978: 54) claims that the initial cluster of Kabardian /t'p'ə n/ is an example of a cluster "which is simultaneously unitary and complex" (for reasons which need not concern us here), and as such should have a representation incorporating the complex segment analysis, as in (15):

(15)
syll	−	
cons	+	+
cont	−	−
lab	−	+
cor	+	−
ant	+	+
const. gl.	+	

while Hoard (1978: 70), following his earlier analysis, suggests that syllabic stops and affricates in Northwest Pacific languages are also complex segments.

Such solutions, then, incorporate a new structural property into the segmental distinctive feature matrix, essentially a structural variable which allows sequential change within the segment. Notice that if this notion were to be directly incorporated into the framework of dependency phonology, we would have to decide whether there were motivations for suggesting a greater degree of structure other than simple linear sequencing between the two elements of a complex segment. In other words, is there reason to suppose that there should be dependency relations within the segment between non-simultaneous elements?

In what follows, I shall investigate this problem, and I shall suggest that there is a structural variable (apart from intra-segmental change) common to the consonantal phenomena mentioned above. Further, I shall claim that this structural variable is such that it isolates the so-called 'complex segments' from other segments and sequences, and as such, removes the need for a decision on the question of a mono- or bisegmental analysis.

4. PRENASALISED CONSONANTS

There have been various proposals concerning the characterisation of the segments in the first column of (16) (from Ladefoged 1971: 34), which displays phonological contrasts involving prenasalised stops in Tiv:

(16) áa mbè   á bèndè   á mènà
      'she suckled'   'he touched'   'he swallowed'

      á ndèrà   á dè   á nèndà
      'he began'   'he left alone'   'he is backward in growth'

      á ndzùùr   á dzèndà
      'he muddled'   'he prohibited'

      á n̲d̲ ɔ́ ɣɔ́ i   á d̲ʒ i ŋgɔ́   á ɲàndè
      'he spoke quickly'   'he searched'   'he urinated'

      á ŋgòhòr   á gèmà
      'he received'   'he turned around'

      á ŋm͡gbahom   á g͡bèr
      'he approached'   'he slashed'

Herbert (1977: 257) notes the existence of the Nyanga pair in (17), which, at the phonetic level, contrasts a syllabic nasal followed by a voiced stop with a syllable-initial prenasalised voiced stop (although the underlying forms, in Herbert's analysis, display a different relationship):

(17) /m + bale/   [m̩bale]   (trisyllabic)   'brother'

      /n + bale/   [m͡bale]   (disyllabic)   'plate'

Herbert, who offers a comprehensive account of the analysis and behaviour of prenasalised consonants in a variety of languages, gives the following "phonetic definition" of a prenasalised consonant:

> A *prenasalized consonant* is formally defined as a necessarily homorganic sequence of nasal and non-nasal consonantal segments which together exhibit the approximate surface duration of 'simple' consonants in those language systems within which they function. (1977: 16).

Complex Segments

At the phonetic level, then, prenasalized consonants have the same length as other single consonantal segments, rather than clusters of two consonants. It is this fact, together with "the homorganicity of their components . . . and various other subtle phonetic adjustments which occur between the two components", which leads Herbert to treat them as units at the surface (phonetic) level. Notice further that prenasalised consonants only occur syllable-initially.

Chomsky and Halle (1968: 317) treat prenasalised consonants as single segments, as does Ladefoged (1971: 35), who suggests, in addition to the feature [nasality], a feature [prenasality], which

> must be defined in terms of the duration of an event. It is the duration of the velopharyngeal opening which occurs before another articulation such as an oral stop or fricative in circumstances which require the whole complex to be considered as one phonological unit.

Thus, prenasalised stops have the values [1prenasality, 0nasality].

These monosegmental solutions are criticised by S. Anderson (1974, 1976), as noted in §3. Much of his distributional argument is based on the tendency of nasality in consonants "to spread into adjacent vowels" (1976: 335). He observes that in Gbeya pure nasal consonants can be followed by nasal vowels, but prenasalised consonants must be followed by oral vowels. Similarly, he observes that Apinayé shows a series of voiced stops which may be nasal, prenasal, postnasal, or oral, depending on the nasality of the preceding and following vowels. The possibilities are:

(18)   [V b V]   [V b d V]
       [Ṽ m͡b V]   [Ṽ m d V]
       [V b͡m Ṽ]   [V b n Ṽ]
       [Ṽ m Ṽ]   [Ṽ m n Ṽ]

Thus, the difference between the four surface varieties of voiced stop is shown to be allophonic. A single intervocalic voiced stop (as in the first column) is oral between two non-nasalised vowels, as are intervocalic clusters of two voiced stops (as in the second column). A single intervocalic stop is prenasalised following a nasal vowel and preceding an oral vowel, and postnasalised if the reverse holds, while the first member of an intervocalic cluster takes its nasality value from the preceding vowel, and the second from the following vowel. This evidence leads Anderson to claim that features such as "[prenasal], [nasal], [postnasal], etc. quite miss the point, in that such features cannot be taken to have the entire segment as their domain". Rather, it is in relative timing (either within the segment or across segment-boundaries) that they differ, and it is for this reason that he proposes the analysis in (12) and (13).

A rather similar case from Sinhalese is cited by Feinstein (1979:251). In Sinhalese, a nasal consonant nasalises a contiguous vowel, rather than the other way round:

(19) mẽe   'this'   ãmmã   'mother, sg. def.'
     dee   'thing, sg. def.'   bõnTə   'to drink'
     mãase   'month, sg. def.'   kãndə   'hill, sg. def.'
     isnãanẽ 'bath, sg. def.'

However, forms with prenasalised consonants show nasalisation only on the preceding, not the following, vowel:

(20) kã^{n}dee 'trunk, sg. def. gen.' ã^{m}bee   'eel, sg. def.'
     ã^{ŋ}gə   'horn, sg. def.'   æ̃^{ŋ}gillə 'finger, sg. def.'

Herbert (1975: 108-109, 1977: 151-152) cites another type of analysis in which prenasalised consonants are treated as single consonants, at least at the surface level, that of Myers (1974). Myers proposes the use of 'vector features', which represent a "changing, vectoring value over the duration of the segment". In particular, she proposes the vector (or movement) feature [early velar closure]: prenasalised consonants ([+nasal, +early velar closure]) are treated as a sub-class of nasal consonants.

Herbert considers prenasalised consonants at the phonological level to be sequences of nasal + consonant. He argues that in, for example, Luganda, the "so-called prenasalized consonants ... function in separate syllables until very late in the application of phonological rules" (1975: 120). At the abstract level, then, the nasal and oral components derive from independent nasal and oral segments in different syllables, while, as we have seen, Herbert considers them to be units at the phonetic level.

In Herbert's system, there are no difficulties in characterising 'prenasalised stops' at the phonological level - they are simply two distinct segments. For their representation at the phonetic level, where they have a unit status, he proposes the incorporation of 'phonetic vector specifications', which differ from the vector features proposed by Myers, in that they "make use of ordinary, motivated features and incorporate the same information as an ad hoc feature posited to account for the movement of articulators within a single segment. Thus, for example, the continuant specification for /nz/ would be [-→+cont]." (1977: 185). Thus, prenasalised voiced stops and fricatives would be represented as (21) and (22):

(21) $\begin{bmatrix} +\text{voi} \\ +{\rightarrow}-\text{nas} \\ -\text{cont} \end{bmatrix}$ (22) $\begin{bmatrix} +\text{voi} \\ +{\rightarrow}-\text{nas} \\ -{\rightarrow}+\text{cont} \end{bmatrix}$

Feinstein (1979) offers a characterisation of the prenasalised consonants in which they are bisegmental sequences, phonetically as well as phonologically. Noting that these consonants can only occur in syllable-initial position, he claims that

> in a theory of phonology which incorporates a direct representation of syllable structure . . . 'prenasalized consonants' and ordinary NC (homorganic nasal-oral consonant) clusters alike are represented as sequences of discrete homorganic nasal and oral consonants. (1979: 246).

Thus Feinstein abandons Anderson's monosegmental approach, and the way in which he distinguishes between the Sinhalese forms in (23) (1979: 247):

(23) ka^{n}də   'trunk, sg. def.'
      kandə   'hill, sg. def.'

Rather, Feinstein distinguishes between the two forms by means of different syllable structures, as in (24):

(24) ka\$ndə
      kan\$də

"The representations . . . involve no purely segmental distinction." Notice that Feinstein observes that, at the phonetic level, the difference in the relative duration of the nasals in the two forms in (23) might have to be characterised; this, however, does not function "in any linguistically significant way".

Feinstein, too, points out the difficulties which Ladefoged's system would have in accounting for data such as (19) and (20), in that all prenasalised stops are [−nas] (as well as being [+prenas]), and so the Sinhalese rule nasalising vowels contiguous to nasal consonants, which he formalises as (25), fails to affect vowels preceding prenasalised consonants:

(25) [+syll] → [+nas] % [+nas] ──────

(where % denotes the use of the mirror-image convention). Indeed, Feinstein claims (1979: 252) that

> monosegmental analyses of this sort all fail to capture the obvious generalisation about 'prenasalized consonants' with respect to vowel nasalisation, namely that they behave as though they are clusters of nasal and oral consonants.

As noted above, Feinstein considers prenasalised stops to be tautosyllabic, and, further, always to form a syllabic onset. He claims, indeed, that this is the defining characteristic of what are usually called prenasalised consonants, while phonetically identical clusters which are not tautosyllabic are not so interpreted.

It seems that various aspects of the models of prenasalisation discussed above (at least of those incorporating some sort of 'complexity' or bisegmentality assumption) can be reconciled by appealing to the model of dependency phonology. The apparent difference between the various analyses is, I suggest, due to a failure to take account of the kinds of structural properties inherent in the dependency model; in particular, the characterisation of the syllable and its structure.

As we saw in §1, the internal structure of the syllable, as far as relative precedence is concerned, generally follows the sonority hierarchy. In the 'normal' syllable, then, the centre of the syllable is the most prominent and the margins least prominent, with any sequentially intermediate segments also intermediate in dependency. Feinstein (1979: 255) notices that the sonority hierarchy theory of syllable structure predicts that a syllable-initial prenasalised stop is unexpected: "in a /$ndV/ syllable ... the sonority of the initial nasal is greater than that of the following stop". Herbert (1977: 87), too, observes that the fact that the order of components in prenasalised consonants is contrary to the sonority hierarchy is "a singly important piece of evidence traditionally cited as pointing to the unitary status of prenasalized consonants". Thus, a syllable which begins with a prenasalised stop violates the general principles of syllable structure. In dependency terms, a nasal is more |V|-like than a voiced stop, and so is expected to occur nearer to the syllabic. In terms of sequence, this is not the case. However, if we maintain the expected hierarchical relation between the nasal and the stop nodes, such that the stop is dependent on the nasal, the representation of, for example, Tiv /mbè/ will be:

(26)

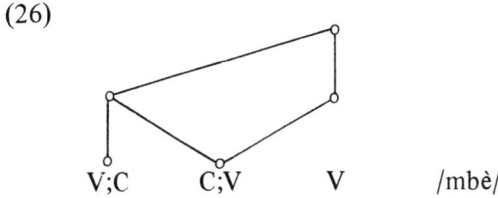

V;C   C;V   V   /mbè/

(26), then, shows a characterisation of the prenasalised stop in which reversed dependency is apparent, in that precedence and dependency are not related in the expected way. Notice that, as well as the nasal node being dependent on the vowel node (the governor of the syllable), the oral

Complex Segments

stop node is dependent on a subjoined copy of the vowel. Thus, the nasal is the governor of the whole onset, but the oral node nevertheless also has a direct dependency relation with the vowel, thus indicating the status of the prenasalised stop as a sub-type of stop. The representation of these consonants, then, which are deviant with respect to syllable structure, involves an extra hierarchical level – analogous with the units discussed in §1.

In this dependency analysis, the difference between Sinhalese /kandə/ (/ka$ndə/ in Feinstein's syllabification) and /kandɔ/ (/kan$də/) would be:

(27) a.   b.

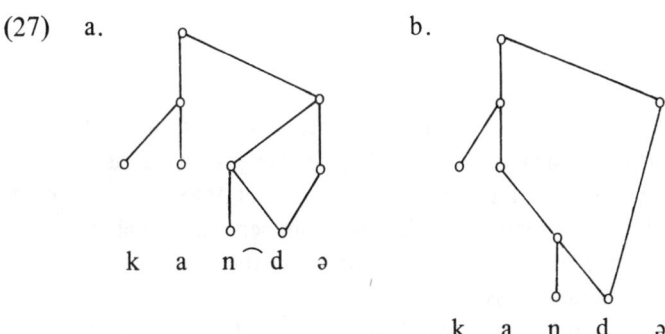

In (27)b, /d/ is ambisyllabic (occurring in foot-internal position), while in (27)a. the prenasalised stop belongs only to the second syllable – as we have seen, these items can occur only syllable-initially.

Thus, prenasalised stops are invariably represented by a reversed dependency structure, while 'normal' N+C clusters are not. What I want to claim, then, is that the structure represented in abstract form in (28) is associated with the deviant status of these elements:

(28)

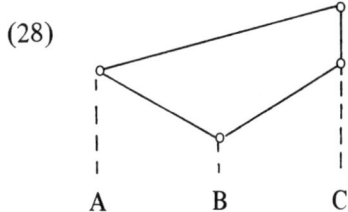

Further, structures like (26) reflect the tendency noted by Herbert for prenasalised stops to be derived from separate syllables. The kind of configuration in (28) is that more usually associated with separate syllables – as it has two sonority 'peaks' (A and C), which, under other circumstances, would correspond to two syllabic elements. The other circumstances, of course, concern the nodes to which B is attached. If B is an intervocalic consonant, then it forms the onset of the second syllable, and is adjoined to the syllabic governor. It also forms the coda of the first syllable, and so is attached to the head of the rhyme, as in (29), the structure for a bisyllabic foot:

(29)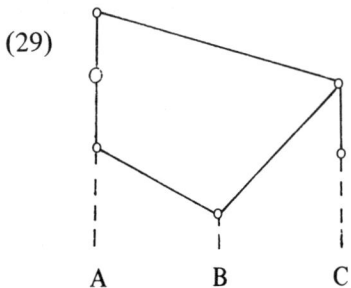

Notice also that C is dependent on A, the governor of the foot.

However, although structures like (26) correctly characterise certain aspects of the behaviour of prenasalised stops (that they are a sub-class of stops, and that they tend to be derived from separate syllables), they do not reflect the fact that prenasalised stops have the length of single segments. (28), as noted above, is formally not very different from normal sequences. In other words, although their representation reflects the fact that they are made up of two sequentially distinct elements, it does not characterise their status as a single phonological unit (or as having the length of a single segment). I suggest that in the course of the derivation of prenasalised consonants, B becomes uniquely dependent on A (cf. the case of ambisyllabic consonants, which become uniquely dependent on the following syllabic if they are foot-initial - Anderson and Ewen to appear). Thus the surface representation for prenasalised consonants is:

(30)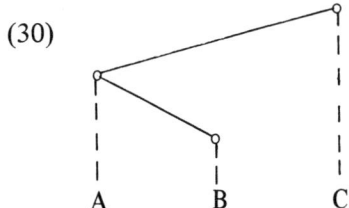

The fact, then, that prenasalised stops behave as single units can now be associated with the counter-sequential dependence of B on A, together with the fact that the syllabic governor has only A directly dependent on it. As we shall see, the operation of the process giving (30) allows us to distinguish prenasalised stops from clusters of [s] followed by a stop, which in other respects show a similar representation, but which do not

Complex Segments

have the length of single segments. The structure in (30), then, as we shall again see in the case of the affricates, correlates with the fact that prenasalised stops have a shorter duration than normal bisegmental clusters.

The characterisation of prenasalised consonants in these terms is, I think, compatible with the evidence for either a unit or a cluster approach. Although the nasal part and the oral part of, say, /n̂d/ are under separate nodes, and may therefore be interpreted as distinct segments, it seems equally possible to suggest that the presence of the reversed dependency structure represents not two phonological segments, but two phonetic events functioning as one phonological unit, or at least showing greater intimacy than in the unmarked case, where relative sequential distance from the syllabic correlates with relative hierarchical distance. The 'deviant' structure, then, characterises the deviant nature of such elements, and the controversy surrounding their segmental status is, in this model, shown to be a function of their structure. Whether we call prenasalised consonants one segment or two, phonologically, is unimportant within the dependency model — their unique status is characterised by making use of the greater richness of phonological structure available within this model than within the frameworks employed by S. Anderson, Herbert, and Feinstein (or indeed by Ladefoged and Chomsky and Halle). Further, notice that the fact that prenasalised consonants occur only syllable-initially is naturally reflected in the framework proposed here — in syllable-final position such sequences would show the regular dependency structure.

The analysis of postnasalised stops such as those in (18) will proceed in a similar fashion. Postnasalised stops have the "distributional and phonological properties of single segments" (S. Anderson 1976: 332), and seem to occur only syllable-finally. In the dependency model, then, we will have the following tree for [kaid̂n], a form created by the partial denasalisation rules of Land Dayak, which have the effect of creating a postnasalised stop in word-final position (Hyman 1975: 256, Herbert 1977: 317):

(31)

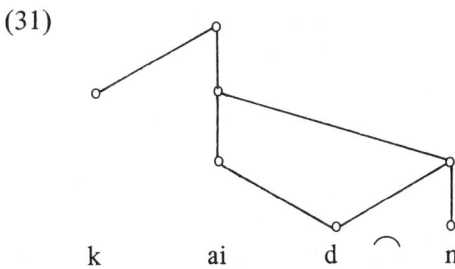

k   ai   d   n

where we again see the reversed dependency structure, this time in postvocalic position, so that the oral stop component precedes the nasal stop component, and is dependent on it. (I ignore here the problem of the representation of the complex nucleus.)

S. Anderson (1976: 335) reports a third type of element, a 'medionasalised' stop [b͡mb], which occurs as a conditioned variant of prenasalised stops in Kaingáng. The representation for these segment-types will follow the same pattern, with both the oral components being dependent on the nasal, which is in turn dependent on both syllabics.

Notice that the difficulties which were noted in a monosegmental analysis of pre- and post-nasalised consonants with respect to the characterisation of the 'spread' of nasality from nasal consonants into contiguous vowels (in the case of Sinhalese) or from nasalised vowels into contiguous consonants (in the case of Apinayé) are not apparent within the dependency model, as in an autosegmental account. Nasal spread is dependent simply on the sequential order of nodes (whether or not these nodes are interpreted as separate segments). Thus, Sinhalese [kã͡ndə] and [kãndə] both show nasalisation on the first vowel because it is contiguous to a nasal node, and not on the second, which is not. Similarly, Apinayé sequences such as [Vb͡mṼ], [VbnṼ], [Ṽm͡bV], and [ṼmdV] show nasalisation spreading into the contiguous stop; if, simultaneously, an oral vowel on the other side of a single consonant or consonant cluster inhibits nasalisation, then nasal spread will be prevented from affecting the whole consonant or cluster, thus giving a pre- or post-nasalised stop in the case of a single consonant, and a cluster of nasal followed by oral stop, or oral followed by nasal stop, in the case of a consonant cluster.

5. *SP, ST, SK* CLUSTERS

The next area which I want to deal with involves the analysis of clusters of [s] followed by a stop, as in English *spate, master, task,* etc. The analysis of these clusters (which I shall transcribe as [sC] for the purpose of the discussion) raises some of the same problems as have been noted with respect to prenasalised consonants. Phonetically, syllable-initial [sC] clusters violate the sonority hierarchy, in that the [s] is more sonorant than the stop. Typically, [s] in such clusters takes a distinct chest pulse, or "burst of muscle drive" (Catford 1977: 90). Phonologically, the clusters deviate in various ways from the normal patterns in languages. They show different distributional properties from other clusters; notably, they can occur both syllable-initially and syllable-finally, whereas (in accordance with the sonority hierarchy) syllable-final clusters in a language are generally the mirror-image of syllable-initial clusters (e.g. /pr-/ *vs.* /-rp/, /kl-/ *vs.* /-lk/). In addition, as Kuryłowicz (1971: 195) notes, [sC] clusters deviate from the normal alliteration rules "in the inherited Germanic verse".

Complex Segments

While initial *p*- may alliterate with clusters such as *pr*- and *pl*-, and *h*- with *hr*-, *hl*-, and *hn*-, *s*- may not alliterate with *sk*-, *sp*-, *st*-, nor *sk*- with *sp*-, *sp*- with *st*-, etc. Rather, "*sk* can alliterate with *sk*, *st* only with *st*, *sp* only with *sp*".

These facts have led some phonologists to analyse [sC] as a single phonological unit, although such sequences have usually been given a bisegmental analysis. In bisegmental analyses, the [s] is generally identified with /s/ in, for example, English *sate*, and the stop is identified either with the /p t k/ series, or with the /b d g/ series, or is treated as an archiphoneme – for discussion, see Davidsen-Nielsen (1975).

The fact that [sC] sequences violate the sonority hierarchy leads Anderson and Jones (1977: 125) to propose that they, like the prenasalised consonants discussed in §4, show a reversed dependency structure, as in (32):

(32)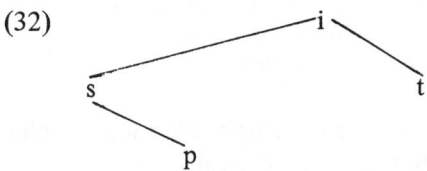

in which "the degree of dependency accords with the prominence of |V|", thus giving a structure in which [s] governs [p].

In what follows, I shall discuss the various arguments put forward for a monosegmental analysis of [sC], arguments which tend to support the reversed dependency structure proposed by Anderson and Jones. This structure, I shall argue, displays the same phonological properties as that proposed for prenasalised consonants (although, as we shall see, the phonetic characterisation is rather different).

Arguments for the unitary status of [sC] clusters come from various sources. Vogt (1942: 14), for example, notes that [sC] in Norwegian, unlike other clusters, can form both initial and final clusters. No other initial *xy* clusters can occur finally, but they *can* occur finally in the reverse order, i.e. as *yx*. "The clusters *sp*- etc. do not behave as the other clusters, they behave in all respects as single phonemes." Thus we find initial and final *st* and *sk*, and also initial *st-r*-, *sk-r*- vs. final *-r-st*, *-r-sk* in Norwegian. This leads Vogt to characterise [sC] clusters as 'composite phonemes'. If they are so treated, then the violations of the syllable structure rules are eliminated; initial [sC]r- (i.e. *xy*) parallels with final -r[sC] (i.e. *yx*), where *x* is the composite phoneme /sC/ and *y* the phoneme /r/. A similar argument is offered by Sigurd (1965: 62), with respect to Swedish.

Kohler (1967: 51) offers rather different reasons for treating [sC] as a unit. He interprets /sp, st, sk/ in English as 'single sequential elements', partly because it would be arbitrary to interpret "the stop section as /p, t, k/", and partly "to separate the inherent structures /sp, st, sk/ from the alien ones /sf, sv/", which *are* interpreted as biphonemic sequences.

Fudge's (1969) arguments are primarily concerned with syllable structure. He claims that the onset of English syllables contains two 'places', the first of which (place 1) may be filled by various phonemes, such as /p t č k/, /b d ǰ g/, /sp st sk/, and the second by /w l r/. Fudge, then, treats [sC] clusters as single phonemes, and claims further that this is preferable to an alternative analysis, in which [sC] clusters are treated as biphonemic, in that

> it avoids the necessity of postulating an extra place in the syllable structure (place 0) at which a system of only one element operates, and which must be filled by zero except when place 1 contains p, t, k, m, n, and perhaps f, v; other advantages include the avoidance of an arbitrary decision on whether to identify the stop portion of [sp] with the stop of series *a* (i.e. [p]) or that of series *b* (i.e. [b]). (1969: 273).

Kuryłowicz (1971) interprets [sC] clusters as being neither unitary phonemes nor biphonemic sequences, but as 'phonological compounds'. He cites evidence to support this claim from various sources, such as alliteration and the behaviour of initial and final clusters. He notes that in Latin, Gothic, and English an opposition exists in word-final position between -sT and -Ts (i.e. [-sC] *vs.* [-Cs]), but in word-initial position only sT- ([sC-]) occurs:

(33)　word-final　　　-sT : -Ts
　　　word-initial　　　sT-

> The phonological status of sT- (taken as a whole, not its components) is therefore different from that of -sT. The latter is, as against the former, *permutable*. The elements of -sT are on an equal footing. Each of them may occupy the first or the second place within the cluster. Not so in sT-, where the order of the elements is rigid. (1971: 197).

This leads Kuryłowicz to draw a parallel between syntactic compounds and sT-; as the defining feature of compounds is their rigid order, sT- is to be treated as a phonological compound. This in turn leads to the claim that clusters of three consonants are to be considered as "dichotomous groups with different degrees of internal cohesion". Thus, initial *str-* in the languages under consideration shows a structure in which *s* and *t* show the greatest internal cohesion, and together form a group with *r*, as in (34):

Complex Segments

(34)   [(s + t) + r]

There is, then, a great deal of evidence to support the view that the elements of [sC] clusters are, at least, more intimately linked than those of normal consonant clusters, whether or not this means that they should be interpreted as single segments, and this evidence tends to support the interpretation of initial [sC] clusters as displaying a reversed dependency structure as in (32). However, the structure offered by Anderson and Jones is not sufficiently rich to bring out all the characteristics of syllable-initial [sC] sequences. Rather, an analysis similar to that for prenasalised consonants seems appropriate:

(35)

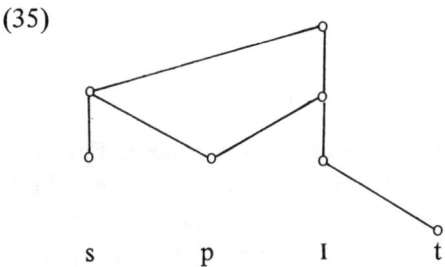

    s   p   I   t

where [p] is simultaneously dependent on [s] and on the vowel. This analysis again allows us to represent the bisegmental phonological status of [sC], and also to characterise the fact that the constraints on [sCL] sequences (where L is a liquid) are typically the same as constraints on [CL] sequences. Thus, in English, we find neither [stl] nor [tl]. A word such as *split*, then, will have the structure:

(36)

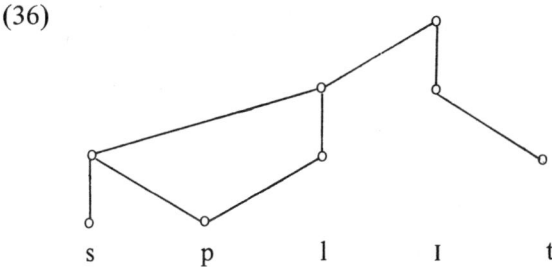

    s   p   l   I   t

in which [p] is again bidependent, this time on [s] and on [l], which is then simultaneously head of the onset, and of a unit which we might label 'sub-onset'.

Notice that in the case of [sC], unlike the prenasalised consonants, the stop remains bidependent; i.e. the dependency are linking [p] and [I] in (35), and [p] and [l] in (36), is not deleted in the course of the derivation.

This, I suggest, reflects the phonetic differences between the two types – the [sC] clusters do not have the length of a single segment, but of a normal consonant cluster. This is not apparent in the various unitary analyses discussed above. This suggests that there is a gradient between segment and cluster – prenasalised consonants are nearer the segment-end of the gradient than the [sC] clusters.

The interpretation of [sC] clusters as having a reversed dependency structure has other advantages. Such structures can occur intervocalically in English feet, as in *fester*. In a theory of syllable structure in which such intervocalic consonants are assigned to syllables according to their potential for syllable-initial and syllable-final occurrence in monosyllables, *fester* would have the following syllable-bracketing:

(37) [fɛ[st]ər]
      1 2 1 2

Words containing intervocalic [sC] clusters are the only ones in English to show syllable boundary placement such that two consonants are ambisyllabic – because of the fact that these are the only clusters which can occur both syllable-initially and syllable-finally. If these clusters are given a reversed dependency structure, then *fester* will have the following representation:

(38)
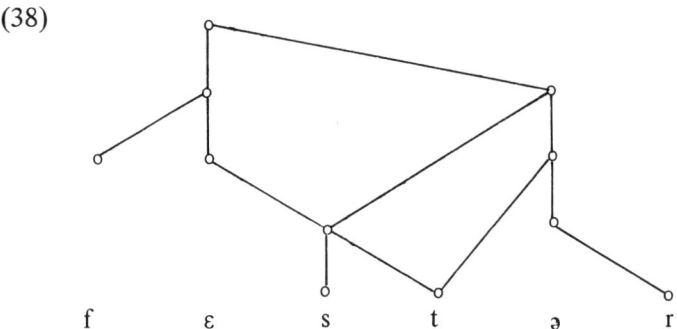

in which only [s] is directly dependent on the two syllabics. Thus, a universal constraint can be maintained that only one consonant can be simultaneously directly dependent on two syllabics. In all other cases where we have more than one intervocalic consonant, only one can be ambisyllabic, as in (39):

(39) [fɛn[d]ər]   [mɛ[t]rɪk]
      1 2 1 2   1 2 1 2

Complex Segments

Notice that this treatment effectively eliminates an objection of Kahn (1976: 20) to the assumption that [sC] may be ambisyllabic. He argues that this assumption means that the representation of *Boston*, in "line-of-association form", will be:

(40)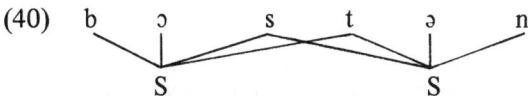

i.e. we have an example of a tree showing 'tangling' – the association lines linking the syllable labels to the segments cross. This objection is removed in the treatment outlined here, in which a non-linear approach to the structure of [sC] is adopted.

Lastly in this section, notice that [sC] clusters in syllable-final position will show a regular structure, as in English *past*:

(41)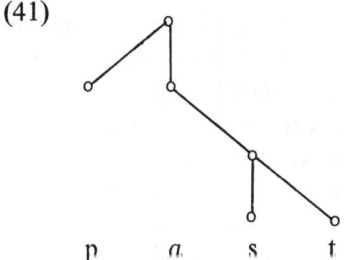

6. AFFRICATES

As noted in §3, the characterisation of affricates with respect to the monosegmental/bisegmental interpretation problem has been a matter of controversy in the literature (see, for some discussion, Sommerstein 1977: 28-29). The differing views are apparent at the level of traditional phonemic transcription systems: as Campbell (1974: 59) notes, affricates in the IPA transcription tradition are given the 'complex symbol' representations /tʃ/ and /dʒ/, while American tradition (as exemplified by Bloomfield 1933) uses the unitary symbols /č/ and /ǰ/.

It is clear that, phonetically, two distinct 'events' are involved in the production of affricates – a closure phase and a friction phase – whether or not these are interpreted as two phonological segments. As such, they are held by many to be identical to those sequences of stop and (homorganic) fricative which are not considered to be affricates. Representative views are to be found in various introductory books: thus Abercrombie (1967: 148) observes:

> When the friction following the stop is sufficiently marked to be considered a separate segment, the cluster of stop and homorganic fricative is usually known as an *affricate* ... the term is only used when it is convenient to treat the cluster as a single phonological unit.

while Catford (1977: 211) remarks:

> Generally speaking, we reserve the term 'affricate' just for those sequences of stop and homorganic fricative that occur within one and the same syllable, and that are regarded, for a variety of reasons, not necessarily phonetic, as representing unit phonemes in a given language. Thus, although the final [ts] in German *Spatz* [ʃpats] and English *cats* [kæts] may be phonetically identical, we generally call the former an 'affricate', but the latter merely a sequence of stop plus fricative.

Finally, Sommerstein (1977: 28) concludes that "it is ... best to proceed on the assumption that the existence of such contrasts [i.e. between affricates and stop/fricative sequences] cannot be determined".

However, Newton (1972: 132-134) makes a phonetic distinction between [t^s] and [ts] in dialects of Modern Greek spoken in Rhodes, as in [peát^{s}i] 'child' from underlying /peðáki/, but [látsi] 'wells' from underlying /lákki/ and [papútsi] 'shoe' from /papútsi/, where [t^s] is a 'voiceless dental affricate'. In many dialects, he observes, 'degemination' (of /kk/) operates to remove the distinction between [t^s] and [ts] (all of the forms turning up as affricates), but "in Rhodes ... the absence of degemination still permits an opposition in terms of length: [t^{s}ilá]:[tsillá]". Similarly, Herbert (1977: 440) gives the following set of Polish minimal pairs, which appear to show a difference between "unit and non-unit stop-fricative sequences":

(42) czech   [č̑ɛx]   'Czech'   trzech   [t̑ʂɛx]   '3' (gen.)
      czysta [č̑Ista]   'clean' (fem.)   trzysta [t̑ʂIsta] '300'
      paczy   [pač̑I]   'warps'   patrzy   [pat̑ʂI]   'look'
      oczyma [oč̑Ima]   'eyes' (instr.) otrzyma [ot̑ʂIma] 'obtains'
      czy   [č̑I]   'whether'   trzy   [t̑ʂI]   '3'

(Notice, however, that, as in the Greek set, the opposition between the affricates and the stop-fricative sequences is often no longer apparent; the 'non-unit' sequences being commonly replaced by the affricates.)

Newton and Herbert's evidence might appear to support an analysis in which affricates are treated as monosegmental, although Catford's argument does not. Let us assume, in any case, that at least phonologically, our system of representation must enable us to make a distinction between the two categories – affricates and sequences of stop + fricative.

Complex Segments

The kinds of solution proposed within feature theory parallel quite closely those put forward for the prenasalised consonants discussed in §4. Chomsky and Halle and Ladefoged have monosegmental analyses: Chomsky and Halle distinguish affricates from stops by means of a feature [delayed release], affricates being [+del rel], by virtue of the fact that the closure phase is released more slowly than in the production of a stop, and from fricatives by being [-cont]. Ladefoged uses two features [stop] and [fricative] to cross-classify the three categories – stops are [1stop, 0fricative], fricatives are [0 stop, 1fricative], while affricates have positive values for both features, thus allowing us to show that "affricates are related to both fricatives and stops" (1971: 55).

Complex segment analyses are proposed by various phonologists, as discussed in §3. One of the areas in which proponents of the complex segment theory claim that monosegmental analyses are inadequate is 'amalgamation' rules, "by which I mean rules in which unit segments are produced by a convergence of underlying separate segments" (Campbell 1974: 61). Campbell claims that a rule such as (43), which amalgamates the sequence [t] + [š] to produce the affricate [tš] fails to reveal the relationship between the two:

(43)
$$\overset{t}{\begin{bmatrix} -\text{continuant} \\ +\text{anterior} \\ +\text{coronal} \end{bmatrix}} + \overset{š}{\begin{bmatrix} +\text{continuant} \\ -\text{anterior} \\ +\text{coronal} \end{bmatrix}} \rightarrow \begin{bmatrix} +\text{delayed release} \\ -\text{anterior} \\ +\text{coronal} \end{bmatrix}$$

> There is no real change in feature composition, for both the articulatory gestures of t and š are still present in the affricate, and the only real change is in their unitary status.

This, however, is not revealed by the formulation in (43). In the complex segment analysis, these amalgamation rules would have the form in (44):

(44)
$$\begin{bmatrix} -\text{continuant} \\ +\text{anterior} \\ +\text{coronal} \end{bmatrix} + \begin{bmatrix} +\text{continuant} \\ -\text{anterior} \\ +\text{coronal} \end{bmatrix} \rightarrow \begin{bmatrix} -\text{continuant} & +\text{continuant} \\ -\text{anterior} & \\ +\text{coronal} & \end{bmatrix}$$

It is not immediately obvious how affricates are to be characterised within dependency phonology. In that they consist of two phonetic units functioning as a single phonological unit, we might expect them to show the same kind of reversed dependency structure as those proposed for prenasalised consonants and [sC] clusters, and, indeed, Anderson and Jones (1977: 126) propose (without defending their choice) (45) as the appropriate representation for (voiceless) affricates:

(45)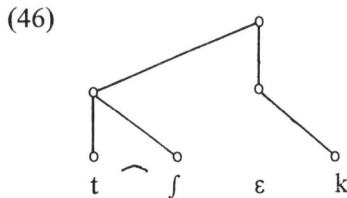

Thus, English *check* might have the categorial representation in (46):

(46)

Similarly, the distinction between (Rhodes) Greek [t^{S}ilá] and [tsillá], or Polish [ʑɛx] and [tʲɕɛx], might be shown as in (47) and (48):

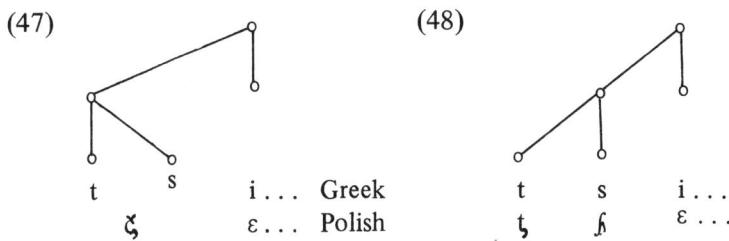

(where I ignore the structure after the first vowel). (47) displays the reversed dependency structure which Anderson and Jones take to characterise affricates, while (48) displays the dependency relations holding within a 'normal' syllable.

However, the structures in (46) and (47) diverge from the normal syllable structure in rather a different way than the structures postulated in §§4 and 5 for prenasalised consonants and [sC] clusters. In setting up the reversed dependency structure for these elements, I argued that this was appropriate in that the more sonorant element preceded the less sonorant element, and as such, should be the governor. However, this is not the case in Anderson and Jones' analysis of the affricates. Rather, (48) displays the expected structure (in that fricatives are more |V|-like than stops), while the suggested structure for affricates deviates from the expected pattern. We may refer to this kind of reversed structure as showing DEPENDENCY REVERSAL, and the kind displayed by prenasalised consonants as SEQUENCE REVERSAL. There appears at first sight to be no phonetic justification for the reversed structure in the case of dependency reversal. If this structure is to be incorporated into the system of representation, then, we must find arguments from other areas.

Complex Segments

We have seen that most of the arguments for the phonological status of affricates have involved the claim that they are phonetically identical to stop + fricative sequences. The arguments for setting up affricates as units, then, are purely phonological; there is no necessary aspect of the phonetic signal to justify the claim (although there may be phonetic support in the case of, for example, Rhodes Greek). Bearing this in mind, it seems that the justification for structures like (46) must be phonological; associated with the claim that a stop + fricative sequence forms a single phonological unit in a particular language is the reversed dependency structure, which appears to be characteristic of 'complex segments'.

I suggest that the representation for affricates differs in one further respect from those previously considered, in that it involves a structure in which, throughout the derivation, the 'fricative' node is dependent only on the 'stop' node, and not on the syllabic governor, i.e. a structure of the form in (49):

(49)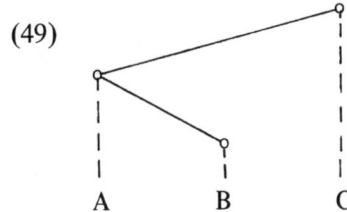

In terms of the segment/sequence gradient, then, they seem to be more segment-like than the prenasalised consonants, which only develop the structure in (49) as a result of the deletion of the dependency arc linking B and C. This appropriately represents the difference in length between [t^s] and [ts] in Greek. The bisegmental [ts] has the structure-pattern in (50):

(50)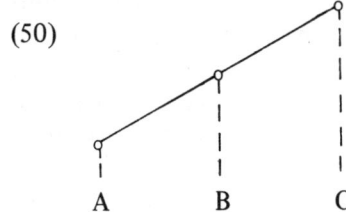

In (49), A, which is temporally more closely related to C than in (50), is also more closely related in terms of the structures involved; the structures, then, predict that the duration of the consonantal structure in (47) is potentially less than the 'normal' structures exemplified by (48).

A further argument for the structure in which |C| governs |V,C| (and, indeed, in which |V,C| is not simultaneously dependent on the syllabic governor — cf. the argument for the prenasalised consonants) would involve the claim that affricates are a sub-class of stops, rather than fricatives. Such a categorisation is inherent in Chomsky and Halle's feature system, where stops and affricates are [-cont], as opposed to fricatives, but not in Ladefoged's system, in which affricates differ 'equally' from stops and fricatives. Herbert (1977: 163-164) appears to suggest that affricates function more often with stops than with fricatives; and it seems likely that affricates typically develop historically from stops (perhaps via aspiration), rather than from fricatives (consider, for example, MdEng *church* < WGmc *kirika* and MdEng *chin* < CGmc *kinn-*).

If the reversed dependency structure is adopted for affricates, MdEng *judge* will have the representation in (51):

(51)

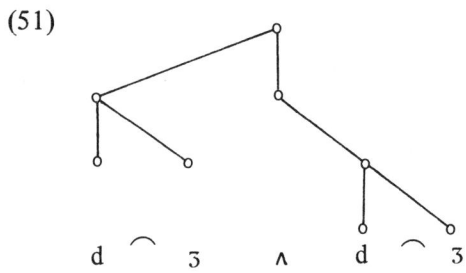

In postvocalic position, then, affricates have the expected dependency shape (relative to distance from the syllabic), in that the final element (the fricative phase of the affricate) is dependent on the penultimate (the stop phase); however, the reversed dependency structure is still apparent, in that the more sonorant element is still dependent on the less sonorant. Thus, we have both sequence and dependency reversal, yielding an apparently 'non-reversed' configuration. Notice, too, that in postvocalic position we do not find contrasts in length between affricates and stop + fricative clusters (of the [t^s] vs. [ts] sort); we have already seen that Catford claims that final /t͡s/ in German is phonetically identical with the final sequence /ts/ in English. In this case, then, it seems appropriate that we do not have a structure in which the element further from the nucleus governs the element nearer to the nucleus — such a structure would imply, on the argument outlined above, the possibility of phonetic shortening.

The question remains, however, as to what exactly the appropriate structure for English final /ts/ clusters should be. These clusters are, phonologically, never interpreted as affricates. In that /s/ is more sonorant than /t/, we might expect (52) to be a suitable structure for English *cats*:

(52)

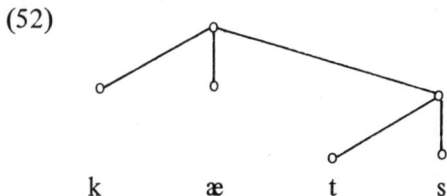

However, (52) implies that /ts/ has a unit status, which contradicts normal phonological analyses of these clusters in final position, and would suggest that /ts/ has the length of a single segment. Similarly, if /s/ is taken to be dependent on /t/, we have the structure already proposed for affricates.

These /ts/ clusters involve dependency reversal, and have the length of a normal cluster. As such, they appear to be mirror-images of initial /st/ clusters, and therefore the representation in (53) seems appropriate:

(53)

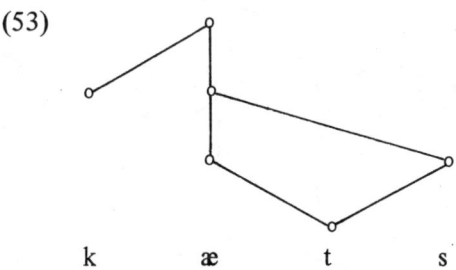

Notice, however, that English /ts/ clusters do not have the same phonological status as [sC] clusters. They (and /dz/ clusters) arise only as a result of morphological processes (plural formation, 3rd person present tense formation, possessive formation). They do not occur intramorphemically (with the exception of a very few words such as *adze*). I suggest, then, that in the operation of these processes, the realisation of the bound morpheme ([s] or [z]) is attached directly to the governor of the rhyme of the free morpheme, while at the same time becoming governor of the /t/.

Given the arguments of this section and §4 above, it is clear that prenasalised affricates, such as those in Tiv /á ndzùùr/, /á nd͡ʒɔ́ɣɔ̀ i/, will be given a representation involving a reversed dependency structure with three nodes. Herbert, using Campbell's complex segment proposal, characterises the prenasalised affricates as (54):

(54) $\begin{bmatrix} +\text{cons} \\ -\text{voc} \\ +\text{voice} \quad +\text{voice} \\ +\text{nasal} \quad -\text{nasal} \\ +\text{ant} \\ +\text{cor} \\ -\text{cont} \quad\quad +\text{cont} \end{bmatrix}$

Phonologically, these will have the dependency representation in (55), showing bidependency of the stop node; phonetically, in accordance with the discussion in §3, and their status as segment-like elements, we find the structure in (56):

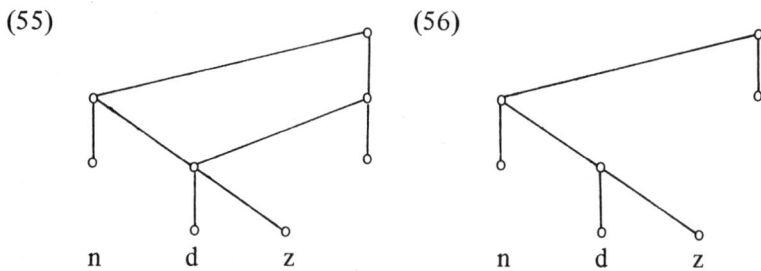

(55)   (56)

n   d   z   n   d   z

7. PREASPIRATION

In this section I consider a phenomenon whose treatment in dependency terms appears to be rather different from those discussed in the previous sections, but whose interpretation, nevertheless, has raised problems with respect to its status as a phonological segment. Various languages show preaspirated consonants, for example, Gaelic, Icelandic, and various dialects of the other Nordic languages, while Welsh provides an example of a language with preaspirated vowels. For a general discussion of preaspiration, see Kylstra (1972).

As in the case of the other phenomena discussed in this paper, there has been some discussion in the literature as to whether preaspirated consonants should be interpreted phonologically as one segment or two. Borgstrøm (1940: 20-21), for example, gives pairs in Lewis Gaelic which show an opposition between preaspirated and unaspirated stops:

(57) glac   [gla^{h}k]   'grasp!' (imper.)
      glag, clag [glàg]   'a bell'
      at   [a^{h}t]   'a fester'
      ad   [ad̦]   'a hat'

Borgstrøm considers the possibility of regarding the preaspirated stops "as groups of consonants (h + occlusive)", but rejects this possibility because, among other reasons, "the preaspiration is shorter than an ordinary h in the same dialect, and shorter than that of the group ht etc. in the southern dialects". Thus, he interprets the Lewis preaspirated stops as single phonemes. However, preaspiration in the other dialects which Borgstrøm (1940, 1941) considers is given a different characterisation. In these dialects, the sequence of preaspiration + stop is treated as a group of two phonemes, partly because of the length of the [h]-segment - "Ross dialects have occlusives preceded by a very distinct and long h" (1941: 100) - and partly because the preaspiration is not realised only by [h], but also by [x] and [ç]. Thus we find the transcriptions in (58) for the Ross-shire forms:

(58) cat   [k'a^{h}t]   'cat'
      boc   [bo̯hk]   'a buck'

As Herbert (1977: 86) points out, the phonetic sequence [k^{h}a^{h}t] is said to be "the realization of three underlying phonemes . . . /k^h/, /a/, and /t^h/" in the Lewis dialect, while in the other dialects the string [k^{h}aht] (which Herbert calls 'phonetically identical') is composed of four underlying phonemes: /k^h/, /a/, /h/, /t/.

Ternes (1973: 57ff), in considering the Applecross dialect of Scots Gaelic, argues that "the sequences resulting from historical preaspiration are interpreted partly monophonemically, partly biphonemically". Thus, 'fricative + stop' sequences occurring medially and finally, which do not have mirror-image counterparts in initial position, are interpreted as biphonemic /çp çf çk̬ xk/. All '[^{h}] + stop' sequences, "which do have mirror-symmetrical counterparts in initial positions", are monophonemic: /p^h t^h t̬^{h} k̬^{h} k^h/. These phonemes have initial 'postaspirated' allophones [p^h t^h], and final 'preaspirated' allophones [^{h}p ^{h}t].

Various views have been put forward with respect to the Icelandic data in (59), presented by Thráinsson (1978):

(59)   *Fem. sg.*   *Neut. sg.*
     feit [fei:t^h] 'fat'   feitt [feiht]
     ljót [ljou:t^h] 'ugly'   ljótt [ljouht]
     sæt   [sai:t^h] 'sweet'   sætt   [saiht]

Icelandic shows two series of voiceless stops - unaspirated *b d g* (known traditionally as 'soft' - Árnason 1980: 9), and aspirated *p t k* (known as 'hard'). The two series can be represented phonetically as [p t k] *vs.* [p^h t^h k^h]. Notice that if the *p t k* is preaspirated, as in the second column of (59), it is not also (post)-aspirated.

Haugen (1958: 72) argues for a treatment of the 'fortis' series of stops (*p t k*) in which both preaspiration and postaspiration are interpreted as "components of fortis stops; in each case the aspiration occurs on the side of the consonant closest to the syllabic". Thus, in Haugen's model aspiration is the defining factor of the *p t k* series. His phonemic representations for the two series are /b d g/ and /p t k/, and (60) shows the phonemicisation in Haugen's system of some words displaying preaspiration (from Thráinsson 1978:6):

(60)   kappi   [k^{h}ahpI]   /kapI/   'hero'
       þakka   [Θahka]   /þaka/   'thank'
       hattur   [hahtYr]   /hatYr/   'hat'

Haugen, then, treats the aspirated series as single phonemes, and considers aspiration to be allophonically statable; thus /p/ may have realisations such as [p^h] and [hp], while /b/ is realised as [p].

Haugen criticises Malone's (1923) analysis of the same phenomena for its "great inconsistency" in treating postaspiration as a component of the stop, but preaspiration as a separate phone. Malone, then, offers a bi-segmental analysis of preaspiration, but a single segment analysis of postaspiration. However, this is perhaps not such an inconsistency as Haugen appears to think. As Thráinsson (1978: 5) points out, preaspiration at the phonetic level "typically has a normal segment length in Icelandic, whereas postaspiration is generally much shorter". Pétursson (1972a:66) notes:

> Sur le plan de la durée, qu'on compare d'une part les chiffres moyens d'*aspiration vs. préaspiration* et d'autre part d'*aspiration +cons. occl. vs. préaspiration+consonne occl.* il est évident que la différence de durée est trop grande pour qu'il puisse s'agir du même phénomène qui se présenterait dans un ordre inverse.

Phonetically, then, preaspiration and (post-)aspiration are rather different phenomena, and this leads Thráinsson (and cf. Árnason 1980: 24) to accept Malone's view, and also to adopt the phonetic notations [hp] *vs.* [p^h]:

(61)   hatur   [ha:t^{h}Yr]   /hatYr/   'hate'
       hattur   [hahtYr]   /hattYr/   'hat'
       haddur   [hat:Yr]   /haddYr/   'hair'

Notice, too, that Thráinsson (1978: 4) points out that "postaspiration is a very common phenomenon, while preaspiration seems to be very rare".

Thráinsson offers a representation of the aspiration phenomena of Icelandic in terms of an autosegmental approach, using in particular Halle

Complex Segments

and Stevens' (1971) laryngeal features. Thus the sequence [ht] in *hattur* has the representation in (62):

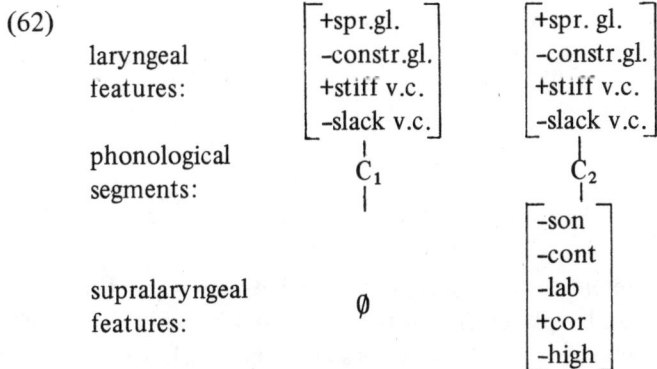

(62)

laryngeal features:

phonological segments:

supralaryngeal features:

where [h] is treated as lacking any specification for supralaryngeal features, but as showing the laryngeal feature specifications for the following stop. A postaspirated stop, however, is treated as a single segment, and has simply the representation in (63) for the laryngeal features, while the unaspirated series has (64):

(63) $\begin{bmatrix} \text{+spr.gl.} \\ \text{--constr.gl.} \\ \text{+stiff v.c.} \\ \text{--slack v.c.} \end{bmatrix}$ (64) $\begin{bmatrix} \text{--spr. gl.} \\ \text{--constr.gl.} \\ \text{+stiff v.c.} \\ \text{--slack v.c.} \end{bmatrix}$

As in the cases of the phenomena discussed in the previous two sections, we are again confronted with a situation where both one- and two-segment analyses have been suggested. An analysis in terms of the dependency model, I suggest, tends to provide support for Thráinsson's two-segment analysis of preaspiration, thus leading to a characterisation of this phenomenon which is in certain respects different from those of the last three sections.

I assume that Thráinsson's monosegmental analysis of the aspirated series /p^h t^h k^h/ is correct; that is, I shall take postaspiration to be a component of the aspirated series, an interpretation which is supported by Pétursson's phonetic analysis. Clearly, however, the elements of the categorial gesture given in §2 are not in themselves adequate to represent the opposition between the voiceless aspirated stop series and the voiceless unaspirated stop series. The appropriate way to characterise this opposition is in terms of a component of GLOTTAL OPENING, |O|; segments with a larger degree of glottal opening show a relatively more prominent |O| than segments with a smaller degree of opening. This component is introduced in dependency phonology to account for, among other things, voiceless sonorants (for discussion, see Ewen 1980a: ch. 9, 1980b). In languages with voiceless sonorants, such as Burmese (cf. Ladefoged 1971: 11), the following representations will be appropriate:

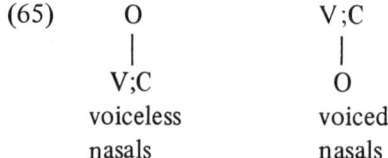

(65)   O   V;C
       | |
       V;C   O
       voiceless   voiced
       nasals   nasals

(For clarity, I represent the dependency relation between |O| and the categorial representation by placement on the graph, and between |V| and |C| by use of the ';' notation.) Thus, voiceless sonorants, which have a greater degree of glottal opening than their voiced counterparts, have more prominent |O|. The |O| governing the |V|, then, overrides the voicing specification inherent in the categorial representation of the nasals, in which |V| governs |C|.

The component |O| is also appropriate for the characterisation of the phenomena I have been discussing in this section, and of aspiration in general. It has been argued in various places that degree of aspiration correlates with degree of glottal opening. Thus Kim (1970: 111) states that "if a stop is *n* degree aspirated, it must have an *n* degree of glottal opening at the time of release", while Catford (1977: 114) observes that "modern techniques of glottography and laryngoscopy show that unaspirated voiceless sounds have a narrowed (though not completely closed) glottis, while aspirated sounds have a more or less widely open glottis". Similarly, Pétursson (1976: 187), in a study of aspiration in Icelandic, concludes:

> L'examen de glottogrammes de consonnes aspirées et non aspirées semble pour l'essentiel confirmer qu'en islandais l'aspiration peut être décrite comme une fonction de l'ouverture glottale au moment de l'explosion.

In dependency terms, then, aspirated segments show a more prominent |O| than corresponding non-aspirated segments.

As noted above, Icelandic has an aspirated and an unaspirated series of stops, both of which are voiceless. In terms of the representations of the categorial gesture, then, both series have the representation |C|. They differ in the relative prominence of |O|: for the aspirated series, |O| is governing, while for the unaspirated series, |O| is dependent, as in (66):

(66)   O   C
       | |
       C   O
       /p t k/ ([pʰ tʰ kʰ])   /b d g/ ([p t k])

The representations in (66) incorporate the monosegmental analysis of aspiration. Notice too that although the series /b d g/ is said to be 'unaspirated', it is not the case that |O| is absent in the representation. Rather, such segments show some glottal opening, and so display (dependent) |O|. The absence of |O| (in a phonological representation which contrasts with segments which do display |O|) would characterise a glottal stop.

The analysis of preaspirated stops, however, is rather different. I assume, following Thráinsson, that preaspirated stops are bisegmental; or at least that they are sequentially distinct in a dependency tree, whether or not such a configuration is to be equated with the occurrence of two segments. How, then, is the period of preaspiration itself to be represented?

As Thráinsson points out, preaspiration in Icelandic is realised phonetically as [h]. It has been argued that [h] can best be characterised as a segment lacking any specification in the articulatory gesture, and should therefore be defined as a voiceless fricative with no articulatory specification (cf. (62), and Lass 1976). However, what I want to argue is that the preaspiration 'segment' in Icelandic has a rather different specification. '[h]' in such cases, then, still lacks the articulatory specification. However, instead of being characterised as |V,C|, it is characterised by the presence of |O| alone, as in (67), which represents the surface form of *feitt* (neuter sg.) 'fat':

(67)

```
              V
           ╱ ╱|
          ╱ ╱ |
         o ╱  |
           o  O
              |
              o   O
                  |
                  o  C
         f   ei   h   t
```

There are two ways of justifying this analysis. Notice first of all that Thráinsson's characterisation of [h] ([+spread gl., -constr.gl., +stiff v.c., -slack v.c.]) is interpretable within this model as |O| alone. On the principles outlined in, for example, Anderson and Jones (1974), in a segment containing a particular property occurring alone, that property is more preponderant than if it occurs in combination with other properties: thus, in this case, the segment shows maximal glottal opening. Secondly, the choice of |O| rather than |V,C| is appropriate because of the nature of the opposition between the /p t k/ and /b d g/ series in Icelandic. As the opposition is one of aspiration, and |O| is already required in the phonological characterisation of the language, the choice of |O| to represent [h] reflects its *phonological* status as a period of aspiration, rather than as a voiceless fricative.

It is also necessary to account for the fact that the preaspiration 'segment' governs the stop in (67). I suggest that aspiration in Icelandic may be viewed as a kind of prosody whose domain is the whole consonant (cluster) forming a syllable onset or coda. (A similar proposal is apparently made by Liberman 1971 - see Pétursson 1972b). This is parallel to Thráinsson's claim (1978: 38-39) that preaspiration is an autosegment which can behave independently, and is "capable of such behaviour as moving or floating from the stop where it originated in phonological specification". If this is so, Thráinsson claims:

> this sort of movement should have two consequences: First, it should make the stop unaspirated, since it would no longer be specified as [+SG]. Secondly, if the preceding segment were voiced, we would expect it to become voiceless, since the feature [+SG] refers to a wide open glottis.

Evidence that this treatment might be appropriate comes from the fact that preaspirated consonants in Icelandic are never postaspirated. Thráinsson (1978: 49) notes that if a vowel follows a preaspirated stop it is not also postaspirated. As we saw above, Haugen (1958: 72) observes that aspiration occurs on the side of the consonant closest to the syllabic: "preaspiration excludes postaspiration . . . the position of this aspiration is a matter to be stated in the allophonic rules". Compare also Pétursson's remark (1976: 174) that "après *h*, la consonne occlusive n'est jamais aspirée". Notice too that there is a general constraint, noted by Árnason (1980: 25), such that in most dialects of Icelandic any consonant intervening between a vowel and an aspirated stop must be voiceless. Thus any (phonologically voiced) sonorant occurring in this environment is devoiced, and will show a phonetic representation with governing |O|. In such circumstances, the stop is deaspirated. This again supports the notion that governing |O| is a prosody whose domain is the whole cluster.

This interpretation means that only one occurrence of |O| need be present in the phonological representation of each cluster, and (67) is therefore inadequate. Rather, (68) appears to be a closer approximation to what is required for the rhyme of a syllable containing an aspirated stop:

(68)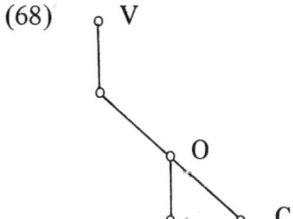

where |O|, as head of the coda, governs the following stop, which is unspecified for aspiration. The claim inherent in (68) is parallel to that made by Thráinsson (1978: §5.4). He notes a number of phenomena which indicate that the "spreading of the glottis that one would expect to go with the stop is absorbed by the preaspiration segment". In other words, the stop itself is deaspirated. This leads Thráinsson to propose the following rule, accounting among other things for the deaspiration of /p t k/:

(69)   [-syll] [+SG] ⇒ [+SG] [-SG]

where the [+SG] specification is transferred to the '[h]' segment.

As we saw in (59), forms such as [feiht], with preaspirated stop in the neuter singular form of the adjective, contrast with words such as [fei:t^h], with an ordinary aspirated stop in the feminine singular form. Representations such as (68), then, contrast with those such as (70), representing the rhyme of the feminine singular form:

(70)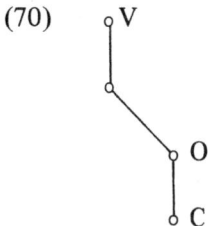

Thus, the forms in (68) and (70) are shown to differ in whether or not strict precedence holds between the |O| and |C| components.

I turn now to the characterisation of the distinction between aspirated and preaspirated consonants occurring intervocalically, as in *mæta* [mai:t^{h}a] 'meet' (inf.) vs. *mætti* [maihtI] 'meet' (past). In the case of the aspirated series, the structure in (71) is appropriate, and for the preaspirated series, (72):

(71) (72)

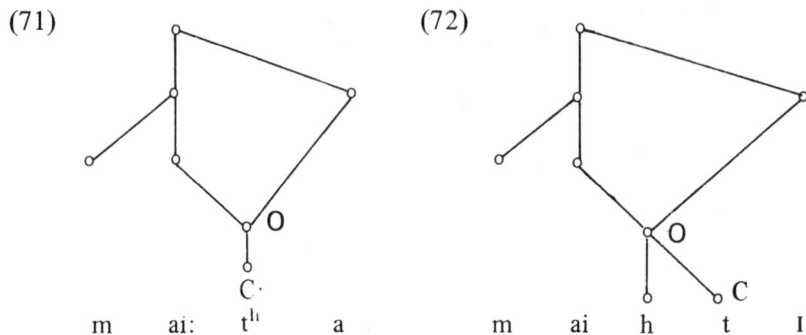

where in (72) we see a structure similar to that for English intervocalic [sC] clusters.

However, even the structure in (68) (and (72)), while correctly capturing the notion that a single occurrence of |O| is sufficient phonologically, still fails to capture its *prosodic* nature: the structure of the coda in (68) is formally no different from any other cluster. I suggest that this may be remedied by the adoption of an extra hierarchical level; thus 'cluster prosodies' would have the structure in (73):

(73)

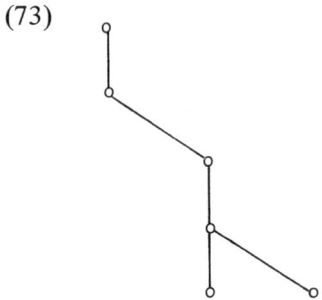

where the governor of the prosody is labelled, and the node which it immediately governs is a copy. Thus [ht] and [nt] in Icelandic would have the structures in (74) and (75) (for rather different approaches to this problem, see Ewen 1980a: §9.4, Belder 1981):

(74)

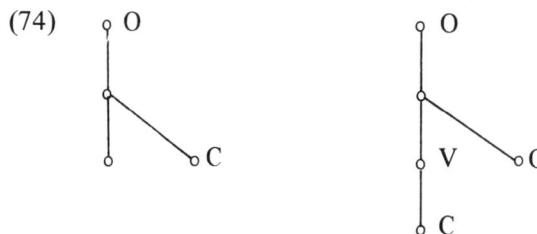

Complex Segments

The representations in (74) and (75) assign to the prosody |O| a different place in the prosodic structure than that occupied by normal segmental labels, in that an unlabelled node intervenes between the prosodic and segmental labels. Thus, the distinction between the two types of node is characterised by their different places in the structure, while the affinity between them is also apparent, in that a prosodic node may bear a label which under other circumstances may be segmental. The label |O|, for example, is associated with a prosodic node in (74), and with a segmental node in the phonetic realisation of the segment as [h]. Consider, too, the roundness and backness prosodies of Turkish. Prosodic nodes in Turkish would be labelled with various combinations of the roundness and frontness vowel components (|u| and |i|), which in other languages function only as segmental labels.

The Role of Vowel Deletion and Epenthesis in the Assignment of Syllable Structure

Steven G. Lapointe and Mark H. Feinstein
Wayne State University and Hampshire College

0. INTRODUCTION

In recent years generative phonologists have shown increasing interest in the study of syllable structure representations and syllable structure-sensitive processes.[1] Among the assumptions which are frequently posited in these recent analyses are the following:

(1)   Phonological derivations consist of the assignment of syllable structure to underlying morphophonemic forms, followed by the application of syllable-sensitive rules which produce surface phonetic syllable structures.

(2)   In phonetic structure, a syllable minimally consists of a vowel (or a vowel-like consonant).

(3)   In phonetic structure, every segment in the segmental string must be dominated by some syllable structure node.

Within analyses which essentially conform to (1) - (3), deletion and epenthesis processes are often taken to be syllable-sensitive rules. However, deletion and epenthesis are in fact problematical for such analyses. To see why this is the case, consider a language L whose grammar contains the (overly-simplified) syllable structure assignment rule (4), and the syllable-sensitive rule (5), where σ is the node label for syllables:

(4)   *Syllable Assignment in L*
      $\sigma \rightarrow C\ V\ (C)$

---

* We wish to dedicate this work to the memory of Mrs. Alice E. Lapointe and to the memory of Mrs. Lily S. Feinstein as a small token of our love and grattitude for all that they have done for us.

(5) Schwa Deletion in L

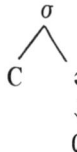

If L contains a morphophonemic string such as *pasədak*, we will obtain the derivation in (6). The problem here is that, while the desired segmental string for this form (namely *pasdak*) is in fact produced by the derivation, the accompanying syllable structure is ill-formed according to assumption (2), since the circled σ contains only consonants.

(6) a. Underlying string   pasədak

  b. Syllable structure
     assignment

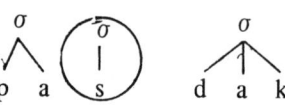

  c. Schwa deletion (5)

Similarly, if the grammar of L contains the syllable-sensitive vowel epenthesis rule (7), we will obtain the derivation in (8) for the hypothetical underlying form *pals+n+do*.

((7) Schwa Insertion in L

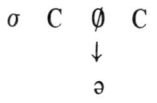

(8) a. Underlying string   pals + n + do
  b. Syllable structure
     assignment

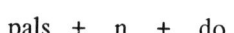

  c. Schwa Insertion (7)

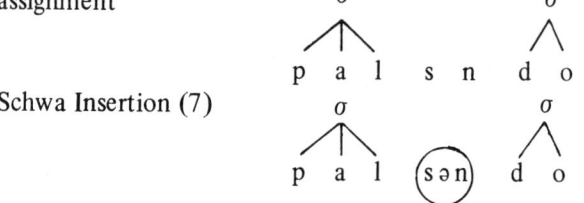

Once again, the desired output string *palsəndo* is produced, but now the accompanying syllable structure is illformed according to assumption (3), since the circled segments of (8)c are not attached to any σ-node.[2]

Vowel Deletion and Epenthesis

In general, then, the problems with the assumptions given above can be summarized as follows: in the case of derivations involving syllable-sensitive vowel deletions, the output syllable structure may contain syllables lacking vowels and hence are illformed according to (2); while in the case of derivations involving syllable-sensitive vowel-insertions, the output structure may contain unattached segments and hence will contravene assumption (3). To resolve these problems, some sort of readjustment system might be introduced to rearrange the output structures of syllable-sensitive rules in such a way that only structures consistent with assumptions (2) and (3) are produced. A system which included the following conditions might suffice for this purpose:

(9)   *Universal constraint on syllable structure assignment*
      Each V must define a σ.

(10) *Reapplication of assignment rules*
      After each syllable-sensitive rule applies, reapply the syllable structure assignment rules of the grammar to the segmental string produced by the rule.

The derivation begun in (6) would therefore continue as in (11) under these conditions, where a new syllable structure is assigned by (4) to the output string *pasdak*, resulting in the desired output structure.

(11) Readjustment of (6)c

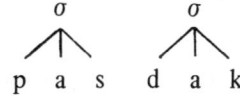

In a similar way, the derivation in (8) would continue as in (12), where the inserted schwa will automatically form the basis of a new syllable, and the syllable structure assignment rules will yield the appropriate structure.

(12) Readjustment of (8)c

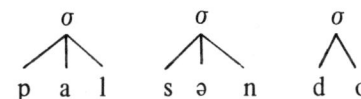

An alternative to this readjustment approach would be to say instead that there is a *syllable-structure preservation condition* restricting the operation of syllable sensitive rules of the sort given in (13):[3]

(13) *Syllable structure preservation condition*
      No rule which is sensitive to syllable structure can operate in such a way as to create or destroy a syllable.

If we were to extend the condition in (2) that a syllable in phonetic structure must minimally consist of a vowel to phonological representations in general, then (13) would have the effect of disallowing vowel deletion or insertion by syllable-sensitive rules. This sort of restriction would, in essence, say that once syllable structure has been assigned, various assimilation, consonant deletion or insertion, or metathesis rules may apply by making reference to the constituents represented in syllable structure, but no such rule can so seriously deform that structure as to require the addition or deletion of syllable nodes. Such a restriction would therefore place severe limitations on the application of syllable-sensitive rules.

As appealing as condition (13) may be, however, it cannot alone answer the question of what is to be done about derivations like (6) and (8), which we might otherwise wish to analyze as involving syllable-sensitive vowel deletion or insertion rules. One potentially interesting approach to this problem would be to assume that phonologically-general vowel deletions and insertions are carried out *as part of the assignment of syllable structure itself*. This might be accomplished by replacing (3) with assumptions along the following lines:

(14) General processes which create or destroy syllables, including the addition or deletion of vowels, operate only as part of the universal syllable assignment algorithm; hence these processes apply at a point (or points) in a derivation before syllable-sensitive rules can apply.

(15) Under certain universal and language-specific conditions, the syllable assignment algorithm need not attach all of the vowels which appear in the underlying segmental string to a syllable; and under further conditions, the algorithm may attach certain vowels to a syllable although these vowels are not present in the underlying segmental string.

(16) Only those segments that are attached to syllables are given phonetic realisations; all elements of the segmental string left unattached to syllable structure are interpreted as phonetically null.

The problem facing the researcher who wishes to pursue this line of inquiry is, of course, to formulate a satisfactory algorithm under these assumptions which will allow only the desired segments to be deleted or inserted when syllable structure is assigned to forms in individual languages. The purpose of the present paper is to construct just such an algorithm.

The paper will proceed in the following way. In Section 1 we will spell out our general assumptions about morphological structures, syllable structures and their interactions, which will allow us to form a theoretical framework in which the syllable assignment algorithm is constructed. In Section 2 we will examine the vowel deletion process in Yawelmani, a language with fairly simple syllable assignment rules, and we will present the first version of the assignment algorithm. In Section 3 we will revise the algorithm on the basis of an analysis of Klamath, a language which exhibits more complex syllable structures and more complex vowel deletion phenomena. Finally, in the fourth section, we summarize the findings of this line of research and consider several open issues of theoretical importance that arise within this approach to syllable structure.

1. THEORETICAL ASSUMPTIONS

The central claim of this paper, embodied essentially in (14) - (16), is that productive vowel deletion and epenthesis processes are not to be accounted for in terms of language-particular rules of deletion and insertion, but are instead a function of the universal processes which relate morphologically-structured segmental strings with syllable structures in those languages. Since these universal processes involve the manipulation of morphological and syllabic structures for words,[4] it is necessary for us to make explicit some of our basic assumptions about these sorts of structures, and their interactions, before proceeding further. In doing so, we will make explicit several issues that were only hinted at in (14) - (16). In particular, we will specify more fully the points in a derivation at which syllable assignment can apply, and we will give a more complete characterisation of what it means for a deletion or epenthesis process to be "general." The problem of formulating the specific conditions under which the algorithm adds or drops vowels from a segmental string will form the main topic of the remaining sections of the paper.

1.1. Morphological Structures.

For the purposes of this paper, we only need to make three assumptions about morphological structure. First, we will follow Selkirk (forthcoming) in assuming that morphological structures follow a modified $\bar{X}$ form (Chomsky, 1970) in which X^0 = word node, X_s = stem node, X_r = root node (X is a major lexical category) Af = affix node. X_r cannot dominate X^0 or X_s, and X_s cannot dominate X^0. An example of a morphological structure (MS) conforming to these conditions which is based on the hypothetical verbform *palsǝndo*, discussed earlier, is given in (17):

(17)

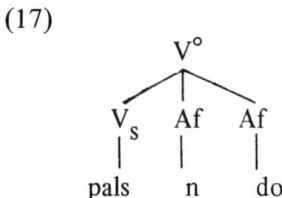

Second, following Stanley (1967) we assume that generalizations about the underlying segmental phonological form of roots, stems and affixes are to be expressed in terms of language-particular Morpheme Structure Conditions (MSCs), and that morphemes which follow the MSCs of a language do not add to the cost of that language's lexicon. Third, following Lapointe (1981), we assume that there is something special about affixation at the $X^°$ level (i.e. affixation where the immediately dominating node is $X^°$) in that inflectional processes occur at this level, and the output of these processes form the input to lexical insertion into syntactic structures. On this view, root and stem forms are stored in the lexicon, whereas word-level forms are generated productively from stems or other words without being stored. We will have more to say about the implications of this assumption in Section 1.3 below.

1.2. Syllable structure.

We assume that Syllable Formation (SF) rules have the universal form given in (18):

(18)   *Universal Form of SF Rules*

a.	σ	→	(On) Ri	σ	=	Syllable
				On	=	Onset
b.	On	→	[-voc]*	Ri	=	Rime
				Nuc	=	Nucleus
c.	Ri	→	Nuc (Cd) (Ap)	Pk	=	Peak
				Sat	=	Satellite
d.	Nuc	→	Pk (Sat)	Cd	=	Coda
				Ap	=	Appendix
e.	Cd	→	[+seg]*			

The rules in (18)a-c essentially follow recent work by Selkirk (forthcoming), Prince (1980) and Cairns and Feinstein (in press). (We are, however, largely ignoring the elaboration of On proposed by Cairns and Feinstein; the details of the Nuc will be discussed at greater length below; and evidence in favor of an Ap constituent will be provided in Section 3.)

The SF rules in (18) define a set of labeled trees of the form given in the schema (19):

(19)
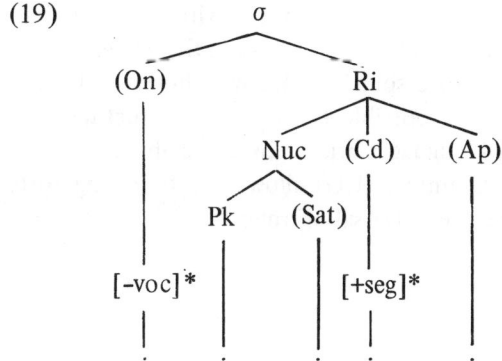

All of the terminal nodes in (19) can dominate consonantal segments (but see fn. 8); and Pk, Sat and in some instances Cd can dominate vocalic segments. We assume that the configuration of consonants within the syllable is governed by a markedness evaluation system, such as that proposed in Cairns and Feinstein (1982; henceforth, the C-F metric). This system has the effect of imposing the well-known sonority hierarchy on the segmental string, from the first C in the "margin core" of an On, to the last C in the Cd; but it also accomodates various syllable-marginal consonant clusters which appear to violate the sonority hierarchy. These are shown to have distinct constituent structures from clusters that "obey" the sonority hierarchy, and are governed by distinct marking conventions. We also assume, with the C-F metric, that a Composite Markedness Value (CMV) is determined for each word by summming the markedness values for each of the syllables of the word, and that the CMV plays an integral role in the assignment of syllable structures to words in those cases where more than one well-formed syllabification is possible for a given form.

Consideration of the structure of the Nuc constituent leads us to an examination of vowel length. Long Vs in languages like Yawelmani and Klamath, discussed below, have been assumed in earlier analyses to be monomoraic, i.e. single segments marked [+long]. On the other hand, languages like Latin and Greek have traditionally been held to contain long Vs that are bimoraic (double V sequences). Furthermore, various phonological phenomena such as compensatory lengthening, geminate clusters across syllable boundaries, and overlong syllables (Ingria, 1980; Prince 1980) seem to be exhibited by languages of the latter rather than the former type. Nevertheless, we would like to be able to make the restrictive claim that long Vs in *all* languages arise from double segment sequences. To do this we must make explicit the range of possible variation among languages along the dimension of vowel length, locate the above types of languages along these dimensions, and correlate the differences in syllabic representation for long Vs in the various types of languages with the differing phonological behaviour that they exhibit. Space limitations preclude us from fully accomplishing this task in the present paper (but see fn. 8 for the beginnings of a solution). We will, however, lay the groundwork for the definition of possible types of Nuc structure, and associate these with the types of languages briefly discussed above.

We assume that Universal Grammar (UG) allows the following sorts of Nuc structures, as defined by the universal SF rules:[5,6]

(20)   *Universally Possible Nuclei*

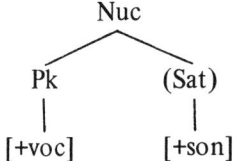

We follow Lowenstamm (1979) in assuming that the feature *vocalic* and not *syllabic* distinguishes vowel segments from all others. (20) then says that a Nuc can consist of a vocalic peak by itself, or a vocalic peak and either a vowel, a glide (G), or a sonorant consonant (R). Viewing (20) as a universal SF rule schema, the particular instantiations of (20) in an individual grammar may add further feature restrictions to the segments appearing under Pk and Sat, thereby constraining the possible types of Nuc structures allowed in that language. The possible variations on (20) are listed in Table 1.

Notice in Table 1 that the ranking of possible nuclei is determined according to two principles: a. the fewer the possibilities of Nuc structures allowed in a given grammar, the more highly ranked is the Nuc type, and b. the closer the Sat segment is to V, the more highly ranked it is. Principle a. leads to the consequence that the ranking is the inverse of the one we would have expected if we were taking into account just the number of features required to specify the Sat element in the SF rule. We have little to add to this observation at present, except to note that some underlying principle like a. appears to govern most of the syllabic markedness considerations that we are familiar with..

Turning now to the issue of how various languages are distributed among the types listed in Table 1, as we will see below, Yawelmani has Nuc structures of Type II, while Klamath has Nuc structures of Type VII. On the other hand, languages like Latin and Greek have Nuc structures of Type I; long vowels in the bimoraic languages would still be represented

Tabel 1:

Type	Nuc Structure	Possible sequences allowed
I	Nuc — Pk — [+voc]	V
II	Nuc → Pk [+voc], Sat ([+son, −cons, +voc])	V, VV
III	Nuc → Pk [+voc], Sat ([+son, −cons, −voc])	V, VG
IV	Nuc → Pk [+voc], Sat ([+son, −cons])	V, VV, VG
V	Nuc → Pk [+voc], Sat ([+son, +cons])	V, VR
VI	Nuc → Pk [+voc], Sat ([+son, −voc])	V, VG, VR
VII	Nuc → Pk [+voc], Sat ([+son])	V, VV, VG, VR

as VV sequences, but here the second V would be dominated by Cd rather than Nuc. Apprantly, long Vs in languages of the six other types cannot be represented in this way, but can only arise through sequences contained solely within Nuc. To capture this distinction between Type I and the other language types, we can posit a universal condition to the effect that a grammar containing Sat (i.e. a SF rule introducing this constituent) can only permit [-voc] segments in the Cd. The differences in the phonological properties of these two types of languages (e.g. the presence or absence of phenomena like compensatory lengthening) would then be a reflection of differences in the representation of long Vs in the two types.[8]

Before leaving this topic, we wish to note that not all of the Nuc structures in (20) are equally marked: a Nuc consisting of a single short V is certainly the maximally unmarked structure; a Nuc with a Sat carries one additional mark; and it is probably correct to say that Gs are less marked when they appear in the Sat than when they appear in the Cd. Various other markedness principles suggest themselves, but we will not pursue the matter further here.

Finally, we must add a few comments on notation. Internal structure (both syllabic and morphological) will frequently be abbreviated when it is irrelevant to the point being discussed. In addition, certain syllable types will often be abbreviated by special indications on a σ node. Among these are σ_o = open syllable (i.e., one with a nonbranching Rime), σ_c = closed syllable (i.e. one with non-null Cd), $\breve{\sigma}$ = short syllable (i.e. one with a nonbranching Nuc), $\bar{\sigma}$ = long syllable (i.e. one with branching Nuc) and σ_h = heavy syllable (i.e. one with branching of any sort in the Rime; thus $\sigma_h = \breve{\sigma}_c, \bar{\sigma}_o, \bar{\sigma}_c$).

1.3. Syllable/Morphology Interactions.

The problem that we now face is to specify how syllable structures are constructed for morphologically structured segmental strings. Given the theory of inflectional morphology proposed in Lapointe (1981), it is reasonable to assume that the Syllable Assignment Algorithm (SAA) forms syllable structures for morphological structures that are the output of the inflectional processes, that is, to assume that the SAA can apply each time a word-level structure is generated by the morphology. This assumption means that in a word with several internal X^o constituents the SAA will have had a chance to apply several times, thus potentially allowing re-syllabification of earlier syllable structures and producing an effect similar to cyclic application. Several remarks need to be made to clarify our conception of how this reapplication of the SAA is to work in light of the discussion in the introduction and how this reapplication differs from the standard assumptions about the segmental cycle.

It is important to note first that the discussion about resyllabification in the introduction was concerned only with the problems raised when syllable structure was reassigned *after the application of particular phonological rules*. Nothing in that discussion suggested that the SAA should not be allowed to reapply after certain morphological processes had applied. Since we still wish syllable sensitive rules to be constrained by (1) and (13), we offer the following organisation of the rules and structures that we have considered so far. Morphological operations in a grammar produce X° (word)-level structures, to which the SAA applies the SF rules of the grammar under the constraint of various universal and language-specific conditions to be discussed in the following sections. The SAA gets a chance to apply as often as the morphological operations produce a new X^0-level structure, and it does this in the following way: the SAA attempts to assign syllable structure first just to that portion of the segmental string that has been added by the last application of the morphological operations and does not currently have syllable structure assigned to it; if for various reasons the SAA cannot assign a well-formed syllable structure to this portion of the string, only under this condition does it reassign syllable structure to the whole word. When the morphological operations cease, the syllable sensitive rules apply to the final resulting syllable structure.[9]

This conception of the reapplication of the SAA differs from the standard assumptions about cyclic application in a number of important respects. Under the present view, the only operations that are cycling are the morphological processes and the SAA; under the standard view, a significant set of phonological rules also applies cyclically. Given that many general non-V deletion or insertion rules are applying *after* the final application of the SAA in the present theory, and hence do not cycle, this theory would seem to place much tighter restrictions on the possible interactions of phonological rules than the standard conception of the cycle allows. Notice further that cyclic interactions of the SAA with previously processed segmental material occurs only when it is not possible to straightforwardly assign syllable structure to newly-added morphological structure, so that in languages with relatively simple syllabic inventories and uncomplicated morphological structures, very little of this resyllabification will be exhibited. Finally, what is left of the cycle in this view is defined by word-level domains only, whereas in the standard view it is defined essentially by all productive morphological boundaries.[10]

We will also assume that the assignment of syllable structure to a segmental string does not eliminate the morphological structure of the string. Rather it pairs a syllable structure with the already-existing morphological representation. The resulting *dual representation* offers certain advantages within the sort of theory we are proposing. In particular, such representations allow us to refer to "deleted" and "inserted" Vs directly, without referring to properties of the derivation that produced such Vs. This can be accomplished by saying that a "deleted" segment in general is one which is attached to a morphological node in the dual representation but not to a syllabic node. Under the phonetic interpretation convention of (16), such "deleted" segments will be given a null phonetic interpretation. The form *pasdak* in example (6) would have the dual representation in (21), where the circled schwa is the deleted V:

(21)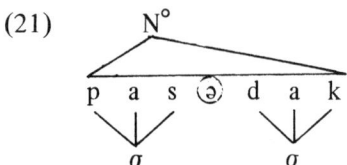

Similarly, an "inserted" segment is one attached to a syllabic node but not to a morphological node in the dual representation of the word. The hypothetical form *palsəndo* above would therefore have the dual representation in (22), where the triangled schwa is the inserted V:

(22)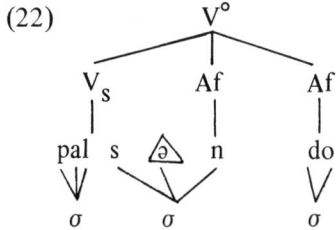

Notice that the orientation of the two parts of these dual representations does not matter; either the syllabic structure or the morphological structure could be placed above the segmental string with the other structure below it. In general we will place the structure which is most relevant to the discussion above the segmental string. In the sections below, this will generally be the syllabic structure. In some cases we will simply leave the morphological structure out of the diagram entirely. The reader should not become confused by such diagrams; we are using them only as unofficial abbreviations for dual representations that contain full morphological structures in addition to the given syllable structure.

We have answered one of the questions set out at the beginning of this section concerning the points in a derivation at which the SAA may apply, but there remains the question concerning the definition of a "general" V deletion or insertion. Broadly speaking, we take a general phonological process to be one which operates only on the basis of surrounding phonological context and is not constrained to apply (or not to apply) as a

Vowel Deletion and Epenthesis

result of the morphological environment that the affected segments appear in. There are of course rules which affect phonological segments which *are* constrained by the surrounding morphological environment, and some of these rules can insert or delete Vs. We assume that such *morphologically-restricted* phonological rules apply in a block after morphological material has been inserted into MSs at *every* level in a MS tree. Since these rules are only of peripheral interest to us in the present investigation, we will not go into detail about the theory of this class of rules.[11] Nonetheless the analyses presented in the following sections do make use of morphologically-restricted rules, sometimes in quite important ways (cf. fn. 11). One major difference that we assume distinguishes such rules from the V deletion and insertion processes that are part of the operation of the SAA is that a morphologically-restricted V deletion (or insertion) rule actually removes (or adds) a V to the morphological structure of the form in question. Thus a language that has a morphological deletion of the sort in (23)a will have the structure in (23)c after the rule applies to the structure in (23)b, and before the SAA applies:

(23)   a.   *a-Truncation*

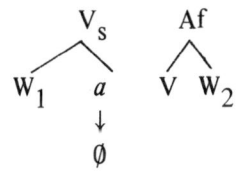

b.

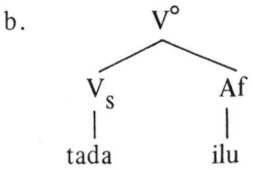

c.

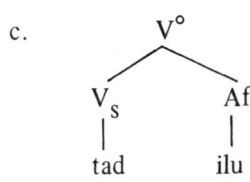

(23)c should thus be contrasted with (21): in (23)c the *a* has actually been removed from the MS, while in (21) the schwa is still attached to the MS in the dual representation, although it is not attached to the syllable structure.

1.4. Summary and plan of attack.

Figure 1 summarizes the general grammatical organization that we have outlined in the preceding section.

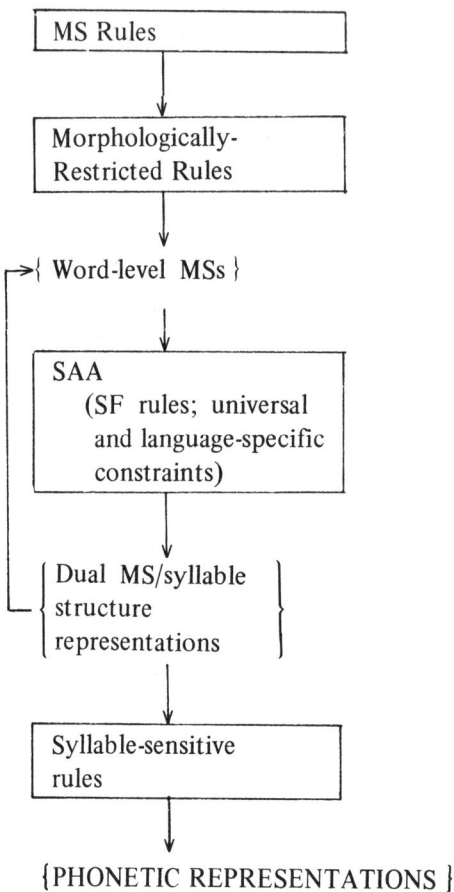

Figure 1

The rest of the paper will be concerned mainly with accomodating V deletion and epenthesis facts from Yawelmani and Klamath in an explicit algorithm governing the association of morphological and syllabic structures. The formulation of the SAA will be guided by two principles. The first is a kind of "minimal distance" principle which says that the greater the distance between the segmental string attached to the MS tree and that attached to the syllable structure tree in a dual representation, the more marked that representation is. As a consequence of this principle, the SAA will be arranged in such a way that it first attempts to assign syllable structures in which all of the Vs attached to morphological nodes are also attached to syllabic nodes, and it only attempts to construct syllable structures with "deleted" or "inserted" Vs if universal or language-specific constraints prevent it from constructing any syllable structures containing only the morphologically determined Vs. The second principle is that, all things being equal, V *deletion* causes a segmental string to deviate from the morphologically determined form to a lesser degree than V *insertion* does. As a result, the SAA will be constructed in such a way that it attempts to construct syllable structures which contain "deleted" Vs before it attempts to construct structures which contain "inserted" Vs, or a mixture of the two. It turns out that considering these possibilities in this order yields the correct results in several complex cases.

2. YAWELMANI V DELETION

In this section we will look at V/∅ alternations in the Yawelmani dialect of the Amerindian language Yokuts. All of the data that we will be using can be found in Kuroda (1967) or Newman (1944). The analysis presented here is based on the analysis given in Lapointe (1978) and will itself form the basis for our syllable assignment algorithm.

2.1. *Syllable Structure*

Let us begin by citing Newman's (1944) comments about possible types of syllable structures in Yawelmani.

> [Yawelmani] syllable structure is simple and uniform. Two types of syllables are found: (1) the open syllable CV and (2) the closed syllable CVC . . . combinations of the CV and CVC syllables cannot result in any bivocalic cluster, or in any triliteral cluster, or in a final cluster; when morphological processes imperil the regularity of the two syllable patterns, these are preserved by [the operation of morphological adjustment rules – SL&MF].
>
> (Newman, 1944, pp. 26-29)

Given these remarks, it is reasonable to assume the following syllable formation rules which will yield syllable structures of the form in (2.5).

(24) *Yawelmani Syllable Formation*
    a.   σ   →   On Ri
    b.   On   →   [-voc]
    c.   Ri   →   Nuc (Cd)

d. Nuc → Pk (Sat)
e. Pk → [+voc]
f. Sat → [+voc]
g. Cd → [-voc]

(25)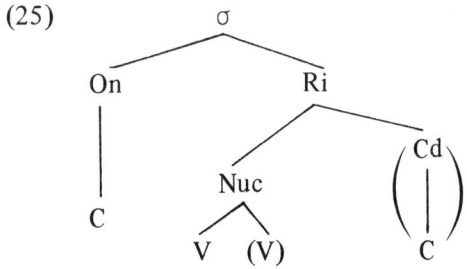

In addition to the rules of (2.4), various language-specific constraints on syllable structures must be added in order for the desired surface forms to arise. Among these are a constraint that guarantee that both Vs appearing in a Nuc must be identical (26)a and a constraint which disallows the fullest expansion of R (26)b.

(26) *Syllable Structure Constraints*

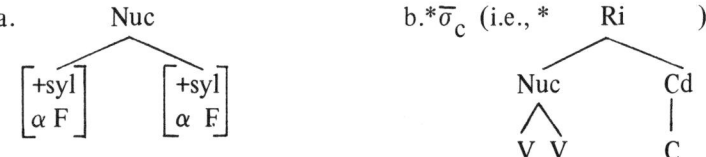

The kinds of syllable structures permitted by these rules and constraints differ from those described by Newman only in that we are assuming that long Vs in Yawelmani arise from double segments in the Nuc by (24)d and (26)a in accord with the theory of Nuc structures given in Section 1, whereas Newman assumed that long Vs consist of single, long segments. Hence, where Newman states that there is a type of open syllable CV, he intends that the V in such syllables may be either short or long; this syllable type corresponds to two types under the rules and constraints given above, CV and CVV, both of which are nonetheless 'open' under the definition of that term stated in Section 1. Furthermore, in the closed syllable type CVC, Newman notes that the V cannot be long. This restriction is stated in the constraint in (26)b. Therefore, the only syllable types allowed by the above rules are CV, CVV, and CVC, in accordance with Newman's description and the treatment of long Vs as double segment sequences.

2.2. Morphophonemics of Verb Forms

A full analysis of the Yawelmani verb morphology must deal with a number of interesting V/∅ alternations of the sort illustrated in (27) taken from Kuroda (1967).

(27)   a. *xaṭ-*   b. *pa?ṭ-*   c. *panā-*
                    'eat'   'fight'   'arrive'

	a.	b.	c.
Aorist	xaṭhin	pa?iṭhin	panāhin
Passive Aorist	xaṭit	pa?ṭit	panat
Commitative Pass. Aor.	xaṭmixit	pa?iṭmixit	panamxit
Mediopassive Aorist	xaṭinhin	pa?ṭinhin	paninhin
Mediopassive Dubitative	xaṭnal	pa?ṭinal	pannal

Before considering these alternations, we must first make explicit some of our assumptions about the underlying forms of Yawelmani verb stems and suffixes, which differ in a number of respects from the assumptions made by Kuroda (1967). We follow here the analysis of Lapointe (1978) in assuming that several fairly general Morpheme Structure Conditions (MSCs) allow us to take the underlying forms of verb stems and suffixes to be less abstract than those posited by Kuroda without adding to the cost of the lexicon. Specifically, Kuroda's Echo and Length Redundancy rules can be built directly into the MSC for the class of verb stems illustrated by (27)c, thus permitting underlying forms such as *panā-* rather than the non-occurring **pna-* proposed by Kuroda. In addition, the underlying forms of the verb suffixes found in (27) can be fully specified with Vs since they all conform to the appropriate MSCs; that is, the verb suffixes can be taken as having the following forms:[12]

(28)   Aorist - *hin*   Mediopassive - *in*
          Passive Aorist - *(i)t*   Dubitative - *al*
          Commitative - *mix*

This is a welcome result, for it clears up certain problems in Kuroda's analysis of the suffixes, as noted in Lapointe (1978). Kuroda assumed that all of the underlying suffixes in (28) except the Mediopassive *-in* are underlyingly represented *without* vowels (i.e. as *-hn, *-t, *-mx, *-1*) and that the Vs are supplied by a general epenthesis rule formulated as in (29):

(29) *Kuroda's Epenthesis*
$$\emptyset \rightarrow i \ / \ C \ \underline{\quad} \ C]$$

However, Kuroda is forced to claim that this rule exceptionally inserts *a* instead of *i* to produce the surface forms *-al* and *-taw* (a gerundive suffix), although he gives no indication of how this sort of exceptional operation is to be included either in the statement of the rule, as a rule feature on the morphemes involved, or both. Furthermore, at least two suffixes, *-in* and gerundive *mi-* must be fully specified for Vs underlyingly even in Kuroda's own analysis. These sorts of problems do not arise if we assume that the verb suffixes have the underlying forms given in (28).

Finally, Kuroda's Epenthesis rule was supposed to apply in a number of cases in which C-final verb stems abutted C-initial suffixes. Given our assumptions about the underlying forms of stems and suffixes, most of these cases disappear. There remains one environment, however, in which some rule like Kuroda's Epenthesis still seems to be required, namely, in verb stems of the type in (27)b, which end in double Cs; this *pa?t+hin* is realised as *pa?ithin* and *pa?t+mixit* is realized as *pa?itmixit*, whereas the surface forms in the remaining cases contain no inserted *i*'s (*pa?tit*, etc.) These facts can be handled by assuming that Kuroda's general epenthesis rule is actually a morphologically-restricted rule which applies in the context given in (30):

(30) *Stem-final Epenthesis*
$$\emptyset \rightarrow i \ / \ X \ C \ \underline{\quad} \ C]_{V_s} \quad C \ Y$$

2.3. Vowel Deletion

Several cases of V/∅ alternations exhibited by the data in (27) remain to be dealt with. The first involves a morphologically-restricted rule of Truncation which deletes the final Vs in stems of the type in (27)c when they are followed by a V-initial suffix (cf. *paninhin<panā+in+hin; pannal< panā+in+al*; see Kuroda (1967) and Lapointe (1978) for a formulation of the rule).

Of greater importance for the present study is the alternation found in the Mediopassive forms *xatnal, pannal* vs. *pa?tinal* and in the Commitative Passive Aorist form *panamxit* vs. *xatmixit, pa?itmixit*. To account for such facts, Kuroda posited the segmental deletion rule in (31):

Vowel Deletion and Epenthesis 87

(31)   *Kuroda's V deletion*
$$V \rightarrow \emptyset \ / \ V \ C \begin{bmatrix} \underline{} \\ -\text{lg} \end{bmatrix} C \ V$$

It is intuitively clear that a rule such as (31) is linked in an intimate way with the syllable structure of the language. Kuroda himself apparently sensed this fact, since he dubbed the environment in which the rule operates a "two-side open syllable", although within the assumptions of segmental phonology in which he was working, there was no way to incorporate such an insight into the rules responsible for the surface absence of underlying vowels in this environment.

How can we build this insight into our analysis of the language under the theoretical assumptions of Section 1? Consider the form *xatnal*, whose morphological form is roughly *xat+in+al*. Following the suggestion made in Section 1, the SAA will attempt to assign a syllable structure to this form in which all of the segments are attached on the basis of the SF rules and constraints of the language (21) and (26). This results in the candidate dual representation in (32).

(32)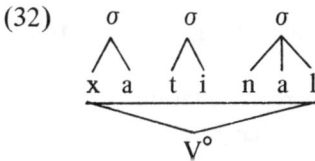

But this is not the syllable structure that we want, since the surface form of the verb is *xatnal*, not **xatinal*. If we were to assume that the grammar of Yawelmani contained a constraint on sequences of syllable structures such as the one in (33), the structure in (32) would no longer be well-formed, since it is exactly of the sort prohibited by the constraint.

(33)   Double Open Syllable Constraint (DOS)

$$* \quad \overset{}{\underset{\circ}{\sigma}} \ \overset{\smile}{\underset{\circ}{\sigma}} \ \sigma$$

Continuing to follow the suggestion made in the previous section, we may assume that the SAA now tries to construct a new candidate syllable structure which is well-formed under the rules and constraints of (21) and (26) but to which not all of the Vs are attached. In this case the resulting syllable structure would be the one in (34) in which the circled *i* is left unattached:

(34)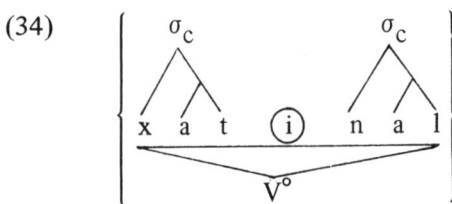

No other structures with unattached Vs are possible given the syllable formation rules and constraints of the language, since leaving any V other than the *i* unattached would require Ons or Cds to contain more than one C each, or would require the absence of Ons. The structure in (34) is of course just the syllable structure we want for the surface form *xatnal* under the interpretation of unattached segments proposed in Section 1. Parallel comments can be made for the construction of syllable structures for *pannal* from the intermediate form *pan+in+al* cf. the comments about Truncation above) and *panamxit* from *panā+mix+it*.

The problem remains of specifying the SAA in such a way that it will be able to carry out the above mentioned operations. The following formulation will serve our purposes for the time being.

(35) *Syllable Assignment Algorithm* (to be revised)
  Step a. Construct a set of candidate dual lexical representations (the *candidate set*) such that
  (i) the syllabic structure of each dual representation in the set is consistent with the SF rules of the language and with the universal and language-specific syllable structure constraints, and
  (ii) the syllable structure of each dual representation in the set meets Condition 1, below.
  Step b. If there is one member in the candidate set, output that complex structure as the dual representation for the word. If there is more than one member in the set, apply the markedness evaluation metric to the syllable structures of the candidate representations, and output the one(s) with syllable structure(s) having the least CMV.
  Step c. If the candidate set is null, go back to *step a* and reapply the algorithm using Condition 2 in place of Condition 1.
  Condition 1. All segments in the morphologically-determined segmental string of the word are attached to some syllable.
  Condition 2. All Cs are attached to some syllable, and at least one word-medial V is unattached.

The SAA has been generalised to construct *sets* of candidate dual representations here in order to accomodate cases in which more than one syllable structure can be assigned to a segmental string on the basis of the formation rules and constraints of the particular language. Although we will not generally be concerned with such cases in the present study, the reader may consult Cairns and Feinstein (in press) for a discussion of several cases of this sort. When such a case does arise, we assume that the C-F complexity metric (or a comparable device) is used to determine which of the candidate representations is most highly valued, and thus to be output. The SAA is arranged, as suggested above, so that the dual representations in the candidate set must *first* contain only syllabically-attached vowels; only if there are no such representations meeting the rules and constraints of the language does the SAA consider candidate dual representations containing unattached Vs.[13]

Applying the SAA (35) to *xat+in+al* in the just-discussed case, we find that the initial candidate set is null, since the only possible dual representation with all segments attached in syllable structure would be the one in (32), and that representation is ruled out by DOS (33). Therefore a candidate set with unattached Vs is constructed, the only possible member of this set is (34), and this representation is the output, as desired.

Before continuing with the discussion of V/∅ alternations in Yawelmani, a few comments need to be made about syllable structure constraints like DOS (33). Unlike the constraints given in (26) which restrict the *internal* structures of individual syllables, DOS constrains possible *sequences of types* of syllables. A plausible universal condition that we might consider imposing on possible language-specific syllable structure constraints would permit them to refer only to syllable-internal structure, thus allowing the constraints in (26), but not DOS, as legitimate syllable structure constraints. How then would we capture the generalizations handled by DOS if this were the case? The most natural solution would be to say that constraints on sequences of syllable types all follow from the metrical structure constraints of the language. This would be a fairly reasonable suggestion since (as noted in McCarthy, 1979) it is well known that constraints on higher metrical structure need to refer to the Ri-structure of syllables occurring within metrical constituents, and this is just the sort of information that constraints like DOS seem to require in order to operate. Adopting this suggestion, we would then need to modify the SAA so that candidate dual representations would be consistent with the metrical constraints of the language as well as the syllable-internal formation rules and constraints.

As appealing as this possibility may be, we have chosen not to pursue it here for two reasons. First, the languages that we are dealing with in the present work do not offer terribly solid support in favor of these suggestions. For example, in Yawelmani, which offers the most promising case, it appears that two constraints on foot-structure assignment are required, but neither is "natural". Second, in order to do justice to the topic, it would be necessary for us to undertake an investigation that would take us far beyond the bounds of the present study. The reason for this is that current theories of metrical structure do not specify the notion "natural foot-structure constraint" in sufficient detail for our purposes, and once we had presented a detailed account of this notion, we would still have to present some convincing cases in which constraints on sequences of syllables were more perspicuously handled in terms of those foot-structure constraints. For these resons, we have decided to continue to assume here that sequence constraints like DOS can appear as legitimate syllable structure constraints in the grammars of particular languages, while anticipating a more tightly constrained future theory of syllable and metrical structures in which constraints like DOS follow from considerations of metrical principles.[14]

2.4. Vowel Shortening

The final process in the language which we will consider involves the shortening of long Vs in cases like *panamxit* from *panaa+mix+it*. Since we are assuming that long Vs are represented in the language as sequences of identical short Vs appearing together under Nuc, this shortening process is most reasonably viewed as a deletion of one of these Vs under the appropriate conditions, namely, when the syllable structure would otherwise be of the illegal type ruled out by (26)b. As it turns out, the mechanisms which we have already set up will automatically allow the deletion of such a V during the construction of syllable structures by the SAA, and hence there is no need for a separate deletion rule to handle these facts. To take one case, consider the morphophonemic form *panaa+mix+it* mentioned above.[15] The candidate set based on this form constructed by the SAA under Condition 1 is null, the only possible candidate syllable structure in this case being (36) which is ruled out by (33).[16]

(36)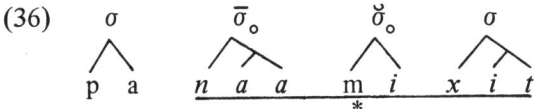

Turning then to Condition 2, the SAA creates the candidate representation in the set in (37).

(37)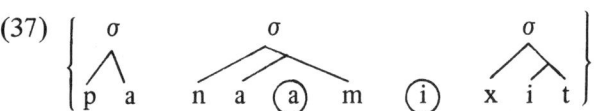

Notice that this is the *only* possible candidate representation in the set;

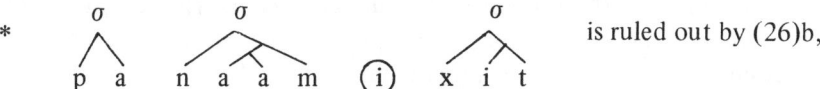 is ruled out by (26)b, and leaving any other Vs unattached will result in violations of (24). The representation in (37) contains just the syllabic structure we want for the surface form *panamxit*, which the SAA correctly outputs. Thus, by setting up the SF rules and syllable structure constraints in Yawelmani as we have in (24), (26) and (33) and by allowing the SAA to leave Vs unattached under the conditions specified in (35), we can account for the V shortening facts as a case of V deletion that occurs during the assignment of syllable structure without being forced to posit further theoretical machinery.

2.5. Summary

Having made assumptions about the general nature of dual lexical representations in Section 1, about the details of the SAA (35), and about the specific syllable formation rules and constraints in Yawelmani, we have been able to provide a fairly elegant analysis of V deletion and V shortening in this language in which both processes arise as a result of the way in which syllable structures are assigned to morphophonemic strings. Specifically, because language-specific constraints rule out certain of the logically possible candidate syllable structures for a word, the SAA is forced to assign trees with unattached (and hence "deleted") Vs in those cases. As a consequence, no additional syllable structure readjustment is required to produce the desired surface syllable structures.

The analysis presented here does not of course exhaust all of the topics of theoretical interest in this language.[17] Numerous researchers have, for example, attempted to provide a further explanation for the kinds of abstract analyses that Kuroda proposed. One well known attempt along these lines was suggested by Kisseberth (1970). He suggested that there was a "functional conspiracy" acting in Yawelmani to prevent the various illegal sequences mentioned in Newman's quote above from appearing in surface forms and that the segmental Epenthesis and V Deletion rules had to have the particular forms that Kuroda had proposed in order to carry out this conspiracy in the language. Within a purely segmental treatment of phonological processes, the theoretical status of such conspiracies is something of a mystery. On the other hand, conspiracies of this sort find a natural explanation within a syllable structure approach to the problem. At least for the coarse C–V structure of words, the SF rules and syllable constraints of a language restrict the possible surface sequences of Cs and Vs in fairly specific ways, and whatever V deletion and insertion processes are at work in the language operate so as to produce surface sequences which conform to those syllable structure constraints. Hence, within syllable structure theory, it would seem appropriate not to view those processes as interacting in a conspiratorial manner but rather as acting in such a way that otherwise syllabically ill-formed morphophonemic strings will in fact have syllabically well-formed surface forms. It is therefore clear that the syllabic treatment of phonological processes offers a straightforward way of explaining the kind of phenomena that Kisseberth's notion of functional conspiracy was trying to capture.

3. KLAMATH VOWEL ALTERNATIONS

In this section, we will consider facts from Klamath, a language with more complex syllable structures and more complex V/∅ alternations, which have a direct bearing on the operation of the SAA. We will proceed below in a fashion parallel to that adopted in the previous section. First, we will examine Barker's (1964) descriptive comments about consonant clustering in Klamath and propose a general picture of the syllable structure for the language. Next, after discussing several morphological processes, we will turn to a set of facts involving V/ə/∅ alternations and show how these facts follow from the theory of V deletion elaborated above if one assumes that the grammar of Klamath contains a simple constraint on open syllables. We will then take up the more difficult problem of accounting for the set of data involving $\bar{V}$/G and $\bar{V}$/VG alternations.

Our analysis of these facts relies on Kean's (1974) insight that the long Vs in such cases arise from G sequences, although the analysis presented here differs from Kean's in a number of important respects. First, the present analysis relies on general principles of syllable structure in explaining a number of the Klamath facts. Next, although certain of the complex alternations in Klamath require us to assume that the SAA applies in the cyclic manner at the $X^°$-level described in Section 1, where the facts from Yawelmani above did not require such reapplication of the algorithm, our use of the cycle is a more restrictive one than the standard conception of the segmental cycle employed by Kean, as noted in that earlier section. Third, the analysis provides a basis for explaining why the G → $\bar{V}$ process ought to be a fairly "natural" phenomenon in terms of the principles of syllable structure and markedness theory. In the process of accounting for the Klamath data, we will extend the SAA (35) to cover cases involving V epenthesis, and we will consider situations in which general V deletion and epenthesis interact.

3.1. Syllable Structure

In the major descriptive work on Klamath, Barker (1964) lists numerous examples of the sorts of consonant clusters that can appear word-initially, word-medially, and word-finally. A consideration of these lists leads to the following general conclusions regarding syllabic margins in the language.

(38) a. Syllable onsets must contain at least one and at most two Cs.
 b. Syllable offsets may contain zero to four Cs, arranged as follows:
   (i) Two-member clusters may consist of a sonorant plus obstruent, or two obstruents.
   (ii) Three-member clusters may consist either of a sonorant plus two obstruents, or two obstruents plus an additional [+coronal] obstruent.
   (iii) Four member clusters consist of a sonorant plus two obstruents plus a [+coronal].

In addition, Klamath exhibits short and long Vs, the latter of which can be either bisegmental V sequences (VV) or diphthongs (VG).

We will assume that Klamath syllable structures are defined by the following set of rules.[19]

(39) *Klamath Syllable Formation*
 a. σ → On Ri
 b. On → C (C)
 c. Ri → Nuc (Cd) (Ap)
 d. Nuc → Pk (sat)
 e. Pk → [+voc]
 f. Sat → [+son]
 g. Cd → [+cons] ([-son])
 h. Ap → [+cor]

The following example shows a monosyllabic word (*lwelpks* 'slaying, Durative') that exhibits the maximally expanded syllable structure permitted by the above SF rules:

(40)

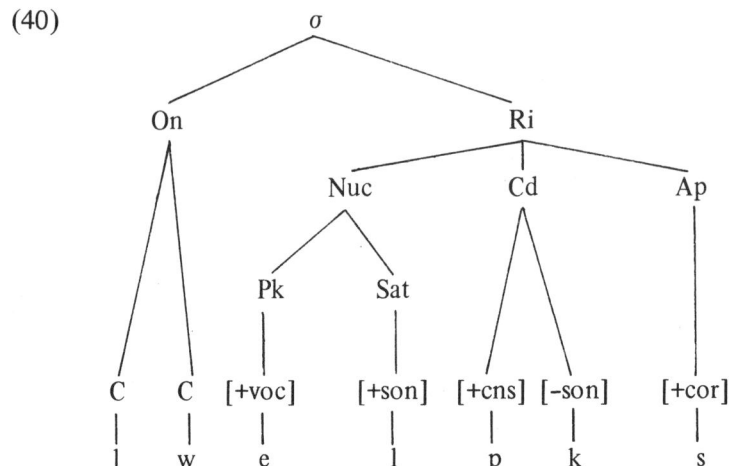

There are a number of co-occurrence facts involving syllable-final Cs which support the appearance of post-vocalic sonorants under Sat. First, there are no syllables of the form *...VVRCC (for example, *...*iiltk*) which we would otherwise expect to occur if sonorants appeared under Cd rather than Sat. Second, there are no syllables of the form *...VGRCC (e.g. *...*oympk*) which again we would expect if sonorants appeared in Cd. Finally, if sonorants appear under Sat as in (39), we would expect syllables of the form ...VVRCT (T= [+cor]) to be permitted, and we do indeed find such sequences (e.g., ...*iilks* in the word *?odiilks* 'dam').

The apparatus defined thus far will handle all case of word-initial and word-final C clusters, but more must be said about clusters appearing word-medially, where the Cs must be apportioned between adjacent syllables ...$\sigma_i \sigma_j$... Sequences of up to five segments can occur in this environment. In general the final two Cs will constitute the On of the second syllable σ_j. However, there are severe constraints on the sequences that can constitute the offset of the first syllable σ_i: if there are two Cs ending σ_i, the first must be a sonorant *or* the second a coronal. Thus we find medial sequences like ...*tspg*... and ...*qtqn*... which can be divided between σ_i and σ_j as ...*ts-pg*... and ...*qt-qn*..., but a sequence like ...*pkql*... cannot be divided as *...*pk-ql*... since *p* is not a sonorant, and *k* is not a coronal, despite the fact that this division is permitted by the SF rules in (39). What happens in this and similar cases is that a schwa is inserted to break up the clusters. For instance, a morphologically well-formed word like [[gepg] [bli]] 'comes back' appears on the surface as *gep-gə b-li*. We will return to this set of facts below after we have dealt with several other issues in the phonology of the language.

3.2. Some morphophonemic processes

Before proceeding to the V alternations which are of special interest to us, we must first consider some morphophonemic processes which interact with these V alternations. First, there is a class of so-called "reduplicative" prefixes (Kisseberth, 1972), including *snV-* 'strong causative,' *hVs-* 'weak causative', *pV-* 'pull causative', *sV-* reflexive', and various stem reduplications which have distributive senses; the Vs in these prefixes are a short copy of the first V in the verb stem or following prefix. We therefore find the following sorts of alternations (from Kean, 1974):

(41) a. čwék'a   'is tough'   snečwēk'a   'cause to be tough'
     b. bonwa   'drinks'   hosbənwa   'cause to drink'
     c. k'atsga   'tooth falls   pak'ətsga   'pulls one's tooth
                     out'   out'

Previous researchers have generally assumed that these data are to be handled by a V Copy rule of some sort. We can formulate the rule as in (42), where [αF] is an abbreviation for all of the features of the copied V, M is any morpheme, and Af* denotes the class of prefixes containing variable vowels.

(42) *V Copy*

$$[W_1 \ [C_o \ \underset{[\alpha F]}{\overset{\downarrow}{V}} \ C_o]_{Af^*} \ [C_o \ \underset{[\alpha F]}{V} \ W_2]_M \ W_3 \ ]_{X^o}$$

Second, there is a class of V-initial stems and locatives whose initial Vs are truncated after any morpheme once V Copy applies. We thus find forms like (43):

(43) a. -ák̇ik̄-   'wring out'   pačīka   'pulls and twists'
     b. -otēg-   'deep into'   gwotēga   'bites deep into'
     c. -adgl-   'picks up'   ʔitgəl   'picks up pl. ob-
                                                   jects'

The underlying form for *pačīka* must therefore be [[pa] [ačik] [a]]] after V Copy applies and before the second *a* is deleted, for, as Kean (1974) has pointed out, if the second *a* were deleted before V Copy has had a chance to apply, we would expect the *next* V in the stem, namely *i*, to be copied by the rule, but this results in the ungrammatical form *pičīka*. Furthermore, we know that it must be the *stem* V and not the final V of the prefix that is deleted, since ʔitgəl is derived from

[[?i] [adgl]], where ?i- is a prefix containing a *fixed* invariant V. In all such cases, the invariant V of the prefix appears on the surface rather than the V in the stem. The following rule will account for the deletion of these stem-initial Vs.

(44)   *Morpheme-Initial Vowel Deletion* (MIVD)
$$[W_1 \text{ Af } [V \quad W_2 \quad]_{V_s} \quad W_3 \quad]_{X^\circ}$$
$$\downarrow$$
$$\emptyset$$

Finally, there is a process by which the first V in a stem or morpheme becomes schwa. This process is at work in forms like *hosbənwa* (41)b. Since this process is intimately linked with the V deletion facts in the langiage, we will return to this phenomenon in the immediately following section.

3.3.   V/ə/∅ Alternations

There are various deletion and reduction processes that occur in prefixed forms in Klamath. The forms in (45)-(47) exemplify the facts:

(45)   *Long V in stem*
    a.   čwēka   'be tough'   snečwēka   'cause to be tough'
    b.   pēnhi   'be naked'   hespēnhi   'cause to be naked'
    c.   twā'qa   'smears'   satwā'qa   'smears oneself'

(46)   *Short V in closed syllable in stem*
    a.   posla   'hatch an egg'   popəsla   'distrib. hatch eggs'
    b.   bonwa   'drinks'   hosbənwa   'cause to drink'
    c.   k'atsga   'tooth falls out'   pak'ətsga   'pulls a tooth'

(47)   *Short V in open syllable in stem*
    a.   ṗaga   'smokes'   snapga   'cause to smoke'
    b.   toq'a   'is scared'   hostq'a   'cause to be scared'
    c.   t'ek'a   'be in pieces'   petk'a   'pull off bit by bit'

The basic generalizations to be gleaned from these facts are: a. when the stem V is long, a full long V appears in the stem when a prefix is present; b. when the stem V is short and in a closed syllable, it appears as a schwa when a prefix is present; and c. when the stem V is short and in an open syllable, the V deletes after a prefix. Generalization a. requires only that we be able to distinguish long from short Vs, a distinction that we are capturing in our assumptions about the Nuc structure of the language.

Vowel Deletion and Epenthesis

In order to account for b. directly and c. indirectly, we follow Kean (1974) and others in assuming that there is a rule of Vowel Reduction which changes the stem V to schwa in an appropriate context. A first approximation to the rule is given in (48).

(48) *Vowel Reduction* (to be revised)

$$[W_1 \quad Af \quad [C_o \quad \underset{\underset{[ə]}{\downarrow}}{V} \quad C \quad W_2]_M \quad W_3 \quad]_{X^o}$$

Notice that this is a rule of the sort mentioned in fn. 11, i.e. a morphologically-restricted rule which operates at the X^o-level and hence can reapply after successive affixations at that level. The importance of this fact will become apparent below. For the moment, however, it is clear that the rule stated in (48) will convert the underlying V in the stems in (46) and (47) to schwa when prefixes are added.

Finally, we must account for generalization c. Given that Vowel Reduction applies to the forms in (47) as well as those in (46), our task can be viewed as trying to account for the failure of schwa to appear in the final form of the verbs in (47). In terms of the theory of general V deletion that we have advanced above, the straightforward assumption to make is that there is a syllable structure constraint in Klamath which disallows schwas in open syllables, as in (49):

(49) *Open Syllable Schwa Constraint* (OSS)

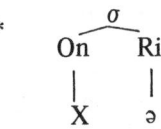

We may now consider the derivations of the forms in (46) vs. those in (47). Taking the forms in (46)a first, *posla* involves the stem *posl*- plus the Indicative suffix *a*, and together these morphemes constitute a word-level form. No morphologically-restricted rules apply, so we attempt to apply the SAA. By step a, using Condition 1, the candidate set will have two members, as in (50).

(50)
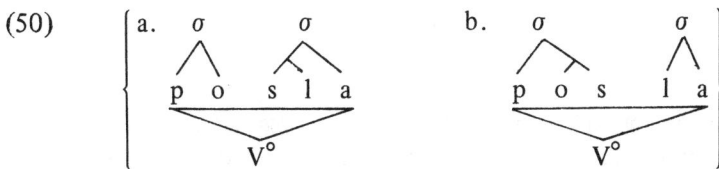

By Step b, the markedness evaluation metric should be applied to these forms and the one with the least CMV should be the output. Unfortunately, both are of equal value as far as the C-F metric (or any other syllable markedness metric, such as that proposed by Kaye and Lowenstamm, 1980) is concerned. For present purposes it does not matter which structure is chosen, although we will pick (50)b because, as we shall see, it yields a correct derivation of the related form *popəsla*.[20] Nothing else of interest happens to this form, and we obtain the correct phonetic output.

The related form *popəsla* is created by reduplicating the initial CV of the stem of *posla* (51)a. Vowel Reduction (48) now applies, converting the second *o* of the word to schwa (as in (51)b) and providing the structure which is input to the SAA.

(51) a.

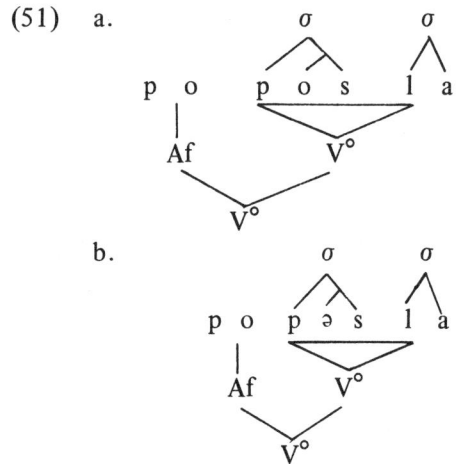

b.

When the SAA applies to the structure in (51)b it need only assign a σ_o structure to the initial *po-* of the word; since there is only one dual representation in the candidate set in (52), that structure is correctly output as the surface form for the word.

(52)

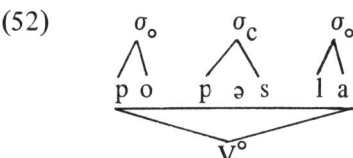

Consider now the forms in (47)a. The form *paga* has the same morphological structure as *posla*; hence the SAA yields the unique syllabification in the candidate set in (53) for this form.

Vowel Deletion and Epenthesis

(53)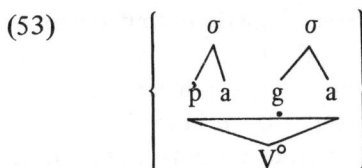

The form *snapga* is created by adding the Causative prefix to *paga*. Again Vowel Reduction applies, leaving the form in (54)b as the input to the SAA.

(54)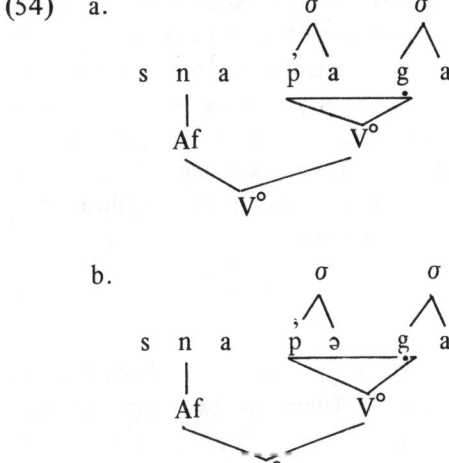

By Step a, the SAA yields a *null* candidate set under Condition 1, since by the OSS (49), the schwa in (54)b cannot remain in the open syllable. By Step c, then, the SAA reapplies Step a using Condition 2; this produces a candidate set with two members, each of which contains an unattached schwa.

(55)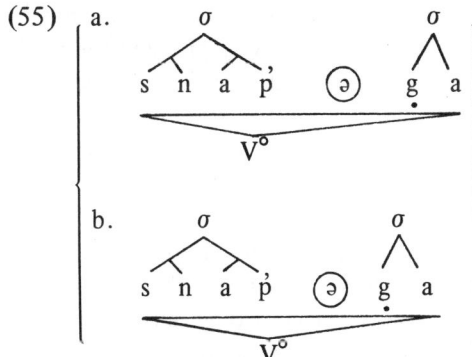

Step b will now choose (55)a as the correct phonetic output representation, since it has the lower CMV (by the C-F metric, an On containing two obstruents is more marked than a Cd and an On each containing one obstruent). Notice that the syllabic affiliation of the *p* in (54)b has been changed in (55)a as a result of the reapplication of the SAA to the entire string. Within the present theory, the only situation in which a segment previously associated with one syllable is reassociated with another is one of the above sort, i.e. one in which the SAA cannot simply add syllable structure to newly added morphological material to yield a well-formed dual representation. Notice furthermore that these forms are not the ones which force us to employ reapplication of the SAA after word-level morphological affixation, since, as noted in earlier versions of this paper, the SAA can also produce the correct outputs for such forms if it were to apply once only at the end of the morphological derivation for each word. There are more complex forms, however, which *do* require that the SAA operate in this manner which we will be discussing below. We will also make explicit at that time the conditions governing the application of the SAA when it does have to reapply to a form.

3.4. *Vowel/glide alternations*

Perhaps the fundamental problem in the phonology of Klamath is the description of long V/glide alternations. There are two types of such alternations; one involves $V_1 G_2 \sim \overline{V}_2$, and the other, $G_1 \overline{V}_1$, where identity of subscript indicates that the segments have the same feature values for height and backness. Examples of each type are given in (56).

(56) a. siwga   'kills'   sisoga   'kills oneself'
     b. čonwa 'vomits'   čononʼapga 'feels like vomiting'

Kean's (1974) insight into these forms was that *both* types can be accounted for in a unitary fashion by saying that the long Vs arise from schwa-glide sequences. It is reasonable to say that this is what is happening in the first sort of case, (56)d, where we have underlying prefixed forms like [[si] [siwga]], which is converted to [[si] [səwga]] by Vowel Reduction leaving the required schwa-glide sequence. For the second type of case one must show that independently-needed schwa-epenthesis processes insert schwas in the appropriate pre-glide positions, thus feeding the process responsible for converting əG into $\overline{V}$.

There are two quite positive aspects to this proposal. First, it accounts for the fact that the glides turn into long Vs rather than short ones, since the length of the surface V would be a direct consequence of the double-segment source. No other analysis of Klamath that we are aware of has this

Vowel Deletion and Epenthesis

feature; every other analysis either has a rule converting single Gs into long Vs, or long Vs into single Gs by fiat. Such analyses are ultimately unsatisfying because there are other languages in which Gs vocalize (or Vs devocalize) but in which the V involved in the alternation is always short.[21] If there were some way to account for the length of the Vs in the Klamath alternation, for instance by saying that they actually arise from underlying əG sequences, then we can eliminate Klamath as a counterexample to the generalization that single-segment glides normally vocalize as *single* short Vs, a generalization that follows form the basic assumptions about syllable structure that we have been making. Second, there is a sense in which it is natural to expect that *schwa* is the vowel involved in this conversion process, since it is, we believe, the universally unmarked reduced vowel, it is the most "easily deleted" vowel, in that many languages, like Klamath, have processes which superficially eliminate schwas, and it is the most "changeable" V, in that many languages have rules reducing full vowels to schwa and converting schwa to various full vowels.

There are however several problems with the particular approach which Kean adopts. First, although she takes a step toward accounting for the length of the V in these alternations in Klamath, she also assumes, following Barker (1964) that long Vs are *single* segments which are simply marked for extra length, and hence her rule of Vocalization (by contraction of schwa and glide) also winds up simply saying that the glide becomes a long V by stipulation in the rule, the schwa being deleted in the process. Second, while there may be something "natural" about the vowel involved in this coalescence being schwa, there is nothing in Kean's analysis to suggest why this should be the case. Finally, the rule which Kean gives to account for the insertion of schwa in forms like (56)b conflates two distinct processes: one involving morphologically governed epenthesis and the other a very general insertion process.

In the following subsections we will take up each of these problems in turn, considering first the matter of V length, and then the question of the various epenthesis processes at work in the language.

3.4.1. Vowel length and Schwa Assimilation

As we suggested in Section 1, Klamath contains Nuc structures of Type VII in Table I, which permits nuclei of the form V, VV, VG, and VR. In the following discussion we will only be concerned with the first three of these Nuc types. In addition to these, the grammar of Klamath contains several syllable-sensitive rules which neutralize VG sequences to VV sequences within the Nuc. The first of these is given in (57).

(57)   *Nuclear Lengthening*

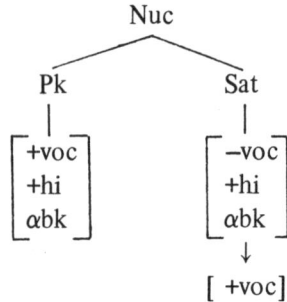

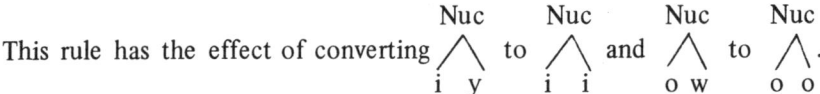

This rule has the effect of converting [Nuc i y] to [Nuc i i] and [Nuc o w] to [Nuc o o].
Notice that this rule must be stated as a part of the grammar of Klamath, since there are languages (e.g. English) which have *iy* and *uw* sequences rather than *ii* and *uu* sequences (non-diphthongal long vowels) in the Nuc. An example of a case which requires such a rule involves underlying [[wo] [wosa]] asurfacing as *wōsa* 'fears, distrib.' The derivation for this form proceeds as follows. On the second application of the SAA, after Vowel Reduction, we have the form *wo + wə̂ sâ* which serves as input to the SAA. We find that there is only one possible candidate structure for the form (the medial syllable cannot remain, as it violates the OSS (49)). This syllabification is given in (58).

(58)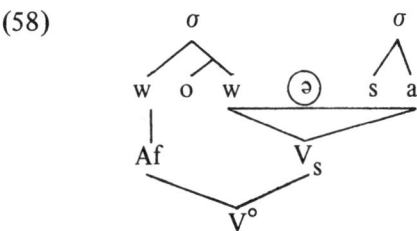

Since this structure is alone in the reduced candidate set, it goes on to become the syllable structure of the word. After the SAA has applied, (57) will convert the nuclear *ow* to *oo*, to produce the long V required in the surface form.

A second process of this type involves the assimilation of glottal stop within the Nuc. Consider a verb stem such as *sleʔ-* 'see'. The simple Indicative form is *sleʔa*, which can only be syllabified as *sle- ʔa*, and this in fact is the correct surface form. If we contrast this with the nominal form produced by adding *-s* to the stem, we will obtain the syllabification in (59).

Vowel Deletion and Epenthesis

(59)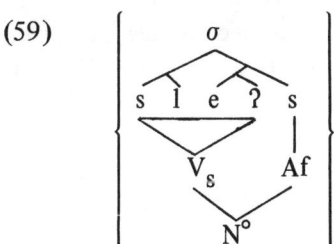

This representation must undergo a rule assimilating the glottal stop to the proceeding V, as given in (60).

(60)   *Glottal Lengthening*

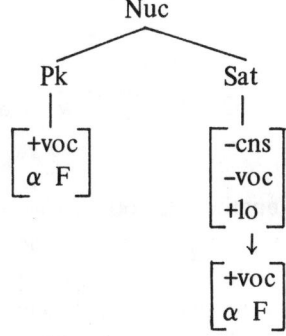

After the application of this syllable-sensitive rule to (59), we obtain a syllabic structure containing the correct surface output *slēs*.

(61)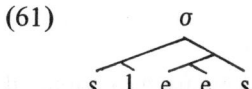

Returning now to forms like *sisōga* in (56)a, the input to the SAA for this form (after the application of Vowel Reduction) is (62)a, and the output of the SAA is (62)b.

(62)   a.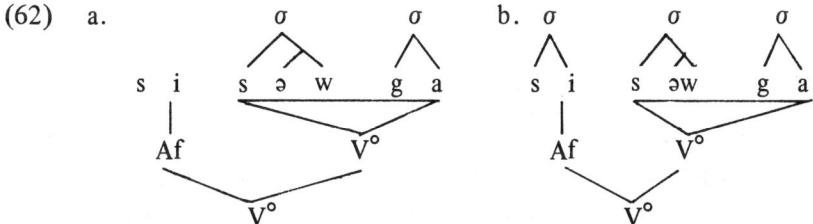

Notice that the second syllable does not contravene the OSS because it does not contain schwa syllable-finally. We now need a rule converting schwa in structures like (62)b into the appropriate full vowel; (63) will accomplish this.

(63) *Schwa Assimilation*

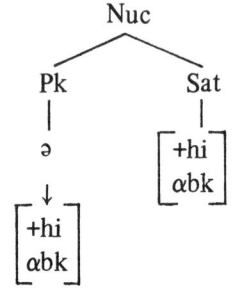

(63) Will convert the second syllable of (62)b to s o w which will in turn become s o o by Nuclear Lengthening (60). In general, then, morphologically determined X C V_1 G_2 Y sequences become X C V_2 G_2 Y sequences through the combined operation of Vowel Reduction – which converts V_1 to schwa – and Schwa Assimilation, which converts schwa to a full V with the same height and backness as the following high glide. The surface string X C V_2 V_2 Y is then produced by Nuclear Lengthening. All of these rules except Vowel Reduction are syllable-sensitive rules that apply after all morphological operations have been accomplished, and after the SAA has finished assigning syllable structure to the representations in question.

Before turning to the second type of long V/G alternation exemplified by (56)b, let us consider some examples which require that the SAA apply after affixation at *each* X^0-level. The first set of forms involve the stem *y̓ooq̓*- 'shave'. Prefixed with the morpheme *ʔV*- 'act on someone', we derive by Vowel Copy (42) and the SAA the straightforward syllabification in (64), which contains the correct surface form.

(64)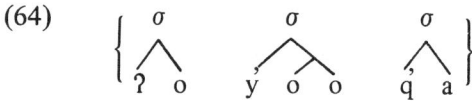

Notice that Vowel Reduction does not apply here because the second *o* is followed by another V (it is part of a long-vowel Nuc). The reflexive of this form is derived by adding the prefix *sV*- to this form, Vowel Copy applies to give the form *so*- for the prefix, and now Vowel Reduction

Vowel Deletion and Epenthesis

can apply to the *o* following the glottal stop, converting it to schwa. By Step a, Condition 1, the SAA produces a null candidate set because the only possible dual representation that could be in the set is the structure in (65), which is illformed because it contravenes the OSS.

(65)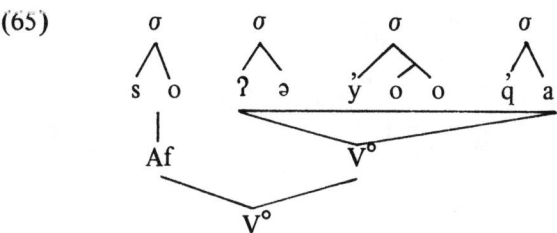

Reapplying the SAA using Condition 2 yields the non-null candidate set in (66), containing a representation in which the schwa is left unattached.

(66)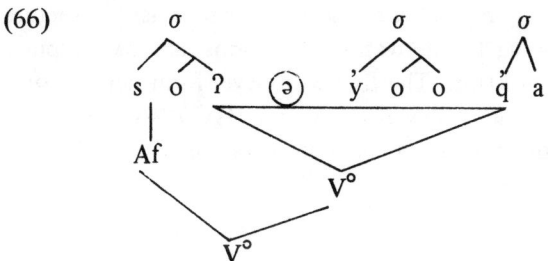

The syllable-sensitive rule of Glottal Lengthening (60) can apply to this structure to produce the correct surface form *sōyō'q'a*.

Finally, a Distributive can be derived from the form in (66) by reduplicating the initial CV, adding an additional *so-* to the beginning of that form. As the analysis now stands, Vowel Reduction should apply to the second *o* in this form; if this were to happen, we would be left with the syllabification in (67).

(67)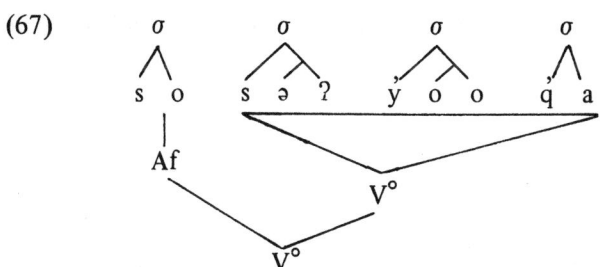

Glottal lengthening would then apply to give the incorrect surface form *sosə́yō̄qá*. We can avoid this result if we restrict Vowel Reduction so that it will fail to apply in cases like this. The revised version of Vowel Reduction in (68) will accomplish this for us.[22]

(68) *Vowel Reduction* (revised)

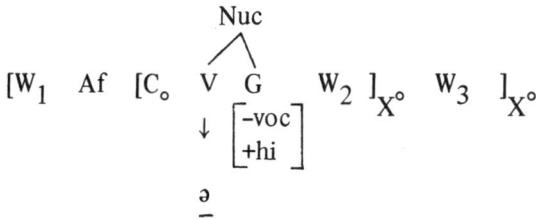

With these modifications, the rule cannot apply to reduce the second *o* in the structure to schwa. Hence Glottal Lengthening will convert *soʔ* into *soo* in the second syllable, and we will arrive at the correct surface form *sosō̄yō̄qá*.

That this morphologically-restricted rule must refer to syllable structure can be shown by examining the derivations for forms like *sosʔīgi* 'put a long object over oneself, distrib.' The first word-level form here is *-oygi* plus the prefix *ʔi-*, which after Vowel Copy and MIVD (44) appears as *ʔoygi*. The SAA will construct the dual representation in (69) for this form.

(69)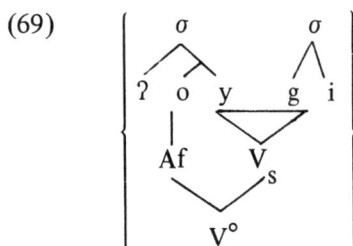

The reflexive prefix *sV-* is then added to this structure; Vowel Copy applies, as does Vowel Reduction, since the *o* in the second syllable *ʔoy* shares the Nuc with a high glide. The SAA yields the following candidate set.

(70)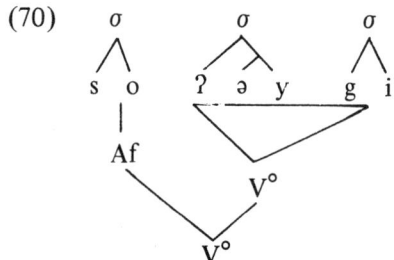

Vowel Deletion and Epenthesis

If this were the end of the derivation, Schwa Assimilation and Nuclear Lengthening would apply to produce the correct surface form *soʔigi*. If, however, the Distributive prefix, a reduplication of the first syllable, is added to the form in (70), then Vowel Reduction will be able to apply again, this time changing the second syllable *so* to *sə*. The SAA will then create a null candidate set, since the only possible representation that could be set is the one in (71), which contains an illegal open syllable.

(71)

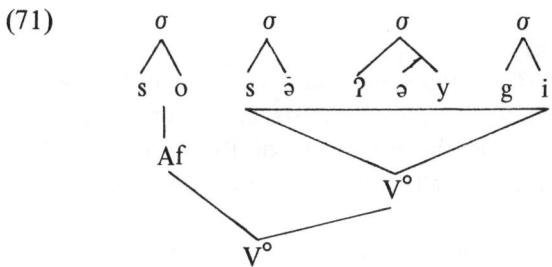

Under Condition II, the SAA is able to create a well-formed representation, namely the one in (72).

(72)

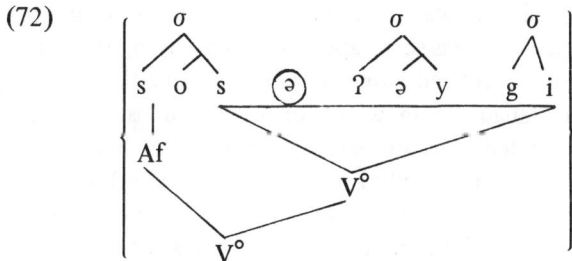

The important point to note about this derivation is that Vowel Reduction can apply to the second *o* here even though it is immediately followed by a glottal stop, whereas in the preceding case involving *sosō̕yō̄qa* Vowel Reduction could *not* apply immediately before this segment. The only difference between these forms lies in the syllable structure assigned to them on the previous application of the SAA. In the case of *sosʔigi* the *o* and the *ʔ* are in separate syllables, while in *sosō̕yō̄qa* the *o* and the *ʔ* are in the same syllable, and both are under Nuc. Referring to this difference in syllable structure in the environment of Vowel Reduction therefore allows us to permit it to apply in cases like *sosʔigi* and to prevent it from applying in cases like *sosō̕yō̄qa*, as desired.[23]

3.4.2. Vowel length and epenthesis.

Returning now to the type of long V/G alternation exemplified by the form in (56)b, it is clear that as long as we can find a way to insert a schwa before the G in these forms, the machinery that we have already motivated will automatically produce the correct long surface V. To do this in the general case, we will follow Lowenstamm (1979) in assuming that when a segmental string consists of a sequence of Cs which cannot be attached in a well-formed manner into the syllable structure being constructed by the SAA, the Cs are grouped together into a syllable with a null Pk, and a V is inserted under this Pk.

(73) *Universal Epenthesis*
   a. If one or more Cs in the segmental string of a word cannot be attached to a well-formed syllable structure, construct a new syllable structure in which at least one Pk in the new structure dominates ∅ until all of the Cs in the segmental string are attached.
   b. Fill all null Pk positions with ə.

A number of remarks must be made about this first approximation to the Universal Epenthesis process. First, the quality of the epenthetic V is to some extent a language-specific property. In general it appears that schwa is the epenthetic vowel in languages where schwa arises as a result of phonological or morphological processes, or appears in underlying segmental strings; otherwise, various "reduced" or other Vs may fill the null Pk. Second, there are some languages in which epenthesis does not apply to insert a V among "stranded" Cs; instead, one of the Cs is deleted. For example, in Sinhala, which permits only single-C Cds, an underlying form like *lind* surfaces with the final segment deleted (i.e. as *liŋ*, see Cairns and Feinstein, 1982). We refer to this process as *syllable-marginal C-deletion*. At present we are not in a position to be able to predict the conditions under which syllable-marginal C-deletion as opposed to Universal Epenthesis will apply. It appears however that epenthesis is employed in languages like Klamath which have relatively complex Ons and Cds, while deletion occurs in languages with generally simpler constructions. Space limitations preclude our further investigating either of these topics here. Finally, although we have relied on the proposals of Lowenstamm (1979) in formulating our version of Universal Epenthesis, the two approaches are quite different in that Lowenstamm adopts a theory which allows resyllabification after the application of all phonological rules, whereas the theory proposed here incorporates this universal process directly into the algorithm which assigns syllable structure, as we are about to see.

To include Universal Epenthesis (and Syllable-Marginal C-Deletion) in the SAA, we need only change (35) so that Step c will allow the algorithm to start over again if neither Condition 1 nor Condition 2 yield a non-null candidate set, this time employing Condition 3 given in (74).

Vowel Deletion and Epenthesis

(74)   *Condition 3* Either (i) all Cs are attached and at least one ə (or other reduced V) is inserted by Universal Epenthesis (73), or (ii) all Vs are attached and there is at least one syllable-marginal C unattached.

The second form in (56)b is now straightforwardly derivable. The underlying morphological representation for the form is *čonw+ńapg+a* containing only one word-level domain. Using Condition 1, the SAA will not produce a non-null candidate set; neither of the structures in (75) are possible because *nw* is not a possible Cd (75)a and *wn* is not a possible word-medial On (75)b.[24]

(75)   a. *

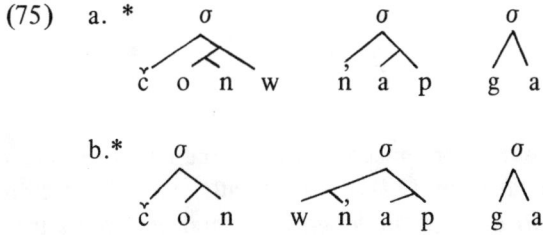

b. *

Using Condition 2 will provide no relief from this situation, since the non-attachment of any V in this form will also fail to produce a well-formed structure. Moving on to Condition 3, the SAA produces the candidate set in (76)a; the structure in (76)b is ill-formed because it contravenes the Open Syllable Schwa Constraint (49).

(76)   a.

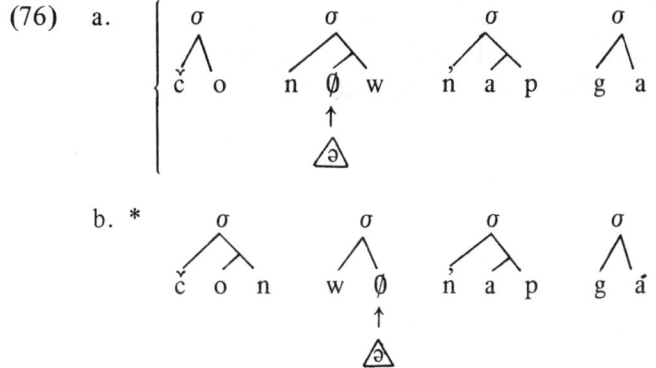

b. *

Schwa Assimilation and Nuclear Lengthening now convert the form in (76)a into the desired surface form.

There are other sorts of forms to which Universal Epenthesis applies during the operation of the SAA which, however, do not involve converting G sequences to VV sequences. The form *gepgəbli* mentioned in Section 3.1 is of this sort. Given the underlying segmental string for this form ([[gepg][bli]]$_{V^o}$) and the constraints on medical clusters noted in that earlier section that disallows sequences like ...*pg-bl*..., there is no way to construct a well-formed syllable structure for the word without inserting a V somewhere. There are in fact two places where a *ə* can be inserted in this form, and both of the resulting representations, shown in (77), turn out to have the same CMV in terms of the C-F metric.

(77)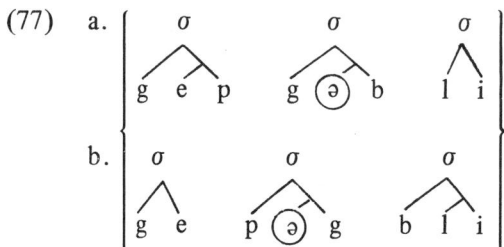

Determining how the SAA must be made to choose the correct form in such cases (in the example at hand, (77)a) is a difficult one which we do not have the space here to consider in detail. In general, it appears that Klamath prefers intermorphemic insertions, as in (77)a, although there are instances recorded by Barker (1964) which contain intramorphemic insertion. These issues, as well as the interesting matter of the proper formulation of the constraint disallowing syllabifications like . . .*pg - bl* . . . word-internally, are considered in more detail in Feinstein and Lapointe (in preparation).

In addition to this general sort of insertion, there are several morphologically restricted rules which epenthesize *ə*. The most important of these for our purposes provides additional sources for long V/G alternations by inserting *ə* after *w* (and *only* after *w*) in the following context.[25]

(78) *w*-Cluster

$$[[W_1 \quad [+son] \; w \; \emptyset \; C_o] \quad W_2]$$
$$\downarrow \quad \left\{ \begin{matrix} X_s \\ X^o \end{matrix} \right\}$$
$$ə$$

This is a modification of Kean's (1974) Idiosyncratic *w* rule which allows the rule to apply when *any* [+son] (either V or C) appears before the *w*, a restriction which seems valid given the forms involved:

(79) a. [[bonw]$_{V_s}$ s]$_{N^o}$ → bonwəs 'drink'

[[delwg]$_{V_s}$ s]$_{N^o}$ → delwəks 'attack'

Vowel Deletion and Epenthesis 111

[[sgoyw]$_{V^s}$ [alčwi]]$_{V^o}$ → sgoywəlčwi   'send someone right up to'

[[sʔaywg]$_{V_s^s}$ s]$_{N^o}$ → sʔaywəks   'knowing'

b. [[sʔoowy]$_{V^s}$ dk]$_{V^o}$ → sʔōwitk   'having passed a tray'

[de [dewy]$_{V^o}$]$_{V^o}$ → dedwī   'shoot bow and arrow, distrib.'

Under this approach, all of the forms which Kean cites as undergoing Idiosyncratic w (79)a will undergo w-Cluster, in addition to forms like those in (79)b. In the first of these forms, the ə is inserted by (78) between the w and the y, giving [[sʔoowəy]$_{V^s}$ dk]$_{V^o}$, which after SAA, Schwa Assimilation, Nuclear Lengthening, and a voice assimilation rule yields sʔoowiitk; the second i is deleted by a shortening rule which leaves the desired surface form.[26] The second form in (79)b has a derivation which proceeds in the following way.

(80)   *Internal word*   dewy
        w-Cluster   dewəy

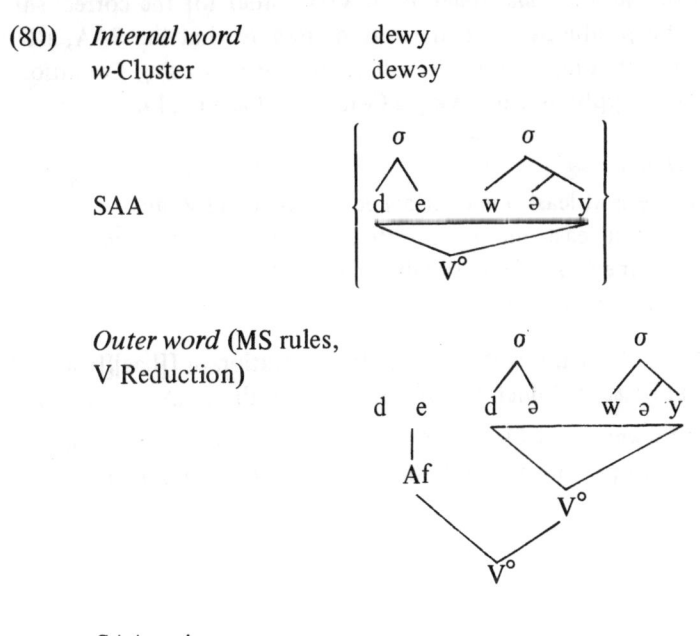

SAA

Outer word (MS rules, V Reduction)

SAA, using Condition 1   ∅

SAA, using
Condition 2

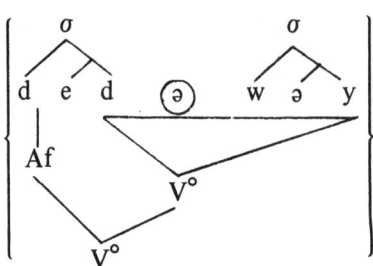

The final form in (80) ultimately surfaces as *dedwi* after application of Schwa Assimilation and Nuclear Lengthening (and Shortening) as desired. Notice that the application of *w*-Cluster in the internal word sets up the preceding V for deletion since it cannot appear in an open syllable.

3.4.3. Deletion/epenthesis interactions

Finally, let us consider a type of derivation which is similar to the one in (80) but in which the ə is inserted by Universal Epenthesis. These cases involve both the addition *and* deletion of Vs in order for the correct surface form to be produced. Such derivations require that the SAA, after finding that it can only construct null candidate sets using Conditions 1, 2, and 3, can reapply by employing a Condition 4 as in (81).

(81)   Condition 4
(i) There is at least one unattached word-medial V, *and*
(ii) either at least one ə is inserted by Universal Epenthesis, or at least one C is deleted syllable-marginally,
and all other segments are attached.

To take an example of this sort, consider the derivation of [[has][[wayʾasg][iys]]]_{N⁰} → *hasōyasgis* 'loincloth'. Application of the SAA on the inner word straight-forwardly yields the structure in (82)a. Addition of the prefix *hVs-*, Vowel Copy, and Vowel Reduction yield the structure in (82)b.

(82) a.

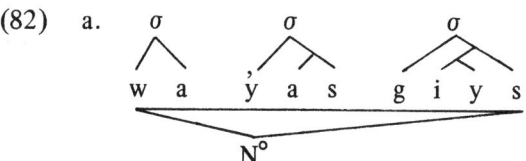

b.

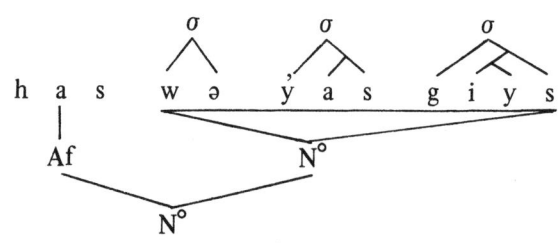

Vowel Deletion and Epenthesis

When the SAA applies to the form in (82)b, the candidate set based on Condition 1 will be null since the only possible structure for that set would have an illegal open second syllable. Similarly, the candidate set based on Condition 2 will be null because there is no way simply to leave a V unattached and obtain a well-formed syllable structure.[27] The conditions for Universal Epenthesis are not met, so no candidate set is produced under Condition 3. The SAA tries Condition 4, and this yields the candidate set in (85) which contains both a deleted and an inserted ə.

(83)

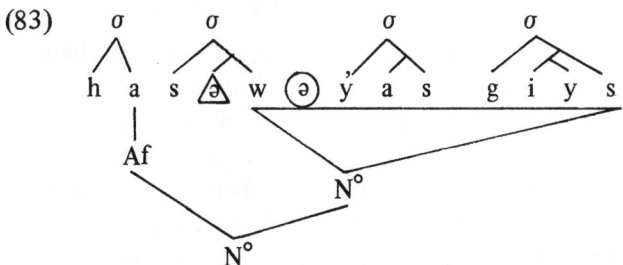

Again, after Schwa Assimilation and Nuclear Lengthening convert the second syllable to *soo*, we obtain the correct surface output.

3.5. Summary

Given the assumptions which we have made about the morphological and syllabic structure of Klamath words, we have constructed a straightforward analysis of the V/ə/∅ and V̄/G alternations in the language in terms of the theory of Sections 1 and 2 which assumes that general V deletion and insertion occur as part of the assignment of syllable structure. This analysis provides a fairly elegant account of the basic phonological processes at work in Klamath, including a. a maximally simple, nonmorphological account of the context in which ə is left unattached (namely, in open syllables), b. a fairly transparent approach to the various epenthesis processes at work in the language, and c. a phonetically plausible account of the conversion of əG sequences to long Vs. Regarding c, our analysis explains the naturalness of the length of the final V, and the naturalness of the insertion of ə by Universal Epenthesis, but it does not address the issue of the naturalness of the appearance of ə, as opposed to any other V, being crucially involved in these conversion processes. The issue essentially hinges on the question of what it is that makes the syllable sensitive rules of Schwa Assimilation and Nuclear Lengthening natural. While only a more detailed specification of the theory of syllable sensitive rules and the role that reduced Vs play in such rules will be able to answer this question satisfactorily, a reasonable first step would be to say that the naturalness of these rules follows from two considerations. First, a Nuc is less marked if both Pk and Sat segments share the values for the features [αhi, βback]; second, a syllable sensitive rule is less marked if it assimilates the features of a *reduced* V to those of an adjacent sonorant rather than the other way around, and it is less marked if it assimilates G to an adjacent *full* V rather than the other way. Although this is a plausible way to proceed, only much further work will allow us to conclude that it is correct. In the meantime, it should nevertheless be clear how the naturalness of these processes can be reflected in a theory of the sort that we are proposing.

In the process of developing our analysis of Klamath, we have found it necessary to modify our theory of the operation of the SAA in several ways. In particular, we have had to allow the SAA to insert as well as delete Vs, and we have relied to a much greater extent on the reapplication of the SAA in the generation of new words. We therefore state below a modified version of the SAA which incorporates these changes, along with the conditions governing its reapplication.

(84) *Syllable Assignment Algorithm* (revised)
The algorithm starts with $n = 1$.
Step a. Construct a candidate set of dual representations for a word such that
> (i) the syllabic structure of each dual representation in the set is consistent with the syllable formation rules of the language and with the universal and language-specific syllable structure constraints, and
> (ii) the syllable structure of each dual representation in the set meets Condition n.

Step b. If there is one member in the candidate set, output that dual representation for the word. If there is more than one member in the set, apply the C-F metric to the syllable structure of the candidate representations and output the one(s) with syllable structure(s) having the least CMV.
Step c. If the candidate set is null, go back to *Step a* and reapply the algorithm using Condition $n+1$.
Condition 1. All segments in the morphologically determined segmental string of the word are attached to some syllable.
Condition 2. All Cs are attached to some syllable, and at least one word-medial V is unattached.
Condition 3. Either (i) all Cs are attached and at least one ə (or other reduced V) is inserted by Universal Epenthesis, or (ii) all Vs are attached and there is at least one syllable-marginal C unattached.

Condition 4. (i) There is at least one unattached word-medial V, *and* (ii) either at least one ə is inserted by Universal Epenthesis or at least one C is unattached syllable-marginally, *and* all other segments are attached.

(85) *Reapplication of SAA*
   a. Whenever new morphological material is added to a dual representation at the $X^°$-level, apply the SAA to the newly added material only, using Condition 1.
   b. If the resulting dual representation contains an ill-formed syllable structure, erase all of the syllable structure for the entire word, go to *Step a* using Condition 2, and apply the SAA as above to the entire word.

4. CONCLUSION

In the preceding sections we have presented fairly straightforward reanalyses for two classical problems of segmental phonology: the distribution of inserted and deleted Vs in Yawelmani, and the distribution of long Vs and Gs in Klamath. The analyses have been formulated within a restrictive theory of the reapplication of the syllable assignment algorithm in which phonologically productive deletion and epenthesis processes operate directly during the application of the SAA to MSs and are not carried out by particular syllable sensitive rules. The success of these analyses suggests that it may well be possible to maintain a syllable structure preserving condition of the sort in (13) and the overall organization of syllable/morphology interactions depicted in Figure 1 when the present theory is tested against facts from a wider range of languages. A considerable amount of research remains to be conducted in these areas, however, especially in the specification of the theories of morphologically-restricted and syllable sensitive rules, as well as in the further modification and extension of the theory of language-specific syllable structure constraints and the C-F metric. Nevertheless, the theory proposed here presents a reasonably constrained and conceptually appealing framework within which these further issues can be considered.

NOTES

1. Some of the recent studies that we have in mind are Hooper (1976), Kahn (1976), Broselow (1976), Lowenstamm (1979), McCarthy (1979), Kiparsky (1979), and Selkirk (forthcoming).

116 Steven G. Lapointe and Mark H. Feinstein

2. For a real example of ə-deletion, see Selkirk (1977); for an example of ə-epenthesis, see Lowenstamm (1978).
3. This approach is similar in spirit to, though quite different in detail from, Emonds' (1976) structure preserving constraint on syntactic transformations. The major difference is that Emonds' theory claims that syntactic PS rules act as constraints on the *application* of transformations whereas (13) is in effect a restriction on the *kinds* of syllable sensitive rules that can appear in a grammar.
4. Among others. The reader should note that we will *only* be concerned with the assignment of syllable structures *within words* here. We ignore the assignment of higher levels of metrical structure in the present discussion (Liberman and Prince, 1977; Selkirk, forthcoming) both within the word and in larger syntactic domains.
5. There are various ways in which vocalic sonorants can be accomodated in this framework. One would be to say that there is a second universally possible Nuc type as in (i), with a universal restriction to the effect that every grammar must at least have a Nuc SF rule of the type in (19) and a markedness condition to the effect that sonorants in the Pk are more marked than Vs.

(i)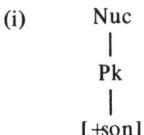

Other possibilities exist, but the choice among these is irrelevant for the subsequent discussion.
6. It is probable that Universal Grammar also allows Sats to the left of Pk's as well as to the right of them in order to handle English $\bar{u}$ (phonetically [yuw], French and Spanish "broken" mid-vowels (French [ye] and [wa]; Spanish [ye] and [we]), and the like.
7. English has either Type III or Type VI Nucs, depending on how one analyzes the various sonorants and their properties in the language. We are still searching for a convincing case of Type V.
8. One possibility is that Universal Grammar makes available to grammars with Nuc Type I two ways of representing long Vs (i) and two ways of representing long Cs (ii).

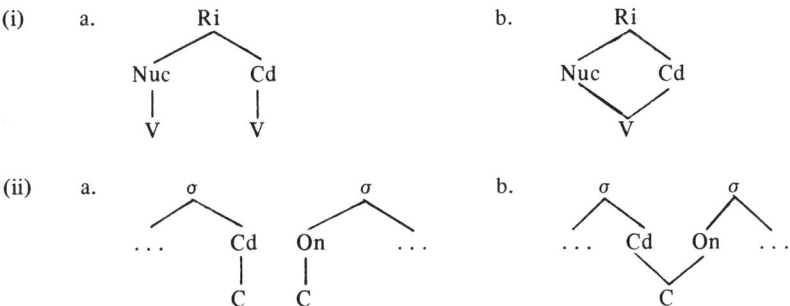

If grammars were to choose freely from among these options, four possible types would arise. The first type would contain (i)a and (ii)a and would not exhibit either compensatory lengthening or gemination as a result of C deletion from Cd. The second type would contain (i)a and (ii)b and should show gemination since it allows doubly attached Cs; the Lesbian/Thessalian dialect of Greek discussed by Ingria (1980) would be of this type. The third type would contain (i)b and (ii)a and should permit compensatory lengthening; the remaining Greek dialects discussed by Ingria would be of this type. The last type would contain (i)b and (ii)b. Since it is not clear which process, if either, would win out when a C is deleted from Cd for this type, it may be that Universal Grammar simply disallows this possibility from being realized in actual grammars.

9. This conception of the interaction between SAA and morphological processes represents a departure from the suggestion put forth in Cairns and Feinstein (1982) and argued for in a widely distributed earlier version of the present paper to the effect that reapplication of the SAA is not needed under *any* circumstances. A number of facts from Klamath, discussed in Section 3, have forced us to retreat from our earlier position.

10. We are following Aronoff (1976) in this regard. Notice however that Aronoff was considering a more standard segmental theory of the cycle in his work.

11. These rules must be severely constrained, since as it stands now they are extremely powerful. Note for instance that morphologically-restricted rules applying at the $X°$-level will in essence be allowed to cycle in a way similar to that allowed in the standard conception of the circle. In fact, a major part of Klamath phonology hinges on one morphologically-restricted rule behaving in just this way. One way to constrain this type of rule might be to make these rules more intimately connected with the actual morphological attachment processes themselves so as to greatly diminish the opportunities for them to apply productively. In the cases of the Klamath example below, we might consider fusing Vowel Copy and Vowel Reduction into a single operation that applied whenever but only when one of the special class of $X°$-level reduplicative prefixes were attached to a word. Regrettably, we cannot go into further detail about this important issue in the present context.

12. Parentheses have been placed around the *i* in the passive aorist suffix to indicate that it is present if and only if a monosyllabic segment precedes it. Thus, when this suffix is added to a stem like *panaa-* in (2.4)c, the *i* will not be presented, exactly as desired. This interpretation of parenthesized morpheme-marginal Vs is assumed to be given universally and hence need not be stated explicitly in the grammar of Yawelmani.

13. The restriction that the unattached Vs in Condition 2 of the SAA must be word-medial has been included for the following reasons. Consider a language which permits syllables to be V-initial, i.e., a language in which Ons are optional, and consider a V-initial word which does not have a well-formed syllable structure in which all segments are attached. It appears that under such conditions, languages typically do not opt for deleting the initial V of the word, even if the resulting syllable structure has a complexity value which is less than that of a candidate syllable structure with a deleted medial V. Similarly, word-final Vs, especially those that are part of regular inflectional endings, seem in general not to be deleted preferentially over medial Vs. Where such Vs *are* deleted, they appear to be deleted under various morphological conditions, and we therefore assume that such cases are handled by language-specific morphologically-restricted rules.

14. Notice that although the DOS constraint in (33) contains what amounts to a syllabic version of the segmental environment appearing in Kuroda's V Deletion rule (31), these theoretical devices make quite distinct claims about the phenomena that they are trying to explain. First, DOS captures the syllabic nature of the phenomena in a way that the segmental rule cannot. Next, there is nothing in the frame-

work underlying the segmental analysis to suggest that the context of (2.6) is a natural one for V deletions to occur in, as opposed to, say, the context in which the Cs and Vs are reversed (i), or that these contexts are more or less natural ones in which to find Cs being deleted (ii) and (iii).

(i)   V → ∅ / C V ___ V C
(ii) C → ∅ / V C ___ C V
(iii) C → ∅ / C V ___ V C

On the other hand, in the syllable structure theory, depending on the language-specific syllable constraints that are involved, these contexts would have rather different degrees of naturalness. Thus, the deletion of a V in the context of (31) is only natural in terms of the present theory if the particular language in question has a constraint like DOS (33); furthermore, a rule such as (i) above would be natural only if it were a Morphological Adjustment rule, i.e., only if a morpheme boundary were included in the SD immediately before or after the affected V. On the other hand, a rule like (ii) would be more natural than (iii), since the latter would produce a V-initial syllable, which is a marked option (cf. Cairns and Feinstein, 1981 and the discussion in Section 1), whereas the deletion of a C in the environment of (ii) would, depending on the syllable structure constraints, yield less complex and hence more highly valued syllable structures. For these sorts of reasons then, it can be seen that the adoption of a constraint like DOS is not simply a restatement of the segmental rule in (31).

15. Kuroda (1967) discusses numerous other cases of the same sort which can be handled in exactly the same way as *panamxit*.

16. Assuming that long Vs are to be represented as double V sequences, examples of this sort suggest that the expansion of Nuc in (24) is correctly formulated. The alternative would be to say that the second of the two Vs appears under Off rather than Nuc, so that syllables with long Vs would have a structure parallel to that of short closed syllables, as in (i).

(i)
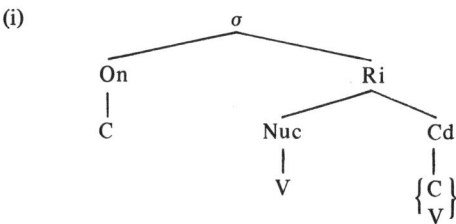

Such a move would have the desirable consequence of not requiring the separate constraint in (26)b to rule out long closed syllables in the language. Unfortunately, this change would also require us to complicate the statement of the DOS (33) considerably. The problem has to do with the first syllable mentioned in that constraint. Cases like (37) show that the *length* of the V in this syllable does not matter (it can be long as in (37) or short as in (32)) so long as it does not end in a C. Given our assumptions about Yawelmani syllable structure and the conventions for referring to syllable-internal structure given in Section 1, we need only stipulate this syllable as σ_o in the constraint. If, however, long Vs were represented as in (i), the only way to refer to this syllable would be by reference to the two kinds of structure it can have, as in (ii).

Vowel Deletion and Epenthesis   119

(ii)   *   Ri   σ̆°   σ
               /\
              X V

(33) Is clearly the more straightforward statement of the constraint, thus lending support to the assumption that both Vs are represented under Nuc in this language.
17. Among these topics is the question of the abstractness of the underlying V system in the language and the status of the rules of Lowering and V Harmony. For considerable discussion, see Kuroda (1967) and Lapointe (forthcoming).
18. All of the Klamath data discussed in this section derive from Barker's grammar or from his dictionary (Barker, 1963, 1964). Notice that it is customary in studies of Klamath to use *o* to represent the high back rounded V in the language, since this V is in fact pronounced with a lowered tongue position.
19. In addition, Klamath also exhibits syllabic sonorants (cf. fn. 5), but these are not relevant to the present discussion.
20. Whether a grammar chooses a form like (50)b over one like (50)a or vice versa in such cases seems to be at least in part a language-specific matter. Thus, Kaye and Lowenstamm (1980a) show that in similar situations Polish also prefers the associations in (50)b, while Cairns and Feinstein (1982) show that Sinhala prefers structures like (50)a. Space limitations preclude us from going into the matter further here, however.
21. See Feinstein (1979), Cairns and Feinstein (1982), and numerous other works for examples of G/short V alternations.
22. Thomas (1974) attempted a purely segmental approach of this sort to restricting the operation of Vowel Reduction in such forms because at the time the theory of syllable structure was not yet available as a way of stating the necessary restrictions. It will become clear immediately below, however, that the only difference between forms like *sosōyōqa* in which Vowel Reduction fails to apply before ʔ and forms like *sosʔigi* where the rule must apply before ʔ is in the syllabic association of the ʔ.
23. Allowing morphologically-restricted rules to refer to syllable structure weakens the theory of such rules even further. Notice though that *only* those rules which can apply at the X°-level can refer to syllable structure since only those morphologically-restricted rules can apply *after* the SAA has assigned syllable structure to an inner word. If, as suggested in fn. 11, these rules are restricted to apply as a more direct consequence of the attachment of morphemes at the various levels of MS, then the restriction of the occurrence of syllable contexts to those morphologically-restricted rules which opreate at the X°-level would be a quite natural consequence of the theory being proposed.
24. Barker (1964) notes that *wC is* possible, but only word-initially. In such cases a reduced V with the same height and backness as *w* is inserted to break up the cluster.
25. In addition, there is a rule of Sonorant Epenthesis (i), which inserts ə before sonorants near morpheme boundaries, and there are several idiosyncratic epenthesis rules; none of these leads to long V/G alternations however.

(i)   *Sonorant Epenthesis*

$$[_{W_1} [_{W_2} C \underset{\downarrow}{\quad} \begin{bmatrix} +son \\ +cns \end{bmatrix}]_{X^i} \; (C \; Z) \;]_{V^\circ}$$
$$\quad\quad\quad\quad\quad\quad ə$$

Kean's (1974) rule of Sonorant Cluster attempted to generalise (i) in a number of ways, but given the existence of Universal Epenthesis and the properties of Klamath syllable and morphological structure, there is really no need to modify the rule in the ways that she has suggested. See Feinstein and Lapointe (in preparation) for discussion.

26. The shortening rule in Klamath seems to have the following form:

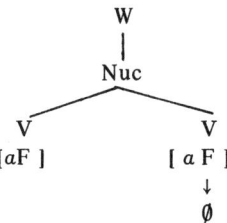

There are however several problems with using this rule; see Feinstein and Lapointe (in preparation) for some discussion.

27. There actually *is* a way to derive a well-formed syllable structure by leaving a V unattached, namely, by disattaching the *a* in the third syllable, leaving the structure in (i).

(i)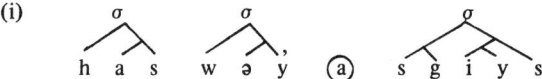

This structure is quite well-formed (*sg* is a possible On) which will lead to the ungrammatical *haswīsgis* as output. To eliminate this possibility, it appears that we need to make the deletion Conditions 2 and 4 in the SAA sensitive to the presence of ə (or other reduced Vs) in a word. Specifically, the condition would seem to be that if there are any ə's or other reduced Vs in a word, the deletion conditions try to leave them unattached, and the SAA tries to leave full Vs unattached *only* if there are no ə's or other reduced Vs in the word. For further discussion of this matter, see Feinstein and Lapointe (in preparation).

Phonological Representation and Action-At-A-Distance

William J. Poser
M.I.T.

0. INTRODUCTION

The formal theory of phonology may be thought of as comprising two interacting but distinct components: the theory of phonological representations and the theory of phonological rules. What is undoubtedly the greatest result obtained thus far in phonology, the theory of distinctive features, belongs to the theory of representations, but in the past twenty years it has been, for the most part, the theory of rules that has attracted the most attention. It is only in the past five years that interest in the nature of phonological representations has returned to the fore. Two major theories have been advanced: the Autosegmental theory of Goldsmith (1976) and the Metrical theory of Vergnaud & Halle (1978). These two theories propose different, though largely compatible, modifications of the theory of representations set out in Chomsky & Halle (1968). The Autosegmental theory is for the most part an enriched theory of distinctive features, obtained by relaxing the constraints on the geometry of distinctive feature representations imposed in *The Sound Pattern of English*. The Metrical theory, on the other hand, proposes the existence of additional, hierarchical structure, such as the syllable and the foot.[1]

One of the classical problems in the formal theory of phonology is the proper treatment of harmony processes and related forms of action-at-a-distance, the discussion of which antedates the publication of SPE (see Lightner 1965). Although neither the Autosegmental theory nor the Metrical theory was originally conceived as a theory of harmony, claims have been made on behalf of both theories on the basis of their treatment of harmonic processes. In the present paper I shall consider the treatment

---

* The research reported here was supported by a Graduate Fellowship from the National Science Foundation, USA. An earlier version of this paper was presented at the GLOW Colloquium, 25 March 1982, Paris, France. Thanks are due to Nick Clements, Morris Halle, Jonathan Kaye, Paul Kiparsky, and Engin Sezer for helpful discussion.

of such processes in the two non-linear theories. In particular, I shall evaluate the claims of the Metrical theory of harmony.

1. The Autosegmental Theory

In the classical generative phonological theory of Chomsky & Halle (1968) a phonological representation consists of a linear sequence of feature matrices. Each matrix is a column-vector consisting of binary specifications of a fixed set of distinctive features, and each matrix corresponds to one quasi-temporal unit or "segment". Equivalently, we may conceive of a phonological representation as a linear sequence of segment "slots", to each of which is linked a specification for every distinctive feature. There are two implicit constraints on the relationship between the feature specifications and the segment slots. First, it is assumed that to every segment there corresponds exactly one specification for every feature, and conversely, that every feature specification corresponds to exactly one segment. This constraint is stated formally in (1).

Secondly, it is assumed that no rule can create a violation of (1). That is to say, deletion rules must affect the entire feature bundle together with the temporal slot that it occupies, and insertion rules may insert only an entire segment, not an incompletely specified segment, or an isolated feature specification. Moreover, no rule may create an association between a single unit of one sort (segment slot or feature) and more than one unit of the other sort. This constraint is stated formally in (2).

(1) *The Bijectivity Constraint*[2]
     The mapping between every string of distinctive feature specifications and the string of segments must be bijective.

(2) *The Integrity Constraint*
     No rule may operate in such a manner as to create a violation of the Bijectivity Constraint

Over the years it has become clear that neither of these two constraints can be maintained. In particular, evidence from African tone languages led Goldsmith (1976) to reject the two constraints, thus replacing the theory of Chomsky & Halle (1968) with the Autosegmental theory of phonology.[3] The violations of the two constraints may be summarized as follows.

Violation of the Integrity Constraint is exemplified by the phenomenon of melody preservation discussed by Goldsmith (1976). In these cases a vowel is deleted but its tone remains and is realized on an adjacent vowel.

Action-At-A-Distance

This is illustrated schematically in (3). If the Integrity Constraint held, we would expect the tone always to be deleted along with the vowel with which it is associated.

(3) $\begin{matrix} T^1 & T^2 \\ | & | \\ V^1 & V^2 \end{matrix} \rightarrow \begin{matrix} T^1 & T^2 \\ \diagdown & \diagup \\ & V^1 \end{matrix}$

Violations of the Bijectivity Constraint take two forms: violations of injectivity and violations of surjectivity. Violations of injectivity occur when a single unit on one tier is associated with more than one unit on another tier. Violations of surjectivity occur when a unit on one tier lacks an association with a unit on some other tier. Both types of violation can occur in two directions, i.e. in the direction from the segment-tier to the melody-tier or in the direction from the melody-tier to the segment-tier. The four possible violations are illustrated schematically below; (4)a and (4)b are violations of injectivity; (4)c and (4)d are violations of surjectivity.

(4)   *Bijectivity Violations*

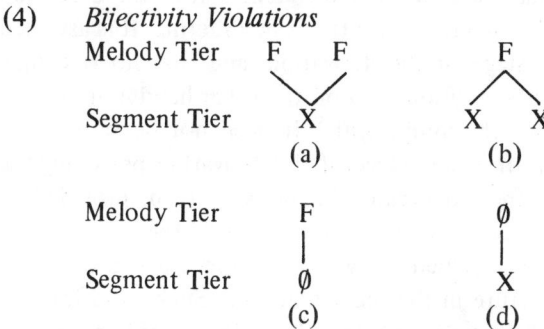

Examples of all four types of bijectivity violation have been provided in the autosegmental literature. Type (4)a is exemplified by the mapping of multiple tones onto a single vowel, producing a phonetic contour tone, discussed in Goldsmith (1976). Type (4)b is exemplified by the association of a single tone to more than one vowel (Goldsmith 1976), by the association of a single set of consonant features to two consonants, yielding a geminate consonant (Schein 1981), and by the association of a single element of a consonantal or vocalic melody with multiple consonant or vowel positions in Semitic languages (McCarthy 1978, 1979, 1981, 1982).

The two types of surjectivity violation frequently occur simultaneously. For example, in many Bantu languages verb stems have no underlying tone, a violation of type (4)d. Instead, the tone pattern of the verb is determined by its tense or aspect; that is to say, the tense/aspect morphemes consist exclusively of tones, a violation of type (4)c. A similar situation arises in Semitic where lexical roots consist exclusively of consonants and derivational "stems" consist of a CV-skeleton, that is to say, a sequence of segments specified only for the feature Syllabic (McCarthy 1978, 1979, 1981, 1982).

The existence of such cases as these led to the abandonment of the Bijectivity and Integrity Constraints. The theory in which these violations are permitted is the Autosegmental theory of Goldsmith (1976).

In Autosegmental phonology each distinctive feature potentially constitutes a separate tier, distinct from the segmental core. The association between each feature tier and the segmental core is governed by the Well Formedness Condition of Goldsmith (1976), given here in modified form.[4]

(5)   *The Well Formedness Condition*
       a. Association lines may not cross.
       b. Every segment must be fully specified.

The two subconditions have a somewhat different status. Subcondition (5)a in effect states that the two tiers have the same ordering. It is assumed that (5)a holds at every stage of the derivation, and that no rule may create a violation of it. Subcondition (5)b on the other hand is an output condition on the phonological component.[5] It need not be satisfied in underlying representation, or at any stage of the derivation preceding the last. Moreover, rules are free to create violations of (5)b, provided of course that such violations are eliminated in the course of the derivation.

Condition (5)b may be satisfied in two ways. First, a segment may be specified for a given feature in the segmental core. Such specifications are available for segments that do not participate in prosodic processes. A segment not specified in the segmental core must obtain its specification by association with an autosegment. Such segments are referred to as P-bearing, and the corresponding autosegments may be referred to as P-segments.[6]

Representations that do not satisfy the Well Formedness Condition must be modified so as to do so. This is accomplished by means of a set of universal association conventions.

(6)   *Association Conventions* (Clements 1981; 138)
       a. Given a continuous string S consisting of one or more free P-segments and an open string T occurring in its domain, associate (free) P-segments in S to (free) P-bearing units in T in a one-to-one manner from left to right.
       b. Given an open string T remaining after the operation of

(6)a, associate each (free) P-bearing unit in T with the P-segment in whose domain it falls (giving precedence to the P-segment associated with a P-bearing unit occurring to the left of T).[7]

A P-segment is said to be free if it is not associated to a P-bearing unit. An open string is an unbroken sequence of unassociated P-bearing units. A P-bearing unit is said to be in the domain of a P-segment if an association line could be drawn between the two without crossing an existing association line.

Although the Autosegmental theory was not originally conceived as a theory of harmony, a large class of harmonic processes fall out without further stipulation from the assumptions of the theory. In any string in which some segments are underlyingly unspecified for a feature (and this is permitted in the Autosegmental theory), the Well Formedness Condition must be fullfilled, and in the absence of language particular rules this will be accomplished by the Association Conventions. The result of application of these conventions will be the association of the unspecified segments to existing autosegmental specifications. Thus, unspecified segments will come to harmonize with fully specified segments. The application of the various clauses of the Association Conventions is illustrated by the case of Turkish vowel harmony.

In Turkish suffix vowels generally harmonize with preceding vowels in backness, and if high, in roundness as well. This is illustrated by the verb forms in (7) in which the unspecified high vowel (written I) of the past tense suffix /dI/ harmonizes with the verb stem.

(7) geldim   "I came"   aštɨm   "I opened"
     durdum   "I stood" güldüm "I laughed"

In these cases the past tense is unspecified for the feature Round whereas the verb stem is specified. Thus, in accordance with Association Convention (6)b the autosegment associated with the vowel of the verb stem is associated to the vowel of the past tense suffix. This is illustrated in (8).

(8)   -R   -R
          | →
        gel dIm   gel dIm

In some cases a suffix vowel is specified for the harmony feature. As a result, an unspecified vowel may find itself in the domain of two autosegments, and, as required by Association Convention (6)b, it is the left-hand autosegment that takes precedence. This is illustrated by the progressive forms in (9), the derivation of which is shown in (10).

(9) geliyorum "I am coming"   atšɨyorum "I am opening"
    duruyorum "I am standing" gülüyorum "I am laughing"

(10) -R +R   -R +R
       | | →   ∖ ∕∖
      gel Iyor Im   gel Iyor Im

Finally, the autosegment with which unspecified segments are associated need not have any underlying association. This situation arises in the case of words that trigger irregular suffix harmony, that is to say, harmony in which the suffixes do not agree with the last vowel of the stem. These may be represented as in (11), with a floating (unassociated) autosegment at the end of the stem. In accordance with Association Convention (6)a, this floating autosegment takes precedence in associating to free P-bearing units.[8]

(11) +B -B   +B   -B   "hour" (definite accusative singular)
       ∕∖   →   ∕∖ |
      saat I   saat I   saati

We see then that the existence of harmony systems of this type follows directly from the possibility of under-specification of segments in underlying representation, together with the Association Conventions. Since this theory of representations and the Association Conventions are motivated quite independently of harmony, this in itself constitutes an argument in favor of the autosegmental analysis.

A number of additional arguments for the autosegmental analysis have been presented in the literature. I will only summarize these here.[9] First, the autosegmental analysis eliminates the arbitrariness of assigning an underlying feature specification to segments which are always in the harmonic domain of some harmony trigger and which always harmonize with it. Second, and closely related, the redundancy of lexical representations is minimized by removing from them feature specifications for segments whose specification for the harmony feature is entirely predictable. Third, the autosegmental representation provides a means of representing a variety of apparently irregular forms, such as the irregular Turkish nouns discussed above. Fourth, the theory makes the correct prediction that segments specified for the harmony feature by a rule will never undergo the harmony. If they are specified at the segmental core, they will be transparent to the harmony, while if they are specified autosegmentally they will be opaque, that is to say, not only will they fail to undergo the harmony but they will themselves be potential harmony triggers. Fifth and finally, the Autosegmental Theory allows the description of non-directional harmony systems such as those of Akan (Clements 1981) and Guaraní (Poser 1981b).

The fact that the autosegmental account of harmony falls out from independently motivated properties of the theory together with the manner in which this account produces the five advantages listed above provides strong motivation for this account of harmony. Consequently, the fact that there exist harmony-like processes that are not describable as purely autosegmental underspecification harmonies should not be taken to indicate that the autosegmental account must be abandoned, *contra* Anderson (1980). Linear accounts of the type proposed by Howard (1972) simply do not meet the challenge of the five arguments mentioned above, nor, for the same reasons, does the metrical account of non-directional harmony of Vergnaud and Halle (1978)[10]. Moreover, since the autosegmental account falls out from the theory without further stipulation, the addition of mechanisms capable of handling non-autosegmental harmony would, at best, yield redundant descriptions of the autosegmental cases, were these mechanisms extended to the autosegmental cases, since nothing would prevent the autosegmental generation of such harmonies. The conclusion is, then, that the existence of non-autosegmental harmony processes motivates the existence of mechanisms in addition to the autosegmental association conventions, not their replacement.

2. THE RESIDUE OF THE AUTOSEGMENTAL THEORY (RES(AS))

I will discuss four types of process that cannot be treated as purely autosegmental underspecification harmonies. The first of these is feature-changing harmony. In the autosegmental account of harmony outlined above only segments that are unspecified for the harmony feature undergo harmony. If it can be demonstrated that a harmonizing segment must nonetheless be underlying specified for the harmony feature, such a harmony cannot be attributed to autosegmental spreading. Some mechanism must be added to the theory to permit features to be changed.

The second type of harmonic process that cannot be described in purely autosegmental terms is local harmony. By local I do not mean that the harmony trigger and the undergoer need be strictly adjacent. Rather, I refer to processes in which only some fixed number of a string of potential undergoers of harmony actually undergo harmony. In typical unbounded harmonies, an unbroken string of harmonizing segments will all undergo harmony. An element will fail to harmonize only if it never harmonizes; whether or not it harmonizes in some particular environment will not depend upon its position in the string. In a local harmony, only some fixed number of potentially harmonizing elements will actually undergo harmony, these being those elements closest to the trigger. Such a harmony cannot be described autosegmentally, since autosegmental spreading is unbounded.

A third class of case that cannot be described in purely autosegmental terms is that of unbounded dissimilation. Autosegmental spreading can produce only assimilation; an unbounded dissimilatory rule can only be described by means of a feature-changing rule.

The last class of case, and the only one that has been offered as evidence for the Metrical theory (Halle & Vergnaud 1981), is that of directional harmony. By this I mean a harmony in which the spreading of the harmonic feature is demonstrably restricted to one direction.

Emphasis must here be put on the word *demonstrably*, for there are harmony systems that are only apparently directional. Consider, for example, the case of Turkish rounding harmony, discussed briefly above. This system has been taken to be an example of a directional harmony by Halle & Vergnaud (1981) on the grounds that the harmony always spreads from left to right. However, this is not due to any explicit statement of directionality; rather, it is due to the fact that the underspecified vowels of Turkish nearly all belong to bound suffixes and hence are nearly always in the domain of an autosegment to their left.[11] Since, by Association Convention (6)b it is the lefthand autosegment that takes precedence when an unspecified element lies in the domain of two autosegments, unspecified vowels nearly always obtain their specification from an autosegment to their left, thus giving the appearance of directionality.[12] As we have seen, and as Clements & Sezer (this vol.) document in great detail, there is nothing in Turkish that is inconsistent with the bidirectional spreading predicted by the Autosegmental theory.

It is also important to note that the priority clause of Association Convention (6)b is not equivalent to making autosegmental harmony strictly directional. Consider the underlying representations in (12)a and (13)a. The Association Conventions predict that in (12)a P-bearing unit X will be associated with autosegment A, while Z will be associated with B, as in (12)b. This case is identical to the Turkish example in (10). A directional account of Turkish would make this same prediction.

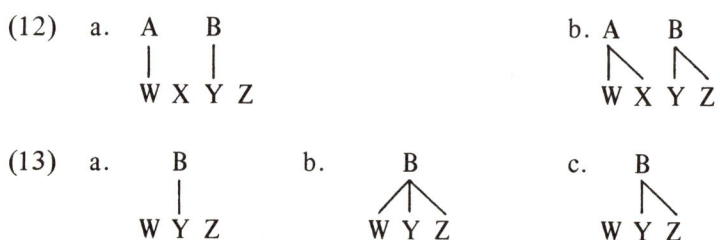

Consider now underlying representation (13)a. The Autosegmental theory predicts that in this case W as well as Z will be linked to B. Since there is no autosegment to the left of B the priority clause does not apply, and W will be linked to the only autosegment in whose domain it lies, which in this case is to its right. This yields the output in (13)b. In a strictly directional account, only Z would harmonize with Y. W would surface with its underlying value (in a feature-changing system) or would be provided with the default value of the harmony feature (in a feature-specifying system). In neither case would W harmonize with Y. In order to establish the existence of strictly directional harmony it is necessary to demonstrate the existence of cases like (13)c.

It is also important to observe that the addition of the priority clause to the association conventions is not an *ad hoc* way of adding directionality to the autosegmental theory. If only cases of the type described in (12) were known, we might conclude that, while there was no necessity of permitting strictly directional rules, there was also no reason to treat such cases as being non-directional. Cases like that in (13)b would however demonstrate conclusively the necessity for a priority clause in a fundamentally non-directional theory. The fact is that such cases have been documented. Clements & Sezer (this vol.) show that this is precisely what happens in Turkish.

As we have seen, almost all unspecified vowels in Turkish occur to the right of some fully specified vowel, so that harmony appears to be directional. In certain cases, however, an epenthetic vowel is inserted to break up impermissible word-initial consonant clusters, and in general this vowel harmonizes in backness and rounding with the following stem vowel. In this case the epenthetic vowel is not preceded by any fully specified vowel, so it associates perforce with an autosegment to its right. This indicates that Turkish vowel harmony is indeed non-directional; directionality comes into play only when two autosegments compete for the same vowel.

A parallel case, though with the priority clause reversed (i.e. righthand autosegment takes precedence), occurs in Guaraní.[13] Guaraní has an interesting system of nasal harmony. Voiceless obstruents are always oral and do not participate in the harmony; they are transparant to it. Of the segments participating in the harmony, only stressed vowels (both oral and nasal) and nasal stops are underlyingly specified for nasality. The remaining segments obtain their nasality specifications from the stressed vowels and nasal stops. This harmony is illustrated by the pairs in (14) and (15).

(14) a. ʔokarú "he eats"
 b. ʔõkãñɨ̃ "it got lost"

(15) a. ⁿderɨvɨ́   'thy brother"
     b. nẽpẽtɨ́   "thy tobacco"

In (14) we see that the third person singular subject prefix /ʔo/ agrees in nasality with the following verb stem. In (15) the second person singular possessive prefix /ne/ is nasal before a nasal stem, and oral before an oral stem. (A nasal stop is prenasalized before an oral vowel.) Of these four cases, only (15)a shows any evidence of directionality, and in this case we have an unspecified element in the domain of two autosegments, a nasal autosegment on the left and an oral autosegment on the right. This demonstrates that in Guaraní the priority clause gives precedence to the righthand autosegment. The same phenomenon is illustrated by (16) and (17).

(16) ʔũmĩ́šaɣʷá   <   /umí + ša + ɣʷá/
     "like those"   those+like+belonging to

(17) rexótã r̃ ã m õ̰   <   /re + xó + ta + ramṍ/
     "if you go"   you+go+future+if

In (16) the /a/ of /ša/ is in the domain of the stressed nasal vowel to its left and the stressed oral vowel to its right, and it is the righthand vowel that wins. In (17) the /a/ of /ta/ is in the domain of the stressed oral vowel to its left and the nasal stop (/m/) to its right, and it is the nasal to the right that wins.

Thus far we have a case like that of Turkish (without word-initial epenthesis) but with the priority clause reversed. If Guaraní nasal harmony were truly directional we would expect to find that no segment would ever harmonize with something to its left. This prediction is false. Consider for example the forms in (18) and (19). In the first case we have an oral verb stem, and in the second a nasal verb stem. As expected, the negative prefix /no/ harmonizes with the verb stem to its right. Note however that the negative suffix /i/ also harmonizes with the verb stem, even though the verb stem is to its left. Since the negative suffix is word-final there is no autosegment to its right and the priority clause does not apply.

(18) ⁿdoroxaɨxúi   <   /no+ro+xaɨ+xú+i/
     "I don't love you"   Neg+1-2+love+Neg

(19) nõ r̃õ ĩnũpã́ ĩ   <   /no+roi+nupã́+i/
     "I don't beat you"   Neg+1-2+beat+Neg

A similar example is given in (20). In (20)a the /a/ of "spouse" harmonizes with the stressed oral vowel of the suffix /ré/, in accordance with the priority clause. What happens when this suffix is removed ? As we see in (20)b the /a/ now harmonises with the nasal stop to its left.

(20) a. mẽⁿdaré   <   /mẽna + ré/
         "widow(er)"   spouse + former
      b. mẽnã   <   /mẽna/
         "spouse"

Just as in Turkish, Guaraní nasal harmony is bidirectional, and directionality only comes into play when two autosegments compete for the same P-bearing unit. These two cases demonstrate the necessity for the priority clause of Association Convention (6)b, since they cannot be treated as strictly directional.

Let us return now to the question of what would constitute a real example of directional harmony. I have indicated that in a truly directional harmony system a representation like (13)a would yield (13)c, not (13)b. This is a necessary condition for a harmony to be truly directional, but it is not sufficient. The failure of W to harmonize in (13)c could be due to its being opaque, i.e. underlyingly fully specified. Thus, we must demonstrate that W is indeed susceptible to harmony, that is to say, that when it occurs to the right of a harmony trigger it does undergo harmony. To summarize, we know that we are dealing with a strictly directional harmony if some element harmonizes with a harmony trigger when it occurs on one side of the trigger, and fails to harmonize with a trigger when it occurs on the other side. To my knowledge, no explicit argument for the existence of a harmony of this type has been made in the literature to date, and thus it remains to be demonstrated that true directional harmony exists. I will present such a case below.

2.1. Directional and Feature Changing Harmony

I will demonstrate the existence of both directional and feature-changing harmony by means of the same example, that of the Ineseño dialect of Chumash, described by Applegate (1972).[14]

Chumash has a harmony system that makes all sibilants in the word, with the limited exception discussed in section Five below, agree in palatality; i.e. they are all /s/ or all /š/. This is illustrated by examples (21) and (22). In (21) the verb stem is /sunon/, and when it is followed by the third person singular object suffix /us/ it retains its underlying /s/. When the stativizing suffix /š/ is added, however, the /s/ harmonizes with this suffix. (/n/ becomes /t/ before /š/.) In (22) the verb "to pay" in its isolation form begins with an /s/; when the suffix /Vtš/ is added this /s/ becomes /š/.

(21) ksunonus   "I obey him"   /k + sunon + us/   (290)
      kšunotš   "I am obedient"   /k + sunon + š/   (290)

(22) saxtun   "to pay"   (255)
      šaxtunitš   "to be paid"   (255)

It is a straightforward matter to demonstrate that this harmony is feature-changing. Since a morpheme containing a sibilant need not be followed by any other such morpheme, it is possible to observe the isolation form of harmonizing segments. If Chumash were not feature-changing, we should expect to find that the isolation form of harmonizing segments was either /s/ in every case or /š/ in every case, since the specification for the harmony feature of underspecified segments would have to be supplied by a default rule that would necessarily assign the same default value to every harmonizing segment. Consequently, if some harmonizing segments surface as /s/ when outside the domain of another sibilant, and others surface as /š/ when outside the domain of another sibilant, we must attribute /s/ from /š/, and therefore we must conclude that the harmony process changes these underlying feature specifications. I shall now show that this is the case.

Consider first the causative prefix, whose isolation[15] form is seen to be /su/ in (23). This prefix harmonizes with the verb stem /šoyin/ in (24).

(23) suwayan   "cause to hang"   /su + wayan/   (151)

(24) kšušoyin   "I darken it"   /k + su + šoyin
                                                           (119)

A similar example is the third person subject prefix, whose isolation form is seen to be /s/ in (25) and (26).

(25) saqunimak   "he hides"   /s + aqunimak/   (15)
(26) sixut   "it burns"   /s + ixut/   (18)

When the following verb stem contains a /š/, the prefix harmonizes with it, as illustrated in (27) and (28).

(27) šilakš   "it is soft"   /s + ilakš/   (7)

(28) šammotš   "they paint it"   /s + am + motš/   (17)
                                       3 + indef.pl.subj. + paint

It is even possible to see /s/ change to /š/ in the same environment depending on what follows. Thus, in (29)a the third person prefix retains its isolation form; when the past tense suffix is added in (29)b the prefix harmonizes. Example (30) is exactly parallel.

(29) a. hasxintila   "his Indian name"   /ha + s + xintila/   (200)
                                        poss.+ 3 +Ind.name

(29) b. hašxintilawaš   "his former Indian name"   (200)

(30) a. skuti   "he sees"   /s + kuti/
     b. škutiwaš   "he saw"   /s + kuti + waš (509)

Consider now the dual subject marker, whose isolation form is seen in (31) to be /iš/.

(31) a. pišanan'   "don't you two go"   /p + iš + al + nan'/
                                                           (109)
                                      2 + dual+neg.imv.+go
(31) b. piš'ik+min   "you two are young"   /p + iš + ʔik+min/ (417)
                                            2 + dual + be young

This prefix becomes /is/ when the rightmost sibillant in the word is /s/, as illustrated in (32).[16]

(32) a. sis^{h}iluleqpeyus "they two want to follow it"   <
        /s + iš + sili + <u>ulu + aq + pey</u> + us/   (333)
         3 du. desid follow   3obj
(32) b. sistisiyepus   "they two show him"   /s + iš + <u>tiši + yep</u>
                                              3 du.   show
        + us/   (71)
        3obj

A similar example is given below. In this case, (33)a shows that the isolation form of the stem "good" is /tš^{h}o/, and indeed this stem causes the subject prefix /s/ to harmonize with it. When this same stem is followed by the third person object suffix /us/ it harmonizes with it.[17]

(33) a. šapits$^{v h}$olit   "I have a stroke of good luck"   <
        /s + api + tš^{h}o + it/   (89)
         3   quick good   1obj
(33) b. sapits^{h}olus   "He has a stroke of good luck"   <
        /s + api + tš$^{v h}$o + us/   (118)
         3   quick good   3obj

We have now seen four morphemes that contain sibilants, all of which undergo harmony. Two of these show /s/ in their isolation forms, while the other two show /š/. This suffices to establish that Chumash sibilant harmony is feature-changing.

Consider now the issue of directionality. In every example that we have so far examined it is the rightmost sibilant that dominates. Is this evidence of true directionality, or is this an artifact of the distribution of harmonizing and opaque segments?

Example (34) below shows that the third person object suffix /us/ harmonizes with the past tense suffix /waš/ to its right. What happens when /us/ is not followed by any sibilant, but is preceded by /š/ ? If Chumash sibilant harmony were non-directional, we should expect /us/ to harmonize with the sibilant to its left, yielding /uš/. As we have already seen in (33)b this is not the case; rather, it is /us/ that triggers harmony in the sibilant to its left. Notice that this behaviour cannot be attributed to the sibilant to the left of /us/ being unable to trigger harmony; example (33)a shows that /tš̌ʰo/ does indeed trigger harmony to its left, when it is not followed by another sibilant. We conclude that Chumash sibilant harmony constitutes a genuine case of right-to-left directional harmony.

(34) šapitš̌ʰolušwaš   "he had a stroke of good luck"
      /s + api + tš̌ʰo + us + waš/   (119)
      3   quick   good   3obj past

This Chumash case is of particular interest because it is a case of unbounded harmony; we might expect that local rules would be directional and feature-changing but that unbounded rules would be feature-specifying and non-directional. In order to establish that Chumash sibilant harmony is indeed unbounded, it remains to show that it is not local cyclic.[18]

This may be demonstrated in two ways. First, consider again example (34). This may be bracketed in three ways, [19] listed in (35). The first bracketing yields the incorrect output *šapitš̌ʰoluswaš: the second and third bracketing yield the equally incorrect *sapitš̌ʰolušwaš. Thus, no matter what the bracketing, (34) cannot be generated by cyclic application of a local rule.

(35) a.   [[[s   [apitš̌ʰo]] us] waš]
      b.   [s [[[apitš̌ʰo]   us] waš]]
      c.   [[s [[apitš̌ʰo]   us]] waš]

The unboundedness of this rule may also be established by considering the effect of following sibilants on single morphemes containing more than one sibilant. If the harmony rule were local, a following sibilant would be able to affect only the rightmost of the sibilants in the stem; only an unbounded rule could affect more than one sibilant on a single cycle. As the examples below demonstrate, in stems containing two sibilants, both harmonize with a following sibilant. Consequently, Chumash sibilant harmony cannot be local cyclic.

(36) šlušišiniwaš   "it is all grown awry"   <
                         /s + lu + sisin + waš/   (291)
                         3 +all + grow awry + past

(37) šitš'iwišutš   "he plays the rattle"   <
                         /s + ts'iwis + Vtš/   (99)
                         3 + rattle + verbaliser
      cf. ts'iwisun   "to make a rattle"   (275)

We conclude that Chumash sibilant harmony is an unbounded, directional, feature-changing harmony-rule.

2.2. Local Harmony

Anderson (1980) has already proposed one example of local harmony. This is the case of Chamorro, described by Topping (1968). As the examples in (38) illustrate, when a word is preceded by a particle containing a front vowel, the initial vowel of the word becomes front and unrounded.

(38) gúmə   "house"   i gímə   "the house"
      tómU   "knee"   i témU   "the knee"
      láhI   "male"   i láhI   "the male"
      húlU?   "up"   sän hílU?   "upward"
      lágU   "north"   sän lägU   "northward"
      túnU?   "to know"   en tínU?   "you know"
      ótdUt   "ant"   mi étdUt   "lots of ants"
      óksU?   "hill"   gi éksU?   "at the hill"

Notice that this harmony does not extend beyond the first syllable; if it did we should obtain *i témI and *sän hílI?. One might claim that this failure of harmony to affect the second syllable was due to a restriction to tense vowels; since the second vowel in the above words is always lax it would not be a candidate for harmony. This way out is not available, however, since Kenstowicz and Kisseberth (1979) show that this harmony rule must be ordered prior to stress placement, and that stress placement must precede the vowel reduction rule that creates the lax vowels in question.

In an attempt to provide an autosegmental analysis we might propose that the harmonizing vowels are unspecified for the features Back and Round, and that we are dealing with a dominant harmony. When the prefixed particle contains a front unrounded vowel these features will be spread to the underspecified vowel of the stem. Such an analysis requires that only the stem initial vowels be underspecified. This is logically possible, and it is not ruled out by any explicit principle of the Autosegmental theory. However, this is a rather bizarre distribution of specified and unspecified segments. Moreover, it has been implicitly assumed in work in the Autosegmental theory that the status of segments is a lexical property. As such, we expect either a random distribution of specified and unspecified elements, subject to such functional principles as the notion that elements that can occur freely are likely to be fully specified, whereas bound forms are likely to be incompletely specified, or a context-free generalization to the effect that every member of a given natural class, subject to lexical exceptions, will be specified or unspecified for a given feature. Context-sensitive generalizations of the type necessary in Chamorro are contrary to the spirit if not the letter of the Autosegmental theory. Nonetheless, since no explicit version of the constraints on underspecification is available, nor has any investigation of the consequences of different theories been made, it is not possible to rule out this analysis of the Chamorro facts *a priori*.

Were we to adopt this analysis we would face a further problem. When no particle precedes, why do the word-initial vowels not harmonize with the following vowel, e.g. why is the isolation form of "male" not *lähI* instead of *lahI*? We might suppose that only vowels in word-initial position or in particles are P-bearing, while those elsewhere are specified at the segmental level, which would prevent them from spreading their feature specifications. This would increase the bizarreness of the distribution of specification types. The alternative would be to make this harmony strictly directional, itself incompatible with a purely autosegmental account. Thus, it is possible to provide a purely autosegmental account of this harmony system, but only at the cost of a bizarre underlying distribution of specification types that ought very likely to be prohibited.

A more solid example of a local harmony is found in Lango, described by Woock and Noonan (1979)[20]. Lango has ten vowels which fall into two harmonic sets in accordance with their ATR specification, as listed in (39).

(39) a. i e ə o u [+ATR]
     b. ɪ ɛ a ɔ ʊ [-ATR]

[-ATR] vowels become [+ATR] when adjacent to [+ATR] vowels, as illustrated in the following examples. In (40) we see that the second person

Action-At-A-Distance

singular alienable possessor suffix /ni/ causes the preceding vowel to harmonise. In (41) we see that the second person plural alienable possessor suffix /wu/ has the same effect.

(40) lʊt   "stick"   lúttí   "your stick"
     màc   "fire"   màccí   "your fire"
     dɛ̀k   "stew"   dèkkí   "your stew"

(41) bɔ́   "net"   bówú   "your net"
     lɛ̀   "axe"   léwú   "your axe"
     jɔ̀   "people"   jòwú   "your people"

When the same suffixes are added to disyllabic stems, only the second vowel of the stem harmonises.

(42) còŋò   "beer"   còŋóní   "your beer"
     bɔ̀ŋɔ́   "dress"   bɔ̀ŋóní   "your dress"

(43) lɛ̀mún   "orange"   lɛ̀múnwú   "your orange"
     bɔ̀ŋɔ́   "dress"   bɔ̀ŋówú   "your dress"
     rɔ̀mɔ̀   "sheep"   rɔ̀mòwú   "your sheep"

This suggests that Lango ATR harmony is local. In principle we could propose an autosegmental analysis along the lines discussed for Chamorro. Specifically, we could say that only the last vowel of the word is P-bearing. Such a proposal would suffer from the same defects as in the Chamorro case, but here it is possible to rule it out empirically.

Consider the plural forms in (44). These show that the plural suffix /i/ triggers harmony in the preceding vowel. The form in (45) show that in certain cases this suffix triggers deletion of the stem final vowel. The forms in (46) show that when as a result of this deletion rule the vowels that fail to harmonize with the suffix /wu/ in (43) come to be adjacent to the suffix /i/, they undergo harmony. this should not occur if these vowels are lexically opaque. Consequently, we may conclude that Lango ATR harmony is indeed local.

(44) gɔ̀t   "mountain" gòdí   "mountains"
     lʊt   "stick"   lùdí   "sticks"

(45) pʊ̀nʊ̀   "pig"   pùní   "pigs"

(46) bɔ̀ŋɔ́   "dress"   bòŋí   "dresses"
     rɔ̀mɔ̀   "sheep"   ròmí   "sheep" (pl.)

2.3. Dissimilation

Although unbounded dissimilations do not appear to be common at least one clear example has been reported from a well studied language. According to Cheng (1973) Mandarin Chinese has a rule that converts a Third toned syllable to Second tone before another Third toned syllable. This is illustrated in (47).[21]

(47) mai² ma³   "to buy a horse"   /mai³ ma³/
      fən² c̣ʰaŋ³   "flour factory"   /fən³ c̣ʰaŋ³/

In these cases the domain of the rule is VP and NP respectively. In slow, careful speech this rule is restricted to maximal projections of lexical categories, but in more rapid, casual speech the domain of the rule becomes the entire sentence. As a result, it is possible to find such examples as (48). Here a sequence of four Third toned syllable dissimilates from the final Third toned syllable.

(48) lau² li² mai² xau² tɕiou³   "Old Li buys good wine"

This rule is clearly dissimilatory, it affects an unbounded string of Third toned syllables, and inspection of the syntactic tree of (48) will show that it cannot be local cyclic.

The examples presented demonstrate the existence of directional, feature-changing, local, and dissimilatory rules.

3. The Metrical Theory

In the Metrical theory of Vergnaud & Halle (1978) and Halle & Vergnaud (1981) it is necessary to set the five parameters listed in (49), the significance of which will be explained in the course of the discussion. The harmony process procedes in four stages, listed in (50).

(49) *Parameters*
      (i) projection
      (ii) direction of branching
      (iii) harmony feature
      (iv) opaque elements
      (v) conditions on feature copying

(50) *Stages*
      (i) projection

(ii) tree construction
(iii) feature copying
(iv) percolation

The operation of projection consists of designating the class of segments on which the harmony tree is to be constructed, that is to say, the elements which will be the terminal nodes of the tree. The projected segments are all those that are in some way relevant to the operation of the harmony: undergoers, triggers and blockers. Segments that do not participate in the harmony are not projected. For example, in a typical vowel harmony the projected class might be all [+syll] segments. A formal definition may be found in Vergnaud (1977).

The second stage consists of the construction of the minimum possible number of metrical trees ont the projected segments. These trees are uniformly left-branching or right-branching, depending upon the setting of parameter (ii), and all are binary-branching. All such trees are in princinple unbounded, so that in a word containing no opaque elements there will be only one tree. Tree construction is subject to the constraint that opaque elements may appear only in the Designated Terminal Position. The Designated Terminal Position is defined to be the most deeply embedded node of the tree, that is to say, the leftmost node in a left-to-right harmony and the rightmost node in a right-to-left harmony.[22]

The next step consists of copying the specification of the Designated Terminal Element (the segment occurring in the Designated Terminal Position) for the harmony feature to the root of the tree. This copying may be unconditional, in the case of an α-harmony, or it may take place only if the DTE is specified +F or −F, in the case of a dominant harmony.

Finally, the feature specification on the root of the tree percolates to all of the terminal nodes of the tree, overriding their existing feature specifications.

We may illustrate this procedure by applying it to the Chumash sibilant harmony described in section 2.1.

The projection consists of the class of sibilants, which it is sufficient to specify as [+strid]. Since this is a right-to-left harmony the direction of branching is to the right. The harmony feature is arguable; let us say that it is the feature Anterior. With the exception of the cases to be discussed in section Five, which we will ignore for the time being, there are no opaque segments. Finally, since this is an α–harmony, there are no conditions on feature copying.

Consider now example (34). The harmony tree for this example is shown in (51). Its terminal nodes are the four sibilants, and it is right branching. As the arrow shows, the specification of the DTE (circled in the illustration) is copied to the root, whence it percolates to the terminal nodes to produce the surface form.

(51)

In an earlier paper (Poser 1981a) I proposed two extensions to the metrical formalism. First, I proposed that harmony trees might be bounded (binary) as well as unbounded. Secondly, I proposed that the opposite of the DTE value of the harmony feature might be copied to the root. This latter modification requires a change in the percolation convention. The value of the harmony feature at the root must now percolate to every terminal node *except* the DTE.

With these extensions the Metrical theory is capable of describing the RES(AS). The Metrical formalism is inherently directional and pays no attention to the underlying specification of the harmonizing segments, so these two problems are solved in the original version of the theory. The addition of bounded feet permits the description of local harmony. Finally, the copying of the opposite of the DTE value of the harmony feature to the root produces dissimilation. The Metrical formalism thus provides, at least *prima facie*, an adequate formalism for the RES(AS). In the following section I will investigate the theoretical properties of the metrical formalism.

4. THE PROPERTIES OF THE METRICAL FORMALISM

A formalism by itself does not constitute a theory; the formalism must be provided with an interpretation in order to be a theory. In discussing the metrical theory this distinction is of particular importance, for while the metrical formalism has remained fairly constant since its inception in Vergnaud & Halle (1978) and Sportiche (1977) the interpretation of this formalism has varied considerably. For example, I have shown above that there exist four classes of process not describable in purely autosegmental terms, and that this RES(AS) can be described in terms of the metrical formalism. I shall discuss this point further below. For the moment, what is important is to observe that of the four properties thus attributed to metrical trees, two (boundedness and dissimilation) were not envisaged at all in the classical Metrical theory, while one property (the ability to change features) was not attributed explicitly to metrical trees, and is indeed explicitly denied them in the "Metrical" theory of Steriade (to appear). Only the property of directionality is part of the original interpretation of the formalism. On the other hand, with the single exception

Action-At-A-Distance

of the issue of directionality, the original arguments for the Metrical theory were based on what I will refer to as the geometric interpretation of the metrical tree. In this interpretation geometric properties of the harmony tree are claimed to play a crucial role. This interpretation is quite different from the interpretation that allows the description of the RES(AS).

4.1. The Geometric Interpretation of the Metrical Tree

Two geometric properties of the metrical tree have been claimed to play a role in harmony processes. These are the depth of embedding and the uniform branching property.

The depth of embedding function is claimed to play two roles. First, recall that the Designated Terminal Element of the harmony tree is defined to be the most (or least, in other versions of the theory) embedded node. On this basis, Vergnaud & Halle (1978) claim that depth of embedding plays a crucial role in determining directionality. Now it is clear that they do not mean to claim that the direction of spreading can in any way be predicted by this device; the direction of branching of the harmony tree does not come from anywhere; it is simply stipulated. The claim must rather be that the depth of embedding function plays a necessary and sufficient role in the mechanism of the harmony process. This claim is false.

First, it is obvious that reference to depth of embedding is not necessary to stipulate directionality. It is more than adequate to draw a pair of brackets delimiting the harmonic domain and to designate either the leftmost position or the rightmost position as the DTE. This is no more arbitrary than stipulating construction of a left- or right-branching tree.

Nor is reference to depth of embedding sufficient to designate the DTE. Since, as Vergnaud & Halle (1978; 4.6-7) state, depth of embedding is "...measured in number of intervening nodes between the root of the tree and the affected segments", it follows that every tree has two "most embedded nodes". To see this, consider the tree in (52). The nodes intervening between the root and terminal node D are S and T. The same nodes, and no others, intervene between the root and terminal node C. Consequently, C and D are equally embedded. In any right-branching tree the rightmost node and its neighbor are equally embedded; in any left-branching tree the leftmost node and its neighbor are equally embedded. Consequently, the DTE is ill-defined if reference is made only to depth of embedding.

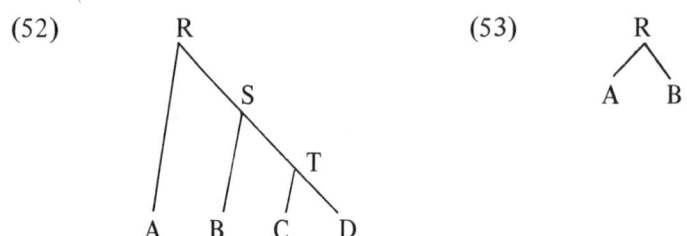

In some versions of the Metrical theory the DTE is defined to be the least embedded node. This definition eliminates the above problem in some cases, for in a tree with three or more terminal nodes there is a unique least embedded node. However, the problem remains whenever there are only two terminal nodes. As is obvious from figure (53) both terminal nodes are equally embedded, so the least embedded node is not unique. Such trees will arise not only in local harmonies where all trees have only two terminal nodes, but also in unbounded harmonies whenever it happens that there are only two elements on the projection, as in example (27), for example.

I conclude that reference to depth of embedding is neither necessary nor sufficient for the specification of the DTE.[23]

The second claim for the role of depth of embedding in harmony is based on the existence of phonetic gradation within the harmony domain. Following the proposal of Sportiche (1977), Vergnaud & Halle (1978) claim that in Guaraní nasality spreads directionally, from right to left. Within the harmony domain there is a decrease in nasalization from right to left, as described by Gregores & Suarez (1967: 66):

> With the unstressed syllables preceding a nasal consonant, N[asalization-WJP] is automatically present and is never strong. Elsewhere, nasalization occurs covering a span of varying length, in which the velum appears to be lowered increasingly from medium to strong, so that the nasal timbre is strongest toward the end of the nasal span.

Vergnaud & Halle (1978:4.6-7) observe that:

> ...this fact is captured directly ... if it is assumed that the degree of nasality varies inversely with the depth of embedding measured in number of intervening nodes between the root of the tree and the affected segment: the larger the number of intervening nodes, i.e. the deeper the embedding of the affected segment, the weaker its degree of nasalization. As noted by Sportiche, this phenomenon is of some theoretical significance because it suggests that there is an advantage to representing nasal harmony in Guaraní by means of left-branching trees rather than by nondirectional trees
> ...Since in the nondirectional tree all terminal nodes are equidistant from the root, differences in the distance from the root cannot be utilised to reflect such facts as the difference in Guaraní nasalization.

Since in more recent versions of the Metrical theory it is a right-branching tree that represents right-to-left harmony, the degree of nasality would have to vary in direct proportion to the depth of embedding.

Vergnaud & Halle are quite correct in their claim that a non-directional tree does not allow the degree of nasalization to be represented as a function of the depth of embedding. However, this is hardly the only way to represent such a nasality cline. The same result would be obtained by defining the degree of nasalization to be a monotonically decreasing function of the distance from the DTE, measured either in terminal nodes, or perhaps in real time. The former proposal would be exactly equivalent to Sportiche's; the latter would differ from it in that it predicts a role in determining the phonetic degree of nasalization. In the absence of instrumental data it is not possible to decide between these two proposals. Clearly no additional structure is necessary.

Moreover, as Vergnaud & Halle themselves point out in the passage cited above, the degree of nasalization cannot be represented as a function of depth of embedding in a non-directional tree. This implies that phonetic gradients are possible only in the case of directional harmony; in non-directional harmony systems phonetic gradients could not occur since such systems lack the requisite directional trees; all terminal nodes are equally embedded. In contrast, the representation of degree of nasalization by a function of distance from the DTE would permit phonetic gradients to exist even in non-directional harmony systems. This is in fact the correct prediction.

Hoenigswald (1948) describes an Urdu dialect in which unbounded sequences of vowels and semi-vowels are nasalized both before and after nasal consonants. This is therefore a case of non-directional dominant harmony. Nevertheless, Hoenigswald notes (p.143) that:

> Phonetically, the nasalized vowel sequences seem to be rather evenly nasalized after *m* or *n* [according to footnote 14, ŋ does not occur before vowels.–WJP]; under all other conditions the velum appears to be lowered increasingly so that the nasal timbre is strongest toward the end.

Here we have a nasality cline just like that described in Guaraní, in a language with a non-directional harmony. This falsifies Vergnaud & Halle's claim.

Indeed as I have argued above, Guaraní nasal harmony is itself non-directional and hence the nasal gradation observed in Guaraní cannot be attributed to metrical tree structure. Sportiche (1977) is aware of the facts presented in section Two that show Guaraní nasal harmony to be non-directional. He claims, however, that the evidence for left-to-right spreading can be ignored on the grounds that such spreading is merely "coarticulatory". Apparently Sportiche means to claim that left-to-right spreading is some sort of low level phonetic process, to be distinguished from right-to-left spreading, which is truly phonological. But it is not clear what this would mean. In the technical sense of Chomsky & Halle (1968) the term *phonetic* refers to rules that assign non-distinctive feature specifications or integer values of features that are, in their binary form, distinctive. In this interpretation of the term, neither left-to-right nor right-to-left spreading can be considered "phonetic", since both modify a distinctive feature. The only other interpretation that seems reasonable is that "coarticulatory" is taken to mean phonetically motivated. But many rules that are normally treated as phonological are phonetically motivated, and on the other hand it is hard to see why nasal spreading in one direction would be more or less phonetically motivated than in the other. In fact, the term *coarticulation* has no technical sense at all. According to Daniloff & Hammarberg (1973:241):

> "Phoneticians apply the term coarticulation to a wide array or phenomena involving intersegmental influences, even to the point of claiming that, in effect, any context sensitive phenomenon involving sounds is an instance of coarticulation."

Consider now Sportiche's criteria for distinguishing left-to-right and right-to-left spreading in Guaraní. He cites two. First, he cites Dixit & MacNeilage (1972) to the effect that, "...the scope of coarticulatory effects is unrestricted by syllable or word boundaries." But this is a study of a single language (Hindi), not a claim about all coarticulatory processes, whatever they may be, and one that has itself been disputed on precisely this point. Ohala (1975:330) says:

> ...their claim that except for pause, other boundaries such as word or syllable did not have much of an effect on nasal coarticulation, was not supported by the data I obtained from two subjects using the nasograph.

In any case, no evidence is presented that all coarticulatory processes have this property, or crucially, that *only* coarticulatory processes have this property.

Moreover, when this criterion is applied to the Guarani facts it fails to distinguish between leftward and rightward spreading. As we have seen, e.g. in (17), nasality spreads leftward across syllable boundaries, so by this criterion leftward spreading should also be "coarticulatory". As far as word boundary is concerned, nasality spreads across word boundary in *both* directions (see Rivas 1974 and Poser 1981b); on the other hand, across word boundary nasality spreads only one syllable, regardless of direction.

Sportiche's second argument is that, "...if coarticulation is at work, it should be inhibited by the presence of stops." (p.21). Observing that

Action-At-A-Distance 145

prenasalized stops do indeed block spreading of nasality across word boundary, he claims that this confirms the coarticulatory nature of rightward spreading. In contrast, he claims, leftward spreading must be phonological since stops are transparent to it. But this argument also is spurious. To begin with, Sportiche provides no hint of why coarticulation ". . .should be inhibited by the presence of stops." Secondly, stressed oral vowels also block spreading across word boundary. Here Sportiche admits that, "We do not know whether this fact has some articulatory basis." (p. 33, ftnt. 12) From this we may conclude that there is not the slightest evidence that the conditions on spreading across word-boundary are diagnostic of coarticulation. Here again, the criterion fails to distinguish between leftward and rightward spreading. In leftward spreading just as in rightward spreading stressed oral vowels and prenasalized stops are opaque. On the other hand, voiceless stops are transparent to spreading in both directions, contrary to Sportiche's implicit claim that they are opaque to rightward spreading.[24]

I conclude that Sportiche has offered no serious argument for disregarding rightward nasal spreading. Guaraní thus constitutes a legitimate case of non-directional harmony, which fact refutes Vergnaud & Halle's claim.

The other geometric property of the metrical tree that is claimed to play a role in harmony is uniform branching. The argument was first raised by Zubizarreta (1979); for reasons explained in the footnote I deal with the version due to Marantz (1980).[25]

Marantz observes that in some languages long vowels are opaque even though their short counterparts are not. This can be dealt with by projecting not the vowels themselves but the syllable nucleus, and letting the branchingness of the nucleus be "visible" to the harmony tree. Since the harmony tree must be uniformly branching the branching nucleus will be capable of insertion only into the Designated Terminal Position of the tree, for in any other position it would disrupt the uniform branching structure. This situation is illustrated in (54). A branching nucleus can be attached in the DTP, labeled A, but not in any other position, for example B.

Insofar as certain technical problems can be overcome, this is indeed a possible means of representing the opacity of long vowels. The technical problems concern the fact that in many, if not all, languages long vowels represent not branching nuclei but branching rhymes. But if it is the rhyme as a whole that is projected, why do not rhymes with a consonantal coda participate in the harmony? A special sort of double projection that has yet to be properly formalized would be required to pick out just those branching rhymes that contain long vowels, and not diphthongs or other syllables with consonant codas.

(54)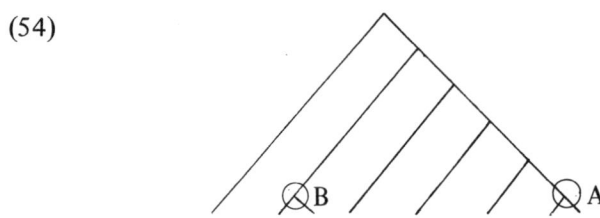

If only long vowels could be opaque this proposal would have some merit, but it is clear that short vowels may also be opaque. For example, in Turkish nonhigh vowels are opaque to rounding harmony, though not to backness harmony. This is illustrated in (55). The accusative singular forms show that the high vowel of the accusative suffix harmonizes in backness and rounding with the stem. But the nonhigh vowel of the plural suffix fails to harmonize in rounding with the noun stem, and transmits its own rounding value to the accusative suffix. Other examples of this sort are discussed by Steriade (to appear). Since, as this example shows, some mechanism for specifying opacity independent of geometric structure must exist, there is no reason to attribute the opacity of long vowels to the branching structure of the harmony tree.

(55) | Nom.Sg. | Acc.Sg. | Acc.Pl. | |
| --- | --- | --- | --- |
| diš | diši | dišleri | "tooth" |
| köy | köyü | köyleri | "town" |
| son | sonu | sonlarɨ | "end" |
| kɨz | kɨzɨ | kɨzlarɨ | "girl" |

Moreover, long vowels may be opaque in situations in which their opacity cannot be attributed to violation of uniform branching. According to Sohn (1971, 1975) Woleaian has a rule that raises /a/ to /e/ between two high vowels. This rule is formalized in (56). The justification for this rule is found in (57) and (58).

(56) $[+\text{syll}] \rightarrow [-\text{low}] \:/\: \begin{bmatrix} +\text{syll} \\ +\text{high} \end{bmatrix} C_o \underline{\quad} C_o \begin{bmatrix} +\text{syll} \\ +\text{high} \end{bmatrix}$

(57) | | | |
| --- | --- | --- |
| ülümej | /würüma + ji/ | 1sg "drinking object" |
| ülümem^w | /würüma + mu/ | 2sg |
| ülümemi | /würüma + mii/ | 2pl |
| ülümal | /würüma + la/ | 3sg |
| ülümaš | /würüma + ca/ | 1plinc |

(58) metaj   /mata + ji/   1sg   "eye"
      metam^w   /mata + mu/   2sg
      metami   /mata + mii/   2pl

      metal   /mata + la/   3sg
      metaš   /mata + ca/   1plinc

The first three forms in (57) show that the stem-final /a/ raises to /e/ when it is surrounded by high vowels. The second two forms in (57) show that a high vowel on the left is not sufficient to trigger raising. The first three forms in (58) show that a high vowel on the right is not sufficient to trigger raising. Of course no raising occurs in the absence of any high vowels.

Since this rule has in effect two DTEs, it cannot be represented by a uniformly branching tree. Consequently, if the only reason for long vowel opacity were violation of uniform branching, we should predict that long vowels could not be opaque to rule (56). This prediction is not borne out. According to Sohn (1975;31), "The double vowel *aa* never changes to *ee* in any environment, as observed in the examples [itaai] 'I...no longer' and [nigaausape] 'area below eye'." Thus, long vowels can be opaque in environments where their opacity cannot be attributed to the uniform branching of harmony trees.[26] Note that this example also shows that not all harmony trees are uniformly branching, which undermines the whole basis for Marantz' argument.[27]

The conclusion to be drawn from the above discussion is that no evidence favors the geometric interpretation of the metrical formalism.

4.2. The Metrical Theory as a Theory of RES(AS)

I hope to have shown that there is no basis for interpreting the metrical formalism as part of a theory of phonological representation. We have however seen that there exists a class of phenomena not describable in purely autosegmental terms, and that it is possible to describe these phenomena in a straightforward way by means of the metrical formalism. It thus seems reasonable to treat the Metrical theory as the theory of the RES(AS).

From this point of view the properties attributed to the formalism are precisely the properties that render the RES(AS) untreatable in purely autosegmental terms. These are: 1. directionality; 2. the ability to change feature specifications; 3. the ability to assign the opposite of the feature specification of the trigger; and 4. the possibility of local application. Of course these are precisely the properties of ordinary linear rules of the SPE sort. Thus, perhaps the more relevant question is how metrical rules differ from ordinary linear rules.

The Metrical Theory imposes a number of constraints on rules that distinguish it from the linear theories. First, the theory of projection, which I will not discuss here, imposes constraints on the use of variables. There are in addition three constraints of importance. First, a metrical tree may have only a single Designated Terminal Element. This rules out the possibility of rules with two-sided environments. Second, since the feature specification that percolates from the root of the tree to the terminal nodes is obtained from the DTE, it follows that only assimilations and dissimilations are possible. No rule can be formulated that arbitrarily assigns a particular feature value to the focus regardless of the value of that feature in the environment. Consider for example rule (59) which is written in the parenthesis-star notation of Chomsky & Halle (1968). This rule makes an unbounded string of vowels round if the last vowel in the word is a high vowel. Suppose further that the language in question has the vowel inventory given in (60), so that some high vowels are rounded while others are unrounded. In this case rule (59) cannot be conceived of as assimilatory, since its effect will be dissimilatory whenever the last vowel in the word is /i/ or /ɯ/. On the other hand, rule (59) is not dissimilatory since its effect will be assimilatory whenever the last vowel in the word is /u/ or /ü/. Consequently, rule (59) has no metrical translation.

(59) $[+\text{syll}] \rightarrow [+\text{rnd}] / \underline{} (C_o V C_o)^* C_o \begin{bmatrix} +\text{syll} \\ +\text{high} \end{bmatrix} C_o \#$

(60) i ü u ɯ
     e   o
       a

Perhaps the most interesting aspect of the Metrical Theory is the constrained theory of harmony domains that it provides. Within this theory there are only two domains available: binary and unbounded. That is to say, a harmony trigger may affect either an unbounded string of identical projected elements, as in (61), or only its immediate neighbour, as in (62). No rule can affect a fixed number of elements greater than one, as in (63).

(61) X X X X Y → Y Y Y Y Y

(62) X X X X Y → X X X Y Y

(63) X X X X Y → X X Y Y Y

This same claim has been made for stress placement rules by Hayes (1980). Hayes claims that stress feet are all binary or unbounded, just like harmony (and disharmony) domains. Indeed, it appears to be possible to extend this claim to all phonological rules, since lengthening rules and shortening rules also obey it, as far as I have been able to determine. It even extends to phonologically arbitrary allomorphy rules, in those cases where such rules refer to position in the string. Such rules occasionally refer to initial or final position, or to second or penultimate position, but never to any higher number of elements from the periphery, e.g. antepenultimate position or third position. The only case of which I am aware in which an allomorphy rule refers to a position other than the four mentioned is a remarkable rule of Shipibo described by Lauriault (1948). In this case a small number of morphemes exhibit a phonologically arbitrary alternation between two forms, one of which appears when the segment in question is an odd-numbered mora, counting from the beginning of the word, the other of which appears when the segment in question is in an even-numbered mora. This example confirms the hypothesis that (morpho-) phonological rules count either by two's or not at all.

To summarize this section, it appears that the properties of the Metrical Theory are not so much those of a theory of representation as of a constrained theory of phonological rules. The principal constraints are the limitation of harmony domains to a single DTE, the claim that the feature value assigned is derived from that of the DTE, and the restriction of harmony domains to two types, binary and unbounded.

5. PROBLEMS IN THE THEORY OF RES(AS)

In the preceding section I pointed out that among the constraints imposed by the Metrical Theory are the limitation of harmony domains to a single DTE, and the derivation of the feature value assigned to undergoers from the feature value of the DTE. Counterexamples to both of these constraints exist.

We have already seen a counterexample to the first of these constraints. Recall the Woleaian rule (56) discussed in section 4.1. This rule raises /a/ to /e/, provided that *both* of the surrounding vowels be high. This rule thus has in effect two DTEs, and is not stateable in metrical terms.

Counterexamples to the second constraint are to be found among rules that are sensitive to boundaries. Any rule that depends exclusively on boundaries will be a counterexample to this constraint, for, since boundaries have no feature specifications, the feature value assigned to the focus cannot be derived from the value of this feature at the DTE.

A wellknown example of this type is the syllable-final devoicing rule of Turkish, stated in (64). This rule devoices oral stops syllable finally. The operation of the rule is illustrated by the alternations in (65). The parallel forms in (66) show that these alternations do not result from a rule voicing oral stops intervocalically.

(64) $\begin{bmatrix} -\text{son} \\ -\text{cnt} \end{bmatrix} \rightarrow [-\text{voi}] \ / \ \underline{\quad} \ \$$

	Nom.Sg.	Acc.Sg.	Dat.Sg.	Abl.Sg.	Nom.Pl.	
(65)	kap	kabɨ	kaba	kaptan	kaplar	"container"
(66)	sap	sapɨ	sapa	saptan	saplar	"stalk"

Although counterexamples to the constraints in question exist in the case of local rules, I do not know of any such counterexamples involving unbounded rules. This may be an accident, but I should like tentatively to suggest that these examples show that local rules and unbounded rules do not involve the same mechanisms. In the remainder of this section I would like to investigate an alternative to the metrical theory of RES(AS).

In the case of local rules, we may consider the existence of rules that directly change features to be firmly established since it is otherwise impossible to account for dissimilation. Within the autosegmental framework a second rule type has been proposed, namely the delinking rule. Delinking rules delete the association between an autosegment and the P-bearing unit with which it is associated. An example of this type is the Rising Tone Simplification rule proposed by Clements & Ford (1979) for Kikuyu, which is reproduced in (67). This rule deletes the association between a low tone and a tone-bearing unit to which a following high tone is also associated, when either a downstepped high tone or a low tone follows.

(67) Rising Tone Simplification

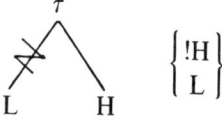

Insofar as it is correct to represent contour tones as sequences of level tones associated with a single tone-bearing unit, the effect of this rule can only be obtained by delinking or outright deletion of the low tone. Clements & Ford show that the latter alternative is incorrect, since in some cases the delinked low tone is also associated to a preceding tonebearing unit, which remains low-toned. As a result, it appears necessary to permit both rules that directly change features and rules that delete associations.

If a delinking rule applies in such a way as to remove the only autosegment linked to a P-bearing unit, the representation will be ill-formed, and the association conventions will apply to rectify this situation. As a result, the P-bearing unit will be reassociated with some other autosegment. Clements & Ford propose a convention that operates correctly in a large number of cases, and is, to my knowledge nowhere falsified, to the effect that when an association is destroyed, the element conditioning the delinking takes precedence in reassociation. Thus, a rule that delinks the only autosegment associated with a P-bearing unit has the ultimate effects of causing the assimilation of that P-bearing unit to the P-bearing unit conditioning the delinking. Thus, delinking rules can change feature specifications, albeit indirectly.

The fact that changes in feature specifications can come about either directly or via delinking raises the possibility that unbounded feature-changing rules might operate not by directly changing features but by unbounded delinking followed by convention-governed reassociation. Such accounts have appeared from time to time in the autosegmental literature. An example is Hayes (1981) in which Russian obstruent voicing harmony is treated by means of unbounded delinking.

This account differs in two respects from direct feature changing. First, it is clear that delinking followed by reassociation can only spread an existing feature value. Consequently, a theory allowing only unbounded delinking, not unbounded feature-changing will have the property that the feature value assigned by unbounded rules will be derived from the value of that feature at the trigger, while local rules need not obey such a constraint. Since this prediction appears to be correct, this is an advantage of the theory.

The second way in which unbounded delinking differs from unbounded direct feature-changing is that it takes place in two steps. As a result, it is possible in principle for a rule to intervene between delinking and reassociation. There is at least one case in which it is possible to argue that this occurs.

Recall that in a pure autosegmental harmony a segment that is associated with an autosegment at the point at which the Well Formedness Condition is fulfilled is opaque. As a result, if a segment is specified for the harmony feature by a rule applying before fulfillment of the WFC, that segment will be opaque. But no such result is expected in a feature-changing harmony. If the feature-specifying rule applies after the harmony rule the result will be a single segment interrupting the harmonizing string. If the feature specifying rule applies before the harmony rule, it should have no effect in any string to which the harmony rule applies; the harmony rule will override any effect it may have had.

Suppose however that feature-changing harmony results from delinking ultimately followed by reassociation. In this case there are three possible orderings of the feature specifying rule rather than two. If this rule is ordered before delinking its effect will be overridden by the harmony rule. If it follows reassociation, it will create an island in the midst of the harmonizing string. But if it is ordered after delinking and before reassociation the feature-specifying rule will create opaque segments. In other words the delinking rule in effect sets up an autosegmental harmony system. Thus, if we can show that in a demonstrably feature-changing harmony segments specified for the harmony feature by rule are opaque, we shall have an argument in favour of the delinking analysis, since this behaviour can be accounted for only by a rule ordering that is not available in the direct feature-changing theory. It appears that just this situation arises in the Chumash sibilant harmony described in section 2.1.

Chumash has a rule that turns /s/ into /š/ before /t,l,n/. This rule is formalized in (68), and illustrated by the examples in (69), all of which involve the third person subject prefix which we know to be underlyingly /s/.

(68) $\begin{bmatrix} +\text{cor} \\ +\text{stri} \end{bmatrix} \rightarrow [-\text{ant}] \;/\; \underline{\quad} \; \begin{bmatrix} +\text{cor} \\ -\text{stri} \end{bmatrix}$

(69) šnan'   /s + nan'/   "he goes"   (18)
      štepu?   /s + tepu?/   "he gambles"   (521)
      šloxit'   /s + lox' + it/   "he surpasses me"   (116)
      šlok'in   /s + lok'in/   "he cuts it"   (117)
      štumun   /s + tumun/   "its egg"   (242)
      šnit^{h}oy   /s + nit^{h}oy/   "it is possible"   (402)

Rule (68) applies only in derived environments. Morpheme internally /s/ may appear before the nonstrident dentals, as illustrated in (70).

(70) stumukun   "mistletoe"   (228)
      slow'   "eagle"   (246)
      wastu   "pleat"   (163)

Of course /š/ is free to appear in the same position morpheme internally. Such morpheme internal /š/ are subject to sibilant harmony, as illustrated in (71)-(73).

(71) /wašti/   "of a flow, of liquid in motion"   (352)
     waštinan'   /wašti + nan'/   "to spill"
     swastilok'inus   /s + wašti + lok'in + us/
                       "the flow stops on him"

(72) /ušla/   "with the hand"   (351)
    ušlok'om   /ušla + k'om/   "to stroke with the hand"
    uslasɨq   /ušla + sɨq/   "to press firmly by hand"

(73) /uqšti/   "of throwing"   (365-6)
    uxštimɨkɨn   /uqšti + mɨk + Vn/ "go far when throwing"
    suxstimes   /su + uqšti + mes/ "throw over to"

In contrast, /š/ derived by rule (68) are opaque.[28] They may trigger harmony themselves, as in (74) and (75), and they do not undergo it, as in (75) and (76). The fact that only those /š/ derived by rule are opaque supports the delinking hypothesis. This cannot be a case of context-sensitive specification of opacity, since in that case underlying morpheme internal /š/ before /t, l, n,/ should be opaque too.

(74) šistɨʔɨ   /s + is + tɨʔ/   "he finds it"   (18)

(75) šišlusisin   /s + iš + lu + sisin/ "they two are gone awry"
                                                                (126)

(76) štiyepus   /s + ti + yep + us/ "he tells him"   (120)

This Chumash example suggests that in at least some cases unbounded feature-changing is performed by delinking rather than directly.

Of course the most interesting hypothesis is that delinking is the *only* mechanism available for unbounded feature-changing, that there are no unbounded rules that directly change features. In this case it is necessary to give an account of unbounded dissimilation, such as the Mandarin Chinese example discussed in section 2.3, in terms of local feature-changing rules and unbounded delinking.

It is clear that the local dissimilation rule must follow unbounded delinking. Suppose not. Then a string of Third tones would first be converted into an otherwise identical string whose penultimate tone had been changed to Second Tone, as in (77). To this representation unbounded delinking would then apply, to be followed, ultimately by reassociation. But in this case we should expect an underlying string of the form 3 3 3 2 3 to be converted to 2 2 2 2 3, which is incorrect, the correct output being 2   2   3   2   3.

(77)   3 3 3 3 3 → 3 3 3 2 3

In the case of an unbounded feature-changing assimilation the most natural delinking rule would have the form (78).

(78) $\begin{pmatrix} F \\ \not{|} \\ \pi \end{pmatrix}_Q \Big/ \begin{array}{c} F \\ | \\ \pi \end{array} \underline{\quad}$

This rule delinks an unbounded sequence of autosegments representing the feature F, leaving only the last such autosegment linked. We might make us of a similar rule to handle dissimilation, in this case requiring that all of the autosegments in the sequence bear the same specification, say + for concreteness.

(79) $\begin{pmatrix} +F \\ \not{|} \\ \pi \end{pmatrix}_Q \Big/ \begin{array}{c} +F \\ | \\ \pi \end{array} \underline{\quad}$

This would be followed by a local dissimilation rule like (80).

(80)   +F → −F / ___ +F

The result will be a derivation like that in (81).

(81)   +F +F +F +F +F   +F +F +F +F +F
        | | | | | → | →
        π   π   π   π   π   π   π   π   π   π

       +F +F +F −F +F
                              |
        π   π   π   π   π

But the reassociation conventions predict that the unlinked P-bearing units will now link to the rightmost autosegment, since it is the one that triggered delinking, and if this takes place there will be no dissimilation. How are we to arrange for the dissimilated autosegment to be the one that links up to the unassociated P-bearing units? The simplest solution seems to be to make use of a somewhat more complicated rule, namely (82).

(82) $\begin{pmatrix} +F \\ \not{|} \\ \pi \end{pmatrix}_Q \Big/ \begin{array}{cc} +F & +F \\ | & | \\ \pi & \pi \end{array} \underline{\quad}$

Action-At-A-Distance 155

This will yield the derivation in (83).

(83)
```
    +F  +F  +F  +F  +F       +F  +F  +F  +F  +F
    |   |   |   |   |    →            |   |       →
    π   π   π   π   π        π   π   π   π   π

    +F  +F  +F  -F  +F
            
                |   |
    π   π   π   π   π
```

Now the no-crossing prohibition prevents linking to the rightmost autosegment, and the penultimate autosegment takes precedence since it is a trigger of the delinking rule. The result is that the unassociated P-bearing units will all associate to the penultimate autosegment, yielding (84), which is the correct output.

(84)
```
    +F  +F  +F  -F  +F
     _____|   |
    π   π   π   π   π
```

Notice that in this framework unbounded assimilation requires only a single rule, but unbounded dissimilation requires two. Although this might appear to be a defect I suggest that it may indeed be an advantage, in that there is some reason to believe that unbounded dissimilation is more highly marked than unbounded assimilation. Rules of unbounded dissimilation appear to be much rarer than unbounded assimilations, and from a functional point of view it makes little sense to convert a long sequence of identical feature specifications into a slightly shorter sequence of the opposite feature specification. Alternating dissimilation makes a great deal more sense.

6. CONCLUSION

We have seen that the Autosegmental Theory is well motivated as a theory of phonological representation, and as such contributes to the description of action-at-a-distance. The Metrical Theory, on the other hand, makes no contribution to the description of action-at-a-distance when taken to be a theory of phonological representation. Rather, it is properly conceived as a theory of phonological rules. Furthermore, the properties of local rules and unbounded rules are shown to be distinct, suggesting that unbounded phenomena should be accounted for by means of special mechanisms. I have suggested that unbounded delinking rules may be the appropriate mechanism.

NOTES

1. It is important to distinguish between the broad and narrow senses of the term "metrical". In the broad sense this term may be taken to refer to the theory of Vergnaud & Halle (1978) and their subsequent publications, taken as a whole. In the narrow sense, the term refers to a theory making use of hierarchical phonological structure, thus including the metrical theory of stress, the theory of syllable structure, and the metrical theory of harmony. These two usages are quite distinct, as the Metrical Theory, in the broad sense, has come to include large parts of the Autosegmental Theory. In particular, Halle & Vergnaud (1980) have adopted the autosegmental theory of non-concatenative morphology of McCarthy (1978, 1979, 1981, 1982), and Halle & Vergnaud (1982) adopt a version of the autosegmental theory of tone. The case of harmony is more complex. Vergnaud & Halle (1978) proposed a completely non-autosegmental theory of harmony; this theory was abandoned, in the case of non-directional harmony, in Halle & Vergnaud (1981), although they still maintain a metrical account of directional harmony. What I discuss in the present paper is the specific question of the role of metrical structure in harmony processes, particularly in directional harmony since Halle & Vergnaud themselves have conceded the autosegmental nature of non-directional harmony.
2. A mapping is said to be bijective if and only if it is both injective and surjective. A mapping F from A to B is injective if, for a and a' in A, $F(a)=F(a')$ implies $a=a'$. A mapping F from A to B is surjective if for every b in B there exists an a in A such that $F(a) = b$.
3. Although the theory was formalized by Goldsmith (1976) many of the basic observations had been known to Africanists for some time. See for example Welmers (1959), who says, "If sequences of two or three tonemes can be crowded into simultaneity with a single vowel, it is equally true that, in some languages, the domain of a toneme may be more than one 'syllable'." (p.6)
4. The original form of the Well Formedness Condition is as follows: a. Association lines may not cross, and b. Every P-segment must be associated with at least one P-bearing unit, and every P-bearing unit must be associated with at least one P-segment. In much recent work the first clause of b. has been abandoned. See Clements & Ford (1979), Halle & Vergnaud (1982). Once b. is reduced to the second clause, this may be stated in the more general form given in the text.
5. Note that the requirement that every segment be fully specified by the end of the derivation need not be stipulated in the phonology since it is an input condition on the phonetics. Every segment must be fully specified at the input to the phonetics; otherwise the state of some of the articulators will be left indeterminate. This is a further reason for adopting the revised version of the WFC, since the requirement of the original WFC that every P-segment be associated with at least one P-bearing unit is not deducible from any other principles and must simply be stipulated.
6. I adopt here the terminology of Clements (1981).
7. This Priority clause must be subject to language-particular variation. Although it appears that most languages give priority to the leftmost of two autosegments in whose domain an unlinked P-bearing unit lies, the Guaraní facts discussed below in the text demonstrate that in this language priority is given to the rightmost.
8. For further discussion of Turkish vowel harmony see Clements & Sezer (this vol.)
9. See Clements (1976, 1977a, 1981), Clements & Sezer (this vol.), Goldsmith (1976) and Poser (1980, 1981b).
10. Since abandoned by them. See Halle & Vergnaud (1981).

11. "Nearly all" since underspecified vowels also arise by epenthesis.
12. "Nearly always" since, in the case of word-initial epenthesis discussed briefly below, the specification is obtained from the right.
13. The best non-autosegmental account of Guaraní is Rivas (1974). For the facts see this paper and the references cited therein, especially Gregores & Suarez (1967). Goldsmith (1976) contains a sketch of an autosegmental account. For a more detailed account, including replies to criticism of Goldsmith's account, see Poser (1981b).
14. All examples are followed by a reference to the page of Applegate (1972) on which they occur.
15. Note that I am using the term "isolation" in the rather special sense of "outside of the domain of a harmony trigger", which in the case of Chumash means "not followed by another sibilant within the same word."
16. The /s^h/ of (32)a is the result of a rule that converts geminate obstruents into aspirates.
17. The /l/ that appears after /$\check{ts}^h$o/ in these forms is epenthetic.
18. I am grateful to Paul Kiparsky for raising this issue.
19. I ignore the possible bracketings of the prefix /api/ since it contains no sibilandts and is thus irrelevant.
20. Okello (1976) also deals with Lango, but her transcriptions are not in accord with Woock & Noonan's. Without personal knowledge of the language it is impossible to determine who is right, or whether perhaps two different dialects are involved, but the fact that Woock & Noonan argue explicitly that this harmony is local together with the fact that they are familiar with Okello's work, inspires hope that their facts are correct.
21. The numbers used here are traditional diacritics. For a feature analysis of Chinese tones see Yip (1980).
22. The definition of the DTE has varied during the history of the Metrical Theory. Vergnaud & Halle (1978) defined the DTE to be the least embedded node, a position argued for also by Zubizarreta (1979). But by Spring 1979 Halle in his class lectures defined the DTE to be the most deeply embedded node.
23. It has been suggested to me that these difficulties might be avoided by assigning the labels (s,w) (in a left-branching tree) and (w,s) (in a right-branching tree) to each pair of sister nodes, and then computing for each terminal node a rank according to the following algorithm, used by Liberman & Prince (1977) to mimic the SPE numerical values for stress.

> If a terminal node is labelled w, its rank is equal to the number of nodes that dominate it, plus one. If a terminal node is labelled s, its rank is equal to the number of nodes that dominate the lowest w dominating it, plus one.

In this system every terminal node receives a distinct rank, so the DTE could be defined as the terminal node of rank one without ambiguity. While this system does make use of depth of embedding, it also makes use of the stipualtion that the tree be labelled (s, w) or (w, s), which, since trees are required to be uniformly branching, is equivalent to stipulating that the DTE be the leftmost or rightmost node, respectively. My claim is not that no adequate algorithm for determining the DTE will make use of depth of embedding. Rather, it is that depth of embedding by itself is insufficient, and that every adequate algorithm makes use of reference to direction, rendering the use of depth of embedding superfluous.

24. For example [kũñãkãraí] "lady" < /kuyã # karaí/ (Gregores & Suarez (1967) p. 69).

25. According to Zubizarreta (1979), Andalusian Spanish has a right-to-left harmony that affects, but does not spread beyond, stressed vowels. These are phonetically long. She argues that if the DTE is taken to be the least embedded node, and if the stressed vowels are treated as branching, they will be able to occur only at the opposite end of the domain from the DTE, since otherwise uniform branching will be violated. Marantz (1980) pointed out that if the DTE is taken to be the most embedded node, the fact that in Telegu long vowels both block and fail to undergo harmony will be accounted for, and that the Andalusian case can then be accounted for by adding a local rule to spread the harmony onto the long vowels that blocked its further propagation. In contrast, he argued, Zubizarreta's account cannot be extended to the Telegu case.

26. It has been pointed out to me that the failure of long vowels to raise could in this case be attributed to their representation as sequences of vowels, i.e. as $\begin{matrix} V & V \\ | & | \\ a & a \end{matrix}$.

Then neither of the /a/s will be surrounded by high vowels. This is true, but it is worth noting that it rests on the assumption that each mora of the long vowel is separately specified, contrary to what is generally assumed. Secondly, the example clearly shows that local rules, at least, cannot be represented by uniformly branching trees. As a result, a second Woleaian rule provides an example of long vowel opacity not attributable to the uniform branching requirement. This is the rule that raises *a* to *e* before another low vowel, which according to Sohn (1973) does not apply to long *a*. In this case no reanalysis is possible.

27. Steriade (to appear) claims that opaque segments tend to be "more prominent" (i.e. more sonorant, stressed, high toned) than undergoers, and that this fact supports a metrical approach. But she admits that this prominence cannot be a geometric property, and since it is precisely this that is at issue, her argument lacks force. Insofar as her generalizations about opaque segments are valid, they can just as easily be stated without a metrical tree as with one.

28. Unfortunately, there are exceptions to this generalization, among them example (32)b. Even so, the fact that such derived /š/ are sometimes opaque supports the analysis presented, in that no other account provides an explanation for the difference in behaviour between derived and underlying /š/. It is also worth noting that Harrington (1974), describing the closely related Ventureño dialect, asserts categorically that derived /š/ is opaque.

The Formal Interaction of Harmony and Accent: The Tone Pattern of Japanese

Maria L. Zubizarreta
M.I.T.

0. INTRODUCTION

As has often been observed, a *stressed syllable* has the unique property of being defined with respect to other syllables — adjacent and non-adjacent — in a phonological string. For example, in *bandanna,* the second syllable *da* is more prominent (i.e. more stressed) than the third syllable *na* and the first syllable *ban*, and *ban* is more prominent than *na*. Likewise, in *Ticonderoga,* the most prominent syllable is *ro*. The second most prominent is *Ti*, and the third most prominent is *con*. There exists no word with only secondary and/or tertiary stress: i.e. with no primary stress. For example, words with a stress pattern such as $\overset{2\ 3}{Ticonderoga}$ or $\overset{2\ \ 2\ 3}{bandanna}$ do not exist. An adequate theory of stress must characterize this "relative" property of stress. Liberman 1975 and Liberman & Prince 1977 proposed to represent relative prominence by means of *hierarchical-binary branching* tree structures, in which each pair of sister nodes is labelled S W or W S, depending on which node is the strongest. Given the hierarchical nature of trees, not only syllables but also non-terminal constituents are specified for relative strength:

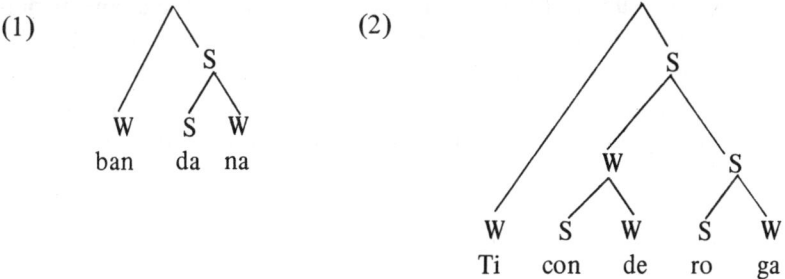

---

*   I would like to thank Morris Halle, Norval Smith and Jean-Roger Vergnaud for comments and discussions.

Notice that the labels *Strong* and *Weak* do not have an intrinsic meaning or value. A node labelled S can only be interpreted with respect to a sister node labelled W, and vice-versa.

The strength of the syllable in a word is determined in the following way:

(3) The stress number of a terminal node t is equal to the number of nodes that dominate the lowest W dominating t, plus one.

Thus the syllable that is dominated by only Ss is interpreted as having the strongest stress: *da* in (1) and *ro* in (2). The W that is immediately dominated by the root of the tree has the second strongest stress: *ban* in (1), *Ti* in (2), and so on.

Since Liberman 1975 and Liberman & Prince 1977, an important amount of research has been dedicated to the construction of a universal theory of stress: the core-grammar (i.e. the set of parameters and principles) which defines the class of well-formed metrical structures. We refer the reader to Vergnaud & Halle 1978, forthcoming, MIT Working Papers - Vol. I, Hayes 1980, and references cited therein. We will content ourselves here with sketching out the parts of the theory that are relevant to the discussion in the following sections.

0.1

It has been noticed for some time that many stress rules draw a distinction between heavy syllables: $C_o\bar{V}$, $C_o VC$ (and heavier ...) and light syllables: $C_o \overset{\circ}{V}$ ($\bar{V}$ stands for long vowel and $\overset{\circ}{V}$ for short vowel). Metrical theory provides a natural solution to this problem by first dividing the syllable into two main subconstituents: an *onset*, consisting of the segments preceding the syllabic prominence peak of the syllable, and a *rime*, consisting of everything else; and furthermore by assigning internal structure to the *rime*. If long vowels are represented as underlying geminate, the distinction can be represented as one of branching versus non-branching rime:

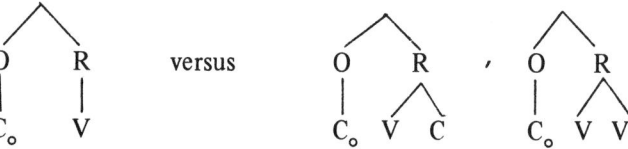

Since the *onset* is non-pertinent for the determination of stress, it is natural to assume that higher metrical structure is mapped onto a *projection of rimes*, in the sense of Vergnaud & Halle 1978.

Harmony and Accent

Some stress rules draw the distinction between $C_o\bar{V}$ and $C_o\breve{V}$, C_oVC. In these cases it may be assumed that the rime is further divided into two sub-constituents: the *Nucleus*, which contains the [+syllabic] segments, and the *Coda*, which contains the [-syllabic] segments; and that only the Nuclei are projected.

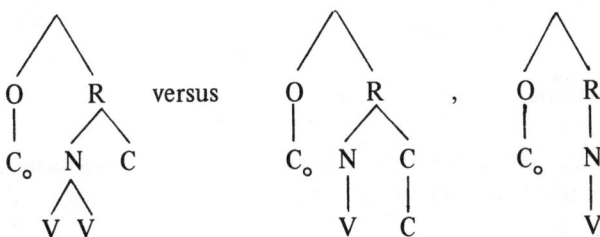

In the Japanese dialects that we will be reviewing, there is no reason to postulate a further division of the rime in terms of Nucleus and Coda. The Japanese rime is either non-branching (it contains one vowel) or it is branching (it contains a sequence of two vowels or a sequence of a vowel and the dental nasal *n*). In some dialects, for example in Osaka, gemination processes create branching rimes. As we shall see, in some dialects all syllabic segments contained in the rime – including nasals – are relevant for the determination of the tone structure of a word. In others, only the rime node is relevant.

Coming back to our initial example *bandanna*, it has been noticed that although this word has the same prominence pattern as the trisyllabic word *banana*, the degree of stress differentiation is different: the difference of strength between the first and second syllables of *bandanna* is definitely smaller than the difference of strength between the first and second syllables of *banana*. Likewise for *Panama* and *Pamela* with respect to the first and last syllable. This fact has motivated, in part, the postulation of an intermediary level of metrical organization between the projection of *rimes* and the *Word* level (i.e. the metrical structure that encompasses the entire word): the *foot*.[1]

(4)   a.   b.

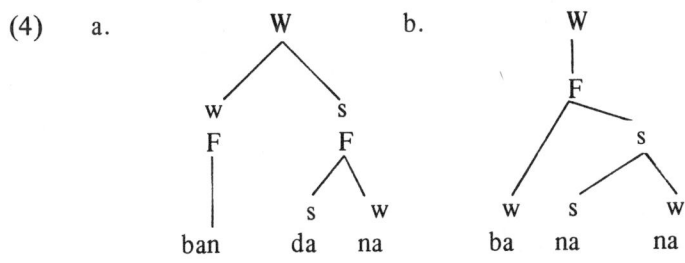

(5) a. 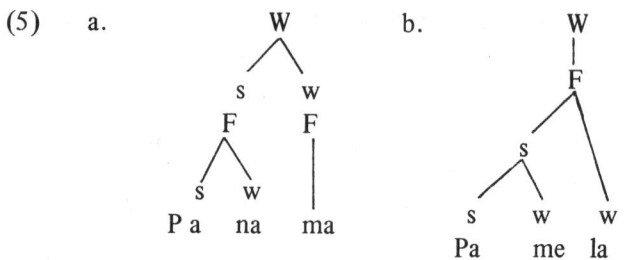 b.

(the internal structure of rimes is omitted)

Convention (3) is no longer sufficient to interpret the prominence pattern of (4) and (5). It is necessary to assume that:

(6) The degree of subordination that apply to syllables within a foot is greater than the degree of subordination that apply between feet.

and (3) has to be modified accordingly.

Instead of assuming (6), we propose a more straightforward solution. Only the *Word tree* is labelled with the labels S and W which encode the notion of relative strength of a node or constituent. The *Foot tree* is labelled with the labels + and -. That is, the internal constituents of a foot have an absolute value: +stress or -stress. We will refer to a foot thus labelled as a *polarized foot*.

(2), (4)a, and (4)b will have the following forms:

(7) a.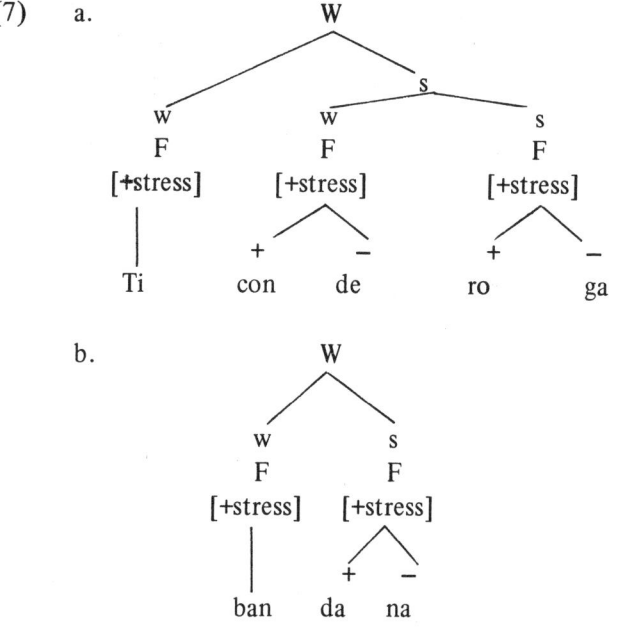

b.

Harmony and Accent 163

c.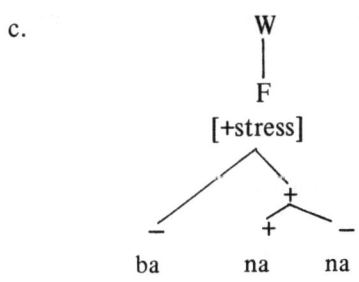

Obviously, convention (3) now applies only to the Word tree (*t* is interpreted as the terminal node of a Word tree, i.e. the topmost node of a foot.)

[+stress] is a feature on the root-nodes of feet, which percolates down onto the terminal nodes of the tree. If the value of a terminal node is +, it is +(+stress) (i.e. +stress). If the value of a terminal node is -, it is -(+stress) (i.e. -stress). Since there is one terminal node labelled + per foot, there is one stressed rime per foot. The terminal node labelled + is the *designated element* of a foot: it defines or determines a domain of metrical organization. In a left-branching tree, the designated element is the left-most terminal node. In a right-branching tree, the designated element is the right-most terminal node.

More motivation for considering a stress-foot to be a polarized foot will be given in later sections.

0.2.

There are at least two questions that a metrical theory of stress has to answer: 1. What are the conditions or properties that define the class of well-formed trees? 2. What are the conditions on the mapping between the different levels of metrical structure?

The answer to question 1 can be divided into two independent but related parts: 1. what are the *geometrical properties* of well-formed trees? 2. what are the conditions on the *labelling* of trees?

The geometrical properties of well-formed trees are the following:

(8)   a.   Trees are *binary-branching* structures:

   b.   Trees may be *recursively* binary-branching: unbounded trees; or *nonrecursively* binary-branching: bounded trees.[2] (word-trees are always unbounded but there exist both bounded and unbounded feet, as we shall see.)

164 *Maria L. Zubizarreta*

c. Trees are *uni-directional*: at a given level of metrical structure: either 1. only the right-nodes (recursively) branch:

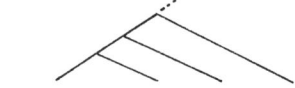

or, 2. only the left-nodes (recursively) branch:

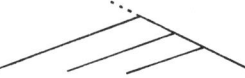

As for labelling, the main (universal) constraint is (9) below:

(9) A branching node may not be labelled W or -.

The simplest labelling convention is (10), defined in terms of the parameter X.

(10) L (X): X-nodes are labelled S (or +), X = "right" or "left".

Given constraint (9), it follows that Labelling Convention L (Right) will never apply to a left-branching tree and Labelling Convention L (Left) will never apply to a right-branching tree:[3]

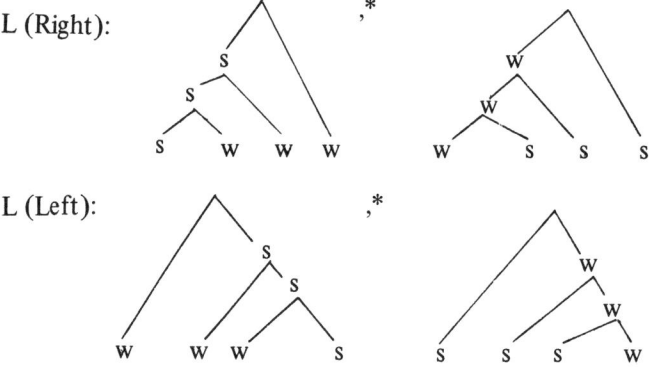

The grammar of a language will state the relevant projection: rimes, nuclei, or [+syllabic] segments, and will fix the parameters discussed above for each metrical level. We restate them:

(11) -bounded/unbounded trees
      -right/left branching
      -right-node/left-node labelled S (or +)

Thus, a particular grammar defines its type of tree for each level.

Harmony and Accent   165

   Recall that the projections of rimes (or nuclei) are mapped onto an intermediary level of metrical organization: the feet. And the feet are mapped onto a higher metrical level: the Word.[4]
   The principles that govern the mapping are:

(12)   1. *The Maximality Principle*: the largest trees compatible with the well-formedness conditions (discussed above) are chosen.
       2. *Constituent Integrity*: the tree-structure of level X^n may not break up constituents of level X^{n-1}.
       3. Trees of a given level may or may not be sensitive to the branchingness of a lower level.

(12)1. and (12)2. are universal. (12)3. is a parameter, the value of which varies among languages. I will assume here without justification that in the unmarked case the word tree is not sensitive to the branchingness of feet and that feet are sensitive to the branchingness of rimes. That is, if a grammar does not specify the contrary, it is to be interpreted in the above manner. But this point will not be crucial to the discussion below. Cf. Vergnaud & Halle 1978, Hayes 1980 for further discussion.
   To illustrate how the theory works, we will depart from English whose stress-system is quite complex and marked, and present two simple but illuminating examples: Eastern Cheremis and Komi, two Finno-Ugric languages discussed in Vergnaud & Halle 1978.
   In Eastern Cheremis:

(13)   a. the accent falls on the syllable containing the last full vowel of the word.
       b. if the word has only reduced vowels, the accent usually is on the first syllable.

Full vowels may be represented as underlying geminates. Consider the following strings of nuclei:

(14)   a. V́ V́ V̂V   V́ V́ V́ V̂V   V́ V́ V́
       b. V́ V́ V́ V́ V́ V́

They are mapped onto unbounded left-branching feet. Hence, left-nodes are labelled +. Given the principles stated in (12), the only possible mappings are:

(15)   a.

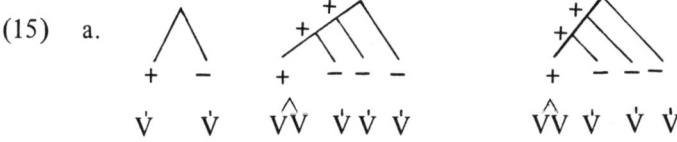

b.

Notice that if (14)a. were mapped onto the following foot-structures, the mapping would be ill-formed because the second foot is not uniformly left-branching:

(16)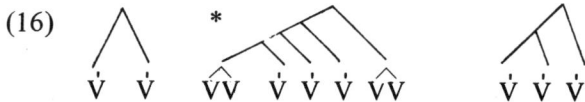

If (14)b. were mapped onto two feet, the Maximality Principle would be violated:

(17) *

Likewise if a syllabic node is skipped:

(18) *

Structures (15)a. and (15)b. are mapped onto a right-branching word tree. Hence, right nodes are labelled S.

(19) a.

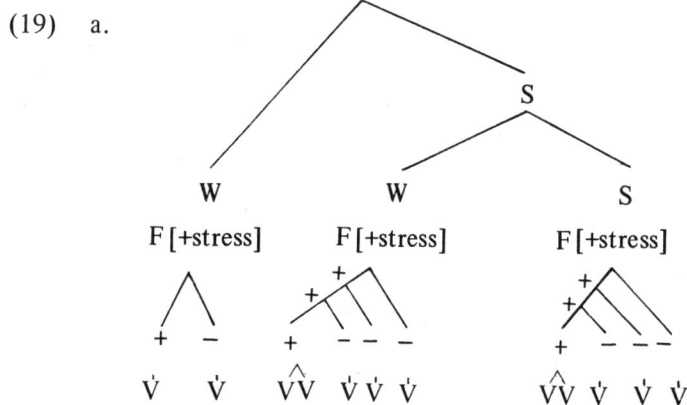

b.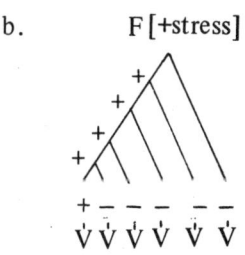

Since (15)b. has only one foot, (19)b. has no word tree (or a degenerate word tree). Some actual examples (cited in Hayes 1980):

(20) a. šiinčáam
     b. slaapáažəm
     c. púugəlmə
     d. kíidəštəžə
     e. təĺəzən

There is no information about subsidiary stress in Eastern Cheremis but this is of no crucial importance for our illustrative purpose.[5]

In the Eastern Permyak dialects of Komi:

(21) a. the accent normally falls on the syllable containing the first heavy vowel of the word.
     b. if the word has only light vowels, the accent is on the last vowel.

Komi is exactly the mirror image of Eastern Cheremis. Feet are unbounded right-branching trees. Hence, right-nodes are labelled +. The word tree is left-branching. Hence, left-nodes are labelled S.

(22) a.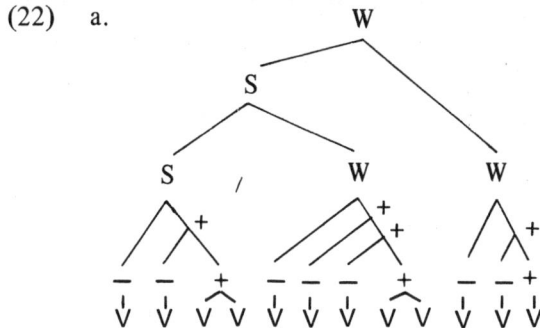

168 *Maria L. Zubizarreta*

b.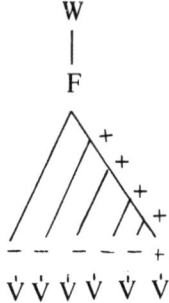

We have illustrated above two cases of unbounded feet. Let us now take a look at bounded feet. Bounded feet characterize alternating stress systems, in which stressed and unstressed vowels alternate in the sequence. An example is Modern Czech discussed in Vergnaud & Halle 1978. In Modern Czech:

(23) main stress is placed on the first syllable of the word and subsidiary stresses are placed on all odd numbered syllables. Hence, feet are bounded and right-nodes are labelled +. The word-tree is left-branching and the right-nodes are labelled S.

Consider a word with an even number of syllables and a word with an odd number of syllables.[6]

(24) a.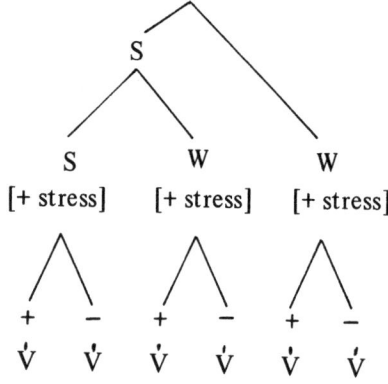

b.

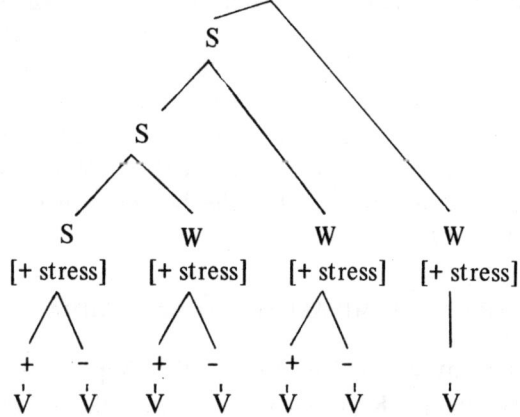

Since there is an odd number of syllables in (24)b, the last syllabic node does not form a constituent with an adjacent node. It stands alone as a *degenerate foot*. Consequently, the final syllable of an odd-numbered syllable word is stressed, unlike the final syllable of an even-numbered syllable word.

Notice that if the string of vowels were mapped onto a feet-structure like the following:

(25) $[_A \ V \ [_B V \ ]_A \ V \ V \ ]_B \ \ldots$

the Constituent Integrity Principle would be violated.

0.3. Given a limited amount of data, how does the language-learner choose the grammar that correctly generates the stress system of the language to which he or she is exposed? The most plausible answer to this question is the same as the one that seems to emerge from recent syntactic work. That is, Universal Grammar will provide a "system of principles" and a relatively small set of "parameters that can be fixed in one or another way, given a relatively small amount of experience. Small changes in the values assigned to parameters in a rich system may lead to what appear to be radically different grammars, though at a deeper level, they are all cast in the same mold." (Chomsky 1981, pag. 8). A stress system which does not fall under core grammar is not necessarily a counterexample to the theory. It may simply be a marked grammar. What is essential is that the theory be rich enough in order to allow for such a grammar and refined or intricate enough to characterize it adequately for its degree of markedness, i.e. that it explains how the language-learner selects a marked grammar over an unmarked one.

It is with the "learnability problem" in mind that we will approach the study of the tone-pattern of several Japanese dialects. It seems plausible that Japanese can be handled by the theory sketched above given that it is a pitch-accent language (a language between tone and accent.) We will limit ourselves to the study of dialects with no subsidiary accent: i.e. dialects with only High and Low tones, with no Mid tone. They are theoretically the most pertinent. All of the data that we will present below are from Haraguchi 1977a, 1977b.

1. SHIMAGAWA, IZUMI, MIYAKONOZYÔ, KAGOSHIMA

We shall start by examining some of the simplest dialects: Shimagawa, Izumi, Miyakonozyô, Kagoshima. Their tone-rules are simple in the sense that there is very little, if any, lexical information that needs to be learned about it. Except for Kagoshima, they are entirely phonological (i.e. non-lexically determined). Each [+syllabic] segment bears a tone: +High or -High (Low). In Shimagawa, Miyakonozyô, and Izumi the tone structure is mapped onto a projection of [+syllabic] segments. In Kagoshima, on the other hand, there is evidence that it is the rime and not the segment which is the elementary unit for the tone structure.

Shimagawa's tone pattern consists of an initial High tone followed by Low tone(s). Examples:

(26) a. e – (ga)   – picture or handle
        H   L
     b. ame – (ga)   – rain or candy
        H L   L
     c. abunai   – dangerous
        H L LL
     d. atumeru   – collect
        H L L L
     ("ga" is the Subject's suffix)

The fact that the accent systematically falls on the initial vowel indicates that the foot is left-branching.[7] Recall that the accented or designated element of the foot is the left-most node in a left-branching tree. It follows that the left-nodes are labelled +. Obviously, the grammar has to indicate that the relevant feature is [+High] (and not [+stress] as in the examples in section 0.). We shall refer to it as the *Percolating Feature*. (26)d, for example, has the following structure:

(27)

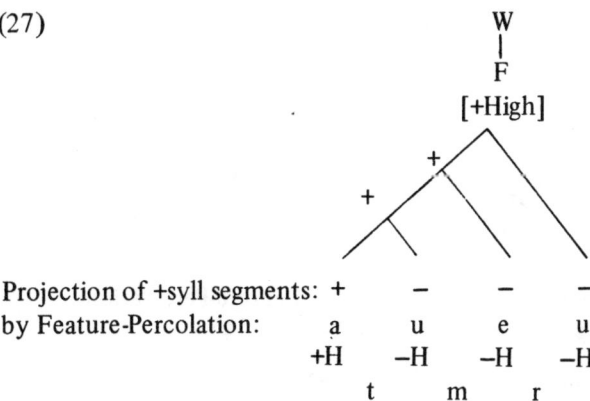

Projection of +syll segments:
by Feature-Percolation:

Shimagawa's tone-rule:
Projection: [+syllabic] segments
Foot: left-branching
Percolating-Feature: [+High]

We assumed above that the projection of syllabic segments is mapped onto a foot structure. The word tree is degenerate. Alternatively, it may be assumed that the syllabic segments are directly mapped onto a word tree, given that an intermediary metrical structure is superfluous. This would imply that word trees may also be polarized, which is conceivable. Cf. footnotes 4 and 5. We leave the issue open.

Miyakonozyô's tone pattern is the inverse of Shimagawa. The accent falls on the final vowel:

(28)   a. ki - ki-ga   'tree or air'
          H   L H

       b. hana - hana-ga   'flower or nose'
          L H   L L H

       c. tamago - tamago-wo   'egg'
          L L H   L L L H

This indicates that the feet are right-branching, and that the right-nodes are labelled +. Recall that the right-most node is the designated element in a right-branching tree. For example, *tamago-wo* has the following tone-structure:

(29)   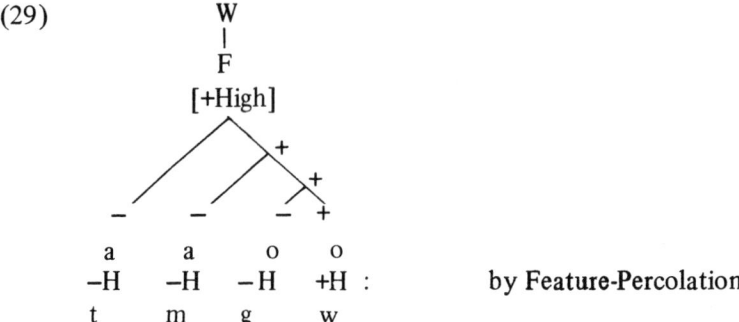   by Feature-Percolation

Miyakonozyô's tone-rule:
Projection: [+syllabic] segments
Foot: right-branching
Percolating-Feature: [+High]

In Izumi, the accent falls systematically on the second mora (except in bisyllabic words):

(30) a. ame   −   ame-ga   −rain or candy
          H L   L H L
      b. abunai   −dangerous
          L H LL
      c. atumeru   −collect
          L H L L

This suggests that the foot starts on the second vowel:

(31)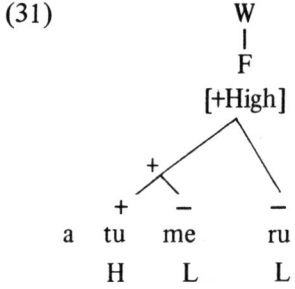

What is then the status of the first vowel? It is *extrametrical*, except in bisyllabic words.

The notion of extrametricality was introduced in Liberman & Prince 1977, where it was motivated for English. It is furthered exemplified in Hayes 1980. An extrametrical element is a peripheral element which is not mapped onto higher metrical structure. It is only later attached to the structure by a general convention. We will adopt here this notion of extrametricality with no further refinements. The extrametricality hypothesis is a marked option. It will only be considered when there is positive evidence against the competing unmarked hypothesis.

After extrametrical segment *a* in (31) is adjoined to the word tree, structure (32) is obtained:

(32)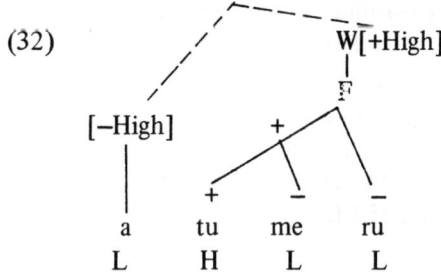

Since the word tree is labelled [+High], it follows that its sister node is labelled [-High].

Izumi's tone-rule:
Projection: [+syllabic] segments (1st segment is extrametrical)
Foot: left-branching
Percolating-Feature: [+High]

In Kagoshima the vocabulary is divided in two. There is a lexical class of words in which the accent falls on the final syllable, as in Miyakonozyô, which indicates that the foot is right branching.

(33) a. na   —   na-ga   —vegetable
         H   L H
     b. hana —   hana-ga   —flower
         L H   L L H
     c. irogami — irogami-ga   —color paper
         L L L H   L L L L H
     d. kookoo —   kookoo-ga   —filial piety
         LL HH   LL LL H
     e. kantan —   kantan-ga   —simplicity
         LL HH   LL LL H

Note that when the last syllable contains a long vowel (cf. (33)d) or a vowel and a nasal (cf. (33)e), the High tone spreads onto both syllabic segments. This constitutes evidence that the relevant projection for tone assignment in this dialect is the rime-projection and not the segment-projection as in the previous dialects.

In another lexical class of words, the accent falls on the penultimate syllable. This constitutes evidence that the final syllable in this class is extrametrical.

(34) a. hana   —   hana-ga   —nose
       H L   L H L
    b. sakura   —   sakura-ga   —cherry
       L H L   L L H L
    c. kagaribi —   kagaribi-ga —watch fire
       L L H L   L L L H L
    d. meirei   —   meirei-ga   —order
       H H L L   L L HH L

    e. kinsen   —   kinsen-ga   —money
       HH LL   L L HH L

As expected, in this lexical class, as in the former, when the rime is branching the High tone spreads onto both segments (cf. (34)d and (34)e). To illustrate, (33)e of Class 1 has the following tone-structure:

(35)

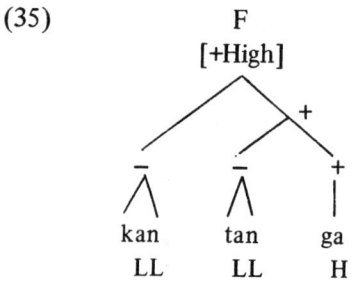

And (34)d of Class 2 has the following structure:

(36)

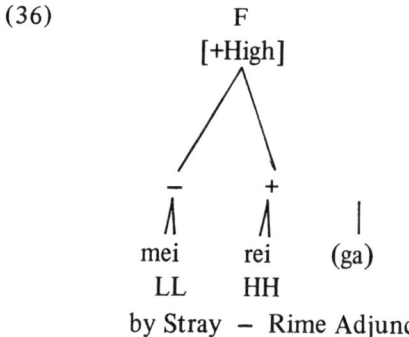

by Stray – Rime Adjunction:

Harmony and Accent

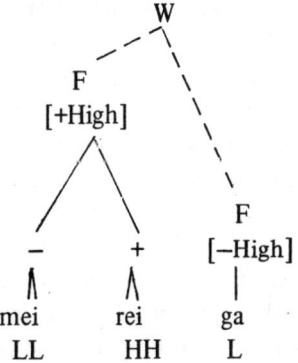

Kagoshima's tone-rule:
Projection: rimes (last rime is extrametrical in Class 2)
Foot: right-branching
Percolating-Feature: [+High]

2. HIROSAKI

One of Hirosaki's tone pattern is entirely predictable, like the tone patterns of the dialects discussed above. It consists of Low tone(s) and a final High tone: ... X X ⌠X

(37) a. e   −   e-mo   -handle
          H   L H
      b. kaze   −   kaze-mo   -wind
          L H   L L H
      c. sakura   −   sakura-mo   -cherry-tree
          L L H   L L L H
      d. tomodati   −   tomodati-mo -friend
          L L L H   L L L L H

("mo" is an enclitic meaning "even, also".)

But the other tone patterns are not entirely predictable. They consist of Low tone(s) followed by High tone(s) and a final Low tone:
... X X ⌠X .. X⌡X

(38) a. usagi   −   usagi-mo   -rabbit
          L H L   L H H L
      b. tebukuro   −   tebukuro-mo -glove
          L H H L   L H H H L
      c. kudamono   −   kudamono-mo -fruits
          L L H L   L L H H L

Where the sequence of Low tones ends and the sequence of High tones starts is not predictable. It varies from word to word. This information must be lexically specified. Haraguchi encodes this information by labelling with a star (*) the first vowel in the sequence of High tones: *usăgi, tebŭkuro, kudamŏno*. When the language-learner learns a word, along with its meaning it must learn the location of the star (if it has one). In metrical theory, the star is equivalent to a *lexically designated element* which defines a foot domain.

Notice that the "predictable" case (the first case mentioned above), already fixes certain parameters. From the data in (37) the language-learner will infer that Hirosaki's foot is right-branching and the percolating or melody feature is High. This tone structure consists of one single foot:

(39)

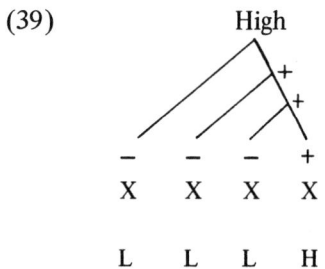

```
      High
       +
       +
- - - +
X X X X

L L L H
```

How does the language-learner discover the tone structure of the second type of tone pattern (cf. 38)? He will know that it consists of more than one foot since it contains a star for the reasons given above. He also knows that the word tree — which combines the feet — is polarized. It is not labelled SW since there is no subsidiary accent, i.e. there is no Mid tone. Notice that the starless tone pattern is properly included in the starred tone pattern, i.e. it is a subpart of the latter. This suggests that the initial foot of the starred tone pattern is identical to the foot of the starless tone pattern. In effect, we have seen that the starless tone pattern already fixes two parameters: the foot is right-branching, which means that the right-nodes are labelled +, and the percolating feature is High. The problem is how does the language-learner discover where the star is on each word. Is it on the Low-tone segment which immediately precedes the first High-tone segment or is it on the first High-tone segment? In other terms, is the star on the last vowel of the initial foot or on the first vowel of the second foot?

Let us postulate the following principle:

(40)   In the unmarked case the "starred" segment has the same value as the percolating-feature.

Harmony and Accent 177

Given this principle and the information provided by the starless tone pattern, under the unmarked hypothesis the "star" must be on the first High-tone bearing segment, i.e. on the right-most segment of the initial foot; and the left-node of the word tree is labelled +:

(41)

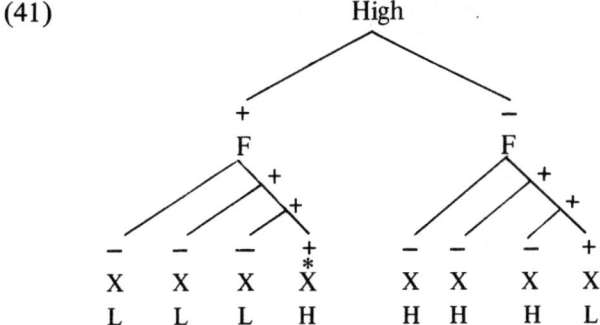

As expected, if the * is on the initial syllable, there is no Low tone preceding the sequence of High tones:

(42) a. kĭtune   —   kĭtune-mo   —fox
        H H L   H H H L
     b. ŭrukome   —   ŭrukome-mo   —nonglutinous rice
        H H H L   H H H H L

(42)b, for example, has tone structure (43). The designated element constitutes a foot by itself.

(43)

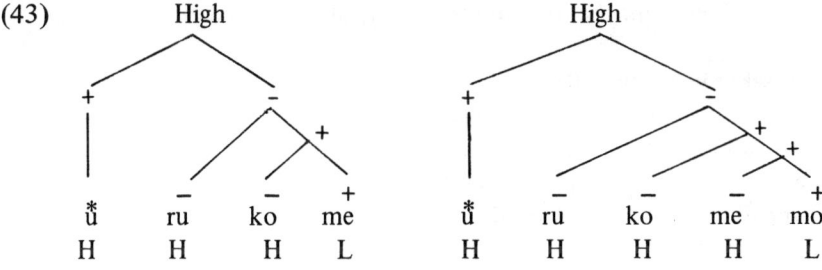

The reader might wonder what is the difference between the tone pattern of a starless word and a word with a final star. As our grammar predicts, if the enclitic "mo" is attached to the end of a word, the starless one still ends in a High tone while the one with a final star ends in a Low tone. Compare (37)d and (44):

(44) a. ĕ   —picture
        H L

178 Maria L. Zubizarreta

  b. otokŏ-mo   —man
    L L H L
  c. kaminarĭ-mo   —thunder
    L L LH L

A word with a final star and an enclitic attached to its right has the following tone-structure:

(45)

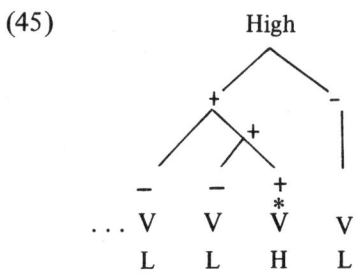

Our grammar also predicts that if an enclitic is not added, the words with a final star will end with a High tone. This is indeed correct in a [—pause] context. But before [+pause] these words end with a falling tone: otokŏ , kaminarĭ , ĕ.[8] The following low-level rule obtains the desired
L L HL L L L HL HL
results:

(46)   H →   HL / ___ # #
             [+pause]

  Condition: the final vowel is a lexical designated element.

Hirosaki's core tone-rule:
Projection: [+syllabic] segments
Percolating-Feature: High
Feet: right-branching
Type of feet: polarized
Word tree Label: + —
The word tree label follows from the conjunction of principle (40) and the other parameters.

  It is interesting that all the dialects described by Haraguchi which have a starred tone-pattern also have a starless tone-pattern. Moreover, the starless tone-pattern is always a subpart of the starred tone-pattern. This cannot be an accident. And in fact in the system proposed above it is not. The starless tone-pattern plays a crucial role in discovering the structure of the starred tone-pattern. It provides positive evidence concerning the per-

Harmony and Accent

colating-feature and the type of feet, which permits the language-learner to fix these parameters immediately without having to consider alternative possibilities. As we have seen, these two parameters being fixed, the discovery of the starred tone-pattern becomes a feasible task, given the principles of universal grammar (in particular, principle (40)).

3. OSAKA

Osaka's tone patterns are very different from Hirosaki's. It has two lexical classes of words with distinct tone patterns. Each lexical class has one predictable (i.e. starless) tone pattern and one not entirely predictable (i.e. starred) tone pattern.

One of the starless tone-patterns is exactly like Hirosaki's, a final High tone preceded only by Low tones: $\underline{\ldots X X \overline{X}}$

Class 1:

(47) a. ee   —   e- ga   —picture
          L H   L H
      b. sora   —   sora-ga   —sky
          L H   L L H
      c. suzume   —   suzume-ga   —sparrow
          L L H   L L L H

As we have seen above, this tone pattern indicates that the feet are right-branching and that the Percolating-Feature is High. For example, (47)c has the following structures:

(48)

The other starless tone pattern consists uniquely of High tones: $\overline{\ldots X X X}$

Class 2:

(49) a. ee   —   e-ga   —handle
          H H   H H

b.	take	–	take-ga	–bamboo
	H H		H H H	
c.	sakura	–	sakura-ga	–cherry tree
	H HH		H H H H	

A tone pattern that consists solely of one type of tone indicates that the foot is not polarized, since there is no contrast in value. The percolating-feature is obviously High, as in Class 1. The starless tone-pattern of Class 2 says nothing about the direction of branching of the foot. But recall that the language-learner knows from the shape of the starless tone-pattern of Class 1 that the foot is right-branching. To illustrate, (49)c has the following structures:

(50)

Since the nodes are not labelled, the feature High percolates onto every terminal node with the same value: i.e. [+High]. We will refer to the non-polarized foot as the *harmony foot*; it defines the domain of spreading of a given feature.

The formalization of harmony processes in terms of trees has been proposed in Vergnaud 1979 and Vergnaud & Halle 1978. They proposed to represent directional vowel and consonant harmony processes by means of binary-branching unlabelled trees.

A harmony rule must define the class of relevant segments (i.e. the segments that undergo or block the harmony). These are projected and mapped onto unbounded feet, modulo the following conditions:

(51) a. The Maximality Principle —cf. (12)1.
      b. The "harmony trigger" or segment that defines the domain of harmony must be immediately dominated by the root of the tree. More precisely, the left-most node (right-most node) must be interpreted as opaque in a right-branching tree (left-branching tree).[9]
      c. The opaque segment must not be specified for a different value than the harmonizing feature (i.e. it must either have the same value as the harmonizing feature or it must be unspecified for the given feature.)

Harmony and Accent

From (51)b it follows that if the opaque element defines a harmony domain to its right, the projected segments are mapped onto right-branching feet. If the opaque element triggers harmony to its left, the projected segments are mapped onto left-branching feet.

Leftward harmony:

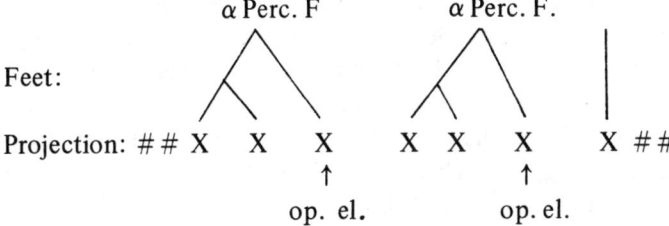

Rightward harmony:

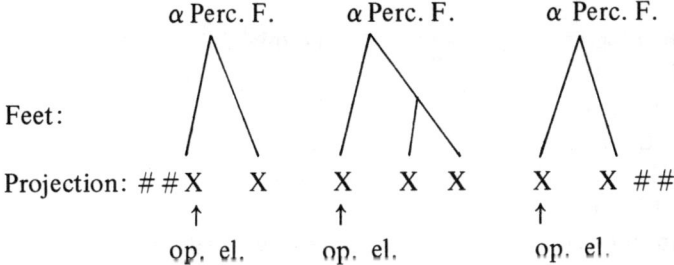

(α = + or −. α Feature specified on the root of the foot percolates unaltered onto each terminal node.)

(51)c is not relevant for the tone harmony discussed here since the segments are unspecified for tone in the lexicon. Hence, the tone value of an opaque element will never be distinct from the harmonizing tone.

In summary, a harmony rule specifies:

– the segments projected
– the type of feet
– the harmony or percolating feature
– the opaque segments.

We will refer to a polarized foot as "accent" foot and to a non-polarized foot as "harmony" foot. To distinguish the opaque element from the designated element we will reserve the symbol * to mark the former and we will refer to the latter as a branching node (∧) from now on. We will continue to use the word "starred" to refer to both of them.

We can consider the designated element and the opaque element to be particular cases of a more general notion: *accessible element*, where accessible element is defined in the following way: it is a terminal node separated from the root of the tree by *no node not labelled* + (i.e. by no node labelled − or unlabelled).

A priori, there is an alternative hypothesis. We may consider the opaque element and the designated element to be formally identical: the rightmost (left-most) node in a right- (left) branching foot. Here we will adopt the former hypothesis. The formal difference between opaque and designated elements makes some interesting predictions as will be shown.[10]

Coming back to Osaka, we have seen that one of the starless tone structures has a polarized, right-branching foot (Class 1) and the other has a non-polarized, right-branching foot (Class 2). And as expected, there are also two starred tone-patterns, one in each lexical class. One of the starred tone-patterns consists of High tone(s) followed by Low tone(s):

$\overline{\ldots X} | X \ X \ X \ldots$.

(52) a. yama (-ga)   −   mountain
H L L
b. inoti (-ga)   −   life
H L L L
c. otoko (-ga)   −   man
H H L L
d. uguisu (-ga)   −   Japanese nightingale
H L L L L
e. kaminari   −   thunder
H H H L

Notice that (52) is partially similar to (49), i.e. (49) is a subpart of (52). From this, it is inferred that (49) and (52) belong to the same lexical class (Class 2). Since the starless tone-pattern of Class 2 consists solely of High tones the language-learner knows that the percolating-feature is High and that the foot is non-polarized. Recall moreover that the starless tone-pattern of Class 1 (cf. (47)) has fixed the parameter 'direction of branching of foot' (i.e. it is right-branching). Given this information it follows that the tone structure of (52) must be (53):

Harmony and Accent

(53)

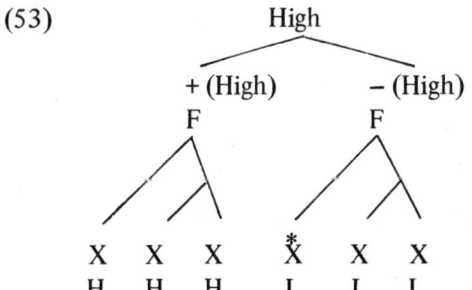

The word tree is labelled + −. There is spreading of High tone in the left-most foot and spreading of Low tone in the right-most foot. Recall that an opaque element in a harmony foot is the node immediately dominated by the root of the tree. Consequently, the "starred" segment in (53) must be the first Low tone-bearing segment of the sequence. This means that structure (53) is marked with respect to principle (40): in (53) the "starred" segment does not have the value of the percolating-feature.

Notice that the term "markedness" is not used here in the sense of "statiscally rare" or "hard to learn". It is a purely theory internal notion: X is marked *with respect to* principle Y of the theory. This means that the language-learner will make the hypothesis that principle Y is correct unless he encounters positive evidence that it is not. If he encounters such evidence he will then modify his initial hypothesis accordingly.

In Haraguchi's system, * is a feature which corresponds to [+accent]. A starred segment always bears a High tone, never a Low tone. Consequently, in the case of Class 2 of Osaka, it is the last High tone-bearing segment which is starred. In the system proposed here the * does not correspond to [+accent]. It is a diacritic with no intrinsic meaning, which serves to indicate how the word is mapped onto a tone structure. It may be High or Low. Interestingly, the two analyses differ empirically with respect to Osaka. We make the following prediction: there is no word in Osaka which consists of only High tones such that if a suffix ("ga" for example) is added, it is Low:

(54)   *...   X X X − (ga)
           H H H   L

To generate tone pattern (54) either 1. the * has to be on the final High vowel as shown in (55)a. But this gives an ill-formed tree: principle (51)b is violated. Or, 2. we have to postulate a "floating" tone which only gets realized when a suffix is added as shown in (55)b. ii. But (55)b. i is meaningless since the * is a diacritic: a lexical idiosyncratic property of a segment.

(55) a.
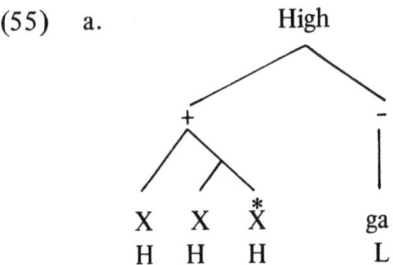

b. i. 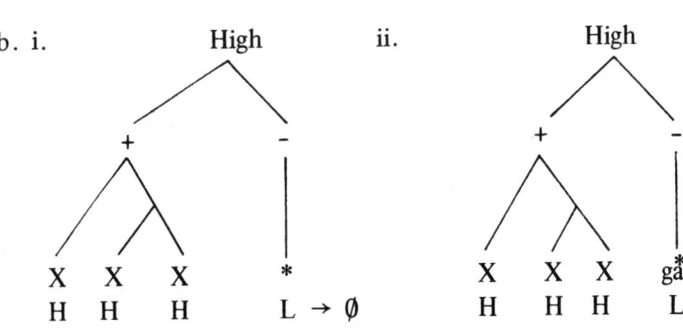 ii.

The prediction is borne out. There is no word with a melody of the form (54) in Osaka.[11] Notice that if there were no formal difference between an opaque and a designated element, the last High tone-bearing segment of the sequence would bear the star. But then, as we have seen, there is no explanation for gap (54) – supposing it is not accidental.[12]

Notice that according to the above analysis, examples (49)a-c are ambiguous between a "starless" form:

(56) a.
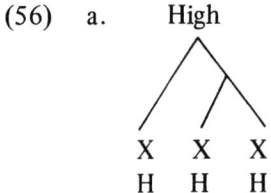

and an "initial-starred" form:

b.
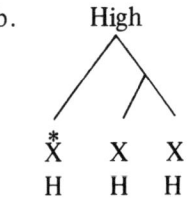

Only a prefix could in principle distinguish them. If a prefix is added, (56)b should be transformed to the following structure:

c.

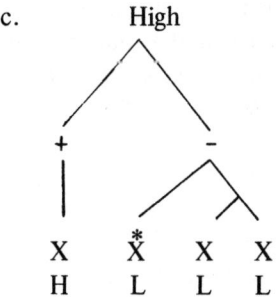

Unfortunately we cannot test this prediction. The only prefix that Haraguchi discusses is the polite prefix "O". This prefix behaves in a particular way. It does not behave simply like one more syllable of the word, unlike the suffixes "ga" and "mo" discussed above. The form "O + stem" always belongs to Class 1. The tone pattern is modified accordingly, as shown in (57).

(57) a. kama   (iron pot)   →   o-kama
        H H   L L H
     b. kao   (face)   →   o-kao
        HH   L LH
     c. tuyu   (soup)   →   o-tuyu
        H L   L H L
     d. mugi   (wheat)   →   o-mugi
        H L   L H L

Turning now to the other starless tone-pattern, we observe that, as expected, it is properly included in the starred pattern of Class 1, namely it consists of a string of Low tones and a single High tone: ..X⌈X⌊X...

(58) a. naa   –   na-ga   – name
        HL   H L
     b. ame   –   ame-ga   –rain
        L HL   L H L
     c. kabuto   –   kabuto-ga   –helmet
        L H L   L H L L
     d. nokɔgiri-(ga) –   –saw
        L L H L L

186 *Maria L. Zubizarreta*

Recall that the "starless" structure of Class 1 is a right-branching polarized foot. The right-nodes of a right-branching foot are labelled +. Hence, the right-most node of the foot is +High given that the percolating-feature is +High. Under the unmarked hypothesis the * will then be on the right-most node of the initial foot. This implies that the tone structure of (58) consists of a left-most "accent" foot and *a right-most "harmony" foot* with −High as the harmonizing feature, as shown in (59):

(59)

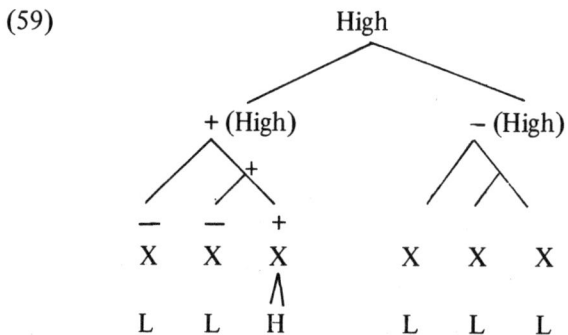

Unlike the other tone-structures examined, tone-structure (59) is a mixed case of harmony and accent.

Notice that a word with an initial High tone followed by Low tones — for example: inoti-ga— is ambiguous. It can belong to Class 1 as shown in
H L L L
(60)a or to Class 2 as shown in (60)b:

(60)

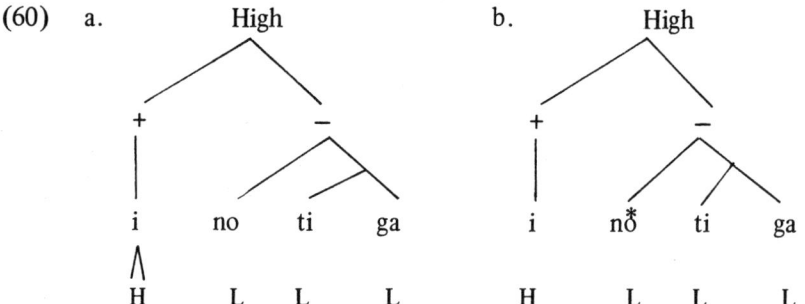

The Compound Formation Rule could distinguish them. When two words are compounded: "A + B", the new word belongs to the lexical class of the left-most word: "A". Unfortunately, very few examples of compounds are given in Haraguchi 1977 where the left-most word has an initial High tone. An example: yama + sakura → yama+zakura (mountain + cherry).
H L   H H H   H H H L L

Harmony and Accent

A careful and detailed investigation of Compounds might prove to be very revealing.

A word remains to be said about the falling tone in cases like (58)a and (58)b. The same low-level rule that takes care of a final falling tone in Hirosaki (cf. 46) will take care of these cases except that in Osaka the rule applies in both [−pause] and [+pause] contexts:

(61) H → HL / ___ ##
   condition: H is a lexical designated element.

To summarize, Osaka's core tone-rule is as follows:
Projection: rimes[13]
Feet: right-branching
Type of feet: harmony feet, except for the initial foot of Class 1 which is an accent foot.
Percolating-Feature: High
Word tree Label: + −

The word tree label follows from the conjunction of principle (51)b and the other parameters.

Osaka shows that the type of foot (i.e. the labelling) may vary between two lexical classes within one same dialect.

4. MARUGAME

Marugame, like Osaka, has two lexical classes of words with distinct tone patterns. But unlike Osaka, the two classes have different percolating-features.

The "starless" tone patterns of Class 1 consist solely of Low tones:

(62) a. tee   −   te-ga   −hand
        LL   L L
     b. kasa-(ga)   −umbrella
        L L L
     c. usagi-(ga)   −rabbit
        L L L L

This indicates that the percolating-feature of Class 1 is Low. The "starless" pattern of Class 2 consists solely of High tones, like Class 2 of Osaka:

(63) a. kii   −   ki-ga   −attention
        HH   H H
     b. tori-(ga)   −bird
        H H H

188 *Maria L. Zubizarreta*

    c. sakana-(ga)   –fish
        H H H H
    d. hinomaru   –(gloss not given)
        H H H H

This indicates that the percolating-feature of Class 2 is High.

Like in Osaka, the "starred" tone pattern of Class 2 consists of High-tone(s) followed by Low-tone(s):

(64) a. kee   –   ke-ga   –hair
           HL   H L
      b. uta-(ga)   –song
           H L L
      c. musume-(ga)   –daughter
           H L L L
      d. asikosi   –(gloss not given)
          H HLL
      e. garasudo-(ga)   –(gloss not given)
          H H H H L

As we have seen in the previous section this tone pattern is composed of two non-polarized feet. But notice that unlike Osaka, Marugame has words of the form (54) (cf. (64)e) which constitutes positive evidence that the feet are left-branching in Marugame, as shown in (65):

(65)

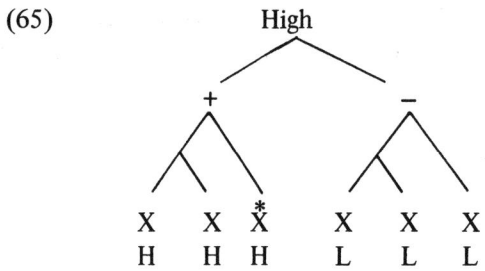

Under the unmarked hypothesis, the opaque segment in (65) is the right-most vowel of the sequence with High tone. (64)e will then have the following structure:

Harmony and Accent

(66)

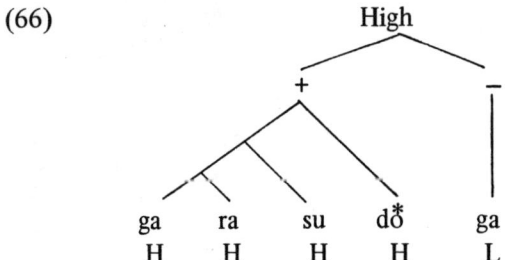

The "starred" tone pattern of Class 1 has one single High tone per word:

(67) a. saru-(ga)   —monkey
        L H L
     b. kabuto-(ga)   —helmet
        L HL L
     c. minna-(ga)   —everyone
        L H L
     d. mayoigo-(ga)   —(no gloss given)
        L LL H L

From the shape of the "starless" pattern the language-learner knows that one foot is non-polarized and that the percolating-feature is Low in this class (cf. examples in (62)). The presence of the High tone in (67) indicates that the second foot is polarized, as shown in (68):

(68)

Given that the percolating-feature is Low, the vowel with Low tone which immediately precedes the vowel with High tone will be interpreted as the "starred" segment. To illustrate, (67)b and (67)d have structures (69)a and (69)b respectively:

(69)

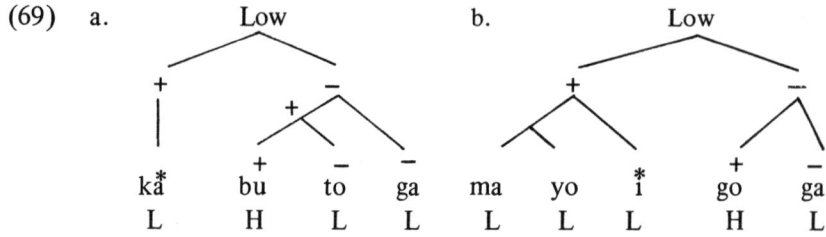

Notice that words with initial High tone (cf. (64)a, b, c) will be interpreted unambiguously as belonging to Class 2.

Marugame's tone rule:[14]

Projection: [+syllabic] segments
Feet: left-branching
Type of feet: harmony feet, except for the second foot of Class 1 which is polarized.
Percolating-Feature: Class 1: Low
Class 2: High
Word tree Label: + —

The labelling of the word tree follows from the conjunction of the above parameters and principle (40).

Marugame shows that not only the type of feet may vary between two lexical classes of one same dialect but also the percolating-feature.

5. KÔSHI

As in Osaka and Marugame, there are two lexical classes of words with distinct tone patterns.

Class 1 is the mirror image of Hirosaki. The "starless" pattern consists of an initial Low tone followed by High tone(s) (if the word is polysyllabic): $\underline{X}\rfloor X \ X \ \dots$

(70) a. te   —   te- ŋa   —hand
          L   L H
          (te = 'hard', ŋa = the Subjects suffix)
      b. umi   —   umi- ŋa   —sea
          L H   L H H
      c. usagi-(ŋa)   —rabbit
          L H H H
      d. dai dai-(ŋa)   —orange color
          L H H H H

Harmony and Accent

The monosyllabic (70)a indicates that the percolating-feature is Low. This fact in conjunction with the rest of the data (70)b-d indicates that the tree is left-branching and polarized:

(71)

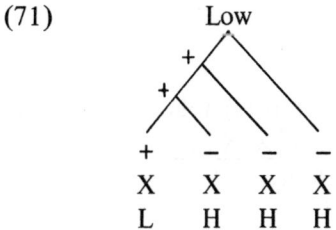

The following "starred" words belong to Class 1, their tone patterns being partially similar to (70): X⏋X X ⎣X X ...

(72)   a. aki   —   aki- ŋa   —autumn
            L H   L H L
       b. nadesiko-(ŋa)   —wild pink
            L HL L L
       c. osiroi-(ŋa)   —powder
            L HH L L

The language-learner knows that the percolating-feature is Low and that the initial foot has structure (69). The second foot of the "starred" tone structure must then be −Low. But the data in (70) shows that there are Low tones in the second foot. This implies that the second foot is also polarized as shown in (73):

(73)

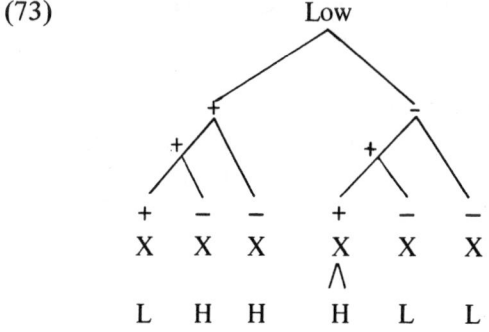

Notice that the designated element in (73) is the right-most segment with High tone. It is a marked structure with respect to principle (40).

Class 2 of Kôshi is like Class 2 of Marugame. The "starless" tone pattern is composed solely of High tones: ‾‾ X X X, which indicates that the percolating-feature in Class 2 is High and the foot is not polarized.

(74) a. to   —   to-ŋa   —door
        H   H H
     b. tori-(ŋa)   —bird
        H H H
     c. saka na-(ŋa)   —fish
        H H H   H

The "starred" tone pattern consists of High tone(s) followed by Low tone(s) (if the * is not on the final vowel): $\overline{X\ X}|X\ X\ldots$, which means that there is Low tone harmony in the second foot.

(75) a. na   —   na-ŋa   —name
        H   H L
     b. asi-(ŋa)   —feet
        H L L
     c. kagami-(ŋa)   —mirror
        H H L   L
     d. asanao-(ŋa)   —morning glory
        H H LL   L
     e. akuruhi-(ŋa)   —next day
        H H H H   L

To illustrate, (74)e and (75)d have the following tone structures:

(76) a.

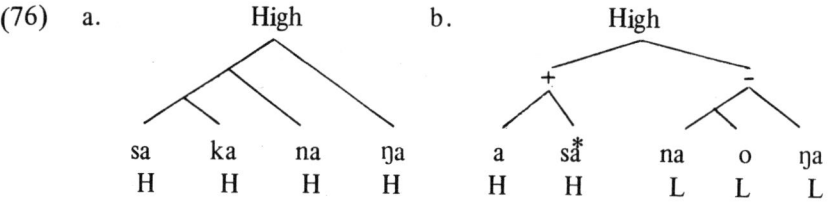

Given that the feet are left-branching, the right-most vowel with High tone is interpreted as the opaque segment. Notice that since the feet are left-branching, we predict that Class 2 has words of form (54) (cf. discussion in section 3). The prediction is borne out as shown by example (75)e.

Kôshi's tone-rule is as follows:

Projection: [+syllabic] segments
Feet: left-branching
Type of feet: Class 1: polarized
                   Class 2: non-polarized
Percolating-feature: Class 1: Low
                   Class 2: High
Word tree Label: + —

Harmony and Accent 193

The labelling of the word tree follows from the interaction of Kôshi's rule and the principles of universal grammar.

Let us now consider the analysis in which the opaque element and the designated element are formally non-distinct. Recall that under this hypothesis the "starred" segment must always be the left-most node in a left-branching tree, and the right-most node in a right-branching tree. We have seen that the tone patterns of Class 1 indicate unequivocally that the feet in Kôshi are left-branching. Hence, according to the hypothesis under consideration, the "starred" segment must be the left-most node of a foot. For example, in tone structure (76)b, the "starred" segment would be the vowel with Low tone which immediately follows the right-most High tone. This creates a problem for the analysis of (75)e, which is of the form (54) (cf. discussion of Osaka). However, since the examples of this type are scarce, we might consider it to be a rare exception.[15] A more serious problem for this hypothesis is that it generates the wrong tone pattern for words composed of a monosyllabic stem and a suffix. Consider example (75)a. It will have the following tone structures:

(77)

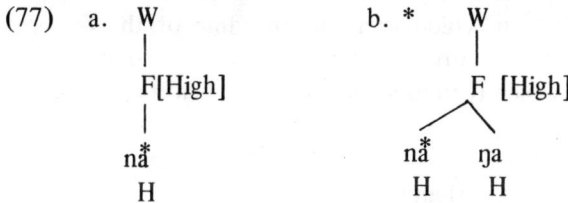

Since the * is on the initial vowel, the word will be composed of one single foot. Consequently, the suffix will be wrongly assigned a High tone.

6. TÔKYÔ

At first sight, Tôkyô's tone patterns are very similar to the tone patterns of Class 1 of Kôshi. The "starless" pattern is composed of an initial Low tone followed by High tones: X̲ X X . .

(78)   miyako   –   miyako-ga   –capital city
         L H H   L H H H

The "starred" pattern consists of an initial Low followed by High tone(s) and Low tone(s): X̲ . . X X̲ X X . . .

(79) a. kokoro   –heart
          L H L
      b. atama(ga)   –head
          L H H L

But there are two pieces of evidence that show that Tôkyô's tone-rule is different from Kôshi's. First, monosyllabic words have a High tone, not a Low tone. Compare (70)a with (80):

(80)   ?e   —   ?e-ga   —handle
         H   L H

Second, there are words with an initial High tone:

(81)   inoti
         H L L

In Kôshi the words with initial High tone belong to Class 2, not to Class 1. The rules of Class 1 of Kôshi cannot generate (81).

Example (81) indicates that the percolating-feature in Tôkyô is High. This means that the initial Low tone in (78) and (79)b (and consequently also in (79)a) must constitute a seperate foot from the rest. The tone structure of Tôkyô then consists of an initial extrametrical Low tone, followed by a harmony foot in which there is spreading of the feature [+High]. In the case of the "starred" pattern, this foot is followed by another harmony foot in which there is spreading of the feature [—High]:

(82)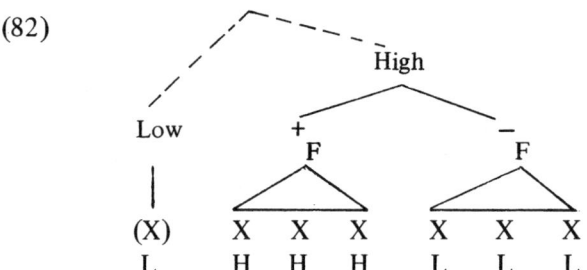

The question which now arises is: are the feet left — or right —branching? The starred tone-patterns (79) and (81) can answer this question. Since the percolating-feature is High, under the unmarked hypothesis the opaque element must be High (cf. principle (40)); i.e. the right-most vowel with High tone in structure (82). The opaque segment defines a harmony domain to its left. Hence, given principle (51)b, the language-learner will conclude that the foot is left-branching:

(83)
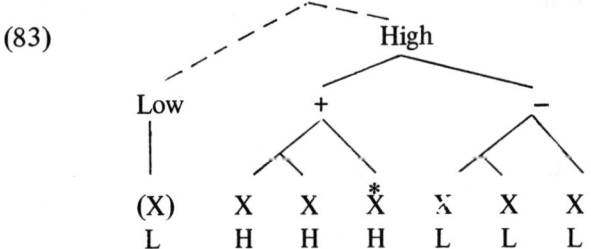

To illustrate, the "starless" word (78) has the following structures:

(84)
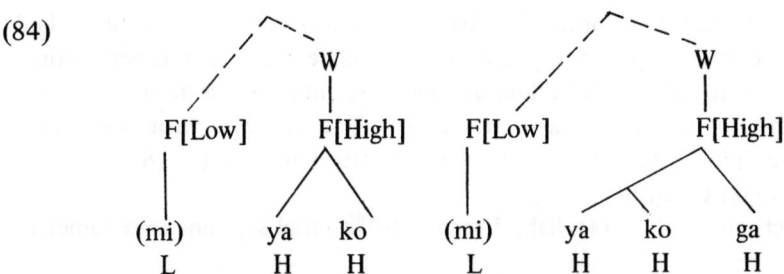

And the "starred" words (79)a, (79)b, and (81) have tone-structures (85)a, (85)b, and (85)c respectively:

(85) a.

b.

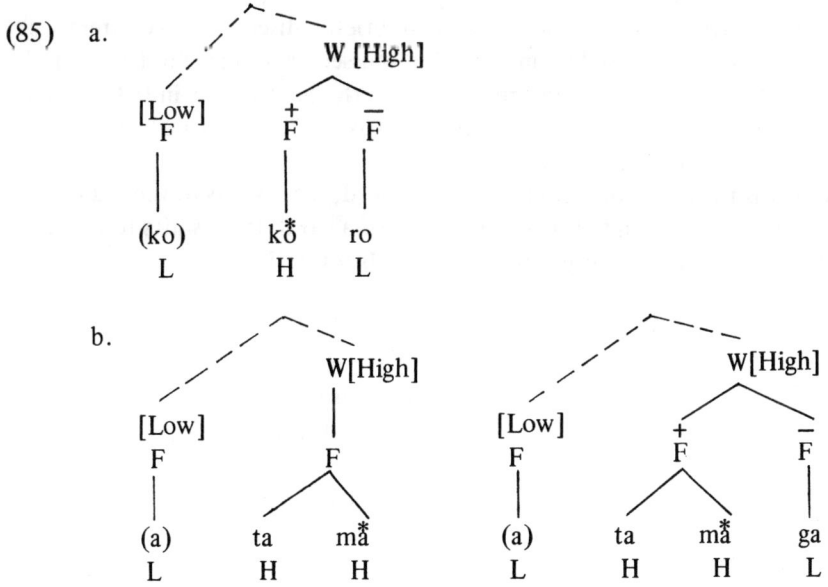

c.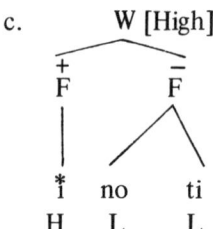

In (85)a and (85)b the initial extrametrical segment is adjoined to the word tree by convention. Given that the feature on the word tree is High, it follows that the extrametrical material is Low.

Notice that given principle (40) — which says that under the unmarked hypothesis the opaque segment has the same value as the percolating-feature — it follows that a lexical opaque segment (i.e. a starred segment) may not be interpreted as extrametrical. It is the case then that words with an initial * (cf. (81)) have no extrametrical material (cf. (85)c).

Tôkyô's tone-rule:

Projection:	[+syllabic] segments.[16] (initial segment is extrametrical)
Feet:	lef-branching
Type of Feet:	non-polarized
Percolating-feature:	High
Word tree Label:	+ −

To conclude this section, we shall briefly discuss a very interesting process of "accent-slide" in Tôkyô discussed in Haraguchi 1977a. It is interesting because it confirms our hypothesis that the initial segment — if it is not starred — is extrametrical in Tôkyô. The facts are as follows:

If a starred vowel is devoiced and
A. if it is the initial or second mora of a word, the * shifts to the right.
B. if it is not the initial or second mora of a word, the * shifts to the left.
(86)ii and (87) exemplify case A and case B respectively.

(86) i. a. tǐkaku   →   b. tikǎku
          H L L   H L
     ii. a. atǔkereba   →   b. atukěreba
          L H L L L   L ° H L L

(87) a. yasasǐkatta   →   b. yasǎsikatta
        L H H L L   L H ° L L

We will examine Case B first. (87)a has the following tone structure:

Harmony and Accent

(88) a.

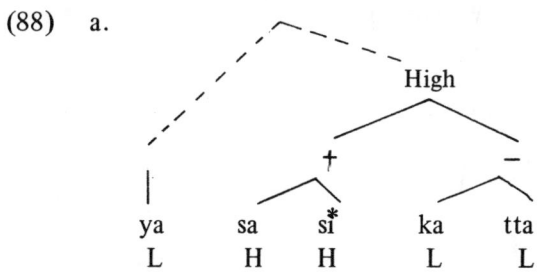

When a vowel is devoiced ($\overset{*}{i}$ in the case of (88)a), it is deleted from the [+syllabic] projection. The tone pattern obtained ((87)b) is exactly the one predicted by the theory:

(89) b.

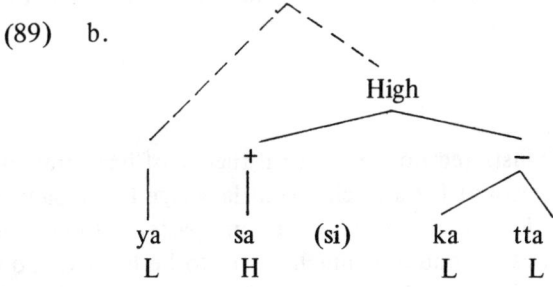

With respect to case A, the question is 1) why does the * "shift" to the right and 2) why do the second-starred mora words behave like initial-starred mora words and not like non-initial-starred mora words (i.e. like case B)? Within the analysis of Tôkyô presented here, there is a straightforward answer to question 2. The second-starred mora words behave with respect to devoicing like initial-starred mora words because the initial [+syllabic] segment is extrametrical: it is not part of the [+High] foot and it is "invisible" to any prosodic process. The answer to question 1 will be tentative. (86)i starts with tone structure (90)a. After devoicing, it has tone structure (90)b.

(90) a.   [+High]   b.   [+High]

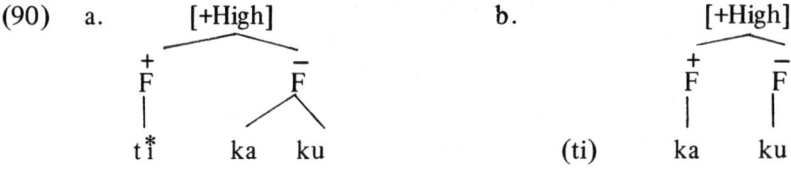

Structure (90)b is unexpected. The expected structure is (91):

(91)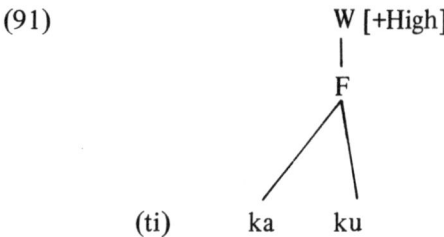

Our suspicion is that there is a principled reason why (90)b and not (91) is obtained. It might have to do with a general principle of "structure-preservation". If structure may not be destroyed, then a reanalysis (90)a→(91) would not be unexpected. We will leave the issue here, hoping that a deeper understanding of the principles that underlie metrical structure will shed light on this question.

7. CONCLUSION

In this paper we have illustrated how a metrical theory of harmony and accent can successfully account for a pitch-accent language like Japanese. It makes correct predictions as to the type of tone patterns found and not found in several cases. Undoubtly, much is yet to be learned about the principles that underlie prosodic processes but it seems to us that metrical theory has the right kind of properties in that it is a highly structured system, which makes it possible to address the "learnability-problem": how is a grammar learned or acquired despite the poverty of the stimulus.

Learning or acquiring the tone-rule of a language like the Japanese dialects consists in fixing three main parameters:

(92) 1. Direction of branching feet:
        I – Left-branching
        II – Right-branching
     2. Type of foot:
        A – Both feet polarized (accent feet)
        B – Only initial foot polarized
        C – Only final foot polarized
        D – Both feet non-polarized (harmony feet)
     3. Melody or percolating feature
        1 – High
        2 – Low

We have seen that the "starless" tone patterns play a crucial role in fixing these parameters. It is consequently not surprising that every dialect with

Harmony and Accent

a "starred" tone pattern also has a "starless" tone pattern where the latter is a subpart of the former. The nature of the "starred" segment (designated or opaque) and the word tree label of the "starred" tone structure follow, in the unmarked cases, from the conjunction of the above parameters and principle (40). An auxiliary parameter provided by the theory is the extrametricality of a peripheral element (segment, rime). A structure that makes use of extrametricality as well as one that does not conform to principle (40) is a marked case. Recall that markedness is a purely theory internal concept. It is built into the theory as part of a "grammar – learning" strategy. See the Appendix for an outline of the unmarked core grammars allowed by the theory.

From our study of several dialects, the following generalization emerges: of the three parameters in (92), only two may vary dialect internally: *type of foot* and *melody or percolating-feature*. The *direction of branching of feet* never varies between two classes of one same dialect. If this constraint is not an accident, it must be incorporated into the grammar.

Let us make the following assumption. Each dialect has a basic tone structure. In dialects with more than two lexical classes of tone pattern, one of them is derived from the other (from the basic tone structure) by a transformation that changes the percolating-feature:

(93)   a.   High → Low   or,
        b.   Low → High

and/or a transformation that changes the type of feet by *polarization*:

(94) a.

b.

c.

d.

(The combination of (93)a and (94)a is found in Marugame. The combination of (93)a and (94)b is found in Kôshi. (94)c is found in Osaka.)

Although it is natural to assume that the basic or simplest tone structure have uniform feet (i.e. that both feet are of the same type), we have no real justification for the moment for choosing harmony feet as basic. This hypothesis might prove to be correct if in fact there exists no dialect in which one lexical class has two accent feet and the other has only one accent foot:

(95) a.*

b.*

c.*

d.*

This point is left open for further empirical research.

We may think of the labelling as an interpretative mechanism of metrical structure. And it is the case that rules only affect the interpretative component of a grammar (i.e. it changes features and labels) but never the structural component: there exists no rule which transforms the geometry of trees. Interestingly, Halle & Vergnaud (forthcoming) reach similar conclusions with respect to the grammar of English stress.

APPENDIX

In this section we will outline the unmarked core-grammars obtained by fixing the parameters in (92).

Let us first consider the grammars in which the feet are left-branching (cf. (92)1.I.).

I.A. If both feet are polarized, the Word tree is labelled − + in the unmarked case. The "starred" segment is the designated element of the second foot.

I.A.1. If the Melody is High, the following tone pattern is obtained:

Harmony and Accent

(1) a.

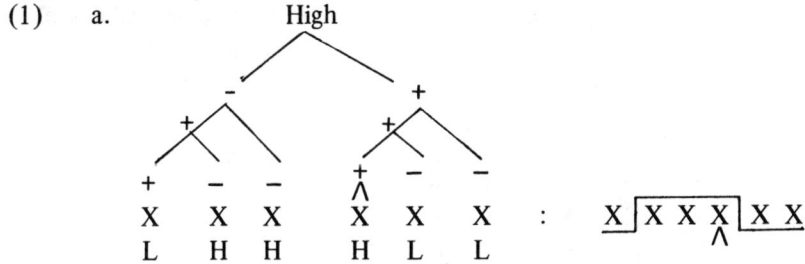

b. If there is no lexical designated element:

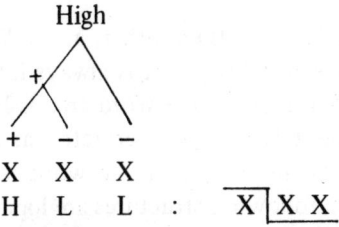

At least one dialect of Japanese has tone-rule *I.A.1: Shimagawa*. Since this dialect has no lexical designated element, its tone-structure is always of the form 1b. *Izumi* also has tone-rule I.A.1 but with an auxiliary parameter: an initial extrametrical syllabic segment.

I.A.2. With a Low melody:

(2) a. Low   b. with no lexical des. el.:

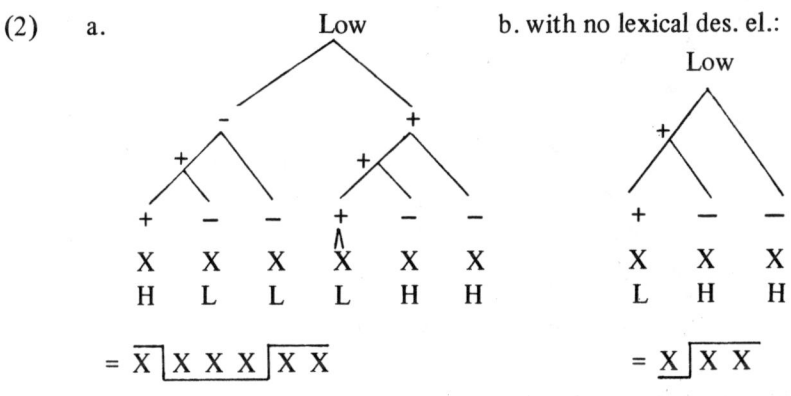

We have not found this particular tone-rule among the dialects that we have studied. But a rule very close to this one exists: *Class 1 of Kôshi*. It has left-branching feet, both feet are polarized, the percolating-feature is Low, but the Word tree is labelled + −. It is a *marked* rule: the lexical designated element has a different value than the percolating-feature as shown in (3).

(3) a. Low   b. with no lexical des. el:
              same as (2)b.

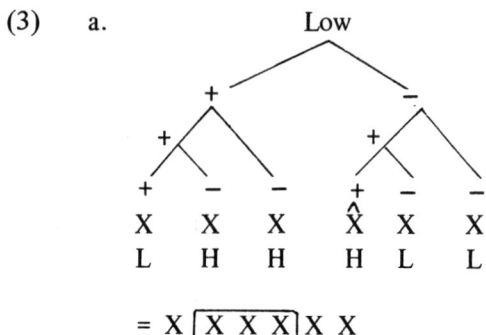

= X ⌠X X X⌡X X

I.B. If only the initial foot is polarized, then either, a. the Word tree is labelled + − and consequently the initial segment is always interpreted as the designated element of the Word or, b. the Word tree is labelled − + and consequently the final segment is always interpreted as the opaque segment of the word. This means, in fact, that the word is "starless", since it is predictable. Hence, the following structures are logically impossible:

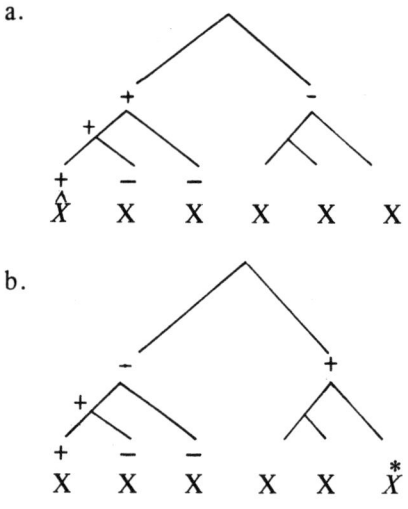

I.B. is then an impossible rule.

I.C. If only the final foot is polarized, *either*:
the Word tree is labelled − + and the "starred" segment is the designated element of the second foot.
I.C.1. With Percolating-Feature High:

Harmony and Accent

(4) a.
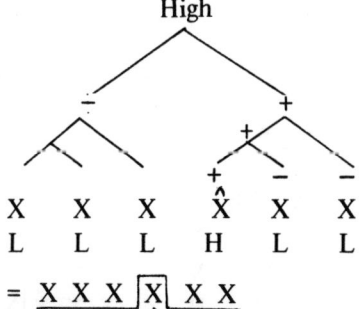

b. with no lexical des. el.:
   i.
   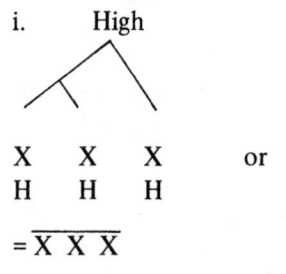
   or
   ii.
   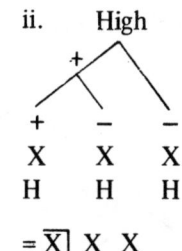

I.C.2. With Percolating-Feature Low:

(5) a.
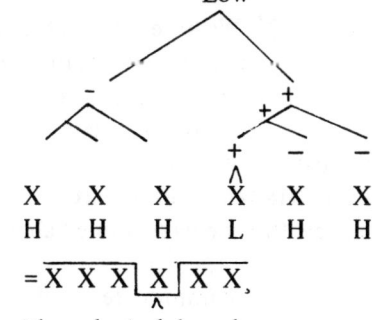

b. with no lexical des. el.:
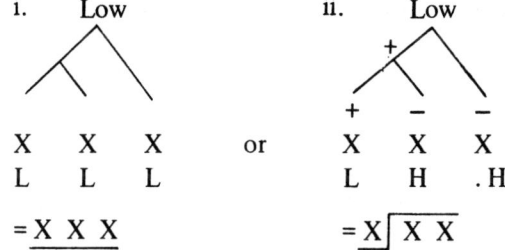

or:
the Word tree is labelled + − and the "starred" segment is the opaque segment of the initial foot.

204   Maria L. Zubizarreta

I.C.1′. With Percolating-Feature High:

(6) a.

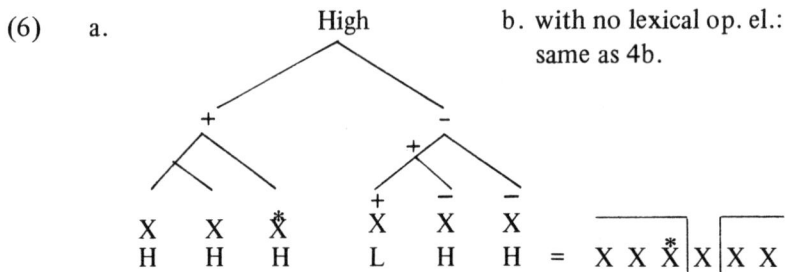

b. with no lexical op. el.:
same as 4b.

I.C.2′. With Percolating-Feature Low:

(7) a.

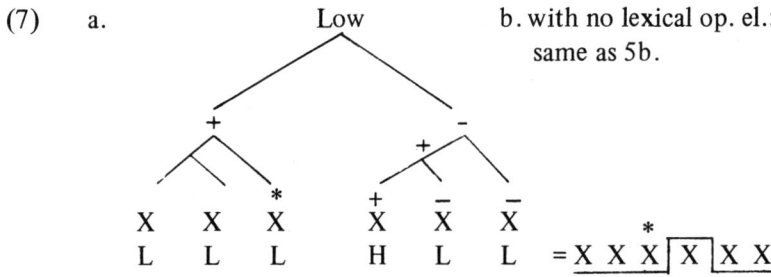

b. with no lexical op. el.:
same as 5b.

Class 1 of Marugame has tone-rule I.C.2′. We have seen that in one lexical class of Marugame, the "starless" tone pattern is a harmony foot (cf. (5)b.i.). But in another lexical class it is an accent foot (cf.(5)b.ii). Our theory correctly allows for both cases. But it is conceivable that in the unmarked case the "starless" pattern is equal to the foot which contains the "starred" segment in the "starred" pattern. (Cf. footnote 14.) This is the case in most of the dialects that we have studied above.

I.D. If both feet are non-polarized (i.e. harmony feet), the Word tree is labelled + − in the unmarked case.

I.D.1. With Percolating-Feature High:

(8) a.

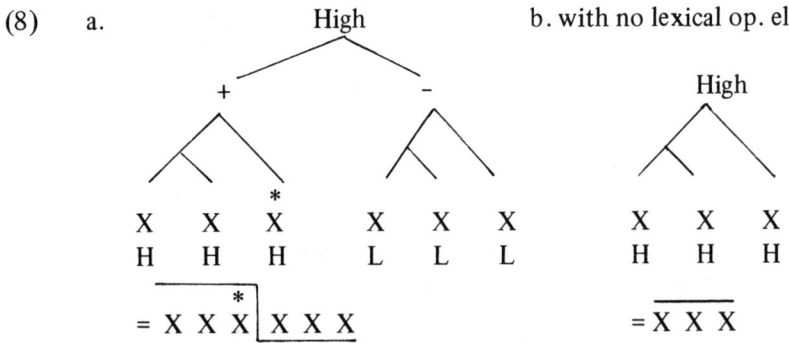

b. with no lexical op. el.:

Class 2 of Marugame and *Class 2 of Kôshi* have tone-rule I.D.1. *Tôkyô* also has tone-rule *I.D.1* but with an additional parameter: the initial segment is extrametrical.

I.D.2. With Percolating-Feature Low:

(9) a.　　　　　　　Low　　　　　　b. with no lexical op. el.:

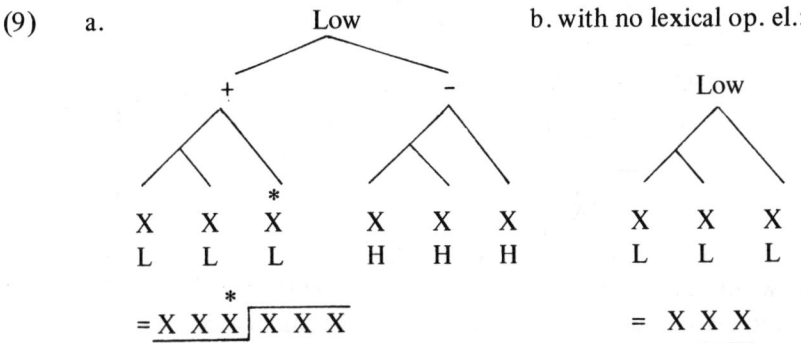

Let us now consider the set of possible unmarked grammars with right-branching feet (cf. 92.1.II).

II.A. If both feet are polarized, the Word tree is labelled + − in the unmarked case, and the "starred" segment is interpreted as the designated element of the initial foot.

II.A.1. If the melody is High, the following tone patterns are obtained:

(10) a.　　　　　　High　　　　　　b. with no lexical des. el.:

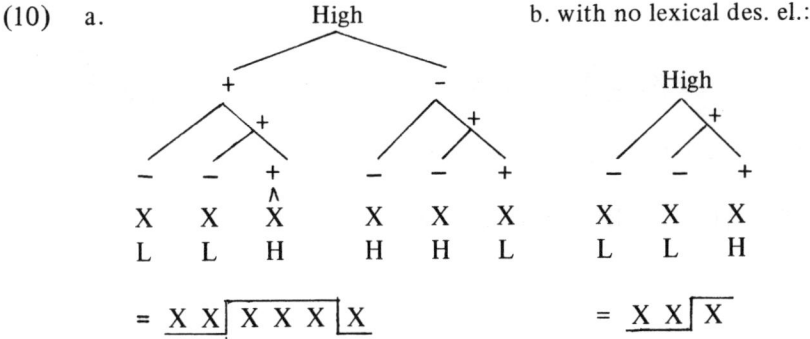

Tone-rule *II.A.1* is found in *Hirosaki*, also in *Miyakonozyô* and *Kagoshima*. But in the latter dialects, unlike the former, there are no words with a lexical designated segment. Hence, its tone pattern is always of the form (10)b. Recall, moreover, that the tone-rule of one lexical class of Kagoshima has an additional parameter: the final segment is extrametrical.

206 *Maria L. Zubizarreta*

II.A.2. With Low melody:

(11)   a.

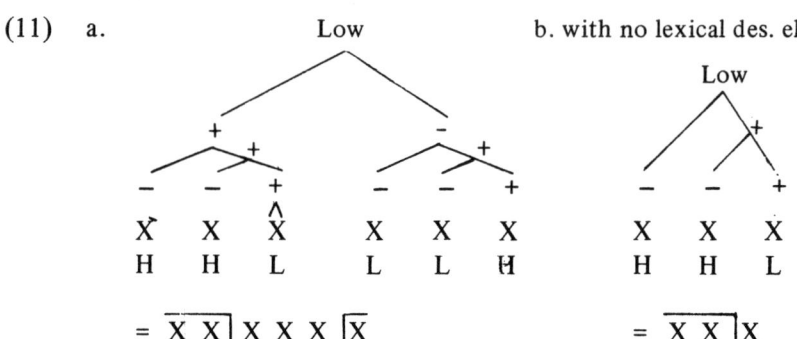

b. with no lexical des. el.:

II.B. If only the initial foot is polarized, *either*:
the Word tree is labelled + − and consequently the "starred" segment is interpreted as the designated element of the initial accent foot:

II.B.1. With Percolating-Feature High:

(12)   a.   High

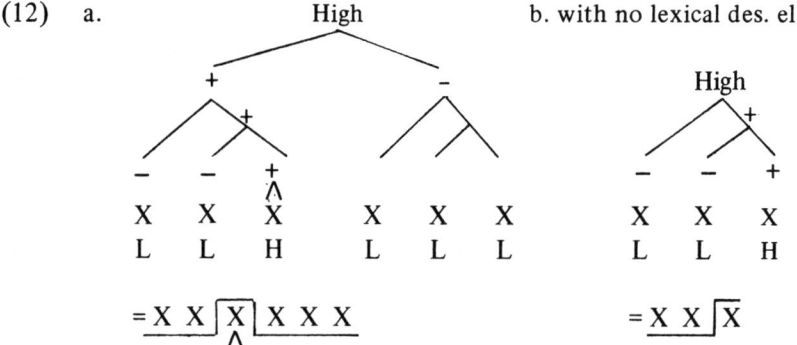

b. with no lexical des. el.:

This rule is found in *Class 1 of Osaka*.

II.B.2. With Percolating-Feature Low:

(13)   a.   Low

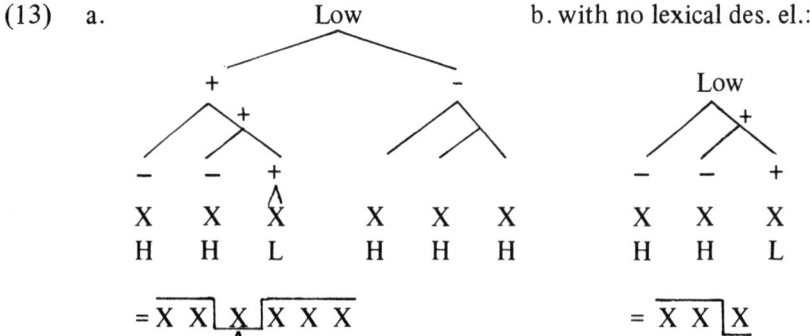

b. with no lexical des. el.:

Harmony and Accent

or:

the Word tree is labelled − + and the "starred" segment is interpreted as the opaque segment of the final foot:

II.B.1'. With Percolating-Feature High:

(14) a.   High   b. with no lexical op. el.:

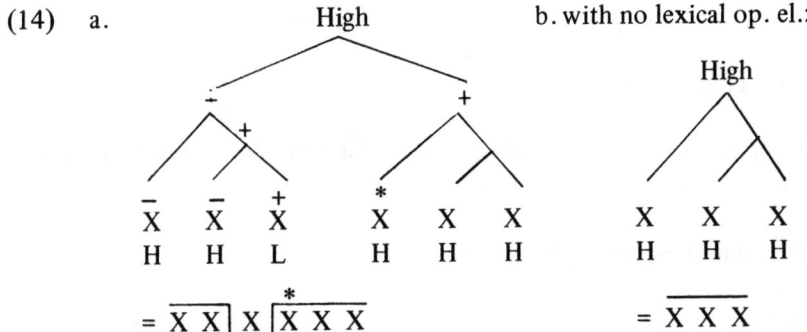

II.B.2'. With Percolating-Feature Low:

(15) a.   Low   b. with no lexical op. el.:

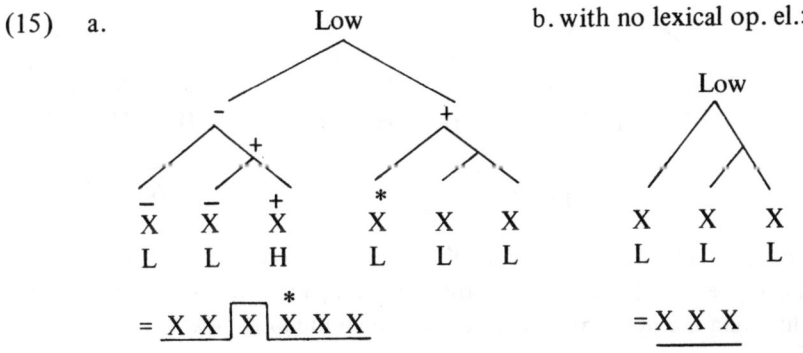

II.C. If only the final foot is polarized, either the Word tree is labelled − + and the last syllabic segment is always interpreted as the designated element of the word, or the Word tree is labelled + − and the initial segment is always interpreted as the opaque element of the word. Since they are predictable, they are not lexically determined. Hence, the following tone structures are logically impossible:

a.

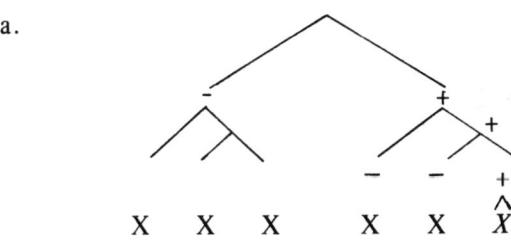

b.

II.C. is an impossible tone-rule.

II.D. If the feet are non-polarized (i.e. harmony feet), the Word tree is labelled − + in the unmarked case.

II.D.1. With Percolating-Feature High:

(16) a. High   b. without a lexical op. segment

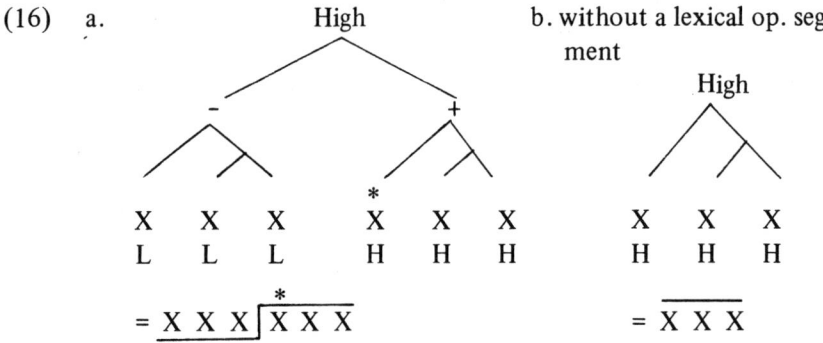

Class 2 of Osaka has a very similar tone-rule except that its Word tree is labelled + −. It is *marked*: the lexical opaque segment has a different value than the percolating-feature, as shown in (17)a.

(17) a. High   b. without a lexical op. segment: (same as 16b)

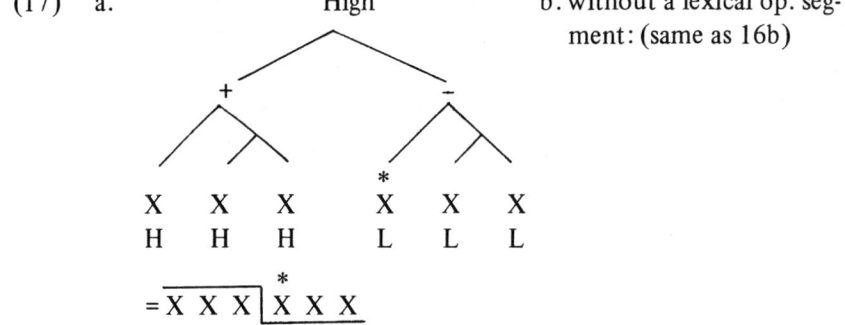

II.D.2. With Percolating-Feature Low:

(18)

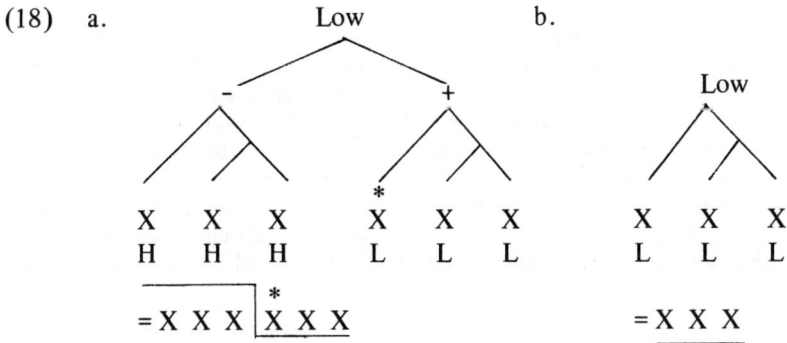

Old Kyoto, a dialect which we have not discussed here, has three lexical classes of words. Two of them have the following tone patterns: "starred": $\overline{X\ X\ X}\lfloor X\ X\ X$, $X\ X\ X\lceil\overline{X\ X\ X}$; "starless": $\overline{X\ X\ X}$, $X\ X\ X$. The tone-rules of these two classes are either, *I.D.1* and *I.D.2* (if feet are left-branching) or *II.D.1.* and *II.D.2* (if feet are right-branching). We do not have the information necessary to decide which are the correct tone-rules. We leave the question open.

NOTES

1. Another motivation for the metrical level foot is that there are segmental rules that have as their domain of application the foot (cf. Kiparsky 1979 on flapping in English), or that are constrained by the foot structure (cf. Zubizarreta 1980 on vowel lengthening, ə-deletion, and consonant gemination in Yuk).

2. Hayes 1980 has shown that Halle & Vergnaud's ternary feet are in fact binary-branching feet (bounded) plus extrametrical material. We will come back to the notion of extrametricality.

3. However, there are stress systems that have somewhat more complex labelling conventions for the Word tree, which refer explicitly to the branching property of a node:

– L'(left)-node is labelled S if and only if it branches (if the left-node does not branch, it is labelled W).

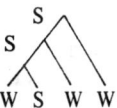

– L'(right)-node is labelled S if and only if it branches (if the right-node does not branch, it is labelled W).

We will not be concerned here with the above Labelling Conventions. For further discussion see the references cited.

4. There are stress systems with more than three metrical levels. See Stowell 1979 in *MIT Working Papers* for a discussion of the level super-foot motivated for Seneca and Passamaquoddy. There are also stress systems with only two metrical levels: the rime and the Word. For example, Aguatec discussed in Halle & Vergnaud 1978, and possibly some Japanese dialects discussed in the text below.

5. Consider a language exactly like Eastern Cheremis but with no subsidiary accent (maybe Eastern Cheremis itself). In this language the Word tree is polarized instead of being labelled S W. Moreover, in this language either the foot structure is exactly like Eastern Cheremis except that only the right-most foot is polarized (the others are unlabelled) or, there is only one foot at the right-most end of the Word:

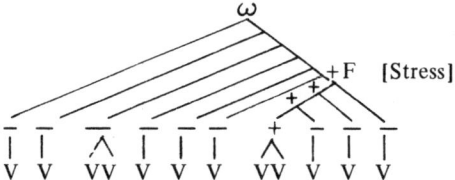

Which is the correct solution is left open.

6. Since long vowels exist in Czech, the grammar must specify that the feet are insensitive to the branchingness of the nucleus.

7. We use the term accent as a cover term for stress and tone.

8. 38, 42, and 44 are the forms before [+pause]. Before [−pause], the final Low tone becomes High. Examples:

a. e-mo. . . .
   H H

b. otoko−mo. . .
   L L H H

c. ki tune. . .   ki tune-mo. . . .
   H H H   H H H H

d. usagi. . . .   usagi-mo. . .
   L H H   L H H H

These tone patterns are obtained by the following Low-level Rule:

$$L \rightarrow H \;/\; \underline{\quad} \;\; \# \# $$
$$[-\text{pause}]$$

Hopefully, though, a better understanding of the principles that underlie prosodic phenomena — i.e. of the interaction of structure and labelling — will permit us to dispense with this type of low-level rules.

9. This more precise definition of opaque element takes care of binary-branching feet:
$\overset{F}{\overset{\diagup\diagdown}{A\;\;B}}$, where both nodes are immediately dominated by the root of the tree.

10. Andalusian laxing-vowel harmony provides empirical evidence in favor of the formal distinction between opaque and designated elements (cf. Zubizarreta 1979 in *MIT Working Papers # 1*). But on the other hand, in Eastern Cheremis the domain of application of the harmony rule is defined by the prosodic foot. And it is

Harmony and Accent

the stressed segment (i.e. the left-most node in a left-branching foot) which triggers harmony. The stressed segment assimilates vowels to its right in roundness and backness. We can assume that in the cases where the domain of harmony rules is defined by prosodic trees (i.e. polarized feet), the embedded segment (i.e. the stressed segment of the foot) becomes "accessible". Notice that in this case the tree is polarized with respect to the feature *stress* but it is non-polarized with respect to the harmonizing feature(s) (*round* and *back* in the case of Eastern Cheremis).

11. Kameyama, which is essentially like Osaka, has some words of the form (54). But according to Haraguchi, such words are very rare. In effect he gives only two examples:

a. akuruhi* —   akuruhi*-ŋa   —   next day
   H H H HL   H H H H L

b. asita* —   asita*-ŋa   —   tomorrow
   HH HL   H H H L

It is possible that something else is going on here. "Akuruhi" is a compound. The monosyllable "hii", which means "day", has a long vowel in isolation, as all monosyllables in Kameyama do. When the compound is formed, generating a polysyllabic word, the vowel is shortened: *akuru+hii* → *akuru+hi*. We may assume that the tone of the deleted vowel attaches to the vowel in the adjacent foot, if it belongs to a degenerate foot:

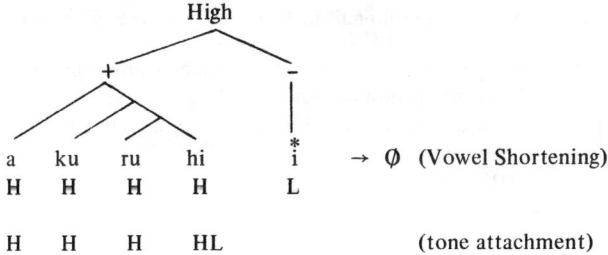

But if the foot branches, the "floating" tone is attached to the adjacent segment, foot internally:

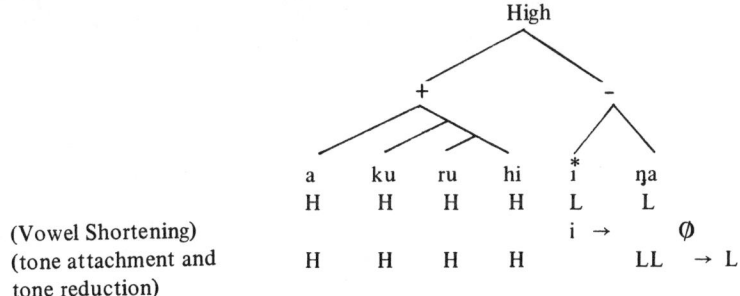

Something similar might be going on in example b.

12. We are here making the implicit assumption that the two lexical classes of one same dialect cannot differ in the direction of branching of their feet. This point is discussed in section 7.

13. Words like the following indicate that the syllabic segment and not the rime is the relevant terminal unit for the metrical tree in Osaka:

a. bentoo   —   lunch   c.   eesi   —   the rich
    HH LL   LH L
b. sendati   —   pioneer   d.   roozi   —   alley
    L H L L   LH L

14. Apparently, the "starless" tone-pattern of Class 1 has some phonetic variation. For example, the word "suzume" is pronounced "suzume" by some speakers
                                     L L L   L H H
and "suzume" by others. There are several speculative hypothesis that can be made
    L L H
to explain this variation. For instance, it may be the case that speakers that pronounce "suzume" are reanalyzing the data in such a way that the "starless" tone-pattern
    L H H
of Class 1 is interpreted as identical to the second foot of the "starred" tone-structure. With respect to "suzume", it might be the case that these speakers are reanalyzing
                               L L H
the foot as right-branching — in both Classes 1 and 2 — and generalizing the percolating-feature High to both classes. The initial foot of the "starred" tone-structure of Class 1 will then be interpreted as polarized. If this is true, we predict that these speakers in fact pronounce "garasudo-ga" and not "garasudo-ga" (cf. 64e), as in
                                               H H H H H   H H H H L
Osaka. Cf. the discussion in section 3. Still other hypothesis come to mind. In any case we will consider this to be a peripheral phenomenon.

15. The tone pattern of "akuruhi-ŋa" in Kôshi cannot be explained in the same
                                    H H H H L
manner as in Kameyama. Unlike Kameyama, monosyllables in Kôshi have short vowels: *hi* — *hii (day). Cf. the discussion in footnote 12.

16. That [+syllabic] segments are the relevant units is indicated by examples like the following: a— kyoo (today),
                                       HL
                          b.—hon (book).
                               HL

Vowel and Consonant Disharmony in Turkish

George N. Clements and Engin Sezer
Cornell University

1. INTRODUCTION

The present study examines a range of phenomena related to the topic of vowel and consonant harmony in Turkish. Its purpose is both descriptive and theoretical. We aim first to bring new empirical data to bear upon the question of the formal treatment of vowel and consonant harmony, and second to show that autosegmental phonology provides an internally consistent account of not only the regularities but also the irregularities and apparent exceptions within the particular system of Turkish.

Turkish is normally thought of as offering a paradigm case of vowel and consonant harmony at its simplest and most transparent. According to textbook descriptions, all vowels and consonants in Turkish words agree in their specification for backness, and all high vowels agree with preceding vowels in their specification for roundness. Moreover, the velar and lateral consonants are described as having back variants in back vowel words and front variants in front vowel words. Closer examination, however, reveals a host of exceptions to these statements. While these exceptions — or cases of disharmony — have not gone unnoticed in the literature, they have not received the attention that their interest for phonological theory merits.

The existence of large numbers of exceptions to proposed rules or principles is often a sign that a system has not been well understood. We believe that this is the case with most recent studies of vowel and consonant harmony, which have been carried out within phonological theories that postulate a principle of linearity in phonological representation. We will show in this study that the apparent exceptions to otherwise general principles of vowel and consonant harmony in Turkish are predictable consequences of the structure of phonological representations, and follow from the independently-motivated assumptions of autosegmental phonology given the optimal set of underlying representations selected by the evaluation metric of the theory. It is both unnecessary and misleading to treat such apparent exceptions in terms of the theoretical devices (rule features and other diacritic symbols) that have been proposed elsewhere for the expression of true exceptionality in phonological rule systems.

More specifically, we will propose that the apparent exceptions to Turkish vowel and consonant harmony are due to the presence of *opaque vowels and consonants* in underlying representations. The notion of "opaque segment," which will be formally characterized below, is well-motivated in autosegmental theory on both theory-internal and empirical grounds. Its theoretical justification derives from the conceptual organization of the theory itself. The primitive units of autosegmental phonology – segments, tiers, association lines – permit the expression of a richer variety of arrangements of distinctive features than is possible under linear theories of phonology. In particular, the units of related autosegmental tiers may be only partially related by association lines. "Opaque" segments can be characterized as consonants and vowels that are underlyingly associated with autosegmentally-represented features. It will be shown that such segments have certain characteristics that are reflected, in surface forms, as apparent exceptions to regular "spreading" processes. A theory that provides natural means for expressing such notions as "opaque segments" embodies the hypothesis that such segments may exist, and creates a strong presumption that they should be instantiated in particular linguistic systems.

The empirical justification for the notion of opaque segment derives from the fact that the recognition of this segment type allows for simple, straightforward descriptions of commonly recurring phenomena that require complicated or ad hoc accounts under alternative theories. Thus, in tone systems it has been found that certain types of consonants ("depressor consonants") function as opaque elements with respect to processes of tone spreading (Laughren, in press; Kisseberth, in press). Opaque segments play an essential role in the description of nasal prosodies (Poser (1981b), Hyman (1982), van der Hulst and Smith (this volume)). Opaque segments have elsewhere proven to be fundamental to an understanding of the vowel harmony system of Akan (Clements (1981)).

The notion of opaque segment cannot, however, be reconstructed within the representational system of standard generative phonology (see e.g. Chomsky and Halle 1968). Under this theory, phonological representations have the characteristics of *linearity, complete feature specification*, and *segmental integrity*. According to the first of these properties, phonological representations are exhaustively analyzable into sequences of segments having no ordered subparts: the phonemes of traditional linguistic analysis. "Suprasegmental" properties such as pitch, stress or length are treated as features of phonemes. Secondly, the criterion of complete feature specification requires that all segments be fully specified for all distinctive features; this condition rules out the possibility of archiphonemes. The third characteristic is related to, but logically independent of the second, and requires that phonological rules may operate only upon phonemes as wholes, and not upon their subparts. Thus, assimilation processes are formally characterized as properties which substitute phonemes, rather than features (see Chomsky and Halle (1968): "Appendix on Formalism").

Many structuralist and generative approaches to the description of vowel and consonant harmony have proposed to eliminate the second of these three criteria, by admitting archiphonemes into the theory (for treatments of Turkish along such lines, see Lees (1961), Crothers and Shibatani (1980)). Advocates of this approach have not so far succeeded in responding to familiar criticism of archisegmental representation such as that of Stanley (1967). In the framework of autosegmental phonology, it has been shown that the rejection of linearity does not entail the rejection of complete feature specification or segmental integrity. Given multilinear representations, it is possible to maintain that all segments on each tier are fully specified for all features, and to disallow rules that operate upon subparts of such autosegmentally-arrayed segments. Now since the assumption of linearity must be abandoned for entirely independent reasons (e.g. the treatment of floating tones, complex segments and the like), the adoption of an autosegmental approach to the analysis of vowel and consonant harmony is the most conservative move one can make. Given the independent need for nonlinear representations, an autosegmental treatment of harmony phenomena need exploit only those principles of phonological theory that are motivated in the treatment of other domains.

The present study focuses on the role of opaque segments in explaining apparent irregularities in the system of vowel and consonant harmony in Turkish. The discussion is organized as follows. Section 2 presents an introduction to the main features of Turkish vowel harmony and to the theoretical framework assumed in this work. Section 3 examines the main cases of disharmony: polysyllabic roots (3.1), exceptional suffixes (3.2), consonant harmony and disharmony (3.3), consonant-conditioned suffix harmony (3.4), and epenthetic vowels (3.5); further problems are discussed in 3.6. In section 4 we summarize our theoretical results.

2. VOWEL HARMONY

By vowel harmony we mean a system of phonological organization according to which all vowels are drawn from one or the other of two (possibly overlapping) sets within harmonic spans in the word. There are two well-defined types of word harmony systems. In *symmetrical* systems, roots do not alternate, and alternating affixes agree with the category of the nearest nonalternating vowel. In *asymmetrical* systems, both roots and affixes alternate; moreover, alternating forms assimilate to a single ("dominant") value of the harmony category if and only if a nonalternating morpheme of that value appears in the word. Examples of symmetrical systems include Turkish, Finnish, Hungarian, Mongolian, Manchu, and Akan. Examples of asymmetrical systems include Nez Perce, Chukchee, Somali, Diola-Fogny, and Kalenjin.

The following forms illustrate regular harmonic alternations in Turkish:

(1)
	nom.sg.	gen.sg.	nom.pl.	gen.pl.
'rope'	ip	ip-in	ip-ler	ip-ler-in
'girl'	kɨz	kɨz-ɨn	kɨz-lar	kɨz-lar-ɨn
'face'	yüz	yüz-ün	yüz-ler	yüz-ler-in
'stamp'	pul	pul-un	pul-lar	pul-lar-ɨn
'hand'	el	el-in	el-ler	el-ler-in
'stalk'	sap	sap-ɨn	sap-lar	sap-lar-ɨn
'village'	köy	köy-ün	köy-ler	köy-ler-in
'end'	son	son-un	son-lar	son-lar-ɨn

(k, l are palatal; see section 3.3). These forms illustrate two intersecting vowel harmony systems, one involving the feature of backness and the other involving the feature of roundness. All the vowel phonemes of Turkish are represented in (1). The system of backness harmony opposes the front vowels /i, ü, e, ö/ to the back vowels /ɨ, u, a, o/, and the system of roundness harmony opposes the rounded vowels /u, ü, o, ö/ to the unrounded vowels /i, ɨ, e, a/. It will be seen that all vowels in the word agree in backness. Suffix vowels alternate according to the category of the root vowel. Moreover, all high vowels agree in rounding with the preceding vowel, whether high or not; nonhigh vowels show no alternation in rounding. Finally, the back consonants /k, l/ appear in back vowel words while the front consonants /k, l/ appear in front vowel words.

It will be seen from the forms in (1) that Turkish displays the characteristics of a symmetrical vowel harmony system. No roots in Turkish alternate, and alternating suffix vowels agree with the nearest (in this case, the only) root vowel.

Previous studies of vowel harmony have shown that an autosegmental analysis permits an explanation for various recurrent properties of vowel harmony systems in the languages of the world (Clements (1977a)). These properties include the fact that vowel harmony is *phonetically motivated* in terms of universal distinctive feature theory; its *bidirectionality* (the fact that roots control the harmony of both prefixes and suffixes); its *obligatory* character (while vowel assimilation rules are optional in many languages, vowel harmony rules are not); and its *unboundedness* within the domain of the word, applying across maximal sequences of harmonic vowels. These properties follow from the formal structure of the theory. Phonetic motivatedness is a consequence of the fact that autosegmental representations are arrangements of distinctive features, rather than arrangements of arbitrarily selected "prosodies" or the like. Bidirectionality, obligatoriness, and unboundedness follow as a consequence of the fact that vowel harmony is characterized as an effect of the universal Well-formedness Conditions of the theory, which have these three properties. It will be noted that none of these properties follow from traditional accounts of vowel harmony, which describe vowel harmony systems in terms of language-particular rules.[1]

It has further been shown that the autosegmental framework allows a substantial reduction in the abstractness and arbitrariness of conventional descriptions, by reducing the emphasis on the role of rules in favor of the specification of a small number of parameters along which individual languages make a selection (Clements (1981)). These parameters appear to include the following:

(2) a. The class of *P-segments* (melody units) which constitute the autosegmentally-represented harmony features;
 b. The class of *P-bearing units* (melody-bearing units) defined as the class of units to which P-segments are associated under the universal Well-formedness Conditions;
 c. The (possibly null) class of *opaque segments*, defined as those which are underlyingly associated with a P-segment;
 d. The (possibly null) class of *transparent segments* which must be formally excluded from the class of P-bearing units;
 e. The *domain* within which the Well-formedness Conditions initially apply.

It seems that several of these parameters can be "set" on a language-independent basis. In all known vowel harmony systems, the class of P-bearing units stipulated under (2b) is the class of vowels. Similarly, the domain identified under (2e) is the (phonological) word, as this is independently defined in each language.[2] Thus these values can be supplied by the theory, and what remains to be specified on a language-particular basis are the classes of P-segments, opaque segments, and transparent segments. As noted above, the P-segments characterizing any vowel harmony system are drawn from the universal set of vowel features, including such features as back, round, advanced tongue root (ATR), high, and perhaps certain others.[3] Opaque segments, insofar as they are predictable, must be specified in the grammar of each language; note that opaque segments may include segment types other than those included in the class of P-bearing units (thus, consonants, in the case of vowel harmony).

Transparent segments are a subset of the segments characterized under (2b) which are "neutral" to the system in the sense that they do not associate with P-segments under the Well-formedness Conditions, but receive their feature values by independent specification. These include the familiar neutral vowels of many Uralic and Altaic languages.[4]

Turkish vowel harmony may be provisionally stated as follows. Each system is stated separately.

(3) backness harmony:
     P-segments: [+back], [−back]

(4) roundness harmony:
     P-segments: [+round], [−round]
     opaque segments: [+syllabic, −high]

(3) and (4) may be taken as the rules of vowel harmony in Turkish. Note that the fact that nonhigh vowels do not participate in the roundness system as P-bearing units is not treated by excluding them as transparent segments under (2d), but rather by identifying them as opaque segments under (2c). We shall see shortly how this treatment accounts for the phonological behavior of these vowels.

The present theory further assumes a set of universal Association Conventions which implement the Well-formedness Conditions. These conventions have the effect of requiring all P-bearing units (vowels) to be associated with one P-segment (harmony feature). The following informal statement is based upon that given in Clements (1981):

(5) Association Conventions

  a. Associate free (i.e. as yet unassociated) P-segments with free P-bearing segments from left to right across the mapping domain, until no further such associations can be made. For example (P = P-segment, π = P-bearing segment):

  $$
  \begin{array}{ccc}
  P_1 & P_2 & P_3 \quad \ldots \\
  \\
  \pi_1 & \pi_2 & \pi_3 \quad \ldots
  \end{array}
  \rightarrow
  \begin{array}{ccc}
  P_1 & P_2 & P_3 \quad \ldots \\
  | & | & | \\
  \pi_1 & \pi_2 & \pi_3 \quad \ldots
  \end{array}
  $$

  b. Associate any remaining free P-bearing units with a P-segment, giving precedence (in case of indeterminacy) to the P-segment on the left:

Disharmony in Turkish

$$\begin{array}{cccc} P_1 & P_2 & & \\ | & | & & \\ \pi_1 & \pi_2 & \pi_3 & \ldots & \pi_n \end{array} \quad \rightarrow \quad \begin{array}{cccc} P_1 & P_2 & & \\ | & | \diagdown & & \\ \pi_1 & \pi_2 & \pi_3 & \ldots & \pi_n \end{array}$$

(mirror image)

Convention (5a) provides for a left-to-right, one-to-one mapping between free (unassociated) P-segments and free P-bearing segments. (5b) insures that all P-bearing units will be associated with a P-segment, though not the converse. (5b) incorporates the following priority clause proposed in Clements (1976):

(6) Given configurations in which one or more free P-bearing units are flanked on both sides by bound P-bearing units, associate from the left. E.g.:

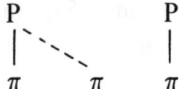

(5a) and (5b) together express the commonly-observed bias toward spreading from left to right. We finally assume the general constraint on autosegmental representations that prohibits the crossing of association lines (Goldsmith (1976)). These conventions act as "monitoring" devices in phonological derivations to preserve well-formed patterns of association between P-segments and P-bearing units. At the phonetic level, these associations are interpreted as patterns of coarticulation. Language-particular association rules, such as are commonly met with in tone languages, may take precedence over these conventions. Thus, the Association Conventions may be regarded as constituting the unmarked basis for mapping between autosegmental tiers. Language-particular rules may override any of these conventions, but only at the cost of adding extra complexity to the grammar.

Given these principles, we may return to the forms given in (1) above. The simplest set of underlying representations required to account for the representative forms *ip* 'rope' and *son* 'end' are the following:

(7)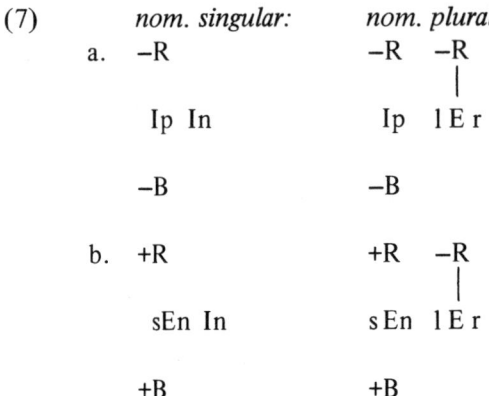

Here, in accordance with (4), nonhigh vowels are represented as opaque on the roundness tier. Otherwise, suffixes have no P-segments in their representation.[5] Each root, on the other hand, has a P-segment in its representation for each autosegmental tier. Since root vowels have not been defined as opaque,[6] there are no underlying associations between root vowels and root P-segments. Association Conventions (5a) and (5b) apply in succession to create the following output forms:

(8)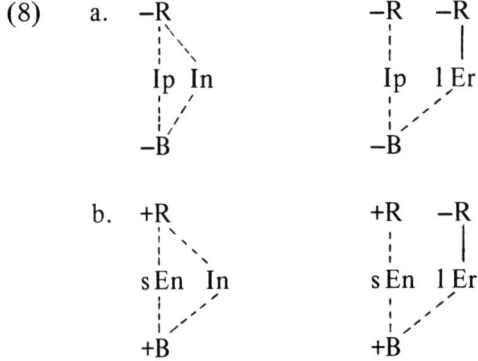

Notice that no rule has applied in deriving the surface forms of (8) from the underlying forms of (7). The rules defining Turkish vowel harmony, as stated in (3) and (4), are structure-building rules rather than feature-changing rules.

The special properties of opaque vowels become apparent if we consider the derivation of the genitive plural of these two forms. The underlying forms are as follows:

(9) a.   −R −R   b. +R −R
         | | | |
         Ip lEr In   sEn lEr In

         −B   +B

Association Convention (5a) applies first to link the single free P-segment on each tier to the first free P-bearing segment:

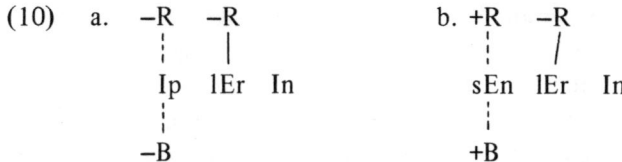

Association Convention (5b) then applies to link remaining free vowels to the first P-segment to their left:

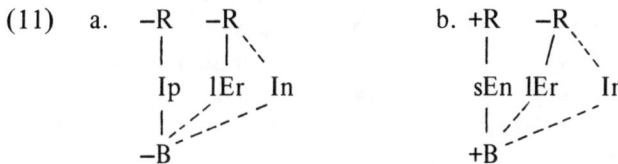

If we observe the roundness tier, we note that the opaque vowel of the plural suffix has three characteristics: (i) it fails to associate with the P-segment of the root to its left, (ii) it prevents the P-segment on its left from associating with any vowel to its right, and (iii) it determines the roundness value of the vowel to its right. These properties are formal consequences of the Association Conventions (5). We may therefore say that opaque segments are "nonundergoers," "blockers," and "spreaders" with respect to the Association Conventions, differing in this respect from true neutral segments (such as consonants[7]) which are nonundergoers but neither blockers nor spreaders. We shall take these three properties as criterial for the identification of opaque segments in our subsequent discussion.

3. A TYPOLOGY OF VOWEL AND CONSONANT DISHARMONY IN TURKISH

In this section we examine various types of exceptions to the principles of vowel and consonant harmony suggested by our preliminary examination of the forms in (1), and show that these follow from the existence of "opaque" vowels and consonants in phonological representations.

3.1. Vowel Disharmony in Roots

Many polysyllabic roots conform to the principles of vowel harmony stated earlier. However there is a large number of exceptions to these principles which any adequate analysis of Turkish must take account of. Representative examples, involving exceptions to backness harmony, are given below.

(12) a. cooccurrence of /a/ and /i/:

vāli	'governor'	kitap	'book'
hamsi	'anchovies'	izmarit	'sea-bream'
dakīka	'minute'	fiat	'price'
vaziyet	'position'	infilak	'explosion'
takvim	'calender'	istakoz	'lobster'
hani	'where is'	silah	'weapon'

b. cooccurrence of /a/ and /e/:

hareket	'movement'	hesap	'bank account'
anne	'mother'	general	'general'
adet	'item, piece'	jevap	'answer'
haber	'news'	jezā	'punishment'
kardeš	'sibling'	mezat	'auction'
katmer	'fold, layer'	selam	'salute'

c. cooccurrence of /o/ and /i/:

bobin	'spool'	pilot	'pilot'
polis	'police'	činko	'zinc'
orkinos	'tunny fish'	čiroz	'dried mackerel'
torik	'blue fish'	limon	'lemon'
politika	'politics'	sifon	'toilet flush'
komite	'committee'	kilo	'kilo'

d. cooccurrence of /o/ and /e/:

otel	'hotel'	petrol	'petrol'
kolye	'necklace'	peron	'railway platform'
rozet	'collar pin'	teleskop	'telescope'
model	'model'	depo	'warehouse'
noter	'notary public'	metot	'method'
dočent	'associate professor'	dekor	'stage scenery'

e. cooccurrence of /u/ and /i/:

billur	'crystal'	hūri	'beautiful girl'
zigurat	'ziggurat'	muzip	'mischievous'
(gap)		kulis	'stage wing'
		mūnis	'easy-going'
		muhit	'neighbourhood'
		zarūri	'necessary'

Disharmony in Turkish

f. cooccurrence of /u/ and /e/:

sūret	'copy'	jesur	'brave'
buket	'bouquet'	mebus	'member of parliament'
kubbe	'dome'	mektup	'letter'
kudret	'power'	mevzū	'topic'
sūre	'chapter of the Koran'	nemrut	'unsociable'
		resul	'messenger of God'
muhterem	'respected'		

We note that while /u...i/ in that order is a common sequence, /i...u/ is very rare. With this exception, we find that exceptions to backness harmony involving vowels from the set /i, e, a, o, u/ are common in Turkish, involving many items of the everyday as well as the learned vocabulary. On the other hand, exceptions involving the vowels /ü, ö, ɨ/ are very rare. Furthermore, these, unlike the previous class of exceptions, are highly unstable and tend to regularize to various extents in different dialects. For example, we find the following examples of disharmonic sequences containing /ü, ö/ in the standard dialect:

(13)
komünizim ∼ kominizim		'communism'
komünist ∼ kominist		'communist'
mersörize ∼ merserize		'mercerized'
püro ∼ puro		'cigar'
nüzul ∼ nüzül		'paralysis'
motör ∼ motor		'engine, motorboat'
kupür ∼ ķupür		'denomination, clipping'
šoför ∼ šöför		'driver'
külot ∼ kilot		'panties'
ķüsur ∼ ķüsür		'fractions'
fütur ∼ fütür		'langour'
nüfus ∼ nufus		'population'
mürur ∼ mürür		'lapse'
zulüm ∼ zulum		'oppression'
nüfuz ∼ nufuz		'authority'
bülū ∼ bulū		'adolescence'
bisküvit ∼ büsküvüt		'biscuit'
šövalye ∼ šovalye		'knight'

Examples such as *külot*∼*kilot* show that regularization need not make an item regular with respect to backness harmony, but may only replace one vowel of the set /ü, ö, ɨ/ with a vowel of the set /i, e, a, o, u/ agreeing with it in backness.

Let us now consider exceptions to the system of roundness harmony.

We may first note that just as in the case of backness harmony, exceptions involving vowels from the set /ü, ö, ɨ/ are rare and subject to regularization; indeed, exceptions consisting of /ɨ/ cooccurring with a rounded vowel are virtually nonoccurrent. As a subregularity, however, we find that /ü/ and /i/ cooccur in several words, in either order:

(14) ümit   'hope'   tifüs   'typhus'
      düzine   'dozen'   virüs   'virus'
      ümmī   'illiterate'   virgül̂   'comma'
      mümbit   'fertile'   nīlüfer   'water lily'
      ünsiyet   'familiarity'   bitüm   'bitumen'

With this set of exceptions, we conclude that /ü, ö, ɨ/ are extremely infrequent in words violating roundness harmony.

In contrast, violations involving vowels from the set /i, e, a, o, u/ are common. Consider first violations with /o/. Since nonhigh vowels are opaque to rounding harmony, the only true violations will involve cases of /o/ followed by either of the high vowels /i, ɨ/; as we have just seen, violations involving /ɨ/ do not exist. Examples of the remaining case, /o/ followed by /i/, were given in (12c).

Let us consider, finally, violations of rounding harmony involving /u/. Since, once again, nonhigh vowels are opaque to the roundness system, violations are of one of two sorts: /u/ followed by /i/, already illustrated in (12e), and /u/ following one of the vowels /i, e, a/. Words with /u/ following /i/ are rare, as shown by the near-total gap in (12e) (two examples were found). Words with /u/ following /e/ are on the other hand not uncommon, as shown in (12f). Our final case is /u/ following /a/, and this deserves special comment.

The /a...u/ type of exception pattern is common in Turkish, and a special status is usually assigned to this sequence. In the traditional analysis, /u/ is found to the exclusion of /ɨ/ after /a/ if the intervening consonant is one of the labials /p, b, m, f, v/ (or if the intervening consonant cluster contains a labial). In generative analysis, this statement is usually formulated as a morpheme structure condition of Labial Attraction (see, for example, Zimmer (1969)), since the rule does not hold across morpheme boundaries, as already illustrated by the form *sap-ɨn* in (1).

Now while many Turkish roots conform to the proposed rule of Labial Attraction, many more do not. Lees (1966) and Zimmer (1969) were able to find 61 roots of the form /...aCu../ where C is a labial consonant or a cluster containing a labial, and 13 which had /ɨ/ in place of the expected /u/. Further examination shows that exceptions of the latter sort are more numerous than Lees and Zimmer believed. We have found the following, all of which are quite common words:[8]

(15)　apɨš (arasɨ)　'crotch'　　čapkɨn　'womanizer'
　　　čarmɨh　　　'cross'　　　kapɨ　　'door'
　　　kaplɨja　　　'thermal spring'　sābɨk　'ex' (prefix and noun)
　　　hāfɨza　　　'memory'　　sarmɨsak　'garlic'
　　　sabɨr　　　'patience'　　yapɨšmak　'to stick to'
　　　kabɨz　　　'constipated'　kamčɨ　'whip'
　　　hāfɨz　　　'Koran reciter'　apɨšmak　'to be shocked'
　　　damɨz (lɨk)　'stag'　　　kamɨš　'reed'
　　　rābɨta　　　'connection'　yapɨnjak　'kind of grape'
　　　damɨtmak　　'to distill'　　sapɨk　'psychotic, pervert'
　　　mutābɨk　　'in agreement'　münāfɨk　'heretic'
　　　muhāfɨz　　'sentry'　　　kɨzamɨk　'measles'

Even more decisive evidence against a rule of Labial Attraction is the existence of a further, much larger set of roots containing /...aCu.../ sequences in which the intervening consonant or consonant cluster does not contain a labial; we have found 61 such roots, of which a representative sample is given below:

(16)　marul　　'lettuce'　　　barut　　'gunpowder'
　　　mālup　　'defeated'　　žaluzi　　'Venetian blind'
　　　hātun　　'lady'　　　　fatura　　'invoice'
　　　sardunya　'geranium'　　mādur　　'oppressed'
　　　fasulya　　'beans'　　　māsum　　'innocent'
　　　arzu　　　'desire'　　　kazūrat　'feces'
　　　anut　　　'sulky'　　　kānun　　'law'
　　　ajūze　　'ugly'　　　　ajur　　　'type of cucumber'
　　　panžur　　'shutter'　　　ašūre　　'kind of dessert'
　　　vakur　　'grave'　　　yakut　　'emerald'
　　　āguš　　　'bosom'　　　mahkum　'convict'
　　　yahudi　　'Jew'　　　　sahur　　'meal before dawn'

We conclude that there is no systematic restriction on the set of consonants that may occur medially in roots of the form /...aCu.../.

Our conclusion is supported by the results of psycholinguistic experimentation carried out by Zimmer (1969). Zimmer found that subjects' reactions to nonsense-word preference tests fell into two categories. One set of speakers consistently preferred nonsense words of the shape /...aCu.../ to nonsense words of the shape /...aCɨ.../, while the other set consistently made the opposite choice. In both cases, the nature of the intervening consonant was found to have no bearing upon the choice. These results support our view that there is no rule of Labial Attraction in the synchronic grammar of modern standard Turkish. The fact that /...aCu.../ sequences were regularly preferred by one group of subjects reflects the fact that this sequence is well-formed in roots, in spite of its apparent violation of roundness harmony.

Let us consider now how our results are to be interpreted. The standard approach to disharmonic roots has been to treat them as exceptions to the otherwise general rules of vowel harmony. Their exceptional status is reflected in the grammar by assigning them diacritic features indicating that they are exceptions to backness harmony, roundness harmony, or both. Yet our results suggest that the burden of proof is on the linguist who wishes to demonstrate that roots are governed by vowel harmony at all.

The traditional analysis has been defended on the basis of the claim that disharmonic roots are loanwords, and thus not subject to the otherwise general and productive rules of Turkish (Lightner (1972)). This account is problematic on two counts. In the first place, no support can be found for this claim in the synchronic grammar of Turkish. Lightner enumerates a number of features that distinguish nonnative words from native words in the Turkish lexicon: (i) occurrence of /ž/, /ä/ as phonemes; (ii) stem-internal ablaut (*kitap* 'book', *kütüp* 'books'); (iii) occurrence of glottal stop; (iv) root-initial consonant clusters; (v) nonfinal stress in morphemes other than adverbs and place names; and (vi) occurrence of palatal /l̡/ in back-vowel words. He suggests that roots having these characteristics are marked [-native], and that nonnative roots are redundantly marked as exceptions to vowel harmony. The fact is, however, that the vast majority of exceptional roots, including most of those cited above, show none of the characteristics listed by Lightner nor other characteristics that would mark them as nonnative. Whatever their historical source (many, though not all[9] disharmonic roots are historical borrowings), there is no basis for the claim that most disharmonic roots involving the vowels /i, e, a, o, u/ show any exceptionality other than their disharmony.

Secondly, even if disharmonic roots were loanwords, there is no reason to suppose that they would not undergo the productive rules of Turkish phonology. Yavash (1980a) cites examples such as the following in support of the claim that loanwords regularly undergo Turkish phonological rules:

(17) Final k-deletion[10]
 biftek   'steak'   biftei   'his steak'   (Fr. *bifteck*)
 tɨrafik 'traffic'   tɨrafii 'its traffic' (Fr. *trafic*)

(18) Final obstruent devoicing
 kitap   'book'   (Ar. *kitāb*)
 istibdat 'despotism'   (Ar. *istibdād*)

Disharmony in Turkish

Yet these and similar roots do not undergo vowel harmony. We conclude that one cannot isolate disharmonic roots as somehow marginal to the regular system of Turkish phonology.

To summarize, we see that the vowels /i, e, a, o, u/ freely cooccur with each other in Turkish roots. The large number of disharmonic roots created by the combination of these vowels is readily attestable in any dictionary of modern Turkish. There appear to be no grounds for treating these sequences as in any way exceptional. Such roots are common in the everyday vocabulary, fail to become "regularized" (as do disharmonic roots involving the vowels /ü, ö, ɨ/), undergo the productive rules of Turkish phonology, and are accepted by native speakers as "well-formed" in psycholinguistic testing. Further evidence for the latter observation has been adduced by Yavash (1980b), who reports on the results of an experiment similar in nature to that carried out by Zimmer. Yavash found the following hierarchy of disharmonic vowel sequences, those at the top of the list being most acceptable to his subjects. The figure in parentheses indicates the number of times the sequence in question was selected in preference to a corresponding harmonic sequence, out of a total of 26 trials.

(19) i...a   (13)
      e...a   (13)
      a...e   (11)
      a...i   (10)
      e...u   (9)
      ü...a   (7)
      u...e   (6)
      o...e   (5)
      ɨ...e   (5)
      a...ü   (1)
      e...ɨ   (1)
      ö...a   (0)

Yavash's results are consistent with our claim that disharmonic combinations involving /i, e, a, o, u/ are well-formed, but those involving /ü, ö, ɨ/ are not. Indeed, the first two disharmonic sequences were selected as frequently as the corresponding harmonic sequences. Only the sequence /ü...a/ occurs higher on the list than expected.

We therefore conclude that within single morphemes, the vowels /i, e, a, o, u/ freely cooccur, while the vowels /ü, ö, ɨ/ may occur only harmonically. In order to state this constraint formally we will assume that all root vowels are opaque. We therefore add the following statement to (3) and (4):

(20)   opaque segments: [+syllabic, +root]

This ensures underlying representations like the following (cf. (12)):

(21)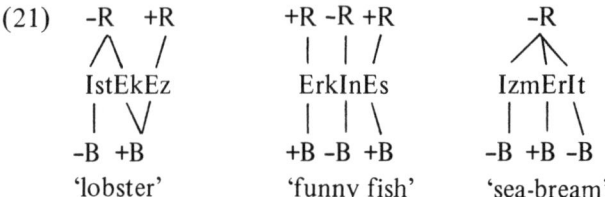

      'lobster'   'funny fish'   'sea-bream'

This treatment is consistent with the analysis of opaque vowels given earlier. Recall that opaque vowels were characterized as "nonundergoers," "blockers," and "spreaders". Root vowels are nonundergoers; thus a root vowel does not harmonize with the preceding vowel. Root vowels are blockers; thus a suffix vowel cannot harmonize with a nonfinal root vowel, except coincidentally. Root vowels are spreaders; thus a final root vowel determines the harmonic category of the immediately following harmonic suffix vowel. The last two points are illustrated in (22) for the genitive singular of *orkinos* 'tunny fish':

(22)   +R −R +R
       │ │ /\.
       ErkInEs In   [orkinosun]
       │ │ \ ⁄
       +B −B +B

It can be deduced from (3), (4), and (20) together with the universal Well-formedness Conditions that harmonic suffix vowels following a root will harmonize with the last root vowel, a claim which is correct for Turkish.

We now introduce the following constraint on vowel cooccurrence within single morphemes:

(23)   The vowels /ü, ö, ɨ/ do not occur disharmonically in VC₀V sequences, except that /i, ü/ may occur in either order.

This statement admits roots of the type /CuCaCɨ/ while excluding roots of the type /CuCɨCa/ and /CaCɨCu/, since only the latter involve harmony violations involving /ü, ö, ɨ/ in disyllabic subsequences. This formulation seems intuitively correct, although we have not found examples of disharmonic roots of the first type. This statement also provides for the subregularities involving /i, ü/ (see (14)). The first part of (23) may be restated formally as an if-then condition holding of single morphemes:

Disharmony in Turkish

(24) if

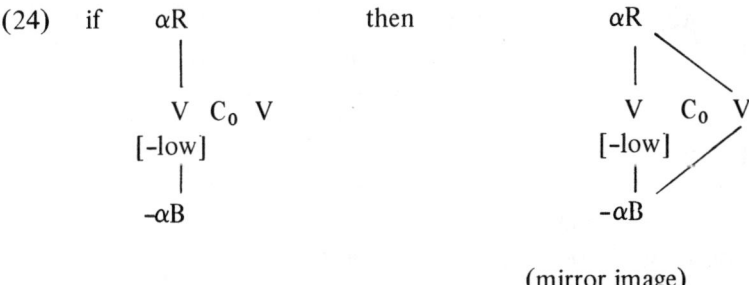

(mirror image)

Or, using the abbreviatory conventions of autosegmental phonology,

(25)

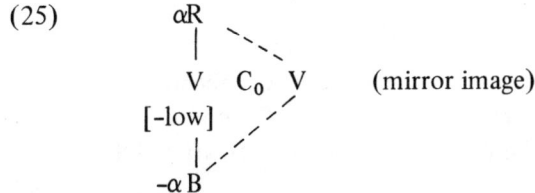   (mirror image)

The exceptional, well-formed subsequences involving /i, ü/ are subsumed under the following further condition:[11]

(26)

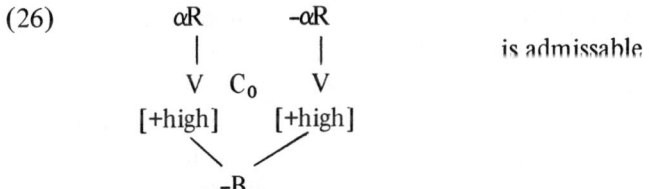   is admissable.

3.1.1. The Status of non-initial /o/

In connection with the distribution of /o/ we would like to comment briefly on a claim that has gained wide currency in the literature, to the effect that /o/ is restricted to initial syllables of roots. Whatever its historical status, this claim is not true of modern standard Turkish, which offers many examples of non-initial /o/; see (12c, d) for a few examples, which can easily be multiplied. Surface exceptions to this alleged regularity arise through two regular processes: (i) partial reduplication of certain adjectives, (ii) a rule of vowel assimilation whereby a high vowel optionally assimilates to an immediately preceding nonhigh vowel with which it agrees in backness and rounding:

(27) a. Adjective reduplication:

bok	'ordure'	bombok	'utterly useless'
dolu	'full'	dopdolu	'full to the brim'
mor	'purple'	mosmor	'bright or dark purple'

b. Vowel assimilation:

aır	∿	aar	'heavy'
böür	∿	böör	'bellow'
yourt	∿	yoort	'yogurt'

Underlying exceptions have a variety of historical sources. The earliest loans introducing noninitial /o/ include loans from the 14th and 15th centuries (28a), and later loans from Byzantine Greek (28b) and Italian (chiefly Venetian) (28c):

(28) a. abanoz   'ebony'   <   Gr. ebenos
        horoz   'rooster'   <   Gr. horus
        afyon   'opium'   <   Pers. afyon (cf. Gr. opion)
        orospu   'whore'   <   Pers. ruspī
        anadolu   'Asia Minor'   <   Lat. Anatolia
     b. anafor   'whirlpool'   <   anafori
        lodos   'southwest wind' <   lotos
        istavros   'cross'   <   stavros
        takoz   'wooden wedge'   <   takos
     c. kalyon   'gallion'   <   galión
        moloz   'debris'   <   molo (<Lat. moles)
        marangoz   'carpenter'   <   marangón
        alabora   'capsize'   <   albora

Examples of more recent loans, coming primarily from French and Italian, are numerous. The following are minimal pairs in which the first member has noninitial /o/:

(29) tablo   'painting' tabla   'tray'
      komplo   'plot'   komple   'complete'
      limon   'lemon'   liman   'harbor'
      balkon   'balcony'   balkan   'Balkans'
      balo   'ball'   bale   'ballet'
      filo   'fleet'   file   'shopping net'

That noninitial /o/ is well-entrenched in modern Turkish is further shown by the fact that many loans have introduced noninitial /o/ in place of an original /u/, a fact which would be surprising if there were a constraint

Disharmony in Turkish

against noninitial /o/. See the examples *horoz* and *orospu* in (28a), as well as the following, which now have /o/ in free or dialectal variation with the original /u/:

(30)　mool　∿　moγol　∿　mogol　∿　mogul　'Mongolian'
　　　soot　∿　soγot　∿　sogot　∿　sogut　'Sogdian'
　　　feylesof　∿　feylesuf　　　　　　　'philosopher'

3.2. Vowel disharmony in suffixes

We may draw a distinction between *harmonic* and *disharmonic* suffixes as follows: harmonic suffixes are those whose vowels show regular alternation involving at least one of the two harmonic features [back] and [round], while disharmonic suffixes contain at least one vowel which fails to alternate under any circumstances. The following examples illustrate words formed with the disharmonic suffixes /-Iyor/ 'progressive', /-gen/ 'noun-forming', /-istan/ 'noun-forming', and /-Edur/ 'verb-forming'. Note that in the first and fourth of these the first vowel alternates regularly while the second vowel does not:

(31)　a.　gel-iyor-um　　　　'I am coming'
　　　　　koš-uyor-um　　　　'I am running'
　　　　　gül-üyor-um　　　　'I am laughing'
　　　　　bak-ɨyor-um　　　　'I am looking'
　　　b.　üč　'three'　　üč-gen-ler　　'triangles'
　　　　　altɨ　'six'　　altɨ-gen-ler　'hexagonals'
　　　　　sekiz　'eight'　sekiz-gen-ler　'octagonals'
　　　　　čok　'many'　　čok-gen-ler　　'polygonals'
　　　c.　arab-istan-ɨ　　'Arabia'　　(acc.)
　　　　　ermeni-stan-ɨ　'Armenia'　　　"
　　　　　mool-istan-ɨ　　'Mongolia'　　"
　　　　　türk-istan-ɨ　　'Turkestan'　　"
　　　d.　gid-edur-sun　　'let him keep going'
　　　　　koš-adur-sun　　'let him keep running'
　　　　　gül-edur-sun　　'let him keep laughing'
　　　　　bak-adur-sun　　'let him keep looking'

It will be noticed that the nonalternating vowels exhibit the characteristics of opaque segments: they are nonundergoers, blockers, and spreaders. Accordingly, we will postulate underlying representations such as the following, for *geliyorum*:

(32)   -R   +R
         | |
        gEl   IyEr   Im
         | |
        -B   +B

Association Convention (5b) is applicable. Notice that the condition of precedence (6), incorporated into the statement of (5b), uniquely determines the pattern of association shown below:

(33)   -R   +R
       / ˋ   / ˋ
      gEl   IyEr   Im   = [geliyorum]
       | ˏˊ   \ ˏˊ
      -B   +B

More generally, we find that (6) is always correct for Turkish: opaque segments, whether vowels or (as we shall see) consonants, always govern the harmonic category of a harmonic vowel to their right. We might call (6) the Principle of Inertia, according to which an articulatory state determined by a particular feature configuration is maintained until a new specification (or set of specifications) is encountered. This principle need not be stated as a condition on rule application. As noted earlier, this principle, together with the left-to-right mapping convention (5a), explains the common phonological bias toward spreading from the left. As a convention (rather than a language-particular rule condition), it expresses the "unmarked" case of spreading which can only be overruled by a language-particular statement taking precedence over it.[12]

The constraint ruling out disharmonic sequences with /ü, ö, ɨ/ in roots holds of polysyllabic suffixes as well. A small number of such suffixes contain two opaque vowels. The suffix /-istan/, illustrated in (31c), is one, and the others are:

(34)   -āne   denominal, adjective-forming
        -vāri   denominal, adverb-forming
        -leyin   denominal, adverb-forming
        -iyet   denominal, noun-forming

In these suffixes the disharmonic vowels are drawn exclusively from the set /i, e, a/. More generally, opaque vowels in suffixes are always one of the following: /i, e, a, o, u/; the vowels /ü, ö, ɨ/ do not occur as opaque segments outside roots. We thus have the following condition holding of suffixes in underlying representation:

(35)   /ü, ö, ɨ/ are prohibited in suffixes.

3.3. Consonant harmony and disharmony

The following chart gives a partial distinctive feature specification of Turkish surface consonants:

(36)	p	b	f	t	d	s	z	č	j	š	ž	k	g	m	n	v	l	r	y	h
coronal	-	-	-	+	+	+	+	+	+	+	+	-	-	-	+	-	+	+	+	-
anterior	+	+	+	+	+	+	+	-	-	-	-	-	-	+	+	+	+	-	-	-
labial	+	+	+	-	-	-	-	-	-	-	-	-	-	+	-	+	-	-	-	-
high	-	-	-	-	-	-	-	+	+	+	+	+	+	-	-	-	+	-	+	-
sonorant	-	-	-	-	-	-	-	-	-	-	-	-	-	+	+	+	+	+	+	+
voiced	-	+	-	-	+	-	+	-	+	-	+	-	+	+	+	+	+	+	+	-
strident	-	-	-	-	-	+	+	+	+	+	+	-	-	-	-	-	-	-	-	-

The high nonstrident consonants k, g, l have two major forms, front (palatal) and back (velar), which occur under conditions which we state below. While the choice between these forms is, as we shall see, partly conditioned by context, it is partly unpredictable, as the following examples show:

(37)   velar /k g l/:   palatal /k̡ g̡ l̡/:
       bol   'abundant'   bo̡l   'cocktail, drink'
       kalp   'counterfeit'   kal̡p   'heart'
       kar   'snow'   k̡ar   'profit'
       gaz   'gas'   g̡avur   'infidel'

In addition to these, an unpredictable palatal /r̡/ has a marginal occurrence in stem-final clusters, and some dialects of modern standard Turkish retain a very restricted occurrence of palatal /t̡/ in absolute stem-final position. We shall see examples of all of these below. Apart from these cases, the feature of backness is not distinctive in consonants.[13]

The selection between /k g l/ and /k̡ g̡ l̡/ is partly determined by the harmonic structure of the word in which they occur. In general – and we shall shortly see that this is an oversimplification – /k g l/ appear in back vowel words and /k̡ g̡ l̡/ appear in front vowel words. This so-called "consonant harmony" cannot be considered a redundant effect of vowel harmony since disharmonic consonants may appear in regular harmonic words while harmonic consonants may appear in disharmonic words.

3.3.1. The velar consonants

The following forms illustrate harmonic velar consonants in monosyllables. The words in (38a) show that syllable-initial velars assimilate to the value of the following vowel, and those in (38b) show that syllable-final velars assimilate to the value of the preceding vowel.

(38) a. kir̂   'dirt'   gür   'abundant'
         k̂el   'bald'   k̂ör   'blind'
         k̂ɨr   'meadows'   kul   'slave'
         gaz   'gas'   kol   'arm'
     b. dik̂   'upright'   yük   'load'
         tek̂   'single'   dök̂   'pour'
         sɨk̂   'often'   ak   'white'
         ok   'arrow'

(Note that /g, ġ/ do not occur syllable-finally.[14]) As a preliminary hypothesis, we might suppose that it is the position of the consonant with respect to the vowel in the linear string of phonemes that determines whether the palatal or the velar is selected, and propose the following rule (cf. Anderson (1974), 211):

(39) [+cons] → [αback] / $\begin{bmatrix} \\ +\text{high} \\ -\text{strident} \end{bmatrix} \begin{bmatrix} +\text{syllabic} \\ \alpha\text{back} \end{bmatrix}$ (mirror image)

Due to the convention related to mirror image rules according to which the given order of elements takes precedence over the mirror image order, this rule also extends correctly to the following data:

(40) sāk̂in   'calm'   raket   'racket'
     vak̂it   'time'   fak̂ir   'poor'
     īk̂az   'warning'   mika   'mica'
     ikon   'icon'   patika   'path'
     sigara   'cigarette'   ištigal̂   'occupation'
     hakīk̂at   'truth'   dikk̂at   'attention'

In sāk̂in, for example, the velar assimilates to the following vowel by the first case of the rule, and since this case takes precedence over the second, the rule cannot reapply. Consider now, however, the following data:

(41) fark̂   'difference'   kɨrk̂   'forty'
     zamk̂   'glue'   burk̂   'sprain'
     sirk̂   'circus'   ilk̂   'first'
     k̂ürk̂   'fur'   denk̂   'equal'

Here the backness of the final consonant is determined by the value of the preceding (and only) vowel. But since rule (39), as stated, does not provide for an intervening consonant it will not account for any of these forms. We must therefore modify the rule to allow for the presence of an intervening consonant:

(42) $[+\text{cons}] \rightarrow [\alpha\text{back}] / \underline{\quad} \begin{bmatrix} +\text{high} \\ -\text{strident} \end{bmatrix} (C) \begin{bmatrix} +\text{syllabic} \\ \alpha\text{back} \end{bmatrix}$

(mirror image)

A serious problem now arises, however, with forms such as the following, which are also perfectly regular:

(43)   nektar   'nectar'   reklam   'advertisement'
       ikram   'offer'   šükran   'gratitude'
       boksit   'bauxite'   akrep   'scorpion'
       daktilo   'typist'   ukte   'ganglion'

Our revised rule will apply incorrectly to these forms due to the principle (required for the forms of (40)) that the first case of a mirror image rule applies disjunctively with respect to the second case. Thus, there appears to be no way of accounting for velar consonant harmony in terms of a rule formulated in terms of the linear string of segments alone.

Let us propose, instead, that the backness value of a harmonizing velar consonant is determined by the *tautosyllabic* vowel – the vowel with which it shares a syllable. We may account for consonant harmony by defining the following autosegmental system, which spreads the backness value of a vowel onto any tautosyllabic high non-strident consonant:[15]

(44)   Consonant Harmony
       P-segments: [+back], [−back]
       P-bearing units: [−syl, +high, −strident]
       domain: σ

This rule, in effect, generalizes the rule of backness harmony (3) to the set of harmonic consonants within the domain of the syllable. The bidirectional and obligatory character of this rule, as well as the irrelevance of intervening consonants, are an automatic consequence of this analysis. (44), defining an autosegmental system, will apply in a derivation whenever its structural description is met. (44) will apply correctly to the following examples, as indicated by the broken lines:

(45)   +B   +B−B+B   −B +B
       /|\ | /| /| |\ /|
       kIrk   hEkIkEt   dIkkEt
       \|/   \| \| \|/   \|/ \|/
       σ   σ σ σ   σ   σ

       [kɨrk]   [hakīkat]   [dikkat]
       'forty'   'truth'   'attention'

There are some occurrences of velar stops in stem-initial and stem-medial position whose values cannot be predicted on the basis of rule (44). Some representative examples follow:

(46)   bekar   'bachelor'   kātip   'clerk'
       ahkam   'judgements'   zekat   'alms'

In traditional analyses within linear frameworks, such consonants must be marked with a diacritic feature indicating that they are exceptions to rule (44). No such diacritic marking is necessary in the present treatment, which regards these forms as regular, though somewhat more complex in structure than forms with harmonizing velars. We need only treat the consonants in question as opaque segments. This will give us underlying representations such as the following, to which no further rules apply:

(47)   −B +B   −B +B −B   +B −B+B   −B +B
       |\ | \| | / | / / |\ /
       bEkEr   kEtIp   EhkEm   zEkEt
       \| \|/   \| \|/   \| \|/   \| \|/
       σ σ   σ σ   σ σ   σ σ

       [bekar]   [kātip]   [ahkam]   [zekat]

3.3.2. The lateral

We now consider the harmonic behavior of the lateral. This consonant has generally been treated in parallel to the velars. However, its harmonic behavior is considerably more complex.

First of all, in the Istanbul dialect the lateral is predictably palatal in word-initial position:

(48)   laf   'expression'   lutuf   'favor'
       lodos   'south wind'   lɨkɨrda−   'gurgle'

In word-final position after back vowels, however, the value of this consonant is unpredictable:

Disharmony in Turkish

(49) a. front 1:

sol	'sol' (musical note)	kalp	'heart'
bol	'cocktail, drink'	ihlal	'violation'
usul	'system'	sual	'question'

b. back 1:

sol	'left'	kalp	'counterfeit'
bol	'abundant'	okul	'school'
bavul	'suitcase'	hamal	'porter'

The lateral is invariably palatal when the first preceding or following vowel is [−back]:

(50)

čelo	'cello'	melun	'cruel'
ilač	'drug'	selam	'hello'
kalem	'pen'	polis	'policeman'
albüm	'album'	islam	'Islam'

Otherwise, word-internal laterals may be front or back, with the front variant strongly favored if either flanking vowel is long (51a) and the nonpalatal favored in all other cases (51b):

(51) a.

mālum	'known'	ālā	'fine'
ulūfe	'soldier's pay'	ukalā	'pedantic'

b.

ɨlɨk	'warm'	balɨk	'fish'
yala	'lick'	balo	'ball'

There is evidence that the predictable occurrence of front /l/ in (50) is lexically determined by a morpheme structure condition, rather than assigned by rule. While predictable occurrences of back laterals are fronted before invariant front vowel suffixes (52a), predictable occurrences of front laterals remain front before invariant back vowel suffixes (52b):

(52) a.

asɨl	'original'	aslī	'basic'	aslen	'basically'
mool	'Mongolian'	moolistan	'Mongolian'		

b.

ādil	'just'	ādilāne	'justly'
sefil	'miserable'	sefilāne	'miserably'

The velar consonants, in contrast, assimilate to a following back vowel across morpheme boundaries:

(53) mālik 'owner' mālikāne 'residence'

These facts are easily accounted for on the assumption that the palatal laterals in (50) and (52b) are determined by a morpheme structure condition having the following form (this statement is to be interpreted as a conditional, as in (25) earlier):

(54)   −B
         ╱‒ ‒ ‒
        V   (C) [+lateral]   (mirror image)

In other words, laterals are lexically associated with any −B harmony segment associated with the first vowel to their left or right.

Laterals which are not opaque are subject to rule (44) given earlier. (44) will therefore not apply to the forms in (50) and (52b), but it will apply to the forms in (52a), just as it does to those in (53):

(55)   +B   +B −B   +B −B   +B −B +B −B
        ╱·.   / ╱| | /| | /|·\ /
       Es I l   Es1 I   mEl I k   mEl I k En E
       | \/   \/ \/   \/ \/   \/ \/ \/ \/
       σ σ   σ   σ   σ   σ   σ σ σ σ

This analysis is confirmed by the fact that the lateral is not palatal before the invariant front-vowel suffix /-gil/ in examples like (56b), in apparent violation of (54); the latter, as a morpheme structure condition, will not apply across morpheme boundaries.

(56)   a.   tombul   (a name)
       b.   tombulgiller 'the Tombuls'

To summarize, we have proposed an analysis of the "harmonizing" consonants of Turkish which parallels the treatment we have given of harmonizing vowels. We have suggested that harmonizing occurrences of the velars and the lateral are underlyingly transparent, while nonharmonizing occurrences are underlyingly opaque. In the next section we turn to some consequences of this analysis.

3.4.   *Consonant-conditioned vowel harmony*

In the preceding section we showed that certain properties of "nonharmonic" consonants could be accounted for in a straightforward way by treating them as opaque segments. Recall that opaque segments are nonundergoers, blockers, and spreaders. Examples such as those of (46) and

(48) show that opaque consonants do not undergo the Consonant Harmony rule (44), and are thus "nonundergoers". In this section we turn to evidence confirming our prediction that nonharmonic consonants are also blockers and spreaders.

Consider first the velars. We have seen examples of disharmonically palatal /k̭/ in initial and medial position in the word, but no examples of this consonant word-finally. Indeed, this is a genuine gap in the surface distribution of this form in the dialects we have examined which remains to be accounted for.

There is a further idiosyncracy regarding roots with opaque palatal /k̭/. We find a small number of Turkish words whose final syllables have back vowels and which govern front vowel harmony, and whose final consonant is [k] word-finally, or before a consonant-initial suffix, and [k̭] before a vowel-initial suffix. A partial list includes the following:

(57)
		nom. sg.	acc. sg.
	'explosion'	infilak	infilāki
	'perception'	idrak	idrāki
	'alliance'	ittifak	ittifāki
	'participation'	ištirak	ištirāki
	'fasting'	imsak	imsāki
	'expropriation'	istimlak	istimlāki
	'real estate'	emlak	emlāki
	'exhaustion'	helak	helāki
	'addiction'	inhimak	inhimāki
	'consumption'	istihlak	istihlāki

Most of these words are ultimately of Arabic origin, and originally ended in nonemphatic velars. In most examples, the penultimate vowel is front and the final vowel is long back /ā/.

Now it will easily be seen that if we permit opaque palatal velars to occur freely in underlying representations — and in particular, to occur finally in the underlying representations of the stems in (57) — the front vowel quality of the suffixes will be instantly accounted for. Thus, assuming the final consonant of *idrak* to be opaque, we have the following representations of the nominative and accusative singulars, respectively:

(58)   −B +B −B   −B +B −B
            \| \| /   \   \| /\
           I dr E k   I dr E k   I

By Association Convention (5b), the P-segment associated with the final consonant of the accusative singular becomes associated with the suffix vowel, as indicated by the broken line. In order to account for the back quality of the final consonant in the nominative singular, where it occurs syllable-finally, we introduce a rule disassociating the P-segment in syllable-final position:[16]

(59) $\quad\begin{matrix} -B \\ \neq \\ [-son] \end{matrix}]_\sigma$

This rule will not apply to syllable-final sonorants, which retain their palatal quality on the surface (see (62) below). Consonant Harmony (44) then applies to spread the backness value of the preceding vowel to the now-transparent consonant:

(60) $\quad\begin{matrix} -B +B -B \\ | \; | \; / \\ I\,dr\,E\,k \end{matrix} \rightarrow \begin{matrix} -B +B \\ | \; | \\ I\,dr\,E\,k \\ (by\,(59)) \end{matrix} \rightarrow \begin{matrix} -B +B \\ | \; \backslash \\ I\,dr\,E\,k \\ (by\,(44)) \end{matrix}$

We here assume that a (nontonal) P-segment left afloat after the operation of a phonological rule is automatically deleted by convention. If it is not left afloat, it is of course retained in the representation, as in the nominative plural:

(61) $\quad\begin{matrix} -B +B \;\; -B \\ | \; | \;\;\; / \\ I\,dr\,E\,k \;\; 1\,E\,r \end{matrix} \rightarrow \begin{matrix} -B +B \;\; -B \\ | \; | \;\;\;\; \backslash \\ I\,dr\,E\,k \;\; 1\,E\,r \\ (by\,(59)) \end{matrix} \rightarrow \begin{matrix} -B +B \;\; -B \\ | \; \backslash \;\;\;\; / \\ I\,dr\,E\,k \;\; 1\,E\,r \\ (by\,(44)) \end{matrix}$

It will be noticed that rule (59) is in no way an artifact of the present analysis; the absence of syllable-final palatal velars after back vowels is a surface gap that must be accounted for in any analysis. Nor can the recognition of underlying word-final palatal velars be considered unnecessarily "abstract", since such representations are justified by alternations (57).

Consider now the behavior of words ending in a back vowel followed by a palatal *l*. These words invariably take front suffixes, as the following examples show:

Disharmony in Turkish 241

(62)
	nom. sg.	*acc. sg.*
'system'	usul	usūlü
'petrol'	petrol	petrolü
'role'	rol	rolü
'question'	sual	suāli
'crescent'	hilal	hilāli
'independence'	istiklal	istiklāli

To this group may be added words ending in back vowels followed by consonant clusters whose first member is palatal *l*:

(63)
'heart'	kalp	kalbi
'golf'	golf	golfü
'waltz'	vals	valsi

All such words contrast in their behavior with back vowel words ending in nonpalatal *l*, which invariably take back vowel suffixes:

(64)
'fork'	čatal	čatalɨ
'school'	okul	okulu
'police station'	karakol	karakolu

The harmonic behavior of a word ending in a lateral is therefore fully predictable: front vowel suffixes are required if the final lateral is palatal, otherwise back vowel suffixes are required. As before, we may represent stem-final palatal *l* as an opaque segment underlyingly associated with the autosegment [−back]. This unit spreads onto any suffix vowel or vowels that follow:

(65)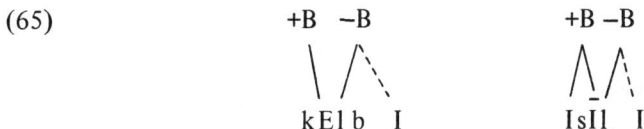

We have now succeeded in verifying our prediction concerning opaque consonants: as the forms in (57), (62) and (63) show, they are not only nonundergoers, but also blockers and spreaders.

In addition to the forms we have examined so far, there is a fairly large set of back vowel stems ending in either a cluster containing /r/, or in one of the consonants /t, d, b/, which require front vowel suffixes. Their Arabic or Persian sources have plain (nonemphatic) consonants in this position. A few examples are given below:

(66)
	nom. sg.	acc. sg.
'war'	harp	harbi
'letter'	harf	harfi
'west'	garp	garbi
'coinage'	darp	darbi
'watch; hour'	saat	saati
'limit'	hat	haddi
'acquittal'	beraat	beraati
'congregation'	jemaat	jemaati
'attention'	dikkat	dikkati
'reading'	kɨraat	kɨraati
'interest'	menfaat	menfaati
'God'	rab	rabbi

It appears that for some speakers, words such as *saat* end in a phonetically palatal *t* in the unsuffixed form (Waterson (1970)). For these speakers, an analysis parallel to that given for palatal *l*-stems is called for. For speakers who do not have palatal *t* in word-final position, we may generalize the solution given earlier for palatal *k*-stems. That is, the final consonant of these stems will be represented as opaque. If a vowel-initial suffix follows, the P-segment attached to the *t* will associate to it; otherwise it will be disassociated by rule (59).

Finally, we turn to a small class of stems which in some idiolects exceptionally take back vowel suffixes although their final syllable contains a front vowel. These stems include the following:

(67)
	nom. sg.	acc. sg.
'desire'	ševk	ševkɨ
'drive'	sevk	sevkɨ
'top'	fevk	fevkɨ
'creator'	hālik	hālikɨ
'confirmation'	tasdik	tasdikɨ
'Mercury' (planet)	utarit	utaridɨ[17]

For those (mostly older) speakers who still retain these forms, the nominative singular ends in a back velar rather than the expected front velar, as our transcriptions indicate. This behavior reflects the historical fact that the Arabic sources of these words ended in a uvular. The behavior of these forms suggests that the final consonant is underlyingly associated with a +B P-segment:

(68)   −B +B   −B +B
              \ | \ |\
              šEvk   šEvk I

For speakers who do not have final opaque consonants in these words, the suffix vowels are front.

In sum, we have seen that the following generalizations hold of the class of exceptions discussed in this section: (i) no roots governing disharmonic suffix values end in a vowel; (ii) all roots ending in disharmonic consonants govern disharmonic suffix values. These generalizations, which do not follow from "diacritic" treatments of exceptions to vowel and consonant harmony, are consequences of a theory treating disharmonic consonants as opaque.[18]

3.5. Disharmonic epenthetic vowels

There are some 200 bisyllabic forms in Turkish in which a high vowel in the second syllable alternates with ∅. Some ten of these forms go back to old Turkic. These refer to body parts except for *oul* 'son', 3. poss. *ōlu* from the older *ogul*. The remaining forms are almost exclusively of Arabic origin. These include many common, everyday words that are heard with great frequency in the present-day language. Some examples follow:

(69)
		nom. sg.	3. poss.	abl.
	'bosom'	koyun	koynu	koyundan
	'idea'	fikir	fikri	fikirden
	'judgement'	hüküm	hükmü	hükümden
	'part'	kɨsɨm	kɨsmɨ	kɨsɨmdan
	'patience'	sabɨr	sabrɨ	sabɨrdan
	'text'	metin	metni	metinden

We see that the vowel in question agrees in backness and rounding with the preceding root vowel.

There are in addition bisyllabic forms that are similar to those in (69), but in which the alternating vowel does not show the expected backness harmony with the root vowel. All these words are of Arabic origin. The following is a representative list.

(70)
		nom. sg.	3. poss.	abl.
	'time'	vakit	vakti	vakitten
	'womb'	rahim	rahmi	rahimden
	'resolution'	azim	azmi	azimden
	'volume'	hajim	hajmi	hajimden
	'tomb'	kabir	kabri	kabirden
	'tribe'	kavim	kavmi	kavimden

Let us consider the question whether the alternating vowels in (69) and (70) are to be treated in terms of epenthesis or deletion. It would appear, on the face of things, that an epenthesis analysis would be difficult to maintain. Under such an analysis, we could not predict whether the epenthetic vowel is back /ɨ/ or front /i/. We could not predict whether an epenthesizing stem governs back vowel suffixes or front vowel suffixes. And finally, there would be no way of capturing the generalization that all and only the stems that take epenthetic front vowels also require front vowel suffixes.

A deletion analysis, on the other hand, can account for all three facts at once. By setting up underlying /sabɨr/ 'patience' and /kabir/ 'tomb', for example, we directly relate the quality of the suffix vowel in the 3. possessive to the quality of the second stem vowel in the nominative singular and ablative. Thus the derivation of *sabɨr*, *sabrɨ*, *kabir*, and *kabri* proceeds as follows:[19]

(71) /sabɨr/   /sabɨr-I/   /kabir/   /kabir-I/
    –   sabɨr-ɨ   –   kabir-i   Vowel Harmony
    –   sabr-ɨ   –   kabr-i   Vowel Deletion

In spite of the apparent attractiveness of this solution, it is quite clearly incorrect. The first problem is that there is a host of exceptions to the proposed rule of vowel deletion which cannot be predicted on phonological grounds. Some representative examples include the following:

(72)
	nom. sg.	3. poss.	abl.
'copper'	bakɨr	bakɨrɨ	bakɨrdan
'food'	azɨk	azɨɨ	azɨktan
'poor'	fakir	fakiri	fakirden
'baby's shoe'	patik	patii	patikten
'coal'	kömür	kömürü	kömürden
'sheep'	koyun	koyunu	koyundan

Thus, vowel deletion would have to be a lexically conditioned rule that will fail to apply to a majority of eligible forms.

Secondly, and more significantly, there is a large class of exceptions to the vowel deletion rule that *can* be predicted on phonological grounds. This consists of the set of stems of the form $C_1VC_2VC_3$ where C_2C_3 elsewhere form a permissable syllable-final cluster. Examples are the following:

(73) 'gunpowder' barut   barutu   baruttan
      'strange'   garip   garibi   garipten
      'ambitious' haris   harisi   haristen
      'outfit'   kɨlɨk   kɨlɨɨ   kɨlɨktan
      'lifebuoy'   simit   simidi   simitten

Permissable syllable-final clusters in Turkish are of the following types:[20]

(74) a. sonorant + obstruent: *türk* 'Turk', *genč* 'young'
      b. voiceless fricative + oral stop: *čift* 'double', *ašk* 'love'
      c. k + s: *raks* 'dance', *boks* 'boxing'

Under the deletion analysis there is no way to capture the relationship between the forms of (73) and the generalizations expressed in (74) short of postulating some sort of transderivational constraint on the deletion rule that would prohibit its operation just in case it would give rise to a cluster that, if syllable final, would be well-formed. Such a solution is clearly unacceptable.

In sum, traditional approaches place us in a dilemma. The epenthesis analysis forces us to introduce independent diacritic features to describe forms that are exceptional both in regard to epenthesis and to suffix harmony, and fails to explain why forms that are exceptional with regard to one are also exceptions with regard to the other. The deletion analysis is unable to relate a phonologically-motivated class of exceptions to deletion to independently-needed constraints on syllable structure.

Under an autosegmental analysis, two solutions are potentially available in the face of data such as this. One solution is to postulate root-final floating P-segments in the case of the forms in (70); the other is to treat the second consonant of each root of (70) as opaque. Both solutions assume the epenthesis rule. Thus, the alternative analyses can be represented as follows:

(75) a. +B −B   b +B −B
          | | /
          vEkt   vEkt

If all else were equal, the evaluation metric would select (75a) over (75b) as the simpler of the two representations. As it happens, however, all else is not equal. A consideration of the ablative forms shows us that only the second solution, positing an opaque consonant in C_2 position, accounts for the surface form:

(76) +B −B   +B −B   +B −B
      | / \   → | / \   → | /\
      vEkt tEn   vEkIt tEn   vEkIttEn
      (by (5b))   (by (78))   (by (5b))

The first solution, positing a floating P-segment, fails:

(77) +B −B   +B   −B   +B   −B   (wrong
      /   \   → | | →   \ | output)
      vEkt tEn   vEkIt tEn   vEkIt tEn
      (by (5a))   (by (78))   (by (5b), (44))

The Epenthesis rule involved in the above derivations is the following:

(78) Vowel Epenthesis

      $\emptyset \rightarrow I \;/\; C \underline{\quad} C'$ (C' = an extrasyllabic consonant)

(78) inserts an epenthetic high vowel, unassociated with any features on the autosegmental tiers involved in harmony, between two consonants if the second can form neither a syllable onset nor a syllable coda by the syllable structure rules of Turkish.[21] The inserted vowel then undergoes the normal operation of the Association Conventions (5).[22]

Given this analysis, then, we see that a further class of monosyllabic noun roots of the structure CVCC must be recognized, where the second C is opaque. But it will be recalled that this is not in fact a new structural type of Turkish root, since such roots have already been motivated: see (63), and in particular (66), where we find a unique set of occurrences of palatal /r̃/. Thus, roots of the type (75b) come cost-free in our analysis, and indeed fill in an otherwise unexplained gap in the distribution of opaque segments.

We have so far examined cases of disharmonic epenthetic vowels inserted into root-final clusters. There is another source of epenthetic vowels in Turkish consisting of root-initial clusters, as the representative forms in (79) illustrate. It will be noted that each word (consisting of uninflected roots) shows two or more variants. The first variant, containing the cluster, generally reflects a careful or learned pronunciation. The second and subsequent forms represent normal or colloquial pronunciations. In the latter forms, which are the more usual, we observe a short epenthetic vowel between the two members of the cluster. Under contrastive emphasis, these short vowels may receive the full value of normal (short) vowels.[23]

Disharmony in Turkish 247

(79)   careful form   colloquial form(s)

a. 'fetters'   pranga   pɨranga
    'prince'   prens   pirens
    'test'   prova   purova
    'Prussia'   prusya   purusya
    'protest'   protesto   purotesto
    'premium'   prim   pirim
    'canvas'   branda   bɨranda
    'bridge' (card game) brič   birič
    'brooch'   broš   bɨroš
    'blue jeans'   blujin   bulujin, bülüjin
    'bromide'   brom   bɨrom, burom
    'brake'   fren   firen
    'France'   fransa   fɨransa
    'frenchified'   frenk   firenk

b. 'banister'   trabzan   tɨrabzan
    'trichinosis'   trišin   tirišin
    'Tripoli'   trablus   tɨrablus
    'transit'   transit   tɨransit
    'direct'   drek   direk
    'Dracula'   drakula   dɨrakula
    'announcer'   spiker   sipiker
    'probation'   staž   sɨtaž, ?sitaž
    'dinner jacket'   smokin   sɨmokin, simokin
    'sports'   spor   sɨpor, sipor

c. 'king'   kral   kɨral
    'credit'   kredi   kɨredi
    'necktie'   kravat   kɨravat
    'crèche'   kreš   kɨreš
    'sketch'   kroki   kɨroki
    'jack'   kriko   kɨriko
    'cruiser'   kruvazör   kuruvazör
    'group'   grup   gurup
    'grippe'   grip   gɨrip
    'strike'   grev   gɨrev

We have divided our examples into three groups. (79a) illustrates the behavior of labial-initial clusters, (79b) that of dental-initial clusters, and (79c) that of velar-initial clusters.

We note first that with a few sporadic exceptions, the epenthetic vowel consistently harmonizes in backness with the following root vowel after labials and dentals, but is invariably back after velars, whatever the category of the following root vowel. There is, however, a second peculiarity of velar-initial clusters: namely, that when these clusters are not broken up by an epenthetic vowel, the velar is invariably back in quality, regardless of the harmonic category of the following root vowel. These two facts can be related if we assume that word-initial velar consonants are assigned the feature [+back] before a following consonant. If epenthesis applies, the inserted vowel will then automatically receive the feature [+back] from the preceding consonant:

(80) +B −B   +B −B
     | /   → |\ | (by (5b))
     grEv   gIrEv

A further set of exceptions to backness harmony consists of *s*-initial clusters, which allow front-vowel epenthesis in the four forms we have found. We assume that an analogous solution positing opaque occurrences of /s/ is possible here, although auditory judgements are more subtle in this case than with the velars. Note that the linking of the acoustically "grave" velars with the feature [+back], and of the acoustically "acute" /s/ with the feature [−back], is a phonetically motivated pairing: it seems quite appropriate to attribute the exceptional quality of the epenthetic vowel in these cases to intrinsic features of the initial consonant.[24]

Apart from these cases, epenthetic vowels are regular with respect to backness harmony. Turning to roundness harmony, there is a single regular pattern of exceptions: the epenthetic vowel may be unrounded before /o/ (though not, in our data, before /ö/). Examples are *broš, brom, smokin, spor,* and *kroki*; compare the expected behavior of *prova, protesto*. In the case of at least the *s*-initial forms, we can observe that the initial consonant is unrounded even in the nonepenthetic variant. Thus compare [sp^{w}or] (not [s^{w}p^{w}or]) with regular words like [s^{w}om^{w}un] 'loaf', where /s/ assimilates in rounding to the following vowel. Apparently, therefore, some consonants occur with an opaque specification for the feature [−round] in word-initial clusters if the root vowel is /o/.

Otherwise, all forms are regular with respect to roundness harmony. In particular, we have found no cases of an epenthetic rounded vowel before an unrounded root vowel. The phonetic value of the epenthetic vowel in regular forms is accounted for by the mirror image case of Association Convention (5b):

(81)   −B   −B
         | →   ´|
      p r E n s   p I r E n s
         | `|
         −R   −R

Disharmony in Turkish

What is particularly instructive about examples like (81) is the fact that it shows that autosegmentally-represented features may spread leftward, if the opportunity arises. Thus epenthesis in initial clusters confirms the prediction of autosegmental phonology that vowel harmony is a bidirectional process. The apparent unidirectional nature of Turkish vowel harmony is a consequence of the fact that Turkish lacks prefixes, and does not reflect any fundamental restriction on the directionality of this process.

3.6. Further problems

The discussion of the preceding sections has not exhausted the cases of disharmony in Turkish. As noted by Lees (1967), in certain varieties of the Istanbul dialect a short vowel is unrounded immediately before a palatal or palatoalveolar consonant within word boundaries if either (i) morpheme-final, or (ii) not in the first syllable of the word, and it is moreover raised if the conditioning consonant is followed immediately by a vowel. This process, as Lees elsewhere noted (1961), is confined to deverbal suffixes. Compare the deverbal suffixes of (82) with the denominal suffixes of (83):

(82) ara-mak   'to search'
      arɨ-yan   'one who searches'
      arɨ-yaǰak   'will search'
      arɨ-yor   'is searching'

(83) ara   'interval'
      ara-ya   'to the interval'
      ara-yɨ   'the interval'

If the unrounded vowel follows a rounded vowel, surface exceptions to roundness harmony are created: thus [üšümiyiš] 'not feeling chilly' from /üšü-me-yiš/, and [okɨyɨp] from /oku-yIp/ 'having read'.

What is particularly problematical about the latter forms is that the unrounding of the vowel preceding the palatal or palatoalveolar consonant induces the unrounding of all subsequent vowels. As Anderson ((1974): 216) points out, this fact offers an apparently insoluble challenge to standard theories of rule interaction. If unrounding precedes roundness harmony, the latter rule should cancel the effects of the former rule: oku-yIp → okɨ-yIp → oku-yup. If roundness harmony precedes unrounding, the final vowel should remain rounded: oku-yIp → oku-yup → okɨyup. There is no solution to this problem within the context of the standard theory that does not introduce unwarranted or ad hoc assumptions about the nature of rule ordering or rule interaction.

Within autosegmental phonology, on the other hand, a straightforward solution is available. It will be noted that the vowel preceding the palatal consonant has the properties of an opaque segment: it does not undergo rounding harmony, it blocks the spread of rounding harmony, and it spreads its own value onto the following vowel(s). Since the ultimate source of the opacity is the palatal consonant, it is reasonable to suppose that it is this element that is opaque in underlying representations. We thus have:

(84) +R −R   +R −R
      ∧   ∧   →   ╱   ╱∧   (leftward spreading)
      E k I y I p   E k I y I p

A local readjustment rule spreads the [−round] value of the opaque consonant onto the preceding vowel, as shown above.[25]

While this analysis seems attractive, there remain certain questions concerning the extensiveness and exact nature of the phonological processes involved. In the dialect spoken by one of the authors (Sezer), the two processes of unrounding and raising are optional and independent of each other. Either, both, or neither may apply, with application in both cases favored in casual speech styles. Furthermore, the raising rule itself appears to have a stylistically marked variant which not only raises, but also rounds the vowel in question if the preceding vowel is round. It seems likely then, that the vowel alternations associated with palatal and palato-alveolar consonants are not yet fully understood.

4. CONCLUSIONS

In this study we have offered evidence that apparent exceptions to vowel and consonant harmony in Turkish should be treated in terms of opaque segments, a category provided by autosegmental representation, rather than in terms of the diacritic (rule exception) features provided by the standard theory. We have shown that in each case where alternative solutions present themselves, the autosegmental solution can be motivated over the diacritic solution on purely empirical grounds.

It has been shown, moreover, that opaque segments are consistently characterized in Turkish by the following three properties: they are non-undergoers, blockers, and spreaders with respect to vowel and consonant harmony processes. These properties follow from the formal structure of the theory itself, and in particular from the formulation of the Association Conventions stated in (5). We offer these results as a contribution to the current discussion concerning the nature and formal characterization of vowel harmony systems (see, for example, Halle and Vergnaud (1981), as well as several contributions to the present volume).

The theory of autosegmental phonology, first formulated in response to a number of problems as diverse as the treatment of tone, accent, and nasalization in a variety of languages unrelated to Turkish, has proven capable of explaining a relatively complex and intricate set of forms in Turkish with no essential modification. This result supports the interest of pursuing a research strategy which seeks a simple and unified account of the deep-seated structural regularities underlying apparently distinct phonological processes, which — taken from the phonetic point of view alone — would appear superficially to have no properties in common across diverse languages.

NOTES

The authors are indebted to Jaklin Kornfilt for much helpful discussion based on a close reading of an earlier version of this manuscript.

1. Certain of these claims have been challenged by Anderson (1980). In particular, Anderson questions the validity of the claim that vowel harmony systems are phonetically motivated, citing Nez Perce and certain dialects of Mongolian as examples of phonetically arbitrary systems. As Anderson points out, the "asymmetrical" system of Nez Perce is not a strict counterexample to the claims of Clements (1977a) which were there formulated to hold of the "symmetrical" type of system. Nevertheless, even "asymmetrical" systems are elsewhere known to be phonetically motivated, and Nez Perce would continue to constitute a puzzling phonological anomaly were it not for the convincing recent demonstration that Nez Perce harmony is based on the feature ATR (Hall and Hall (1980)). The Mongolian dialects cited by Anderson have yet to receive satisfactory descriptions within modern phonological frameworks, and phonetic information regarding them is still sparse. Assuming, however, that Anderson's sources are correct in essential respects, it would be incorrect to consider these systems as phonetically arbitrary; they are quite clearly based on the feature category "back" as demonstrated by regular suffix alternations. The problem raised for phonological analysis by these systems derives from the fact that certain nonalternating vowels belong phonologically to the category of back vowels but (due to regular processes of historical change) phonetically to the category of front vowels. Eventual analyses of these systems will have to select between the options of treating these vowels "abstractly" by deriving them from underlying back vowels, or "concretely" by deriving them from underlying front vowels. Either type of analysis will, in spite of this additional complexity, treat these systems as based on the feature "back", and thus as phonetically motivated.

Anderson's second objection concerns the claim that vowel harmony is bidirectional. The claim here, of course, is not that vowel harmony is always both progressive and regressive in all languages, but rather that it is progressive in suffixing systems, regressive in prefixing systems, and bidirectional in systems that employ both prefixing and suffixing. Anderson has offered no counterevidence to this claim. Rather, he cites examples from Turkish and other languages showing that (to adopt our terminology) opaque segments control harmony domains to their right. Such a bias toward spreading from the left is characteristic not only of vowel harmony systems but also of tone systems, and is expressed in the theory assumed here in the formulation of the Association Conventions (5).

2. Some vowel harmony systems appear to show spreading of the harmony feature beyond the domain of the word. However, it seems that such spreading should be treated in terms of independent mechanisms. In Akan, such spreading involves a phonetic "cline:: effect rather than the assignment of a simple plus- or minus-value of the harmony feature (Clements (1981)). In Somali, whose vowel harmony system is of the "asymmetrical" type, spreading beyond the domain of the word is a variable phenomenon, depending on phrasing and rate of speech, while word-internal vowel harmony is obligatory (Farnetani (1981), 55-8).

3. The phonetic basis of certain Nilotic vowel harmony systems remain to be identified. See e.g. Jacobson (1980).

4. The treatment of neutral vowels assumed here is different from that of Clements (1977b), in which neutral vowels were treated as P-bearing units.

5. Except, of course, in the case of non-alternating vowels, which we will discuss in 3.2., below.

6. We shall find reason to revise this treatment in the next section. For the moment, the forms in (8) will serve to illustrate the usual operation of the Association Conventions.

7. Except in the case of opaque consonants. See 3.4., below.

8. The last four examples could be removed from this list if Labial Attraction were formulated to apply to the first two syllables of a root only. This formulation, however, would predict that we should find /...aCɨ.../ to the exclusion of /...aCu.../ in the second and third syllables of trisyllabic roots. This claim is inconsistent with examples such as the following:

kɨlavuz	'guide'
palamut	'type of fish'
salamura	'brine for pickling'
salapurya	'large boat; small lighter'
arnavut	'Albanian'
firavun	'pharaoh'
telaffuz	'pronunciation'

9. Examples like *hani* 'where', *hangi* 'which', *kardeš* 'sibling', and *elma* 'apple' are native Turkish words often cited in traditional grammars.

10. See Sezer (1981) for discussion of this rule.

11. This rule, stated as an admissability condition (Akers (1981)), takes precedence over (25) under the Elsewhere Condition (Clements (in press)).

12. For an example in Shona, see Odden (in press)). A further example, cited from Guaraní by Poser (1981b), seems susceptible to reanalysis (Van der Hulst and Smith (this volume)). It should be noted that (6), as a condition on the operation of the Association Conventions, is not inconsistent with the existence of rules of regressive (right-to-left) assimilation, which do not directly involve the operation of the Association Conventions but rather of rules operating on autosegmentally-specified features.

13. This feature is not needed to distinguish /y/ from other consonants, given the

feature characterization of (36), since /y/ is the only nonanterior high sonorant. Unlike the velars and the lateral, backness is always predictable in /y/.

14. The only genuine exception to this that we know of is *lig* 'sports conference'. In most cases the orthography has *g* where the pronunciation has [k]:

ürolog   'urologist'
katalog   'catalogue'
vantrilog   'ventriloquist'

15. The treatment of consonant harmony proposed here is based on a suggestion by Toni Borovsky (personal communication). Note that rule (44), as formulated, will apply to laterals as well as to velars; this treatment is motivated in section 3.3.2.

It would be phonetically plausible to suppose that not only laterals and velars, but all consonants undergo Consonant Harmony (44). Presumably, the phonetic effects of this rule are less salient in the case of labials and dentals than in the case of laterals and velars. Rule (44) can be extended to the remaining consonants simply by eliminating the features [+high, −strident].

16. This rule, as formulated, will disassociate the feature [−back] in front vowel syllables as well as back vowel syllables. This instance of overapplication is harmless, since Consonant Harmony (44) will subsequently apply, restoring the original configuration which is subject to no further rules:

$$\begin{array}{ccc} -B & -B & -B \\ \diagdown & | & \diagdown \\ E\ k & E\ k & E\ k \\ & \text{(by (59))} & \text{(by (44))} \end{array}$$

17. This form is highly suspect, since dictionaries old and new cite *Utarid* as a perfectly regular root Develioğlu and Kiliçkan (1975), Redhouse (1890), Hony (1972)). This word, which is now obsolete, was borrowed from Arabic and originally ended in a non-emphatic consonant.

18. As a check on the validity of the descriptive generalizations summarized in this section, based upon standard dictionaries and grammars, the authors conducted a survey of university-aged Turkish speakers resident in Cambridge, Massachusetts. Five subjects were presented with a randomized list of unsuffixed Turkish nouns. They were asked first to eliminate from the list any words unfamiliar to them, and then to read the remaining items on the list, first in the uninflected form and then in the accusative plural form (X-1ER-I). Nouns of three types were included:

A: palatal-*l* stems (*usul*)
B: other consonant-final stems reported as taking exceptional front-vowel harmony (*iştirak*)
C: consonant-final stems reported as taking exceptional back-vowel harmony (*ševk*)

In addition, regular nouns were included as distractors. Each subject was tested separately.

The results of this survey were as follows. All subjects invariably assigned front vowel suffixes to all ten test words of class A (*usul, petrol, rol, mahsul, alkol, sual, hal, hilal, general, istiklal*). Of the ten test words of class B (*kalp, garp, harp, harf, infilak, idrak, iştirak, saat, kabahat, hat*), only the latter received front vowels suffixes uniformly; the others showed variation among subjects with *infilak* and *idrak* showing the greatest tendency toward back vowel behavior (four out of five subjects). Six words of class C were included (*ševk, sevk, fevk, tasdik, halik, Utarit*), and all were assigned front vowel suffixes by all speakers, except for four cases which had to be eliminated due to their unfamiliarity (*halik* twice, *fevk* and *Utarit* once).

These results may be taken to reflect the different degrees of integration of opaque consonants in contemporary Turkish. The palatal *l*'s of the class A words are the most fully integrated into the Turkish system, occurring initially, medially, and finally. In the latter environment they offer phonemic contrasts with non-opaque (harmonic) *l*'s (see (49)). The opaque consonants of the class B words are less well integrated, since none occur freely as surface disharmonic consonants in all positions in the word. Indeed, *t* never occurs disharmonically anywhere in the word except for marginal occurrences in final position in the dialect reported by Waterson (1970). Finally, not only do the opaque consonants of class C words never occur as surface disharmonic consonants anywhere in the word, but more significantly, most varieties of modern standard Turkish have *no* surface back-velar consonants in front-vowel words at all; hence one would expect this class to be the most unstable, and the first to undergo regularization, in conformity with our results.

19. Such an analysis is proposed in Foster (1969). See, in contrast, Pyle (1974) and Yavash (1980c), whose arguments for an epenthesis analysis are incorporated into the following discussion.

20. In the learned dialect, we also find *alarm* 'alarm', *titr* 'academic title', etc.

21. There are a few forms in which the epenthetic vowel breaks up clusters which are otherwise permissible in Turkish. These include the following:

ufuk	/ufk/	'horizon'
akis	/aks/	'echo'
kâyït	/kayt/	'record'
lahit	/laht/	'sarcophagus'
ahit	/aht/	'testament'

Compare the well-formed *čift* 'double', *raks* 'dance', *taht* 'throne'. Some of the words in this class have regularized in some dialects: thus *beyit* 'line of a poem' may appear in the 3. possessive as either *beyti* or *beyiti*. We assume that the exceptionally epenthetic words are distinguished from normal words in the lexicon in that their final consonants are (unpredictably) extrasyllabic, that is, unaffilated to the syllable:

$$
\begin{array}{ccc}
\sigma & & \sigma \\
\wedge & \text{vs.} & \wedge\!\!\!\wedge \\
\text{laht} & & \text{taht}
\end{array}
$$

The extrasyllabic consonant of the first form triggers Vowel Epenthesis (78).

22. Notice that in forms to which Vowel Epenthesis (78) cannot apply, such as the 3. possessive, rule (59) is applicable:

$$
\begin{array}{ccc}
\begin{array}{cc} +B & -B \\ / & \diagup \end{array} & \begin{array}{cc} +B & -B \\ / & | \end{array} & \begin{array}{cc} +B & -B \\ \wedge & | \end{array} \\
\text{vEkt} \quad I & \rightarrow \quad \text{vEkt} \quad I & \rightarrow \quad \text{vEkt} \quad I \\
(\text{by (5b)}) & (\text{by (59)}) & (\text{by (44)})
\end{array}
$$

23. See Yavash (1980a,c) for further examples. The variety of Turkish reported on in this study appears to be similar to that of Yavash in respect to the quality of the epenthetic vowels.

24. Less understandable from this point of view is the possible, though generally dispreferred occurrence of disharmonic front vowels in /fl/ clusters:

      'banner'   flama   fɨlama, ?fil ama
      'flush' (poker) floš̌   fɨloš̂, ?fil ôš

In contrast, only back epenthetic vowels are found in /fr/ clusters: *fransa* 'France', *frak* 'frock', *frank* 'French currency', *franjala* 'type of bread'. Apparently, /l/ may optionally replace /l/ in /fl/ clusters. A further, isolated occurrence of palatal /l̂/ is in *bluz* 'blouse'; palatal /ṛ/ occurs exceptionally in *traž* 'circulation'.

25. We could alternatively suppose that it is the preceding vowel, rather than the consonant, that is opaque. Under this analysis, a context-sensitive rule would assign opacity to any vowel preceding a palatal or palatoalveolar consonant. The treatment given in the text, however, seems preferable, for two reasons. First, it seems that opaque segments can elsewhere be characterized entirely in terms of context-free rules; the recognition of context-sensitive rules of opacity assignment would allow a degree of latitude into the theory that seems at present unwarranted. Second, rules similar to the raising and unrounding rule given here are not infrequent in Altaic languages (see Johnson (1980) for further examples). In all such cases of "preemptive" harmony, the feature value associated with the class of opaque consonants represents the unmarked value of the feature category for that class of consonants. In the present case, for example, the unmarked value of the feature category *round* for palatal consonants is [−round]. This relationship can be most naturally explained if we regard the consonant, rather than the vowel as the opaque element.

Syllabification and Syllable Changing Rules in French*

Roland Noske
University of Amsterdam/Z.W.O.

0. INTRODUCTION

In this paper, a proposal will be formulated concerning the assignment of syllable structure in French. It will be proposed that syllabification takes place according to the following principles:
- the prohibition against violating the notion of 'possible French syllable'
- the tendency to achieve the lowest possible syllabic markedness.

A new concept of syllabic markedness will be developed, which also takes into account the number of syllables of a given form.

Then, a principled account will be given concerning two syllable changing processes in French, viz. the deletion of schwa and the change of high vowels into glides. It will be shown that these processes, which take place in apparently disparate contexts, can be accounted for in a principled and natural way if one assumes that they are governed by precisely the same conditions as those that govern syllabification, viz. the prohibition against violating the notion of 'possible French syllable' and the tendency to achieve the lowest possible syllabic markedness.

In section 1, a proposal for syllabification will be formulated. The notion of 'possible French syllable' will be expressed by means of a syllable template and a set of conditions on the cooccurrence of segments. There will be several digressions in order to account for apparent counterexamples to my proposal.

In section 2, the following two rules will be formulated accounting for the processes of schwa-deletion and the change of high vowels into glides (semivocalization):

(1) *Schwa-Deletion*
     ə → ∅

---

* This paper is a revised version of Noske (1981). I would like to thank Irene Vogel and Norval Smith for giving me many valuable suggestions and much of their time. I am also indebted to Wus van Lessen Kloeke and Jaap Spa. I would like to thank Deirdre Wheeler for supplying a number of suggestions for the final version, as well as for corrections to my English. This work has been partially supported by the *Stichting Taalwetenschap*, which is subsidized by the Netherlands Organization for the Advancement of Pure Scientific Research (*ZWO*).

(2) *Semivocalization*
$$\begin{bmatrix} +\text{syll} \\ +\text{high} \end{bmatrix} \rightarrow [-\text{syll}]$$

These two rules will be assumed to be members of a class of rules without environment, to which the following two conditions are applicable. These conditions reflect the same tendencies as those that govern the syllabification process.

(3) *The Syllabification Condition*
    The output of the environmentless rules must be exhaustively syllabifiable.

(4) *The Markedness Condition*
    The environmentless rules *may not* apply if the syllabic markedness value of their output would be higher than that of their input; they *can* apply if the syllabic markedness value of their output is equal to that of their input; they *must* apply if the syllabic markedness value of their output is lower than that of their input.

Many cases of schwa-deletion and semivocalization will be treated, illustrating the working of the rules and the conditions. Also, some other proposals will be critically examined demonstrating that in those proposals certain facts have to be explicitly stated, while in my theory they can be explained in a natural way.

In an appendix, it will be shown that the metrical proposals put forth by Selkirk (1978) and Vergnaud and Halle et al. (1978) contain a number of inconsistencies.

1. THE ASSIGNMENT OF SYLLABLE STRUCTURE IN FRENCH.

As is commonly known, the syllabic structure of a given string of segments is highly predictable in a great many languages. This had led linguists to devise syllabification mechanisms which assign syllabic structure to phonological strings.[1] Most of these theories are based on the well-known *onset-rime* bipartition, advocated by Selkirk (this volume), Kaye and Lowenstamm (1982) and Vergnaud and Halle et al. (1978), among others. According to this assumption the syllable is divided into two parts: the *onset*, containing all material prior to the syllabic *peak* (or *nucleus*, usually consisting of a vowel; however in some languages other segments may function as a syllabic peak) and the *rime*, containing the remainder of the material in the syllable.

Syllabification in French

(5) σ   (σ = syllable
    /\   O = onset
   O R   R = rime)

Another feature of most syllabification proposals is the notion of a 'possible syllable' in a given language. This notion is embodied in one way or another in the proposals of Kuryłowicz (1948), Vennemann (1972), Hooper (1972), Kahn (1976), Vogel (1977), Broselow (1979), Lowenstamm (1979), Selkirk (this volume), among others. In my syllabification proposal for French, I will assume the *onset-rime* bipartition as a universal of syllable structure. I will also assume that the notion of 'possible syllable' plays an important role in the assignment of syllabic structure. For this reason, I will discuss the notion of 'possible French syllable' in detail. During that discussion I will postulate the existence of monophonematic diphthongs in French, i.e. diphthongs which constitute a single phoneme.

I will then show that syllabification does not take place at the underlying level in French, but at some intermediate stage in the derivation after the application of at least one phonological rule.

Finally, I will propose a syllabification mechanism for French, making use of the principle of syllabification to lowest possible markedness.

1.1. The notion of 'possible French syllable'.

In addition to the universal *onset-rime* bipartition mentioned in (5), I will assume a language specific part of the syllable structure. It will be expressed by means of a syllable template as in Selkirk (this volume), as well as by a set of conditions on the cooccurrence of segments. The following template will be assumed:

(6) 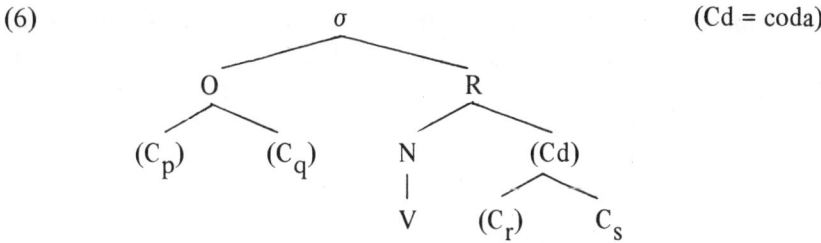   (Cd = coda)

It should be noted that according to this template, the onset may be empty, but the rime must contain at least one segment. Some phonologists allow for empty rimes in which segments are inserted (see, e.g., Lowenstamm (1979) for Old English and Yiddish and ter Mors (1981, 1982) for Klamath). For French, however, there is little or no evidence for such extensive epenthesis processes. There is thus no reason to assume that a French rime may be empty at any stage of the derivation.

Another thing to be noted is that the rime may contain an optional coda, but that this coda, if present, cannot be empty.

In addition to the template given in (6), I will adopt an auxiliary template. This template will account for the sequences of *s* + obstruent which can occur in French onsets and codas. These sequences would otherwise be excluded by the conditions on the cooccurrence of segments which will be given in (10), below. The auxiliary template expresses the fact that an *s* + obstruent cluster may be analyzed as one obstruent.

(7) *auxiliary template*

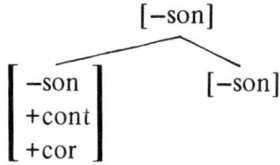

This template is to be interpreted in accordance with the Feature Percolation Convention (FPC) proposed by Vergnaud (1979):

(8) FPC: If a node in a tree is labelled with a particular feature or feature complex, then all segments dominated by the node in question must possess the feature or features.

As the reader will notice, the auxiliary template (7) is rather like the auxiliary template proposed by Selkirk (this volume) in order to account for similar phenomena in English.

The set of conditions on the cooccurrence of segments applicable to the main syllable template (6) will refer to the following strength hierarchy which I will assume for French. This hierarchy is similar to the language-universal strength scales proposed by Jespersen (1920) and de Saussure (1915), rather like the strength scale Hooper (1976) proposes for Spanish, and identical to the one proposed by Vogel (1977):

(9) *a strength scale for French*
obstruents/nasals/liquids/glides
    4   3   2   1

The following conditons on the main syllable template (6) will refer to the above strength scale:

Syllabification in French

(10) a set of conditions on the main syllable template
    i. $p > q$
    ii. if $q = 2$, then $p = 4$
    iii. $r = 2$
    iv. if $r = 2$, then $s = 4$

Note that C_r is optional, thus condition iii. does not imply that condition iv. is automatically fulfilled. Conditions i. and ii. express the fact that a French *onset* can consist of a cluster of obstruent+nasal[2], obstruent+liquid, or nasal+glide, as well as liquid+glide, but not of a cluster of two obstruents[3], two nasals, two liquids, two glides, nasal+liquid. Conditions iii. and iv. express the fact that a French *coda* may consist of a cluster of liquid+obstruent[4], but cannot consist of two obstruents[5], two nasals, two liquids[6], two glides, liquid+nasal[7], nasal+obstruent[8].

1.2. Monophonematic diphthongs.

The syllable template (6) and the set of conditions (10) exclude onsets consisting of a stop+liquid+glide cluster. Yet these onsets seem to appear abundantly in French. Examples are given in (11).

(11) a. [trwa]   'three'   (trois)
       b. [trɥit]   'trout'   (truite)
       c. [plɥi]   'rain'   (pluie)
       d. [brɥi]   'noise'   (bruit)
       e. [grwɛ̃]   'muzzle' (groin)

I will argue here that the phonetic glide+vowel sequences in these forms are in fact single phonemes, just as e.g. affricates are often considered single phonemes. There are two arguments for this assumption.

The first argument concerns the fact that glides followed by a vowel are normally in free alternation with a homorganic high vowel in French, cf. (12).

(12) a. [lue] ~ [lwe]   'to rent'   (louer)
       b. [nier] ~ [nje]   'to deny' (nier)
       c. [ilia] ~ [ilja]   'there is' (il y a)
       d. [luɛst] ~ [lwɛst] 'the West' (l'Ouest)

In the forms in (13) however, where the high vowel is preceded by a tautosyllabic obstruent+liquid cluster, the pronunciation with a glide is not possible[9]:

(13) a. [griɛf] *[grjɛf] 'grievance' (grief)
       b. [adriɛ̃] *[adrjɛ̃] 'Adrien'   (Adrien)

262   Roland Noske

In my theory this is accounted for by the fact that the forms in (13) are not in line with the notion of 'possible French syllable' as expressed by the syllable template (6). The forms in (11) do not seem to obey the syllable template nor do they display the otherwise normal alternation between the glide and an homorganic high vowel, cf. the impossible pronuciations in 11'[10]:

(11')   a.   *[trua]
        b.   *[tryit]
        c.   *[plyi]
        d.   *[bryi]
        e.   *[gruɛ]

It can thus be established that the glide-vowel sequences in (11) differ from other glide-vowel sequences in two ways:

   (i) they occur in the environment OL___;
   (ii) their glides do not alternate freely with a homorganic high vowel.

The apparent aberrations in the behaviour of these glide-vowel sequences can be explained in a natural way if it is assumed that these sequences are single phonemes.

   Part of the argument above is in fact a classic argument for analyzing a sequence of sounds as a single segment. Cf. the following rule established by Trubetzkoy (1969:58):

(14)   *Trubetzkoy's rule IV for monophonematic evaluation*:
       "a potentially monophonematic combination of sounds (...) must be evaluated as the realization as a single phoneme, if it is treated as a single phoneme; that is if it occurs in those positions in which phoneme clusters are not permitted in the language."

The second argument for postulating the existence of diphthongal phonemes in French can be found in the existence of alternations like those in (15):

(15)   a.   ɛ~wa   : verra   – voir   '(he) will see – to see'
       b.   {ø/u}~ɥi   : peux   – puisse   '(he) can   – (he) can (sub-
                          pouvons   (we) can   junctive)'
       c.   ə~jɛ   : tenir   – tienne   'to hold – (he) holds (subjunctive)'

Syllabification in French

This argument is used by Kaye and Lowenstamm (1980, 1981a) in connection with a slightly different assumption[11]. They also note that it is only wa~wɛ̃, ɥi, jɛ~jɛ̃ that can be found in the environment OL___ or that can be found in words where the glide does not alternate freely with a homorganic high vowel. It can thus be inferred that these sounds must form part of the phoneme inventory of French.

1.3. The point in the derivation where syllabification applies.

In this subsection, I will argue that syllabification does not take place at the underlying level in French, but at a later stage, after the application of at least one rule. For the sake of the argument, we first have to consider some examples of the working of the well-known process of consonant truncation in French. Consider the forms in (16):

(16) a. petit ami   /pətit#ami/   [pətitami]   'little friend'
      b. petit papa /pətit#papa/ [pətipapa]   'little papa'
      c. cher ami   /ʃɛr#ami/   [ʃɛrami]   'dear friend'
      d. cher papa   /ʃɛr#papa/   [ʃɛrpapa]   'dear papa'

In the phonetic form of (16b) the second *t* has been deleted. Confronted with these data, one may think that they are the result of a syllable sensitive rule which deletes obstruents in syllable-final position. Spa (1975) takes this position, but also indicates two important problems connected with the analysis of the truncation process as a syllable sensitive rule.

For the first problem we must look at the form in (17) (Spa (1975:81)):

(17)   petit rat   /pətit#rat/   [pətira]   'little rat'

In (17) the word-final *t* of /pətit/ has been deleted (as well as that in /rat/ but this latter deletion does not concern us here), due to the process of consonant truncation. If this process were indeed a syllable sensitive process, it could be inferred that the word-final *t* of /pətit/ is in syllable-final position at the point of the derivation at which the truncation process applies. Now look at the forms in (18) and (19):

(18)   petit trou /pətit#tru/ [pətitru] 'little hole'

(19)   petite roue /pətit+ə#ru/ [pətitru] 'little wheel'

These forms receive the same pronunciation and in both cases native speakers locate the syllable boundary to the left of the *tr* cluster[12]. In fact an intervocalic *tr* cluster is always incorporated in the onset of the second syllable in French. Returning to the form in (17), we see that the second *t* of /pətit#rat/, which is part of an intervocalic *tr* cluster, cannot be in the onset of the latter syllable at the point in the derivation at which the truncation process takes place, if it is assumed that this process is a syllable sensitive process consisting of the deletion of syllable-final obstruents. This contradiction between the distribution of syllabic structure in the phonetic forms in (18, 19) and the intermediate structure at which the (allegedly) syllable sensitive truncation process applies in (17) could be resolved by assuming that word boundaries are initially boundaries for syllabification, and that a resyllabification process ignoring word boundaries takes place after the truncation process has applied. This latter assumption, however, would produce another problem: it would imply that the second *t* in (16a), /pətit#ami/, would find itself in syllable-final position at the point in the derivation at which truncation applies because there is a word boundary following it. This would result in the deletion of this *t*, thus incorrectly yielding *[pətiami].

The second problem connected with the analysis of French consonant truncation as a syllable sensitive rule concerns the fact that no instances can be found of the truncation process taking place morpheme internally. This fact in itself is not surprising because morpheme-internal syllable-final obstruents would always be deleted and would consequently be lost in the lexicon. The real problem, however, is that there are many everyday words in French which *are* pronounced with a morpheme-internal syllable-final obstruent, e.g. *rester* [rɛste] 'to stay', *espérer* [ɛspere] 'to hope'.

The two problems mentioned above disappear if it is assumed that the process of consonant truncation in French is not the result of a syllable sensitive rule, but rather of a rule referring to morpheme and word boundaries[13].

Having shown that it is better to assume that the truncation phenomena in French are the result of a rule referring to morpheme and word boundaries rather than to syllable boundaries, I will now give an argument against the assumption that syllabification takes place at the underlying level. Consider the form in (20):

(20)   ils sont petits   /pətit+z/

If the syllabification applies prior to the application of the truncation rule (which deletes the *t* as well as the *z*) the syllabification of *petits* would be as in (21):

(21)

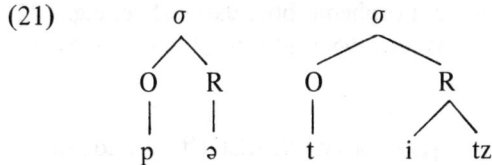

This would mean that *tz* would form the coda of the second syllable. Such a coda however, never shows up at the surface in French[14]. The notion of 'possible French syllable' (as defined in section 1.1.) would thus have to be extended to include a coda consisting of a *tz* cluster, which would only occur in underlying syllables. This is far from elegant, especially since *tz* would constitute a rather marked coda because it violates the well-known sonority or strength hierarchy as proposed by Jespersen (1920), Saussure (1915) and Hooper (1976): a fricative is considered to be less 'strong' or more 'sonorous' than a voiceless stop. Its unmarked position with regard to the voiceless stop is on the nucleus side of the stop, i.e. to the left of the stop. But in a *tz* coda, the position of the fricative is on the other side of the stop, next to the syllable boundary. Thus French would have to be marked for this exception to the sonority hierarchy, purely on the grounds that an underlying syllable, not a phonetic one, displays this order of segments. This would lead to a complication of the grammar.

If one adopts Lowenstamm's position, which is that syllabic structure is present in the lexicon, the argument dealing with the extension of the notion of 'possible syllable' no longer holds because Lowenstamm does not use this notion in his theory. But the fact remains that underlyingly the rather marked *tz* coda has to be assumed.

All these problems can be solved if one assumes that the initial syllabification takes place later in the derivation, a position adopted by Broselow (1979) for Egyptian Arabic. In her article, Broselow shows that two sandhi rules of this language are not at all simplified if their environment is described in terms of syllable structure. She thus shows that there is no need for syllabification rules to apply at the underlying level. I refer the reader to her article for the details; she also gives an ordering hypothesis to which I will return below. In Noske (1981) I showed that the data given by Broselow *force* us to assume a late syllabification in Egyptian Arabic.

The fact that syllabification must take place at a later stage than the underlying level in French as well as in Egyptian Arabic may not be coincidental. In both languages, syllabification takes place across word boundaries and segments belonging to two different words may be syllabified together — a phenomenon traditionally called *enchaînement* by French grammarians. In this respect, French and Egyptian Arabic appear to be very different from, e.g., German in which syllabification is blocked by word boundaries and even some morpheme boundaries. See, e.g., (22) and (23), in which the glottal stops have been inserted by a process triggered by a syllable initial vowel:

(22) Zahnarzt /t^{s}an#art^{s}t/ [tsan ʔartst] 'dentist' ('tooth doctor')

(23) Verabredung /vər+ap+red+uŋ/ [vərʔapreduŋ] 'appointment'

The relationship between late initial syllabification and syllabification across word boundaries may be due to the fact that this syllabification takes place at a point in the derivation at which syntactic and morphological information is no longer available to phonological rules.

We now come to the question of whether syllabification should take place once only or whether there is resyllabification. Broselow (1979) formulates the following ordering hypothesis (p. 368), which she assumes would replace the hypothesis that syllabification takes place at the underlying level:

(24) Rules which insert, delete, or change the position of vowels in a string must precede rules of syllable structure assignment and therefore must also precede all rules which crucially refer to syllable structure.

A counterexample to this hypothesis is provided by the French forms in (25):

(25) a. bon /bɔn/ [bɔ̃] 'good' (masc.)
     b. bonne /bɔn+ə/ [bɔ̃n] 'good' (fem.)

The rule of nasalization in French, which deletes a nasal consonant in syllable-final position and nasalizes the preceding vowel, has applied in (25a). This rule does not apply in (25b) even after the deletion of the schwa. It should be inferred, then, that the rule of nasalization which crucially refers to syllable structure is ordered before the rule which deletes the schwa. Thus syllable structure has to be present at the point of the derivation at which the rule deleting the schwa applies, which means that the assignment of the syllable structure has already taken place at this stage of the derivation. Because the rule deleting the schwa destroys part of the syllable structure, it has to be assumed that a resyllabification takes place after the application of the rule deleting the schwa. It thus has to be assumed that syllabification has to take place more than once. It must also be concluded that Broselow's ordering hypothesis, however attractive, must be rejected.

1.4. The syllabification rules.

Now that the notion of 'possible French syllable' has been defined and that we have seen that syllabification cannot take place at the underlying level in French, we can proceed to define the syllabification process. Apart from a proposal by Basbøll[15] and one by Lowenstamm which I will discuss below, essentially only one principle has been proposed to govern the process of syllabification: the Maximal Cluster Approach (MCA), as it is termed by Lowenstamm (1979, 1981). The principle is based on a claim by non-generative phonologists, e.g. Kuryłowicz (1948), according to whom consonant clusters are possible syllable onsets and codas only if they are observed word-initially and word-finally respectively. It has been formalized in different versions by Kahn (1976), Vogel (1977) and Selkirk (this volume), among others. The essence of these proposals is that a given string is syllabified in three stages:

(i) one syllable is associated with each [+syll] segment of the string.
(ii) a maximum number of consonants preceding each [+syll] segment is associated with the syllable containing the relevant [+syll] segment. The consonants must form a permissible word-initial cluster.
(iii) the remaining consonants are associated with the syllable containing the [+syll] segment preceding them. These consonants must form a permissible word-final cluster[16].

It has been pointed out by Lowenstamm (1979: 38; 1981: 589) that this approach is inadequate for French. The MCA would syllabify words like

(26) aspirer   [aspire]   'to breath'

(27) ausculter [ɔskylte]   'to auscultate'

(28) astuce   [astys]   'wit'

as (. indicates a syllable boundary):

(26') .a.spi.re.

(27') .ɔ.skyl.te.

(28') .a.stys.

These syllabifications, however, are incorrect. The correct ones are:

(26″) .as.pi.re.

(27″) .ɔs.kyl.te.

(28″) .as.tys.

Lowenstamm uses the rule of Closed Syllable Adjustment (which changes e and ɔ to ɛ in closed syllables) to motivate this distribution of syllable boundaries. He shows that this rule apparently functions to produce ɛ in the second members of pairs as:

(29) a. étudiant   [etydjã]   'student'
     b. estudiantin [ɛstydjãtɛ̃]   'typical of students'

(30) a. gérer   [ʒere]   'to manage'
     b. gestion   [ʒɛstjɔ̃]   'management'

(31) a. fêter   [fete]   'to celebrate'
     b. festin   [fɛstɛ̃]   'festive'

It can be seen that in forms like (29b), (30b) and (31b) the s must belong to the first syllable because the rule of Closed Syllable Adjustment has applied. Lowenstamm provides additional motivation for the syllabification in (26″), (27″) and (28″) by mentioning the fact that there are many French words starting with ɛ followed by s + stop, as in (32), but no words starting with e followed by s + stop.

(32) a. Esquimau   [ɛskimo]   'Eskimo'
     b. espoir   [ɛspwar]   'hope'
     c. estomac   [ɛstoma]   'stomach'

The MCA wrongly syllabifies (26), (27) and (28) as (26′), (27′) and (28′) respectively because *sp, st* and *sk* are possible French word-initial clusters as can be seen in (33):

(33) a. spécial   [spesjal]   'special'
     b. station   [stasjɔ̃]   'station'
     c. scandale   [skãdal]   'scandal'

This type of onset is provided for in my definition of 'possible French syllable' by the auxiliary template (7). A possible remedy for the wrong predictions made by MCA could be provided by assuming a readjustment rule, transferring the s from the onset to the coda of the previous syllable

Syllabification in French

if it is preceded by a vowel and followed by a plosive. This solution has been adopted by Selkirk (this volume). Unfortunately no independent motivation can be found for such a readjustment process[17].

As an alternative to the MCA Lowenstamm (1979: 97) proposes two principles, given here as (33):

(33) a. Principle I – minimize the number of syllables
  b. Principle II – minimize the degree of markedness of each syllable.

Lowenstamm uses these principles in his language universal syllabification proposal, which is in fact a *re*syllabification proposal because Lowenstamm assumes syllabic structure to be present in the lexicon. He also assumes that syllabification takes place persistently. In section 1.3. I showed that syllabic structure cannot be present at the underlying level in French, but has to be assigned later in the derivation. Hence it cannot be present in the lexicon[18]. I have also shown that syllabification in French has to take place more than once during the derivation. Given this state of affairs, I will adopt the intuitively sound idea of a persistent syllabification, but I will change it to the hypothesis that syllabification is persistent *once it has first applied*.

Let us now return to the principles in (33). Lowenstamm proposes Principle I because his framework allows for zero rimes. Without Principle I, a word like *iti* could have a structure like:

(34)
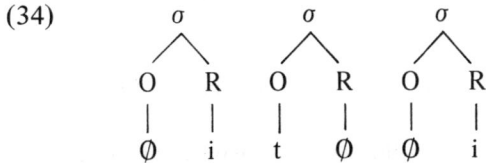

If one rejects the possibility of zero rimes in French, as I do, Principle I appears to become superfluous. I will use the idea behind this principle, however, in my syllabification proposal for French which I will give shortly, for reasons that will be explained.

But first, consider Principle II in (33). Concerning this principle, the question can be asked how one is to decide about the markedness of a given syllable. The following markedness metric is given by Kaye and Lowenstamm (1981b:292) (also in Lowenstamm (1979:62)):

(35) onset   rime   markedness
      C   V   0
      ∅   ∅   1
      CC   VC   2
      CCC   VCC   3
      $C_1...C_n$ $VC_1...VC_{n-1}$ n

This metric treats onsets and rimes separately. Kaye and Lowenstamm claim that the markedness for syllables should not be computed by adding the markedness of the onset to that of the rime. Yet, Kaye and Lowenstamm used the concept of syllabic markedness, by which they mean an ordered pair whose first member is the markedness specification of the onset and the second the markedness specification of the rime (Kaye and Lowenstamm (1981b:295), Lowenstamm (1979:67))[19].

It is unclear, however, how the markedness metric in (35) should evaluate the syllabification of the forms in (26), (27) and (28), which are used by Lowenstamm himself in order to show the inadequacy of the MCA. The correct syllabification of (26), displayed in (26"), would have the following markedness values for onsets and rimes according to the markedness scale in (35):

(36)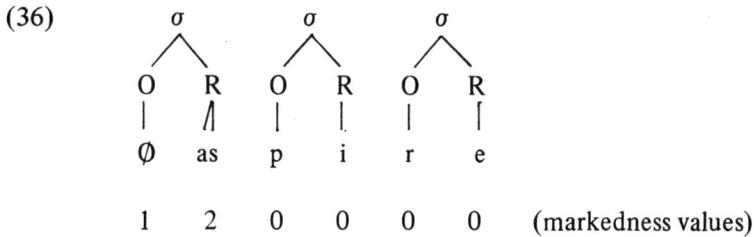

The syllabification that is predicted by the MCA (displayed in (26')) would have the following markedness values for onsets and rimes:

(37)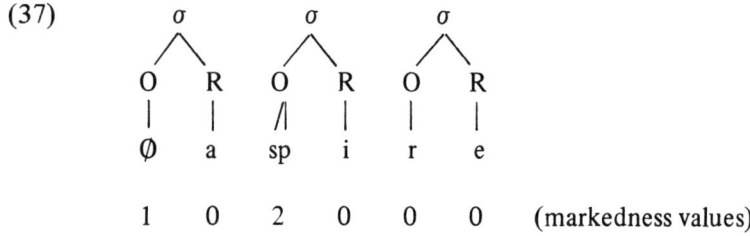

The difference between (36) and (37) is that in (36), the coda of the first syllable has markedness value 2, and the onset of the second syllable markedness value 0, while in (37), the situation is reversed. Principle II

Syllabification in French

in (33) cannot predict the correct syllabification, because it says nothing about the way the markedness values are spread over the word (or the higher prosodic unit which constitutes boundaries for syllabification). Thus Principle II makes no prediction with respect to the correct syllabification of words like [aspire].

This might lead the reader to the conclusion that this principle should be rejected. I think, however, that such a conclusion would be premature. The idea that syllabification is governed by a tendency to achieve the lowest possible markedness is a potentially insightful principle. It allows us to account for the syllabic divisions within a string of segments without resorting to otherwise unmotivated readjustments. Rather than trying to define yet another principle governing the syllabification process, it seems better to focus our attention on the markedness scale in (35). This markedness scale treats a VC rime on a par with a CC onset. There are however many languages that can have VC rimes, but not CC onsets. The reverse situation, however, does not occur. This suggests that a VC rime is less marked than a CC onset. Also, there is no case in which the rime will receive markedness value 1, because the syllable template in (6) does not allow for zero rimes. I therefore tentatively assume the following markedness scale, which replaces Kaye and Lowenstamm's markedness scale in (35):

(38) | onset | rime | markedness value |
|---|---|---|
| C | V | 0 |
| ∅ | VC | 1 |
| CC | VCC | 2 |
| CCC | VCCC | 3 |
| $C_1...C_n$ | $VC_1...C_n$ | n |

Principle II in (33) can now predict the correct syllabification of [aspire]. According to the markedness scale in (38), the markedness of the onsets and the rimes in (26') and (26") will be:

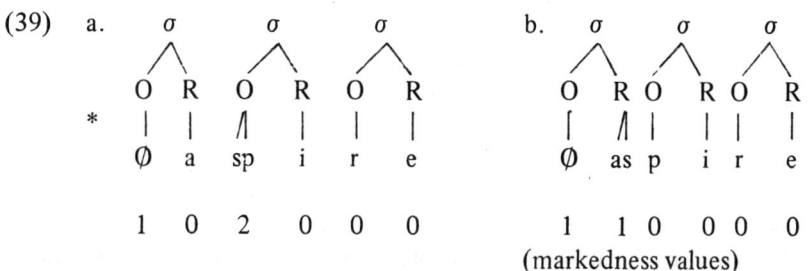

(markedness values)

As one can see, the syllabification in (39b) only has two onsets or rimes with markedness values 1, while (39a) has a rime with markedness value 1 and an onset with markedness value 2. Because of the lower marked markedness, Principle II in (33) will select (39b) as the correct syllabification.

At this point, something must still be decided about Principle II. Probably, Lowenstamm proposed this principle only in view of cases like the French form /lav+e/ 'to wash'. Because of this assumption that syllable structure is present in the lexicon, the structure of the lexical part of this form will underlyingly be as in (40):

(40)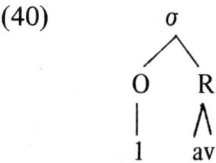

A morphological rule will now create the form in (41) (with markedness values according to Kaye and Lowenstamm's markedness scale in (35):

(41)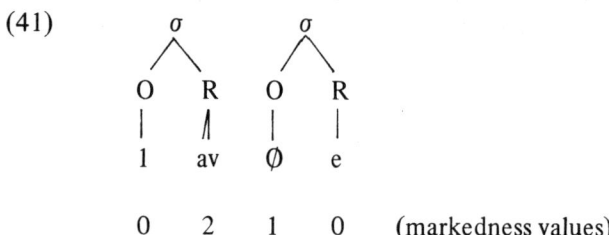

Because of Principle II, the string will be resyllabified as:

(42)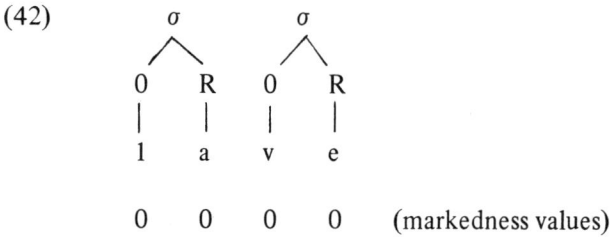

In this case, the markedness values of all onsets and rimes have decreased or remained the same. In the case of the choice between (39a) and (39b) however, the markedness value 2 of the onset of the second syllable in (39b) has to be evaluated in terms of the markedness value 1 of the rime of the first syllable in (39b). As a result, it may be concluded that it is the sum of the markedness values of the onsets and rimes of a given form

Syllabification in French

that must be considered. This is why I introduce here the notion of *syllabic markedness of the prosodic unit*. The prosodic unit meant here is the unit that constitutes the boundaries for syllabification, and which as we have seen above can vary considerably from language to language.

(43) The syllabic markedness of the prosodic unit can be computed in the following way:
    i. determine the markedness of all onsets and rimes by means of the markedness scale in (38);
    ii. add the markedness values together and add 1 to the sum of the markedness values for each syllable.

The second clause in (43ii) is based on the assumption that a form consisting of *n* syllables is less marked than a form consisting of *n*+1 syllables, other things being equal (e.g. in the case of a string of CV syllables). In fact, this clause just incorporates Principle I of (33) (reduction of the number of syllables) into the principle of syllabification to lowest possible markedness. The idea will receive further motivation in section 2 when I discuss schwa-deletion and semivocalization.

The syllabic markedness values for the two possible syllabifications of [aspire] are:

(44) a.

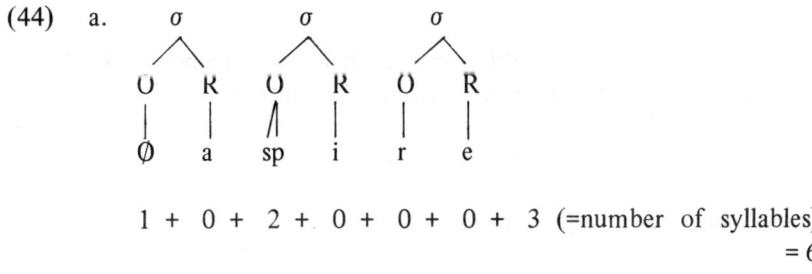

$1 + 0 + 2 + 0 + 0 + 0 + 3$ (=number of syllables)
$= 6$

b.

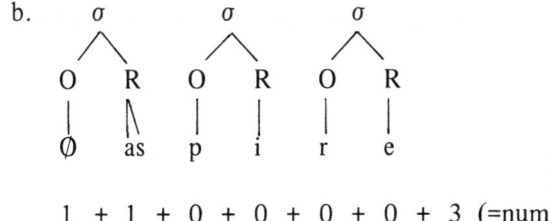

$1 + 1 + 0 + 0 + 0 + 0 + 3$ (=number of syllables)
$= 5$

The principle of syllabification to lowest possible markedness correctly predicts that (44b) is the correct syllabification.

274   *Roland Noske*

1.5.   A summary of the syllabification proposal.

At this point, it seems useful to give a summary of the proposals on syllabification made above. I propose that syllabification in French takes place as follows:

(45) i. Syllabification does not take place at the underlying level, but at a later stage, after the application of the truncation rule;
      ii. once the initial syllabification has taken place, (re-)syllabification takes place persistently.

(46) Syllabification takes place according to the following principles:
      i. syllabification must be wellformed according to the templates in (6) and (7), subject to the conditions in (10) (which refer to the strength scale in (9);
      ii. minimize the syllabic markedness (determined by the markedness scale (38) and the number of syllables) of the prosodic unit which constitutes the domain for syllabification.

1.6.   Stop+liquid clusters and resyllabification under the influence of stress.

The proposal on syllabification in French has still to be modified and elaborated on two points. The first one concerns the behaviour of stop+liquid clusters. The syllabification proposal that I have made above would predict the wrong syllabification for words like (47):

(47) librement   /librəmã/   'freely'

According to the proposal, (48a) would be selected as the correct syllabification, because its syllabic markedness is lower than that of (48b):

(48) a.

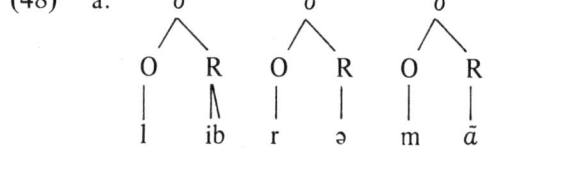

0 + 1 + 0 + 0 + 0 + 0 + 3 (=number of syllables)
= 4

b.

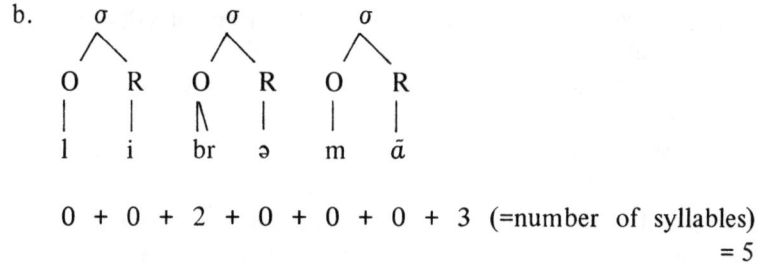

0 + 0 + 2 + 0 + 0 + 0 + 3 (=number of syllables)
= 5

This is clearly the wrong prediction. There are no instances in French in which segments of a stop+liquid sequence are not tautosyllabic[20]. I will hypothesize, therefore, that the two segments in such a sequence cannot be split up into two different syllables. Moreover, I will hypothesize that a stop+liquid cluster receives markedness value 1 instead of the 2 which it would get according to the markedness scale in (38). The major reason for this will be given in section 2.1. (on schwa-deletion), but at this point some motivation can be given. Pillinger (1982) has shown by means of evidence from stress and metre that CLclusters in Latin behave differently from clusters consisting of a consonant followed by another consonant that is not a liquid. This can be seen in (49), which is reproduced from Pillinger's article:

(49)   –CC   –CL
stress: renders penultimate heavy   does not render penult. heavy
metre: renders syllable heavy   does not render syll. heavy
degemination: occurs if one C is part does not occur if C is part
              of a geminate ciuster   of a geminate cluster

An illustration of the different behaviour by CL clusters from that of CC clusters in the case of degemination is provided by the forms in (50) and (51):

(50)
    a.   ascendō   [askendoo] (←asskendoo←) /ad+skendoo/ 'to ascend'
    b.   agnoscō   [agnoskoo] (←aggnoskoo←) /ad+gnoskoo/ 'to become
                                                                                                                  acquainted with'

(51) a.   acclamō   [akklamoo]   /ad+klamoo/ 'to cheer'
     b.   effringō   [effringoo]   /eks+frangoo/ 'to break off'

This evidence from Latin provides motivation for the assumption that a CL cluster is less marked than a CC cluster, and that under certain circumstances it acts as a single consonant[21].

Here, a word must be said about the concept of syllabic markedness developed above. It might strike the reader as odd that it is only the number of segments of a given form that determines the syllabic markedness of a given form. Indeed, as the above case from Latin shows (as well as the French case in (81), see section 2.1., below) the nature of the segments might also be a factor in determining the syllabic markedness of a given form. In fact a more elaborated concept of syllabic markedness than the one put forth in the present article may have to express the interaction of several, sometimes conflicting, tendencies like: (i) the tendency to achieve a CV syllable, and (ii) the tendency to achieve a maximal onset[22]. The exact nature of this interaction may or may not be different for individual languages.

We come now to the second point where my syllabification proposal needs to be modified. Like Selkirk (this volume), I will assume that a specified resyllabification takes place under the influence of stress. This resyllabification will apply once the stress has been assigned. I will assume that like the general syllabification process, this resyllabification will apply persistently once it has first applied. I will also assume that this resyllabification process takes precedence over the general syllabification process during its reapplications. Also, for reasons that will become clear in section 2.1., I will assume that the syllable templates can be violated by this resyllabification process. Thus in a sense this resyllabification process is 'stronger' than the general syllabification process.

The nature of the resyllabification process is as follows: a stressed syllable will attract segments from the onset of the following syllable, if this latter is unstressed. Selkirk (this volume) makes a similar proposal for English, while Hoard (1971) and Basbøll (1972) have integrated the attraction of segments under the influence of stress in their accounts of syllabification in English and Danish respectively. I will tentatively formulate this resyllabification as follows:

(52)
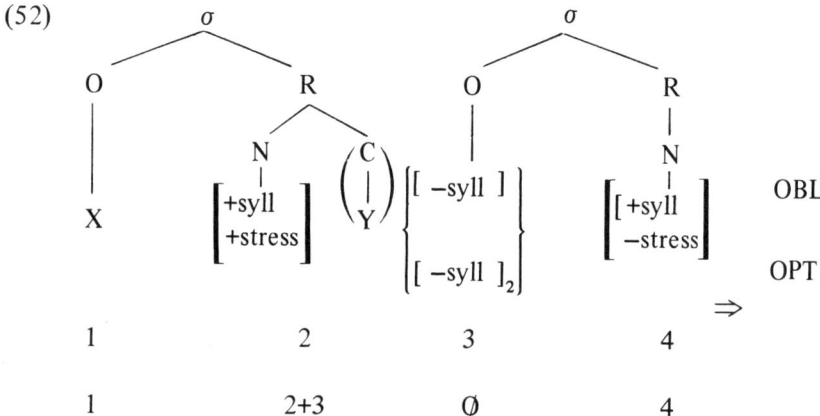

Syllabification in French

In (52) the numbers in the structural analysis and change refer to the material in the onsets and the rimes. The full motivation for this resyllabification rule will be given in section 2.1., in the account of the obligatory deletion of the schwa in (53) and the optional deletion of the schwa in (54):

(53) elle est petite /pətit+ə/ 'she is small'
    ↓
    ∅

(54) astre /astrə/ 'star'
    ↓
    ∅

2. SCHWA-DELETION AND SEMIVOCALIZATION IN FRENCH: A MODULAR APPROACH

In this section I will concentrate on two processes in French: the deletion of schwa and a (semivocalization) process which changes high vowels into glides. It will be shown that the various phenomena of schwa-deletion and semivocalization, which at first sight appear to be of a disparate character, can be accounted for with just two phonological rules which are formulated without an environment. They simply express the fact that a schwa is deleted and that a high vowel turns into a glide. The application of these extremely simple rules will be subject to two conditions which reflect exactly the same principles as the ones that governs the syllabification process, viz. the prohibition against violating the notion of 'possible French syllable' and the tendency to achieve the lowest possible markedness. The idea that there are rules which are stated without an environment and which are subject to certain conditions has proved useful in syntax (see, e.g., Chomsky and Lasnik (1977)).

2.1. French Schwa-Deletion.

Dell (1973, 1980) Selkirk (1978) and Vergnaud and Halle (1978) have all given accounts of the phenomena of schwa-deletion in French. Of these three accounts, that by Dell is by far the most complete as far as the data that have to be accounted for are concerned. Unfortunately, he needs no less than ten rules[23], some of which include quite complicated environments. His account does, however, constitute a good inventory of the facts that have to be accounted for and I will consequently refer to his rules in the course of my account of French schwa-deletion.

The analyses by Selkirk (1978) and Vergnaud and Halle (1978) are of a more principled character. They are based on the metrical theory developed by Liberman and Prince (1977). These analyses are not of primary concern to us here, but will be treated in the appendix to this article.

I now come to my own proposal. As mentioned above, I will assume only one rule of schwa-deletion. The analysis will account for the fact that only schwa, and no other vowel, can be deleted in French, apart from three isolated cases[24]. In fact, it is just this that is expressed by the rule:

(55) *Schwa-Deletion*:

ə → ∅

The rule, which is formulated without an environment, will be assumed to be a member of a class of rules without environments (to which, as will be shown in section 2.2., the rule of Seminvocalization also belongs), to which the following conditions are applicable:

(56) *The Syllabification Condition*:
The output of the environmentless rules must be exhaustively syllabifiable.

(57) *The Markedness Condition*:
The environmentless rules *may not* apply if the syllabic markedness value of their output would be higher than that of their input, they *can* apply if the syllabic markedness value of their output is equal to that of their input, they *must* apply if the syllabic markedness value of their output is lower than that of their input.

The Markedness Condition in (57) can also be expressed by means of the α convention, if it is assumed that the rules of the class of environmentless rules are optional, just as the rules in the Chomsky and Lasnik framework in syntax (like free deletion in Comp, etc.):

(57') *The Markedness Condition* (formalized):
if $S(\alpha A(R)) < S(-\alpha A(R))$, then $* -\alpha A(R)$,
in which S = syllabic markedness value
        A = application
        R = member of the class of environmentless rules.

I will first discuss the Syllabification Condition in (56). This condition need not be stated as an independent condition, because it is in fact a consequence of the persistent character of the syllabification mechanism.

Syllabification in French

In section 1.4., motivation was provided for the assumption that syllabification is persistent once the initial syllabification has applied. In addition, it was shown in section 1.3. (see the forms in (25)) that the rule of Schwa-Deletion is applicable at a place in the derivation where the syllabic structure is already present. Hence, the syllabification mechanism automatically applies to the output of the rule of Schwa-Deletion. The Syllabification Condition in (56), then, follows from the straightforward assumption that if the syllabification mechanism fails to syllabify a given string then any further derivation of that string is blocked. The working of the condition can be seen in the contrast between the possible deletion of schwa in forms like those in (58) and (59) versus the non-deletion of schwa in (60):

(58)
a. pudiquement /pydikəmã/ [pydikmã] 'chastely'
b. bombement /bõbəmã/ [bõbmã] 'bombing'
c. froidement /frwadəmã/ [frwadmã] 'coldly'

(59)
a. débarquement /debarkəmã/ [debarkmã] 'debarcation'
b. escarpement /ɛskarpəmã/ [ɛskarpmã] 'steep slope'
c. heurtement /œrtəmã/ [œrtmã] 'collision'
d. énervement /enɛrvəmã/ [enɛrvmã] 'excitement'
e. renversement /rãvɛrsəmã/ [rãvɛrsmã] 'reversal'
f. émergement /emɛrʒəmã/ [emɛrʒəmã] 'emergence'
g. écorchement /ekɔrʃəmã/ [ekɔrʃmã] 'flaying'
h. sveltement /svɛltəmã/ [svɛltmã] 'slimly'
i. burlesquement /byrlɛskəmã/ [byrlɛskmã] 'burlesquely'
j. manifestement /manifɛstəmã/ [manifɛstmã] 'manifestly'

(60)
a. probablement /prɔbabləmã/ [prɔbabləmã] 'probably'
b. simplement /sẽpləmã/ [sẽpləmã] 'simply'
c. aveuglement /avœgləmã/ [avœgləmã] 'blindly'
d. encerclement /ãsɛrkləmã/ [ãsɛrkləmã] 'encirclement'
e. librement /librəmã/ [librəmã] 'freely'
f. âprement /aprəmã/ [aprəmã] 'rudely'
g. tendrement /tãdrəmã/ [tãdrəmã] 'tenderly'
h. autrement /otrəmã/ [otrəmã] 'differently'
i. maigrement /mɛgrəmã/ [mɛgrəmã] 'meagrely'
j. médiocrement /mediɔkrəmã/ [dediɔkrəmã] 'in a mediocre way'
k. ivrement /ivrəmã/ [ivrəmã] 'in a drunk way'
l. exactement /ɛgzaktəmã/ [ɛgzaktəmã] 'exactly'

The forms in (58) and (59) can also be assumed to contain a schwa underlyingly, because they can also be pronounced with a schwa[25]. The contrast between the forms in (58) and (59) and the forms in (60) is a direct consequence of the Syllabification Condition. This becomes clear if one compares the consonants preceding the schwa in the underlying forms in (58) and (59) to those in (60). In the underlying forms in (59), the schwa is preceded by a liquid+obstruent cluster or an s+obstruent cluster, while in the underlying forms in (58), the schwa is preceded by only one consonant. In both cases the consonant or consonants preceding the schwa constitute a possible coda in French, while the consonant clusters in the forms in (60) do not form a possible French coda[26].

Another example of the working of the condition can be found in the forms in (61) and (62) (these examples are taken from Dell (1973: 231):

(61)   insistera   /ɛ̃sistə+r+a/ [ɛ̃sist(ə)ra] 'will insist'

(62)   soufflera   /suflə+r+a/ [sufləra] *[suflra] 'will whistle'

In the phonetic form in (62), the schwa is obligatorily present, because *fl* does not constitute a possible French coda (except in utterance-final position, this case will be treated below, see (74)).

Additional motivation for the Syllabification Condition is provided by the forms in (63) and (64), which are taken from Dell (1973: 229):

(63)   Henri devrait partir   /ɑ̃ri#dəv+r+ɛ#part+ir/ [ɑ̃rid(ə)vrɛpartir]
        'Henri would have to leave'

(64)   Jacques devrait partir / ʒak#dəv+r+ɛ#part+ir/ [ʒakdəvrɛpartir]
        *[ʒakdvrɛpartir]   'Jacques would have to leave'

The difference between these forms is that in the case of (63) the syllable containing schwa is immediately preceded by a vowel (abstracted away from the syllable boundary), whereas in (64) it is preceded by a consonant. The result of the deletion of schwa in the underlying form would be the consonant sequence *kdvr*. This sequence cannot be analyzed into a possible coda followed by a possible onset, hence the derivation is blocked by the Syllabification Condition. In (63) on the other hand, the deletion of schwa results in the consonant sequence *dvr*, which *is* analyzable into a possible coda (*d*) followed by a possible onset (*vr*).

The Syllabification Condition is partially reflected in the output condition OLICONS proposed by Dell (1976:85; 1980: 215)[27]:

(65)   *OLICONS*:

$$*[-son] \begin{bmatrix} +son \\ +cons \\ -nas \end{bmatrix} [+cons]$$

Syllabification in French

This condition replaces the condition in Dell's rule E-FUT prohibiting OL clusters in the input of this rules (see note 23) and it also accounts for the impossibility of (67b) as a phonetic realization of (66)[28].

(66)　estre nouveau 'new star'

(67)　a. [astrənuvo]　　　b. *[astrnuvo]

Dell's condition OLICONS can be dispensed with by assuming the Syllabification Condition, which as we have seen does not need to be stated independently (in contrast with OLICONS), but follows from the assumption of the persistent character of the syllabification mechanisms.

Coming now to the working of the Markedness Condition, I will give examples of cases in which the rule of Schwa-Condition is made obligatory by the working of the Markedness Condition, then of cases in which Schwa-deletion is optional, and finally of a case in which the Markedness Condition prohibits the deletion of schwa.

First, three cases of obligatory schwa-deletion will be exemplified. In each case, the Markedness Condition blocks the derivation of the string if the rule of Schwa-Deletion does not apply. The first example concerns the form in (68):

(68)　l'or /lə#ɔr/　[lɔr] *[ləɔr] 'the gold'

The resulting syllabic markedness values of the phonetic forms in the case of application and non-application of Schwa-Deletion can be seen in (69a) and (69b) respectively:

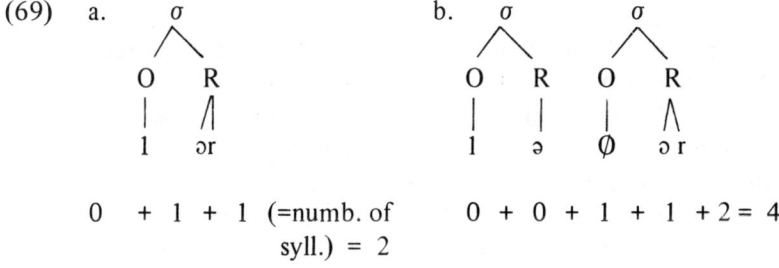

The Markedness Condition prohibits the derivation of the form in (69b), where Schwa-Deletion has *not* applied, because its syllabic markedness value is higher than that of the form in (69a) (the form in which Schwa-Deletion *has* applied). Another example can be found in (70):

(70)　jolie maison / ʒoli+ə#mɛzɔ̃/ [ʒolimɛzɔ̃] *[ʒoliəmɛzɔ̃] 'bonny house'

The resulting syllabic markedness values of the phonetic forms in the case of application and non-application of Schwa-Deletion can be seen in (71a) and (71b) respectively.

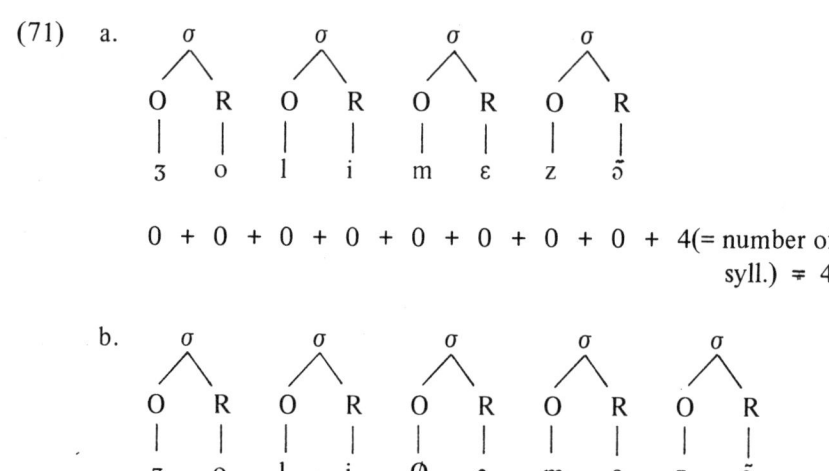

(71) a.

0 + 0 + 0 + 0 + 0 + 0 + 0 + 0 + 4(= number of syll.) = 4

b.

0 + 0 + 0 + 0 + 1 + 0 + 0 + 0 + 0 + 0 + 5
(= number of syll.) = 6

The Markedness Condition prohibits the derivation of the form in (71b) because its syllabic markedness value is higher than that of (71a).

The third example of obligatory schwa-deletion has already been mentioned in (53) and is repeated below:

(72)   elle est petite /ɛl#ɛ#pətit+ə/ [ɛlɛpətit] *[ɛlɛpətitə]

It was hypothesized earlier that the second t in this form is retracted to the preceding syllable by a specified resyllabification which overrules the general principle of syllabification to lowest possible syllabic markedness. This hypothesis was put forward by analogy with similar proposals for English and Danish. Further motivation is provided by the structures for (72) given below in (73). The assumption that the second t in this form has been restricted to the preceding syllable makes it possible to account for the obligatory deletion of schwa here. Compare the two syllabic markedness values derived from deletion and non-deletion of schwa respectively:

Syllabification in French

(73) a.
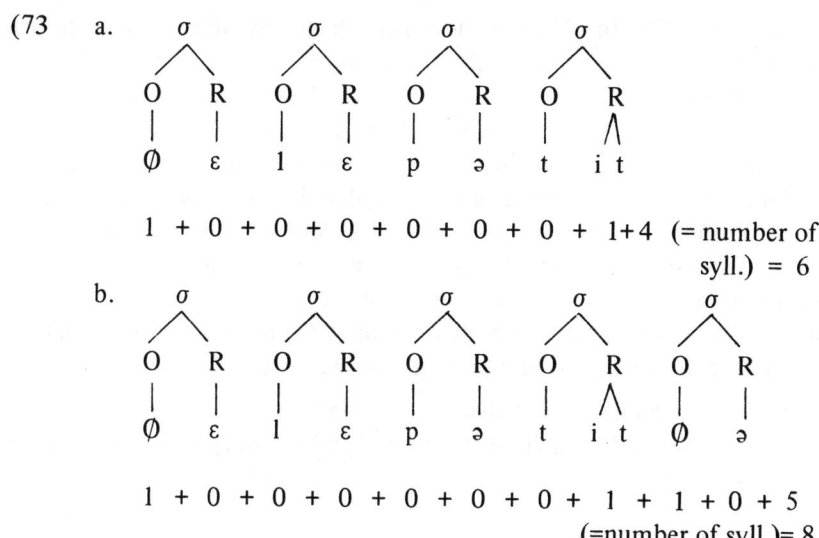

Here again, the Markedness Condition blocks the derivation of the form in (73b) because its syllabic markedness value is higher than that of (73a). If it was not assumed that the second *t* in *petite* was restructured, the deletion of schwa would wrongly be predicted to be optional because the increase in the degree of markedness of the rime of the last syllable by 1 (due to the incorporation of the *t*) would be compensated for by the decrease in the number of syllables by 1[29].

We should now look at the form in (54), repeated here as (74):

(74) astre /astrə/ [astr(ə)] 'star'

In this form the deletion of schwa is optional. The optionality is not due to the Markedness Condition, but rather to the fact that the specified resyllabification under the influence of stress by (52) is optional if there are two consonants following the rightward boundary of the stressed syllable. Thus the two possible syllabic configurations of this form are:

(75)
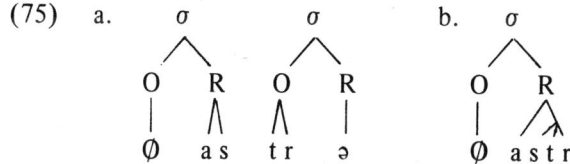

In the form in (75b) the specified resyllabification has applied (recall that this specified resyllabification may violate the syllable template) and the schwa has consequently been obligatory deleted, analogous to the deletion of schwa in (73). In (75a), on the other hand, the deletion of schwa is not possible because the normal syllabification process does not allow for the *tr* cluster to be included in the coda of the previous syllable and the nucleus can also not be empty according to the template in (6). It is the fact that both (75a) and (75b) are possible syllabic configurations associated with the form in (74) that makes the deletion of schwa in (74) appear to be optional. As mentioned, the syllabic configuration in (75b) constitutes a violation of the syllable template and, in this case, of the sonority hierarchy as well. Indeed it is only in cases like these that codas like the one in (75b) cannot occur, i.e. at the end of the prosodic unit which constitutes the domain for syllabification. Compare (76a, b) and (77a, b):

(76) a. probable /prɔbablə/ [prɔbabl(ə)] 'probably'
b. probablement/prɔbablə+mã/ [prɔbabləmã] *[prɔbablmã] / 'probably'

(77) a. (ce train est) le vôtre /lə#vɔtrə/ [ləvɔtr(ə)] '(this train is)yours'
b. votre train /vɔtrə#trɛ̃/ [vɔtrətrɛ̃] *[vɔtrtrɛ̃] 'your train'

The forms in (76a) and (77a) display an optional schwa-deletion analogous to that in (74), but in (76b) and (77b) the schwa which would be deleted is not preceded by a stressed syllable. Since the schwa is not preceded by a stressed syllable, the resyllabification rule (52) cannot apply.

We come now to cases in which the working of the Markedness Condition makes the deletion of schwa optional. Most of the forms in which the deletion of the schwa is optional have the following structure:

(78)   σ   σ
           ╱╲   ╱╲
        X C_o V   C ə Y

The deletion of the schwa in these cases decreases the number of syllables by one, but adds a segment to the rime of the preceding syllable, the result being:

(79)   σ
                 ╱─╲
        X C_o V   C   Y

The result of the deletion of schwa in cases like these is that the syllabic markedness value remains the same, because decreasing the number of syllables by 1 means decreasing the syllabic markedness values by 1, but adding a consonant to the rime increases it by 1. The Markedness Condition thus predicts that the deletion of schwa in cases like these is op-

Syllabification in French

tional. An example can be found in (63) above. More examples are given in (80):

(80)   a. derechef   /dərəʃɛf/   [dər(ə)ʃɛf]   'once more'
       b. revenir   /rə+vən+ir/   [rəv(ə)nir]   'to come back'
       c. je ne crois pas / ʒə#nə#krwa#pa/ [ʒən(ə)krwapa] 'I do not believe'
       d. tu le verras /ty#lə#vɛr+a/   [tyl(ə)vɛra]   'you will see him'

Another example in which schwa-deletion is optional can be found in (61) repeated here as (81):

(81)   insistera   /ɛ̃sistə+r+a/   [ɛ̃sist(ə)ra]   'will insist'

The Markedness Condition would normally block the deletion of schwa in this form, because the deletion would cause the onset of the last syllable to be doubly filled, which increases the markedness value by 2, while the number of syllables only decreases by one, so the overall increase in the syllabic markedness value is 1. Cases like these, however, are accounted for by the provision for stop+liquid clusters made in section 1.6., by which such clusters are assigned syllabic markedness value 1 instead of 2. The above case provides additional motivation for this provision, c.f. the syllabic configurations displayed in (82)[30]:

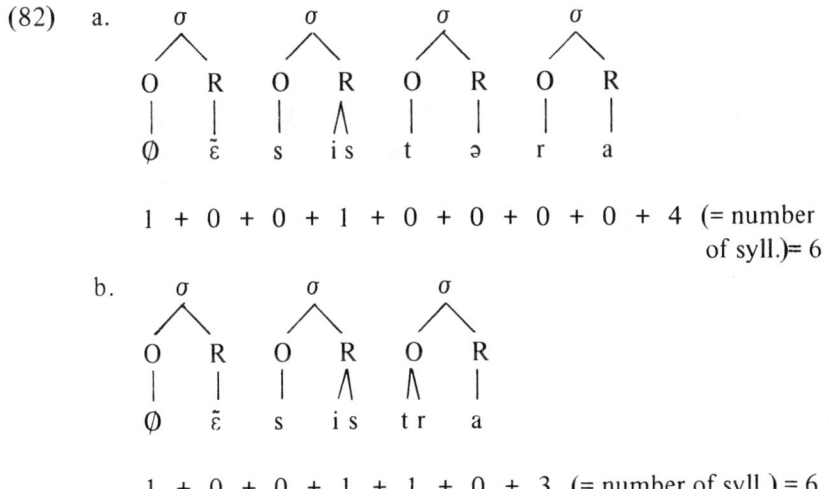

Finally, I will give an example in which the deletion of schwa is blocked by the working of the Markedness Condition. For this, we must consider the underlying form in (83):

(83)   tu devenais   /ty#dəvənɛ/

the three possible phonetic realizations are:

(84)   a. [tydəvənɛ]   b. [tydəvnɛ]   c. [tydvənɛ]

The form in (85), however, is impossible:

(85)   *[tydvnɛ]

The derivation of this form is blocked because its syllabic markedness value is higher than those of (84a, b, c) cf. (86) and (87):

(86) a.

```
     σ         σ         σ         σ
    / \       / \       / \       / \
   O   R     O   R     O   R     O   R
   |   |     |   |     |   |     |   |
   t   y     d   ə     v   ə     n   ɛ
```

0 + 0 + 0 + 0 + 0 + 0 + 0 + 4 (= number of syllables) = 5

b.

```
     σ         σ         σ
    / \       / \       / \
   O   R     O   R     O   R
   |   |     |   /\    |   |
   t   y     d  ə v    n   ɛ
```

0 + 0 + 0 + 1 + 0 + 0 + 3 = 4

c.

```
     σ         σ         σ
    / \       / \       / \
   O   R     O   R     O   R
   |   /\    |   |     |   |
   t   yd    v   ə     n   ɛ
```

0 + 1 + 0 + 0 + 0 + 0 + 3 = 4

(87)

```
      σ           σ
     / \         / \
    O   R       O   R
    |   /\     /\   |
    t   yd    vn   ɛ
```

0 + 1 + 2 + 0 + 2 = 5

Syllabification in French

Having illustrated the working of the Syllabification and Markedness Conditions in the case of schwa-deletion, I will now briefly discuss four cases in which the theory outlined above does not give the right predictions. In two of these cases possible solutions will be given.

The first case concerns examples like the ones in (88), which are taken from Vergnaud and Halle (1978:5-7):

(88) a. souvenir   [suv(ə)nir]   'souvenir'
     b. jalousement [ʒaluz(ə)mã]   'jalously'
     c. passera   [pas(ə)ra]   'will pass'
     d. volera   [vɔl(ə)ra]   'will fly'

Although Vergnaud and Halle claim the schwa deletion as optional, it is obligatory according to Dell (1983; 1980) and most of the native speakers I have been able to consult. Indeed for most speakers of standard French, the deletion of schwa seems to be obligatory if only one intervocalic consonant precedes the schwa, and if there is no word boundary between the consonant and the preceding vowel.

The obligatoriness can be accounted for in two ways. The first one is that the markedness value of the rime does not increase by 1, but by a lower value. This amounts to saying that the decrease in the syllabic markedness value in the forms in (88) caused by the decrease in the number of syllables is not completely compensated for by the increase in the markedness values of the rimes preceding the schwa.

Another solution would be to postulate a resyllabification applying every time a full vowel is followed by a schwa. This means that the idea of a specified resyllabification proposed in section 1.6. (see (52)) is generalized to include resyllabifications under the influence of secondary stress. The schwa then finds itself in a syllable of which the onset is empty. Consequently, the deletion of the schwa decreases the syllabic markedness value of the form as is the case with the forms in (70), (72) and (75b), cf. (89):

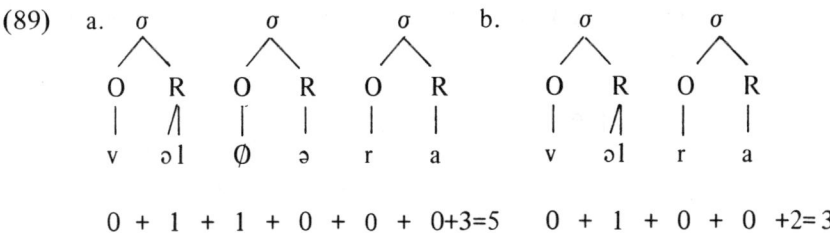

The idea of syllabification according to this principle has been suggested by Basbøll (1978). The contrast between the obligatoriness of the schwa-deletion within one word and the optionality of the schwa-deletion if the syllable preceding the schwa belongs to a different word, may be the result of the optional treatment of a word boundary as a boundary for syllabification. If it *is* a boundary for syllabification, it is consequently also a boundary for the computation of the syllabic markedness values, because the notion of syllabic markedness developed in section 1.4. crucially relates to syllabification. In that case the deletion of schwa would be forbidden. On the other hand, deletion of the schwa would be obligatory if the syllabification process did not respect the word boundary. Unfortunately, the two solutions suggested above are not compatible with other features of my proposal, such as my treatment of the contrast in behaviour between *probable* and *probablement*.

A second problem concerning schwa-deletion has been noted by Dell (1973: 232; 1980: 208). It concerns the forms:

(90) a. hésiteriez /ezitə+r+iez/ [ezitərje] *[ezitrje] 'would hesitate'
    b. volerions /vɔlə+r+iɔ̃z/ [vɔlərjɔ̃] *[vɔlrjɔ̃] 'would fly'

The problem here is that the schwa in these conditional forms cannot be deleted, while the deletion is possible and obligatory for most speakers for some in the corresponding forms of the future:

(91) a. hésiterez /ezitə+rez/ [ezit(ə)re] 'will hesitate'
    b. volerons /vɔlə+r+ɔ̃z/ [vɔl(ə)rɔ̃] 'will fly'[31]

For this problem a straightforward solution can be found. It must be assumed that the morphemes *-ions, -iez* contain underlyingly a glide instead of a high vowel. Evidence for this can be found in the minimal pair:

(92) a. à Lyon /a#liɔ̃/ [aljɔ̃]~[aliɔ̃] 'in Lyons'
    b. allions /al+jɔ̃z/ [aljɔ̃] *[aliɔ̃] '(we) went'

While the form in (92a) can be pronounced with both a high vowel and a glide (the second pronunciation being the result of the application of the rule of Semivocalization, to be treated in section 2.2.), the form in (92b) can only be pronounced with a glide, because it contains a glide underlyingly. The deletion of schwa in (90a), which is now assumed to have as underlying form /ezitə+r+jez/, would cause the onset of the last syllable in this form to become *trj*. This is not a permissible onset, because the syllable templates proposed in (6) and (7) do not allow for an onset consisting of three segments (except if the first and second segments are an *s* and an obstruent respectively), thus the derivation is filtered out by the

Syllabification in French

Syllabification Condition. The deletion of schwa in the form in (90b), now assumed to have as underlying form /vɔlərjɔ̃z/, is blocked by the Markedness Condition. Deletion of the schwa would increase the syllabic markedness value of the form:

(93)

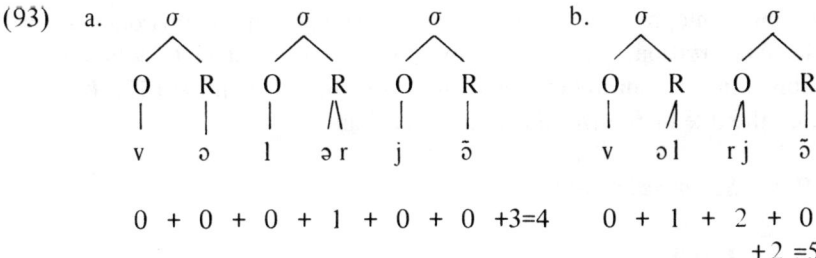

I will come back to the problem involving the verb-endings *-ions, -iez* in section 2.2. when I discuss Semivocalization.

The third problem concerning schwa-deletion is the fact that the deletion of the schwa in the negative particle *ne* takes precedence over the deletion of another schwa. This fact is noted by Dell (1973: 255); 1980: 236). Compare the forms in (94) and (95):

(94) je le demande /ʒə#lə#dəmãdə/ [ʒəldəmã́d]~[ʒələdmã́d]
                                                                                                        'I ask it'

(95) je ne demande pas /ʒə#nə#dəmãdə#paz/ [ʒəndəmã́dpa]
   *[ʒənədmã́dpa] 'I do not ask'

In (94) either the schwa in *le* or the one in the first syllable of *demande* can be deleted, but in (95) only the schwa in *ne* can be deleted. For this problem (for which Dell has formulated a rule that seems entirely adhoc[32]), I see no phonological solution. It can only be stated that the schwa in *ne* is more accessible for deletion than other schwas.

The fourth problem concerns the deletion of schwa in utterance-initial position, in examples like:

(96) a. venez ici /vən+ez#isi/ [vneisi] 'come here'
    b. te fais pas de bile /tə#fɛ#paz#də#bil/ [tfɛpadbil] 'don't worry'
                                                                                                     (slang)

In these cases, the deletion of schwa appears to violate the Markedness Condition, and in the case of (96b) even the Syllabification Condition. Unfortunately, I see no direct solution to this problem, but it may be related to the observation that languages generally allow a wider range of syllable types word-initially and word-finally than word-medially.

2.2. SEMIVOCALIZATION

I now come to the second rule formulated without environment, viz. Semivocalization, and I will show how this rule interacts with the Syllabification Condition (56) and the Markedness Condition (57). I assume that the rule of Semivocalization is stated as:

(97) *Semivocalization*:

$$\begin{bmatrix} +\text{syll} \\ +\text{high} \end{bmatrix} \rightarrow [-\text{syll}]$$

The facts that have to be accounted for are given in (98)[33]:

(98) i. no glide can be preceded by a tautosyllabic OL cluster;
ii. in other cases there exists a free alternation between high vowels and glides in prevocalic position; if a prevocalic glide is preceded by a vowel or if it is in utterance-initial position, however, it cannot alternate with a high vowel.
iii. there are exceptions to the statements in (i) and (ii) in words whose phonetic forms always contain a glide.

I will give examples of each of these cases and I will show how my theory accounts for them. The case in (98 i.) is very straightforward. The Syllabification Condition forbid the application of the rule of Semivocalization because an OLG cluster does not constitute a permissible French onset (cf. the templates in (6) and (7)). Examples are given in (99):

(99) a. Adrien /adriɛ̃/ [adriɛ̃] *[adrjɛ̃] 'Adrien'
b. grief /griɛf/ [griɛf] *[grjɛf] 'grievance'
c. influence /ɛ̃flyãs/ [ɛ̃flyãs] *[ɛ̃flɥãs] 'influence'
d. trouer /tru+e/ [true] *[trwe] 'to punch a hole'
e. publier /pybli+e/ [pyblie] *[pyblje] 'to publish'

Examples of the first clause in (98 ii.), i.e. cases in which the high vowel is in prevocalic position, can be found in (100)[33]:

(100) a. l'ouest /lə#uɛst/ [luɛst]~[lwɛst] 'the west'
b. nier /ni+e/ [nie]~[nje] 'to deny'
c. nuage /nyaʒ/ [nyaʒ]~[nɥaʒ] 'cloud'

Syllabification in French 291

    d.   tu as vu   /ty#a#vy/   [tyavy]~[tɥavy]   'you have seen'
    e.   skier   /ski+e/   [skie]~[skje]   'to ski'
    f.   il y a   /il#i#a/   [ilia]~[ilja]   'there is'

In these cases, the syllabic markedness values resulting from application and non-application of Semivocalization are the same. Hence the Markedness Condition renders the application of Semivocalization optional. Cf. the syllabic configurations in (101):

In (101b), the increase of the syllabic markedness because of the inclusion in the onset of a second segment is compensated for by the decrease in the number of syllables of the form, as well as by the fact that there is no longer an empty onset.

The second part of (98 ii) is exemplified by forms like the ones in (102):

(101) a.   σ   σ   b.   σ

          O R   O R   O   R
          | | | /\   /\ /\
          l   u   ∅ ε s t   l w ε s t

        0 + 0 + 1 + 2 + 2 = 5   2 + 2 + 1 = 5

(102) a.   Paris-Ouest /pari#uɛst/   [pariwɛst] *[pariuɛst] 'Paris-West'
        b.   ouest   /uɛst/   [wɛst] *[uɛst] 'west' (spoken in isolation)

In these cases, non-application of Semivocalization would result in a higher syllabic markedness value than application, cf. (103) and (104):

(103) a.   σ   σ   σ   σ

        O R   O R   O R   O   R
        | | | | | | | /\
        p   a   r   i   ∅   u   ∅ ε s t

      0 + 0 + 0 + 0 + 1 + 0 + 1 + 2 + 4 = 8

    b.   σ   σ   σ

        O R   O R   O   R
        | | | | | /\
        p   a   r   i   w ε s t

      0 + 0 + 0 + 0 + 0 + 2 + 3 = 5

(104) a.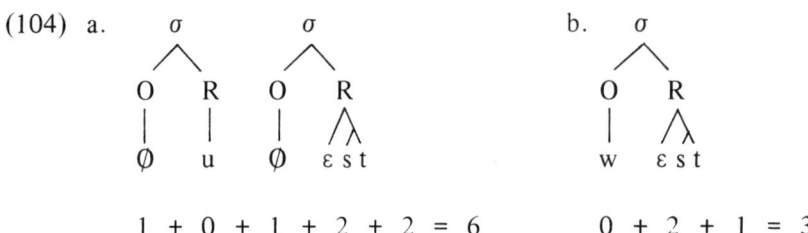

b.

1 + 0 + 1 + 2 + 2 = 6   0 + 2 + 1 = 3

Because of the higher syllabic markedness in the case of non-application of Semivocalization, the Markedness Condition blocks the derivation of (103a) and (104a).

Cases like the ones referred to in (98 iii.) have already been mentioned in (11), where it was argued that the diphthongs in these forms in fact constitute single phonemes. The forms in (11) are repeated here as (105), with their underlying forms (the arcs under the diphthongs in the underlying forms indicate the monophonematic status of these diphthongs)[34]:

(105) a. trois   /trwa/   [trwa]   *[trua]   'three'   y
      b. truite /trɥitə/ [trɥit] *[tryit] 'troute' y
      c. pluie   /plɥj/   [plɥi]   *[plyi]   'rain'   y
      d. bruit   /brɥi/   [brɥi]   *[bryi]   'noise'   y
      e. groin   /grwɛ̃/   [grwɛ̃]   *[gryɛ̃]   'muzzle' y

As already pointed out in section 1.2., these forms do not display an alternation glide/high vowel because of the fact that the diphthongs here are single phonemes. This is also why these diphthongs can be preceded by a tautosyllabic OL cluster — a configuration otherwise disallowed by the template in (6). Other examples of cases mentioned in (98 iii.) can be found in:

(106) a. voir   /vwar/   [vwar]   *[vuar]   'to see'
      b. puisse   /pɥis+ə/   [pɥis]   *[pyis]   '(he) can (subjunctive)'
      c. tienne   /tjɛn+ə/   [tjɛn]   *[tiɛn]   '(he) holds (subjunctive)'
      d. bois   /bwa/   [bwa]   *[bua]   'wood'
      e. bien   /bjɛ̃/   [bjɛ̃]   *[biɛ̃]   'well' (adv.)
      f. puits   /pɥi/   [pɥi]   *[pyi]   'well' (n.)

At this point a few words must be said about an apparent counterexample to my proposal. De Kok and Spa (1978:72) note that the forms in (107) do not display a free alternation vowel/glide:

(107) a. antieuropéen /ãti∅ropeɛ̃/ [ãti∅ropeɛ̃] *[ãtj∅ropeɛ̃] 'anti-European'
      b. semi-aride   /səmi+aridə/ [səmiarid]   *[səmjarid]   'half-dry'
      c. milliampère   /mili+ãpɛr/   [miliãpɛr]   *[miljãpɛr]   'milliampere'

Syllabification in French

The non-application of Semivocalization in these cases can be accounted for by assuming that the boundary between the two formatives in these words is a boundary for syllabification. In that case, the Syllabification Condition blocks the derivation, because *tj* and *lj* are not possible French codas.

I will also briefly discuss here the behaviour of the verb-endings *-ions*, *-iez*. The high vowel/glide alternations in these forms display a pattern different from other high vowel/glide alternations. It was argued in section 2.1. (see (90) and (92)) that these forms contain a glide underlyingly[35]. However, there is one case in which these verb-endings show up with a high vowel at the surface: in the case where they are preceded by an OL cluster. An example can be found in (108)[36]:

(108) entrions /ãtr+jõz/ [ãtriõ] *[ãtrjõ] '(we) entered'

This pattern of high vowel/glide alternation is by no means limited to the verb-endings *-ions*, but also occurs with the noun-endings *-ier*, *-ion* (Jaap Spa, personal communication). For example:

(109) a. poirier   [pwarje]   *[pwarie]   'pear tree'
      b. couturier   [kutyrje] *[kutyrie] 'tailor'
      c. espion   [ɛspjɔ]   *[ɛspiɔ̃]   'spy'
      d. camion   [kamjõ]   *[kamiõ]   'lorry'

(110) a. ouvrier   [uvrie]   *[uvrje]   'worker'
      b. encrier   [ãkrie]   *[ãkrje]   'inkpot'
      c. histrion   [istriɔ̃]   *[istrjɔ̃] 'bluffer'
      d. amphitryon [ãfitriɔ̃] *[ãfitrjɔ̃] 'host (at a dinner)'

The intriguing fact about this type of alternation is that the high vowel occurs only in a position where a glide would not have been possible because it would violate the notion of 'French possible syllable', viz. in a position after an OL cluster. This change from a glide into a high vowel may be the result of a separate process applying before, or during, syllabification. It cannot apply after syllabification because an OLG cluster is disallowed by the syllable template in (6). The process of semivocalization, on the other hand, has to apply after syllabification has taken place. This can be seen by looking at the form in (100a), repeated here as (111):

(111) l'ouest /lə#uɛst/ [luɛst] ~ [lwɛst] 'the west'

Schwa-Deletion has to be ordered before Semivocalization, otherwise it would not be able to apply in (111) if Semivocalization has applied[37].

3. CONCLUSION

I have proposed an alternative theory of Syllabification for French on the basis of an idea proposed by Lowenstamm (1979), viz. syllabification to lowest possible markedness. It was shown that the concept of markedness as developed by Kaye and Lowenstamm is unable to yield the correct predictions for French if we accept the principle of syllabification to lowest possible markedness. I therefore developed a concept of syllabic markedness which involves a somewhat different markedness scale from the one proposed by Kaye and Lowenstamm and which also takes into account the number of syllables in each given form. Another feature found in many syllabification proposals has been retained, viz. the requirement that the syllables conform to a syllable template.

It was then shown that two processes in French, Schwa-Deletion and Semi-Vocalization, depend on precisely the same principles as the ones that govern syllabification, viz. the prohibition against violating the notion of 'possible French syllable' and the tendency to achieve lowest possible syllabic markedness. Schwa-deletion and semivocalization are both syllable changing processes and so it is not surprising that principles governing syllabification should play a role in conditioning their application. In fact, we may go one step further and claim that we have actually been able to explain restrictions on the application of schwa-deletion and semivocalization by means of independently needed syllabification conditions. As a result, the rules of Schwa-Deletion and Semivocalization (and perhaps syllable-structure-changing rules in general) can be stated in a maximally general form. That is, no environments need to be specified for these rules at all. It has thus been shown that the approach involving simplification of the rules as such, connected with the development of a system of (preferably language-independent) conditions, which has been paramount in EST syntax for the last few years, can also be fruitful in generative phonology.

In this article, I have confined myself to French. It is very likely, however, that given the generality of the processes discussed here, an account involving the same principles as the ones proposed here can be given of syllable changing processes in other languages.

APPENDIX

In this appendix, I will discuss two proposals inspired by the metrical theory proposed by Liberman and Prince (1977). These two proposals – Selkirk (1978) and Vergnaud and Halle (1978) – include accounts of some of the cases of schwa-deletion in French. I discuss the two proposals here because they are often referred to. There is a general failure to realize, however, that their analyses contain some inconsistencies, as will be shown below.

Selkirk (1978) uses the notion of *foot* in her analysis of schwa-deletion. This term is borrowed from Liberman and Prince (1977). The *foot* is a higher order unit composed of syllables, just as the syllable is a higher order unit composed of segments. The principles governing the composition of feet in particular languages are thought to be partly universal, partly language specific.

According to Selkirk, French is different from a language like English where feet normally consist of two, perhaps three, syllables. In French the feet consist generally of one syllable (Selkirk mentions that the traditional distinction between syllable-timed languages like French and stress time languages like English can perhaps be viewed as following from the difference in the general definition of foot in the two languages). There are cases, however, in which the French foot can consist of two syllables. According to Selkirk, in addition to a general principle that makes a foot out of each syllable, a second principle is at work, by which a foot that consists of a syllable whose vowel is a schwa can be merged with the preceding foot, cf. the principles of French Foot Formation in (112) (Selkirk 1978: 144); Σ is the symbol used for foot):

(112) Selkirk's *French Foot Formation*:

I. *The Simple Foot*

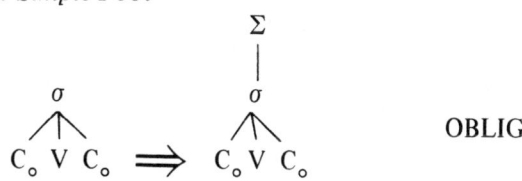

OBLIG

II. *The Derived Foot*

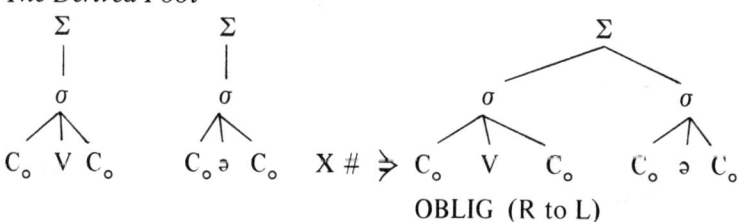

OBLIG (R to L)

296   Roland Noske

B.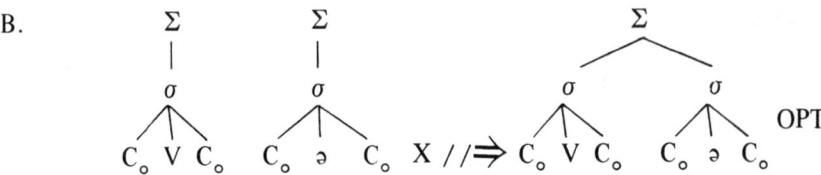

Rules (I), (IIA) and (IIB) apparently apply in the given order. (IIA) differs from (IIB) in two ways: (IIA) operates between word boundaries, and is obligatory, while (IIB), has the entire utterance as its domain, and is optional.

Somewhat later in her article (p. 145), Selkirk gives a rule of schwa-syncope, which refers to the notion of foot:

(113)   Selkirk's ə-syncope:

$$ə \to \emptyset \ / \ [\underset{\Sigma}{\ldots \text{VC}} \underset{\Sigma}{\ldots}] \quad \text{OBLIG}$$

This rule accounts for the deletion of schwa in forms like those in (114):

(114)   a.   *souvenir*   b. *promène*

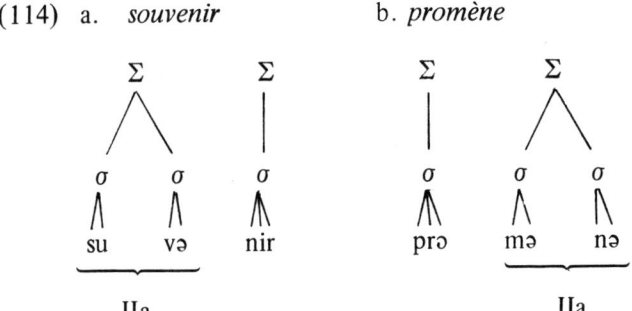

[suvnir] 'to remember'   [promɛn][38] 'walk'

c.   *promener*

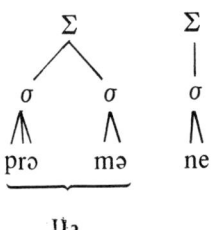

[promne] 'to walk'

Syllabification in French

The rule cannot delete the schwas in forms like those (115) because of the two preceding consonants:

(115) a. *couleuvre*   b. *exactement*

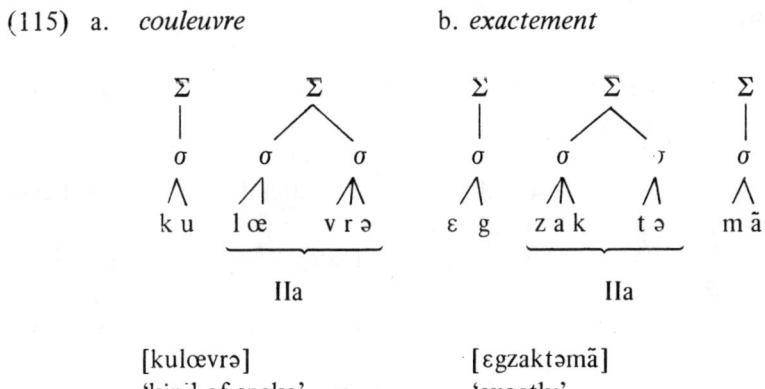

[kulœvrə]   [εgzaktəmã]
'kind of snake'   'exactly'

In (115a), the schwa can be deleted depending on other factors, in particular the stress pattern of the sentence, as indicated by Dell (1973) and others (cf. my account of this phenomenon in section (see (74) and (75)). The deletion of schwa in forms like those in (114) is obligatory because both rule (IIA) of (112) (which forms bisyllabic feet in the form of (114)) and the schwa-syncope rule in (113) are obligatory. However, if a word boundary occurs between a syllable containing a schwa and the preceding syllable, the deletion of schwa is optional, because in that case a bisyllabic foot can only be formed by the application of rule (IIB), which is optional, and the SD of the rule of schwa-syncope in (113) properly includes a bisyllabic foot. The sentence in (116) thus has five possible realizations, which are displayed in (117)[39] (Selkirk (1978: 146)):

(116) Il a envie de te revoir   /il#a#ãvi#də#tə#rə+vwar/ 'he feels like seeing you again'

(117) a. [ilaãvidətərəvwar]
       b. [ilaãvidǝtərǝvwar]
       c. [ilaãvidətǝrəvwar]
       d. [ilaãvidǝtərəvwar]
       e. [ilaãvidətərǝvwar]

Selkirk also makes use of the French Foot Formation in order to account for two other phenomena in French: stress assignment and the change of *e* and *ə* to *ε* in certain environments.

For stress assignment she simply posits the rule: 'stress the last foot in a word', cf. (118):

(118) Σ → [+stress] / ___ #

She then gives two examples of the functioning of this rule (p. 148), cf. (119):

(119) a. mari 'husband'   b. ouvre vite 'open quickly'

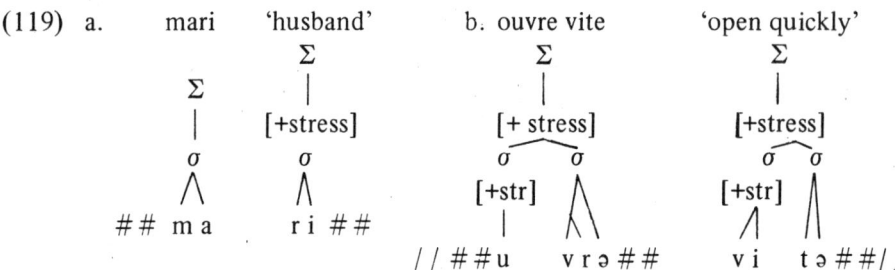

In the formulation of rule (118), no mention of ə needs to be made, because the realization of stress on the first syllable inside each foot in forms like (119b) follows automatically from the fact that it is in some sense the 'nucleus' of the foot or 'supersyllable'. Put in terms of the framework of Liberman and Prince (1977), the syllable on the left is stressed because it is the strong member of an S-W pair:
  For the change of e and $ə$ to $ε$, Selkirk posits the rule:

(120) $\begin{Bmatrix} e \\ ə \end{Bmatrix} \to ε \ / \ [\ C_o \underline{\quad} W\ ]$
           $\quad\quad\quad\quad\quad\ \ Σ \quad\quad\quad Σ$
           $\quad\quad\quad\quad\ \ W \neq \emptyset$

This rule can account for the alternation $e/ε$ and $ə/ε$ in the pairs of (121):

(121) a. cédait   [sedε]/   cède   [sεd]   'gave in/gives in'
       b. célébrait [selebrε]/ célèbre [selεbr] 'celebrated/famous'
       c. insérait   [ɛ̃serε]/   insère [ɛ̃sεr], insertion [ɛ̃sεrsjɔ̃]
                                 'included/includes, inclusion'
       d. sevrait   [səvrε]/   sèvre   [sεvr] 'weaned/weans'

This rule can also account for the occurrences of $ε$ in forms like those in (122), where it is not in a closed syllable:

(122) a. céderiez   [sεdərje]   'would give in'
       b. sèvrerez   [sεvrəre]   'will wean''
       c. (elle est) célèbre donc [selεbrədɔ̃k] 'so (she is) famous'
       d. sèvre-le   [sεvrələ]   'wean it'

Syllabification in French

Selkirk concludes that she has given a unified account of the phenomena involving schwa in French by using a prosodic approach: according to her, the special status of French "mute *e*" follows from its special status in prosodic structure.

However, I will demonstrate that this conclusion is overly optimistic. For this, I will give instances of schwas that are maintained in places where they should be deleted according to Selkirk's proposal, and of schwas that are deleted in places that Selkirk's proposal does not account for. It will be shown that in these latter cases, the deletions of schwa have certain features in common with schwa-deletions that Selkirk does account for. In other words, it will become clear that Selkirk has captured a spurious generalization. I will also show that Selkirk's rule in (120) makes the wrong predictions. In addition, I will show that if one tries to resolve the problems, one gets into more trouble.

The first instance I wish to discuss concerns the apparent optionality of the deletion of schwas which according to Selkirk's proposal of French Foot Formation would be part of the second syllable of a bisyllabic foot. As we have seen in section 2.1. (cf. (83)), the form in (123) has the three possible phonetic forms given in (124):

(123) tu devenais   /ty#dəvanɛ/   'you became'

(124) a. [tydəvanɛ]   b. [tydəvnɛ]   c. [tydvanɛ]

Selkirk's proposal can only account for (124b) because rule (IIA) of the rules of French Foot Formation in (112) obligatory makes a foot out of the first two syllables of /dəvanɛ/, and the rule of schwa-syncope in (113) is also obligatory. How can this situation be dealt with if one wishes to maintain the essence of Selkirk's proposal? (124a) could be derived by making the rule of schwa-syncope optional. In that case the rule cannot account anymore for the obligatoriness of the schwa-deletion in (114b) /prɔmənə/ [prɔmɛn]. This is not a problem in itself, because a rule deleting the final schwa is needed anyhow for the deletion of schwa in words like (115a) /kulœvrə/ (cf. my treatment of this phenomenon in (74) and (75) of section 2.1.).

It is more difficult to revise Selkirk's proposal in order to account for (124c). It could be accounted for by not assuming (IIA) but only (IIB). Bisyllabic feet would then only optionally be formed out of two monosyllabic feet, the second of which has a schwa as its vowel. Another possibility would be to reverse the order of rules (IIA) and (IIB). But in both these cases other problems arise: the rule of stress assignment in (118) would not be able to account for the stress in (125):

(125) il sèvre   /il#səvrə/   [ilsɛvr]   'he weans'

In (125), the first schwa of the underlying form has been changed to ɛ by application of rule (120). If one assumes only rule (IIB), which is optional, no bisyllabic foot would need to be formed out of /səvrə/, and the stress assignment rule in (118) would assign stress to the final syllable of the word, which has a schwa as its vowel. This is clearly the wrong result. As indicated by Selkirk, the final schwa is deleted depending on the stress pattern, so the stress assignment rule will have to apply before the deletion. Reversing the order of rules (IIA) and (IIB) would present the same problem. Because of the optionality of (IIB), a possible outcome would be:

(126) [ilsə] [vrə]
        Σ   Σ Σ   Σ

Rule (118) would assign stress to the second foot in (126), which would again mean stressing the final syllable containing schwa. It has to be concluded, then, that Selkirk's proposal cannot be adapted to account for the deletion of schwa of the type displayed in (124c), unless the rule of stress assignment in (118), which occupies a central place in Selkirk's proposal is dropped.

In addition to the problems concerning the deletion of schwa, another objection may be raised against Selkirk's proposal. For this we must look once again at the underlying form in (123) *tu devenais* /ty#dəvənɛ/. According to Selkirk's rules of Foot Formation in (112), the division in feet must be as in (127):

(127) [ty] [dəvə] [nɛ]
        Σ Σ Σ   Σ Σ   Σ

Rule (120), the rule which changes *e* and *ɔ* to ɛ if these vowels are preceded by a consonant and followed by non-null material within the same foot, would have to apply to the foot [dəvə], making it [dɛvə]. However,
                                             Σ   Σ   Σ   Σ
the phonetic form *[dɛvənɛ] does not occur. Other forms to which rule (120) apparently does not apply can be found in (128):

(128) a. derechef   /dərəʃɛf/   [dər(ə)ʃɛf]   *[dɛr(ə)ʃɛf]   'once more'
       b. démesure   /deməsyrə/ [dem(ə)syr] *[dɛm(ə)syr] 'excess'
       c. développer /devəlɔpe/   [dev(ə)lɔpe] *[dɛv(ə)lɔpe] 'to develop'
       d. revenir   /rəvənir/   [rəv(ə)nir]   *[rɛv(ə)nir]   'to come back'

Syllabification in French

In the forms in (128), a foot can optionally be formed out of the two syllables containing schwa (by virtue of rule (IIB) of (112). Rule (120) would have to apply subsequently, but would produce the wrong outcome:

(129) a. je ne crois pas /ʒə#nə#krwa#pa/ [ʒən(ə)krwapa]
*[ʒɛn(ə)krwapa] 'I do not believe'
b. tu le reverras /ty#lə#rəvɛra/ [tyl(ə)rəvɛra]
*[tylɛrəvɛra] 'you will see him again'

I see no way that rule (120) could be modified in order to account for its non-application to the forms in (128) and (129). The rule has been devised by Selkirk to replace the well-known rule of Closed Syllable Adjustment (which changes e, and ə to ɛ in closed syllables), in order to account also for the phonetic forms in (122). Because of the counter-examples in (128) and (129), rule (120) has to be rejected and one may fear that the occurrences ɛ in the phonetic forms in (122) can only be accounted for by a morphological rule, which *historically* may have had a phonetic motivation.

As a conclusion to this criticism of Selkirk's proposal, it can be said that Selkirk's proposal can only account for a fairly limited number of cases of schwa-deletion in French, that the metrical rule she proposes in order to account for the phenomena of the alternations e/ɛ and ə/ɛ is empirically inadequate, and that if one wishes to broaden Selkirk's analysis in order to account for more cases of schwa-deletion, another feature of her proposal, viz. the rule of stress assignment, cannot be maintained.

The proposal by Vergnaud and Halle (1978: 5.2.) involves an account for certain types of schwa-deletion in French in which they "lean heavily on the solution advanced by Selkirk (1978) (. . .)" (p. 5-7). According to their proposal, full vowels and schwas in the context CC___ are represented by branching nodes, while other vowels may or may not be branching. As an illustration, they give all possible representations of *tu devenais*, given here as (130):

(130)   /ty   də   və   nɛ /

    a. ∧ | | ∧
    b. ∧   ∧ | ∧
    c. ∧ | ∧   ∧
    d. ∧   ∧   ∧   ∧

They assume that it is the branching or non-branching character of rimes that is relevant for foot formation, and that feet are not sensitive to the branching character of any other constituents of the syllable (p. 5-5).

Furthermore, they assume that "in French words a non-branching syllable is paired into a binary foot with its neighbor on the left and that this pairing is done by scanning the word from right-to-left in a maximal fashion" (p. 5-9). In the case of (130), the following sequences of feet are formed:

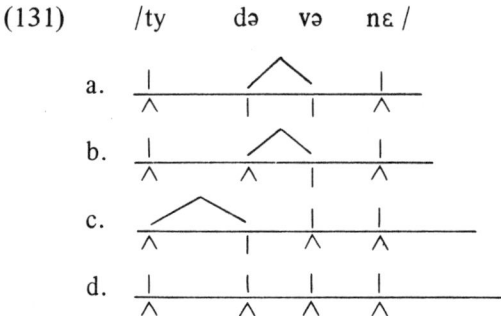

The line in each one of the representations in (131) seperates the foot level from the syllable level. Vergnaud and Halle posit as their rule of 'e-muet-elision' the rule:

(132) ə → ∅ / ⋀ __

Vergnaud and Halle can thus account for the following three phonetic forms of *tu devenais*:

(133) a. [tydəvənɛ]   b. [tydəvnɛ]   c. [tydvənɛ]

The shortcomings of the proposal by Vergnaud and Halle are much the same as the ones of Selkirk's. First a word must be said about the data given by the authors on page 5-8. They contrast the words in (134) in which schwa-deletion is possible, with those in (135), in which according to them, schwa-deletion is not possible (p. 5-7, 5-8):

(134) a. souvenir   [suv(ə)nir]   'souvenir'
      b. jalousement [ʒaluz(ə)mã]   'jalously'
      c. passera   [pas(ə)ra]   'will pass'
      d. volera   [vɔl(ə)ra]   'will fly'

(135) a. parvenir   [parvənir]   'to arrive'
      b. exactement [ɛgzaktəmã]   'exactly'
      c. percera   [pɛrsəra]   'will pierce'
      d. soufflera   [sufləra]   'will whistle'

Syllabification in French

These data are, however, incorrect. (135a) and (135c) *can* be pronounced without schwa. For (135a) confirmation of this fact can be found in Martinet and Walter (1973) (who in fact do not list [parvnir], but do list [parvnõ] and [parvny] (we 'arrive', 'arrived'). For (135c) Dell proposes his rule E-FUT (see note 2). It should be noted that the group of consonants preceding the schwa in the forms in which the schwa can be deleted (135a, c) form a possible French coda, whereas the group of consonants preceding the schwa in forms where it cannot be deleted (135b, d) do not.

Secondly, it should be noted that because of the fact that only schwas preceded by a single consonant may be non-branching, bisyllabic feet cannot be formed in forms like (125), repeated here as (136):

(136) il sèvre   /il#səvrə/   [ilsɛvrə]   'he weans'

This makes Vergnaud and Halle's analysis incompatable with the one by Selkirk discussed above (recall that Vergnaud and Halle declare that their analysis "leans heavily" on Selkirk's). Selkirk's rule of stress assignment in (118) cannot assign stress to the syllable containing ɛ in (136), but will assign stress to the syllable containing schwa. Also, in forms with only one intervocalic consonant preceding the schwa like (137), a bisyllabic foot is only optionally formed according to Vergnaud and Halle's proposal, because a schwa preceded by only one consonant may or may not be branching.

(137) fine   /finə/   [fin]   'delicate'

This means that stress will not be unequivocally assigned to the first syllable in the underlying form in (137).

Thirdly, Selkirk's rule (120), which changes *e* and *ə* to ɛ, will not be able to change the leftmost schwa in the underlying form in (136) to ɛ, because it is not followed by material within the same foot as rule (120) requires. In the case of only one intervocalic consonant as in (138), a bisyllabic foot is only optionally formed (exactly as in (137)), so rule (120) cannot always apply. Vergnaud and Halle's analysis incorrectly predicts that *[ilmənə] should be a possible phonetic representation.

(138) il mène   /il#mənə/   [ilmɛn]

It must be concluded that although Vergnaud and Halle declare that their proposal "leans heavily" on Selkirk's, it in fact deprives Selkirk's analysis of a major part of its (alleged) motivation, viz. The account of the phenomena concerning the distribution of stress and the alternations between *e*/ɛ and *ə*/ɛ.

Even though Selkirk's and Vergnaud and Halle's analysis of French are cited frequently they do not in fact account for the data. The analysis of syllabification and syllable-concerning rules which I have presented in this paper is able to account for the data of schwa-deletion discussed in this appendix. My analysis differs from Selkirk's in that schwa-deletion is not considered as following from metrical structure, but rather as a consequence of the persistent application of the principles that govern syllabification.

NOTES

1. Some linguists, e.g. Lowenstamm (1979), assume that syllabic structure is present in the lexicon.
2. There are just a few French words that have an onset consisting of an obstruent + nasal cluster, e.g. *pneu* [pnø] 'tyre', *snob* [snɔb] 'snob' and *smaragdite* [smaragdit] 'emerald'. These words are mostly of foreign origin, thus it is debatable whether an obstruent+nasal cluster constitutes a possible French onset.
3. Above a provision has been made for onsets and codas consisting of s+obstruent by means of auxiliary template (7).
4. This can be seen in *embarquement* [ãbarkəmã]~[ãbarkmã] 'embarcation, *renversement* [rãvɛrsəmã]~[rãvɛrsmã] 'reversal' and *département* [departəmã]~[departmã] 'department'. Not all French native speakers accept the pronunciation of these words without a schwa, it may thus be that their internalized notion of 'possible French syllable' does not contain a possible second segment in the coda.
5. There are codas consisting of s+obstruent, as accounted for by the auxiliary template (7). Codas like these can be found in one of the realizations of words like *brusquement* /bryskəmã/ 'suddenly', which according to Juilland (1965) can be pronounced as both [bryskəmã] and [bryskmã]. According to this and other sources on French pronunciation however, exactement /ɛgzaktəmã/ cannot be pronounced as *[ɛgzaktmã]. For the word-final codas in words like *exact* [ɛgzakt], as well as *parle* [parl] 'speak' and *vacarme* [vakarm] 'tumult', an explanation will be provided in section 1.6..
6. Cf. note 5.
7. Cf. note 5.
8. It will be shown in section 1.3. that the Nasalization rule, which deletes the nasal consonant and nasalizes the preceding vowel, applies before the rule which deletes the final schwa (Schwa-Deletion). This implies that if an underlying nasal consonant is assumed in a word like *plante* [plãt] 'plant' the underlying form thus being /plantə/, the nasal consonant is not in the same syllable as the *t* at any level of the derivation at which it is present. Hence it is not necessary to allow for a coda consisting of a nasal consonant + obstruent. It is of course debatable whether a word like *plante* really contains an oral vowel + a nasal consonant underlyingly, because there is no alternation between the (phonetic) nasal vowel and an oral vowel + a nasal vowel in this form; in other words, it is debatable whether French has nasal vowels underlyingly or not. In this paper I will not go into this matter but will assume for the ease of exposition that where there is no alternation, the vowel is underlyingly nasal.
9. The forms in (13) can also be pronounced as [grijɛf] and [adrijɛ̃] respectively. Similarly, the forms in (12) can also be pronounced as [luwe], [nije], [ilija] and [luwɛst]. These forms however are not of concern to us here.
10. The form in (11'a) *is* a possible realization of *(il) troua* /tru+a/ '(he) punched a hole'.

11. Kaye and Lowenstamm assume that syllabic structure is present in the lexicon. They also claim that diphthongs like those in (11) and (15) consist of two segments each of which is dominated by the nucleus. In order to account for the fact that there is no alternation high vowel/glide in these cases they posit the Nuclear Integrity Constraint (NIC) which says:

NIC: a. Material may not be resyllabified into a non-null nucleus:

b. Resyllabification of the nucleus must involve the entire nucleus:

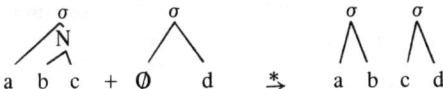

NIC can be dispensed with if it is assumed that the diphthongs in question are single phonemes.

12. The underlying schwa in (19) is deleted by a process which I will discuss in section 2.

13. In spite of the problems with the analysis of truncation as a syllable sensitive process, Spa nevertheless adopts this analysis because of the environment in the truncation rule proposed by Dell (1973: 258; 1980: 157), which does refer to syntactic and morpheme boundaries:

$$\text{TRONC:} \quad [-son] \rightarrow \emptyset \; / \; \underline{\quad} \left\{ \begin{matrix} \left\{ \begin{matrix} + \\ \# \end{matrix} \right\} C \\ \# \# \end{matrix} \right\}$$

Spa points out that the environment stated in this rule is usually taken as an argument for a syllable sensitive process. He solves the problems connected with the form in (17) by assuming for words like those in (17) idiosyncratic markings in the lexicon (i.e. reversal of the ordering of resyllabification and truncation or blocking of resyllabification). For words with morpheme-internal syllable-final obstruents like *espérer* and *rester* he refers to the *pronunciation savante*, 'scolary pronunciation' which is a notion from French historical linguistics. The pronunciation of words like these may indeed have been introduced artificially, but nowadays these pronunciations are not felt as artificial. If they were artificial one would be able to notice a tendency to omit the syllable-final obstruents. There is not the slightest tendency among French speakers however, to pronounce *espérer* and *rester* as *[εpere] and *[rεte] respectively.

14. Apart from words like *axe* [aks] 'ax'. I assume that the coda in this form is the result of a specified resyllabification under the influence of stress, in which the syllable template can be violated. I will treat this specified resyllabification in section 1.6.

15. In a proposal for French syllabification, Basbøll (1978) assumes that consonants that find themselves between a full vowel and a schwa are attracted to the syllable containing the full vowel. He thus follows a proposal made by Hoard (1971) for English. The difference between Basbøll's and Hoard's proposal, however, is that Basbøll assumes that *every* full vowel is stressed as compared to a schwa.

16. Vogel (1977) proposes as her 'Law of codas' that the remainder of the consonants must be associated to the syllable containing the [+syll] segment preceding them, regardless of whether or not they form a permissible word-final cluster.

17. One could argue that such readjustments represent the language-specific part of the syllabification process, while MCA represents the language-universal part. Still, the readjustments would have to be related to other phenomena in the language in question.

18. The assumption that syllabic structure is present in the lexicon is also questionable for another reason: the fact that the syllabic structure is generally predictable. The lexicon is generally thought of as a repository of idiosyncracies, not of regularities.

19. Kaye and Lowenstamm (1981b: 297) (also in Lowenstamm (1979: 69)) base the markedness scale in (35) on the following markedness convention:

$$[\text{u segment}] \rightarrow [\text{+segment}] / [_{O/R} \underline{\quad}]$$

According to Kaye and Lowenstamm, this markedness convention should be interpreted in accordance with Kean's (1975) complement convention and is considered to be the collapsing of four specifications:

    a. $[\text{u segment}] \rightarrow [\text{+segment}] / [_{O/R} \underline{\quad}]$
    b. $[\text{m segment}] \rightarrow [\text{-segment}] / [_{O/R} \underline{\quad}]$
    c. $[\text{u segment}] \rightarrow [\text{-segment}] / \sim[_{O/R} \underline{\quad}]$
    d. $[\text{m segment}] \rightarrow [\text{+segment}] / \sim[_{O/R} \underline{\quad}]$

By $\sim[_{O/R} \underline{\quad}]$ Kay and Lowenstamm mean a branching onset or rime. This is a rather strange deviation from Kean's complement convention, because it is hard to see why a branching onset or coda should be considered as the *complement* of an onset or coda. In other words, it is unclear why a branching onset or coda does not remain an onset or coda all the same.

20. Except for the sequences *tl* and *dl*. In a word like *atlas* 'atlas', the syllabic boundary is located between *t* and *l*. The sequences *tl* and *dl* do not form permissible French onsets. This exclusion will have to be stated in the notion of 'possible French syllable', which means that it has to be included in the set of conditions on the main syllable template in (10). However, the condition prohibiting *tl* and *dl* onsets cannot refer to the strength scale in (9), because obstruent+liquid clusters should not be excluded in general. The impossibility of *tl* and *dl* as onsets, however, seems to be of an isolated character and all other conditions on the syllable template *are* expressible by means of the strength scale in (9).

21. Simon Dik has brought to my attention that the well-known *muta cum liquida* provision in Attic Greek metre (an obstruent-liquid sequence does not render the preceding syllable heavy) in fact constitutes a parallel case. The fact that this provision does not apply to verse written in other dialects of Ancient Greek appears to provide motivation for Vennemann's (1972: 13) statement that 'different syllabification is a possible dialect difference'.

22. See Cairns and Feinstein (1982) for an analysis concerning syllabic markedness in Sinhalese.

23. These rules are in the 1973 version of Dell's book (p. 258-9):

Syllabification in French

ELIS: ə → ∅ / ___ ([−seg]) [+syll]　　　　　OBL

V–E: ə → ∅ / V___　　　　　　　　　　　　OBL

PAUS: ə → ∅　VC₀ ___ §　　　　　　　　　OBL
　　　　　　　　　　　　(§ indicates a pausal boundary)

E-FIN: ə → ∅ / VC₀ ___ #　　　　　　　　　OBL

NE-EX: ə → $\begin{bmatrix}-\text{rule INI} \\ -\text{rule VC E}_1\end{bmatrix}$ $\left\{\begin{array}{c}\_\_\_\#\text{nə}\# \\ V\#_1\text{ nə }\#C\_\_\_\end{array}\right\}$　　OBL

INI-EX: ə → [−rule INI] $\begin{bmatrix}-\text{son} \\ -\text{cont}\end{bmatrix}$ ___ #₀ $\begin{bmatrix}-\text{son} \\ -\text{cont}\end{bmatrix}$　　OBL

INI: ə → ∅ / ʃ C ___ (#) C　　　　　　　　　OPT

VCE₁: ə → ∅ / V#₁C ___ (#) C　　　　　　　OPT

VCE₂: ə → ∅ / VC ___ (#)C　　　　　　　　　OBL

E-FUT: ə → ∅ / X ___ +r+　　　　　　　　　OPT
　　condition: X ≠ OL

In the 1980 version of his book the formulations of some rules were somewhat altered and the output constraint OBLICONS was added (p. 239-41):

FIN-DEL_b: V → ∅ / VC₀ ___ #

VCE₁: ə → ∅ / V#₁C ___ ([−seg]) [+seg]　　　　OPT

VCE₂: ə → ∅ / VC ___ ([−seg]) [+seg]　　　　　OBL

FUT-DEL: ə → ∅ / ___ +r+　　　　　　　　　OPT

(replace E-FUT)

OBLICONS:　*[−son] $\begin{bmatrix}+\text{son} \\ +\text{cons} \\ -\text{nas}\end{bmatrix}$ [+cons]

24. These cases are: the obligatory deletion of the vowel in the feminine definite singular article *la* /la/, the optional deletion of the vowel in the second person singular pronoun *tu* /ty/, both in prevocalic position, and the obligatory deletion of *i* in *si* /si/ before *il* /il/.
25. The tendency to omit the schwa is generally greater in forms where the schwa is preceded by a single consonant, as in (58), than in forms where it is preceded by more than one consonant (as in 59). Some speakers do not accept the pronunciations in (59), which may be explained by the assumption that the internalized notion of 'possible French syllable' does not allow for a second segment in the coda (see note 4).
26. Except in utterance-final position, for which an explanation will be provided below (see (74) and (76).
27. In Dell (1980) this condition is called OBLICONS.
28. According to Dell the underlying form is: /astr##nuvo/ and an optional epenthesis rule is applicable to this form. In the case of non-application of this epenthesis rule the derivation is blocked by OLICONS. OLICONS does not block the deriv-

ation of *astre* /astr/, pronounced in isolation or at the end of a sentence, in the case of non-application of the epenthesis rule. As a result, the phonetic form can be both [astrə] and [astr].
29. In the form in (72), the first schwa can also be deleted (optionally), but that deletion is not of concern to us here.
30. According to Dell, a schwa can be deleted in the environment CC___r only in the case of a future form (the deletion is not possible if CC = OL). He cites some non-future forms in which a schwa in the environment CC___r cannot be deleted, e.g. *fumisterie* [fymistəri] 'hoax'. According to Lerond (1980) and Dubois (1960) however, this form can also be pronounced without a schwa. It thus appears that there is no morphological conditioning involved here, contrary to Dell's suggestion.
31. For many speakers the deletion of schwa in (91b) is obligatory.
32. i.e. rule NE-EX in note 22.
33. The facts as they are stated here have been extracted from de Kok and Spa (1978), except for the second clause in (90ii), which is from my personal observation, but has been confirmed by Spa and native speakers.
De Kok and Spa propose the following two rules (1978: 68-69).

$$\text{DIER:} \quad [+\text{cons}] \rightarrow [-\text{cons}] / \cdot C_2 \begin{bmatrix} \overline{} \\ +\text{voc} \\ -\text{round} \end{bmatrix} \quad \text{OBL}$$

$$\text{SEMI-VOC:} \quad [+\text{voc}] \rightarrow [+\text{cons}] \begin{bmatrix} +\text{high} \\ -\text{mid} \\ -\text{stress} \end{bmatrix} \text{V} \quad \text{OPT}$$

In addition to these rules they propose the following global constraint:

$$\cdot \ [-\text{son}]_1 \begin{bmatrix} +\text{son} \\ +\text{cons} \\ -\text{nas} \end{bmatrix} \begin{bmatrix} -\text{son} \\ +\text{high} \\ -\text{mid} \end{bmatrix} \bigg/ \supset \cdot [-\text{son}]_1 \begin{bmatrix} +\text{son} \\ +\text{cons} \\ -\text{nas} \end{bmatrix}_1 \begin{bmatrix} -\text{cons} \\ +\text{high} \\ -\text{mid} \end{bmatrix}$$

What this condition says is that (1978: 70):

> "if at the underlying level a syllable boundary is followed by the sequence: one or more obstruents, one or more non-nasal sonorant consonants (=liquid or glide), and a closed vowel, then the syllable boundary must also be followed by this sequence at the surface level".

they assume a word like *grief* [griɛf] to contain a glide underlyingly which seems strange because the phonetic form of this word always contains a high vowel.
Most of the examples used in section 2.1. are from de Kok and Spa's article.
34. The underlying forms in (105) and (106) are questionable on other grounds. E.g., the question can be asked whether *bruit* contains an underlying word-final *t* or not and whether *bien* and *groin* contain a nasal vowel underlyingly or an oral one followed by a nasal consonant. These questions, however, are not of concern to us here.
35. The question may be asked whether there are underlying glides in French at all. Kaye and Lowenstamm (1981a) do not assume them, but hypothesize that the phonetic nature of a high vowel is determined by its place in the syllable. I think that underlying glides do exist in the verb-endings *-ions, -iez* in the noun-endings *-ier*,

Syllabification in French 309

-*ion* (to be mentioned below), as well as in a limited number of other forms which are mostly of foreign origin:

    a.   le whisky   /lə#wiski/   [lə wiski]   *[lwiski]   'the whisky'
    b.   le yaourt   /lə#jaurt/   [ləjaurt]   *[ljaurt]   'the yoghurt'
    c.   le huit   /lə#ɥit/   [lə ɥit]   *[lɥit]   'the (number) eight'

These forms can be contrasted with:

    d.   l'ouest   /lə#uɛst/   [luɛst]~[lwɛst]   'the west'

As is displayed in the underlying forms given here, I assume that the contrast in application vs. non-application of Schwa-Deletion between (a, b, c) and (d) is due to the fact that in forms in which the deletion of schwa does not take place, there is underlyingly a glide, while in forms where Schwa-Deletion does apply, the schwa is followed by a high vowel.
36. As is the case with all forms where a high vowel is followed by another vowel, a homorganic glide can be epenthesized after the high vowel, if the high vowel has not turned into a glide itself. This epenthesis process, however, is not of concern to us here.
37. Cf. the forms in (a, b, c) in note (35) where a glide is assumed to be present underlyingly and where Schwa-Deletion cannot apply.
We have already seen in section 1.3. (see example (25)) that Schwa-Deletion has to follow Nasalization. Nasalization has to follow the initial syllabification, because it crucially refers to syllable structure. It was also argued in section 1.3. that the rule of truncation has to precede initial syllabification. We thus come to the following ordering of rules: Truncation, Initial Syllabification, Nasalization, Schwa-Deletion, Semivocalization.
38. The first schwa in this form is changed to by the application of rule (120), to be given below.
39. In my analysis given above the five possible phonetic realizations of (116) are accounted for by the fact that they all receive the same syllabic markedness value:

a.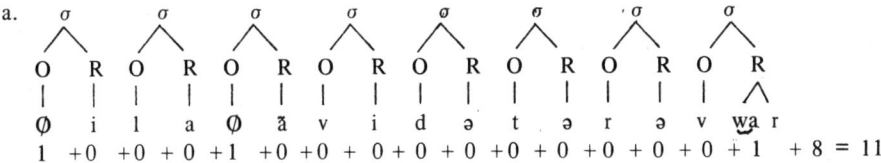

b.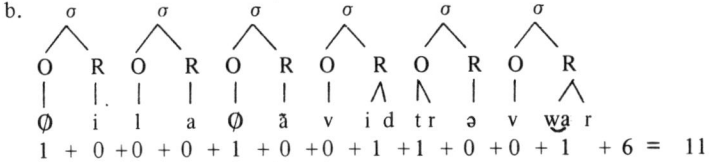

c.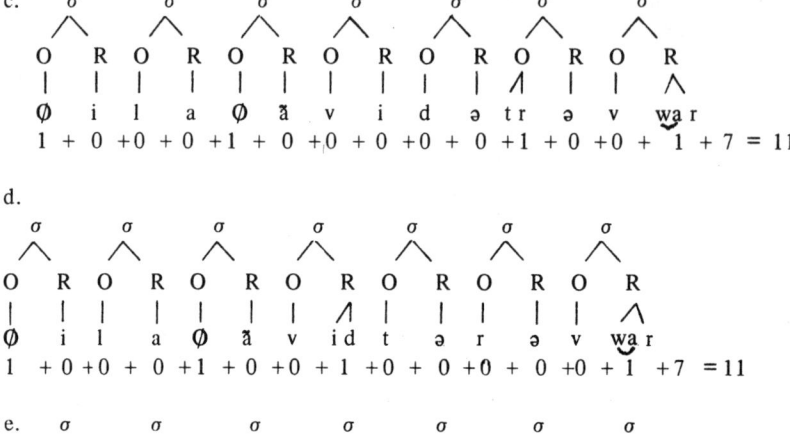

d.

e.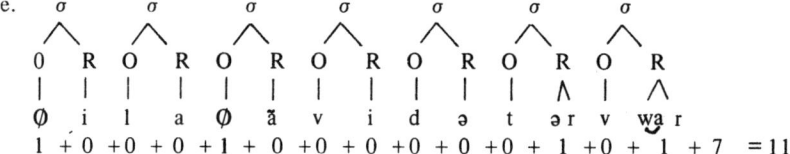

In (b) and (c) the *tr* cluster in the onset of the penultimate syllable receives markedness value 1 instead of 2 (which it would normally get according to the markedness scale in (38)) because of the provision for stop+liquid clusters made in section 1.6. The *d* in (b) and (d) is devoiced due to assimilation with the following *t* (the *d* is shown here in its original form, for reasons of clarity); it does *not*, however, degeminate.

In (116) not all schwas can be deleted. In my analysis this is accounted for by the fact that the resulting *dtrv* cluster cannot be analyzed in a possible coda followed by a possible onset. Hence, the derivation is blocked by the Syllabification Condition (56).

Prosodic Domains and Opaque Segments in Autosegmental Theory

Harry van der Hulst and Norval Smith
INL, Leyden and University of Amsterdam

1. INTRODUCTION

An autosegmental analysis of any suprasegmental phenomenon involves at least the following five parameters (cf. Clements & Sezer, this volume):

(1)   a.   the set of P-bearing segments
      b.   the set of P-segments
      c.   the set of neutral segments
      d.   the set of opaque segments
      e.   the domain of association

In this article we will be concerned with a number of issues concerning opaque segments and domains.

Most studies carried out within the framework of *autosegmental phonology* (henceforth AP) have involved phenomena for which parameter e could be interpreted as "word"; whether this meant grammatical word or phonological (or prosodic) word has not always been made explicit. Some examples can also be found, however, in which the domain of association is not the word but the metrical foot, i.e. a prosodic domain that is independently defined in terms of the metrical theory of stress. In Hayes (1980) for example it is claimed that vowel harmony in Eastern Cheremis is bound to the domain of the stress foot and in Zubizarreta (1979) a similar situation is shown to hold for Laxing Harmony in Andalusian Spanish. That the metrical foot can be an autosegmental domain has also been suggested by Safir (1979) and Yip (1980) in their studies of Capanahuan and Chinese tonology.

Examples like these show that in the analysis of some cases of harmony at least we need both the autosegmental *theory of association* and a *theory of phonological domains*. In the area of segmental rules Selkirk (1981) has clearly demonstrated that *metrical phonology* (henceforth MP) can be utilized successfully as a theory of phonological domains (or phonological constituency structure). She develops a richly articulated typology of phonological rules in terms of the way they make reference to grammatical and phonological domains. The examples we have already quoted show that autosegmental rules too must refer to prosodic domains and this suggests that Selkirk's typology, proposed within a purely segmental framework, carries over to a theory that makes use of autosegmental rules. The main part of this article is devoted to substantiating and illustrating this point. The examples that we will provide show that autosegmental association can be bound to various phonological domains, both smaller and larger than the foot.

In section 3 an autosegmental treatment of emphasis in Arabic will be given, showing the relevance of the syllable as the domain of association. In section 4 an example of the foot as the relevant domain is discussed involving nasalization in Applecross Gaelic. Finally, in section 5, we will analyze nasalization in Guaraní. We will claim that a general treatment of the issue of *precedence of association* (in cases where there are two potential spreaders) can only be given if we view nasalization in Guaraní as being bound to the "stress group", a domain which is larger than the foot but smaller than the phonological word.

In our analysis of nasalization in Applecross Gaelic and Guaraní we will encounter *opaque elements* and in section 6 we will deal with the behaviour of these separately. We will argue that it cannot be maintained that such elements are not subject to spreading (as Halle and Vergnaud 1981 do). On the contrary, we will provide analyses of nasalization in Capanahua and Sundanese that show that opaque segments are subject to spreading due both to the general association convention and to language specific rules.

2. TOWARDS AN INTEGRATED MODEL

The emergency of both AP and MP has led to drastic changes in our conception of phonological representations. Taken independently we can schematicize these changes as follows. Within AP uni-linear representations such as those under (2) have been replaced by multi-linear representations such as those under (3). MP, on the other hand has brought about a replacement of type (2) representation by type (4) representations.

(2) unilinear, non-hierarchical
$$\begin{bmatrix} +F_1 \\ -F_2 \\ +F_3 \\ \vdots \end{bmatrix} \begin{bmatrix} -F_1 \\ +F_2 \\ +F_3 \\ \vdots \end{bmatrix} \begin{bmatrix} +F_1 \\ -F_2 \\ +F_3 \\ \vdots \end{bmatrix} \begin{bmatrix} -F_1 \\ +F_2 \\ +F_3 \\ \vdots \end{bmatrix} \begin{bmatrix} +F_1 \\ -F_2 \\ +F_3 \\ \vdots \end{bmatrix}$$

(3)   multi-linear, non-hierarchical

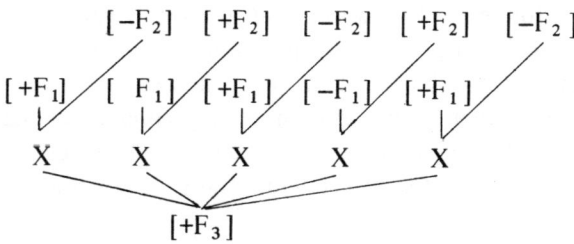

(4)   uni-linear, hierarchical

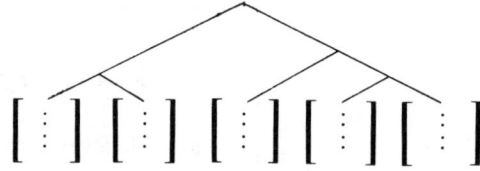

Given the necessity of both types of change the obvious question is what the theory will look like if both are combined. Can different hierarchical structures be found at all levels or is there only one such hierarchy defined at some central tier, the most likely candidate being the X-tier? It is the latter, more restricted position that most phonologists have adopted.

But what does it mean to say that the spreading of some feature is bound to a particular domain? Here we must distinguish between two cases. The spreading autosegment may or may not be lexically bound to a P-bearing segment. If it is lexically bound there is no problem. When we say that the spreading is bound to domain D_i this means, of course, the D_i that contains the P-bearing unit to which the autosegmental is lexically bound. But a string may comprise several D_i's and we will therefore run into problems if an autosegment is not associated with a particular segment in the underlying representation while its spreading is bound to a particular domain. To illustrate this point, how do we derive (5b) from (5a):

(5)   a. $[+F_1]$ b. $[+F_1]$

                (x x x)$_\sigma$ (x x x x)$_\sigma$ (x x x)$_\sigma$ (x x x x)$_\sigma$

In real life (5) would be an example in which whole syllables are characterized by the absence or presence of a particular feature, such that it would be arbitrary to associate this presence or absence with one of the segments constituting the syllable. In this article we will not provide detailed examples of cases like (5), though the possibility exists that this is precisely the right approach to emphasis in at least some dialects of Arabic (cf. section 3). We suspect, however, that more examples will be found once we look for them. If this turns out to be the case we must be able to say not only that a particular sequence of x's belongs to a domain D_i but also that a particular (sequence of) autosegment(s) belongs to this same D_i, without there being any underlying connection between both sequences. The following figure visualizes the overall conception of phonological representation that such a state of affairs presupposes:

(6)

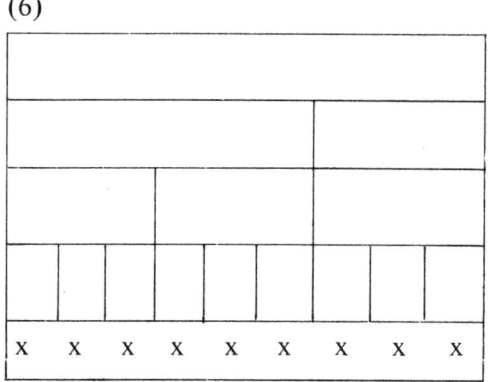

word level autosegments

foot level autosegments

syllable level autosegments

segment level autosegments

The strongest claim is that autosegments within each domain are associated with their P-bearing units according to the same universal association conventions.

As an alternative to this view it might be proposed that autosegments are assigned to the nodes in the phonological hierarchy and that the autosegments *percolate* to the x slots. This is in fact the view of Hart (1981) who defends a version of the autosegmental theory that shares a number of properties with the present proposal. There are, however, several reasons for rejecting such an approach. First, it will be impossible, given the percolation device, to manipulate the connections between autosegments and P-bearing segments in the way that is familiar (and motivated) in many autosegmental studies. Secondly, it is unclear how opaque segments could be handled, and thirdly, it is equally unclear how the parts of whole melodies (e.g. tonal melodies) can percolate to the right P-bearing elements.

The model adopted here allows for the possibility that a given feature is represented as an autosegment at various levels simultaneously. We do not know at present to what extent this must be restricted. Hart adduces one example (concerning nasalization in Parintintin) in which a feature is present at three levels: the segmental level, the syllable level and the word level. We think that the data are not conclusive in this case and we therefore hypothesize that a given feature can occur at no more than *two*

Prosodic Domains and opaque segments

prosodic levels simultaneously, and only if one of these levels is the segmental level. We will make use of this possibility in our analyses in the characterization of so-called *neutral* segments.

3. THE SYLLABLE AS THE RELEVANT DOMAIN: EMPHASIS IN ARABIC

In all Arabic dialects whole syllables can be characterized by the presence or absence of a phonetic property referred to as *emphasis*, involving the secondary articulations of velarization or pharyngealization. In most dialects the presence of emphasis is conditioned by the presence of a particular emphatic consonant in the syllable. If one such consonant is present all segments in the same syllable are emphatic.

The following triggering segments, which Broselow (1979) terms *independent emphatics* occur in all major dialects: *T, D, S, Z, L, R* (and, though the sound is used rarely, *q*). "Furthermore, most of these dialects exhibit additional contrasting pairs, especially in the labial series" (Lehn 1963, 31). Next to the emphatic set there is a set of non-emphatic (plain) consonants, including the six plain consonants corresponding to the emphatic series above. For this phenomenon of emphasis the following treatment will be proposed.

Independent emphatics have a phonological representation consisting of two tiers. On one tier we find the 'feature' emphasis (or whatever set of features is necessary to characterize the corresponding phonetic property) and on the other tier we find all other features. The so-called true pharyngeals ħ and ʕ are "inherently" emphatic, i.e. they are associated with [+E] at the segmental level and not at the syllable level. This then means that the true pharyngeals are formally *neutral* segments.

Using capitals to symbolize independent emphatics we get the following underlying representations (the examples, involving (near) minimal pairs, are taken from Lehn 1963, 32-3):

(7)

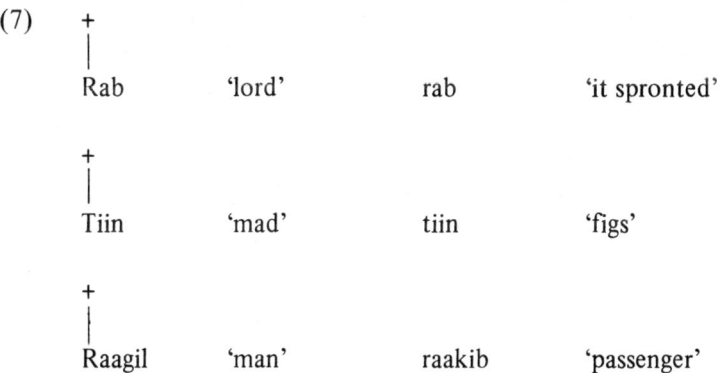

+
|
bukRa   'tomorrow'   fikra   'idea'

+   +
| |
RaaʕiD   (military rank)   raaʕid   'sleeper'

To get the correct surface forms the autosegment [+E] must be spread to all other segments present in the syllable. This fact must be stipulated in the grammar by fixing the five parameters as follows:

(8)   *Emphasis in Arabic*
    a. the set of P-bearing segments: all segments
    b. the set of P-segments: [+E]
    c. the set of neutral segments: ħ, ʕ
    d. the set of opaque segments: ∅
    e. the domain of association: the syllable

The result is as follows

(9) a. +   b. +
         /|\   /|\
        (Rab)ₒ   (Tiin)ₒ

     c. +   d. +   e. +   +
         /|\   /| /| |\
        (Raa)ₒ (gil)ₒ   (buk)ₒ (Ra)ₒ (Raa)ₒ (ʕiD)ₒ

Segments that are not associated with an autosegment will surface as non-emphatic, due to a redundancy rule. This move embodies a deviation from standard autosegmental phonology, but one that is convincingly motivated in Halle & Vergnaud (1982). The alternative analysis would involve assigning an autosegment [−E] to one of the consonants that constitute non-emphatic syllables. The choice of a particular consonant would be arbitrary, however. Avoiding such arbitrariness we could also assign [−E] to all consonants that do not belong to the set of independent emphatics. Such a move forces us to adopt one of the following rules:

(10) a. [−E] → ∅ / [+E]

or:

(10) b. [−E] → [+E] / [+E]

The derivation would then involve two steps rather than one:

(11) a.
$$\begin{matrix} + & - \\ | & | \\ R\,a\,b \end{matrix} \;\text{—(10a)→}\; \begin{matrix} + \\ | \\ R\,a\,b \end{matrix} \;>\; \begin{matrix} + \\ /|\backslash \\ R\,a\,b \end{matrix}$$

b.
$$\begin{matrix} + & - \\ | & | \\ R\,a\,b \end{matrix} \;\text{—(10b)→}\; \begin{matrix} + & + \\ | & | \\ R\,a\,b \end{matrix} \;\rightarrow\; \begin{matrix} + & + \\ \backslash & | \\ R\,a\,b \end{matrix}$$

It seems to us that rules like (10a) or (10b) duplicate the effect of the universal association conventions and we therefore prefer to make use of the 'unmarked' feature value approach. Note, however, that we deviate here from Halle & Vergnaud in one respect. We cannot assume that all segments are segmentally specified with the unmarked feature value, since we have utilized segmental specification for the characterization of neutral segments. We therefore assume that segments not belonging to the set of independent emphatics are *unspecified* at the segmental level. Unmarked values are assigned by rule at the end of the derivation.

Lehn (1963) claims that there are dialects of Arabic in which the opposition emphatic versus non-emphatic has been extended to all consonant types. Given this type of situation it is arbitrary to assign the auto segment [+E] to any one of the consonants that constitute an emphatic syllable. It would be more straightforward to assign the autosegment to the syllable, without any underlying association line. Our model allows for such representations, as we have demonstrated in section 2, and it therefore predicts the possibility of the dialect difference that seems to be involved here.

We conclude that the above analysis represents a clear case of syllable domain association (cf. Selkirk 1980, 577).

4. THE FOOT AS THE RELEVANT DOMAIN: NASALIZATION IN APPLECROSS GAELIC

In Applecross Gaelic primary stress is assigned to the initial syllable of all except a few root morphemes. Affixes or clitic elements never receive primary stress. Compare the following examples:

(12) a. /kʰə́nʸi/ 'meeting'
    /ã́jət̪/ 'angel'
    /mã́.r + içə/ 'mothers'
  b. /γa+ɛ̃çkʸənʸ/ 'seeing him'
    /kʰɔ+vĩa.t/ 'how much'
    /kʰatʰrĩanə/ 'Catherine'

The type (12a) examples, which include as we have indicated the vast majority of monomorphemic words, and also their inflected forms, can be seen as constituting a single foot, i.e.:

(13) a.   b.   c.

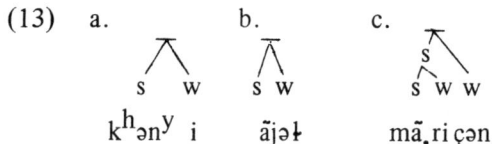

   kʰənʸ i   ã́jət̪   mã́.riçən

Foot trees are left-branching in other words. The forms under (12b), which comprise for the most part prefixations and precliticizations, but also a very few monomorphemic words, appear as follows:

(14) a.   b.   c.

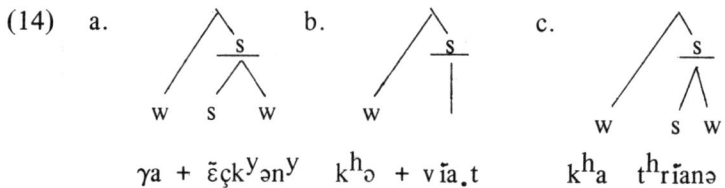

   γa + ɛ̃çkʸənʸ   kʰɔ + vĩa.t   kʰa tʰrĩanə

Pre-stress syllables are considered as extrametrical; they are joined as weak sisters to the feet in the word tree.

The occurrence of nasalization in Applecross Gaelic is subject to the following conditions (Ternes 1973):

(15) a. "the centre of nasal assimilation lies in the vocalic nucleus of the stressed syllable of a stem ... From the centre, nasalization extends in a forward and backward direction unless or until checked by one of the conditions below".
  b. "in the backward direction, nasalization comprises the consonantal onset of the stressed syllable, but never extends beyond". It is this restriction that is to be explained by the fact that nasal assimilation is *foot*-bound.
  c. "in the forward direction, nasalization extends as far as the end of the word, including suffixes ...". All syllables following the stressed syllable will be included in the same foot as the stressed syllable.

d. "nasality does not extend beyond stops" (in either direction).
e. "the vowel phonemes /e, o, ə/ never function as the centre of nasalization. They are never nasalized, whether stressed or unstressed, nor does nasality extend beyond one of these phonemes".

Examples of nasalization are:

(16) a. *Complete nasalization*
   /ʃɛ́nɛ.var/ → [ʃɛ̃́nɛ̃.ṽãr̃]   'grandmother'
   /fría.v/ → [fr̃ía̰.ṽ]   'root'
b. *Nasalization blocked by stop to the left*
   /tʰrɨ́iʃar/ → [tʰrɨ́iʃãr̃]   'plate'
   /strái.γ/ → [str̃ãí·γ̃]   'string'
c. *Nasalization blocked by a stop to right*
   /sNányd ʸan/ → [s̃Nányd ʸan]   'thread'
   /kʰɔ́ispaxk/ → [kʰɔ́ḭ̃s̃paxk]   'wasp'
d. *Nasalization blocked by e/o/ə*
   /sáuLəxkənʸ/ → [s̃ã́ũLəxkənʸ]   'to compare'
   /mã́.riçən/ → [mã́.r̃ĩ́çən]   'mothers'
e. *Nasalization blocked by margin of foot*
   /kʰɔ + vía.t/ → [kʰɔ + ṽĩá̰.t]   'how much'

It is important to note that nasals themselves have nothing to do with nasalization synchronically. Compare the following contrast:

(17) mũxk   'pig'   —   mur   'sea'
     mã́.har 'mother' —   mára.v   'dead person'

Hence we will assume that nasal consonants are associated with [+N] at the segmental level but not at the autosegmental level. Stops and high mid vowels will have an autosegment [−N] associated with them in the lexicon: this is the way in which *opaque* segments are characterized (cf. Clements & Sezer, this volume). The predictability of this will be captured in terms of redundancy rules.

All root morphemes can be lexically classified as [+N] or [−N]:

(18) a. +   −   b. −   c. −   −   +   −
         | | | |
        muxk   mur   kʰatʰ rianə

     d. −   e. − + − −   f. +
                            | | |
        mara.v   kʰɔispaxk   ma.har

The rule of nasalization can now be formulated as follows:

(19) *Nasalization in Applecros Gaelic*
 a. the set of P-bearing segments: all sonorants
 b. the set of P-segments: [+N], [−N]
 c. the set of neutral segments: nasal consonants
 d. the set of opaque segments: obstruents, *e, o, ɔ*
 e. the domain of association: the stress foot

The following examples show the result of the rule:

(20) a. + −   b. −   − + −   c. −   + − −
       |\ |\ | |\ | | /|\ |
     (muxk)_F   (kʰa)_σ (tʰrianə)_F   (kʰ ɔ ispaxk)_F

   d.   +
        |\
     (ma.har)_F

A technical problem must be dealt with here. The free autosegment must be so located that it can be associated with the mainstressed vowel, without violating the condition that lines may not cross.

For example in (18e) the floating [+N] must be placed "above" the first vowel /ɔ/ and not above the /a/. However, if stress is predictable (as it in fact is in most cases), the information where to place the floating segment is not available in the lexicon. To solve this problem we suggest that lexical items are classified in terms of a *morphological feature* [±N]. After stress has been assigned a rule will introduce the appropriate autosegment at the appropriate place. It is important to note that it would be insufficient for such a rule to introduce the autosegment in the domain of the strongest (or unique) foot (as a floating autosegment) for such a foot may contain an opaque segment. In that type of situation the floating autosegment must be linearly ordered before or after the opaque segment, depending on the position of the stressed vowel with respect to the opaque segment. In other words, the rule would have to introduce the autosegment so that the stressed vowel is 'accessible' to it. It appears to be more straightforward then to assume that the rule simply says: associate the appropriate autosegment with the stressed vowel. The difference between the two possibilities is not insignificant for the following reason.

Once the autosegment has been introduced certain P-bearing segments are in the scope of two autosegments, which results in an ambiguity with respect to their association:

(21) a.   +   −   b.   +   −   c.   +   −
        | \ | | /
    m u x k   m u x k   m u x k

Since only (21b) satisfies the actual form, we want to be able to rule out (21c) on principled grounds. Given (21a) as our point of departure we can assume (22) (as has been suggested in the autosegmental literature):

(22) *Precedence Convention I*
     The spreading of a free autosegment takes precedence over the spreading of a bound autosegment.

(22) will not be any use, however, if we take (23) to be the representation that feeds the association conventions:

(23)   + −
        | |
      muxk

It will not be any help to say that in addition to (or in place of) (22) there is a second convention (as has also been suggested):

(24) *Precedence Convention II*
     Rightward spreading takes precedence over leftward spreading

Though this will give the correct result in the case of (23) it will produce the wrong form in the case of (25):

(25)   − − +
     | | |
   k^{h}at^{h}ɾianə

The /r/ must come out nasalized, and (24) would result in an oral sound.

The conclusion seems to be that we must prefer the first possibility, i.e. a rule that introduces the appropriate autosegment at the right spot, but without an association line. We will accept this conclusion for the moment, but return to the issue in section 5, where we will be confronted with the same problem in our analysis of nasalization in Guaraní.

Let us note two other aspects of our analysis that deserve mention. Firstly, we could assume that nonnasal morphemes are simply unmarked and that they will surface with the unmarked value for the feature nasal, i.e. [−nasal]. This is, after all, the kind of approach we choose in the case of emphasis in Arabic (see section 3). It is indeed true that this is possible, but it should be noted that this would not lead to any simplification in the analysis as far as the rule component is concerned. We will leave this issue undecided here.

Secondly, we could follow Halle & Vergnaud (1981) and say that opaque (i.e. lexically bound) segments are not subject to spreading. This would solve our ambiguity problem, without making use of any precedence convention whatsoever. We think, however, that it is incorrect to say that opaque segments need never spread. It will be shown that in the case of Guaraní opaque segments do spread, and we also refer to Clements & Sezer, this volume. We will come back to this issue in section 6.

5. THE STRESS GROUP AS THE RELEVANT DOMAIN: NASALIZATION IN GUARANÍ

The facts of nasalization in Guaraní have been analyzed by various authors both in metrical terms (Sportiche 1977; Vergnaud & Halle 1978) and in autosegmental terms (Goldsmith 1975; Hart 1981; Poser 1981, this volume). Standard segmental treatments have been offered as well in Lunt (1973), Rivas (1974). We will analyze the facts in autosegmental terms. At the appropriate points we will compare our analysis with other autosegmental treatments (especially that of Poser 1981, this volume).

The basic facts of nasalization in Guaraní, as reported in Gregores and Suárez (1967), are as follows. Each utterance can be partitioned into oral and nasal spans, which typically comprise several segments. Nasal spans consist of contiguous strings of sonorants, possibly interrupted by (voiceless) obstruents, which "remain unaffected by the opposition nasal versus nonnasal" (G&S, 67). Except for a few cases each nasal span contains either a nasal consonant ([m], [n] or [ŋ]) or a stressed nasalized vowel. Oral spans on the other hand always contain a stressed oral vowel.

Confining ourselves to monomorphemic utterances for the moment let us consider the following examples:

(26) a. [tũpã́]   'god'   b. [tupá]   'bed'
     [pũrũʔá]   'navel'   [puruʔá]   'to be pregnant'
  c. [mãrõ̃]   'never'
     [mẽnã́]   'husband'
  d. [kʷĩmbaʔé] 'man', 'male'
     [kũmãndá] 'bean'

Within the autosegmental framework we could assume underlying representations as in (27):

(27) a.

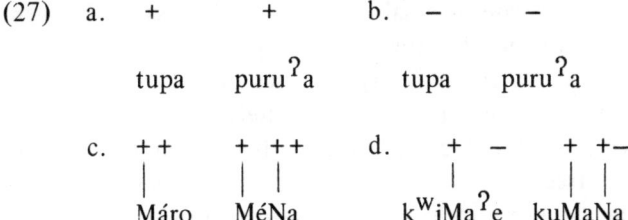

c.   + +   + + +   d.   +   −   + +−
      │ │   │ │ │   │   │ │
      Máro   MéNa   kʷiMaʔe   kuMaNa

The surface forms result from application of the general association convention supplemented by one language-particular rule to derive the prenasalized consonants (cf. the postoralization rule in Goldsmith 1975):

(28)   [−N]
         ┌--¬
         C   V

(29) a.

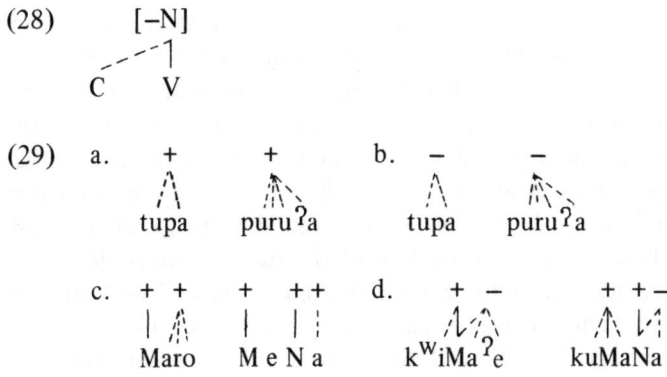

Obstruents are not affected by the nasality flow. They are specified as [−nasal] at the segmental level; they are thus *neutral*. Nasal consonants on the other hand are lexically bound to an autosegment; they are *opaque*.

We have to assume precedence convention I (see (22)): association with floating autosegments takes precedence over association with bound ones, as we have already seen in the case of Gaelic. It is, moreover, quite clear that opaque segments (i.e. nasals) *must* spread. Finally, one must note that the present approach toward the prenasalized consonants presupposes that both [+N] and [−N] are taken as autosegments.

The rule of nasalization can now be formulated as follows:

(30) *Nasalization in Guaraní*
   a. the set of P-bearing segments: all segments
   b. the set of P-segments: [−N], [+N]
   c. the set of neutral segments: obstruents
   d. the set of opaque segments: nasals
   e. the domain of association: ?

Before we turn our attention to the domain specification we must first discuss one other aspect of the analysis proposed so far.

Just as in the previous case of nasalization in Applecross Gaelic there is a technical problem relating to stress and the position of the floating autosegment. Stress falls in the majority of cases on the final syllable, in some cases on the penultimate (cf. 26c) and rarely on the antepenultimate. We have expressed this fact in our underlying representations in (27) by leaving out stress, except in (27c). This means that we cannot, strictly speaking, decide where to locate the floating autosegment in morphemes that have regular stress and in addition contain opaque segments. The floating segment must come to rest to the right of the rightmost opaque segment, but by stipulating this fact we repeat essential information that is also expressed in the stress rule. We propose to solve this problem in the same way as in the case of Applecross Gaelic. Morphemes are classified in terms of a *morphological* feature [±N]. After stress placement a rule will assign the appropriate autosegment to each morpheme.

One will recall that we discussed two possible formulations for such a "spell-out" rule in the previous section. The rule may introduce the autosegment, in such a way that it floats at the right spot (i.e. so that the stressed vowel is accessible) or it directly associates the autosegment with the stressed vowel. In section 4 we chose the first possibility, because it was only under this formulation of the rule that we could handle the fact that spreading of autosegments that are associated with stressed vowels takes precedence over spreading of autosegments that are associated with other segments. We will now show that we can make the same choice here *only* if we specify the domain of spreading to be the stress group, i.e. a constituent defined in terms of metrical structure, that is smaller than the phonological word, but somewhat larger than the foot.

Let us first see what happens if we choose the second possibility: the spell-out rule introduces a bound autosegment. In that case the following intermediate representations will result:

(31)

```
        +         +    ++        +  -      + + -
        |         |    ||        |  |      | | |
       tupa     puruʔa  Maro    kʷiMaʔe   kuMaNa
```

The correct surface forms result if we assume that:

(32)   *Precedence Convention III*
       Leftward spreading takes precedence over rightward spreading

Poser (1981, this volume) makes use of (31) and (32) in his analysis of Nasalization in Guaraní. But since there are cases in other languages where (24) (i.e. rightward precedence) leads to the correct result (cf. rounding harmony as discussed in Clements & Sezer, this volume) Poser assumes that the precedence convention is parametrized.

Prosodic Domains and opaque segments

We will now discuss the consequences of chosing the first possibility. There will be no problems in monomorphemic forms. The rule that introduces the autosegment leads to intermediate representations as in (27). Problems arise, however, if we consider polymorphemic words.

Prefixation introduces no complications. Prefixes are always unstressed and as a result they have no (morphological) specification for nasality. Sonorants of prefixes will therefore be associated with the leftmost autosegment of the stem:

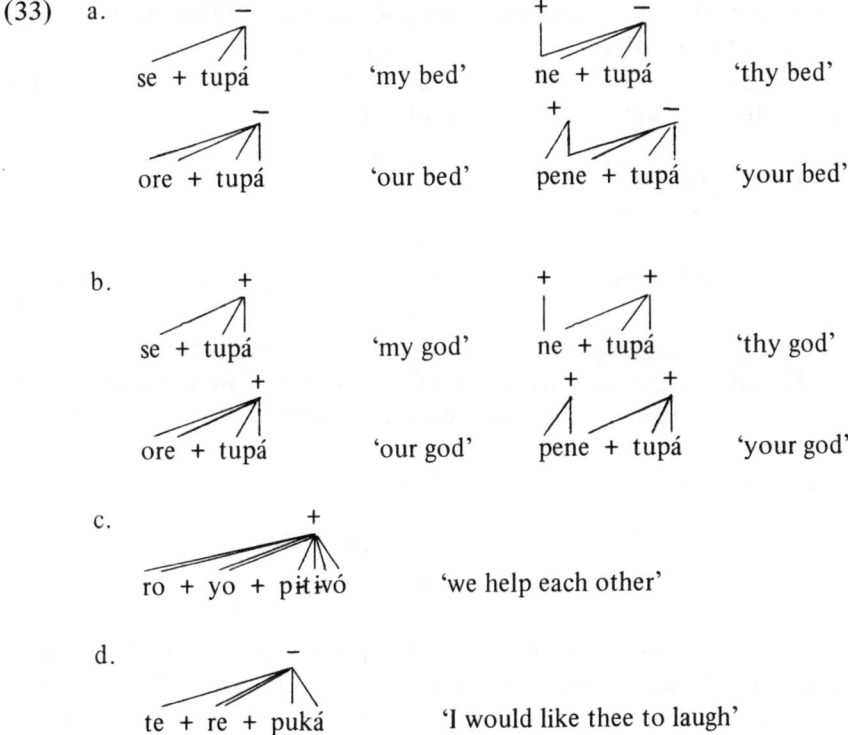

These cases show that the domain of spreading is in any case not the morpheme.

Suffixes may be stressed or unstressed. The latter category poses no problems. Like prefixes stressless suffixes harmonize with the stem. Gregores and Suárez mention only three suffixes that belong to this category, all unproductive. Nearly all the productive suffixes that they mention are stressed. Let us now consider a few examples with stressed suffixes:

b.   −   −

hešá + vé   'to see better' (cf. [hešá] 'to see')

It will be immediately clear that we run into trouble here. The spell-out rule has introduced two floating autosegments and this leads to an ambiguity with respect to association. There is no possibility of solving this ambiguity without making use of a rule that associates the autosegments with 'their' stressed vowels, but such a move would make an analysis that uses the second formulation of the spell-out rule virtually identical to an analysis using the first formulation.

A possible way out might be to assume that we derive the surface forms cyclically. This will work in the case of (34):

(35)   a. *1st cycle*   b. *2nd cycle*

$$+ \quad + \qquad\qquad + \quad + \quad -$$
$$[\eta^W \ aiví] \qquad\qquad [[\eta^W \ aiví] \ vé\ ]$$

(The general spreading convention will only *add* lines of course).

We will get less satisfactorily results, however, if we consider derived words containing stems that have penultimate stress:

(36)   a. *1st cycle*   b. *2nd cycle*

$$+ \quad + \qquad\qquad * \quad + \quad + \quad -$$
$$[m\ á\ r\ o] \qquad\qquad [\,[m\ á\ r\ o]\ v\ é\ ]$$

The correct surface form is not [mãrõvé], however, but: [mãrové]. The orality of the suffix spreads *into the stem* up to the stressed vowel of the stem. Facts like these have been considered problematic for an autosegmental analysis by Goldsmith (1975), though they form no problem in Poser's solution:

(36)   a.   +   +   −

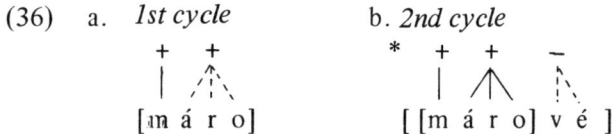

         η^W aiví + vé
    b.   + +   −
         máro + vé

We are now faced with the following problem. In the case of Applecross Gaelic we had to assume that the spell-out rule introduced a *floating*

Prosodic Domains and opaque segments

autosegment to get the precedence facts right. In the case of Guaraní we have to assume that the spell-out rule introduces a *bound* autosegment and, in addition, we have to assume that the spreading convention must be parametrized, laying an extra burden on the language-specific grammar. It seems to us that it would be preferable if the spell-out rule takes the same form in both analyses, whichever of the two formulations comes out as being the preferred one. We will now show that this result can be obtained only if we assume that the domain of association in Guaraní is not the (phonological) word but a smaller metrical constituent, usually equal to the foot.

Since the vast majority of native lexical words in the language have final stress, we assign a right-dominant unbounded foot at the right edge of each word. If we assume that this foot assignment procedure is cyclic we explain why adding prefixes leads to no change whatsoever in the placement of main stress and we also predict that suffixation leads to a rightward shift of the stress. The same result would also be obtained if metrical structure was assigned postcyclically, but in that case we would not predict the secondary accents that Gregores and Suárez give in their phonemic representations. Words that have penultimate or antepenultimate stress have to be handled as exceptional, somehow or other. We will assume here that poststress syllables are marked as extrametrical. In the case of the unstressed suffixes this means that these suffixes are, as a whole, extrametrical. In (37) we give some examples of words with their metrical structure:

(37) a.

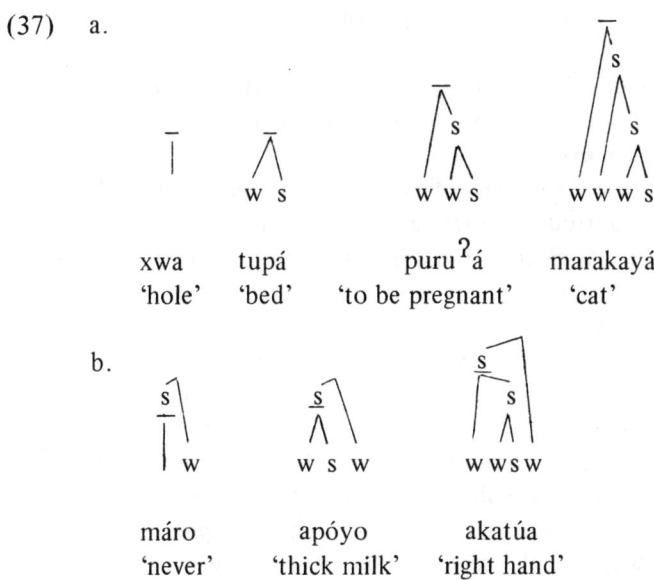

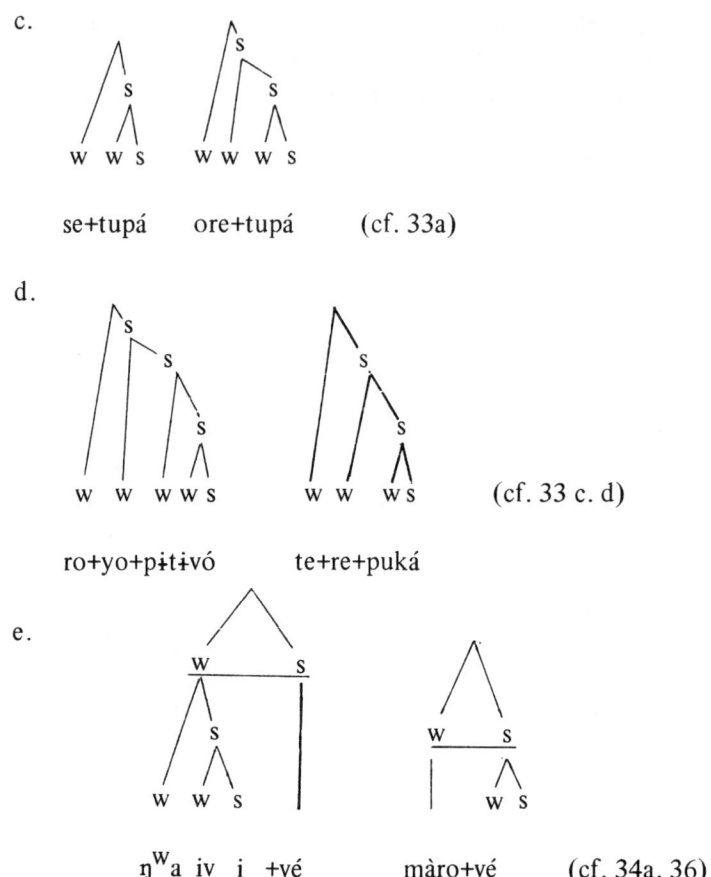

Comparing the metrical structure of *máro* (in 37b) and *màrové* (in 37e) one will see that the post-stress 'stray' syllable in *máro* becomes part of the second foot in *màrové*.

If we now say that the domain of association in Guaraní is the foot, our spell-out rule can introduce *floating* autosegments into the appropriate foot domain (as in Applecross Gaelic). The ambiguity that we noted in (34) can no longer arise since the two floating autosegments will always belong to *different* feet. We also explain why the orality or nasality of the suffix only spreads into the stem if it has penultimate stress, as can be seen by examining the forms in (37e). All remaining cases where an ambiguity exists involve at most *one* floating autosegment. This means that we can appeal to precedence convention (22) for those cases. Of course we will also have cases in which two bound autosegments are involved (cf. 27d). It is not clear whether leftward or rightward precedence applies here since both will give the same result. Since rightward precedence is independently motivated on the basis of other languages and leftward precedence is not, it is clear that we can dispense with the latter. This leads to the interesting result that we do not require to assume (as Poser does) that the precedence convention is parametrized.

We conclude that nasalization in Applecross Gaelic and Guaraní can be handled in the same terms *if* we assume that harmony in the latter language is not bound to the word domain, but to a smaller metrical domain, so far assumed to be the metrical foot. Let us now look somewhat more closely at the precise characterization of this metrical domain.

In our analysis it is the case that word final, post-stress syllables fall outside the scope of any foot; they are stray syllables that are adjoined in the word tree as weak sisters to the preceding foot. It turns out, however, that the sonorants in those post-stress syllables receive the same value for nasality as the sonorants belonging to the preceding foot. The domain of spreading is apparently the foot *plus* any following stray syllables. Let us call this constituent (following Gregores & Suárez) the *stress group*.

It is important to note the following. We claim that nasalization in Guaraní is bound to the *stress group* and we therefore put forward our analysis as an example showing the relevance of both metrical and autosegmental phonology for the treatment of harmony. Unlike the examples in the previous sections, however, association in Guaraní is not bound to one of the familiar metrical domains (such as syllable, foot etc.). The crucial point is that the span over which nasality spreads must be defined in terms of metrical structure: a stress group comprises of all syllables that are minimally governed by a stressed syllable.

Let us finally remark that our analysis arrives at the same interpretation of the domain of spreading as that of Gregores & Suárez. They say: "By delimiting the nasal spans in this way, their boundaries coincide with – and confirm – those of the stress groups delimited at the previous level". (p. 68). 'Stress groups' are defined as follows: "each stressed syllable in a macrosegment belongs in the same constitute with all the immediately preceding unstressed syllables, and – if it is the last stressed syllable in the macrosegment – with the following one (or more, up to three) syllables. A stressed syllable flanked by other stressed syllables stands, of course, alone. We may call each of these structural units a *stress group*; in it, the stressed syllable must be interpreted as the nucleus, and the unstressed syllables, in coordinate construction with each other, as the satellite". (p. 65).

6. PRECEDENCE CONVENTIONS, OPAQUE SEGMENTS AND LANGUAGE-SPECIFIC RULES

Our study of nasalization in Applecross Gaelic and Guaraní has affirmed the claim (already extensively discussed in Goldsmith 1976) that the general association convention must be supplemented by general precedence conventions, since cases arise in which P-bearing segments are in the scope of more than one P-segment. We have made use of Precedence Convention I, repeated here for convenience:

(22) *Precedence Convention I*
The spreading of a free autosegment takes precedence over the spreading of a bound autosegment

In this section we will discuss some of the alternative approaches for dealing with the precedence facts. We will furthermore address a claim advanced by Halle & Vergnaud (1981), which involves a more radical version of (22):

(38) spreading conventions only apply to free autosegments

We will show that this claim cannot be upheld, referring to our analysis of Guaraní, where opaque elements are spread due to the general association convention. In addition we will give an analysis of nasalization in two other languages (Capanahua and Sundanese) in which we make use of language-specific association rules that stipulate *uni*directional spreading of opaque elements.

We found that (22) leads to the right result provided that nasalization in the two languages is bound to the foot and the stress group respectively. The possibility of generalizing over the two cases of nasalization does not crucially depend, however, on our decision to introduce *floating* autosegments. Earlier we expressed the opinion that it seemed more straightforward to associate such autosegments directly with the stressed vowels, not in the least because the spell-out rule that introduces floating segments must also locate the stressed vowel to guarantee accessibility. Suppose then that we select the more direct formulation of the spell-out rule, how could we in that case explain the precedence relations in the two cases. We suggest that then the following precedence convention is needed:

(39) *Precedence Convention IV*
The spreading of metrically stronger autosegments takes precedence over the spreading of metrically weaker autosegments

(39) predicts that the spreading of the autosegment that is associated with the stressed vowel takes precedence and this is precisely what happens in both Gaelic and Guaraní. It is important to note that an

analysis that makes use of this convention still requires that nasalization in Guaraní be bound to the stress group.

The alternative treatment of nasalization in Applecross Gaelic and Guaraní shows that the interaction between autosegmental and metrical phonology is even more intricate than we have suggested thus far. We think, however, that a larger number of cases is required before we can decide whether (39) is really a principle of universal grammar. Assuming that (22) is independently motivated (for example by the analysis of tonal systems) we therefore favour the floating analysis at this point. Let us now address (38).

Halle & Vergnaud (1981) claim that harmony processes "fall into two distinct types depending on whether the harmonic features propagate in one direction only, or whether the propagation occurs in both directions" (H&V, 1). They propose handling bidirectional harmony in autosegmental terms and unidirectional harmony in metrical terms. Apart from the directionality there is another difference between the two types of harmony systems. In bidirectional harmony systems "a distinction is made between triggering and opaque elements. The general association convention only applies to the triggering element which must always be a floating autosegment. Opaque elements, i.e. autosegments that are lexically associated with a P-bearing unit are not subject to spreading. "No such distinction is made in the case of directional harmony: all triggering elements are opaque, and each opaque element induces a harmony of its own" (H&V, 9).

We do not agree with the distinction that H&V make. Take for example the case of Guaraní. We have seen that opaque elements (the nasals) are subject to spreading. This would imply that the harmony is metrical in the framework of H&V. However, spreading in Guaraní is bidirectional (see the forms in 29c & d where nasality spreads in both directions). Our analysis, moreover, makes use of floating autosegments, which would imply that the harmony is autosegmental. But this would be incompatible with the fact that opaque elements are subject to spreading.

If we conclude for this (and other) reason(s) that all harmony should be analyzed autosegmentally, it can no longer be upheld that opaque elements are not subject to spreading. It may be true though that there is a difference between opaque elements and floating elements in the sense that only the opaque elements may be referred to by language-specific association rules, whereas floating autosegments cannot.

Suppose language-specific rules can prescribe three kinds of behaviour for opaque elements: spread leftward, spread rightward or don't spread at all. In the absence of any language-specific rule the general association convention will guarantee that an opaque element spread in both directions. Let us furthermore assume that the general association convention applies after the language-specific spreading rules (this follows from the Elsewhere Condition). We will now give two examples where a theory along these lines seems to be required to handle cases of nasalization in other languages than Applecross Gaelic and Guaraní.

Our first example concerns nasal spreading in Capanahua. It is also discussed in H&V and in Anderson, this volume. In the descriptive source (Loos 1969) the following facts are reported.

A contiguous sequence of vowels and glides (w, y, ʔ, h) is nasalized if it precedes a nasal consonant (n, m). Nasal consonants, however, are deleted before a continuant strident consonant, glide, liquid or word boundary. If a nasal is deleted the nasalization on the preceding vowels and glides remains, but, and this is the surprising feature, vowels and glides that stand after the deleted nasal are also nasalized. Consider the following example:

(40) a. /poyan/ 'arm' [põỹã]
    /bawin/ 'catfish' [bãw̃ĩ]
    /ciʔin/ 'by fire' [cĩʔĩ]
    /boon/ 'hair' [bõõ]
 b. /waran/ 'squash' [warã]
    /ciponki/ 'downriver' [cipõnki]
 c. /bimi/ 'fruit' [bĩmi]
    /banawi/ 'plant it' [bãnawi]
 d. /wïranwï/ 'push it' [wïrãw̃ ï]
    /wïranyašaʔnwʔï/ 'push it sometime' [wïrãỹãšãʔw̃ĩ]

The forms in (40a) show the non-local character of nasal spreading and the effect of nasal deletion before a word boundary. The forms in (40b) show the blocking character of consonants (i.e. r and p in this case). The forms in (40c) show spreading to the left. Finally, the forms under (40d) show the bidirectional nature of spreading following nasal deletion before a glide. We propose the following analysis.

All consonants are autosegmentally specified as [+N] or [−N] at the word level. There is a language-specific rule that prescribes the leftward spreading of [+N] and, ordered before this, a rule that deletes nasals before glides and word boundary, setting the [+N] autosegment afloat. We explain, given this analysis, why spreading is bidirectional after nasal deletion has applied: the language-specific spreading rule cannot apply to a floating autosegment (its SD is simply not met). Thereafter the general association convention takes over, leading to bidirectional spreading. In (41) we give some sample derivations:

Prosodic Domains and opaque segments

(41)

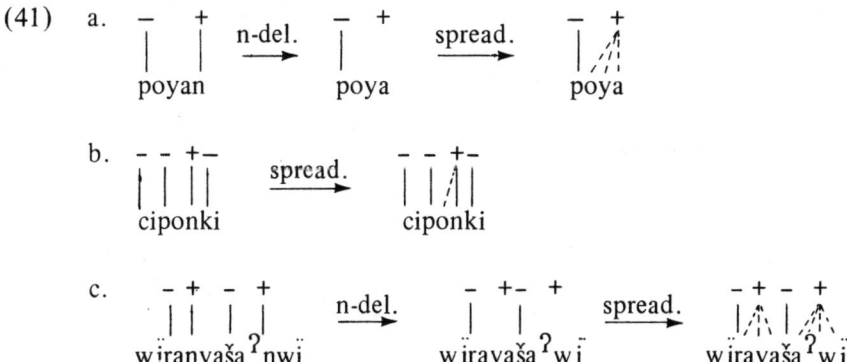

The leftward spreading rule could also be an alpha-rule. The facts of Capanahua are not conclusive in this respect. Note in any case that the "−"value may be allowed to spread bidirectionally due to the general conventions.

The present analysis makes crucial use of a rule that stipulates leftward spreading (cf. Anderson, this volume). Let us now look at a case where we require rightward spreading: nasalization in Sundanese. Nasalization in Sundanese is discussed in Anderson (1972) in segmental terms. Hart (1981) gives an autosegmental analysis, that differs from the one we are going to propose. The descriptive source is Robins (1957) who reports the following facts.

A string of contiguous vowels, possibly interrupted by h or $ʔ$, is nasalized if a nasal consonant ($m, n, ɲ$ or $ŋ$) precedes. The following examples serve as an illustration of this rightward nasal spreading:

(42) a. /ɲiar/ 'to seek' [ɲĩãr]
/ɲaian/ 'to wet' [ɲãĩãn]
b. /maro/ 'to halve' [mãro]
/moekɤn/ 'to dry' [mõẽkɤn]
c. /ɲaho/ 'to know' [ɲãhõ]
/bɤŋhar/ 'to be' [bɤŋhar]

The forms in (42a) show the non-local character of spreading, those in (42b) the blocking character of supraglottally articulated consonants. The forms in (42c) show both the transparency of /h/ and (in the second form) the fact that spreading is not leftward. The analysis we propose is as follows.

All supraglottally articulated consonants are autosegmentally specified as [−N] or [+N] at the word level. There is a language-specific rule that prescribes the rightward spreading of [+N]. It is easy to see that this will give the desired result:

(43) a.

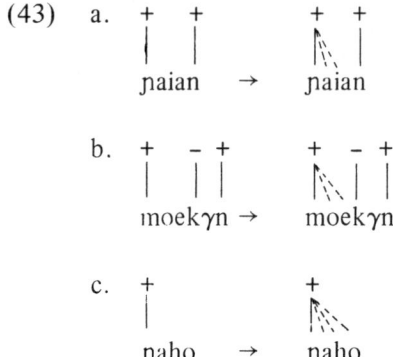

ɲaian → ɲaian

b. ɲoekɣn → moekɣn

c. ɲaho → ɲaho

As in the case of Capanahua we will assume the spreading of [−N] is due to the universal spreading convention. Vowels that remain unassociated will be assigned the unmarked value, i.e. [−nasal]. There is, however, one seemingly complicating factor in the case of Sundanese that relates to the occurrence of infixes.

Robins (1957) mentions three infixes, one without a nasal (*−ar−*), and two containing a nasal (*−um−*, *−im−*). Both categories are extremely interesting for their own reasons. We will first look at forms of the first category (we have italicized the infix):

(44) /ɲaraian/   (cf. 42a)   [ɲãraĩãn]
      /maroekɣn/   (cf. 42b)   [mãroẽkɣn]
      /ɲaraho/   (cf. 42c)   [ɲãrahõ]

The surprising fact about the forms in (44) is that the vowels following the *r* of the infix are nasalized except for the first one. This is odd for two reasons. First we have seen that *r* blocks spreading (cf. the form in 42b) and secondly, even if the *r* of the infix were specified as neutral, why should the vowel immediately following it be nonnasal?

The explanation of these two facts leads us to assume that the rightward spreading rule applies cyclically and that there is a second rule that spreads [−N] to a tautosyllabic vowel. We cannot collapse this second rule with the rule that spreads [+N] precisely because this latter is not bound to the syllable domain but to the word domain. This shows that the word domain rule cannot be an alpha-rule, since this would result in denasalizing all vowels following the /r/ of the infix. We obtain the following derivations:

(41) a. *1e cycle*

moekɣn [−N]–spread. → moekɣn [+N]–spread. → moekɣn

b. *2e cycle*

+ - + -+   [-N]-spread.   + - +- +   [+N]-spread.   + - +- +
| |ʌ∧| → | ∧ |∧ | → |˜∧|∧|
mɑroekɣn   maroekɣn   maroekɣn

The spreading rules are not crucially ordered. Applying them in the reverse order, or simultaneously will lead to the same result. The fact that at least [+N] spreading *must* be cyclically ordered also follows if we look at the second category of infixes, i.e. those containing a nasal:

(42) a. gəde   'to be big'   [gəde]   →   guməde   [gumə̃de]
         dɣhɣs   'to approach'   [dɣhɣs]   →   dumɣhɣs   [dumɣ̃h̃ɣ̃s]
     b. paɲgih   'to find'   [paɲgih]   →   pinaɲgih   [pinã̃ɲgih]

These forms illustrate that the vowels following the nasal of the infix must be nasalized. At first sight one might propose that this is due to the local rule (formulated as an alpha-rule). The second form in (42a) shows, however, that this cannot be true: nasal spreading after the nasal of the infix extends here over two syllables. This must be due then to the word domain rule (Anderson 1972 points out the significance of the crucial form in 42a).

We think that the two analyses given above clearly show the need for language-specific rules that stipulate the direction of spreading of opaque, i.e. lexically bound autosegments. This is an interesting conclusion given the claim advanced in Halle & Vergnaud that opaque elements do not spread. We have not given a crucial example showing the need to stipulate that an opaque element *must* not spread. The facts of Capanahua were seen to be inconclusive on this point. A possible example might be found in Mongolian vowel harmony (as discussed in Chinchor 1979), Chinchor argues that high round vowels block rounding harmony (coming from the left), but all vowels after the round blockers are themselves nonround. This example requires further study, however, so we will not discuss it in any detail here.

7. CONCLUDING REMARKS

We have addressed ourselves to two topics that relate to the spreading of autosegments. Firstly, we have shown that various prosodic categories constitute domains for such spreading, either as the result of general or language-specific association rules. It is of some importance to note that, though we have employed the metrical theory of phonological domains, nothing in our analyses depends crucially on the fact that phonological domains have a binary branching structure in this theory, rather than an n-ary branching structure as suggested in Clements & Keyser (1981) and Leben (1982). Our findings are compatible with either approach to domain characterization.

Secondly, we have discussed the behaviour of opaque segments. We found that such elements are subject to spreading, either as a result of general or of language-specific rules.

The second part is somewhat more speculative than the first, but we hope that on the whole some progress has been made here towards the proper formal treatment of suprasegmental processes, in particular of those involving nasalization.

The Syllable

Elisabeth O. Selkirk
University of Massachusetts, Amherst

English provides a particularly good illustration of the proposition that the syllable is a linguistically significant unit which must have its place in phonological theory. The reasons generally given in support of the syllable as a theoretical construct are threefold, and English provides pertinent evidence in each of these areas. First of all, it can be argued that the most general and explanatory statement of phonotactic constraints in a language can be made only by reference to the syllabic structure of an utterance. Second, it can be argued that only via the syllable can one give the proper characterization of the domain of application of a wide range of rules of segmental phonology. And third, it can be argued that an adequate treatment of suprasegmental phenomena such as stress and tone requires that segments be grouped into units which are the size of the syllable. The same three reasons leading to the postulation of the syllable can be shown to motivate the existence of privileged groupings of segments within the syllable which must be thought of as constituent-like linguistic units themselves.[1] The notion of the syllable that will emerge from this examination of English is therefore one of a hierarchical unit; an internally structured tree quite analogous to a tree representing syntactic structure.

1. THE REPRESENTATION OF THE SYLLABLE

1.1 In what follows, special attention will be given to the question of the representation of the syllable and especially to the hypothesis that the syllable is an element of a hierarchically organized prosodic struc-

---

*This article was written in 1978, and has been circulated informally since then. It was intended that it should form part of my book *Phonology and Syntax: The Relation between Sound and Structure*, forthcoming from MIT Press. I have decided to publish it separately now, unrevised, for it will not now fit in the book. My views on the nature of syllable structure have changed somewhat since 1978, as have the views of other scholars, but I feel that there is enough of value in the present piece to merit its publication at this time.

ture. One of the main sources of support for this hypothesis comes from the demonstration that the syllable has internal structure, and for this reason we will dwell at some length on questions of syllable constituency. The other main source of support for the hypothesis, is the demonstration that there exists a higher order hierarchical prosodic structure of which syllables must be seen as building blocks.[2] Being structured within and forming an integral part of a larger structure without, how can the syllable be anything but a structural, suprasegmental, prosodic unit itself?

In our view, the phonological representation of an English monosyllabic word like *flounce* is structured as in (1).

(1)
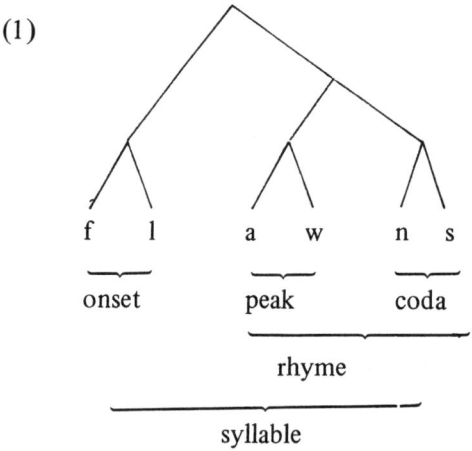

(where the letters should be taken as standing for the corresponding distinctive feature matrices). There is a first major bipartite division of the syllable - into *onset* (the initial consonant cluster) and *rhyme* (the rest). The rhyme in turn divides into two parts - the *peak* (containing the syllabic nucleus) and the *coda* (the final consonant cluster).[3] Of course not all syllables in English are so rich in internal structure: *cow* [kaw] has only a simple (non-branching) onset, a complex peak, and no coda at all; *fat* [fæt] has a simple onset, a simple peak and a simple coda; *aye* [aj] has a complex peak, but no onset and no coda.

Before moving to a defense of this particular analysis of English, it will be useful to address the question of syllable-internal structure in somewhat more general fashion. Pike (1967) has argued that it is a universal of syllable composition that a constituent structure break exists between a syllable nucleus (our "peak") and its margins (our "onset" and "coda"). The argument for constituency is based, in part, on distributional or phonotactic considerations:

"The possibility of substitution of one phoneme for another in a parti-

The Syllable

cular slot in the margin, for example, is likely to be more dependent upon the particular phonemes manifesting other slots in that margin than it is by the particular phonemes manifesting the nucleus of such syllables. I.e., if a formula CCV is manifested by /s/ in the first consonant slot, and the nucleus slot is filled by the phoneme /a/, the list of phonemes which fill the second consonant slot are more likely to be controlled by the presence of the /s/ then they are by the presence of the /a/ - e.g., they may be limited to voiceless consonants after the voiceless /s/, etc. Such considerations indicate that a closer relationship exists between the two consonants than exists between either consonant and the vowel." (Pike 1967, 386-7)

The claim thus is that the likelihood of the existence of phonotactic constraints between the position slots in the syllable (as well as the strength or inviolability of those constraints, one might add) is a reflection of the immediate constituent (IC) structure relation between the two slots: the more closely related structurally (in the obvious sense), the more subject to phonotactic constraints two position slots are. We will call this the IC principle of phonotactics. According to this principle, therefore, onset, peak and coda are units within which the tightest phonotactic constraints obtain.

The grouping of peak and coda into a constituent is advocated as a universal of syllable composition by Kuriłowicz (1948), one reason for this being similar to Pike's. The claim made is that co-occurrence restrictions between peak and coda are always more likely to exist (and indeed are quite common) than are restrictions between either peak or coda and the onset. The explanation offered is that the former two comprise a constituent.

As any detailed analysis of the phonotactics of the English syllable shows,[4] it is within the onset, peak and coda that the strongest collocational restrictions obtain. By contrast, there are no phonotactic restrictions at all for the language which involve onset and peak, for example. The existence of this array of restrictions follows from a single principle, the IC principle of phonotactics, if one assumes an IC analysis of the syllable.

A theory giving an IC analysis of the syllable, and incorporating this principle, is clearly superior to one where syllable structure is defined merely in terms of a sequence of segments (which is the approach of Hooper (1976), for example), for it allows for quite a restrictive characterization of the notion "possible phonotactic constraint of language L". A purely linear representation of the syllable *flounce* might look like (2):

(2) $\$ f_1 \; l_2 \; a_3 \; w_4 \; n_5 \; s_6 \; \$$

The fact that strong phonotactic constraints existed between positions

1 and 2, 3 and 4, or 5 and 6, but not between other pairs, would be given no significance by the linear syllable theory, unless explicit provisions were incorporated to the effect that "syllable-initial consonant clusters, the sonorant elements of syllable centers, and syllable-final consonant clusters tend to exhibit phonotactic constraints among themselves." But, still, the statements remain ad-hoc, for they follow from no more general principle of grammar. The IC approach to the syllable, on the other hand, permits a single eminently simple statement that will cover the same facts. We conclude from this that phonotactic considerations do indeed support an IC analysis of the syllable.

More telling even than these phonotactic arguments for internal structure in the syllable are those provided by phonological rules, for phonological rules must "look at", i.e. operate in terms of, the properties of phonological representation. In this sense, phonological rules are analogous to transformations of the syntactic component, whose operations on syntactic representation are dependent on, and therefore may provide arguments for, the particulars of syntactic constituent structure. One would of course hypothesize that the constituency of the syllable in phonological representation that is revealed by the operation of phonological rules would be the same as that motivated by phonotactic considerations. And, indeed, if it can be shown that there is a systematic coincidence of the constituent units required by rules of the phonology and those required for phonotactics, then in the absence of direct evidence from phonological rules, the investigator would be justified in relying on phonotactics alone in assigning an internal analysis of the syllable.

The arguments of Pike and Kuryłowicz in favor of a hierarchical conception of the syllable have not been limited to phonotactics. They have shown that an internal structural analysis makes available a superior treatment of phonological processes in languages. For example, Pike (1947c, 142) argues for the nucleus (= peak) on the grounds that it serves as a unit with respect to suprasegmental phenomena such as pitch and stress. Pike and Pike (1947) adduce evidence from numerous phonological rules, suprasegmental and segmental, for a particular IC analysis of the syllable in Mazateco. In addition, as a point in favor of the rhyme constituent, Kurylowicz (1948), Pike (1967, 391) and Newman (1972, 303) have observed that it makes possible a unified treatment of the heavy-light syllable distinction which plays such an important part in stress systems. The light syllable CV can be characterized as one whose rhyme is simple, non-branching, while the heavy syllable, be it CVC or CVV (a long vowel) is one with a complex, or branching, rhyme. Other phonological, or shall we say phonetic, phenomena such as duration and closeness of transition between segments might also be taken as revealing of the immediate constituent structure of the syllable.[5] We touch on some of these phenomena below.

The Syllable

There is one additional general question for the theory of the representation of the syllable that we wish to pose. We have argued thus far that the syllable has immediate constituent structure. The next logical question is whether the nodes of this constituent structure are labelled. Or, to put the question in broader terms, is there anything to be said about the nature of syllable-internal constituents aside from the fact that they may branch? We are inclined to believe that the answer is yes, and specifically, that a case can be made for associating two distinct types of information with the nodes, i.e., the constituents as a whole. The considerations giving support for including each of these will be reviewed in turn.

One might first want to ask whether the labels syllable, onset, rhyme, peak and coda, which we have so far used merely as descriptive terms, should be assigned to their respective nodes in a representation. That is, should the representation (1) be recast as (3)?

(3)

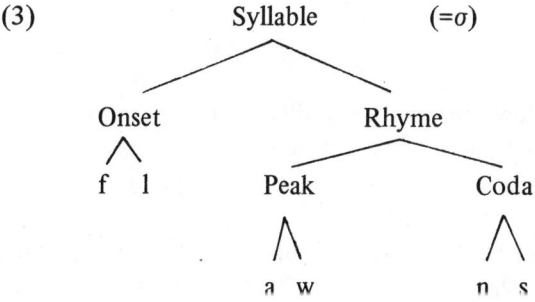

The preliminary answer we have to offer is that while the prosodic category label "syllable" is required in representations, support for naming its internal constituents in this way is currently lacking. The evidence pointing to the need for the 'syllable' label emerges in the examination of higher order prosodic structure. See Selkirk (1980), for example, where it is shown that the label is necessary in order to identify the syllable as a unit distinct from any other branching structure (be it "larger" or "smaller" than the syllable).

A second suggestion is that the nodes be characterized as a complex of distinctive features, that is, that selected distinctive features may be assigned to a node of syllable structure, with the interpretation of this being that any segment or constituent dominated by a node labelled [+F] is characterized as [+F]. This suggestion may be thought of as a particular implementation of the theory of Vergnaud (1976) according to which adjacent segments bearing the same specification α for some feature F_i are to be represented as being dominated by a tree labelled αF_i. In general, it seems reasonable to entertain the possibility that, by convention, any features shared by the segments or constituents immediately dominated by some node be assigned to that node itself. (McCarthy (1977) hints at a convention of this sort in assigning the node dominating a coronal cluster like *st* in English the feature [+coronal].) Following this convention, the representation (1) would be recast as (4):

(4)
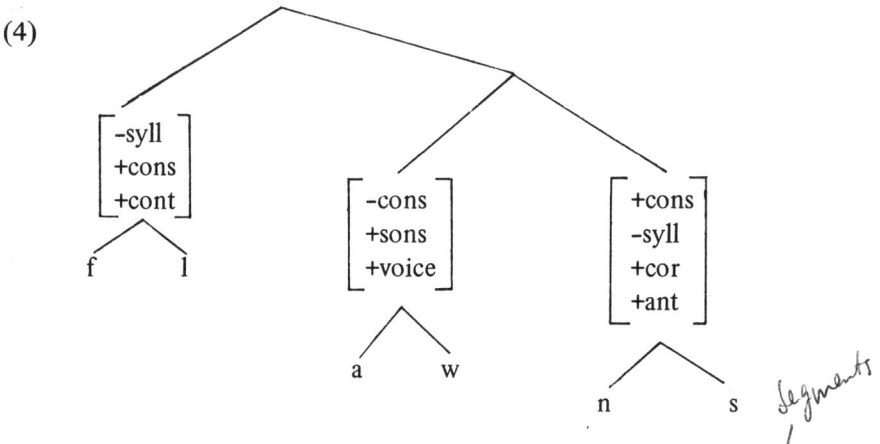

Such a representation allows for the possibility that some phonological rules may operate not in terms of the feature matrices of particular but instead in terms of the features of constituent nodes. (This, in essence, is Vergnaud's suggestion.) For example, it would permit an elegant characterization of the fact that in Arabic and Berber the domain of so-called emphasis (i.e., pharyngealization) is the syllable;[6] the rule pharyngealizing the syllable when it contains a pharyngeal phoneme can simply be seen as assigning the feature [+Constricted Pharynx] to the syllable node.

Similarly, vowel nasalization in French can be conceived of as the attribution of the features of nasality to the constituent (VN), with consequent replacement of the consonantal segment by the features of the vowel. The result is a compensatorily lengthened nasal vowel: ($\widetilde{VV}$). These two examples are simply indicative of the importance of representing the features borne in common by a sequence of segments for the characterization of phonological rules.

A final suggestion concerning node-labelling within the syllable will be entertained. It builds on the observation that in a binary branching constituent of the syllable, one member tends always to be "weaker" than other. Pike and Pike (1947) described this relation as the "subordination" of one to the other. Extending the theory of hierarchical prosodic structure of Liberman (1975) and Liberman and Prince (1977) to the syllable, this relation can be given a formal representation, by labelling the "subordinate" node *w* and the other *s*.[7] With nodes labelled in this fashion, the representation (1) would take on the shape of (5) (ignoring the other two types of node-related information just discussed):

The Syllable

(5)

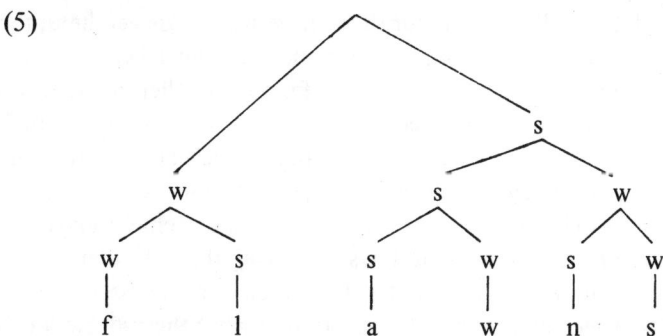

The peak is of course strong (*s*), i.e., more sonorous, than the onset. And within each of the other constituents, the *s* has been assigned to the more sonorant element. This approach incorporates the suggestion made by Pike (1967, 387 ff.) and McCarthy (1977) that the assignment of *w* (= "subordinate" status) vs. *s* can be made, at least partly, on the basis of the relative ranking of the two segments (or constituents) on a universally defined sonority hierarchy.[8]

It has been claimed, by Hooper (1977, 15) for example, that syllable-final position (the coda) is universally "weak." According to the s/w node labelling theory, this need not be stipulated at all: it immediately follows from the s/w theory, on the assumption that syllables always branch into onset and rhyme, and rhyme into peak and coda. The coda is weak (with respect to its sister peak), and is lower in the tree than the onset (which is weak with respect to the rhyme). The strength hierarchy which can be assigned to these constituents, according to the Liberman and Prince algorithm (1977, 259) is thus peak, onset, coda.

Note that not all constituents are composed of members of differing sonority, in which case a language particular specification of the s/w relation may have to be made. Consider, for example, a hypothetical peak composed of the vowels *i* and *u*, which have the same rank on the sonority hierarchy. The constituent could be either ($\overset{s}{i}\ \overset{w}{u}$) or ($\overset{w}{i}\ \overset{s}{u}$). In the first case, one would expect the phonetic outcome to resemble [iw] (a falling diphthong) and in the second [yu] (a rising diphthong). Thus, whether a language has diphthongs that are falling or rising can be seen as resulting from the language-specific assignment of *sw* vs. *ws* to its complex peak. Note that the idea of having gliding result from the s/w relation allows one to consider the possibility that a distinctive feature such as [±syllabic] is not necessary to the capturing of the glide-vowel distinction. (Indeed, one should ask whether such a feature as [±syllabic] is at all required, once the notion of syllable is introduced into phonological theory).

It should be noted that the three separate suggestions for the characterization of nodes in syllable structure that have been reviewed here, the first of which will be adopted only with respect to the label 'syllable', are mutually compatible. They are not different, conflicting, theories about how nodes should be labelled. Rather, they are theories which touch on different aspects of the representation, which all require some treatment in the phonology. Because the graphic representation of these three types of information, alone or all together, is extremely ungainly, we will make the practice in what follows of leaving this information out of syllable structure representation, unless it is crucial for the discussion.

Now it must be recognized that the question of what the syllable looks like in phonological representation is a distinct one, logically, from the question of how the grammar of a language is to give expression to the notion 'possible syllable of L', and, specifically, to the notions possible onset, peak, coda and rhyme. That is, individual representations of syllables do not state generalizations about syllable structure any more than individual noun phrases in a syntactic representation state generalizations concerning the notion 'possible noun phrase' in a language. A grammar must therefore provide for some statement of the notion 'possible syllable of L', this statement being distinct from any phonological representation of the language. Let us suppose that for each language this statement is in the form of a template and an accompanying set of phonotactic constraints somewhat in the spirit of Fudge (1969), and Hooper (1976), but with differences that will become apparent. These together specify all the possible syllable types of the language, and can be thought of as serving as well-formedness conditions on the syllabic structure of the phonological representations of a language. They are, in essence, tree-checking devices.

Suppose, for example, that the syllable template for English looks something like (6):

(6)
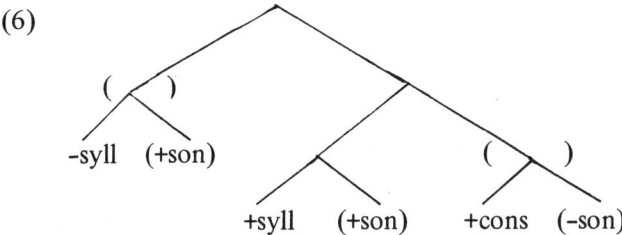

The function of the template is to encode the gross characteristics of syllable structure: (i) the composition of the syllable in terms of segment types identified by the major class features [±syllabic], [±sonorant] [±consonantal], (ii) the order of these segment types within the syllable,[9] (iii) the structural relations between the segment types (defined in IC terms), and (iv) the optionality of segments or groups of segments (= constituents) within the syllable. The role of the template in the grammar will be discussed in latter sections of this paper. Suffice it to say here that it contributes to defining the well-formedness of the syllable structure of particular phonological representations. A necessary condition for the well-formedness of a representation is that, within a syntactic domain specified for the language, the syllabic structure of the representation be *non-distinct* from the template. Roughly speaking, a syllable tree of a phonological representation is said to be non-distinct from the template if its branching matches the branching of the template, and the distinctive feature matrices of its segments are not distinct from the corresponding feature matrices of the template.[10] It is easy to see that the representation of *flounce* given in (1) is non-distinct from the template (6). Note, furthermore, that the template includes provisions for optionality. Thus, the entire onset is optional (cf. *as, aye, in,* etc.), and, if present, may contain just one consonant (cf. *pie, fate, so,* etc.), the second being optional. Clearly, if a syllable in phonological representation contains only the non-optional member of a pair within a constituent, it is not to be considered to be distinct from the template.

The template on its own does not give a characterization of English syllable structure that is sufficiently restrictive, though. Formulated as in (6), it allows for more types than are ever evidenced in English. For example, in the onset, if the first consonant is a labial then it may not be followed by *w*, or if it is an *s*, it may not be followed by *r*. And in the peak, for example, only a limited variety of diphthongs are available: *j* is not possible after any back vowel except ɔ and *a*. These further restrictions do not find a natural expression in a template like (6). Following Fudge (1969), we acknowledge that another type of formal device is required in the grammar to express such phonotactic constraints. Fudge calls them collocational restrictions, and gives them the form of an implication on the order of "if a second position in onset is *w*, then first position is not [+labial]." (Alternatively, one could think of them as filters on the output of an "overgenerating or overly permissive template."[11] They might have the form, cf. * [+labial] *w*. We will take no firm position on this matter here.) Clearly, then, a second condition on the well-formedness of the syllabic structure of a representation is that it not be ruled out by the collocational restrictions of the language.

1.2. An examination of English reveals evidence that supports the approach to the representation of syllable structure that has been outlined here. Motivation for internal constituency on the basis of phonotactics is particularly strong (following the IC principle), and while the operation of phonological rules and their relation to syllable constituency in English has not received much attention in the framework of generative grammar, some very suggestive work pointing to internal constituency has been carried out by phoneticians, and will be referred to.

Let us first look at the onset constituent. According to template (6), any consonant in the phoneme repertory of English may serve alone as the onset. This is correct, except for ž and ŋ which will have to be excluded in a separate statement. The template also says that the onset contains at most two consonants, and that if it does contain two, the second must be a sonorant.[12] One could consider not specifying that the second place consonant has to be a sonorant, and change the onset in (6) to -syll(-syll). But since the more restrictive -syll(+son) of (6) does not exclude any possible onsets, and removes the need for mentioning an additional collocational restriction in the grammar, we retain it. Note that the template does not state a further restriction on onsets that must find expression in the grammar: that when there is a second sonorant consonant in the onset, the first consonant must be a non-sonorant. This information could conceivably be incorporated into the template itself, by modifying the onset portion to look like the following: (-son) (+son). But it seems undesirable to make this modification: first, because, with it, the template no longer says in direct fashion that *any* consonant (i.e. [-syll]) can be the sole element of the onset, and second, because the fact that the first must be a non-sonorant when there is a sonorant that follows should quite likely be seen as following from some universals of syllable structure and therefore not require direct expression in the grammar.[13] So we propose instead that the grammar of English contain a collocational restriction associated with the template to the effect that if there is a second consonant in the onset, the first must be an obstruent.

A fair number of additional collocational restrictions on possible onset combinations must be stated. These must express the fact that (i) only stops and voiceless fricatives appear as the first member, (ii) that *j* never appears as a second member, (iii) that only *s* may appear with *m* or *n*, (iv) that *w* never appears after labial consonants, or š or *st*, (v) that *r* never appears after *s* or *h*, and (vi) that *l* never appears after *t, d, š, h* or *sk*.[14] Given the IC principle espoused by Pike and Kuryłowicz, and adopted by us, the existence of these constraints between first and second consonants, and the absence of any between these consonant positions and the vowels that follow, indicate a grouping of the consonants into a constituent.

Looking now at clusters with initial *s*, we see that they provide the sole instances of onsets where the second consonant may be an obstruent (e.g. *stay, spite, sky, sphere*)[15] and of onsets with three consonants instead of two or one (cf. *split, spry, stray, scream, square*). Should the statement about possible onsets in English, which we have expressed in the template

The Syllable

(6), be modified so as to include an additional place for *s*? The answer is no, for to do so would fail to give recognition to the fact that clusters of *s* plus obstruent form a unit that may occupy a single obstruent slot, wherever that slot may appear in the syllable. In the coda as well, as we shall see, *s* plus obstruent clusters may appear where otherwise only a single obstruent would be allowed. To include a provision for an extra *s* in both onset and coda would be to deny that they are really the same fact.[16] What we propose to account for the special status of these *s* clusters is what we will call an *auxiliary* template, a sort of corollary to the general template in (6). It would be formulated as (7):

(7)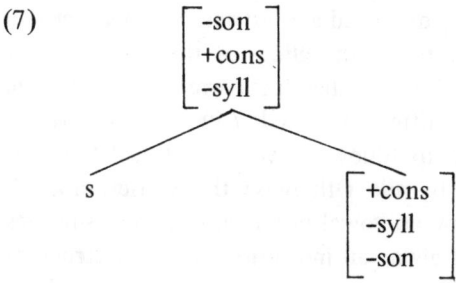

and says, essentially, that *s* plus obstruent may qualify as a single obstruent in English. A phonological representation of English is ruled well-formed, if it is non-distinct from the general template (6), taken in conjunction with the auxiliary template (7) (and obeys the appropriate restrictions). For example, the representation of the word *splint* (8) is ruled well-formed because the circled segments and nodes are non-distinct from the general template (6), while the remaining (squared) segments, unaccounted for by (6), are allowed by the auxiliary template:

(8)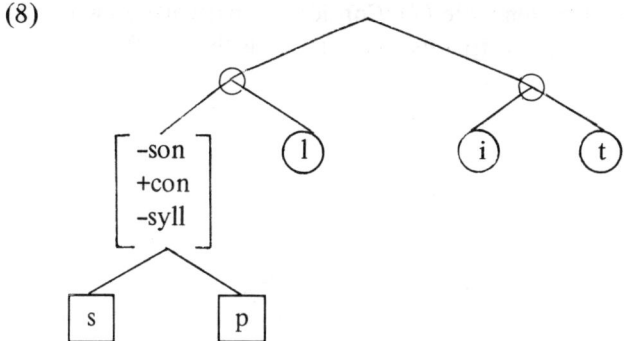

Turning next to the peak, we see that it must contain a single syllabic element, be it a single vowel (cf. *pat, kiss, hex,* etc.) or a syllabic sonorant (cf. *stir* [str̩], *muddle* [mʌdl̩], *chasm* [kæzm̩], etc.). Making use of the addi-

348   *Elisabeth O. Selkirk*

tional [+son] place, one finds the diphtongs *aj, aw*, and *ɔj* (cf. *kite, cow, toy*). One might also wish to contend that the offglides *j* and *w* of the diphthongized tense vowels in English (e.g. *beat, boat, boot*, etc.) occupy that second sonorant position in the peak, though it is not obvious that they do so in underlying representation, that is, if the glide is introduced by a phonological rule.[17] We will also be claiming that the other sonorant consonants *r, l*, and the archiphoneme *N* may occupy second position in the peak, under certain circumstances. This claim will be defended in the context of our discussion of the coda.

There are strong restrictions on what segments may cohabit the peak. Thus, if the second element is *j*, the only preceding back vowels allowable are *ɔ* and *a*. The restrictions being discussed are restrictions on *underlying* segment combinations. Consequently, if the glides of the diphthongized tense vowels *ij* and *ej* are derived by rule, then it is correct to say that the *a* and *ɔ* are the only vowels permitted to precede *j* in the peak. And similarly, the glide *w* may be said to follow no vowel but *a*, if the diphthongized *uw* and *ow* are derived by rule. Otherwise, the restriction would have to state that *w* could follow no vowel but *a, o, u*. Again, such restrictions as these can be taken as giving an indication of a close structural tie between the two elements. By contrast, no such restrictions obtain between a vowel and a following obstruent, which we claim to belong to the coda constituent.

As for the coda, the template (6) states (i) that it is optional (cf. *cow, bee, aye*, etc.), (ii) that it may contain any single consonant (cf. *cat, dog, seem, ease, off, feel, wane*, etc.), (iii) that it contains at most two consonants, and (iv) that if there are two consonants in the coda, the second must be an obstruent (cf. *wax, waft, adze, glimpse*, (=ms), *fifth, apt, James*, etc.). There is a limited class of apparent exceptions to the third claim about the general template, but these are explainable in terms of the auxiliary template (7). Consider, in particular, a word like *next*, with three post-peak obstruents. Its structure is that of (9):

(9)

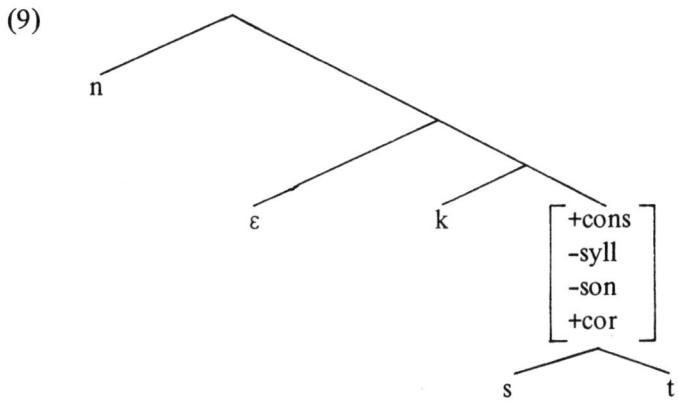

The *st* combination is able to qualify as a single obstruent, however, according to (7), so that this monosyllable does indeed conform to the general syllable template (6).[18]

One extremely important collocational restriction on the coda in English is this:

(10)   The second consonant of the coda must be a coronal.

It is this restriction which describes the absence in English of words such as *rifk* (vs. *rift*), *sipf* (vs. *six*), etc. Again, apparent counterexamples to (10) like *wasp* and *ask* can be explained in terms of the auxiliary template (7). According to (7), *s* plus obstruent groups can qualify as single consonants; because of this, *wasp* and *ask* will not be ruled out by (10).

Reconsidering the representation (9) in view of restriction (10), it is to be noted that here the convention that the features shared by the segments of a constituent become associated with the immediately dominating node plays a crucial role. It is this convention that induces the feature [+cor] on the node dominating *st*, thereby allowing the representation (9) to conform to the [+cor] requirement on consonants occupying second place in the coda. Accordingly, we predict (correctly) that *sk* and *sp*, which do not share the common specification for coronality, will not be permitted as second and third consonants in a coda cluster (cf. **eksp*, **ipsk*, etc.).

The templates (6) and (7), in conjunction with (10), would in principle permit the existence of complex codes with *s* groups in first position. But these do not seem to be possible cf. **nespt*, **lisks*, etc., unless the final coronal is interpreted as an inflectional element, and it will be argued immediately below that such elements do not "count" in determining the well-formedness of syllables in English. Appeal must therefore be made to an additional collocational restriction, which will explicitly rule out *s* groups as first members of a two consonant coda.

In sum, the claim being made by the conjunction of the templates (6) and (7), and the collocational restrictions alluded to, is that the only bi-consonantal codas permitted in English are those with coronal second elements, that the only tri-consonantal codas are those with *st* (or *sθ*) in second or third place, and that codas of more than three are absolutely excluded.

What then of words like *acts (kts)*, *texts (ksts)* or *sixths (ksθs)*? The first has a tri-consonantal coda of a type that is not allowed, and the second and third contain quadri-consonantal codas, impermissible according to our analysis. Should the template (6) be modified so as to allow for yet another [+cons] position? (Note that the consonants extending the codas beyond the predicted limits are always [+cor]). Fudge's (1969) answer to this question is in the affirmative. The position of Fujimura and Lovins (1978) and that of McCarthy (1977) is that an unlimited number of [+cor] positions should in principle be allowed in the coda. But the correct answer, we claim, is no. The analysis should remain as it stands. Observe first of all that the only forms seeming to require an extension of the template's coda include inflectional endings. To extend the template would be to predict, incorrectly, we believe, that monomorphemic forms in English could appear with the codas, e.g. *kts* and *ksəs*. Furthermore, general considerations having to do with the syntactic domain of the template in English, i.e., the domain over which well-formed syllable structure is defined, would require that, in underlying representation, the inflectional suffixes *not* be taken into consideration. Inflectional affixes are *word* affixes, and as such are outside the basic domain of syllabification, which is the word-initial category *root*. (On the root-word distinction, see Selkirk (1982a, 1982b).)[19] And finally, even if *phonetically* a word with an inflectional ending is sometimes indistinguishable from a monomorphemic word (cf. *find* vs. *fined*), the operation of certain phonological rules, such as voicing assimilation, suggests that at a more abstract level the endings do not have the same relation to preceding segments of the syllable as do consonants contained within the coda (compare, for example, *width*, with regressive voicing assimilation ([wɪtə] < /wɪdə/) to *kits* [kɪts] and *lids* [lɪdz], with progressive assimilation). We conclude that the inflectional endings are outside the domain of syllabification, and therefore that they require no modification of the template. (These points will be developed at greater length in the last section of the chapter.)

There are a number of quite strong additional collocational restrictions affecting the coda, and these can be taken as further support for a coda constituent. To cite just one: if there is a second consonant in the coda, the first may not be *b, g, v, č, ǰ, š,* or *ž*.

Turning now to the rhyme as a whole, we must discuss first the question of the place of post-vocalic sonorants in syllable structure. As was mentioned above, the template (6) states that the sonorant liquids *l, r,* and nasals, *n, m* and *ŋ* may cohabit the peak with a vowel. However, this cohabitation is possible only if the vowel is simple, i.e., occupying only the first position in the peak. When a vowel is complex, as in the case of diphthongs, and as we shall see, the tense diphthongized vowels, post-vocalic nasals and liquids must be analyzed as part of the coda (which they can be, in their capacity as consonants). So, for example, the words *while* [wajl], *wire* [wajr] and *wine* [wajn] consist of a complex peak *aj* and a coda consonant *l, r,* or *n*. But the words *Paul* [pɔl], *pour* [pɔr] and *pawn* [pɔn] with simple vowels may be given two analyses - as containing a complex peak and no coda, or as containing a simple peak and a coda consonant. With this in mind, we can now see that the template, combined with restriction (10), makes the following interesting prediction: that within the same syllable, the sequence simple vowel plus sonorant may be followed by *any* consonant, whereas the sequence complex vowel plus sonorant can be followed only by a coronal consonant. (These restrictions are pointed out by Fudge (1969).) The former array of possibilities, exemplified partially in (11),

(11)
land	lam(b)	ban(g)		lunge	—	—
lard	orb	—		purge	warm	barn
bald	—	—		bulge	elm	kiln
lint	lamp	ink	month	hunch	prince	—
heart	harp	lark	hearth	arch	purse	wharf
hilt	help	elk	health	gulch	pulse	elf

follows from the fact that simple vowel and sonorant can act as a peak, leaving the following consonant alone in the coda, and the fact that the template puts no restrictions on single consonant codas. The restrictions in the latter case, exemplified for nasals in (12), have their explanation in the fact that a complex vowel occupies the entire peak, requiring that a following sonorant plus consonant be treated as a complex coda, and the fact that in a complex coda the second consonant must be [+cor].

(12) a.
	nt	nd	nk	mp
aj	pint	find	*	*
aw	mount	mound	*	*
ɔj	point	—	*[20]	*

b.
ij	—	fiend	*	*
ej	paint	—	*	*
uw	—	wound	*	*
ow	(won't)	—	*	*

(12)a shows examples of the "real" diphthongs with various finals, and supports our claim. (12)b is instructive as well. Here we see that the tense vowels place the same restrictions on the following coda that the real diphthongs do. These facts can be taken as evidence that in the underlying representation, where the template is applicable, the tense vowels are either long, i.e. geminate (VV) and therefore complex, or diphthongal. As for clusters with *l* or *r* plus coronal following a complex peak, they are far less common, but those that are attested are compatible with our claim: *wild, whilst, field, Gould, old, weird, pierce*.

The fact that sonorants must form part of the peak when followed by non-coronals indicates that the collocational restriction which must be stated to exclude syllable-final combinations of n (or m) plus v or f, for example, cannot be stated as restrictions on possible *codas*; rather they are restrictions on possible *rhymes*. Moreover, because combinations including the liquids l, r plus z are permitted as possible peak plus coda combinations, the collocational restriction excluding them must be stated at the level of the rhyme. Here, then, are instances of phonotactic constraints on peak plus coda. Since none are attested on peak and onset, we would conclude, following the IC principle, that it is correct to join peak and coda in the rhyme constituent.

This concludes our review of the phonotactics of English syllables. Basing ourselves on facts concerning phonotactics, i.e., the distribution of segment types, we have been led to draw conclusions concerning the nature of the phonological representation, in particular concerning units internal to the syllable. In adopting this approach, we follow in the footsteps of numerous scholars who have argued for the larger unit syllable as a part of phonological representation on the grounds that the notion of possible "word" or morpheme in a language is definable, in large part, on the basis of syllables: a possible "word" is simply a sequence of possible syllables. (The term *word* is placed in quotations at this point since we do not intend to imply that the domain of syllabification in English is the word (cf. Selkirk (1982)). At present, we employ it to indicate, vaguely, the notion of a domain over which syllable structure is defined.) For example, to use an example from Kahn (1976, 57ff), *atktin* is not a possible "word" of English. Assuming a syllabic analysis of "word" in English, the non-existence of *atktin* is predicted simply from the fact that it cannot be "parsed" as a sequence of well-formed English syllables. (*tk* cannot close a syllable, nor can *kt* begin one.) The matter is not so simple in a theory not making use of the syllable, as Kahn demonstrates: the statements required to rule out such a form are cumbersome, and fail to express the appropriate generalizations. A theory incorporating the syllable is therefore preferable, the argument goes, for it allows for a natural and explanatory statement of the phonotactics of words. Our argument, which has drawn heavily on the insights of Fudge (1969), within a framework roughly corresponding to that of Pike and Pike (1947) and Pike (1967), has been that the phonotactics of the syllable itself lead to the postulation of units of representation within the syllable, that the syllable has an internal immediate constituent structure with labelled nodes.

It would be reasonable to ask that phonological, rule-related evidence be adduced for this particular hypothesis concerning the internal structure of syllables, before it is adopted with any degree of certainty. We are unfortunately not in a position here to answer in full to that demand, but will point out in the course of our examination of English which areas seem to offer promising leads in the search for confirming evidence. One of these areas is the phonetic study of duration in relation to the hierarchical organization of the utterance.[21] For example, work on the duration of English vowel-glide combinations, which in our analysis together comprise the peak of the syllable, seems to show that they function as a unit on a par with simple vowels, which in our theory are also peaks. Lehiste and Peterson (1960) report that the length of simple vowels and complex vowels (branching peaks) is affected in the same way by the voiceless/voiced property of a following obstruent: vowel length before voiceless vs. voiced is in the ratio of 2:3 in both cases. Fujimura and Lovins (1978) report on additional very promising durational evidence suggesting that vowel and glide form a unit. Evidence such as that provided by Chen (1970), who claims that there is a constancy (approximate) in the length of vowel plus stop combinations, could be taken as supporting the existence of the rhyme. According to Chen, a lengthening of the vowel (as before voiced stops) coincides with a shortening of the consonant. That is, one could say that within a constituent like the rhyme the duration of one element is adjusted in function of another.[22] Other areas which bear examination in the light of syllable-internal structure are nasalization,[23] voicing assimilation, and so on.

1.3. The conception that we are espousing here of the syllable as a linguistic unit having internal structure and entering moreover into a higher order prosodic structure is at variance with a number of other conceptions of the syllable which have had some currency in present and past work in phonology. Consider first the commonplace view that the syllable is merely that sequence of segments in a representation that is delimited by syllable boundaries or juncture elements. Advocates of the syllable boundary approach to representing the syllable may differ in their ideas about whether syllable boundaries are part of underlying phonological representation, and, if not, about just how they are assigned to the representation, but all agree that, once syllabified, the representation would look something like (13), where a selected symbol, be it "$" or ".", serves as the boundary:

(13) $ CVC $ CV $ or   . CVC . CV .

This non-hierarchical conception of the syllable has been an extremely popular one in phonological works that do give a place to the syllable in phonological representation. To name just a few of the more prominent adherents of the boundary approach to the syllable we might cite Bloch and Trager (1942), Trager and Smith (1951), Jones (1956), Hockett (1955), Haugen (1956), Pulgram (1970), Hoard (1971, 1977),[24] Venneman (1972), Hooper (1972, 1976, 1977) and Bailey (1978). This view of the representation of the syllable is perhaps the most obviously available one within the theory of phonological representation which has been prevalent in work in phonology in the last five decades and which is assumed by the above mentioned, that is, that phonological representation consists of a strictly linear arrangement of phonemes and boundary or juncture elements.[25] According to this theory, all information relevant to the functioning of phonological rules (or to the statement of phonotactic constraints) must be encoded in the sound segments (= phonemes) or in the boundary or juncture markers which are located between the segments.[26] Syllables are therefore defined in terms of their boundaries.

In the preceding discussion, we have already mentioned some of the drawbacks of a non-hierarchical approach to the syllable. These include its inability to provide an explanation for the sorts of phonotactic constraints on syllable composition that one typically finds in languages. In the absence of an IC analysis of the syllable, many generalizations about the phonotactics of the syllable cannot be given descriptively adequate expression. And the same goes for generalizations concerning phonological processes. The notion heavy syllable cannot be given a unitary characterization along the lines suggested by Pike, Kuryłowicz and Newman. A general hypothesis concerning the relation between durational constancy and linguistic units longer than, smaller than or equal to the size of the syllable, such as that advocated by Lehiste (1971), could not even be entertained. No straightforward way of representing the syllable or its subparts as units over which "suprasegmental" features such as emphasis, nasalization, backness, etc. could be predicated could be made available. There would be no means of representing that special relation of relative strength (*s* vs. *w*) which one might reasonably claim to obtain between pairs of segments or groups of segments. And finally, no means is afforded of fitting the syllable into a conception of a higher order hierarchical organization of the utterance which has been shown to be necessary for the proper treatment of such phenomena as stress and rhythm. These reasons in and of themselves are sufficient to justify the rejection of the boundary approach to the representation of the syllable in favour of a hierarchical approach. There is one additional, rather important, reason which *could*, in principle, be adduced, and it involves the phenomenon of ambisyllabicity.

The term *ambisyllabic* or some comparable term such as *interlude* has been employed by phoneticians and phonologists alike[27] to describe consonants which are considered to belong to both a preceding and a following syllable at the same time, as in words like *happy, butter, coming, college*, etc. It has been observed, first of all, that no clear break between the syllables is perceptible in these cases, and, secondly, that the consonants in this context seem to display a special sort of phonological behavior (to be reviewed below). These peculiarities are best explained, the claim goes, by considering the consonants to be ambisyllabic – neither just syllable-initial, nor just syllable-final, but both at the same time. Clearly, ambisyllabicity, if it exists, would provide a further argument against the boundary approach to the syllable: a syllable boundary cannot be simultaneously before and after some segment of the string.[28] Were ambisyllabicity not to exist, another, superior, explanation having been found for the special behavior of the consonants in the examples cited, the syllable boundary theory would not be much better off, however, for there still are too many other reasons for rejecting it.

The issue of whether or not these consonants are indeed ambisyllabic is not important just because it may make available yet another argument against syllable boundaries. It is important for the theory of the representation of the syllable that we are developing here and for the theory of hierarchical prosodic structure as a whole, for ambisyllabicity would constitute the sole instance we know of where the tree structures of phonological representation are not well-formed, in the formal sense that a node of the tree (in this case, a terminal element) is immediately dominated by two separate nodes, giving overlapping constituents. We believe that ambisyllabicity does not exist, however, and that the phenomena claimed to result from ambisyllabicity can be expressed eminently well in other terms. (See Section 2).

The most important set of arguments in favor of ambisyllabicity and its role with respect to phonological rules has been put forth by Kahn (1976), and we will examine his analysis as well as the theory of the representation of the syllable within which it is couched. Kahn develops an approach to the syllable which is suprasegmental in the sense that the syllable is a linguistic unit on a level of the phonological representation distinct from the segmental level, and an association between syllable and segments must be defined. But this theory of the syllable is significantly different from ours. To be more precise, Kahn conceives of his as an "autosegmental" theory of the syllable which is quite analogous to the "autosegmental" theory of tone elaborated by Goldsmith (1976) and others. (In Goldsmith's theory, tones are represented on an autosegmental level distinct from the segmental level, and certain universal laws, as well as language-specific rules, govern the association of these tones with the segmental level). Given Kahn's theory, the representation of *flounce* would be (14):

(14)

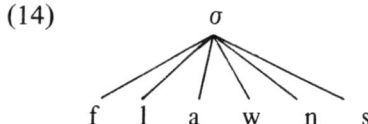

As for the representation of *study*, which is claimed to contain an ambisyllabic consonant, it would be converted from the basic (15)a into (15)b, where the medial consonant is associated with two syllables.

(15) a.

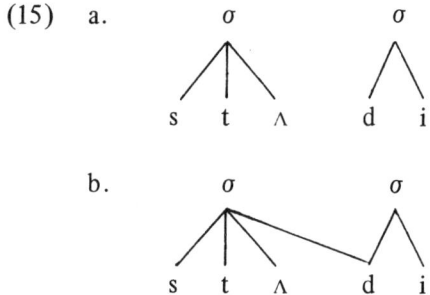

   b.

But this autosegmental theory of the syllable suffers from the same shortcoming, as the boundary theory of the syllable, and so must be rejected.[29] In an autosegmental framework, it is impossible to view the syllable as a structural unit of a fully ramified prosodic structure. There is no sense in which autosegmental entities like tones (or syllables) are arranged in a hierarchy with respect to each other. Thus, the syllable could not be viewed as having an internal structure, nor could it be represented as part of a higher order prosodic tree. Given this, the same criticisms that were levied against the boundary approach can be levied against Kahn's.[30]

To sum up, we have argued in this section that the syllable has a structure that is to be represented as a well-formed bracketing, in the way described. In the following section we treat the issue of how syllable structure is assigned in the language, and in treating the issue of resyllabification, we present arguments against the notion of ambisyllabicity.

2 The Principles of Syllabification

The questions we wish to address in this section are these: How does syllable structure become associated with the phonological representations of a language? What is the nature of the principles of syllabification? In answering them, we must make a distinction between principles of *basic syllable composition* (BSC) and principles of *resyllabification*. The principles of BSC take the form of a template and an accompanying

The Syllable

set of collocational restrictions, as discussed and exemplified in sections *1.1* and *1.2*. We will not assume that the principles of BSC "apply", in the sense that they participate in a phonological derivation, converting a phonological representation consisting of a sequence of segments into a syllabified phonological representation. Rather, we think of them as well-formedness conditions on underlying phonological representation, which thus is to be thought of as having syllabic structure. As for the principles of resyllabification, which we present below, they may be thought of as participating in a derivation, in the sense that they perform operations on the (already syllabified) phonological representation, modifying it in particular ways.

2.1. Recall that in the grammar of English, there is a general template (repeated here as (16)), which specifies the gross features of BSC in the language, an auxiliary template (repeated here as (17)), which permits combinations of *s* plus obstruent to function like a single obstruent with respect to the general template, and a rather detailed set of collocational restrictions, which enumerate the particular co-occurrence restrictions that are not expressible in template form.

(16)

(17)

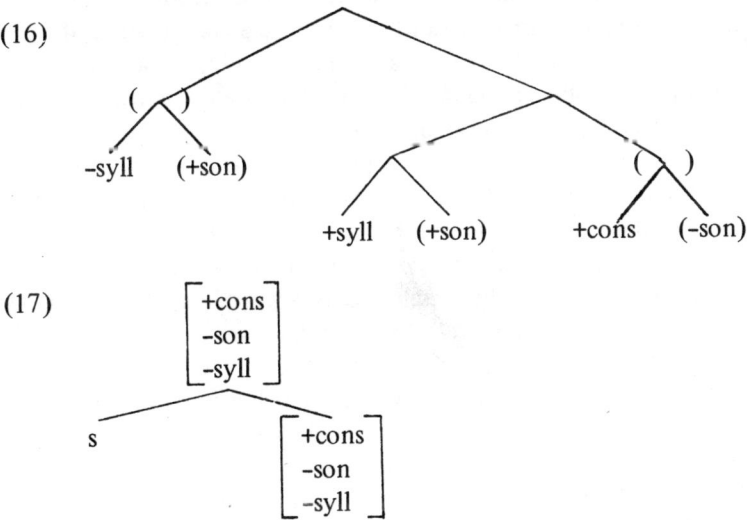

Taken all together, these define the basic syllable composition of the language. As we suggested in *1.1.*, a phonological representation will be ruled well-formed if it is non-distinct from the template(s) and does not violate the collocational restrictions. To put it another way, one could say that the grammar rules a phonological representation well-formed if its syllable structure can be *parsed* according to the templates, and also satisfy the collocational restrictions.

Consider, for example, the well-formed English monosyllables of (18), in contrast to their un-well-formed counterparts of (19).

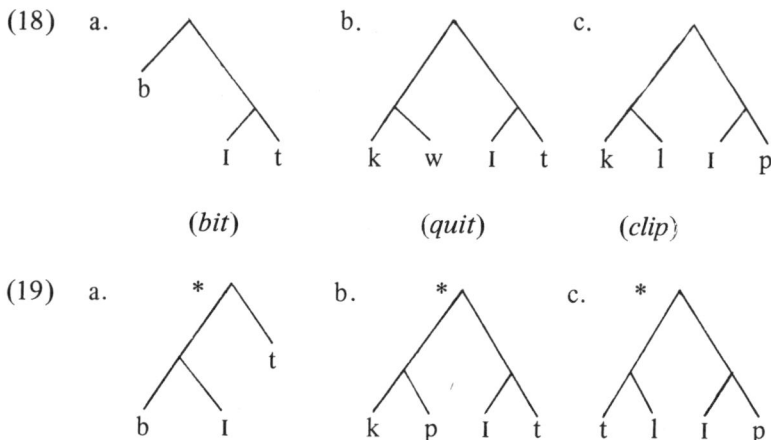

(18) a. b I t (*bit*)   b. k w I t (*quit*)   c. k l I p (*clip*)

(19) a. *b I t   b. *k p I t   c. *t l I p

(19)a is ruled out because of incorrect branching: a [+syll] element may form a constituent only with a consonant that follows, according to template (16). (19)b is out on the grounds that in a biconsonantal onset, the second consonant must be [+son], unless it is a combination of *s* plus obstruent; following templates (16) and (17). Finally, (19)c is ruled out because there is a collocational restriction which states that in the onset an *l* may no follow a [+cor] consonant.

Turning next to a consideration of polysyllables, it will become clear that several additional conditions must be imposed in defining the well-formedness of the syllabic structure of an utterance. Parsability with respect to the templates and satisfaction of the collocational restrictions is not enough. First, consider the simple case of a word like *allow*. There are two syllable structure analyses of the word that are consistent with the principles of BSC: ʌ.*law* or ʌl.*aw* . (Note that here we adopt the convenience of employing the period to indicate the limits of syllables, since the internal bracketing is irrelevant to our present point.) But only the first is correct (as can be seen from the fact that *l* is pronounced with its light, syllable-initial version). To cite a few additional examples, the syllabifications *pro.strate, ac.tress, ar.cane* are clearly the only correct ones, though *pros.trate, prost.rate, act.ress* and *arc.ane* would all be permissible, given the principles of BSC in English. In general, when a medial consonant or consonant cluster may be analyzed as either a coda or an onset according to BSC, it is the onset analysis which prevails. A number of scholars have proposed that in syllabification (in our terms, the determination of the well-formedness of some syllabic structure) the following universal principle be respected:

(20) *Maximal Syllable Onset Principle*
In the syllable structure of an utterance, the onsets of syllables are maximized, in conformance with the principles of basic syllable composition of the language.[31]

And we concur in considering this principle to be part of linguistic theory.

The (near) minimal pair *pattern* [pæDr̩n] from /pǽtrn/) vs. *patron* [péjtr̩n] offered by Bloomfield (1933, 122), would seem to suggest that, internal to the syllable, the principle of onset maximalization is not at play. If one assumes that the syllabicity of sonorants comes about as a result of their being accorded the status of peak in the syllable, then we see that in the first case the underlying *trn* is analyzed as (21)a, and in the second as (21)b:

(21) a.   b.

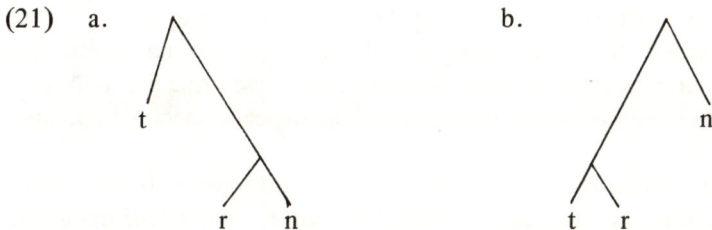

If this interpretation of these facts is correct, then the principle stated in (20) is to be interpreted as one promoting the maximalization of an onset only *with respect to the coda of the preceding syllable*.

Another issue which arises when considering polysyllables, though not in the case of English, has to do with the fact that BSC principles may differ according to the place a syllable happens to occupy in the word. In French, for example, a greater range of onset types is available for word-initial syllables than for syllables placed elsewhere in the word. So, while *sl* or *ps* are permissible onsets in *slave* or *psychologie*, within the word they must belong to separate syllables: *Is.lande, cap.sule*. We will not have anything more to say on the subject here, confining ourselves to the observation that in a general theory of the syllable and syllabification, the principles of BSC may not be identical for all parts of the word.

Finally, a consideration of polysyllables in English brings to the fore the question of the syntactic (i.e. morphological) domain of syllabification. We wish only to point out here that this domain may vary from one language to another, and will therefore have to be specified for each language. In English, this domain is smaller than the word, as is shown by such pairs as *incline* [ɪn.kʰlajn] vs. *inklike* [ɪŋk.l̥ajk]. As we shall see in 2.3. the aspiration of *k* and voicelessness of *l* in the former case testify to the syllabification that we would expect according to the principles outlined above. *Inklike*, however, does not obey principle (20): the *k* is syllable-final (and therefore non-aspirated), and the *l* is voiced (hence syllable-initial). The limits of the syllables correspond to the limits of the suffix *-like*, and the preceding stem. The generalization, we claim, is that the limits of the highest root or, equivalently, the lowest word always coincides with the limits of a syllable, and that the limits of word affixes always coincide with a syllable limit as well (cf. Selkirk (forthcoming)). Note, furthermore, that from this it follows that word limits always coincide with syllable limits.

To sum up, we conceive of the principles of basic syllable composition of a language as consisting of a template (with auxiliary templates possible in addition) and a set of collocational restrictions. To be defined as well-formed, the syllable structure of an underlying phonological representation must of necessity satisfy these basic principles. It must moreover satisfy the (universal) principle favoring maximal onsets. And, of central interest to us, it is required to satisfy these principles only within the limits of certain syntactically or morphologically specified domains.

2.2.   In English one observes that there exist divergences from syllabification according to the Maximal Onset Principle. They occur under precisely defineable conditions, the most important being the stress pattern of the word. Examples of words exhibiting such divergences are *money, butter, particle, college, heaven, actor, aspen, digital, permissive, Hecate*. It is to be noted that in all instances the underlined consonant, which violates the Maximal Onset Principle, precedes a stressless vowel. It is consonants in this context which, according to some, are ambisyllabic, belonging to both the preceding and following syllables. (Such a syllabification would be in violation of the Maximal Onset Principle in the sense that the consonant was not exclusively an onset but also in the preceding coda.) We will show in section *2.3* that the assumption of ambisyllabicity is unnecessary, that it does not contribute to the proper statement of the phonological rules said to depend on it, and that it even complicates their expression. As for the "intuition" that the medial consonants of examples such as those above are ambisyllabic, we suggest, again in *2.3.*, that there is an explanation for it that does not require that ambisyllabicity be allowed in phonological representations. In our view (and the view of certain others)[32], consonants in the context illustrated must be thought of as belonging only to the preceding syllable, i.e. forming the coda of that syllable, and not the onset of the following one. As such, they constitute a flagrant violation of the principle of Maximal Onset.

It is our contention (as well as that of Kahn) that divergences from *normal* syllabification, i.e. the syllabification determined by the principles of BSC and Maximal Onset, are brought about by processes of *resyllabification*, which operate on a representation syllabified according to the normal principles. In Kahn's analysis, what is produced is ambisyllabicity. In our analysis, it is an association of a consonant with a preceding syllable, accompanied by a *complete dissociation* of the consonant from its syllable of origin.

The rules of resyllabification are transformational in character, in that they define a mapping from one (structural) representation to another. Rule (22) provides an example of an "adjunction" transformation of the type described.

(22)   Resyllabification I

$$\begin{array}{cccccc} X & [-\text{cons}] & [-\text{syll}] & \begin{bmatrix} +\text{syll} \\ -\text{stress} \end{bmatrix} & Y & \\ 1 & 2 & 3 & 4 & 5 & \rightarrow \\ 1, & 2+3, & \emptyset, & 4, & 5 & \end{array}$$

This transformation will map the syllable sequences of (23) into those of (24).

(23)   a. 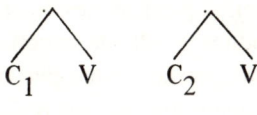   b.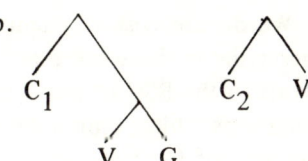

(24)   a. 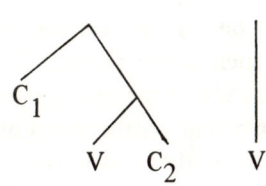   b.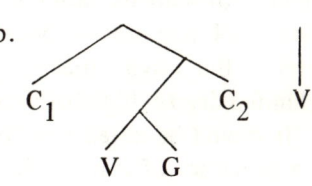

It should be clear from an examination of (24) that we are assuming that resyllabification transformations are structure-preserving in the sense that their output conforms to the basic template. A wealth of possible adjunctions are in principle available. Thus, the second C in (24)b could, logically, be adjoined in any of these other configurations as well.

(25)   a. 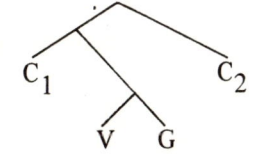   b.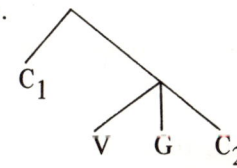

362 *Elisabeth O. Selkirk*

c.

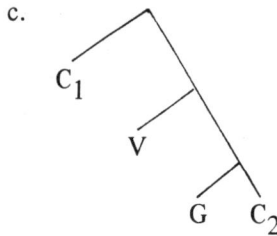

None of these correspond to the BSC of the language, however.

Our hypothesis that only (24)b is a possible output of the operation of (22) on (23)b receives some support from the fact that, in so far as tautosyllabic phonological rules such as vowel lengthening, nasalization, etc. are concerned, the consonant-final syllable created through resyllabification seems to behave in the same way as an underlying consonant-final syllable. For example, the length of the diphthongs of *writer* and *rider* parallels that of those in *write* and *ride*. (See also *2.3*). To the extent to which the length phenomenon is dependent on syllable constituency, and not merely on the linear arrangement of segments within the syllable, it offers support for the structure-preserving conception of resyllabification.

We do not wish to claim that all phonological processes are structure-preserving in the sense that they all produce a syllable structure that conforms to the BSC of the language. Clearly, certain rules give rise to representations which cannot be syllabified according to the BSC, cf. Kahn's example of the fast speech pronunciation of *potato* [pt^hejDo]. Indeed, a number of scholars have pointed out that the syllables attested at the phonetic level may not be those which must be motivated at the phonological level.[33] But resyllabification processes such as we propose do testify to a limited degree of globality in the application of the principles of BSC.

It should be noted that, in being dependent on the stress of a syllable, the processes of resyllabification distinguish themselves from the principles of BSC. The basic syllable composition of an utterance in English does not depend on stress. In fact, stress assignment is itself dependent on, i.e., sensitive to, the syllable structure of an utterance as the BSC (and the Maximum Onset Principle) define it. (See Hoard (1971), Anderson and Jones (1974) and Kahn (1976) for arguments in favor of this point.) There is therefore a logical ordering that is intrinsic to stress assignment and the various processes of syllabification:

(26)   Basic Syllable Composition (following the Maximum Onset Principle)
       Stress
       Resyllabification

The Syllable 363

As well-formedness conditions, of course, the principles of BSC do not, strictly speaking, apply. They merely characterize the underlying phonological representation. Stress is conventionally thought of as being assigned by rule, however.

So what (26) depicts is the fact that the stress rules apply in function of BSC, and the rules of resyllabification apply in terms of stress *and* BSC.

Kahn argues for a further difference between the principles of BSC (and Maximal Onset) and the principles of resyllabification. He says that while the latter are only optional, and may be suspended under various conditions, having to do with style, speed, etc., the former are always at play. Thus, overprecise slow speech will always obey the principles of normal syllabification, while resyllabification may be suspended in this case. (We tend to agree with this observation.)

Thus, we see, there is motivation for two types of principles of syllabification in the grammar: principles of basic syllable composition and principles of resyllabification. To provide support for our particular conception of resyllabification (as not involving ambisyllabicity), and of just what the rules of resyllabification are, we will have to examine certain rules of English phonology. This we do in the next section.

2.3 It has been increasingly acknowledged that the realization of particular allophones of English sound types may depend on the position of those segments within the syllable. Thus, an investigation of such sorts of allophonic variation may give a key to syllabification in the language. This is especially true of the processes affecting the realization of the voiceless stops *p, t, k*, and especially of the phenomenon of aspiration.

As a wide range of workers in the field have observed, voiceless stops are aspirated in syllable-initial position in English. Formalized, the rule could read as follows:

(27) *Aspiration*[34]

$$\begin{bmatrix} +\text{cons} \\ -\text{cont} \\ -\text{voire} \end{bmatrix} \rightarrow [+\text{aspirated}] \ / \ _\sigma(\underline{\quad} \cdot \cdot \cdot)_\sigma$$

(we will make the practice of employing parenthesis to denote the bracketing corresponding to prosodic structures, in order to readily distinguish it from the square brackets of the syntax.) Given the principles of BSC for English, in conjunction with the Maximum Onset Principle, rule (27) is able to capture in quite simple fashion the fact that aspiration is found in the following types of contexts:

(28) a. initial in a word: *Toronto, pathetic, calamity*

b. before a stressed vowel, except if *s* precedes: *ho̱tel, repair, reca̱nt* vs. *Este̱lle, despair, aska̱nce*
c. before a sonorant plus a stressed vowel, except if *s* precedes or it is *t* followed by *l* (or any other combination ruled out as an onset): *a̱trocious, a̱pply, a̱ccretion, incline, improve, betwixt, a̱cquaint* vs. *destroy, display, discreet* or *Atlantic*, etc.
d. before a sonorant plus stressless vowel, except if *s* precedes, or it is *t* followed by *l*, etc.:
actress, acrimony, countrified, implication, acclamation, April vs. *mistress, miscreant, explicate* or *antler, atlas*, etc.

These are all contexts in which, according to normal syllabification, the stops are syllable-initial. An array of facts such as this provides a rather striking example of the advantages of a phonological theory which gives representation to the syllable, and allows the syllable to serve as a domain for phonological rules. Without the syllable to refer to, the statement of the rule would be ungainly in the extreme, having to mention explicitly each of the contexts enumerated above.

Stops found immediately before unstressed syllabics are not (usually) aspirated:

(29) before unstressed vowels: *wacky, attitude, happen, Hecate, interpolate, elliptical, actor, wimpy*.

The reason we offer, which is also that put forward by Hoard (1971) and Bailey (1978), is that non-aspirated consonants in this environment are not syllable-initial at all, and hence not subject to aspiration. Resyllabification has (usually) put them in final position in the preceding syllable. (A more precise characterization of resyllabification will be made directly below). *Wacky*, for example, has the syllable structure (w(æk)) (i). Thus we take issue with the reason given by Kahn for the lack of aspiration in (29). His explanation is that a process of resyllabification (or "ambisyllabification") has rendered the consonants ambisyllabic in this context, and the status of ambisyllabicity is said to prevent aspiration. In order that this be so, Kahn must state the aspiration rule so that it affects consonants that are syllable-initial, *and not also syllable-final*. This of course amounts to a complication in this statement of the rule, and is a first indication that the approach to resyllabification that we advocate is superior to Kahn's.

The non-aspirated allophones fall into two classes:

(30) (i) (unaspirated), released and unglottalized, as in *stir, spinach*,

The Syllable 365

skate; biting, wiping, liking; (optionally) cat, pack, map in isolation.

(ii) (unaspirated), unreleased and glottalized (to varying degrees, according to the consonant)[35], as in act, actor, activity, Atkins, napkin, ichthyosis; (optionally) cat, pack, map in isolation.

Furthermore, a *t* displaying the characteristic features of class (i) may be changed into a tap, [D], under certain conditions. That is, a *t* displaying the characteristic features of class (i), which concern release and laryngeal activity, may also be changed in its manner of articulation.[36] We have already shown how the grammar accounts for aspiration vs. non-aspiration. It remains to account now for the phenomena of release vs. non-release, glottalization vs. non-glottalization, and tapping vs. non-tapping. Our claim is that these phenomena can be explained insightfully in a theory which does not incorporate the notion of ambisyllabicity. This explanation will nevertheless rely on the notion of resyllabification, and so before proceeding to an analysis of the rules for release, glottalization and tapping, we must provide for a fuller description of the processes of resyllabification in English. The phenomenon of aspiration equips us with an indispensible tool in this endeavour.

2.4 Our hypothesis is that there is essentially just a single process of resyllabification in English, which divides into two sub-rules. The first is Resyllabification I, which is repeated here:

(31) *Resyllabification I*

$$X \quad [-\text{cons}] \quad [-\text{syll}] \quad \begin{bmatrix} +\text{syll} \\ -\text{stress} \end{bmatrix} \quad Y$$
$$1 \quad\quad 2 \quad\quad\quad 3 \quad\quad\quad\quad 4 \quad\quad\quad\quad 5 \;\to\; 1, 2+3, \emptyset, 4, 5$$

This applies when the preceding syllable is not consonant-final. The second sub-rule applies when there is a consonant terminating the preceding syllable:

(32) *Resyllabification II*[37]

$$X \quad [+\text{cons}] \quad [-\text{syll}] \quad \begin{bmatrix} +\text{syll} \\ -\text{stress} \end{bmatrix} \quad Y$$
$$1 \quad\quad 2 \quad\quad\quad 3 \quad\quad\quad\quad 4 \quad\quad\quad\quad 5 \;\to\; 1, 2+3, \emptyset, 4, 5$$

The two rules differ in the extent to which they apply under normal speaking conditions. Resyll I seems to be obligatory: aspiration (i.e., lack of resyllabification) is distinctly unnatural in the examples of (33).[38]

(33) ha_pp_y, migh_t_iest, a_cc_olade, bea_k_er, goi_t_er, wa_ck_y, a_tt_itude, He_c_a_t_e, digi_t_al.

Here the resyllabified consonant is preceded by a vowel or a glide. The distinct unnaturalness of aspiration in words with syllables ending in *r* lead us to favor Kahn's suggestion that *r* be considered to be a glide:

(34) par_t_icle, or_ch_estra, tur_p_itude

When any other non-vocalic elements end the preceding syllable, resyllabification is subject to much greater variability. We therefore consider the rule responsible, Resyll II, to be optional, under normal speaking conditions. Note, for example, that either the non-aspirated or aspirated version of the stop is permissible when it is preceded by another obstruent, a nasal, or *l*:

(35) ellip_t_ical, ap_t_itude, ac_t_or, af_t_er, ic_t_us, hef_t_y, restric_t_ive, produc_t_ive, nap_k_in, A_t_kins, Rif_k_in, Lef_k_owitz

(36) con_t_emplate, pan_t_omine, win_t_er, cen_t_er, wim_p_y, ampersand, contem_p_orary, an_ch_or, lan_k_y, lin_k_age, In_c_a, boun_t_iful, plain_t_ive.

(37) fil_t_er, al_t_itude, hel_t_er, skel_t_er, pol_t_ergeist, al_c_ohol, El_k_a, Wil_k_ins

(Some resyllabifications are less likely than others here. The *k* of *napkin* may aspirate more readily than the *t* of *Acton*; the *t* of *filter* is undoubtedly more often aspirated than the *k* of *alcohol*. The rule Resyll II cannot encode these differences, and at the moment we have no explanation for them.) Despite these differences in applicability, Resyll I and Resyll II are clearly part of the same rule, though, for they share two important characteristics: the first is that they operate only when the second syllable is stressless, and the second is that they resyllabify only segments which are alone in the onset. These shared characteristics permit a collapsing of the rules:

(38) Resyllabification

$$X \quad \left\{ \begin{matrix} [-\text{cons}] \\ [+\text{cons}] \end{matrix} \right\} \quad [-\text{syll}] \quad \begin{bmatrix} +\text{syll} \\ -\text{stress} \end{bmatrix} \quad Y \quad \begin{matrix} \text{OBL} \\ \text{OPT} \end{matrix}$$

$$\begin{matrix} 1 & 2 & 3 & 4 & 5 \\ 1 & 2+3 & \emptyset & 4 & 5 \end{matrix} \implies$$

The Syllable

In the preceding section, the claim was made that Resyll I is structure-preserving. By this it was meant that, out of the numerous ways in which a consonant could conceivably be adjoined to a preceding syllable which ended in a glide or vowel, only an adjunction conforming to the template structure of the language was actually produced. What then of instances where resyllabification adjoins a consonant to a syllable ending in a consonant? The structure preservation hypothesis makes predictions about derived structure. For example, it predicts, that when an obstruent adjoins to a syllable already containing a coda, the obstruent will join the coda:

(39) *hefty*

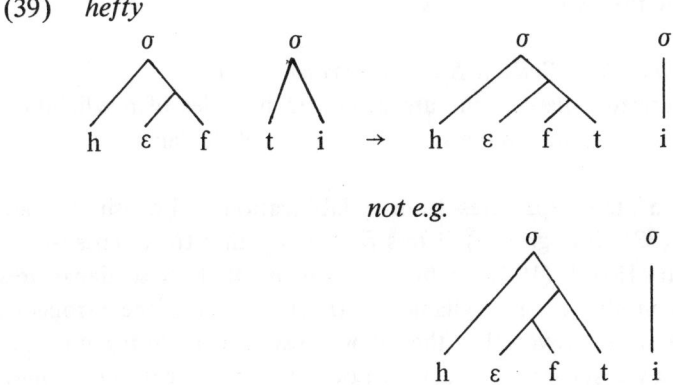

not e.g.

This hypothesis also predicts that certain resyllabifications will not be possible, if they would produce syllables not in conformity with the template. Recall that there are no restrictions on single consonant codas, hence if prior to Resyllabification the syllable has no coda, any consonant will be able to be adjoined. But if the syllable already has one consonant in the coda, then only an obstruent should be permitted to resyllabify. We know that obstruents do resyllabify in such cases (cf. *after, bountiful, poltergeist*, etc.) The question is whether non-obstruents do or do not. The prediction is that in words like *pygmy* or *refreshment*, with obstruent-final first syllable codas, the *m* must remain syllable-initial. (Our verification of this prediction is rendered difficult by our ignorance of the syllable-sensitive allophonic variation of a sound such as *m*, and so will have to await further research on this topic.) It is also predicted that since sonorant-final syllables with complex peaks must be analyzed as having a consonant in the coda, only obstruent resyllabification should be permitted. Thus in *ailment* or *endearment*, the *m*, again, should remain syllable-initial. Cases such as this can be contrasted to the relevant syllables in *fulfillment, Elmer, filmic, garment* which have simple vowels and end in sonorants which can therefore be analyzed as part of the peak. Structure preservation would permit the adjunction of *m* here. And, indeed, there is evidence available for a difference in syllabification, for it seems correct to say that an *l* becomes non-consonantal when followed in the same syllable by another consonant (cf. *help, elk, Elba*, etc.), but tends more to keep its consonantal, apical articulation when syllable-final *ill, fell, fail, Alpine*, etc.) And there is a contrast in the pronunciation of *l* in *Elmer* and *ailment*. The consonantal character of *l* in the latter example is attributable to the syllable-final status which the structure preserving hypothesis predicts it would have. On the basis of this, and given its general appeal as a restrictive hypothesis concerning possible derived syllabic structure, we propose to include the principle of syllabic structure preservation in the theory of phonology:

(40) *The Principle of Syllabic Structure Preservation*
The derived syllable structure produced by rules of resyllabification must conform to the syllable template of the language.

This analysis of the departures from syllabification in English that are evidenced in (33) through (37) differs from two other treatments of the same problem. Hoard (1971), while recognizing that these departures arise only when the second syllable is stressless, makes the erroneous claim that the stressless vowel of the following syllable is *always* immediately preceded by a syllable boundary. In our terms this means two things. First, that no provision is made for optionality in syllabification. The preceding discussion has shown this to be necessary, however. Second, that an onset of whatever size or composition is associated with the preceding syllable. In the case of onsets consisting of obstruent plus sonorant, this claim is clearly in error. As the examples in (28)d indicate, a syllable-initial stop before a sonorant before a stressless vowel is aspirated, except in the case of *t* plus *l*, which do not form a permissible onset. Moreover, the sonorants (except for *l* of *tl*) are voiceless in these circumstances, a trait attributed to their being preceded in the same syllable by a voiceless consonant (compare the liquids of *mattress* and *atlas*). Observe furthermore that the behavior of nasal consonants preceding voiceless stop plus sonorant sequences supports our view that they must remain the onset of the following syllable. Making a voiceless stop part of the preceding syllable has the effect of causing an extreme nasalization of the vowel, and a virtual elimination of the consonant as such. Thus, *winter* has either one or two phonetic realizations: a non-resyllabified one [wɪn.t^{h}r̩] and a resyllabified one [wĩDr̩]. (This is what normally happens when a nasal consonant is followed by a tautosyllabic voiceless stop coda (cf.Malecot (1960)). In *wintry*, however, the nasal consonant is never fully lost (*wĩt^{h}ri , * wĩDri), because it is final in its own syllable. (Compare the examples of *Nantucket* or *quintuplet*, where *t*, syllable initial because pre-stress, does

The Syllable

not cause the *n* to disappear.) The evidence thus converges against an analysis syllabifying the entire voiceless stop-sonorant onsets, or the stop alone of such onsets, with the preceding syllable.[39]

The only other sort of complex onset in English consists of *s* plus obstruent, and it is not clear whether there is resyllabification in this case or not. In words like *westerly, aspen* and *Tuscaloosa* the stop is unaspirated. There are of course two possible reasons for this, the first being that there has been no resyllabification and that the stop is therefore not in syllable-initial position, and the second being that the entire cluster has been resyllabified, so that the stop is in syllable-final position. (The third option, that only the *s* resyllabifies, is excluded on the grounds that the stop would as a consequence be in the context for aspiration.) Since the stop allophones do not provide unambiguous evidence for syllabification in this case, one must look to other phonological processes such as might apply within a syllable before a tautosyllabic *s* group. Unfortunately, we do not have information on hand that might help decide the question. (The reformulation of Resyllabification that would be in order, were it ascertained that the group *s* plus obstruent did resyllabify, would be (41).)

(41) *Resyllabification (possible revision)*[40]

$$X \quad \left\{ \begin{array}{c} [-\text{cons}] \\ [+\text{cons}] \end{array} \right\} \quad \underline{(s) \quad [-\text{syll}]} \quad \begin{bmatrix} +\text{syll} \\ -\text{stress} \end{bmatrix} \quad Y \qquad \begin{array}{c} \text{OBL} \\ \text{OPT} \end{array}$$

$$\begin{array}{cccccc} 1 & 2 & 3 & 4 & 5 & \Longrightarrow \\ 1 & 2+3 & \emptyset & 4 & 5 & \end{array}$$

To sum up, Hoard's factual claim concerning the resyllabification of obstruent plus sonorant onsets is untenable, but in the case of *s* plus obstruent onsets his claim cannot be rejected out of hand. Further research is required to help decide.

Kahn's approach to resyllabification involves positing two rules which operate on a representation syllabified in normal fashion to produce ambisyllabicity. The first is the analogue to our Resyll I, though, as written, it will incorrectly re(ambi)syllabify the stop of voiceless stop-sonorant onsets. Kahn's formulation, (42), could be modified to overcome this deficiency, by eliminating the C_0 factor from the rule.[41]

(42) *Rule III (normal-rate and faster speech only)* (Kahn 1976,55)[42]

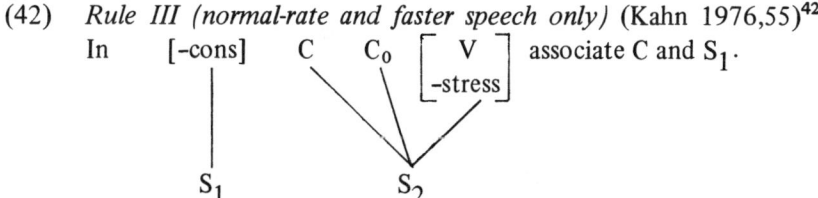

Kahn's second rule for ambisyllabicity is (43). It, too, would require modification in view of the voiceless stop-sonorant facts (a change of the C_0 to C would be enough.):

(43) *Rule IV* (normal rate and faster-speech only) (Kahn 1976)

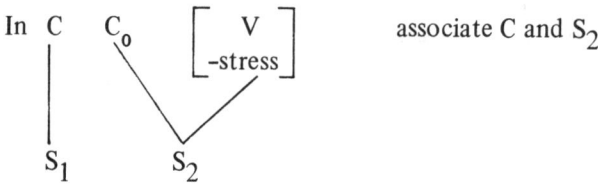

associate C and S_2

Condition: CC_0 must not be a member of the set of universally-prohibited clusters; certain highly marked clusters not universally proscribed may be excluded also.

(The condition associated with the rule is intended to reflect that some syllabifications are more likely than others.) This rule is not exactly the analogue of Resyll II, for it associates a syllable-final consonant with the stressless syllable that follows, rather than associating a syllable-initial consonant with a consonant-final syllable, as Resyll II does. In the case of syllable-final *l* and *n*, the resyllabification it produces will be an incorrect one. As our discussion of *winter* and *Elmer* showed, resyllabification must produce a derived syllable structure which makes the *t* and *m*, respectively, part of the former syllable, with the consequent nasalization and *l*-vocalization effects. What this means is that Kahn's Rule III would have to be modified still further, to allow a syllable-initial consonant to become ambisyllabic when the preceding syllable ended in *l* or *n*, as well. This could be accomplished easily enough, by changing the [−cons] designation to [+son]. At this point one might ask why there needs to be a Rule IV at all, ambisyllabifying in the direction that it does. Kahn's argument for it is based on his observation that "in ordinary speech the syllabic structure of *after* seems entirely parallel to that of *Astor, Haskins.*" (p.49). If this observation is indeed accurate, and we believe it is, then a separate Rule IV is required in Kahn's system, for the only way to produce a resyllabified structure for *after* that is parallel to that for *Astor* (44) is by associating the *f* with the following syllable, not the *t* with the preceding. Compare (44) to (45), produced by Rule IV, and (46), produced by a potentially revised Rule III.

(44)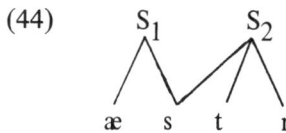

(45)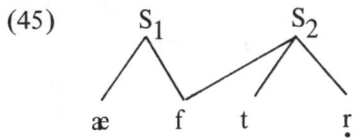

(46)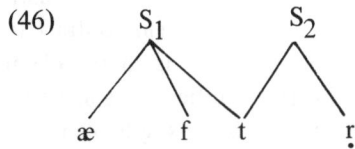

If the observation is not accurate, then all the word-internal resyllabification discussed could, in Kahn's framework, be accompanied by the single Rule III, appropriately revised. This in fact would be a desirable state of affairs, from the point of view of an adherent of ambisyllabicity, for if Rule IV is in fact necessary, the grammar would not be able to treat resyllabification as a unitary process — a distinct disadvantage. The necessity for a distinct Rule IV is an artifact of Kahn's framework, however: Rule IV is the sole means of encoding his factual observation. In the framework we adopt, this observation can be seen as merely revealing that the entire onset *st* or *sk* becomes syllabified with the preceding syllable, creating *Ast.or* or *Hask.ins*, quite on a par with the syllabification *aft.er*, which we already predict. All this means, in our analysis, is that the grammar should include the revised Resyll of (41), instead of that of (38). To conclude, then, in requiring the existence of the two uncollapsible resyllabification rules III and IV, Kahn's theory is preventing the expression of a significant generalization. Subject to the same conditions concerning stress and onset, Rules III and IV are clearly the same process. It is only the assumption of ambisyllabicity (as opposed to the type of resyllabification we advocate) that keeps them apart.

2.5   In this section we take up the question of whether there might exist other sorts of considerations which would nonetheless favor the adoption of a theory of prosodic structure which permitted ambisyllabic overlap. We will first examine additional syllable-sensitive phonological processes that are relevant to this issue.

Our Resyllabification and Kahn's Rule III (appropriately revised) have in common that they cause a syllable-initial consonant to become syllable-final. Both can thus account for the fact that the variety of phonological rules in English which apply within a syllable which is closed by a consonant apply as well in a syllable to which a consonant is said to have been adjoined under the conditions described. In what preceded we have mentioned that the vowel length phenomena of *writer* vs. *rider* parallel those of *write* vs. *ride* (and contrast with those of *italic* and *idyllic*, where the length distinction does not appear). We have also mentioned that the nasalization effects in *winter* are parallel to those in *lint* (and unlike those in *wintry* or *Kentucky*), and that the *l*-vocalization of *Elmer* and *elm* is not found (as readily) in *ailment* or *Elmira*. To these facts, one might add the observation, due to Fujimura and Lovins (1978), that the dark syllable-final *l* allophone appears in *college* just as in *doll* (in contrast to *collegial*, for example). Where the two accounts differ is in the claim (made by Kahn and rejected by us) that the resyllabified consonant remains associated with the following syllable, and is thus syllable-initial in addition to being syllable-final. If there is no evidence for the syllable-initial character of the resyllabified consonant, then the notion of ambisyllabicity is deprived of support.

Kahn's crucial argument for ambisyllabicity comes from his analysis of the rules of English grammar producing the voiced tap [D] as an allophone of *t* (and *d*), as well as the glottalized allophones of the voiceless stops *p, t, k*. It is Kahn's claim that ambisyllabicity is a necessary condition for the tap rule:

(47) (Kahn 1977)

$$[-\text{cons}] \quad \begin{bmatrix} t, d \\ +SI \\ +SF \\ \Downarrow \\ D \end{bmatrix} \quad V$$

(The features ± Syllable Initial (SI) and ± Syllable Final (SF) are employed to indicate the position of a segment in a syllable.)[43] As for the rule glottalizing voiceless stops, Kahn's rule specifies that the consonant involved must not be syllable-initial:[44]

(48) (Kahn 1977)

$$[-\text{cons}] \quad \begin{bmatrix} p, t, k \\ -SI \end{bmatrix} \\ \Downarrow \\ p^?, t^?, k^?$$

Our intention is to show that these formulations do not capture the proper generalizations concerning the appearance of [D] or of glottalized stops in the language, and that the correct representation of the facts need not, and indeed must not, make use of the notion of ambisyllabicity. We will proceed by first giving what we regard as the correct account and will then criticize the ambisyllabic analysis.

The Syllable

On our account, the tapped *t* is always in syllable-final position (and is not syllable-initial). This position is a necessary but not sufficient condition for the tapping of *t*, though. It is enough to note that a syllable-final *t* may also be realized in its glottalized version or as a glottal stop (*atlas*= [æt⁽ʔ⁾ ɔs], [æʔl ə s]) to see that some additional conditions are involved. The most important condition, we claim, has to do with whether or not the consonant is released. What we will argue is that a voiceless stop (including *t*) is glottalized when it is not released, and that the tap allophone arises when i) a *t* is syllable-final, (ii) it is released, and iii) it is preceded by a [-cons] element. In offering this description of the facts, we must rely on a feature [±release], and equipped with this feature can give the following formulation to the rules:

(49)   *Tap*

$$t, d \rightarrow D \ / \ (\ldots [-cons] \begin{bmatrix} \\ +release \end{bmatrix})_\sigma$$
(syllable-final σ)

(50)   *Glottalization*

$$p, t, k \rightarrow p^? , t^? , k^? \ / \ \begin{bmatrix} \\ -release \end{bmatrix}$$

Since in this formulation of the tap rule only the syllable-final character of *t* (or *d*) need be mentioned, it will, if shown to provide the correct account of the facts, make the notion of ambisyllabicity totally unnecessary. The viability of our account relies on a. being able to treat release as a feature which plays a role in phonological rules, and b. being able to provide an adequate description of the facts concerning release in English.

We say that a consonant is released if immediately following the articulation and not during or after the articulation of a following segment, the closure is reopened. A complete and accurate phonetic description of any language requires a specification of the release of consonants, for languages may differ in this respect. The facts concerning release in French are different from those in English, for example. All voiceless stops are usually released in French, except if followed by a homorganic consonant (cf. Grammont 1914, 81-98; 1933, 36-45, 359-361). In particular, one may cite as being significantly different from English the fact that a stop not of the syllable onset is always released before another consonant, be it in the same syllable, e.g. *ac̱t(e)*, in a different syllable, e.g. *ac̱teur*, or in a different word, e.g. *un roc̱ très dur*. (Contrast this with the instances of nonreleased stop in *le bec̱ crochu* or *le cap̱ Matapan*, where a homorganic consonant follows.) In English, as we shall see below, stops are not released in these contexts in normal speech. Furthermore, a pre-pausal stop is (generally) released in French, e.g. *le bec, c'est un marteau qui tap(e)*. Grammont (1914, 85; 1933, 37) explicitly contrasts this state of affairs with English and Vietnamese, where release is generally not made in comparable cases. This constitutes a significance difference in the pronounciation of the two languages, and inasmuch as it is one which cannot be said to follow from the more global characteristics distinctive of the pronunciation of the languages, such as the overall tension of the articulatory musculature or the position of the lower mandible, we assert that an account of a phonetic feature such as release must form part of the grammar of the individual languages. Our proposal is that this be done by rules assigning a specification for the feature [±release]. We do not at present have evidence that a feature such as this ever plays a role in distinguishing the phonemes (sound types) of a language. It is therefore with a certain degree of tentativeness that we propose that it occupy a place in the set of universal distinctive features. Yet even if it were to turn out that no evidence ever became available that release played a *distinctive* role, one cannot deny that it has a role to play in a phonetic description incorporating linguistically significant generalizations. That is, whether or not release is a *distinctive* (i.e. phonological) feature, it is arguably a feature at some level of description. We therefore contend it is possible to allow it to play a determining role in the operation of phonological rules.

It will be assumed that [+release] is the unmarked specification for the feature in underlying representations in English. It is the task of the grammar to capture, in the form of a rule, the conditions for *non*release. All vowels, semi-vowels and continuants are [+release] once and for all. Among the stops, the rule for nonrelease will affect only syllable-final consonants: it goes without saying that consonants of the syllable onset are of necessity released. The question of release vs. nonrelease arises therefore only with syllable-final stops, and it depends on the nature of both the following and preceding contexts. We find the following array of facts:

(51) a. After [−cons] and before [−syll], nonrelease is OBL:

A*t*kins	a*t*las	a*t* Lynne's
a*p*titude	an*t*ler	ba*ck* down
a*c*tual	a*c*tivity	Pa*t* would like it
a*c*tion	surre*p*titious	ta*k*e your pick
ca*p*sule		sto*p* yelling
a*cc*ident		a*t* once
infe*ct*		
ra*p*t		
wi*d*th		

b. After [−cons] and before pause, nonrelease is OPT:

Did you see the ha*t*; take the ta*b*; take the ca*k*e;
They were in a big figh*t*; That's not ba*d*.

When a consonantal element precedes the stop in question, the facts are a bit more complex:

(52) a. After [+cons] and before [+cons], non release is OPT, and depends heavily on the type of consonant that follows:[45]

    exac*t*ly   ac*t* like them
    enac*t*ment   ac*t* nice
                              ac*t* silly
                              Amhers*t* College
                              las*t* night
                              rif*t* between
                              lef*t* me
                              was*p*-tailed
                              as*k* me
                              tas*k* force

b. After [+cons] and before $\begin{bmatrix} -\text{cons} \\ -\text{syll} \end{bmatrix}$, nonrelease is possible but definitely not preferred:

    lef*t* Yalta
    lef*t* one
    las*t* year
    las*t* one
    ac*t* your age
    ac*t* really nice

c. After [+cons] and before pause, nonrelease is possible, but definitely not preferred:

    We saw the second ac*t*.
    He's a was*p*.
    Why not as*k*?

We will not trouble to formulate the rule which ascribes the specification [−release] to segments; the contexts to be specified are obvious from (51) and (52), and the rules clearly have the entire utterance as their domain (they look beyond the limits of the word). In all instances where [−release] is assigned to a voiceless stop, our glottalization rule will bring about a closure at the glottis. If there is a [+release] specification, on the other hand, there will be no glottal closure. [−release] is thus a necessary and sufficient condition for the appearance of the glottalized allophones of the voiceless stops, and the glottalization rule (50) we may thus formulate in our system is significantly simpler than that provided by Kahn (48).

Observe next that when [−release] is *not* assigned to the syllable-final stops in (51), and (52) (in the optional cases), the allophone that appears is the predicted nonaspirated, nonglottalized one. To the above set of cases where release is optional should be added the cases where stops of a coda are *obligatorily* released. Release of syllable coda consonants is obligatory (understandably) when a vowel follows immediately, at the beginning of the next syllable, be it within the same word, as in (53), or in the following word in the utterance, as in (54).

(53) a. wa*c*ky, ha*p*py, wa*t*er, to*t*al
b. ac*t*or, Lef*k*owitz, nap*k*in, hef*t*y
(54) a. sto*p* Ellen, look out, it too*k* a while, sni*p* a few off
go*t* a match, ge*t* out of here, bough*t* Ellen tha*t* album
b. las*t* a long time, a contac*t* of mine, wrappe*d* in silk

(Recall that in the examples of (53), the prevocalic consonant is rendered syllable-final by Resyll. In the examples of (54), the prevocalic stop is syllable-final because it is word-final (see section 3.3)). In these instances, too, the nonglottalized nonaspirated allophones always appear, with the tapped version of *t* being limited to a subset of them. The (nonambisyllabic) formulation (49) of the tap rule sets three preconditions for converting *t* (and *d*) to [D]: that it be syllable-final, released, and preceded by a [−cons] segment. The first two conditions are satisfied by all the examples of (53) and (54), but the latter only by those of the *a* sets, and as we see, [D] is restricted to these. The *t* allophone of the *b* sets is merely the untapped voiceless nonglottalized nonaspirated variety.

It is reasonable to ask at this point how the observed allophones of *p*, *t*, *k* in (54) may be accounted for in Kahn's system. In these examples, the stops in question are word-final and thus according to the principles of normal syllabification in English, they are syllable-final. Yet the particular realization of these phonemes indicates, in Kahn's analysis, that they must be ambisyllabic (in order to *prevent* glottalization, and to *permit* tapping). Kahn's proposal is to introduce another rule of re(ambi)syllabification, this one connecting up a syllable-final consonant with a vowel-initial syllable that follows in the utterance.

(55) Trans-Word-Boundary Ambisyllabification (Kahn 1977)

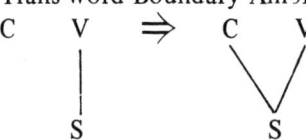

The Syllable

The rule will derive (57) from the more basic (56) (using Kahn's "autosegmental" mode of representing the syllable):

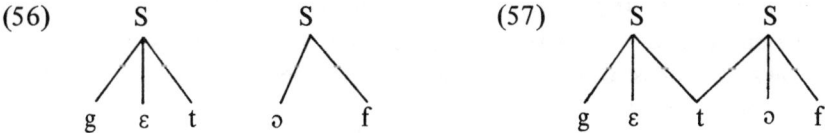

As a result of the resyllabification, the tap rule may, and, in this instance, will, convert /t/ to [D], producing (58):

(58)   *get off*   [g ɛ̀ D ɔ́ f]

(Note that an additional resyllabification such as this is unnecessary in our system, which does not rely on ambisyllabicity. This is not to say, in general, that we believe resyllabification not to take place between words, but only that in English the facts, viewed from our perspective, do not support it.)

Kahn claims TWA to be optional. When it does not apply, a syllabification such as (56) will be left intact, and Kahn's glottalization rule, applying to stops that are not syllable-initial, will give rise to the representation (59):

(59)   [g ɛ̀ t ˀ ɔ́ f] (or [g ɛ̀ ʔ ɔ́ f])

Kahn claims (59) to be the alternative pronunciation to (58), which comes about as a result of TWA. The application or non-application of TWA allows one to explain the appearance of the phonetic variants, in Kahn's view. Were it indeed the case that (59) were a possible realization of underlying /g ɛ t ɔ f/, the analysis we defend here would be in trouble, for according to our rule, glottalization arises only when a stop is not released, yet release is always a characteristic of prevocalic stops. It seems to us, though, that in English there is no phonetic representation possible like (59), where a syllable-final glottalized stop immediately precedes a vowel. The alternative to (58) is instead (60), where a glottal stop is serving as the onset of the following (underlyingly) vowel-initial syllable:

(60)   [g ɛ̀ t ˀ ʔ ɔ́ f]   (or [g ɛ̀ ʔ ʔ ɔ́ f])

(This glottal stop is inserted through the offices of a quite general process in English, which affects word-initial vowel-initial syllables under certain conditions of emphasis.) In terms of our analysis, this means that when a ʔ

is added to a vowel-initial syllable, the preceding syllable-final stop is assigned the feature [−release] (as expected), and is thus glottalized. If ʔ is not added, the final stop is of course prevocalic, released, and therefore not glottalizable. If t, it may be tapped. In terms of Kahn's analysis, this representation of the facts means that TWA is obligatory: when a vowel follows, it applies; when a consonant follows, be it ʔ or any other, it does not apply.

Let us next see how our account handles the facts concerning tapping in the earlier set of examples (51) and (52). We see that in (52), though the syllable-final condition is always satisfied, and the release condition is satisfied optionally (and even preferentially), the tap never appears, because [+cons] precedes in all the examples. In the prepausal context of (51)b, however, release of the syllable-final stop is optional, and since [−cons] precedes, a tap may appear, as the released variant of the nonreleased t'/ʔ, or d. (The tap does happen to be voiceless in this prepausal context; requiring an additional rule $D \rightarrow$ [-voice] / ___ Pause. [46] It is important to note that the appearance of a tap in a prepausal environment produces an important argument against kahn's claim that ambisyllabicity is a precondition for tapping. (Obviously, a prepausal consonant can never be ambisyllabic.) The tap rule of his system will have to be complicated to include an unrelated subcase:

(61) t, d → D / [−cons] $\left\{ \begin{bmatrix} \underline{} \\ + \text{SI} \\ + \text{SF} \end{bmatrix} \text{V} \quad \text{OBL} \atop \underline{} \text{ PAUSE} \quad \text{OPT} \right\}$

The prepausal context requires no such modification to our rule (49), as the reader can see.

Summarizing, it has been argued that an analysis not making use of the notion of ambisyllabicity can provide an adequate and even superior account of the range of data in English that has been thought of as giving support to the notion. The particular analysis put forward makes crucial use of a feature [±release] in providing a statement of the rules for the syllable-final allophones of the voiceless stops. (In Kahn's framework, too, this device is potentially available, for, we have argued, any grammar must include a set of rules specifying the release feature.) By comparison to ours, Kahn's analysis gives a less simple and straight-forward statement of the rules involved. Not only has the notion of ambisyllabicity not permitted an elegant statement of the tap rule (cf. (61)), in the case of glottalization (cf. (48)), it actually introduces a complication. The feature specification [−SI] in the rule is required in order to indicate that the consonant glottalized must *not* be ambisyllabic. A similar situation arises with respect to Kahn's rule for aspiration, which cannot say simply (as ours does) that a syllable-initial stop is aspirated. Given the assumption of ambisyllabicity, it must also be stated that the stop affected is *not also syllable-final*. It would seem then that the theoretical framework which employs the notion of ambisyllabicity enjoys no advantages at all over one, like ours, which does not. Ambisyllabicity is not required for, and in fact inhibits, the most satisfying statement of the generalizations involved. Given that no other support for the notion is available (from English), we permit ourselves to conclude that ambisyllabicity need not be defined in a general theory of prosodic structure.

One final issue we must contend with before closing discussion on ambisyllabicity concerns the fact that numerous phoneticians claim to have the "intuition" that a medial consonant in the contexts discussed is ambisyllabic. This intuition may be characterized as an impression that the boundary between the two syllables "falls within the consonant" or is "doubtful" (Kenyon 1950, 75), or that the consonant "belongs phonetically" to both syllables (Smalley 1968, 154), or that it is in "double syllable-function" (Pike 1967, 382). It would seem that the intuition could be explained in a number of ways, none of them requiring that at the phonetic level such consonants be represented as ambisyllabic. According to these lines of explanation, the intuition would be seen not as one about phonetic representation itself, but as one being determined by the phonetic syllabification in conjunction with some deeper, not strictly phonetic, principles of syllabification. It could be seen as resulting from a combination of the "perception" of the consonant as syllable-final phonetically and the "knowledge" that it is syllable-initial at some deeper level of representation. Or, it could be attributed to a conflict between the perceived syllable-final character of the consonant in phonetic representation and the universal tendency to assign pre-vocalic consonants to the following syllable, in phonological as well as phonetic representation. And so on. All these explanations seem perfectly plausible, and unless the case can be made that intuitions concerning syllable boundaries are made solely on the basis of the phonetic input, we will not accept intuitions of ambisyllabicity as disconfirming our hypothesis that linguistic representation need not give a place to ambisyllabicity.

NOTES

1. We are certainly not alone in ascribing internal constituent structure to the syllable. See Pike (1967), Lehiste (1971), Fudge (1969), Fujimura and Lovins (1978), McCarthy (1977) on English syllable structure, and especially Pike and Pike (1947), Newman (1972), Fudge (1969) and McCarthy (1977) on other languages as well.

2. The primary sources of the notion of hierarchical structure within the tradition of generative grammar are Liberman (1975) and Liberman and Prince (1977). See also Lehiste (1970) and Pike (1967).
3. The terms *onset, peak* and *coda* are due originally to Hockett (1955). In employing rhyme to name the constituent including peak and coda, we are following Fudge (1969).
4. See, for example, Bloomfield (1933); Whorf (1940); O'Connor and Trim (1953); Fudge (1969).
5. For some interesting remarks concerning the relation between close transition and syllable constituency in Estonian, see McCarthy 1977.
6. See, for example, Lehn (1973) and Broselow (1976) on Cairo Arabic, and Saib (1978) on Berber.
7. The idea for labelling syllable-internal structure in this way has been attributed to P. Kiparsky.
8. Pike (op. cit.), drawing on E. Pike (1954), suggests the ranking according to sonority:

```
p  t  k
   ç  č
b  d  g
m  n
f  s  x  h
   i  u
      a
```

The liquids *r, l* should presumably find their place somewhere near the vowels.) Hierarchies such as these have received quite a bit of attention in recent work on the syllable in phonological theory. (See Hankamer & Aissen (1974), Hooper (1976) among others), for the observation has been made that sounds nearer the extremities of the syllable tend to be less sonorous, according to some such hierarchy, then sounds nearer the center of the syllable. For some discussion of how this observation can be built into a theory of the internally structured and s/w – labelled syllable, see McCarthy (op. cit.)
9. Some of the ordering may be predictable according to a universal sonority hierarchy, stipulating that the more sonorous segment types are closer to the center of the syllable, but not all, cf. Hooper (1977).
10. On the distinctness and non-distinctness of feature matrices, see SPE, n.7.
11. Cf. Chomsky and Lasnik (1977) on the notion 'filter'.
12. Below we shall see that *sp, st, sk, sf, spl, str*, etc., apparent counterexamples to these claims about the template, must be accounted for by a special provision, an auxiliary template which does not form part of the general template (6).
13. Fudge (1969) also argues against (-son) (+son) on the grounds that a sonorant which is the sole consonant in an onset does not exhibit the same kinds of restrictions with respect to the composition of the rhyme that a second-position sonorant does. For example, he points out that syllables with *l* in second position of the onset resist having an *l* inside the rhyme, e.g. **flilt* (but *flint, flit, flirt*), whereas an *l* alone in the onset can occur with a later *l*, e.g. *lilt, loll*. Fudge is quite correct in observing that if such constraints were to be viewed as restrictions on what can co-occur in the various "slots" of the syllable template, no principled distinction between the status of the two *l*'s can be made if the onset of the template is of the form (-son) (+son).

14. We consider *sclerosis, schlitz* and others to be nonrepresentative.

15. The orthographic *sv*, occurring just once in the English language (*svelte*) is pronounced [sf] and is therefore to be treated as /sf/ phonologically. Note that /sf/ is itself of limited use in the language: it is found in only four or five roots, all of Greek origin.

16. We are indebted to Fudge (1969) and McCarthy (1977) for signalling the importance of this fact.

17. For discussion of the much disputed matter of the phonemic, i.e. phonological, representation of tense vowels *i, u, e, o* in English, see Bloomfield (1933), Trager and Bloch (1941), Swadesh (1947), Pike (1947), and *SPE*, among others.

18. Note that the existence of the [ksə] coda in *sixth* (the sole one of its kind) requires us to consider that the auxiliary template allows for *sə* clusters to occupy a single consonant slot. The fact that *sə* never appears initially would therefore have to be considered as merely accidental. The situation with *sə* is in a sense the converse of that with *sf*. Initial *sf* clusters are allowed only because of the auxiliary template, just like *sp, st* and *sk*. But *sf* does not appear in codas. Again, this must be considered to be accidental.

19. These points are developed at greater length in Selkirk (forthcoming, chapter three).

20. There is one form, the onomatopoetic *oink*, which includes a complex non-coronal coda preceded by a complex peak. We do not consider it to be representative.

21. See, especially, the work of Lehiste (1971).

22. Cf. Chen (1970) and discussion in Fujimura and Lovins (1978).

23. Cf. Malecot (1960), Raphael et. al. (1975), Fujimura and Lovins (1978).

24. In earlier work, however, Hoard (1971) seems to advocate a view of the syllable closer in spirit to that of Pike (1967), whereby the syllable forms part of the hierarchical organization of the utterance.

25. This is the theory put forth in generative phonology, see especially *SPE*, with the difference that generative phonology also considers the syntactic labelled bracketing of a sentence to form part of its phonological representation. Note that *SPE* gives no place to the syllable in phonological theory.

26. In a radical critique of this theory of phonological representation, same members of the London school of prosodic analysis, inspired by Firth (1948), have rejected the segment entirely as a unit of representation, replacing it with the syllable, of which such feature as place and manner of articulation are predicted. See, for example Henderson (1949). In their recent work on the syllable, Fujimura and Lovins (1978) again pose the question of whether the segment need find a representation, once the syllable is given a place in linguistic theory. Their approach is to reject the segment, but to still allow for a sequential ordering of feature specifications within the syllable.

27. See, for example, Bloch and Trager (1942), Jones (1956), Pike (1967), Hockett (1955), Rischel (1964).

28. Any suggestions that the boundary be placed in the "middle" of the segment in such cases (as has been advanced by Hyman (1977), for example) is incoherent, given the theory of phonological representation in which it is concluded, and vitiates the whole boundary approach.

29. Note that the autosegmental theory of the syllable is by no means merely a notational variant of the syllable boundary theory, as Hooper (1977) declares. One major difference is the possibility of representing ambisyllabicity.

30. The syllable theory of Anderson and Jones (1974) and Jones (1976) can be taken to be similar in some respects to that of Kahn's, insofar as the syllable is viewed

as a suprasegmental entity, and non-wellformed trees are allowed. In their system, medial consonant sequences are systematically ambisyllabic: as long as a consonant sequence is a permissible syllable-initial sequence as well as a permissible syllable-final sequence, it is always treated as ambisyllabic. There are some serious drawbacks to this approach, as Vogel (1977) and Hoard (1971) have pointed out.

31. In some form or other the principle is assumed or explicitly stated, by Hoard (1974), Hooper (1976), Kahn (1976), among others.

32. E.g. Hoard (1971, 1977), Bailey (1977).

33. Cf. Fudge (1969), Rosetti (1963) and works cited there, Hooper (1976).

34. The equivalent of this rule formulated in syllable boundary terms would be written as

$$\begin{bmatrix} +\text{cons} \\ -\text{cont} \\ -\text{voice} \end{bmatrix} \rightarrow [+\text{aspirated}] \;/\; .\underline{\quad}$$

35. t has the strongest tendency to glottalization in standard American, and is often entirely substituted for by [?] ; k is the next most strongly glottalized and in some dialects disappears in favor of [?] as well; p is the least glottizable of all, and often one has the impression that there is no glottal closure at all.

36. A d will also take on the tap allophone when found in the syllabic context which governs the appearance of class (i) allophones.

37. Note that, as formulated, the rule will also join the second element of a syllable-initial consonant cluster to the first element. We will allow for this, since the syllable structure derived by such an operation would be none other than the underlying syllable structure. That is, joining r to t in (tr) can only produce (tr).

38. There is nonetheless a contrast to be made between the naturalness of aspiration in *glitter* vs. *editor*. In the latter case, where the t is one syllable away from the stressed syllable, an aspiration of t is more acceptable. Such a difference is not to be reflected in the (re)-formulation of Resyll I, we would argue. Rather, following McCarthy (1978), we see it as following from the (general) fact that a rule such as Resyll I is more likely to apply when the two syllables involved are sisters in a higher order prosodic tree than when they are not. According to the Liberman-Prince conception of the (prosodic) organization of words in English, to which we turn in the next chapter, *glitter* is bracketed as (i) (before Resyll I applies) and *editor* as (ii):

(i)   ((glI) (tr))   (ii)   ((ε) (dI)) (tɔr))

39. Given this, the greater propensity for n to assimilate in place to the following consonant in *congress* than in *congressional* cannot be attributed to the fact that in the first case the g is tautosyllabic with the nasal, as Hoard argues. Instead, we would argue that the likelihood of nasalization depends on how closely the sounds are related in higher prosodic structure. Note that in *congress* the syllable with n is sister to the following syllable within the same foot. But in *congressional*, *con* is sister to a complex foot which includes the remaining three syllables. The distance, structurally speaking, between *con* and *gress* is therefore far greater in this instance.

40. Note that, written in this way, the rule will resyllabify *any* syllable-initial s cluster, including those like *sn*, *sm*, and *sl*. Were this to prove incorrect, and were it correct to resyllabify *sp*, *sk*, *st*, then we would conclude that Resyll should not be rewritten as in (41), and instead interpret the facts as showing that *sp*, *sk*, *st* are treated as a single consonant by resyllabification processes as well and that the original version (38) was adequate to the task.

41. Note that such a reformulation would not be adequate, though, if *s* plus obstruent clusters permitted *s* to re(ambi)syllabify.
42. In Kahn (1977) this rule is given the name of Medial Ambisyllabification Rule.
43. In general, we believe that an approach which seeks to encode relations between segments, and particularly relations which are structural in character, in the distinctive feature matrices of the segments is a dubious one.
44. Actually, Kahn restricts his discussion to $t \sim t^?$, but we generalize it here to $p \sim p^?$, $k \sim k^?$, recognizing that the degree to which *p, t, k* glottalize may vary considerably.
45. In many of these examples, a nonreleased *t* or *k* will be elided completely.
46. An additional environment allowing for release that was not mentioned above involves syllable-final stop before *h*. Note that in the following instances, the released nonglottalized nonaspirated varieties of *p* and *k* are *de rigeur*, as is the tap variety of *t* (in a voiceless version):

        Sto*p* Helen from doing that.   Do you li*k*e history?
        The weather go*t* hellishly bad.   Helen go*t* hers.

(Note also the tapped version of *d* in *ad hominem, sad history, adherence*). Because release is obligatory here, these examples may be taken as indicating that what is represented in phonetic transcription and orthography as *h* is not in fact a consonant but merely an indicator that the following vowel is breathy or 'aitchified' (cf. Jones (1950)). Given this interpretation of *h*, the above examples are merely instances (albeit special ones) of release before vowel, comparable to those of (54). Note finally that the voicelessness of the tap here will require that the tap devoicing rule applies before "h" — vowels as well as before pause.)

Harmony Processes in Vata*

Jonathan D. Kaye
U.Q.A.M.

0. Harmony processes have been the object of much study from a variety of theoretical approaches in recent years.[1] If one is to draw a conclusion from this work, it is that linear phonology, that is a phonology with one layer of structure at a given level of representation, is not the appropriate framework to represent such processes. This conclusion is by no means novel, nor is it limited to generative phonology. Linguists of the prosodist school[2] and American structuralists[3] arrived at similar conclusions concerning the inadequacies of the more traditional approaches to harmony processes.

Within the generative framework, two models have been employed: the autosegmental theory and metrical trees. In a recent article Halle and Vergnaud (1980) have suggested that indeed both models are necessary. They distinguish two sorts of harmony processes: dominant harmony, which they propose to treat with a revised autosegmental approach and directional harmony, for which they use metrical trees. This theory is quite new and accordingly needs "fleshing out" in various areas. It is my belief however, that the distinction between dominant and directional harmony is fundamentally sound and it is this line of research that I will pursue in this paper.

Halle and Vergnaud give examples of both types of processes from a variety of languages. If one were to judge from these examples, one might come to the conclusion that a complementarity exists between dominant and directional harmonies: languages may have one or the other, or neither, but not both. In fact, such a complementarity is merely the result of the paucity of examples which have been analyzed in this approach. Halle and Vergnaud never claim that the harmony types are mutually exclusive, nor is this entailed in any way by their theory. Indeed the pre-

---

* Research on Vata is supported in part by a grant from the Social Sciences and Humanities Research Council of Canada #410-81-0503. Many thanks to Hilda Koopman, Monik Charette, Dominique Sportiche and G.N. Clements for their useful comments. I am grateful for the collaboration of Doua Blé Siméon and Doua Yao Adolphe.

sence of both harmony types in one language would provide strong support for their theory as well as providing us with a unique opportunity to study their interaction. I will show that Vata is just such a language. In the sections to follow I will discuss both harmony processes in Vata. I will also present in some detail the theoretical approach of Halle and Vergnaud (which I adopt here) since it is quite new and has not (as of this writing) appeared in print.

1. Vata is an Eastern Kru language spoken in the Ivory Coast.[4] It has a system of ten vowels as seen in (1). In fact, as we shall see, Vata distinguishes five vowels at the segmental level each of which may or may not be associated with an autosegmental feature +*A* (for ATR).

(1) advanced   retracted
     i   u   ɪ   ʊ
     e   o   ɛ   ɔ
        ʌ   a

For expository convenience I will use this "linear" ten-vowel system for transcription purposes. Vowels in non-linear representations will be transcribed in upper case (A, E, I, O, U). Vata has four lexical tones which are transcribed as in (2).

(2) v́ high   v̏ mid-high   v̄ mid   v̀ low

Contour tones are transcribed and analyzed as sequences of level tones. Other aspects of the transcription follow the general practices for West African languages.

2. DOMINANT HARMONY

Halle and Vergnaud use a modified version of autosegmental theory to deal with dominant harmony. Dominant harmony has the following properties:

    i.   it is non-directional (it may propagate in either direction)
    ii. there is no identifiable triggering *segment*
    iii. opaque segments do not trigger their own harmony

The version of autosegmental theory utilized here has the following properties:

i. the autosegmental tier contains floating (non-attached) and associated (attached) features
ii. only one feature value (plus or minus) is available for floating autosegments. This is the marked value of the autosegment. Associated autosegments may have either value.
iii. Only floating autosegments may spread; associated autosegments remain linked to their segment.
iv. Each appropriate segment has a specification for the autosegmental feature at the segmental tier. This specification is the unmarked value of the feature.
v. Autosegmental features take precedence over segmental features.

The nature and application of these properties will become clearer as we proceed with the discussion of the facts of Vata.

2.1. Dominant harmony in Vata

In Vata all unanalyzable native morphemes exhibit vowels belonging to the same harmonic class (±ATR). Examples are given in (3) below.

(3) retracted   advanced
    lɛ̄tɛ̀   iron   ménʌ́   nose
    nɔ̄gbɔ̀fà skull   fúlù   rat
    nɛ́nɩ́   walk   kō̩sù   fire
    gɔ̀lɔ̄   dugout   bidō   wash

Non-native morphemes (mainly loanwords from Baoulé, an Akan language spoken just to the east of the Vata region) may be disharmonic as seen in (4).

(4) èlùwà   dog   èflúwá   paper, book

The harmonic domain is bounded by a #. The ATR autosegment does not spread beyond such a boundary. Accordingly, compound nouns may be disharmonic.

(5) bō̄gɔ̀gòdʌ̀ thigh   bɩ̄zàpòpʌ̀   bat
    dúkúnlɛ̀   goat   nlánlàgòdʌ̀   pipe
    zēgògbá   pangolin   ɲʌ̀glògbàzà   grasshopper

In this version of autosegmental theory the two harmonic classes have the

388 Jonathan D. Kaye

representations shown in (6). One example from each class has been chosen.

(6)   retracted   advanced
     autosegmental tier   +A
     segmental tier   g O l U⁵   b I d O⁵
                                   | |
                             [gòló] dugout   [bídō] wash

The representation of [gòló] contains no feature at the autosegmental level. All the vowels are specified [−ATR] at the segmental tier (represented by the minus found under each vowel at this level). Thus, both vowels are realized as retracted for this form. To the right we see an advanced form. Here the autosegmental feature +A (for ATR) appears at the autosegmental level. The vowels nonetheless are represented [−ATR] at the segmental level. Following the normal practice in autosegmental phonology the autosegmen +A will be associated with every appropriate element in its domain. For the feature ATR, vowels are the appropriate segments. Once the association lines are supplied, we have the representation as in (7).

(7)   +A
                      / \
                     /   \
                    b I d O

Each vowel in (7) has two specifications for the feature ATR: [+ATR] by association with the autosegment, and [−ATR] at the segmental level. As we noted above, the autosegmental feature takes precedence and the vowels are realized as advanced.

It was noted above that the domain of the autosegment A is any sequence contained within # boundaries. It is also true that the autosegment +A is available only to major category items (±N, ±V) and certain verbal particles generally derived from body parts. Pronouns, affixes and postpositions are all [−ATR]. Putting these two facts together, it follows that affixation involving a boundary weaker than # will always involve vowel harmony and indeed such is the case in Vata.

(8) a. Instrumental/locative   lɛ̄ – lē (imperfective forms)
     kla̅   sieze   kla̅lɛ̄   sieze with   pī prepare   pīlē   prepare with
     ŋɔ̀nɔ́ sleep   ŋɔ̀nɔ́lɛ̄   sleep in   bī walk   bīlē   walk with
     ɓlī   sing   ɓlīlɛ̄   sing in   sū crash   sūlē   crush with

Harmony in Vata

b. Passive   lɔ̀ – lò   (base form)

klá	cut down	klálɔ̀	be cut down	lī	eat	līlò	be eaten
ɲɛ̀	give	ɲɛ̀lɔ̀	be given	dì´	cut	dì´lò	be cut
ɓīī	sing	ɓīīlɔ̀	be sung	nú	understand	núlò	be understood

c. Singular of collective nouns yɛ̀ – yè

ɲí	hair	ɲíyɛ̀	a hair	nòvó	bees	nòvóyè	a bee
sūgbɔ̀	fruits[6]	sūgbɔ̀yɛ̀	a fruit	zlē	fish	zlēyè	a fish
wīī	fingers	wīīyɛ̀	a finger	vē	palm grains	vūyè	a palm grain

I assume that each of the above suffixes is seperated from its stem by a weak boundary. Thus, affixed forms of the type found in (8) have the representation as in (9).

(9) a.   b.

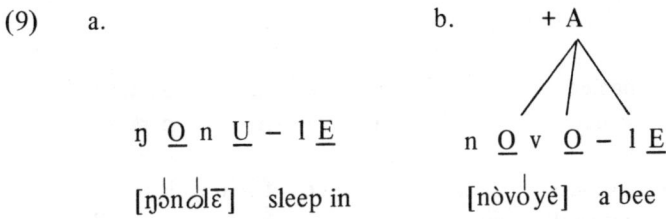

ŋ O n U – l E   n O v O – l E

[ŋɔ̀nɔ̀lɛ̄] sleep in   [nòvóyè] a bee

In (9a) neither the verb stem nor the suffix have a feature at the autosegmental level. The resulting form is entirely [–ATR], the specification at the segmental level. In (9b) the verb stem is +A. This feature is associated to every vowel within its domain. Thus every vowel is advanced in this form. This process will extend indefinitely to as many suffixes as there are in the form in question. In (10a) we see two examples of a verb stem followed by two harmonizing suffixes: the passive and the instrumental/locative, respectively. The representation of each is given in (10b). The hatched lines represent the associations after the universal conventions have applied.

(10) a. sū klálɔ̄lɛ̄   làlùkú` mlí 'one cuts down a tree with a machete'
         tree cut down machete with

        saká līlōlē   ɲīdʌ mlí 'rice is cooked in a pot'
        rice be eaten pot   in

(10) b.

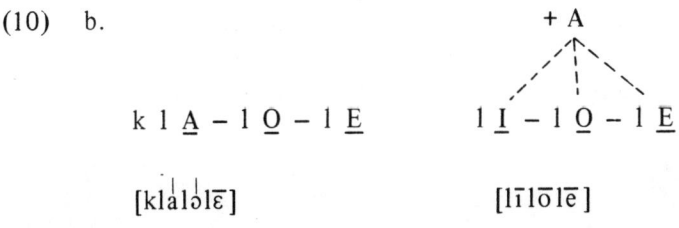

k l A – l O – l E   l I – l O – l E

[klálɔ̄lɛ̄]   [līlōlē]

This concludes the general description of dominant harmony in Vata. We have seen that an autosegment +*A* spreads to every relevant segment within its domain. The domain is the phonological string bounded by a # (or, necessarily a ##) boundary. Thus, dominant harmony is limited to the word, or more precisely to major categories and their affixes. In the case of a word containing two or more major category items (i.e. a compound), dominant harmony does not spread beyond the compound boundary #. The harmony described to this point is strikingly similar in most relevant respects to vowel harmony in Akan as described in Clements (1981). Several important questions remain to be discussed. In the next section I will discuss in detail nominal compounds in Vata.

2.2. *Compounds and vowel harmony in Vata.*

In this section we consider the first class of disharmonic words in Vata: nominal compounds. Examples are provided in (11) below.

(11)
ɲákpɪ̀ɲɔ̀	healer	ɲákpɪ̀	medicine	ɲɔ̄	person
ŋā nɔ̀ɲɔ̀	scared	ŋā nɔ̀	fear	ɲɔ̄	person
lɪ̄lɪ̄zɛ̀	food	lɪ̄	eat	zɛ̀	thing
vɛ̀dàflɔ̄	fromager	vɛ̀dà	fromager	fɔ̄flɔ̄	leaf
sū nɔ̀	caterpillar	sū	tree	nɔ̀	caterpillar
jlàyò	lion cub	jlà	lion	yò	child
gō sù	kola tree	gō lè	kola	sū	tree
zásù	coconut palm	zá	nuts	sū	tree
bɔ̄gɔ̄pòpʌ	sole of foot	bɔ̄gɔ̄	foot	pòpʌ	broom
ɲlūyò	chick	ɲlū	chicken	yò	child

Compounding is an extremely common and productive process in Vata. Among the examples of (11) we find each of the four logical possibilities for compounds of two elements with respect to the feature *ATR*: [−ATR] − [−ATR] (ɲákpɪ#ɲɔ), [+ATR] −[−ATR] (sū#nɔ), [+ATR] − [+ATR] (gō#sù), [−ATR] − [+ATR] (za#sù). I should state here that the representations of *zásù* and *jlàyò* represent an extremely stilted and pedantic pronounciation of these forms. In normal speech one hears *zʌsù* and *jlʌsù*, respectively.[7] These latter forms manifest the application of another harmony process to be discussed in a latter section.

The reader will note that certain tone changes occur in these constructions. In fact such changes are observed in a variety of contexts all of which appear to be nominal compounds of one sort or another. These forms are frequently referred to as "associative constructions" in the literature. What interests us here is that aside from a difference in vowel harmony behaviour, several other traits distinguish the forms in (11) from the examples of affixation given in (8): the existence of the elements as independently occurring forms and the associated tone changes characteristic of associative constructions. This distinction hardly seems controversial and I will not discuss the many other syntactic and morphological differences separating (8) from (11).

In our theoretical framework these compounds are to be represented as in (12).

(12)   ##ɲAkpI#ɲO## [ɲákpìɲɔ̀]   ##sU#nO## [sū̄nɔ̀]
       +A   +A +A

       ##ɓOgU#pOpA## [ɓɔ̄gɔ̀pòpʌ̀]   ##gO#sU## [gō̄sù]

In (12) we see that the compound boundary # constitutes a barrier to the propagation of the floating autosegment. The overwhelming majority of apparently disharmonic words can be explained in this way. This analysis makes the further prediction that if the compound has a suffix (there are no prefixes in Vata), it will harmonize with the last element of the compound. This prediction is confirmed as is seen in the following examples:

(13) a. n̄   dlá'   ɟlàyʌ̀ʌ̀ʌ̀   (ɟlá#yò+àà)   'did you kill a lion cub?'
          you kill-perf lion cub-quest.
      b. n̄   lì   sū̄nàáà   (sū#nɔ̀+àà)   'did you eat a tree cater-
                                                    pillar?'
          you eat-perf tree cater.-quest.

Direct questions are formed by suffixing the question particle $-\overline{aa}$ to the last word of the sentence. Various assimilation rules affect the ultimate realization of the resulting vowel sequence.[8] What interests us here is that the suffix agrees with the preceding word in ATR-ness. If we posit a morpheme boundary + between the final word and the question suffix, the facts of (13) follow automatically as is seen in (14a, b).

(14) a. ##ɟlA#yO+AA##   ##ɟlA#yO+AA## [ɟlàyʌ̀ʌ̀ʌ̀]
          +A   +A

      b. ##sU#nO+AA##   ##sU#nO+AA## [sū̄nàáà]

The underlying forms of the two compounds-cum-question suffix are given in the left column. At the segmental level all vowels are specified as $-ATR$. Certain major category items such as sū̩, yó̩, have a floating autosegment $+A$ as part of their lexical representation. This autosegment spreads to all vowels within its domain. The compound boundary # is opaque to this feature while the morpheme boundary + is transparent. Thus, in the first example (14a), the feature $+A$ spreads to the right up to the word boundary but not to the left. In the second example the autosegment $+A$ cannot spread to the right because of the # boundary. The question suffix is accordingly realized phonetically as a $-ATR$ vowel sequence.

My account differs somewhat from the Goldsmith-Clements version of autosegmental theory. In cases where the question particle is $+ATR$, I assume that an autosegmental feature has spread to this suffix. In cases where the resulting form is $-ATR$, the source of this specification is the segmental level where every vowel carries a $-ATR$ specification. Appearances notwithstanding, the $-ATR$ specification never spreads. In such cases it is always the feature of the segmental tier which is manifested. The implications of this claim will be explored in later sections.

2.3. Pseudo-disharmonic stems.

As far as I can determine, all monomorphemic stems in Vata are harmonic, i.e. one finds no mixtures of advanced and retracted vowels within a single morpheme. Furthermore, Vata has neither neutral vowels — vowels which occur indifferently with either harmonic set (as happens in certain Finno-Ugric languages) — nor opaque vowels — vowels occurring with either set and blocking the propagation of a harmonic feature (such as the vowel *a* in Akan, Clements (1981)). Vata has a fair number of loan words from a variety of languages: Baoulé, an Akan language spoken to the north and east of the Vata region, Dioula, a Mandé language which is the language of the marketplace in the Ivory Coast, French, English, etc. While the vast majority of the loanwords are harmonic, a few words give the impression of being disharmonic.

(15) èlùwà   dog
     èflúwá   paper
     sìka̩`   gold

A number of possible analyses come to mind. It would be possible to treat the disharmonic vowel *a* as an opaque vowel. In terms of our theory this involves a bound autosegment $-A$ as in (16).

Harmony in Vata

(16)

The autosegment bound to the last vowel prevents the floating autosegment to its left from associating with that vowel. Furthermore, any following suffix will not receive the value +*ATR* because of the constraint against crossing association lines. Recall that in this version of autosegmental theory, bound autosegments do not propagate. The floating +*A* autosegment is free to associate with the first vowels of the word. This is precisely the state of affairs which obtains as seen in (17a, b).

(17) a. ǹ   kà   èlùwààà   'do you have a dog?'
         you have dog-quest.
     b.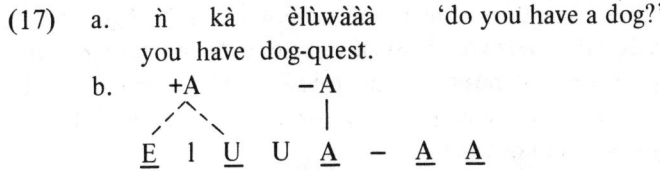

The first two vowels receive the value +*ATR* because of the association with the floating +*A* autosegment. The stem final *a* is −*ATR* because it is bound to a −*A* autosegment. Finally, the suffix −*aa* is −*ATR* because of its specification at the segmental tier.

While the above analysis enjoys a certain plausibility, I will claim that it is incorrect. For reasons to be discussed in later sections it will be impossible to claim that there is an autosegment lexically bound to the final vowel of these words. In fact, true cases of bound autosegments exist in Vata but they will be shown to have rather different properties from the forms under discussion here. If we reject the above analysis we are obliged to consider the forms of (16) as compounds.

(18)   +A   +A
       ╱╲   ╱ ╲
      ╱ ╲   ╱   ╲
     E l U # U A   E f l U # U A
     [èlùwà]   [èflúwá]

        +A
        ┊
     s I # k A
     [sìkà`]

It should be clear that the analysis in (18) will account for the same facts as that of (16-17). Below I will offer an explanation for the preference of this latter solution over the former one. In any event, in the absence of a better alternative I will maintain the compound analysis over that of a bound −*A* autosegment.

It should be pointed out that there is no semantic basis for the proposed compounds, i.e. they are not decomposable into any recognisable recurring elements. For the moment the only justification for the compound boundary in these forms is their behaviour with respect to vowel harmony. In defense of this proposal let me add that Vata contains a considerable number of native (historical) compounds whose components remain synchronically obscure, e.g. *bà-ylɛ̀* 'peppers', *dèglì-mɛ́* 'cameleon', *nōkɔ̀--gbàlʊ́* 'firewood', etc. Aside from their disharmonic nature these compounds betray other phonological aberrancies. For example, *bàylɛ̀* 'peppers' is to be analyzed as *bà#ylɛ̀*. Normally, resonants other than *l* are limited to morpheme-initial position. In verbs, where compounding is almost inexistant, one never finds medial *w* or *y*. Note also that disharmonic verbs of any sort do not exist.

To return to our forms of (15), aberrancies other than lack of vowel harmony can be seen. The first two examples contain a *w* following our postulated compound boundary. I have already noted that *w* does not occur in morpheme medial position. The form *sikà`* displays an atypical tonal pattern − atypical for a monomorphemic bisyllabic noun in Vata. In view of these facts I conclude that a compound analysis for the forms of (15) is not without some independent justification.

2.4. *True disharmonic stems.*

There exists in Vata an extremely small set of forms which I claim are truly disharmonic. These forms may well have the status of unassimilated or partially assimilated loan words. Up to now I have found two such forms which are not simply French words inserted into Vata discourse.

(19)   làlùkú`   'machete'
       àlàdio`   'radio'

I posit the following representations for these forms:

(20)   −A   +A   − A   + A
           | ⁀⁀⁀   ⁀⁀⁀ |
         l A l U k U   A l A   d I O [9]
         [làlùkú`]              [àlàdio`]

The floating −*A* autosegment will spread rightward to the suffixed question particle in the usual way.

(21) ǹ   kà   làlùkú`ʌ̀ʌ̀   'do you have a machete?'
      you have   machete-quest.

```
      −A      +A
       |    ╱━━━━━━
    l  A  l U  k U  −  A  A
       ─    ─    ─     ─  ─
```

Although a compound analysis *là#lùkú`* might seem possible, the forms of (19) display a different behaviour with respect to the directional harmony to be discussed below.

Forms such as those in (19) are abnormal for other reasons. The second example *áládió`* should probably simply be eliminated from consideration. A variety of pronunciations exist: *làdió`*, *ràdió`*, *àràdió`*, *àràdiu`*, etc. Note that *r* is not part of the phonemic inventory of Vata.

The form *làlùkú`* is extremely local in use. While this form is used in Zaroko, one finds *zɔ̀gblɔ̀* at Gogobro, a neighbouring village. The moral of all this is that the forms of (19) represent highly atypical phonological behaviour and should be so represented in the phonology.

With this section I conclude the discussion of disharmonic forms in Vata. We have seen that there exists a system of dominant harmony. An autosegment +A spreads to all relevant elements within its domain. Weak boundaries are transparent to this process while strong boundaries, # or ##, block it. Disharmonic words are analyzed as either compounds (*lī lī#zὲ* 'something to eat') or as elements containing a bound −A autosegment (*làlùkú`* 'machete'). With this analysis and the modified version of autosegmental theory adopted here, we have accounted for a variety of facts in a rather simple manner. No rules are necessary. One specifies the autosegment +A, the domain and the pertinent segments being in all probability specified by universal grammar, and the rest follows. In the following section we consider the behaviour of vowel sequences. Their study will have important implications for the analysis presented thus far.

3. VOWEL SEQUENCES IN VATA.

Vata contains only open syllables. As a result, each time a word is followed by a vowel-initial element, a vowel sequence is created. Certain processes are involved in the realization of these sequences. The organisation of the next sections is as follows: sequences across word boundaries, sequences of verb forms plus object pronouns, sequences of nouns plus definite article, sequences involving the question particle, and finally, miscellaneous sequences.

3.1. Sequences across word boundaries.

Native major category items are invariably consonant-initial in Vata. Trans-word vowel sequences result from either loan words such as those in (22),

(22) àdáɓlá   market   èɓètè   banana
      àjá`   inheritance   éfó   herrings
      àslà   tobacco   èflɪ̩   albino
      àɓà   proper name   èkʊ̩fú   proper name

or pronominal forms such as those in (23).

(23) ɔ̩ nó   his mother   à có   our father
      ɛ̩ ɓōgʊ̩   its leg   ɩ̩ yuʌ́   their children
      ʊ̩glā   its teeth

Loan words may begin with either *a* or *e* [10]. The pronominal forms provide us with the full set of retracted vowels. The forms of (23) include third person pronouns of the various noun classes. The details do not interest us here.[11] Suffice it to say that the vowels ɩ, ɛ, ʊ, ɔ, a are represented in this set. Consider now the following data:

(24) a. second vowel – *a*

initial vowel	verb	verb – vowel	resulting sequence
i	yì know	ŋ̩ yì àɓà I know Aba	ia
ɩ	mlɩ̩ went	ŋ̩ mlɩ̩ àdáɓlá I went to the market	ɩa
u	nu` heard	ŋ̩ nú` àɓà wlú I heard Aba	ua
ʊ	zʊ̩ ` put	ŋ̩ zʊ̩ ` àslà táɓlʊ̩ kʊ̩ I put tobacco	ʊa
e	lē eat	ŋ̩ lā àɓʊ̩dʊ̩ I eat sugar cane	aa
ɛ	mlɛ̄ leave	ŋ̩ mlā àdáɓlá I go to the market	aa
o	nò hear	ŋ̩ ná àɓà wlú I hear Aba	aa
ɔ	zɔ̀ put	ɔ̀ zá àslà táɓlʊ̩ kʊ̩ he puts tobacco	aa
ʌ	fótʌ pierce	ɔ̀ fóta àɲa ɲeflíɔ̩ he pierces ears	aa
a	pà throw	ŋ̩ pá àslà I throw tobacco	aa

b. second vowel – ɔ

i	lì ate	ŋ̩ lì ɔ̩ nlɛ̄ I ate his meat	iɔ
ɩ	ɓlɩ̩ sang	ŋ̩ ɓlɩ̩ ɔ̩ lóɔ̩ I sang his song	ɩɔ
u	nu` heard	ŋ̩ nú` ɔ̩ nó wlú I heard his mother	uɔ
ʊ	wɔ̀lʊ̩ washed	ŋ̩ wɔ̀lʊ̩ ɔ̩ t lànɛ̄` I washed his shirt	ʊɔ
e	lē eat	ŋ̩ lɔ̀ ɔ̩ zā I eat his food	ɔɔ
ɛ	ɲɛ̄ give	ŋ̩ ɲɔ́ ɔ̩ nó I give his mother ...	ɔɔ
o	nò hear	ŋ̩ nó ɔ̩ nó I hear his mother	ɔɔ

Harmony in Vata 397

ɔ	wɔ̄lɔ̄ wash	n̄ wɔ̄lɔ̄ ɔ̀ t lànɛ́	I wash his shirt		ɔɔ
ʌ	fótʌ́ pierce	n̄ fótɔ̀ ɔ̀ dlóò	I pierce his pearls		ɔɔ
a	pā throw	n̄ pó ɔ̀ zā	I throw his food		ɔɔ

c. second vowel – ɛ

i	lì ate	n̄ lì ɛ́ bɔ̄gɔ̀ɔ̀	I ate its leg		iɛ
ɩ	plɩ̋ passed	n̄ plɩ́ ` ɛ́ bùdùɔ̀ kɔ̄	I passed its tracks	ɩɛ
u	nú heard	n̄ nú ` ɛ mlɩ́pɛ̀lìɔ̀	I heard its cry		uɛ
ʊ	nɔ̀ made	ɛ nɔ̀ ɛ lulóò	it made its nest		ʊɛ
e	lē eat	n̄ lɛ́ ɛ bɔ̄gɔ̀ɔ̀	I eat its leg		ɛɛ
ɛ	plɛ́ pass	n̄ plɛ́ ɛ bùdùɔ̀ kɔ̄	I pass its track		ɛɛ
o	nó hear	n̄ né ɛ mlɩ́pɛ̀lìɔ̀	I hear its cry		ɛɛ
ɔ	nɔ̄ make	ɛ nɛ ɛ lulóò	it makes its nest		ɛɛ
ʌ	fótʌ́ pierce	n̄ fótɛ́ fúɔ̀	I pierce its skin		ɛɛ
a	plā sell	n̄ plɛ́ ɛ nɔ̄kpìɔ̀	I sell its feathers		ɛɛ

d. second vowel – ɩ

i	lì ate	ɔ̀ lì ɩ fóò	he ate their bones		iɩ
ɩ	plɩ̋ ` passed	ɔ̀ plɩ́ ` ɩ bùdùɔ̀ kɔ̄	he passed their tracks	ɩɩ
u	nú ` heard	ɔ̀ nú ` ɩ mlɩ́pɛ̀lìɔ̀	he heard their cry		uɩ
ʊ	nɔ̀ made	ɩ nɔ̀ ɩ lulíó	they made their nests		ʊɩ
e	lē eat	ɔ̀ lɩ́ ɩ bɔ̄gɩ̀ɔ̀	he eats their legs		ɩɩ
ɛ	plɛ́ pass	ɔ̀ plɩ́ ɩ lulíó kɔ̄	he passes their nests	ɩɩ
o	nó hear	ɔ̀ nɩ́ ɩ mlɩ́pɛ̀lìɔ̀	he hears their cry		ɩɩ
ɔ	nɔ̄ make	ɩ nɩ́ ɩ lulíó	they make their nests		ɩɩ
ʌ	fótʌ́ pierce	ɔ̀ fótɩ́ ɩ fɔ̄kpɔ̀ɔ̀	he pierces their hides	ɩɩ
a	plā sell	ɔ̀ plɩ́ ɩ nɔ̄kpìɔ̀	he sells their feathers	ɩɩ

e. second vowel – ʊ

i	lì ate	ɔ̀ lì ʊ́ bɔ̄gɔ̀ɔ̀	he ate its leg		iʊ
ɩ	plɩ̋ ` passed	ɔ̀ plɩ́ ` ʊ bùdùɔ̀ kɔ̄	he passed its trail	ɩʊ
u	nú ` heard	ɔ̀ nú ` ʊ mlɩ́pɛ̀lìɔ̀	he heard its cry		uʊ
ʊ	wɔ̀lʊ̀ washed	ʊ wɔ̀lʊ̀ ʊ nɔ̄kpìɔ̀	it washed its feathers		ʊʊ
e	lē eat	ɔ̀ lʊ́ ʊ bɔ̄gɔ̀ɔ̀	he eats its leg		ʊʊ
ɛ	plɛ́ pass	ɔ̀ plʊ́ ʊ bùdùɔ̀ kɔ̄	he passes its trail	ʊʊ
o	nó hear	ɔ̀ nʊ́ ʊ mlɩ́pɛ̀lìɔ̀	he hears its cry		ʊʊ
ɔ	wɔ̄lɔ̄ wash	ʊ wɔ̀lʊ ʊ nɔ̄kpìɔ̀	it washes its feathers		ʊʊ

ʌ	fótʌ́	pierce	à fótɷ	ɷ́ fɷ̄kpàá	we pierce its hide	ɷɷ
a	plā		à plɷ̄	ɷ́ nɷ̄kpì̍ɷ̀	we sell its feathers	ɷɷ

The results of the juxtaposition of the five retracted vowels are given in table (25) below.

(25)

a. i − a ia   b. i − ɔ iɔ   c. i − ɛ iɛ   d. i − ɩ iɩ   e. i − ɷ
   ɩ − a ɩa   ɩ − ɔ ɩɔ   ɩ − ɛ ɩɛ   ɩ − ɩ ɩɩ   ɩ − ɷ
   u − a ua   u − ɔ uɔ   u − ɛ uɛ   u − ɩ uɩ   u − ɷ
   ɷ − a ɷa   ɷ − ɔ ɷɔ   ɷ − ɛ ɷɛ   ɷ − ɩ ɷɩ   ɷ − ɷ
   e − a aa   e − ɔ ɔɔ   e − ɛ ɛɛ   e − ɩ ɩɩ   e − ɷ
   ɛ − a aa   ɛ − ɔ ɔɔ   ɛ − ɛ ɛɛ   ɛ − ɩ ɩɩ   ɛ − ɷ
   o − a aa   o − ɔ ɔɔ   o − ɛ ɛɛ   o − ɩ ɩɩ   o − ɷ
   ɔ − a aa   ɔ − ɔ ɔɔ   ɔ − ɛ ɛɛ   ɔ − ɩ ɩɩ   ɔ − ɷ
   ʌ − a aa   ʌ − ɔ ɔɔ   ʌ − ɛ ɛɛ   ʌ − ɩ ɩɩ   ʌ − ɷ
   a − a aa   a − ɔ ɔɔ   a − ɛ ɛɛ   a − ɩ ɩɩ   a − ɷ

A glance at (25) shows a clear pattern governing these vowel sequences: a non-high vowel assimilates to all the features of the following vowel including the feature *ATR*. The question is by what mechanism can we account for both the apparent assimilation and the apparent spread of the feature *−ATR* to the left. According to our analysis this is quite impossible. To see this consider a putative assimilation rule (26).

(26)
$$\begin{bmatrix} +\text{syll} \\ -\text{high} \end{bmatrix} \rightarrow [\alpha F] / \_\_ \#\# \begin{bmatrix} +\text{syll} \\ \alpha F \end{bmatrix}$$

This rule reflects our informal description of the behaviour of the vowel sequences given above. A non-high vowel receives a copy of all the features of a following vowel across an intervening word boundary. This rule works well enough in cases where the first vowel is *−ATR*.

(27)   pʌ̱ ##Ǫ ##zʌ̱   'throw his food (indef.)'

(26) pǪ##Ǫ##zʌ̱

   [pɔ́   ɔ̄   zā]

What is more difficult, is to account for cases where the first vowel is advanced.

(28)
```
    +A                              +A
    |                                |
    |           —(26)→               |
    |                                |
 1 E  ## A  b  U  d  U         1 A  ## A  b  U  d  U
```

In (28) a derivation of the $e - a$ sequence is given. Rule (26), a rule of the segmental tier, will change all the segmental features of e, including the vacuous change from $-ATR$ to $-ATR$, to those of the following a. One should not forget that *all* vowels are specified as $-ATR$ at the segmental tier. The rule has no effect on the autosegmental level and one would expect that the association of the autosegment $+A$ with the assimilated vowel would yield the form *[lā̀ àbōdò]. In fact the correct form is [lā̀ àbòdò]. Why is the first vowel $-ATR$? In our version of autosegmental theory the $-ATR$ feature cannot float and consequently cannot spread. One could propose that a segmental rule of assimilation simultaneously deletes an autosegment. This would be an unprecedented and certainly unwelcome move. Such an increase in the descriptive power of autosegmental theory is to be avoided if at all possible. Conceptually, a breach in the relative autonomy of the respective tiers goes directly against the grain of the theory. Finally, strong evidence exists that the autosegment is not deleted but rather remains unassociated in the representation as shown in (29).

(29)
```
    +A

 1 A  ## A  b  U  d  U
```

Now the question is why the autosegment does not associate to the vowel within its domain. One could propose that autosegments fail to associate to a non-high vowel followed by another vowel. Aside from being observationally inadequate, as we shall see below, the proposal contains a worrysome redundancy: the specification *–high* is mentioned both in the rule (26) and in the proposed principle given above. Surely this cannot be a coincidence. It would be equally conceivable that *all* vowels fail to associate with an autosegment when followed by another vowel. The analysis fails to provide a reason why precisely the vowels which assimilate are those which fail to associate with an autosegment. It is clear that the assimilation-cum-dissociation analysis is hopelessly inadequate. In fact, to describe what is going on here we must consider some further refinements to autosegmental theory.[12]

A number of linguists have noted the importance of a skeleton, a core level, in a non-linear phonology.[13] The skeleton consists of a series of points. These points are organized and interpreted by the various tiers which intersect with the skeleton. Elements of the segmental tier are mapped onto the skeleton. The syllabic interpretation of these elements is provided by the syllabic tier in the form of a branching structure whose terminal elements are points of the skeleton. To render phonological notation, which has now become complex and "three-dimensional", more comprehensible, I have collapsed the syllabic tier onto the skeleton. In this format elements of the skeleton are represented as C's and V's rather than as points. By convention skeletal elements dominated by the nucleus node of the syllabic tier are designated by V's. All other elements (those dominated by the onset or coda nodes) are represented as C's in the skeleton (Kaye and Lowenstamm, 1981a, 1981b, 1982). It must be remembered that C's and V's enjoy no theoretical status. Unlike other versions of non-linear phonology which employ a C-V tier, in our version they are merely abbreviatory conventions.

Let us turn now to the relationship between the segmental tier and the skeleton. Segments may be associated with the skeleton in a one-to-one fashion (30a), a one-to-many fashion (30b), or a many-to-one fashion (30c).

(30)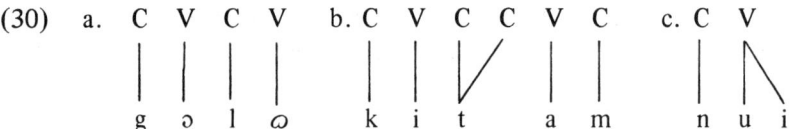

(30a), the one-to-one association, represents the normal state of affairs: each segment has its individual interpretation at the skeletal level. (30b) represents a hypothetical case of gemination. A single segment occupies both a coda position and an onset position of two successive syllables. This consonantal segment is thus realized as a geminate. The representation in full is that of (31).

(31)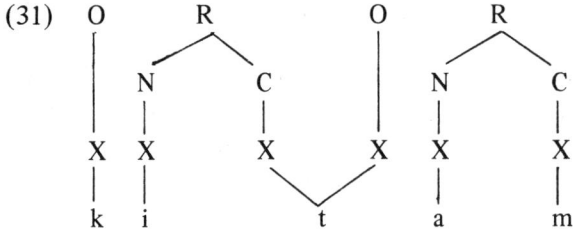

The symbols O, R are the syllabic constituents ONSET and RIME. The rime is composed of the constituents N (NUCLEUS) and C (CODA). The segment *t* is associated with two points of the skeleton. Each of these points occupies a particular syllabic position as defined by the syllabic tier. In this way we may represent processes such as gemination.

Harmony in Vata 401

Taking a less hypothetical example, consider the case of Western Ojibwa. In this language a glottal stop may not occupy the coda position of a syllable. If such a situation arises the glottal stop is deleted (or, simply fails to associate) and the following consonant moves in to occupy the vacant coda position. The derivation of the forms [takoššin] 'he arrives' and [ki·ttakoššin] 'he arrived' demonstrates the creation of geminate consonants as the automatic result of the loss of the glottal stop.

(32)

The past tense form appearing at the right of (32) combines the past tense marker *ki·ʔ* and the verb stem *takoššin*. As is seen in the derivation, the glottal stop must dissociate from the coda position. The segment *t* then propagates to this position yielding the geminate *tt* of the phonetic form.[14]

(30c) represents the other logical possibility. The segmental tier contains one more element than the skeleton. Consequently, the last two segments are associated with a single syllabic element resulting in a "light" diphthong, i.e. a diphthong which behaves exactly like a short open syllable from a metrical point of view. In Dida (Lakota), another Kru language of the Ivory Coast, we find that a skeletal element dominated by the node nucleus in the syllabic tier (a *V* in our abbreviated format) is deleted when it is not linked to a tone, and when it is preceded or followed by another nuclear element with no intervening consonantal element on the segmental tier. Let us informally express this process as in (33).

(33)   V → ∅

Rule (33) states that a *V* (≠ vowel) of the skeleton is deleted. In its present form (33) will overapply in a substantial number of cases. General principles whose exact nature do not interest us here will serve to eliminate most instances of overapplication. Suffice it to say that (33) should only apply in cases where two consecutive vowel segments are found on the segmental tier, and only in those cases where the skeletal element to be deleted has no associated tone. Thus, a representation as in (34)

(34)   H
            |
        C   V   +   V   'plug them'
        | | |
        n   u   i

will undergo rule (33) yielding (35).

(35)
```
      H
      |
   C  V        [nuí]
   |  |\
   n  u i
```

These examples illustrates the relative autonomy of the different tiers. It is, of course, possible to have a deletion process resulting in the loss of elements at both the segmental and skeletal levels. What is important is that elements at either level may independently undergo deletion.

Returning now to the problem of Vata vowel sequences, we have seen that an assimilation analysis will not do. The inclusion of a skeletal level provides us with a solution to this problem. I will suppose that the appropriate rule to treat the data of (24) is a rule of truncation. This rule, given in (36) deletes an element at the segmental tier only – the skeleton remains unchanged.[16]

(36) General Truncation

$$\begin{bmatrix} + \text{vocalic} \\ - \text{high} \end{bmatrix} \rightarrow \emptyset \,/\, \underline{\quad} \#\# \,[+\text{vocalic}]$$

It should be obvious that the truncation analysis will account for all sequences whose first member is $-ATR$. One derivation is given in (37).

(37)
```
   C V ## V ## C V              C V ## V ## C V
   | |    |    | |    —(36)→    |  \___|    | |
   l A    O    n O              l      O    n O
       'call his mother'             [ lò ò nó]
```

What is less obvious but equally true, is that this analysis provides a principled way of dealing with sequences whose initial member is $+ATR$. In order to pursue this point I must first provide some extensions to the theoretic framework employed here.

In the model proposed here there are at least four levels of structure: the autosegmental tier containing the feature A (as well as other features involved in harmony processes to be discussed in later sections), the syllabic tier providing the syllabic organization in terms of a branching structure containing onsets, rimes, and their constituents, the segmental tier containing the remaining phonological features as well as the "default values" of features found on the autosegmental tier, and the skeleton,

Harmony in Vata

a series of points found at the intersection of the various tiers.[17] For the purposes of the present study our representations will include the autosegmental and segmental tiers and the skeleton which includes information from the syllabic tier (C's and V's instead of points). These levels are organized as in (38).

(38)   AUTOSEGMENTAL TIER
        SKELETON-CUM-SYLLABIC TIER
        SEGMENTAL TIER

According to (38) autosegments are not directly associated to segments but rather to the skeleton which is in turn associated to the segments. At the autosegmental tier, *contiguous* autosegments are gathered into n-ary branching trees whose top node is the autosegment.[18] Thus, (39a) will be represented as (39b) and (39c), as (39d).

(39) a.

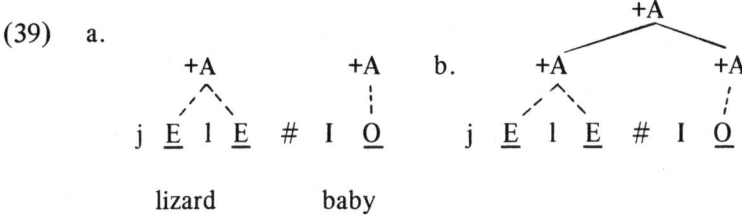

lizard   baby

(39) c.

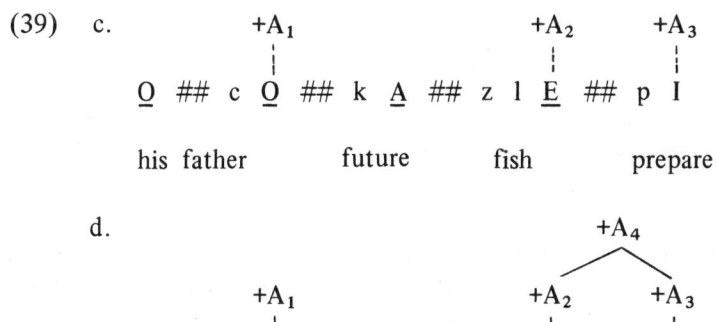

his father   future   fish   prepare

d.

In (39b) two contiguous autosegments are gathered into a binary tree. In (39d), the last two autosegments, A_2 and A_3, are gathered into a tree, A_4. The autosegment A_1 does not form part of this tree since it is not contiguous to the two autosegments to the right.

I will now offer some definitions to facilitate the ensuing discussion.

404 Jonathan D. Kaye

(40) a. The domain of an autosegment is the stretch of skeletal structure (or some projection thereof) which may be associated to it, or to some autosegment which it dominates.
b. The maximal domain of an autosegment is the domain of the topmost node of the autosegmental tree with which the autosegment is associated.
c. Two autosegments are contiguous iff their domains are contiguous.
d. A segment is associated with an autosegment iff it is bound to a skeletal element within the domain of the autosegment.

Looking again at example (39d), we see that the domain and the maximal domain of A_1 are the portion of the skeleton to which *có* is associated. The domain of A_2 is the skeletal structure associated with *zlē*. Its maximal domain is the portion of the skeleton associated with *zlē pī*, i.e. the domain of A_4. The precise display for (39d) is given in (41).

(41)
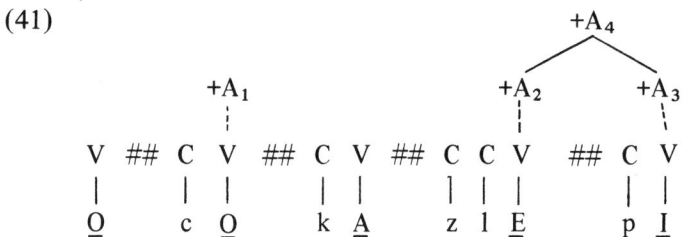

To these definition I add the following well-formedness convention.

(42) Well-formedness Convention
A segment associated with an autosegment must fall entirely within its maximal domain.

Convention (42) may be interpreted in two ways. It may block associations to a floating autosegment which would result in illicit configurations, or it may block applications of phonological rules which would have this same effect. We shall see that both interpretations are indeed necessary, but for the moment it is the first interpretation that is of interest.

Consider now vowel sequences whose first member is an advanced vowel. One example is given in (43).

(43) ń lɔ́ ɔ́ nlɛ̄ɛ̄ 'I eat his meat' (</ ń lē ɔ́ nlɛ̄ – 6ɔ́/)

The sequence *e##ɔ* yields phonetic [ɔɔ]. Rule (36) and convention (42) give exactly this result. The derivation is given in (44).

Harmony in Vata

(44) a. +A   b. +A   c.   +A
                                                 ✳
       C V ## V   C V ## V   C V ## V
       | | | | ⌐┘ | ⌐┘
    ...| E   O... | Ǫ | Ǫ

(44a) gives the initial representation of the form . . .*Ie* ##ɔ́. . . . In (44b) rule (36) has applied deleting the first vowel. At this point the autosegment may no longer associate with the V element in its domain. To do so would violate (42). This is seen in (44c). After truncation the segment O is associated with two elements in the skeleton. The autosegment has the skeletal element to the left in its domain. The ## boundary prevents its spreading to the right. Thus, if the autosegment is associated with the V in its domain, (42) is violated. The skeletal domain of the segment O does not fall within the maximal domain of the autosegment. The boundary falls between the two V elements. Thus, the autosegment may not associate and we correctly derive ɔɔ as the output of this derivation. If we assume that (42) or some version thereof forms part of universal grammar, we can derive all of the forms of (24) with our general truncation rule (36). The problem of the apparent regressive ATR-assimilation is resolved by convention (42). As the complexity of our theory increases in terms of the number of tiers involved in a phonological representation, it is quite natural to have severe restrictions on how these tiers may intersect. The well formedness conventions of autosegmental theory (association lines may not cross, bound autosegments may not spread, etc.) provide such restrictions. Convention (42) is but another example.[19]

Continuing our study of (42), let us consider a vowel sequence involving a bisyllabic verb followed by a vowel-initial word.

(44)   zí zà àslà 'hide some tobacco'   (< /zízò##àslà/)
       hide   tobacco

The derivation of this form is provided in (45)

(45)   +A   +A
                                                 ╱
       C V C V ## V C C V —(36)→ C V C V ## V C C V
       | | | | | | | | | | | ⌐┘ | |
       z I z Ǫ   A s l A   z I z   A s l A

In (45) we have a bisyllabic verb stem followed by a vowel-initial object. Once (36) has applied deleting the verb-final vowel, the +A autosegment may no longer be linked with the final *V* because of (42). This autosegment is still free to associate with the first vowel of the verb since the skeletal domain of this vowel is entirely within the domain of the autosegment. (42) is accordingly not violated. Since the general truncation rule does not apply to a high vowel our analysis predicts that no ATR changes are observed in such cases. This is confirmed by the data of (24). The relevant derivation follows.

(46) ń lì ɔ̀ nlɛ̄ɛ̄   'I ate his meat'
      I ate his meat-def.

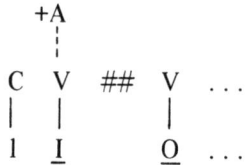

Since (36) does not apply, the autosegment is free to associate with its skeletal domain. Convention (42) is not violated because the vowel *I* associated with the autosegment falls entirely within its domain (and, of necessity, its maximal domain).

In sum, with a simple rule of truncation (36) and a well-formedness convention (42) all the facts of (25) follow. It remains to explain why sequences with an initial high vowel fail to undergo (36). I will pursue this question in a later section. I will turn now to the analysis of object pronouns.

3.2. Sequences involving object pronouns.

Vata possesses a set of object pronouns given in (47).

(47) a. àmí' me   mɔ̀ you sg   b. mɔ́ mέ mɔ̃́
          àɲī us   àɲì you pl   mí má ŋɔ̃á

In (47a) I have presented first and second person object pronouns. These forms will not interest us further. Third person pronouns are given in (47b). The different forms represent the different noun classes of Vata (Kaye, 1981a). These pronouns may be pronounced as in (47b) but a more typical pronunciation involves deleting the initial *m* of these forms. It is crucial to understand that no cliticization is involved here. The forms without the initial *m* have exactly the same status as those in (47b). The operative process is phonological and not syntactic. In fact, Vata has no verbal clitics, subject or object.[20] The loss of *m* results in vowel sequences.

These sequences receive the identical treatment as the cases studied in section 3.1. Sample sequences of two pronouns, ɔ́ and ı́ are given in (48).

(48) a. pronoun ɔ́   b. pronoun ı́
i   ɛ lì ɔ́   it ate him   ɔ̀ lì ı́   he ate them
ɩ   ɔ̀ plí ` ɔ́ kɔ̄   he passed him      à plı́ ` ı́ kɔ̄   we passed them
u   ɔ̀ nú ` ɔ́ wlú   he heard them      à nú ` ı́ wlú   we heard them
ɷ   ǹ kɔ̀lɷ̀ ɔ́   you scratched him à wɔ̀lɷ̀ ı́   we washed them
e   ɛ́ lɔ̀ ɔ́   it eats him   ǹ lī ı́   you eat them
ɛ   wà plɔ́ ɔ́ kɔ̄   they pass him   à ɲı̀ ı́   we give them
o   à nɔ̀ ɔ́ wlú   we hear him   à nı̀ ı́ wlú   we hear them
ɔ   ɔ̀ kɔ̀lɔ̄ ɔ́   he scratches him   ǹ wɔ̄lī ı́   you wash them
ʌ   ǹ fɔ̀tɔ̀ ɔ́   you pierce him   ɔ̀ fɔ́tı̀ ı́   he pierces them
a   à lɔ̀ ɔ́   we call him   ǹ sī ı́   you gather them

Comparing (48) with (24) reveals that the vowel sequences behave in an identical fashion. It is worth noting here that truncation is usually optional across word boundaries. In the examples of (48) however, truncation is obligatory. This may be due to the fact that the slower speech required to impede the application of rule (36) is incompatible with the loss of the initial *m* of these pronouns. Thus, we find (49a) or (49b) but not (49c).

(49) a. ǹ wà mɔ́   'I like him'
      b. ǹ wɔ̀ ɔ́
      c. *ǹ wà ɔ́

Finally, the object pronoun does not necessarily follow the verb. It may appear in a variety of positions, with or without its *m*. In such cases, exactly the same behaviour is observed.

(50) ǹ nıkā zıkà   mɔ́   ɓátı̀   'I will look for him tomorrow'
      I future tomorrow him look for

      ǹ nıkā zıkɔ̀ ɔ́ ɓátı̀

It is clear that exactly the same analysis given in 3.1. will handle the examples of object pronouns. We turn now to the definite article in Vata.

3.3. The definite article

In Vata the definite article is postposed to the noun. The article is separated from the noun by a single # boundary. Its underlying form is ɓɔ́, but in normal speech the ɓ is deleted, probably by the same rule which deletes the *m* of the object pronoun. Two indications of a closer tie between the article and its noun are: (a) the article undergoes tone changes and (b) nothing can intervene between the noun and its article. Consider (51a) and (51b).

(51) a. dí   villages   díɔ̂   the villages
          fì   skins   fìɔ̀   the skins
          sī   trees   sīɔ̄   the trees
          glì   pebbles   glìɔ̂   the pebbles
      b. dí tā   three villages   díɔ̂ tā   the three villages
          *dí tāā (< tāɔ̄)

In (51a) it is seen that the tone of the article assimilates to a preceding tone lower than it. Otherwise it remains unchanged. Recall that object pronouns, with or without *m* never undergo tone changes. In (51b) the article cliticizes to the noun and not to the numerical expression following the noun. Object pronouns, on the other hand, have no such restrictions on their occurrences. I conclude then that a definite noun has the initial structure in (52).

(52)   NOUN # ɓɔ̂

When the ɓ is elided vowel sequences result. These sequences undergo somewhat different changes which are given in (53).

(53)   dí   villages   díɔ̂   the villages
       lɪ́   songs   lɪ́ɔ̂   the songs
       ɲú   water   ɲúɔ̂   the water
       nō   beverage   nōɔ̄   the beverage
       lé   spear   léɛ̄   the spear
       tlɛ̄   snake   tlɛ̄ɛ̄   the snake
       yó   child   yóɔ̂   the child
       sō   arm   sōɔ̄   the arm
       kpʌ̄   chair   kpɔ̄ɔ̄ ~ kpʌ̄ʌ̄   the chair
       gà   lianes   gàà   the lianes

Abstracting away from the data of (53) we have the pattern of sequences shown in (54).

(54)   i — ɔ   iɔ   ɪ — ɔ   ɪɔ
       u — ɔ   uɔ   ʊ — ɔ   ʊɔ
       e — ɔ   εε   ε — ɔ   εε
       o — ɔ   ɔɔ   ɔ — ɔ   ɔɔ
       ʌ — ɔ   ɔɔ ~ ʌʌ   a — ɔ   aa

Sequences beginning with a high vowel behave exactly as inter-word sequences, i.e. nothing happens. Other vowel sequences display the application of a phonological process. This process is clearly different from general truncation in that the same vowels result in different sequences as seen in (55).

(55) a. n̄ lɔ̄ ɔ́ 'I eat him' (< n̄ lē ɔ́)   b. lɛ̄ɛ̄ 'the spear' (<le#ɔ)

A different rule of truncation can handle all the sequences of (54) with the exception of ʌɔ.

(56) Definite truncation
$$[+\text{vocalic}] \rightarrow \emptyset \: / \: \begin{bmatrix} +\text{vocalic} \\ -\text{high} \end{bmatrix} \: \# \: \begin{bmatrix} \underline{} \\ [+\text{def.}] \end{bmatrix}$$

Once again the feature [−high] figures in the formulation. In our two rules of truncation a high vowel to the left prevents the application of the rule. It is hardly likely that this restriction forms part of the rule. The proper formulation of the truncation rules (36) and (56) is certainly along the lines of (57).

(57) a. General truncation

$$[+\text{vocalic}] \rightarrow \emptyset \: / \: \underline{} \: \#\# \: [+\text{vocalic}]$$

b. Definite truncation

$$[+\text{vocalic}] \rightarrow \emptyset \: / \: [+\text{vocalic}] \: \# \: \begin{bmatrix} \underline{} \\ [+\text{def.}] \end{bmatrix}$$

These rules will overgenerate, i.e. they will allow deletion in sequences whose initial member is a high vowel. Such erroneous deletion will be prevented, as we shall see, by general principles. Thus, we will be able to eliminate an annoying redundancy from our rules. It is equally obvious that (36) and (56) are two variants of the same rule. They both delete a segmental element of a sequence of two vowels. The morpho-syntactic context serves to determine which of the vowels is deleted.[21]

Applying (56) to the forms of (53) we correctly derive all the sequences save ʌɔ, which will be discussed below. Illustrative derivations are given in (58).

410   Jonathan D. Kaye

(58) a.

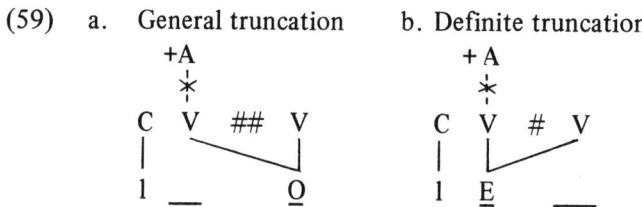

In (58a) rule (56) applies deleting the final vowel. The autosegment can no longer associate with the V in its domain since the associated segment E would not fall entirely within the domain of the autosegment, violating (42). As formulated (42) succesfully blocks association for both types of truncation as desired. The two instances of its effects, general truncation and definite truncation are given in (59).

(59) a. General truncation   b. Definite truncation

In (58b) no truncation occurs, the first vowel being high. The autosegment is free to associate since the segment *I* falls entirely within its domain. Finally, in (58c) deletion takes place as before. No autosegment is involved and the vowel *A* is simply spread over two skeletal slots.

Let us now consider the sequence ʌɔ. According to our rules we should get *aa*. In fact, either ɔɔ or ʌʌ obtains. By any conceivable analysis, this sequence is exceptional. The problem is to pinpoint the exact nature of its exceptionality. We begin with the version ɔɔ. Notice that this is the sequence which would result if general truncation applied rather than definite truncation. If we add a condition to (56) to the effect that it does not apply to the sequence, ʌ#ɔ, we could then assume that this rule undergoes rule (36) slightly modified as (60).

(60)   General truncation (revised)
       [+vocalic] → ∅ /___[-seg] (#) [+vocalic]

Harmony in Vata 411

The form *slɔ́ɔ̀* (<slábɔ̀) 'the house' can now be derived as follows:

(61)
```
       +A                              +A
   C C V # V    (56)  N.A. —(60)→  C C V # V
   | | |   |                       | |     |
   s l A   ɔ                       s l     ɔ
```
                                                                                                       [slɔ́ɔ̀] 'the house'

The other form *slʌ́ʌ́* is more perplexing. The crucial point is that the vowel of the article is +*ATR*. How could the suffix have acquired this feature? Since a # boundary is an absolute barrier to the spread of +*A*, this form could not conceivably be derived from *slʌ́#ɔ̀*. One possibility would be to assume that the boundary separating the article from the noun is optionally reduced to + following ʌ. Assume also a generalized version of definite truncation.[22]

(62) Definite truncation (revised)
      [+vocalic] → ∅ /[+vocalic][−seg] $\begin{bmatrix} \underline{} \\ [-\text{def.}] \end{bmatrix}$

      condition: does not apply to ʌ#ɔ.

We now derive the form *slʌ́ʌ́* as follows:

(63)
```
       +A                              +A                       +A
   C C V # V                       C C V + V                C C V + V
   | | |   |   boundary change     | | |   |    —(62)→      | |     |
   s l A   ɔ                       s l A   ɔ                s l     A
```

The replacement of # by + is at present rather ad hoc, but once we have swallowed this somewhat bitter pill, the rest follows quite neatly. Once the boundary substitution has been made, the domain of the autosegment is increased to *(C) V + V*. This at once explains how the article is realized as a +*ATR* vowel and how the autosegment can associate at all. The skeleton portion bound to +*A* (V + V) falls entirely within the domain of the autosegment and accordingly, (42) does not block the association here. The sequence ʌ+ɔ will not fall under the exception condition to rule (62) since that condition excludes ʌ#ɔ but not ʌ+ɔ.

A major problem remains as to how one can express this exceptionality at all. It clearly applies at the segmental level. If ʌ is specified in the exception condition as opposed to say, *A* (the low vowel of the segmental level) we have to involve the autosegment +A. This mixing of tiers goes against the autonomy of levels inherent in autosegmental theory. If not to be excluded outright, it certainly represents a highly marked case. In section 3.5.3 I will explore this question further.

In sum, the exception condition to (62) and the boundary weakening process are admittedly clumsy, but I see no obvious way of rendering them more natural. This concludes the analysis of the definite article in Vata. We have seen that a single rule of truncation, which is probably a variant of the general truncation rule, along with an optional boundary weakening process and an exception condition suffice to handle all cases of definite nominal forms. One should not lose sight of the truly exceptional nature of the behaviour of ʌ in this regard. If my analysis is awkward with respect to this vowel, it is the reflection of its aberrant behaviour. It remains to be seen if I have expressed this aberrancy in the most perspicuous way. I turn now to a discussion of the question suffix.

3.4. The question suffix.

In Vata direct questions are formed by suffixation to the last word of the sentence. The following vowel sequences result from this process.

(64)

ǹ lì	you ate	ǹ lìʌ [2,3]	did you eat
ǹ ɓlì lí	you sang songs	ǹ ɓlì líā	did you sing songs
ɔ̀ nlá ˋ ɲú	he drank water	ɔ̀ nlá ˋ ɲúʌ̄	did he drink water
ɔ̀ sà wō	he gathers mushrooms	ɔ̀ sà wōā	does he gather mushrooms
wà dì ˋ vē	they cut palm grains	wà dì ˋ vēē	did they cut palm grains
à dlá ˋ tlɛ̄	you killed a snake	à dlá ˋ tlɛ̄ɛ	did you kill a snake
ǹ tō yō	you tell a lie	ǹ tō yʌ̄ʌ	do you tell a lie
ǹ wlɔ́	you return	ǹ wlāā	do you return
ɔ̀ kà kpʌ̄	he has a chair	ɔ̀ kà kpʌ̄ʌ̄	does he have a chair
wà mlì àdáɓlá	they went to market	wà mlì àdáɓláā	did they go to market

The resulting vowel sequences are summarized in (65)

(65)
vowel	vowel-question suffix	vowel	vowel-question suffix
i	iʌ	ɩ	ɩa
u	uʌ	ʊ	ʊa
e	ee	ɛ	ɛɛ
o	ʌʌ	ɔ	aa
ʌ	ʌʌ	a	aa

Harmony in Vata

For the moment let us set aside the vowels e, ε. In all cases the suffix agrees with the stem in ATR-ness, a clear indication of a + boundary. The alternation involves chiefly a and ʌ. I will assume the suffix to have the form -ā: A rule, probably the same that determines the tone of the definite article, will lower the suffix tone following a low tone.[24] With the form of the suffix determined, nothing further need be said. The rule of general truncation (60) along with the association of the autosegment will correctly derive the forms.

(66) a.

```
       +A
      ╱ ╲
     ╱   ╲
  C  V + V      [lìʌ]
  |  |   |
  l  I   A
```

b.
```
  C C V + V  —(60)→  C C V + V        [wlāa]
  | | |   |          | |    ╲ |
  U l O   A          U l      A
```

c.
```
     +A                +A
    ╱╲                 ╱╲
  C V + V  —(60)→   C V + V           [yʌ̄ʌ]
  | |   |           |    ╲ |
  I O   A           I      A
```

In (66a) the initial vowel is high. Thus, (60) does not apply. The autosegment associates to the syllables in its domain and the resulting form is derived. Rule (60) applies in (66b) deleting the initial vowel. The final vowel a is associated to two V's accounting for the occurring form. In (66c) general truncation applies again. Notice that convention (42) is not violated since the syllabic domain of +A is within the maximal domain of the autosegment. The + boundary being transparent to the dominant harmony, the feature +A is free to spread to the end of the word.

Returning now to the case of e and ε we see that the sequences are not as predicted by our analysis. The regular forms would be ʌʌ and aa rather than ee and εε, respectively. It is clear that these forms exceptionally undergo definite truncation (62) rather than rule (60).

(67) a.

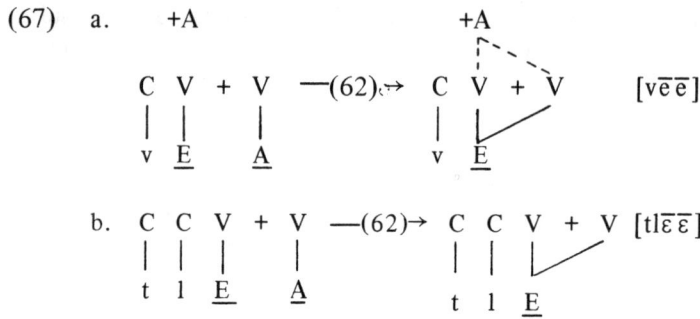

b. C C V + V —(62)→ C C V + V [tlɛ̄ɛ̄]
   | | | | | | |⌐
   t l E   A   t l E

The derivations procede in the same fashion as before. This time the second vowel deletes. The autosegment spreads to the suffix in (67a) and (42) is accordingly not violated. I have no insightful way of representing this exceptionality other than by stipulation – the vowel *E* plus the question suffix exceptionally undergo definite truncation.

3.5. Miscellaneous particles.

Vata contains a variety of particles with an initial labial sonorant (*ɓ* or *m*). This segment is optionally (and preferably) deleted resulting again in a vowel sequence. I shall consider briefly three of these particles in this section: the relative demonstrative *ɓɔ́*, the demonstrative *mɛ̀*, and the adverbial marker *ɓɛ́*.

3.5.1. The relative marker presents no particular problems. It attaches to a verb in relative clauses. The tonal pattern is as in the definite article. The relevant rule is that of general truncation. The forms are given in (68).

(68)   vowel   vowel – ɔ́   vowel   vowel – ɔ́
       i   ǹ yìɔ̀ that you arrived   ɩ   mlìɔ̀ that you left
       u   ɔ́ gūgūɔ́ that he thinks   ʊ   à nɔ̀ɔ̀ that we made
       e   wá pòɔ̀ that they cooked   ɛ   à mlɔ̄ɔ̄ that we leave
       o   ɔ́ bidɔ̄ɔ̄ that he washes   ɔ   ǹ kɔ̀lɔ̄ɔ̄ that you scrape
       ʌ   ǹ fófòɔ̀ that you pierce   a   wá klòɔ̀ that they sieze

3.5.2. The adverbial marker *ɓɛ́* typically follows a verb. It also functions as a locative pronoun. It follows the same tonal pattern as the definite article and the relative demonstrative. The forms are given below.

(69) vowel vowel – ɛ́   vowel vowel – ɛ́
   i   lī ɛ̄   eat there   ι   mlī ɛ̄   go there
   u   dúɛ́   a village there   ω   ɔ́ kɔ̀ɛ̀   he is there
   e   n lɛ́ɛ́   I eat there   ɛ   wa mlɛ́ɛ́   they go there
   o   ɛ́ dlɛ́ɛ́   it leaks there   ɔ   ɔ́ wɔ̄lɛ̄ɛ̄   he washes there
   ʌ   ɔ́ ɓlɛ́ɛ́   he disposes there   a   à lɛ̄ɛ̄   we carry there

As before the rule of general truncation has applied. Convention (42) handles the *ATR* association and all is well.

3.5.3. The most interesting of the forms considered in this section is the demonstrative *mɛ̀* 'here'. It associates with nouns to the meaning 'this N' and with verbs, giving the meaning 'here'. Deletion of *m* results in the vowel sequences shown below. The tone of this marker is always low.[25]

(70) vowel vowel – ɛ̀   vowel vowel – ɛ̀
   i   líɛ̀   these spears   ι   líɛ̀   these songs
   u   ɲúɛ̀   this water   ω   ɔ́ kɔɛ̀   he is here
   e   lɛ́ɛ̀   this spear   ɛ   vɛ̀dɛ̀ɛ̀   this manioc
   o   yɛ́ɛ̀   this child   ɔ   sɛ̄ɛ̀   this arm
   ʌ   {kpʌ̄ʌ̀ / kpɛ̄ɛ̀}   this chair   a   zāà   this food

The low vowels aside, we have here the familiar pattern of general truncation. The first vowel of the sequence is deleted if possible and the rest follows as before. The low vowels ʌ and *a* are interesting here. The form *kpɛ̄ɛ̀* is regular but the other possibility *kpʌ̄ʌ̀* along with *zāà* are not derivable from our analysis. Both these forms have undergone definite truncation (loss of the second vowel). In addition *kpʌ̄ʌ̀* has undergone the boundary weakening process. This assumption is necessary to account for the advanced suffix vowel. It would be simplest to assume that both forms *kpʌ̄ʌ̀* and *zāà* have undergone boundary weakening (from # to +). In the case of *zāà* this has no visible effect since the feature +*A* is not involved in its derivation. This move obviates the mention of a segment *A* with an associated autosegment as the exceptional context. Now one need only stipulate that low vowels behave exceptionally independently of their advanced or retracted status. The derivations are given below.

(71) a.

```
      +A                +A                      +A
      |                 |                       ˆ- -.
                                                |    |
  C V # V  —(62)→  C V # V   bound.   →   C V + V  [kpʌ̄ʌ̀]
  | |   |          | |  ⌣    weak.        | |   |
  kp A  E          kp A                    kp A
```

b.

```
C V # V  —(62)→  C V # V  bound. weak.  →  C V + V
| |   |           | |                       | |
z A   E           z A                       z A
                                            [zāà]
```

We conclude that low vowels behave exceptionally in the context of (m)è. Let us now compare this exceptionality with that already observed in the case of the definite article. The relevant forms are repeated below.

(72)
    a. kpᴧ̄ chair   kpᴧ̄ᴧ ~ kpɔ̄ɔ̄ the chair   zā food   zāā the food
    b. kpᴧ̄ chair   kpᴧ̄ᴧ ~ kpɛ̄ɛ this chair   zā food   zāà this food

There is an obvious parallelism here. Suppose we say that low vowels are exceptional in a number of contexts. They undergo boundary weakening from # to +. This weakening in turn implies the application of definite truncation rather than general truncation. In the case of the definite forms, this is the normal state of affairs: definite truncation applies anyway. In the case of the demonstrative (m)è, low vowels are doubly differentiated from other vowels in that they have a different boundary and they undergo a different rule. How much of all this must be stipulated is unclear to me at the moment.

Returning now to the second form of (72a), we saw above that $z\bar{a}\bar{a}$ was the expected outcome of $z\bar{a}\#\mathrm{ɔ}$. On the other hand if the parallelism is to hold water and if we wish to eliminate mixing segmental and autosegmental contexts as triggering exceptions, $z\bar{a}\bar{a}$ ought to be exceptional. In fact $z\bar{a}\bar{a}$ is exceptional. If it undergoes exactly the same treatment as the exceptional $kp\bar{\Lambda}\bar{\Lambda}$ the only possible result is $z\bar{a}\bar{a}$. This is illustrated in (73).

(73)   a.

```
   +A              +A                        +A
                                            ┌---
C V # V  —(62)→  C V # V  bound. weak.  →  C V + V
| |   |           | |                       | |
kp A  O           kp A                      kp A
                                            [kpᴧ̄ᴧ̄]
```

b.
```
C V # V  —(62)→  C V # V  bound. weak.  →  C V + V
| |   |           | |                       | |
z A   O           z A                       z A
                                            [zāā]
```

There is the annoying detail that $z\overline{a\,a}$ has all the appearances of being perfectly regular. How could it be learned as an exceptional form? Our theory provides the answer. A system which requires autonomous levels forces us to consider only a segmental class of exceptions. A grammar with exceptional *ʌ* but not *a* would be unlearnable and hence unlearned. A learner confronted with the definite forms of Vata must construct a grammar in which, appearances notwithstanding, $z\overline{a\,a}$ is exceptional.

A second parallelism exists between the definite and the demonstrative forms. A second form exists for the advanced version of *A* but not for the retracted vowel. I do not believe this is accidental. It is unlikely that the same rather peculiar irregularity should recur in two independent paradigms without having some underlying motivation. I am unable to explain this fact at the moment.

4. THE STATUS OF HIGH VOWELS IN VATA.

High vowels in Vata display certain suprasegmental properties. The treatment of these vowels is critical to the analysis, yet I cannot claim to understand completely all the intricacies of their behaviour. Consequently, the discussion will be somewhat speculative.

I propose that high vowels have a bound autosegment *+HI* attached to their skeletal domain. The feature being lexically bound, cannot spread. In other terms, there is a marked difference in behaviour between the feature *+A* and the feature *+HI*. Unlike ATR-ness, vowels are not uniformly high or non-high within a morpheme as is seen in (74).

(74) kōsù   fire   gólɔ́   dugout
      ɓūkʌ̀   scrotum   kɔ̀kɔ̀tɛ́   nape
      nīdʌ̀   pot   ŋōmɔ́   hunger

It is clear that the feature *HI* does not behave like a floating autosegment. What then are the indications of its non-segmental nature? For one thing, it has already been shown that neither rule of truncation applies when the first member of the vowel sequence is a high vowel. Treating *HI* as a bound autosegment offers a way of explaining this seemingly ad hoc restriction. Let us consider two forms: *lī ɛ́* 'eat it' and *lī ɔ́* 'the songs'. The first form is subject to general truncation (loss of the first vowel), the second, to definite truncation (loss of the second vowel). In neither case do the rules apply. To see why consider the derivation below.

(75)

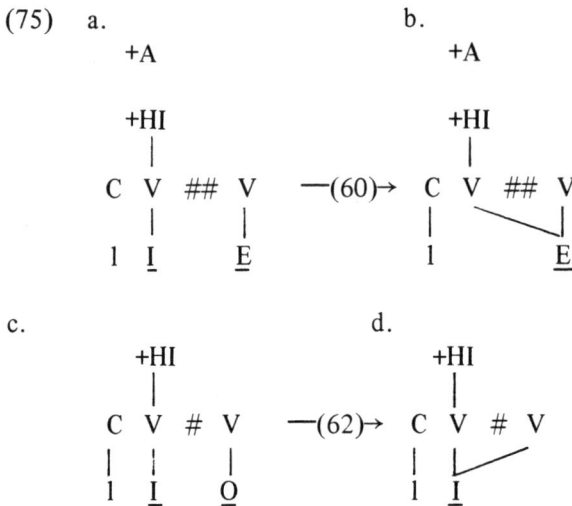

The first derivation (75a, b) shows the effect of applying general truncation to a form with an attached autosegment. In (75c, d) the derivation involves definite truncation. In both cases the result is ungrammatical. By what principle can we exclude (75b, d)? Consider convention (42) and the cases it was designed to exclude. We repeat derivations involving rules (60) and (62): ń lē # # ε [ń lε ε] 'I eat it' and lé #ɔ [lεέ] 'the spear'.

(76) a.
+A

C V ## V —(60)→ C V ## V
| | | | |
1 E   E   1   E

b.
+A
 ⋮
 ✶

c.
+A

C V # V —(62)→ C V # V
| | | | |
1 E   O   1   E

d.
+A
 ⋮
 ✶

Convention (42) prevents the association of the −A autosegment in (76b, d). The similarity between (76b, d) and (75b, d) is unmistakable. If convention (42) excludes the former, then it should exclude the latter as well. Recall that this convention is a general well-formedness condition on phonological representations. It is not to be violated by any means. In one case it prevents the association of an autosegment which would have resulted in its violation. Now suppose that such an option is not available, i.e. that an autosegment were already attached to its skeletal domain. In such a case, if a phonological rule threatened to violate (42), the sole manner of preventing such an outcome would be for the rule not to apply. Now this is precisely the case with respect to high vowels. According to the analysis they come with a lexically bound autosegment +*HI*. What the lexicon hath bound, let no convention rend asunder. Now rule (60) and (62) threaten to create segments whose skeletal domains do not fall within the maximal domain of an associated autosegment *HI*. One cannot block association – the autosegment is already bound in the lexicon. If (42) is not to be violated, the only possibility is that the rules of truncation not apply. The postulation of an attached autosegment *HI* leads automatically to the right results in the cases considered so far.

To this point I have shown that the feature *HI* does not function as a floating autosegment. I have also shown that positing a bound autosegment *HI* can explain why truncation rules do not apply to high vowel-initial sequences. In fact such a conclusion – that high vowels have an attached +*HI* autosegment – is required on entirely independent grounds. To demonstrate this we must now look at plural formation in Vata.[26]

Vata possesses a number of plural markers. Here we are interested in the one which involves a high front vowel suffix. Singular-plural pairs are given in (77).

(77)
Singular	Plural	Gloss
gbàzà	gbàzì	hedge-hog
gɔlɔ́	gɔlí	dugout
ɲéflú	ɲéflí	ear
lé	lí	spear
sū	sī	tree
slʌ́	slí	house
tlàlɛ̀	tlàlì	shirt

Following Travis, Doua and Doua (1980), I will assume that this plural marker is *I*. It triggers a rule of truncation which has the property of deleting an element at the segmental level and at the skeletal level.[27] Other changes internal to the noun stem may be triggered by the addition of the plural suffix –*I* as shown below.

(78)
bōvʌ̀	būvì ~ bōvì		crab
gòlò	gùlí ~ gòlí		mound
jèlè	jìlí ~ jèlí		lizard
gòdʌ̀	gùdì ~ gòdì		mortar
kpóngbó	kpúngbí ~ kpóngbí		plate
ménʌ́	mìní ~ mèní		nose

420   Jonathan D. Kaye

In (78) we see that following the addition of the plural suffix *I*, the antepenultimate stem vowel may be raised. There are a precise set of circumstances necessary for this raising to take place. These circumstances give us an intriguing insight into the interaction of autosegmental elements. The conditions necessary for the application of raising become clearer with the presentation of the data in (79).

(79) a. bɔ̄gʌ̀   bɔ̄gì   *bōgì   foot
         dɔ̄là   dɔ̄lì   *dōlì   hatchet
         gɔ̀zɛ̀   gɔ̀zì   *gōzì   rifle
         kɔ̀là   kɔ̀lì   *kōlì   turtle
         pɔ̄lɛ̀   pɔ̄lì   *pōlì   heart
         pɛ́lʌ́   pɛ́lí   *pɨ́lí   half

      b. ɲéflú   ɲéflí   *ɲíflí   ear
         ŋlōkòsù ŋlōkòsì *ŋlōkùsì claw
         dègʌ̀fófù dègʌ̀fófì *dègʌ̀fúfì lung
         gbòtú   gbòtí   *gbùtí   mat

      c. ʌ́bʌ̀tè ʌ́bʌ̀tì *íbìtì   banana
         zʌ̀gʷʌ̀ zʌ̀gʷì *zìgʷì   agouti
         tʌ̀kʷʌ̀ tʌ̀kʷì *tìkʷì   basket
         tʌ̄kpʌ́ tʌ̄kpí *tīkpí   jaw

In (79a) we see that *–ATR* stems never undergo raising. Advanced stems which end in a high vowel do not undergo raising (79b).[28] Finally, only mid vowels (*e, o*) raise. The low vowel *ʌ* does not. So much for the facts. Let us now consider the analysis. In the examples where raising takes place it is clear that the feature *HI* is spreading. It was also made clear above that it does not spread like a floating autosegmental feature. As a first approximation we may claim that high vowels initiate metrical trees. These are right-branching structures whose top node is labelled +*HI* by the normal percolation conventions. Every element dominated by the tree will, accordingly, be specified +*HI*. The derivation of *jìlí* (sg. jèlé) follows.

(80)

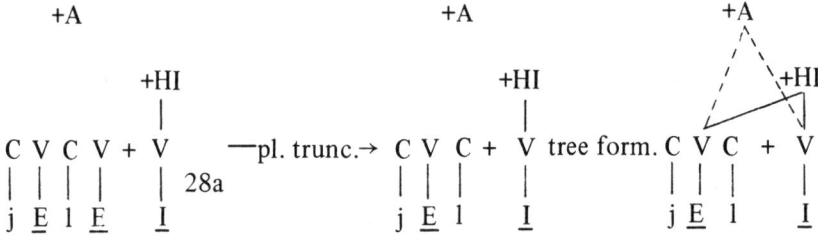

The derivation of (80) begins with the initial representation of the noun stem plus the plural suffix. The latter contains the attached feature +*HI*. The entire form is within the domain of the autosegment *A*. The next step of the derivation involves the deletion of the stem vowel along with the skeletal *V* element to which it is attached. In the final phase of the derivation a right-branching metrical tree is constructed starting from the high vowel suffix. The initial vowel is now dominated by a metrical tree headed by the node +*HI*. It is thus realized as a high vowel accounting for the form [jilí]. I should note here that the construction of these metrical trees is optional. The second plural forms of (78) are simply the result of choosing not to construct these trees.[29]

Let us consider now the forms of (79a). If we take the example dɔ̄là, its plural will have the representation as in (81a).

(81)   a.   b.   c.

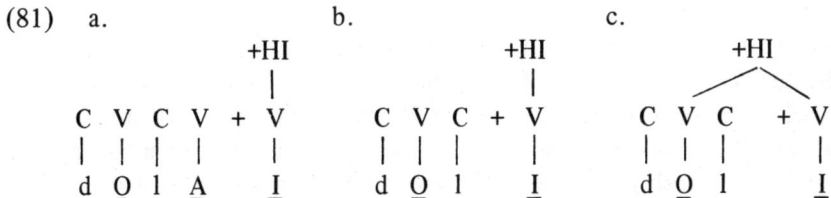

Plural truncation has applied in (81b) giving, in effect, the final step of the derivation. In (81c) we see the representation that would underlie a putative plural *[dɔ̄li]. In fact, this form is impossible. In our account this means that a metrical tree involving the feature *HI* cannot be constructed for this form. Why?

First it can be shown that the impossibility of a metrical tree has nothing to do with the vocalic melody. Compare dɔ̄là – dɔ̄li with bōvʌ̀ – būvi ~ bōvi. The initial representation of the latter form is given in (82a). This form is compared with that of dɔ̄li, repeated in (82b).

(82)   a.   b.

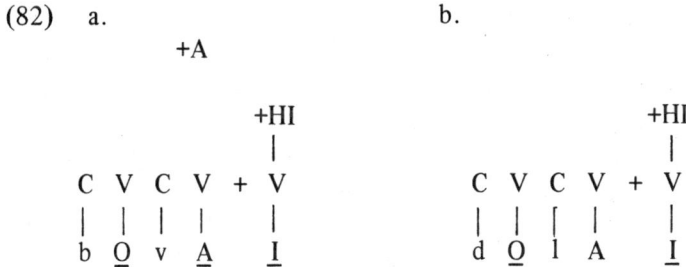

In the two cases the segmental and skeletal levels are for all intents and purposes identical. The only significant difference is the presence of an autosegment in (82a). Let us suppose that the metrical trees based on the feature *HI* are *parasitic*.[30] They do not grow spontaneously but rather require the presence of another metrical structure in order to propagate. In the case at hand the additional structure is that created by the association of the autosegment +*A* to its skeletal domain. Thus, the autosegment +*A* is a required "growth medium" for the propagation of the feature *HI*. The claim is, then, that the feature *HI* does not spread by the construction of a directional tree for this feature. Rather the feature *HI* may percolate to the top node of a metrical structure already in place. The association lines going to the feature +*HI* serve as a trellis for the vine-like spreading of the *HI* feature. This supposition implies that retracted stems never undergo height harmony which is indeed true in Vata.

This state of affairs provides a striking confirmation of the Halle-Vergnaud version of autosegmental theory. The asymmetry imposed by that theory is exactly reflected by the facts discussed here. Only one value of an unattached autosegment appears at the autosegmental tier. In the case of the feature *A*, only the advanced value is represented at this level. Now we see that the feature *HI* may propagate only in advanced stems. It is hard to imagine how a symmetrical autosegmental account could treat such a situation. The two plural forms of (82) would be represented as in (83) in a theory which permitted *both* values of an autosegment to float.

(83)

```
        +A                          −A

        +HI                         +HI
         |                           |
   C V C V + V              C V C V + V
   | | | |   |              | | | |   |
   b O v A   I              d O l A   I
```

Now the difference between the two forms resides in the fact that in one case we have a floating +*A* autosegment, while in the other, the autosegment is −*A*. But why should the feature *HI* spread only in the presence of +*A* and not −*A*? The univalued approach to floating autosegments provides a more satisfactory account for these facts.[31] To illustrate the nature of parasitic spreading a derivation is provided in (83bis).

Harmony in Vata						423

(83 bis)

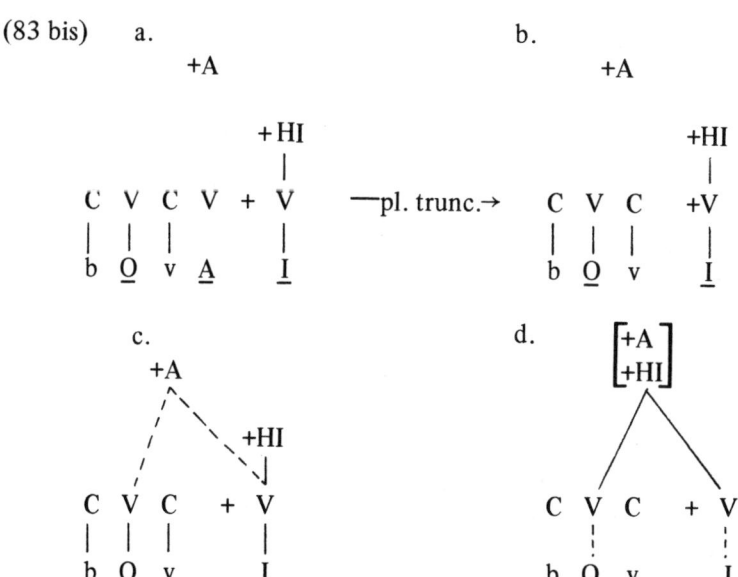

The derivation proceeds as follows: the initial representation of the form [būvì] 'crabs' appears in (83 bis a). The rule of plural truncation applies next resulting in the elimination of both the stem final vowel and the stem final *V* of the form. In (83 bis c) the floating autosegment *+A* associates to the elements of the skeleton in its domain. Finally, in (83 bis d) the bound feature *+HI* percolates up the association structure joining *+A* on the top node of the tree. All the vowels dominated by this structure are interpreted as advanced and high. The parasitic spreading of the *HI* feature is optional. What this means in terms of our analysis is that (83 bis c) may be the final step of a derivation. In this case both vowels are advanced but only the final vowel is high, there being no percolation in this case. The resulting form is [bōvì].

Let us pass now to the forms of (79b). A final high vowel in the singular prevents the parasitic spreading of the *HI* feature in the plural forms. One may first raise the question as to why the final vowel of the singular forms does not trigger this harmony, i.e. why ɲeflú 'ear' is not realized as *ɲiflú. A reasonable explanation is that the height harmony is a cyclic phenomenon and as such could not apply to a non-derived form like ɲeflú. Excluding a putative plural form *ɲiflí is more challenging. Height harmony not applying to forms whose singulars end in a high vowel deleted in plural derivations smells of globality. Let us consider the derivation of ɲeflí to see the form of a possible solution.

(84) a.   b.

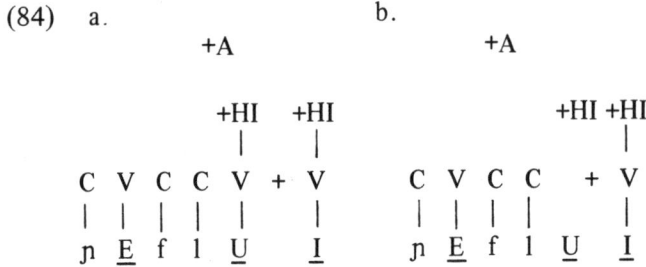

c.

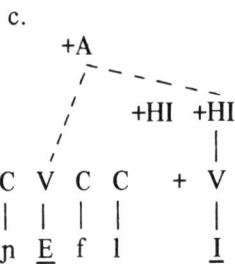

In (84a) the initial solution of ɲéflí 'ears' is given. To the stem ɲéflú is added the plural suffix –I. In (84b) a syllabic element has been deleted from the skeleton as is normal in plural forms. Recall that this element had an autosegment *HI* bound to it. What is the fate of this autosegment once it is "cut adrift" by the loss of the V element to which it was attached? The most plausible assumption is that nothing happens – the autosegment remains unassociated. Following the loss of the skeletal element the stem final vowel is no longer associated to a syllabic element with a bound autosegment. Thus, the vowel is subject to the general truncation rule that we have been calling "plural truncation" up to now. It is deleted as shown in (84c). If we compare this derivation where no high spreading may take place, with that of jìlí 'lizards' (80) where it may, the sole difference is the *+HI* autosegment cut adrift in the former case.

(85) a.   b.

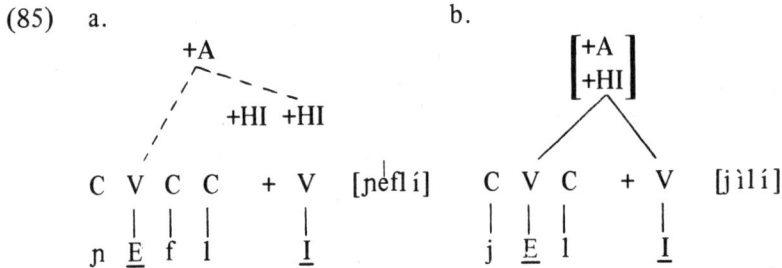

Harmony in Vata

In (85b) the *HI* autosegment can percolate up the dominant harmony structure and in this way spread to the first vowel of the stem. The presence of the unattached *HI* feature in (85a) prevents this percolation. The exact nature of the principle that excludes *ɲifli is not clear, but the presence of the additional *HI* feature is clearly a factor.

A remarkable fact is that certain speakers give *i---i* as the plural for singulars in *o---u*, e.g. *gbòtú* 'mat' *gbòti* ~ *gbìti* 'mats' **gbùti*. Let us take up the derivation of this form after the two deletion processes (syllabic and segmental) have applied.

(86)

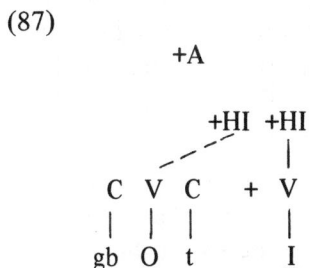

Suppose now that the *HI* feature cut adrift by the deletion of the skeletal element attaches itself to the first vowel as in (87).

(87)

```
              +A

           +HI  +HI
         ⟋       |
       C  V  C  +  V
       |  |  |     |
       gb O  t     I
```

At this point the derivation becomes identical to that of the forms listed in note 31 (*dúlù* – *díli* 'debt') and the plural *gbìti* is derived. If the floating *HI* does not associate, the plural *gbòti* is derived. This possibility is limited to the vocalic patterns *o. . . .u*. *HI* spreading is quite impossible in forms with *e. . . .u*.[32] In sum, whatever principle is to exclude high spreading in nouns whose singulars end in a high vowel, it will surely make reference to an unattached high feature. This problem, even without the ultimate solution provides further evidence for the autosegmental nature of high vowels.

The final property of plural forms to be accounted for is the failure of stems with low vowels (79c) to undergo high spreading (*zàgʷà* – *zàgʷi* 'agouti'). This can be handled quite simply in our analysis. The *III* autosegment cannot land on a syllabic element dominating a low vowel. The resulting vowel would be both [+low] at the segmental level and +*HI* because of the association with the autosegment. While autosegments may override segmental specifications *with respect to the same feature* (cf. the case of dominant harmony discussed above), a vowel will not lose its [+low] specification because of an association with a +*HI* autosegment. Thus, any attempt to associate this autosegment with a low vowel would result in the creation of a vowel which is simultaneously [+high, +low], clearly an impossibility. Hence, no such association can take place.

4.1. High spreading in compounds.

The propagation of the feature *HI* is not limited to the plural cases examined in the previous section. This phenomenon occurs as well in noun-noun compounds.

(88) a. vō#yò   dog   vù#yuʎ   ~ vò#yuʎ   dogs
          zlē#yò   baby fish zlī#yuʎ ~ zlē#yuʎ   baby fishes
          ló   gazelles   lú#wl ì ~ ló#wl ì   gazelle skulls
      b. vó   horns   vó#nò̇   *vó̇#nò̇   horn drink
          tlē   snake   tlē#lì   *tlī#lì   snake songs
          ló   gazelles   ló#lì   *lú#lì   gazelle songs
      c. ń ká ló pī   I will cook gazelles   *ń ká lú pī
          ń kà ló#wl ì   I have gazelle skulls   ń kà lú#wl ì

In (88a) we see that the feature *HI* may spread rightward across a compound boundary. This spreading is parasitic in the sense discussed above. Both terms of the compound must carry the feature +*A* for the spreading to take place. The compound *lú#wl ì* has the initial structure given in (89) below.

(89)

$$\begin{array}{ccccc}
 & +A & & +A & \\
 & & & +HI & \\
 & & & | & \\
C & V & \# & C\ C & V \\
| & | & & |\ \ | & | \\
1 & \underline{O} & & U\ 1 & \underline{I}
\end{array}$$

Autosegments with adjacent domains may form an adjacency tree (cf. (39)) as in (90).

(90)

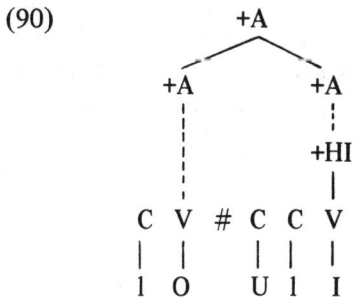

The feature *HI* can percolate up this structure giving the final representation in (91).

(91)

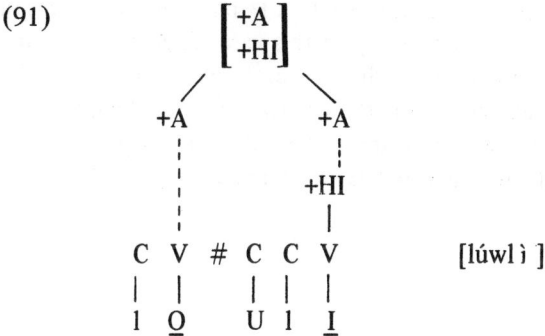

The feature *HI* is transmitted to the first syllable of the forms of (88a) in this way.

The failure of such spreading to take place in (88b) is due to the requirement that both terms of the compound be advanced. In (88c) we see that *HI* cannot spread beyond the word. In the first example, the vowel of *ló*, the direct object, is unaffected by the following verb *pī*. A compound noun is present in the second example and in this case *HI* spreading may occur. The two sentences are close to being a minimal pair in so far as other phonological factors are concerned. Consequently, a word boundary (##) constitutes an absolute barrier to this phenomenon, while a compound boundary (#) or a morpheme boundary (+) do not. In a later section it will be shown that the feature *A* may spread across word boundaries. This constraint holds specifically for the *HI* feature and is not a general property of such spreading processes.

428 Jonathan D. Kaye

5. VOWEL SEQUENCES ACROSS WORD BOUNDARIES REVISITED.

In section 3 we noted that transword vowel sequences could be handled with a rule of general truncation deleting the first of two consecutive vowels. This rule does not apply to high vowels because they are represented as having a bound autosegment associated to their skeletal element. Deletion of a high vowel would result in the illicit structure of (92)

(92)   +HI
            |
         C V ## V
         | |_____/
         β α

where a lexically bound autosegment is attached to the left member of a structure involving the association of a segment to two skeletal elements. Since this configuration is illicit according to the convention, the result is that general truncation does not apply in this case. This much is quite straightforward. We also noted that when general truncation did apply, if the left-most syllabic element is in the domain of a +A floating autosegment, this segment may not associate to the syllabic element for exactly the same reason: the illicit structure (93) would be created.

(93)   +A
            ⋮
         C V ## V
         | ____/
         α   β

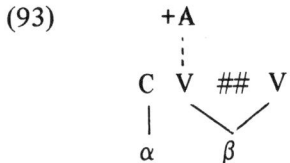

Thus, no association takes place and all seems well. But there is a hidden assumption in this analysis with no apparent justification: the vowel truncation process applies before the association of the floating autosegment. Once this truncation process has applied, association of the autosegment must lead to the ill-formed structure in (93). Accordingly, the association is blocked. But why should a truncation rule take precedence over an association of an autosegment? This seems to follow from nothing in our framework. It is quite conceivable that the association could be made first, with the rule applying subsequently. If such were the case advanced vowels would behave exactly as high vowels. They would block general truncation (as well as definite truncation in the case of the postposed definite article).

Consider now the forms in (94).[33]

(94)

stem-final vowel	verb + pronoun a	gloss	sequence
i	ɔ̀ lì á	he ate it	ia
ɩ	ɔ̀plɩ̀ˋá kɔ̀	he passed it	ɩa
u	n̍ nú ˋá	I heard it	ua
ʊ	ɔ̀ nʊ̀ á	he made it	ʊa
e	ɔ̀ lé á	he eats it	ea
ɛ	ɔ̀ plá á kɔ̀	he passes it	aa
o	ɔ̀ nó á	he hears it	oa
ɔ	ɔ̀ nɔ́ á	he makes it	aa
ʌ	ɔ̀ fótʌ á	he pierces it	ʌa
a	ɔ̀ pá á	he throws it	aa

The pronunciation given in (94) represents a somewhat more pedantic style than the pronunciation given for the same sequences in (25a). In the above forms the initial vowel "assimilates" completely to the second (i.e. is deleted if it is neither high (as in (25a)), nor advanced (unlike (25a)). If the first vowel is either high or advanced, no change takes place. Notice that it would be wrong to claim that in deliberate, pedantic speech, the rule of general truncation is suppressed. This rule must apply in all cases where the initial vowel is neither high nor advanced. Thus, *n̍ nɔ́ á 'I make it' is impossible even in the most pedantic of styles; only n̍ ná á is correct.

Of course the pattern of (94), and only this pattern, is precisely what we obtain if association takes place before truncation. Consider the derivation of n̍ lé á 'I eat it'.

(95)   a.   +A   b.   +A
               | |
        C V ## V   C V ## V
           | | |
           l E   A   l   A

In (95a) association takes place with the stem-final vowel. Application of truncation in (95b) leads to the association of the segment *A* with the syllabic element at the left. This structure is ill-formed and consequently the rule is blocked. Our analysis provides the means to distinguish the patterns (25) and (94). In the former case, truncation precedes association, while in the latter case, association precedes truncation. The simplest conceivable hypothesis regarding the relative ordering of these two processes is that there is none that is theory-imposed. Indeed this is exactly what the facts show to be the case.

6. DIRECTIONAL HARMONY IN VATA.

In section 2 a harmony system involving the feature [ATR] was described and analyzed. This does not, however, exhaust the discussion of the feature and its behaviour in Vata. The dominant harmony process involves the propagation of the floating autosegment +A within the word. Another quite distinct harmony process involves the spread of this feature across word boundaries. This latter harmony has the following properties:

(96) i. it applies across # and ## boundaries.
 ii. it is unidirectional right-to-left.
 iii. it is optional.
 iv. it is subject to certain vowel height constraints.

Let us begin the analysis of this phenomenon with the sentences in (97).

(97) a. kɔ̀ dlá tlɛ̄   'a man kills a snake'
 man kill snake
 kɔ̀ ~ ko̒ lē tlɛ̄   'a man eats a snake'
 man eat - snake
 b. n̩ nó kɔ̀   'I hear a man'
 I hear man
 *n̩ nó ko̒
 n̩ nɩkā kɔ̀ ~ ko̒ nú   'I will hear a man'
 I fut. man hear
 c. ɔ̀ ká zā pī   'He will cook food'
 he fut. food cook
 ɔ̀ ká zʌ̄ pī
 ɔ̀ kʌ́ zʌ̄ pī
 o̩ kʌ́ zʌ̄ pī
 d. n̩ dlá ~ dlʌ́ vōyò   'I kill a dog'
 I kill dog
 n̩ slá ~ slʌ́ sl í   'I build houses'
 I build houses
 n̩ ká ɲī ~ ɲī lī   'I will eat yams'
 I fut. yams eat
 n̩ nɔ̀ /*nù kpʌ̄   'I made a stool'
 I made stool
 n̩ nɔ̀ ~ nù kpī   'I made stools'
 I made stools

Harmony in Vata

In (97a) we see the application of this process across a word boundary. The second example shows that the subject kɔ` may undergo this harmony when followed by a verb that is advanced. The unidirectional character of this process is illustrated in (97b). Here we have the word kɔ`` in object position following an advanced verb nó. In this case the propagation of the advanced feature to the right is absolutely impossible. If the verb follows the object (the underlying order, cf. Koopman 1982) as in the third example, the propagation may take place from right to left and accordingly, it can appear with an advanced vowel. It is worth noting here that this harmony process may take place independently of the categories involved. In (97a, b) nouns underwent the process which was triggered by a verb. The opposite effect is equally possible if a +A noun follows a nonadvanced verb as in (98).

(98)   ń lá`~lʌ` yó   'I called a child'
       I called   child
       ń ká ~ kʌ́ dlù flō`   'I will buy a skirt'
       I fut   skirt buy

The optional nature of the process is clear from the previous examples. In addition, the propagation may be optionally extended indefinitely to the left, subject to constraints to be discussed below. This is shown in the examples of (97c).

In (97d) the behaviour of high vowels with respect to this harmony is illustrated. This behaviour may be summed up in the following way: let A represent any non-high vowel and I, any high vowel. The following combinations permit the propagation of the advanced feature. The triggering element is underlined.

(99)   A <u>A</u>   (e.g. ń dlʌ́ v̄ōyò)
       A <u>I</u>   (e.g. ń slʌ́ sl í)
       I <u>I</u>   (e.g. ń ká ɲī ɲī)
       *I <u>A</u>   (e.g. ń nɔ̀/*nù kpʌ̄)

This harmony may be triggered in a non-high vowel by any advanced vowel; a high may only have an advanced *high* vowel trigger.

These facts bear a remarkable resemblance to those uncovered in Steriade (1981) for roundness harmony. Steriade noted that across languages vowels could undergo roundness harmony in the following contexts.[34]

(34)   <u>A</u> A A;   <u>I</u> I I;   <u>A</u> I I;   *<u>I</u> A A

The Steriade cases are exactly the mirror image of the Vata case under discussion (replace *A* by *I*, *I* by *A*, and change the directionality from right-to-left to left-to-right). This suggests that both the roundness harmony restrictions and those noted here for ATR harmony should fall out from the same general principle, whatever it is.

The mechanism with which I choose to analyze this phenomenon is that of a binary right-dominant metrical tree. This tree will bear the label +*A* at its root. The opaque element with respect to this harmony process is the +*A* floating autosegment. This is the element that triggers the construction of these harmony trees. To see how tree construction works, consider the sentence below.

(100) a. ń ká sū zò zì zò   'I will hide under a tree'
      I fut tree under hide

With the application of the directional harmony we have the pronunciation as in (100b).

(100b).b. ń ká sū zò zì zò

The lexical representation of this sentence is given in (100c) and the effects of association and tree construction are shown in (100d).

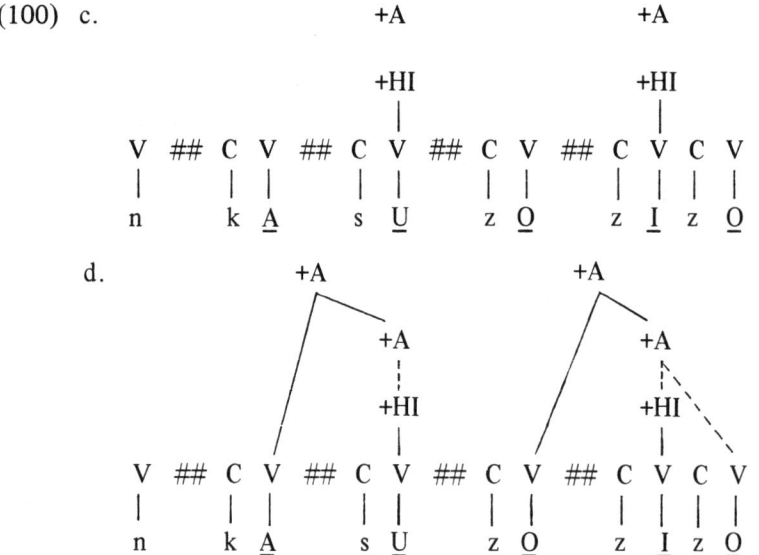

Given that these trees are right-dominant and that they are only constructed off the floating +*A* autosegment, it follows that the spreading of the advanced feature may only proceed from right to left. It also follows that a retracted vowel may become advanced because of this harmony but an advanced vowel may never become retracted. The examples of (101) show that this is indeed the case.

Harmony in Vata

(101) a. kɔ̰   gʷó   'a man runs'
       man run
  b. kɔ́` gʷó
  c. yó   mlɛ̄   'a child leaves'
      child leave
  d. *yɔ́ mlɛ̄

The sentence (101a) contains a noun with a retracted vowel followed by a verb with an advanced vowel. Directional harmony is possible as shown in (101b). In (101c) we have the opposite situation: a noun with an advanced vowel is followed by a verb with a retracted vowel. Any modification of the vowel of the noun is quite impossible as is indicated by the ungrammaticality of (101d). A comparison of the representations of (101a, c) shows quite clearly why this should be so.

(102) a.   b.

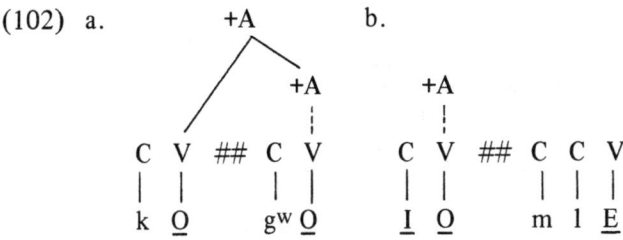

In (102a) a tree may be constructed between the verb and the noun. This is out of the question in (102b). The opaque element (the floating +A autosegment) is on the left and the tree must be right-dominant. Since retracted stems are those characterized by the absence of a feature on the autosegmental tier, and since the directional trees are constructed at this level, a retracted stem cannot trigger a directional harmony because there is literally nothing to propagate. The asymmetrical nature of this directional harmony ([+ATR] spreads, [−ATR] does not) provides still more support for the asymmetrical approach to dominant harmony.

5.1. The behaviour of polysyllabic words.

Given the analysis presented thus far, it is clear that polysyllabic words should act exactly like monosyllabic ones in triggering the directional harmony process. It is the floating +A autosegment that triggers this process and whether it associates to one syllable, or to many, or to none at all (as we shall see later) is of absolutely no importance for directional harmony. This point is illustrated below by the examples in (103a) with their accompanying representations in (103b).

(103) a. ń klá̀ ~ klʌ̀ lé   'I grab a spear'
         I grab   spear
         ń klá̀ ~ klʌ̀ bōvʌ̀   'I grab a crab'
         I grab   crab

b.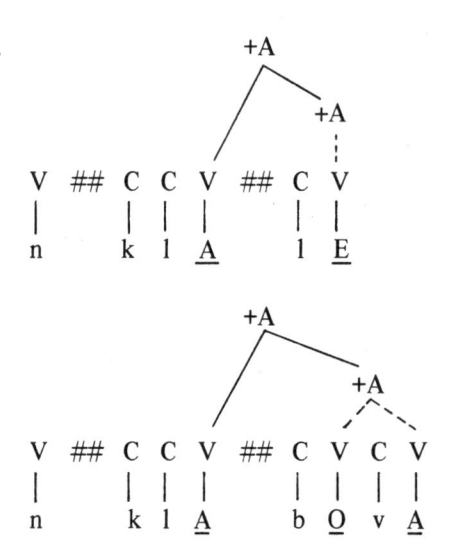

When polysyllables *undergo* the directional harmony, they are subject to the constraint that only the final syllable may undergo this process.

(104) a. ɔ̀ nì zā ~ zʌ̄ pì   'he didn't cook food'
         he neg food   cook
      b. ɔ̀ nì sáká ~ sʌ́kʌ́ pì 'he didn't cook rice'
         he neg rice   cook
      c. ń ká zā pī ~ ń kʌ́ zʌ̄ pī 'I will cook food'
         I fut food cook

A monosyllabic word precedes the verb in (104a). It undergoes the harmony. In (104b) the word in question is bisyllabic (*sáká*). Its final syllable may undergo the harmony but the process goes no further. The example of (104c) has a monosyllabic noun preceded by an auxiliary. In this case the harmony may extend from the verb to the noun to the auxiliary. No such possibility exists for the previous case. The forms of (105a, b, c) are equally ungrammatical. The only possible application of directional harmony is that of (105d).

(105) a. *ń ká sʌ́kʌ́ pī 'I will cook rice' b. *ń kʌ́ sʌ́kʌ́ pī
        I fut rice cook
      c. *ń kʌ́ sáká pī   d. ń ká sáká pī

Harmony in Vata

These facts may be explained if we assume that the directional harmony trees are binary.[35] The essential feature of these trees is that they must be constructed across a word or compound boundary (## or #). Having constructed a binary tree the process may be extended by treating the first construction as a unit and constructing a further binary tree (if possible) containing the first tree as the right member and the preceding syllable as the left member, as in (106).

(106) a.
```
                                        +A
                                        ⋮
                                        +HI
                                        |
        V  ##  C  V  ##  C  V  ##  C  V
        |      |  |      |  |      |  |
        O      k  A      z  A      p  I
```

b.
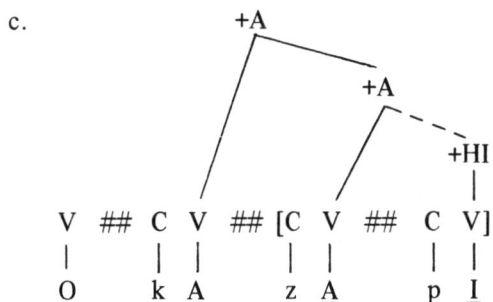

c.
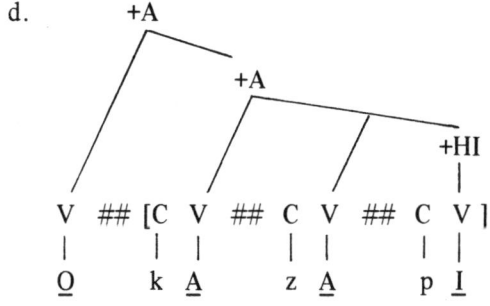

d.
```
            +A
           ╱
          ╱     +A
         ╱     ╱
        ╱     ╱        +HI
        |    |          |
        V ## [C V ## C V ## C V ]
        |     |  |     |  |    |  |
        O     k  A     z  A    p  I
```

436 Jonathan D. Kaye

The forms (106a, b, c, d) represent all and only the possible pronunciations of this sentence, viz.,

(107) a. ɔ̀ ká zā pī b. ɔ̀ ká zʌ̄ pī c. ɔ̀ kʌ́ zʌ̄ pī
      d. ò kʌ́ zʌ̄ pī

respectively. Consider now the sentence ɔ̀ ká sáká pī.

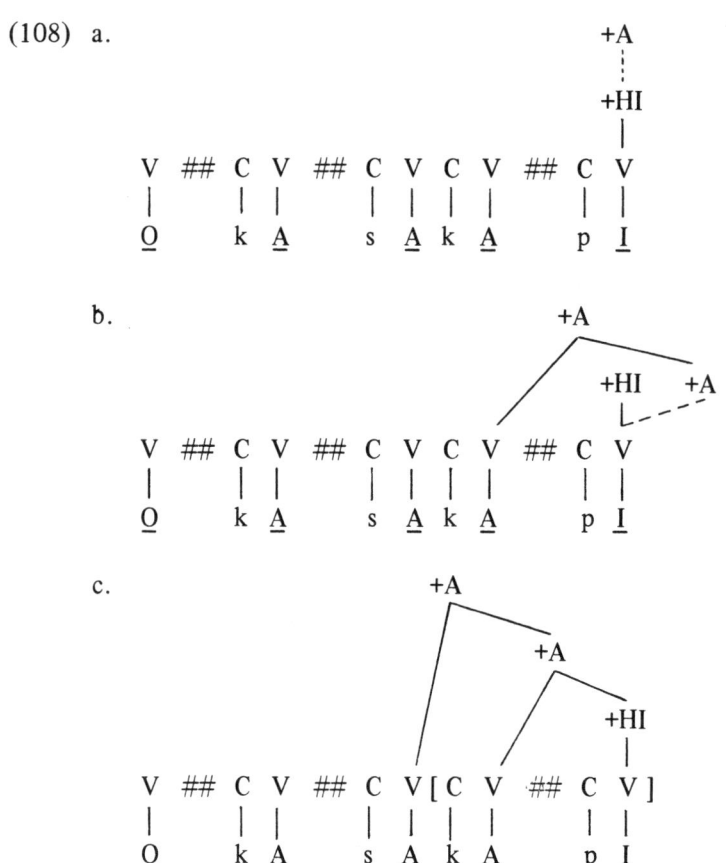

(108a, b) are the two possible versions of this sentence. At most the final vowel of sáká can undergo the directional harmony. Further spreading of any sort is excluded. The reason for this may be seen in (108c). In order to spread the +A feature to the initial syllable of sáká, a binary tree must be constructed with the complex [...ká pī] considered as a unit. But it has already been noted that a binary tree must cross a strong boundary, and there is no boundary at all between the two syllables of sáká. Nor can we simply skip the first syllable and construct our tree be-

Harmony in Vata 437

tween the auxiliary *ká* and the final syllable . . . *ká*, because of a condition on tree construction noted by Halle and Vergnaud, (1981): "All elements in a string must be incorporated into branching structures."

5.2. Compounds.

Compound nouns provide an enormous number of examples of the application of directional harmony.

(109) jlà   lion   jlʌ́#yò   lion cub
       ŋlɔ́   woman   ŋlɔ́#lè   woman's spear
       saká   rice   sakʌ́#ɲù   rice water
       nlɛ̄   animal   nlē#gò   animal tail
  cf. ɓɛ̄lì#gò   deer tail   ɓɛ̄lì#gì   deer tails
       nō#kpʌ   drink stool   nū#kpì   drink stools

We note here the same constraint that was observed in cases of inter-word directional harmony, to wit that a high vowel may undergo the process only if the triggering element is also a high vowel. The same unidirectionality obtains in compounds, i.e. only an advanced noun as the right member of a compound can trigger the harmony. This effect is seen in (110).

(110) sū#ɲɔ̀   wooden man   *sū#ɲò
       līlī#nlɛ̀   animal to eat   *līlī#nlè
       sū#gbɔ̀   (tree) fruit   *sū#gbò

Finally, if a compound both of whose members have retracted vowels appears before an advanced vowel, once again only the final syllable can change

(111) vɛ́#ɲɔ̀   a crazy person   ń gà vɛ́#ɲò yé   I see a crazy per-
                                   I see crazy p. part.   son
       ń gà vɛ́#ɲò yé   *ń gà ve#ɲò yé

The representation of the relevant parts of this sentence appears below.

(112) a.   +A   b.   +A
                            ⋮
      C V # C V ## C V   C V # C V ## C V
      | | | | | | | | | | | |
      v E   ɲ O   I E   v E   ɲ O   I E

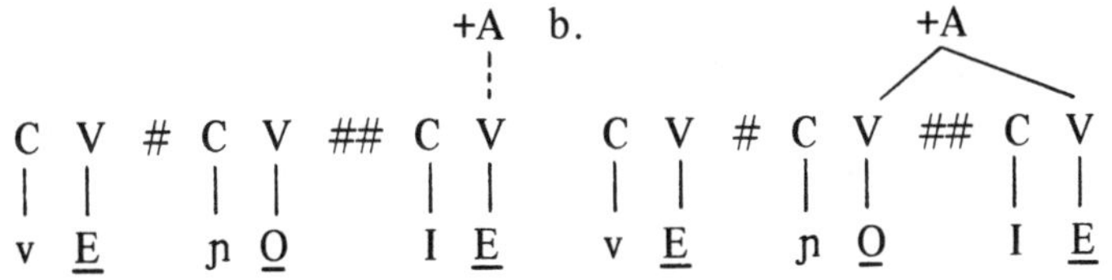

c.

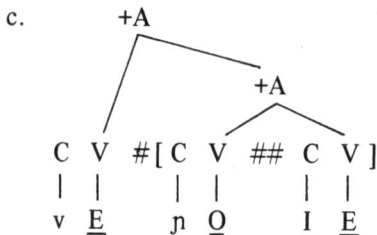

In (112b) a binary tree has been constructed between the particle *yé* and the final syllable of the compound *ɲɔ̀*. In order to repeat this process as in (112c) one must consider the elements *ɲɔ̀* and *yé* as a unit. In this case a strong boundary does appear to the left of *ɲɔ̀*. Nevertheless, tree construction cannot be extended. It appears that the integrity of a word (including a compound word) may not be violated in this way. Hence, [vɛ́#[ɲɔ̀##yé]] is not a possible analysis of the sequence *vɛ́ɲɔ̀ yé* and propagation to the initial syllable is impossible. Following this line of argument it is interesting to compare the two compounds in (113).

(113) a. ɓɔ̄tlɛ̀ viper ɓɔ̄tlèyò baby viper [[ɓɔ̄#tlɛ̀]#yò] *ɓɔ̄t lèyò
 b. gà lianes gàsù liane tree kʷlá bush
 kʷlÁgàsù bush liane tree {kʷlá#[gà#sù]]

In these examples the possibility of constructing binary directional trees depends precisely on the structure of the compound in question. The compound of (113a) consists of a compound *ɓɔ̄#tlɛ̀* as its left member followed by the element *yò* meaning 'child'. Propagation of the advanced feature may proceed to the penultimate syllable, and no further, since . . .*tlɛ̀ yò* cannot constitute a unit. In (113b) the compound consists of *kʷlá* 'bush' plus another compound *gàsù* as its right member. In this case propagation to the first syllable is possible, *gà#sù* corresponding to a unit ('liane tree').

I will conclude this section with a rather interesting example which combines the propagation of both vowel height and advancedness. Consider the forms of (114).

(114) ɓɔ̄gɔ̀pòpʌ̀ 'sole of the foot' ɓɔ̄gùpùpì 'soles of the feet'

This compound derives from *ɓɔ̄gɔ̀* 'foot' and *pòpʌ̀* 'broom'. In the singular form no propagation of the advanced feature is possible. The final vowel of the first term is high and is followed by a non-high vowel. The plural suffix sets of a chain of events which involves the raising of the penultimate vowel which, in turn, permits the advanced feature to spread onto the antepenultimate vowel. The derivation of this form is shown in (115).

(115)

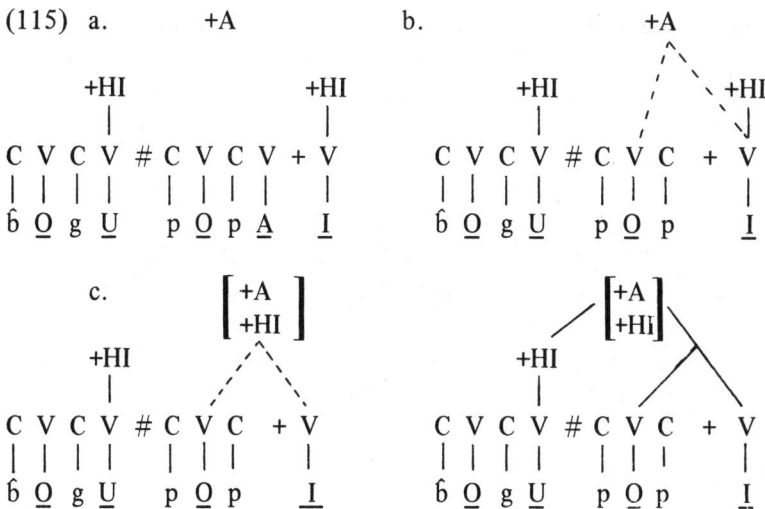

The lexical representation of the plural form of the compound appears in (115a). The rule of general truncation applying at the segmental level, the loss of a syllabic element of the skeleton, and the association of the floating +A autosegment have all applied in (115b). The parasitic spreading of the feature HI has taken place in (115c). Finally, directional harmony can now apply, modifying the antepenultimate vowel since all the vowels to its right are dominated by the feature HI as required. The above example clearly shows the interplay of the association of the floating autosegment, the parasitic propagation of the HI feature, and the construction of a directional tree of the resulting autosegmental feature complex.

5.3. *Disharmonic stems and directional harmony.*

In sections 2.3 and 2.4 I discussed two classes of stems which appeared to be exceptional with respect to dominant harmony. For words of the type èlùwà 'dog', a compound analysis was proposed: èlù#wà, while words like làlùkú̀ were analyzed with a bound -A autosegment.

(116) a.

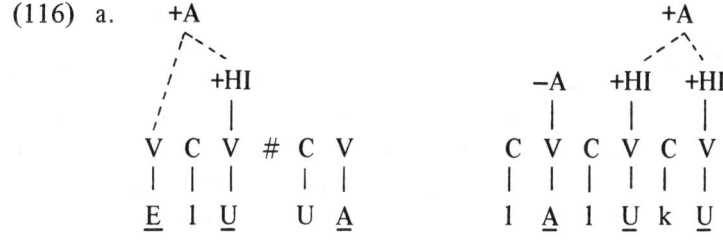

440 *Jonathan D. Kaye*

Given the representations for these forms, one predicts different behaviour with respect to the directional harmony under discussion. Disharmonic words analyzed as compounds, (116a) should undergo the harmony under the appropriate conditions. This is indeed the case as seen from the following examples.

(117) èlùwà   dog   ń gè èlùwʌ́ yé   I see a dog
       èflúwá   paper ɔ́ ɲé èfluwʌ́ kòfí   he gives paper to Koffi
       sìká`    gold   ń nɩ̀kā̄ sìkʌ́`zízò   I will hide gold

These results are hardly surprising given the representation in (116a). The harmony takes place in the manner shown below.

(118)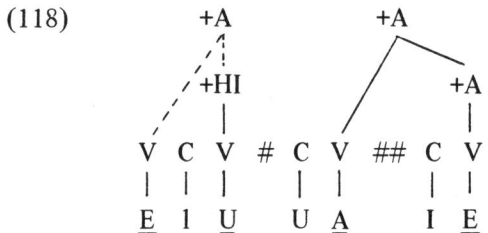

The true disharmonic stems of section 2.4 cannot be analyzed as compounds. A form like *làlùkú* 'machete' with a compound structure *là#lùkú*` should undergo directional harmony in exactly the same way as *jlà#yò* 'lion club'. The latter case yields *jlʌ̀yò* as expected while in the former case \**lʌ̀lùkú*`is incorrect. Thus, these forms cannot be compounds. The analysis in (116b) provides the correct results. If we assume that all segments associated to a *A* autosegment, whatever its value, are opaque with respect to the directional harmony, then a vowel with a lexically bound −*A* autosegment should never undergo the harmony, which is precisely the case. Further, the opaque vowel should block any further propagation of the advanced feature to its left. This is likewise true as seen in (119).

(119) ń ká làlùkú` γlé  'I will steal a machete'   \*ń kʌ́ làlùkú`γlé
       I fut machete steal

Following the Halle-Vergnaud theory of directional harmony one expects that every opaque element triggers its own harmony. In the case under study, the simplest assumption is that a bound −*A* autosegment as well as a floating +*A* triggers directional harmony. This assumption has no untoward results since it could never be the case that a word with a bound −*A* autosegment causes a change in a preceding advanced vowel. Advanced

Harmony in Vata 441

vowels are all opaque by definition. A *–A* harmony can only be constructed on a vowel not associated with an ATR autosegment, whatever its value. Consequently, there are never any visible effects of *–A* directional harmony as the following examples show:

(120) a. ń   γlé   làlùkú`   'I steal a machete'
          I   steal machete
      b. ń   ká   làlùkú` γlé 'I will steal a machete'
          I   fut   machete steal

c.

In addition the examples of the *làlùkú`*-type must include the first and second person plural subject pronouns, *à* and *á*. These forms likewise have a lexically bound *–A* autosegment. They may never undergo directional harmony as do the other subject pronouns.

(121) ɔ́ mlέ   he leaves   ó lé   he eats
       wá mlέ   they leave   wʌ́ lé   they eat
       à mlɛ̄   we leave   à l̄e   we eat
       á mlέ   you leave   á lé   you eat

In the above examples the pronouns *ɔ́* and *wá* undergo the harmony before a verb with an advanced vowel. This possibility does not exist for the pronouns *à* and *á*. Thus, the forms *ʌ̀ l̄e and *ʌ́ lé are ungrammatical. The bound autosegment is the appropriate mechanism to account for this behaviour.

5.4. *Diphthongs and the feature HI.*

In the analysis presented here, all diphthongs are of the light variety, i.e., they involve two vocalic segments associated to one element of the skeleton in the nucleus position of the syllabic structure. These diphthongs are assumed to behave like high vowels with respect to the harmony processes. Accordingly, their representation includes the bound *HI* autosegment giving a display as in (122).

(122) +HI

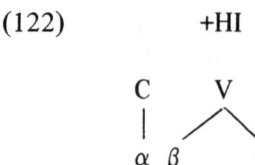

By convention the high feature is transmitted only through the left branch of the diphthong: only the vocalic element on the left is necessarily high. In fact, Vata diphthongs behave exactly like high vowels with respect to the directional harmony.

(123) a. ń ɲɛ́ ɲī̄/*ɲī yó   'I gave yams to a child'
         I give yams   child
         ń ɲɛ́ ɲī   yuʌ́   'I give yams to some children'
    b.   ń ɲɛ́ ŋʊ̰á/*ŋʊ̰ʌ́ kpʌ̄ 'I give them a chair'
         I give them   chair
         ń ɲɛ́ ŋʊ̰ʌ́   kpī   'I give them some chairs'

It has already been noted that a high vowel may only undergo directional harmony if the trigger is also high. In (123a) we see that a diphthong as well as a high vowel can have this effect. The principle works in exactly the same way when it is a diphthong that undergoes the harmony. Only a high vowel (or another diphthong) will permit the transmission of the advanced feature to the diphthong.

6. TRUNCATION AND DIRECTIONAL HARMONY.

In the discussion in section 3 it was noted that following any rule of truncation, an autosegment could not associate to the left syllabic element of two syllabic elements linked to a single vocalic segment as in (124a).

(124) a.   +A   b. +A
            ⋮
           *V # V   V # V
             \ /   \ /
              α   α

It was assumed that the floating autosegment was not deleted but rather remained unassociated, or associated to other vowels if the stem in question was polysyllabic. In the case of monosyllabic stems, the autosegment was to remain unlinked (124b) and hence have no direct surface manifestation. Directional harmony provides striking evidence for the

Harmony in Vata

correctness of this analysis. I have assumed that all features referring to advancedness, +A or −A, can trigger directional trees. Accordingly, we would expect even an unassociated +A feature to fulfill this role. It should be possible to find cases of directional harmony where there is no phonetically advanced triggering vowel. We see in (125) that this is quite true.

(125) a. sō arm sōō the arm yó child yóò the child
     b. ń ká sōō klā I'll grab the   ń ká yóò klā I'll grab the
                               arm   child
        I fut arm-def grab   I fut child-def grab

     c. i.   +A   ii.   +A

```
      C V ## C V # V         C V ## C V # V
      | |    | | | |         | |    |  L_
      k A    I O O           k A    I  O
```

     iii.   +A
               /\
                 +A

```
      C V ## C V # V
      | |    |  L_
      k A    I  O
```

In (125a) we see that the definite forms of stems in −o and −ɔ yield identical sequences, viz., −ɔɔ. Nevertheless, directional harmony is sensitive to the underlying distinction: yɔ́ɔ̀ may trigger it while sɔ̄ɔ̄ cannot, in spite of the surface identity of the vowel sequences. The analysis of this directional spreading is given in (125c). The initial representation of the sentence fragment ká yɔ́ɔ̀ appears in (125ci). In (125cii) definite truncation has deleted the final vowel segment. The remaining vowel spreads over two syllabic elements. The floating autosegment may not associate since to do so would result in the illicit structure (124a). Finally, a binary directional tree is constructed off the unassociated autosegment harmonizing the preceding vowel. A form like sɔ̄ɔ̄ can never induce such behaviour since there is no +A autosegment involved in its representation, hence nothing to spread.

These two definite forms display further differences when they appear on the receiving end of directional harmony.

(126) ń gà sɔ̄ɔ̄/*sōō/*sɔ̄ō yé   'I see the arm'
       I see arm-def   particle
       ń gà yɔ̀ɔ̀ ~ yòó   yé   'I see the child'
       I see child-def   particle

A glance at the phonological representations of these two sentences offers an insight into this behaviour.

(127) a.

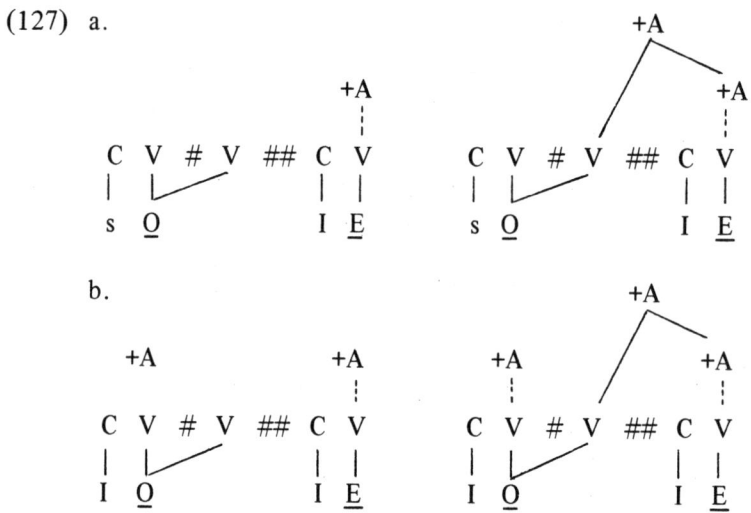

b.

In (127a) the sentence fragment... sɔ̄ɔ̄ yé is analyzed. The representation is shown following the application of definite truncation with the remaining vowel spreading to the vacated syllabic slot. Attempting to construct a directional tree results in a violation of principle (42) since the sequence of V's associated to the vowel O are not wholly within the (maximal) domain of the autosegment +A. One cannot recuperate the ill-formed structure of (127a) by extending the directional tree to the first syllable. In this case the V sequence would indeed be within the domain of the autosegment but given the binary character of tree construction, it is reasonable to assume that each binary subtree must be well-formed, i.e., must obey principles such as (42).[36]

The forms with an unattached +A autosegment do not exhibit the same behaviour. In these latter cases, such as (127b) a directional tree may be constructed. With the construction of the directional tree, the hithertofore unassociated autosegment must now be linked to the initial element of the V-V sequence. The resulting structure is well-formed in the sense that condition (42) is respected: both V elements of the skeleton are within the maximal domain of the autosegment.

It should now be noted that no appeal to supposed constraints on se-

Harmony in Vata

quences of advanced or retracted vowels can adequately handle these facts. Throughout this study we have seen examples of non-ATR-agreeing vowel sequences in abundance. An additional example of this sort appears below.

(128) ń gà ɲīɔ̄ ~ ɲīō yé   'I see the yams'
      I see yams-def. particle

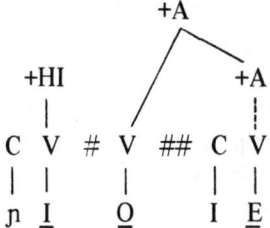

The example of (128) shows the application of directional harmony resulting in a sequence which contains a retracted vowel followed by the vowel rendered advanced by the harmony process. What distinguishes this case from that of (127a), where directional harmony is impossible, is the fact that here the sequence begins with a high vowel. Consequently, general truncation cannot apply for reasons already discussed. Since each vowel of the sequence remains attached to its own syllabic element, a directional tree can be constructed without violating principle (42). We conclude that it is indeed (42) which is the operative constraint in these cases, and not some phonetic condition regarding possible vowel sequences.

7. THE CONVENTIONS.

It has been shown that certain phonological rules approaching maximal simplicity (DELETE α) suffice to account for the wide variety of Vata facts presented in the previous sections. Obviously rules of such simplicity in themselves are inadequate to the task. They must be accompanied by general conventions governing the form of phonological representations. Rule applications resulting to ill-formed structures are blocked. Associations from one level to another are likewise excluded if their output does not conform to these conventions. I have assumed that conventions of various kinds are needed to account for the following facts:

(129) a. The +A autosegment does not associate following the application of a truncation rule.
b. High vowels are not deleted by truncation rules.
c. Vowels following high vowels are not deleted by truncation rules.
d. A high vowel undergoing directional harmony must have a high vowel trigger.
e. The final vowel of a vowel sequence may not undergo directional harmony unless the first vowel belongs to an advanced stem.

The general strategy for dealing with these cases was to show that the application of an otherwise general rule or process would result in an ill-formed structure as defined by the principles. Violation of the points in (129) result in the ill-formed structures below.

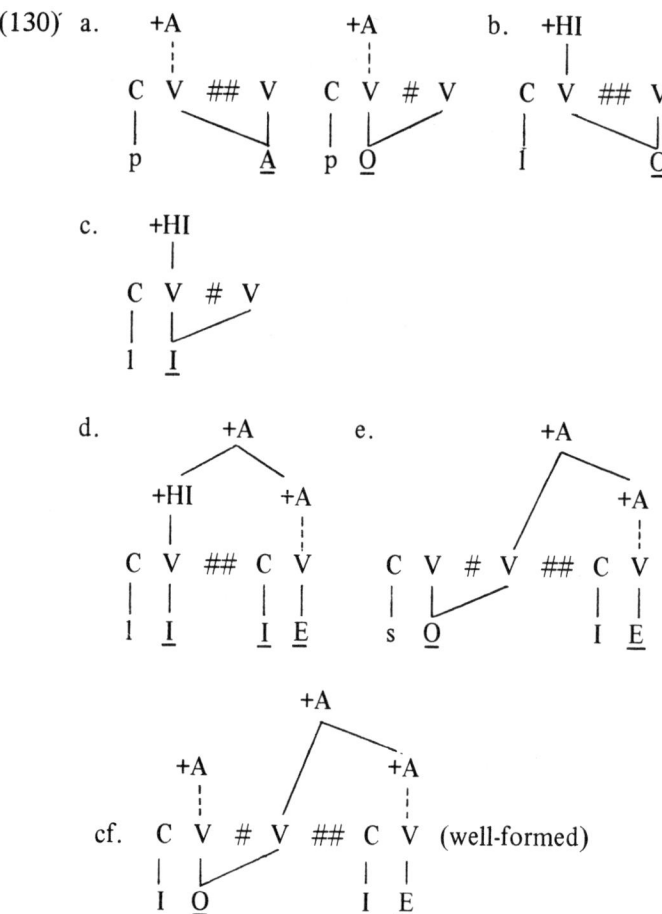

Harmony in Vata 447

All of the above structures (except the example on the bottom in (130e)) should be ill-formed for one reason or another. Convention (42), repeated below, was proposed to handle some of these cases.

(42)   A segment associated with an autosegment must fall entirely within its maximal domain.

This convention succesfully excludes structures (130a, b, c, e) while remaining mute on the question of (130d). Problems arise, however, with respect to vowel truncation. The constraint should rule out the form and structure in (131).

(131) [ɔ́ pí í] 'he throws them'/<ɔ́ pá í/

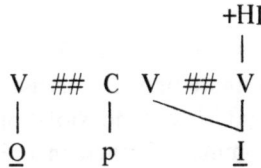

In fact, the above representation is well-formed. Comparing (131) and (130b), we see that the only difference is the placement of the bound *HI* autosegment on the left versus the right syllabic element. The former case is ill-formed while the latter is fine. Since convention (42) excludes both (131) and (130b), this convention needs to be modified or discarded altogether.

Suppose that we weaken (42) slightly by having it only apply in the cases involving a *floating* autosegment. There are many possible implementations of this proposal. I present one in (132).

(132)   A segment associated with a floating autosegment must fall entirely within its maximal domain.

Convention (132) rules out (130a) as desired, permits (131) as desired, and, interpreting directional trees as a variety of floating autosegment, might work for (130e). It also permits, however, (130b) which is not desirable at all. As suggested above, we need a convention which distinguishes the relative position of the autosegment. One such convention has been proposed by Halle and Vergnaud (1981).

(133)   The subordinate or recessive branch of a binary structure may not dominate a node that is branching or *that is specially marked by being linked to an autosegment on a seperate tier*. (Emphasis mine/ JDK).

This convention, with a minor modification, neatly handles the cases of high vowels in directional trees (130d). Recall that in Vata the following possibilities exist:

(134)   A A̲   A I̲   I I̲   *I A̲ (= (130d))

These patterns have the representations as in (135).

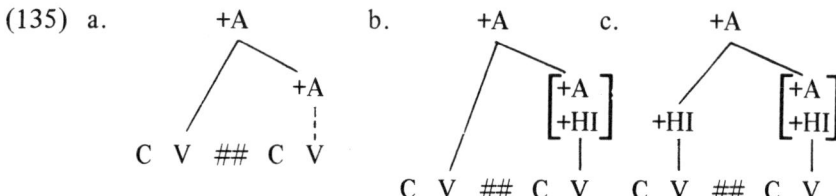

(135a, b, c) are all possible. Since these structures are all right dominant, the left branch is the recessive or subordinate branch referred to in (133). In (135a) there is no linked autosegment: hence no violation of (133). The linked autosegment falls on the dominant branch in (135b) and so this structure is wellformed. (135c) requires some discussion. There is a bound autosegment linked to the recessive (left) branch of this form. Applying (133) would appear to exclude this form. This situation can be remedied, however, by adding a condition of "proper domination".

(136) i. A node is properly dominated if all its A-features appear at the root of the minimal constituent containing it.
ii. All nodes in a branching structure must be properly dominated.

The consequences of (136) are that a high vowel (having a bound autosegment in Vata) may appear in a recessive position as long as every segment to its right in the tree is also a high vowel. Given the uniformly right-branching character of Vata directional trees and the normal conventions for percolation, it follows that the node dominating the high vowel and the d.t.e. of the tree will contain the A-feature in question. The proper domination requirement is satisfied.

If one were to assume that in certain languages non-high vowels are opaque i.e., have a lexically associated −HI autosegment, the constraints on roundness harmony noted by Steriade (1981) fall out as a consequence of (136).

Returning now to (130b) and (131), we see that the convention (133) makes exactly the right predictions, if we assume that the structure linking the segment O̲ to the two syllabic slots is binary right-dominant. In that

Harmony in Vata

case the recessive node is not properly dominated. In (131) the bound autosegment appears in the "head position" of the tree (cf. 135b) and so, no problem of proper domination arises.

A question remains as to the behaviour of two consecutive high vowels across a word boundary. At first glance it appears that the first vowel should be deletable. The sentence (137a) would have the structure (137b) should truncation apply in this case.

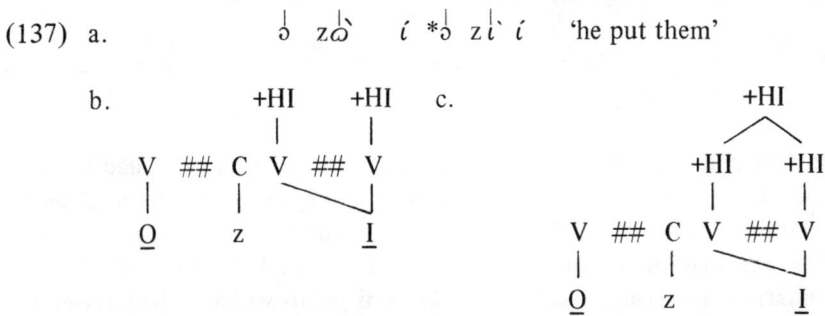

If we are to prevent an infelicitous application of truncation in the above derivation, we need to explain why the construction of an adjacency tree (137c) does not satisfy the proper domination condition. One possible solution is that adjacency trees involving the feature *HI* may not be constructed across a word boundary. It was noted above that the parasitic spreading of the feature *HI* cannot take place across a ## boundary, although it is possible in compounds having a # boundary. Thus, the step (137c) needed to satisfy the proper domination condition is disallowed. This leaves us with (137b) which will be excluded by (133) and (136).

The above proposal predicts that if a high vowel were separated by a weaker boundary, say, # from another high vowel, the deletion of one or the other vowel should be possible. Unfortunately such a situation never arises in Vata and so such evidence is not available. Evidence from other languages indicates that this approach may not be the correct one. A further condition on metrical structure seems to be required.

(138) Opaque elements may not delete.

An opaque element is defined as a segment associated to a skeletal element having a bound autosegment. This constraint can account for the failure of a high vowel to delete as in (130b). It does not account for the failure of any element to delete following a high vowel as in (130c). Thus, (138) by itself is insufficient to account for all the cases under consideration.

Turning to (130e), convention (42) seems to be the only one considered here capable of excluding the ill-formed case while allowing the grammatical form to its right. Taking the conventions (42), (133), (136) and (138) as a group, one finds a disturbing amount of redundancy, suggesting that one or more of these conventions may be derivable from the others. In sum, although no completely satisfactory set of principles has been found as yet, the analysis under discussion at least offers us an idea of the form that such conventions should take. I remain optimistic that further study following the line of research adopted here will ultimately resolve many of these problems.

8. CONCLUSIONS.

In this study we have seen that a reasonably rich and detailed array of facts can be treated in a satisfactory way employing the basic elements of three dimensional phonology and the extensions thereof suggested here. The explanation for these facts lies in the model of phonological representations involving a skeleton: a series of points which is the intersection of the various phonological tiers. These tiers serve to interpret and analyse the points of the skeleton. Two types of association with differing properties were shown to be needed in the above account: an autosegmental approach for the directional harmony. It may well be the case that the actual geometry of the metrical structures discussed here is not the appropriate device from which to derive different properties of each process. Indeed, this point is made in a recent study by Poser (this vol.). It is clear that even with certain amendments to the theory involving an elimination of the distinction between autosegmental and metrical trees, the cluster of properties involved in each structure will have to be derived from some aspect of the modified theory.

Our ultimate aim should be to arrive at a general theory which may account for such harmony processes, stress systems, tone systems, etc. by a small set of general principles which define well-formed phonological structures. These principles along with a now impoverished rule component, conceivably reduced to such elementary processes as "DELETE α" should be able to provide insightful analysis for the rich systems now under study. It is my hope that the present work will contribute in some measure to this enterprise.

NOTES

1. E.g., Halle and Vergnaud (1981), Clements (1981), Steriade (to appear) and Vago (1980) among many others.
2. Firth (1948).
3. Harris (1944).
4. See Kaye (1980, 1981a, 1981b).
5. Tones are not represented here to avoid confusion between association lines and tone markings.
6. sūgbɔ̀ is a compound ('tree-fruits') which explains its disharmonic nature.
7. Alternatively, one finds zésù and jlèyò. See Kaye (1980) for discussion.
8. These are discussed in Kaye (1980). I incorrectly assumed that the underlying form of the question particle was $-\bar{\text{A}}\bar{\text{A}}$.
9. Alternatively, one might propose $\quad$ −A $\quad$ +A $\quad$ as the display for [àlàdió̀].

$$\underline{A} \ l \ \underline{A} \ d \ \underline{IO}$$

I can find no immediate emperical consequences to this choice. The representation in (20) has two vowels lexically bound to a −A autosegment. It is important to keep in mind that lexically bound autosegments cannot spread.

10. ʌ for those speakers who have not phonetically merged e and ʌ.
11. For a discussion of pronoun selection see Kaye (1981a).
12. The approach which I will follow here was suggested to me by G.N. Clements.
13. Cf. Clements (1981), Clements and Keyser (1981), Halle and Vergnaud (1980), McCarthy (1979).
14. This account, which is extremely sketchy, leaves aside a number of important questions. The reader is referred to the sources of note 13 for a more comprehensive discussion.
15. See Kaye and Charette (1981).
16. The disappearance of the mid tone does not interest us here.
17. A tonal tier comprises still another level.
18. Recall that in our model only *one* value (the marked value) of an autosegment may float. Accordingly, all nodes of an autosegmental tree, including the topmost will be labelled +A in the case at hand. The construction of adjacency trees may produce similar effects to those involving the "obligatory contour principle".
19. It is quite possible that a more perspicacious formulation of (42) exists. This problem is discussed in section 7 below.
20. See Koopman (1982) for discussion.
21. A general constraint against vowel sequences may be independently required for Vata. Pushing the analysis to the limit, we could plausibly arrive at the rule: DELETE VOWEL. Certain morpho-syntactic information might be required as well. The rest would follow from general principles.
22. In the following section we shall see that this modification is independently motivated.
23. The question suffix vowel is often realized by a distinctly longer vowel. I will assume this to be a low-level stylistic rule. This decision changes nothing in the analysis.
24. The mid tone may be optionally raised to high following a high tone. Thus, both [líā] and [líá] 'songs?' are possible.
25. The example in (70) ɔ́ kʊ̀ɛ̀ 'he is here' provides an interesting contrast with that of (69) ɔ́ kʊ̀ɛ̀ 'he is there'. The pronunciation of the latter is as transcribed.

The former, however, undergoes a rule of low tone attraction whereby a low tone receives a copy of the preceding tone. This form is pronounced diphthongally, i.e., [ɔ kʊɛ̂]. The contrast is clear in the case of a preceding low tone, cf. [ǹ kʊ̀ɛ̀] 'you are there' and [ǹ kʊɛ̂] 'you are here'. A following vowel blocks the rule of low tone attraction. In the case of a diphthong the attraction persists accounting for the tonal difference between 'he is there' and 'he is here'. I will not pursue the intriguing question of diphthongization here.

26. A preliminary analysis of plural formation is found in Travis, Doua and Doua (1980).

27. My feeling is that this too should not be stipulated but should follow from something more general. I will set aside this point, however, and concentrate on the issue at hand.

28. The high advanced vowel *i* does not occur as the final vowel of native singular forms. Thus, all our examples contain stem-final *u* .

29. The optionality of metrical trees in Vata is confirmed in other cases to be discussed below. If, in other languages, these trees are obligatory for the same features, "optional-obligatory" must be a parameter according to which languages may vary.

30. See Steriade (to appear) for a very similar notion of "parasitic".

31. The feature *back* is involved in a similar sort of process. Nouns containing successive high vowels in their singular forms show a fronting when the plural suffix is added.

dùlù	dìlì	debt	lùlù	lìlí	raphia
kùkú	kìkí	room	kpʊ̀kpʊ̀	kpɪ̄kpɪ̀	slice
mkʊ́kʊ́	mlíkí	worm			

Note that in this case the propagation of the features [aback, around] occurs in both advanced and retracted stems. The consecutive high vowels supply the metrical structure necessary for this parasitic spreading in the form of adjacency trees. This offers further support for the autosegmental status of the feature *HI*.

32. A possible explanation for this fact is that the stem final *−u* has the bound autosegmental feature complex [HI, +ROUND]. When cut loose this matrix may attach itself to a syllabic element dominating a high or non-high vowel. The vowel must be round.

33. I have chosen to give only sequences whose second member is *a* to illustrate this pattern. Sequences terminating in other vowels behave in an identical fashion.

34. These possibilities are not necessarily all found together in every language with rounding harmony. Steriade discussed left-to-right cases and so the left element is underlined.

35. This approach was suggested to me by Donca Steriade.

36. In this example such an extension would be excluded anyway since the constituent structure of the sentence fragment is clearly [sɔ̄ #ɔ̄] yé. Eliminating this factor as in a sentence like ń gò ɔ́ yé 'I see him' (< ń gà ó yé) leaves the conclusion intact: directional harmony is still impossible here. Recall that a verb stem and an object pronoun are separate words. Indeed directional harmony can be extended in precisely this context as in ń gà zā̄ yé 'I see food' (< ń gà zā yé). Such factors illustrate the binary nature of the directional trees: each binary construction must be well-formed.

References

Abercrombie, D. (1967), *Elements of General Phonetics*. Edingburgh: University Press.
Akers, G. (1981), Admissability Conditions on Final Consonant Clusters in the Jamaican Continuum. In P. Muysken (ed.), *Generative Studies on Creole Languages*. Dordrecht-Holland: Foris Publications.
Anderson, S.R. (1972), On Nasalization in Sundanese. *Linguistic Inquiry* 3, 253-268.
Anderson, S.R. (1974), *The Organization of Phonology*. New York: Academic Press.
Anderson, S.R. (1976), Nasal Consonants and the Internal Structure of Segments. *Language* 52, 326-344.
Anderson, S.R. (1978), Syllables, Segments, and the Northwest Caucasian Languages. In Bell, A. and J.B. Hooper (eds.), *Syllables and Segments*. Amsterdam: North-Holland Publishing Company, 47-58.
Anderson, S.R. (1980), Problems and Perspectives in the Description of Vowel Harmony. In R. Vago. (ed.), *Issues in Vowel Harmony*. Amsterdam: Benjamins 1-48.
Anderson, S.R. (1981), Why Phonology isn't 'Natural'. *Linguistic Inquiry* 12, 493-540.
Anderson, S.R. (1982), Shwa in French, or How to Get Something for Nothing. *Language* 58, 534-574.
Anderson, J.M. (1980), On the Internal Structure of Phonological Segments: Evidence from English and its History. *Folia Linguistica Historica* 1, 165-191.
Anderson, J.M. and C.J. Ewen (eds.) (1980), Studies in Dependency Phonology. *Ludwigsburg Studies in Language and Linguistics* 4.
Anderson, J.M. and C.J. Ewen (to appear), *Principles of Dependency Phonology*.
Anderson, J.M. and C. Jones (1974), Three Theses Concerning Phonological Representations. *Journal of Linguistics* 10, 1-26.
Anderson, J.M. and C. Jones (1977), *Phonological Structure and the History of English*. Amsterdam: North-Holland Publishing Company.
Applegate, R.B. (1972), *Ineseño Chumash Grammar*. Unpublished Ph.D. dissertation, University of California, Berkeley.
Arnason, K. (1980), *Quantity in Historical Phonology*. Cambridge: University Press.
Aronoff, M. (1976), *Word Formation in Generative Grammar*. Cambridge, MA: MIT Press.
Bach, E. (1968), Two Proposals Concerning the Simplicity Metric in Phonology. *Glossa* 2, 128-149.
Bailey, C.J. (1977), The Syllable: Syllabization and Markedness. Paper presented at the Symposium on Syllable and Segment Organization, University of Colorado at Boulder, October 1977.

Barker, M. (1963), *Klamath Dictionary*, Berkeley, CA: University of California Publications in Linguistics, Vol. 31.

Barker, M. (1964), *Klamath Grammar*. Berkely, CA: University of California Publications in Linguistics, Vol. 32.

Basbøll, H. (1972), Some Conditioning Phonological Factors for the Pronunciation of Short Vowels in Danish with Special Reference to Syllabification. *ARIPUC* 6, 185-210.

Basbøll, H. (1978), Schwa, Jonctures et Syllabification dans les Représentations Phonologiques du Français. *Acta Linguistica* 16, 147-182.

Belder, S. (1981), *A Dependency Account of the Prosodic Structure of Heavy Syllables in Carib*. Dissertation, University of Leiden.

Bell, A. and J. Bybee Hooper (eds.) (1978), *Syllables and Segments*. Amsterdam: North Holland Publishing Co.

Bloch, B. and G.L. Trager (1942), *Outline of Linguistic Analysis*. Linguistic Society of America Special Publication, Baltimore: Waverly Press.

Bloomfield, L. (1933), *Language*. New York: Holt.

Borgstrøm, C.Hj. (1940), A Linguistic Survey of the Gaelic Dialects of Scotland: Vol. 1 – The Dialects of the Outer Hebrides. *Norsk Tidsskrift for Sprogvidenskap* Suppl. 1.

Borgstrøm, C.Hj. (1941), A Linguistic Survey of the Gaelic Dialects of Scotland: Vol. 2 – The Dialects of Skye and Ross-shire. *Norsk Tidsskrift for Sprofvidenskap* Suppl. 2.

Broselow, E. (1976), *The Phonology of Egyptian Arabic*. Unpublished Ph.D. dissertation, University of Massachusetts at Amherst.

Broselow, E. (1979), Cairene Arabic Syllable Structure. *Linguistic Analysis* 5, 345-382.

Cairns, C. and M. Feinstein (1982), Markedness and the Theory of Syllable Structure. *Linguistic Inquiry* 13, 193-226.

Campbell, L. (1974), Phonological Features: Problems and Proposals. *Language* 50, 52-65.

Catford, J.C. (1977), *Fundamental Problems in Phonetics*. Edingburg: University Press.

Chen, M. (1970), Vowel Length Variation as a Function of the Voicing of the Consonant Environment. *Phonetica* 22, 129-159.

Cheng, C.-C. (1973), *A Synchronic Phonology of Mandarin Chinese*. The Hage: Mouton.

Chinchor, N. (1979), On the Treatment of Mongolian Vowel Harmony. *Cunyform Papers in Linguistics* 8, 171-187.

Chomsky, N. (1965), *Aspects of the Theory of Syntax*. Cambridge, MA: MIT Press.

Chomsky, N. (1970), Remarks on Nominalization. In Jacobs and Rosenbaum (eds.) *Reading in English Transformational Grammar*. Waltham, MA: Ginn and Co.

Chomsky, N. (1972), Some Empirical Issues in the Theory of Transformational Grammar. In S. Peters (ed.), *Goals of Linguistic Theory*. Englewood Cliffs, N.J.; Prentice-Hall.

Chomsky, N. (1980), On the Representation of Form and Function. *The Linguistic Review* 1, 3-40.

Chomsky, N. & M. Halle (1968), *The Sound Pattern of English*. New York: Harper & Row.

Chomsky, N. and H. Lasnik (1977), Filters and control. *Linguistic Inquiry* 8, 425-504.

References

Clements, G.N. (1976), *Vowel Harmony in Nonlinear Generative Phonology: an Autosegmental Model*. Published in 1980 by Indiana University Linguistics Club.
Clements, G.N. (1977a), The Autosegmental Treatment of Vowel Harmony. In W.U. Dressler and O.E. Pfeiffer (eds.), *Phonologica 1976*. Innsbrucker Beiträge zur Sprachwissenschaft, vol. 19.
Clements, G.N. (1977), Neutral Vowels in Hungarian Vowel Harmony: an Autosegmental Interpretation. In *North Eastern Linguistic Society* 7, 49-64.
Clements, G.N. (1981), Akan Vowel Harmony: a Nonlinear Analysis. In G.N. Clements (ed.), *Harvard Studies in Phonology* vol. 2, Indiana University Linguistics Club, Bloomington, 108-177.
Clements, G.N. (in press), A Remark on the Elsewhere Condition. *Linguistic Inquiry*.
Clements, G.N. & K.C. Ford (1979), Kikuyu Tone Shift and its Synchronic Consequences. *Linguistic Inquiry* 10, 179-210.
Clements, G.N. and J. Keyser (1981), A three-tiered theory of the syllable. *Occasional Paper* #19. Center for Cognitive Science, MIT.
Crothers, J. and M. Shibatani (1980), Issues in the Description of Turkish Vowel Harmony. In R.M. Vago (ed.) *Issues in Vowel Harmony*. Amsterdam: Benjamins, 63-88.
Daniloff, R.G. & R.E. Hammarberg (1973), On Defining Coarticulation. *Journal of Phonetics* 1, 239-248.
Davidsen-Nielsen, N. (1975), A Phonological Analysis of English *sp, st, sk* with Special Reference to Speech Error Evidence. *Journal of the International Phonetic Association* 5, 3-25.
Dell, F. (1973), *Les règles et les sons*. Paris: Hermann.
Dell, F. (1976). Schwa précédé d'un groupe obstruante-liquide. *Recherches Linguistiques* 4, 75-112.
Dell, F. (1980), *Generative Phonology and French Phonology*. Cambridge: Cambridge University Press.
Dixit, R.P. & P.F. MacNeilage (1972), Coarticulation of Nasality: Evidence from Hindi. Paper presented at 83d Annual Meeting, Acoustical Society of America, Buffalo, N.Y., 19 April 1972. Abstracted in *Journal of the Acoustical Society of America* 52, 131.
Dubois, M.-M. (1960), *Dictionnaire moderne Français-Anglais*. Paris: Larousse.
Emonds, J. (1976), *A Transformational Approach to English Syntax*. New York: Academic Press.
Ewen, C.J. (1977), Aitken's Law and the Phonatory Gesture in Dependency Phonology. *Lingua* 41, 307-329.
Ewen, C.J. (1980a), *Aspects of Phonological Structure*. Ph.D. thesis, University of Edinburgh.
Ewen, C.J. (1980b), The Characterisation of Glottal Stricture in Dependency Phonology. *York Papers in Linguistics* 8, 35-47.
Ewen, C.J. (1980c), Segment or sequence? Problems in the analysis of some consonantal phenomena. In J. Anderson and C. Ewen (1980), 157-204.
Farnetani, E. (1981), Dai tratti ai parametri: introduzione all'analisi strumentalle della lingua somale. In G.R. Cardona, F. Agostine (eds.), *Studi Somali 1: Fonologia e lessico*. Ministerio degli Affari Esteri: Dipartimento per la Cooperazione allo Sviluppo (Repubblica Democratica Somala). Roma, 27-108.
Feinstein, M.H. (1979), Prenasalization and Syllable Structure. *Linguistic Inquiry* 10, 245-278.
Feinstein, M. and S. Lapointe (In preparation), Syllable Structure and Klamath Phonology.

Firth, J.R. (1948), Sounds and Prosodies. *Transactions of the Philological Society*, 127-152.
Foster, J.F. (1969), *On Some Phonological Rules of Turkish*. Unpublished Ph.D. dissertation, University of Illinois, Urbana.
Fudge, E.C. (1969), Syllables. *Journal of Linguistics* 5, 253-286.
Fujimura, O. and J. Lovins (1978), Syllables as Concatenative Phonetic Units. In Bell and Hooper (eds.), 107-120.
Goldsmith, J. (1976), *Autosegmental Phonology*. Indiana University Linguistics Club. Also published in 1979 by Garland Press, New York.
Goldsmith, J. (1976a), An Overview of Autosegmental Phonology. *Linguistic Analysis* 2, 23-68.
Goldsmith, J. (1979), The Aims of Autosegmental Phonology. In D. Dinnsen (ed.), *Current Approaches to Phonological Theory*. Bloomington: Indiana University Press, 202-222.
Grammont, M. (1914), *Traité pratique de prononciation française*. Paris: Delagrave.
Grammont, M. (1933), *Traité de phonétique*. Paris: Delagrave.
Gregores, E. & J.A. Suárez (1967), *A Description of Colloquial Guaraní*. The Hague: Mouton.
Hall, B. and R.M. Hall (1980), Nez Perce Vowel Harmony: an Africanist Explanation and some Theoretical Questions. In R.M. Vago (ed.), 201-236.
Halle, M. and K. Stevens (1971), A Note on Laryngeal Features. *MIT Quarterly Progress Report* 101, 198-213.
Halle, M. and J.-R Vergnaud (1980), Three Dimensional Phonology. *Linguistic Research* 1, 83-105.
Halle, M. and J.-R. Vergnaud (1981), Harmony Processes. In W. Klein and W. Levelt (eds.), *Crossing the Boundaries in Linguistics*, Reidel, 1-22.
Halle, M. & J.-R. Vergnaud (1982), On the Framework of Autosegmental Phonology. In H. van der Hulst & N. Smith (eds.), *The Structure of Phonological Representations. Part I.* (Dordrecht: Foris) 65-83.
Halle, M. and J.-R. Vernaud (forthcoming).
Hammond, M. (1982), Foot Domain Rules and Metrical Locality. Unpublished paper, UCLA (preliminary version read at West Coast Conference on Formal Linguistics, Stanford University, January, 1982).
Hankamer, J. and J. Aissen (1974), The Sonority Hierarchy. In A. Bruck, R.A. Fox and M.W. Lagaly (eds.), *Papers from the Parasession on Natural Phonology of the Chicago Linguistic Society*, 131-145.
Haraguchi, S. (1977a), *The Tone Pattern of Japanese: An Autosegmental Theory of Tonology*. Tokyo: Kaitakusha.
Haraguchi, S. (1977b), Tonology of Japanese Dialects. In G. Bedell, E. Kobayashi and M. Muraki (eds.), *Explorations in Linguistics*. Tokyo: Kenyusha, 125-146.
Harrington, J.P. (1974), Sibilants in Ventureño. *International Journal of American Linguistics* 40, 1-9.
Harris, Z. (1944), Simultaneous Components in Phonology. *Language* 20, 181-205.
Hart, G.W. (1981), Nasality and the Organization of Autosegmental Phonology. *Indiana University Linguistics Club*.
Haugen, E. (1956), The Syllable in Linguistic Description. In M. Halle et al (eds.), *For Roman Jakobson*. The Hague: Mouton, 213-221.
Haugen, E. (1958), The Phonemics of Modern Icelandic. *Language* 34, 55-88.
Hayes, B. (1980), *A Metrical Theory of Stress Rules*. Unpublished Doctoral dissertation, MIT; distributed by *Indiana University Linguistics Club*.
Hayes, B. (1981), The Phonetics and Phonology of Russian Voicing Assimilation,

Paper presented at Winter Meeting, Linguistic Society of America, 28 December 1981, New York City.
Henderson, E.J. (1948), Notes on the Syllable Structure of Lushai. *BSOAS* 12, 713-25.
Henderson, E.J. (1949), Prosodies in Siamese. *Asia Minor* (New Series) I, 189-215. Also in F.R. Palmer (ed.), *Prosodic Analysis*. London: Oxford University Press, 1970.
Herbert, R.K. (1975), Reanalyzing Prenasalized Consonants. *Studies in African Linguistics* 6, 105-123.
Herbert, R.K. (1977), *Language Universals, Markedness Theory, and Natural Phonetic Processes: the Interaction of Nasal and Oral Consonants*. Ph.D thesis, Ohio State University.
Hoard, J.E. (1966), Juncture and Syllable Structure in English. *Phonetica* 15, 96-109.
Hoard, J.E. (1967), *On the Foundations of Phonological Theory*. Ph.D thesis, University of Washington.
Hoard, J.E. (1971), Aspiration, Tenseness and Syllabicization in English. *Language* 47, 133-140.
Hoard, J.E. (1975), The new phonological paradigm. In Goyvaerts, D. and G. Pullum (eds.), *Essays on the Sound Pattern of English*. Gent: Story-Scientia, 21-61.
Hoard, J.E. (1978), Remarks on the Nature of Syllabic Stops and Affricates. In Bell, A. and J.B. Hooper (eds.), *Syllables and Segments*. Amsterdam: North-Holland Publishing Company, 59-72.
Hockett, C.F. (1955), *A Manual of Phonology*. Indiana University Publications in Anthropology and Linguistics, No. 11, *IJAL* International Journal of American Linguistics 21(4), Part 1.
Hoenigswald, H. (1948), Declension and Nasalization in Hindustani. *Journal of the American Oriental Society* 68, 139-44.
Hooper, J.B. (1972), The Syllable in Phonological Theory. *Language* 48, 525-40.
Hooper, J.B. (1976), *An Introduction to Natural Generative Phonology*. New York: Academic Press.
Howard, I. (1972), *A Directional Theory of Rule Application in Phonology*. Doctoral dissertation, MIT; published as University of Hawaii *Working Papers in Linguistics* IV, 7.
Hulst, H. van der (1981), De Structuur van Fonologische Representaties. *Glot* 4, 1-33.
Hyman, L.M. (1975), Nasal States and Nasal Processes. In Ferguson, C.A., L.M. Hyman and J.J. Ohala (eds.), *Nasálfest: papers from a symposium on nasals and nasalization*. Stanford: Language Universals Project, 249-264.
Hyman, L. (1977), On the Nature of Linguistic Stress. In L. Hyman (ed.), *Studies in Stress and Accent*. SCOPIL 4, University of Southern California Linguistics Dept., Los Angeles.
Hyman, L. (1982), The Representation of Nasality in Gokana. In H. van der Hulst and N. Smith (eds.), *The Structure of Phonological Representations. Part I*. Dordrecht: Foris Publications.
Ingria, R. (1980), Compensatory Lengthening as a Metrical Phenomenon. *Linguistic Inquiry* 11, 465-496.
Jackendoff, R. (1977), $\bar{X}$-*Syntax: a Study of Phrase Structure*. Linguistic Inquiry Monograph 2, MIT.
Jacobson, L.C. (1980), Voice-quality Harmony in Western Nilotic Languages. In R.M. Vago (ed.), 183-200.
Jakobson, R. (1968), *Child Language, Aphasia and Phonological Universals*. The Hague: Mouton.

Jensen, John R. (1974), A Constraint on Variables in Phonology. *Language* 50, 675-686.
Jespersen, O. (1920), *Lehrbuch der Phonetik*. Leipzig.
Johnson, C.D. (1980), Regular Disharmony in Kirghiz. In R.M. Vago (ed.), 89-99.
Jones, C. (1976), Some Constraints on Medial Consonant Clusters. *Language* 52, 121-130.
Jones, D. (1931), The 'word' as a phonetic entity. *Le Maître Phonétique*, 3rd series, no. 36, 60-65.
Jones, D. (1956), The Hyphen as a Phonetic Sign - a Contribution to the Theory of Syllable Division and Juncture. *Zeitschrift für Phonetik and Allgemeine Sprachwissenschaft*. Band 9, Heft 2, 99-107.
Juilland, A. (1965), *Dictionnaire inverse de la langue française*. The Hague: Mouton.
Kahn, D. (1976), Syllable-based Generalizations in English Phonology. Doctoral dissertation, MIT. Also distributed by The Indiana University Linguistics Club.
Kahn, D. (1977), Syllable-structure Specifications in Phonological Rules: Evidence from American English Aspiration, Glottalization and Voicing. [published in M. Aronoff and M.L. Kean (eds.), *Juncture*. Saratoge, Calif.: Anima Libri (1980)].
Kaye, J.D. (1980), The Mystery of the Tenth Vowel. *Journal of Linguistic Research* 1, 1-14.
Kaye, J.D. (1981a), La Sélection des Formes Pronominales en Vata. *Revue québécoise de linguistique* 11, 117-134.
Kaye, J.D. (1981b), Les Diphtongues Cachées du Vata. *Studies in African Linguistics* 12, 225-244.
Kaye, J.D. and M. Charette (1981), Tone sensitive rules in Dida. *Studies in African Linguistics*. Supplement 8, 82-84.
Kaye, J.D. and J. Lowenstamm (1980), A Reanalysis of the Role of Syllabicity. Paper read at GLOW colloquium, Nijmegen, April 12, 1980.
Kaye, J.D. and J. Lowenstamm (1981a), Syllable Structure and Markedness Theory. In A. Belletti, L. Brandi and L. Rizzi (eds.), *Theory of Markedness in Generative Grammar*. Pisa, 287-316.
Kaye, J.D. and J. Lowenstamm (1981b), De la syllabicité. Unpublished paper. UQAM.
Kaye, J.D. and J. Lowenstamm (1982), On the Internal Structure of the Rime. GLOW VII. Paris.
Kean, M.-L. (1974), The Strict Cycle in Phonology. *Linguistic Inquiry* 5, 179-203.
Kean, M.L. (1975), The Theory of Markedness in Generative Grammar. Ph.D diss. MIT.
Kenstowicz, M. & C. Kisseberth (1979), *Generative Phonology*. New York: Academic Press.
Kenyon, J.S. (1966), *American Pronunciation*. 10th ed., Ann Arbor: Wahr.
Kim, C.-W. (1970), A Theory of Aspiration. *Phonetica* 21, 107-116.
Kiparsky, P. (1978), Issues in Phonological Theory. In J. Weinstock (ed.), *The Nordic Languages and Modern Linguistics*. Vol. 3, University of Texac Press, Austin, Texas.
Kiparsky, P. (1979), Metrical Structure Assignment is Cyclic. *Linguistic Inquiry* 10, 421-442.
Kisseberth, C. (1970), On the Functional Unity of Phonological Rules. *Linguistic Inquiry* 1, 291-306.
Kisseberth, C. (1972), Cyclical Rules in Klamath Phonology. *Linguistic Inquiry* 3, 1-34.

Kisseberth, C. (in press), Digo Tonology. In G.N. Clements and J. Goldsmith (eds.), *Autosegmental Studies in Bantu Tone*. Dordrecht: Foris Publications.
Kohler, K. (1967), Modern English Phonology. *Lingua* 19, 145-176.
Kok, A.C. de and J.J. Spa (1978), Semivoyelles, Diérèse et Olisem. *Linguistics* 213, 65-77.
Koopman, H. (1982), Word Order and $\bar{X}$-Theory in Kru Languages. Unpublished paper. UQAM.
Kuroda, S.Y. (1967), *Yawelmani Phonology*. Cambridge, MA: MIT Press.
Kuryłowicz, J. (1948), Contribution à la théorie de la syllabe. *Biuletin Polskiego Towarszistwa Jezyko-Znawaczego* 8, 80-113.
Kuryłowicz, J. (1971), A problem of Germanic Alliteration. In Barahmer, M., S. Helsztyński and J. Kryżanowski (eds.), *Studies in language and literature in honour of Margaret Schlauch*. New York: Russell & Russell, 195-201.
Kylstra, A.D. (1972), Die Präaspiration im Westskandinavischen und Lappischen. *Orbis* 21, 367-382.
Ladefoged, P. (1971), *Preliminaries to Linguistic Phonetics*. Chicago: University Press.
Lapointe, S. (1978), Yawelmani Revisited: a Transparant Solution to an Abstract Problem. Unpublished paper, Johns Hopkins University.
Lapointe, S. (1981), The Representation of Inflectional Morphology within the Lexicon. Burke and Pustejofsky (eds.), NELS XI. Amherst, MA.
Lass, R. (1976), *English Phonology and Phonological Theory*. London: Cambridge University Press.
Laughren, M. (in press), Tone in Zulu Nouns. In G.N. Clements and J. Goldsmith (eds.), *Autosegmental Studies in Bantu Tone*. Dordrecht: Foris Publications.
Lauriault, J. (1948), Alternate-Mora Timing in Shipibo. *International Journal of American Linguistics* 14, 22-24.
Leben, W. (1980), A Metrical Analysis of Length. *Linguistic Inquiry* 11, 497-510.
Leben, W. (1982), Metrical or Autosegmental? In H. van der Hulst & N. Smith (ed.), *The Structure of Phonological Representations. part I*. Dordrecht: Foris publications.
Lees, R.B. (1961), *The Phonology of Modern Standard Turkish*. Indiana University Publications. Uralic and Altaic Series vol. 6, Bloomington.
Lees, R.B. (1966), On the Interpretation of a Turkish Vowel Alternation. *Anthropological Linguistics* 8.9, 32-9.
Lees, R.B. (1967), Turkish Vowel Harmony and the Phonological Description of Assimilation. *Turk dili avastırmaları yilligi-belletin, 1966' dan ayrıbasım*. Ankara Universitesi Basimevi, Ankara, 279-97.
Lehiste, I. (1970), *Suprasegmentals*. Cambridge, Mass.: MIT Press.
Lehiste, I. (1971), Temporal Organization of Spoken Language. In L.L. Hammereich, R. Jakobson, and E. Zwirner (eds.), *Form and Substance: Phonetic and Linguistic Papers Presented to Eli Fischer-Jørgensen*. Akademisk Forlag, 159-169.
Lehiste, I. and G. Peterson (1960), Duration of Syllable Nuclei in English. *Journal of the Acoustical Society of America* 32, 693-703.
Lehn, W. (1963), Emphasis in Cairo Arabic. *Language* 39.1, 29-39.
Lerond, A. (1980), *Dictionnaire de la prononciation,* 3ième éd. Paris: Larousse.
Liberman, A.S. (1971), *Islandskaja prosodika: k fonologiceskoj xarakteristike sovremennogo islandskogo jazyka i ego istorii*. Akademija Nauk SSSR, Institut jazykozanija.
Liberman, M. (1975), *The Intonational System of English*. Ph.D dissertation, MIT.

Liberman, M. and A. Prince (1977), On Stress and Linguistic Rhytm, *Linguistic Inquiry* 8.2, 249-336.
Lightner, T. (1965), On the Description of Vowel and Consonant Harmony. *Word* 21, 244-50.
Lightner, T. (1972), *Problems in the Theory of Phonology, vol. 1: Russian Phonology and Turkish Phonology.* Linguistic Research Inc., Edmonton/Champaign.
Loos, E. (1969), *The Phonology of Capanahua and its Grammatical Basis.* Norman, OK: Summer Institute of Linguistics.
Lowenstamm, J. (1978), Remarks on syllable structure. In R. Saez (ed.), *University of Massachusetts Occasional Papers in Linguistics.* Vol. 3, Amherst, MA: GLSA, University of Massachusetts.
Lowenstamm, J. (1979), Topics in Syllabic Phonology. Ph.D. diss., University of Massachusetts, Amherst.
Lowenstamm, J. (1981), On the Maximal Cluster Approach to Syllable Structure. *Linguistic Inquiry* 12.4, 575-604.
Lunt, H.G. (1973), Remarks on Nasality: the Case of Guaraní. In: S. Anderson & P. Kiparsky (eds.), *A Festschrift for Morris Halle.* New York 1973.
Malecot, A. (1960), Vowel Nasality as a Distinctive Feature in American English. *Language* 36, 222-229.
Malone, K. (1923), *The Phonology of Modern Icelandic.* Menasha, Wis.
Marantz, A. (1980), A Metrical Treatment of Telegu Vowel Harmony. Unpublished manuscript, Massachusetts Institute of Technology.
Martinet, A. and H. Walter (1973), *Dictionnaire de la prononciation français dans son usage réel.* Paris: France-Expansion.
McCarthy, J. (1977), On Hierarchic Structure Within Syllables. Unpublished ms., MIT.
McCarthy, J. (1978), An Autosegmental Account of Classical Arabic Vocalism. Unpublished manuscript, Massachusetts Institute of Technology.
McCarthy, J. (1979), *Formal Problems in Semitic Phonology and Morphology.* Doctoral dissertation. MIT.
McCarthy, J. (1981), A Prosodic Theory of Nonconcatenative Morphology. *Linguistic Inquiry* 12, 373-418.
McCarthy, J. (1982), Prosodic Templates, Morphemic Templates, and Morphemic Tiers, In H. van der Hulst & N. Smith (eds.) *The Structure of Phonological Representations. Part I.* Dordrecht: Foris.
Mors, C.H. ter (1981), Klamath ə-insertion in Empty Syllable Nuclei. Paper presented at the LSA Winter Meeting, New York, N.Y.
Mors, C.H. ter (1982), Directional Syllabification. ə-insertion as a Syllabificiation Process. *Doktoraal skriptie,* Rijksuniversiteit Groningen.
Myers, A. (1974), On Prenasalized Stops. *Papers from the 5th Annual Meeting, North Eastern Linguistic Society,* 129-133.
Newman, S. (1944), *Yokuts Language of California.* New York: Viking Fund Publications in Anthropology, No. 2.
Newton, B. (1972), *The Generative Interpretation of Dialect: a Study of Modern Greek Phonology.* Cambridge: University Press.
Newman, P. (1972), Syllable Weight as a Phonological Variable: the Nature and Function of the Contrast between "Heavy" and "Light" Syllables. *Studies in African Linguistics* 3.3, 301-323.
Noske, R.G. (1981), Theoretical Issues in Syllabic Phonology. A critical Study of The Theories of Syllabification and a Proposal Concerning the Interaction of Syllab-

References

ification and Syllable Changing Rules in the Phonology of French. *Doktoraal skriptie,* Universiteit van Amsterdam.

O'Connor, J.D. and J.L.M. Trim (1953), Vowel Consonant, Sylabble – a Phonological Definition. *Word* 9.2, 103–122.

Odden, D. (in press), Stem Tone Assignment in Shona. In G.N. Clements and J. Goldsmith (eds.), *Autosegmental Studies in Bantu Tone.* Dordrecht: Foris Publications.

Ohala, M. (1975), Nasals and Nasalization in Hindi. In C. Ferguson, L. Hyman & J. Ohala (eds.), *Nasálfest* (Stanford: Stanford University Linguistics Department), 317–32.

Okello, B. (1976), *Some Phonological and Morphological Processes in Lango.* Unpublished Ph.D. dissertation, University of Michigan at Ann Arbor.

Orešnik, J. and M. Pétursson (1977), Quantity in Modern Icelandic. *Arkiv för nordisk filologi* 92, 155–171.

Palacas, A. (1971), Simultaneous vs. Iterative Rules in Phonology. Unpublished paper read at winter LSA meeting, St. Louis, Mo.

Pétursson, M. (1972a), La Préaspiration en Islandais Moderne. *Studia Linguistica* 26, 61–80.

Pétursson, M. (1972b), Review of Liberman (1971). *Phonetica* 26, 89–128.

Pétursson, M. (1976), Aspiration et Activité Glottale. *Phonetica* 33, 169–198.

Pike, K. (1947), On the Phonemic Status of English Diphthongs. *Language* 23, 151–159.

Pike, E.V. (1954), Phonetic Rank and Subordination in Consonant Patterning and Historical Change. *Miscellanea Phonetica* 2, 25–41.

Pike, K. (1947), Grammatical Prerequisites to Phonemic Analysis. *Word* 3, 155–172.

Pike, K. (1967), *Language in Relation to a Unified Theory of the Structure of Human Behavior,* 2nd ed., The Hague: Mouton.

Pike, K. and E.V. Pike (1947), Immediate Constituents of Mazateco Syllables. *IJAL International Journal of American Linguistics* 13, 78–91.

Pillinger, O.S. (1982), Latin Degemination: an Autosegmental Approach. In Pinkster, H. (ed.), *Latin Linquistics and Linguistic Theory.* Papers from the First International Colloquium on Latin Linguistics, Amsterdam, 1981. Amsterdam: Benjamins.

Poser, W. (1980), Two Cases of Morphologically Induced Nasal Harmony. Unpublished manuscript, Massachusetts Institute of Technology.

Poser, W. (1981a), Harmony Domains. Paper presented at Trilateral Conference on Non-Linear Phonology, University of Texas, Austin, Texas, 11 April 1981.

Poser, W. (1981b), Nasalization in Guaraní and the Autosegmental Theory of Phonology. Unpublished manuscript, Massachusetts Institute of Technology.

Prince, A. (1980), A metrical Theory for Estonian Quality. *Linguistic Inquiry* 11, 511–562.

Pulgram, E. (1970), *Syllable, Word, Nexus, Cursus.* The Hague: Mouton.

Pyle, C. (1974), Why a Conspiracy? *Papers from the Parasession on Natural Phonology.* Chicago Linguistic Society, 275–84.

Raphael, L.J., M.F. Dorman, F. Freeman and C. Tobin (1975), Vowel and Nasal Duration as Cues to Voicing in Word-final Stop Consonants: Spectrographic and Perceptual Studies. *Journal of Speech and Hearing Research* 18, 389–400.

Rischel, J. (1964), Stress, Juncture and Syllabification in Phonemic Description. In *The Proceedings of the Ninth International Congress of Linguists, Cambridge, Massachusetts 1962.* The Hague: Mouton, 85–93.

Rivas, A. (1974), Nasalization in Guaraní. In *Papers from the Fifth Annual Meeting*

of the North Eastern Linguistic Society (Cambridge: Harvard University Department of Linguistics), 134-43.
Robins, R.H. (1957), Vowel Nasality in Sundanese: A Phonological and Grammatical Study. In: *Studies in Linguistic Analysis.* Basis Blackwell, Oxford.
Rosetti, A. (1962), La syllabe phonologique. *PICPhS* 4, 490-499.
Safir, K. (1979), Metrical Structure in Capanahua. In K. Safir (ed.), MIT Working Papers in Linguistics. Vol I. 1979, 95-115.
Safir, K. (1979) (ed.), *MIT Working Papers in Linguistics.* Vol 1. Cambridge, Mass.
Saib, J. (1978), Segment Organization and the Syllable in Tamazight Berber. In A. Bell and J. Hooper (eds.), 93-106.
St Clair, R. (1972), Compound Phonological Segments. *Lingua* 29, 120-127.
St Clair, R. (1973), Affricates as Compound Phonological Segments. *Linguistische Berichte* 26, 21-24.
Sapir, E. (1922), The Takelma Language of Southwestern Oregon. In F. Boas (ed.), *Handbook of American Indian Languages* (BBAE 40, vol. II).
Saussure, F. de (1915), *Cours de linguistique générale.* Paris.
Schein, B. (1981), Spirantization in Tigrinya. In H. Borer & Y. Aoun (eds.), *Theoretical Issues in the Grammar of Semitic Languages* (MIT Working Papers in Linguistics III). (Cambridge: MIT Department of Linguistics), 32-42.
Selkirk, E.O. (1978), The French Foot: on the Status of French "mute" *e. Studies in French Linguistics* 1.2, 141-150.
Selkirk, E.O. (1980), The Role of Prosodic Categories in English Word Stress. *Linguistic Inquiry* 11.1.
Selkirk, E.O. (1980a), On Prosodic Structure and its Relation to Syntactic Structure. *Indiana University Linguistics Club.*
Selkirk, E.O. (1982), *The Syntax of Words.* Linguistic Inquiry Monograph Series, Cambridge, Mass. MIT Press.
Selkirk, E.O. (forthcoming), *Phonology and Syntax: The Relation between Sound and Structure.* Cambridge, Mass.: MIT Press.
Sezer, E. (1981), On the k/∅ Alternation in Turkish. In G.N. Clements (ed.), *Harvard Studies in Phonology.* vol. 2. Indiana University Linguistics Club, Bloomington.
Sigurd, B. (1965), *Phonotactic structures in Swedish.* Lund: Uniskol.
Sohn, H.-M. (1971), A Raising in Woleaian. *University of Hawaii Working Papers in Linguistics* 3.8, 15-35.
Sohn, Ho-Min (1975), *Woleaian Reference Grammar.* Honolulu: University of Hawaii Press.
Sommerstein, A.H. (1977), *Modern phonology.* London: Edward Arnold.
Spa, J.J. (1975), Les accolades, la liaison, la syllabe. *Rapports* 45.3, 76-83.
Sportiche, D. (1977), Un fragment de phonologie du Guaraní. Unpublished manuscript, Massachusetts Institute of Technology.
Stanley, R. (1967), Redundancy Rules in Phonology. *Language* 43, 393-436.
Steriade, D. (to appear), Parameters of Metrical Harmony Rules. *The Linguistic Review.*
Swadesh, M. (1947), On the Analysis of English Syllabics. *Language* 23, 137-150.
Ternes, E. (1973), *The Phonemic Analysis of Scottish Gaelic.* Hamburg: Helmut Buske Verlag.
Thráinsson, H. (1978), On the Phonology of Icelandic Preaspiration. *Nordic Journal of Linguistics* 1, 3-54.
Thomas, L. (1974), Klamath Vowel Alternations and the Segmental Cycle. Doctoral dissertation, University of Massachusetts, Amherst.
Topping, D. (1968), Chamorro Vowel Harmony. *Oceanic Linguistics* 7, 67-79.

Trager, G.L. (1942), The Phoneme "t": a Study in Theory and Method. *American Speech* 17, 144-148.
Trager, G.L. and B. Bloch (1941), The Syllabic Phonemes of English. *Language* 17, 223-246.
Trager, G.L. and H.L. Smith, Jr. (1951), *An Outline of English Structure*. Studies in Linguistics, Occasional Papers, no. 3, Norman: Oklahoma Battenberg Press.
Travis, L., Doua, B.S. and Y.A. Doua (1980), Le pluriel en vata. Unpublished paper. UQAM.
Turbetzkoy, N.S. (1969), *Principles of Phonology*. Berkely and Los Angeles: University of California Press.
Vago, R.M. (1980) (ed.), *Issues in Vowel Harmony*. Amsterdam: John Benjamins, B.V.
Vennemann, Th. (1972), On the Theory of Syllabic Phonology. *Linguistische Berichte* 18, 1-18.
Vergnaud, J.-R. (1977), Formal Properties of Phonological Rules. In J. Butts & J. Hintikka (eds.), *Basic Problems in Methodology and Linguistics*. Dordrecht: Reidel, 299-318.
Vergnaud, J.-R. (1979), A Formal Theory of Vowel Harmony. In *Univ. of Mass. Occasional Papers in Linguistics*, Vol. 5.
Vergnaud, J.-R. and M. Halle et al. (1978), Metrical Structures in Phonology. Fragment of a Draft. Unpubl. paper, MIT.
Vine, B. (1981), Remarks on African 'Shadow' Vowels. In G.N. Clements (ed.), *Harvard Studies in Phonology*. vol. 2, Indiana University Linguistics Club, Bloomington.
Vogel, I. (1977), *The Syllable in Phonological Theory with Special Reference to Italian*. Unpublished Ph.D. dissertation, Stanford.
Vogt, H. (1942), The Structure of the Norwegian Monosyllable. *Norsk Tidsskrift for Sprogvidenskap* 12, 5-29.
Waterson, N. (1970), Some Aspects of the Phonology of the Nominal Forms of Turkish Words. In F.R. Palmer (ed.), *Prosodic Analysis*. London: Oxford University Press.
Welmers, W. (1959), Tonemics, Morphotonemics, and Tonal Morphemes. *General Linguistics* 4, 1-9.
White, R. (1973), Klamath phonology. Doctoral dissertation, University of Washington.
Whorf, B.L. (1940), Linguistics as an Exact Science. In J.B. Carroll (ed.), *Language, Thought and Reality*. Cambridge, Mass.: MIT Press, 220-232.
Wilkins, W. (1980), Adjacency and Variables in Syntactic Transformations. *Linguistic Inquiry* 11, 709-758.
Woock, E. & M. Noonan (1979), Vowel Harmony in Lango. *Papers from the Fifteenth Regional Meeting of the Chicago Linguistic Society* (Chicago: University of Chicago, Department of Linguistics), 20-29.
Yavash, M. (1980a), *Borrowing and its Implications for Turkish Phonology*. Unpublished University of Kansas Ph.D. dissertation.
Yavash, M. (1980b), Some Pilot Experiments on Turkish Vowel Harmony. *Papers in Linguistics* 13.3, 543-561.
Yavash, M. (1980c), Vowel and Consonant Harmony in Turkish. *Glossa* 14.2, 189-211.
Yip, M. (1980), *The Tonal Phonology of Chinese*. Unpublished Ph.D. dissertation, Massachusetts Institute of Technology.
Zimmer, K. (1969), Psychological Correlates of some Turkish Morpheme Structure Conditions. *Language* 45, 309-21.

Zubizarreta, M.-L. (1979), 'Vowel Harmony in Andalusian Spanish. In K. Safir (ed.), *MIT Working Papers in Linguistics* (Cambridge: MIT Department of Linguistics) Vol. I, 1-11.

Zubizarreta (1980), A Review of "On Syllable Modification and Quantity in Yuk Phonology" by Miyaoka, Unpublished ms., MIT.

Index of Names

Personal index:

Abercrombie, D. 51
Aissen, J. 380
Akers, G. 252
Anderson, J. 27, 29, 30, 32, 44, 47, 49, 52, 55, 63, 362, 381
Anderson, S. 1, 4, 15, 17-8, 20, 21, 23-4, 36-7, 39, 41, 45-6, 127, 135, 234, 249, 251, 332-3, 335
Applegate, R.B. 131, 157
Árnason, K. 59, 60, 64
Aronoff, M. 117

Bach, E. 20
Bailey, C.-J.N. 354, 364, 382
Barker, M.A.R. 92, 93, 107, 110, 119
Basbøll, H. 267, 276, 287, 305
Belder, S. 66
Beukema, F. 27
Bloch, B. 353, 381
Bloomfield, L. 36, 51, 359, 380-1
Borgstrøm, C.H. 58-9
Borovsky, T. 253
Broselow, E. 115, 259, 265-6, 315, 380

Cairns, C.E. 74-5, 89, 108, 117-9, 306
Campbell, L. 35, 51, 52, 57
Catford, J.C. 46, 52, 56, 62
Charette, M. 385, 451
Chen, M. 353, 381
Cheng, C.-C. 138
Chinchor, N. 335
Chomsky, N. 2, 4, 18, 24, 32, 39, 45, 52, 56, 73, 121-2, 144, 148, 169, 214-5, 277-8, 380-1
Clements, G.N. 121, 124, 127-9, 150, 156, 214, 216-9, 251-2, 311, 319, 322, 324, 385, 392, 451
Crothers, J. 215

Daniloff, R. 144
Davidsen-Nielsen, N. 47
Dell, F.C. 277, 280-1, 287-8, 297, 303, 305-8
Devellioğlu, F. 253
Dickel, G. 1
Dik, S.C. 306
Dixit, R. Prakash 144
Dorman, M.F. 381
Dova, B.S. 385, 419, 451
Doua, B.S. 385, 419, 451
Dubois, M.-M. 308
Dupuis, M. 27

Emonds, J. 116
Ewen, C. 27, 29, 30, 32-3, 44, 62, 66

Farnetani, E. 252
Feinstein, M.H. 40-3, 45, 74-5, 89, 108, 110, 112-20, 306
Firth, J.R. 381, 451
Ford, K.C. 150, 156
Foster, J.F. 254
Freeman, F. 381
Fudge, E. 48, 344, 350, 352, 379, 381-2
Fujimura, O. 350, 353, 372, 379, 381

Goldsmith, J. 1, 10, 37, 121-4, 156-7, 322-3, 326, 330, 355, 392
Grammont, M. 373-4
Gregores, E. 142, 157-8, 322, 325, 327, 329

Hall, B. 251
Hall, R.M.R. 251
Halle, M. 2, 4, 7-8, 10-1, 15, 18-20, 24, 32, 39, 45, 52, 56, 60, 121-2, 127-8, 138, 140-4, 148, 156-7, 159-60, 165, 168, 180, 200, 209-10,

214-5, 251, 277-8, 287, 295, 301-4, 312, 316-7, 322, 330-2, 335, 381, 385-6, 437, 440, 451
Hammarberg, R.E. 144
Hammond, M. 10, 24
Hankamer, J. 380
Haraguchi, S. 120, 126, 178, 183, 186, 196, 211
Harrington, J.P. 158
Harris, Z. 451
Hart, G.W. 37, 314, 322, 333
Haugen, E. 60, 64, 354
Hayes, B. 4, 19, 148, 160, 165, 167, 172, 209, 311
Henderson, E.J. 381
Herbert, R.K. 38, 40, 42-3, 45, 52, 56-7, 59
Hoard, J.E. 35, 37, 276, 305, 354, 362, 364, 369, 381-2
Hockett, C.F. 354, 381
Hoenigswald, H. 143
Hony, H.C. 253
Hooper, J. Bybee 115, 259-60, 265, 339, 343-4, 354, 380, 382
Howard, I. 7, 127
van der Hulst, H.G. 37, 214, 252
Hyman, L. 45, 214, 381

Ingria, R. 75, 117

Jackendoff, R. 32
Jacobson, L.C. 252
Jakobson, R. 33
Jensen, J.R. 7
Jespersen, O. 260, 265
Johnson, C.D. 255
Jones, C. 29, 32, 47, 49, 52, 55, 63, 362, 381
Jones, D. 354, 381, 383
Juilland, A. 304

Kahn, D. 51, 115, 259, 267, 352, 355-6, 360, 362-4, 366, 369-70, 372, 376-9, 381-3
Kaye, J.D. 98, 119, 121, 258, 263, 269-72, 294, 305-6, 308, 400, 406, 451
Kean, M.L. 94-5, 100-1, 110-1, 120, 306
Kenstowicz, M. 135
Kenyon, J.S. 379
Keyser, J. 451

Kılıçkan, N. 253
Kim, C.-W. 62
Kiparsky, P. 27, 34, 115, 121, 157. 209, 380
Kisseberth, C.W. 91-92, 95, 135, 214
Kohler, K. 47
de Kok, A.C. 292, 308
Koopman, H. 385, 451
Kornfilt, J. 251
Kuroda, S.Y. 83, 85-7, 118-9
Kuryłowicz, J. 40, 48, 259, 267, 339-40, 346, 354
Kylstra, A.D. 58

Ladefoged, P. 38-9, 41, 45, 52, 56, 62
Lapointe, S. 74, 78, 83, 85-6, 110, 119-20
Lasnik, H. 277-8, 380
Lass, R. 63
Laughren, M. 214
Lauriault, J. 149
Leben, W. 1, 3-4, 7, 9-14, 16-22
Lees, R.B. 215, 224, 249
Lehiste, I. 353-4, 379, 380-1
Lehn, W. 315, 317, 380
Lerond, A. 308
van Lessen Kloeke, W.U.S. 257
Liberman, M. 4, 27, 64, 116, 157, 159-60, 172, 278, 295, 298, 342-3, 380
Lightner, T.M. 121, 226
Loos, E. 15, 24, 332
Lovins, O. 350, 353, 372, 379, 381
Lowenstamm, J. 76, 98, 115-6, 119, 258-9, 263, 265, 267-72, 294, 304-6, 308, 400
Lunt, H.G. 322

McCarthy, J.J. 89, 115, 123-4, 156, 342-3, 350, 379, 380-2, 451
MacNeilage, P.F. 144
Malecot, A. 381
Malone, K. 60
Marantz, A. 145, 147, 158
Martinet, A. 303
ter Mors, C.H. 259
Myers, A. 40

Newman, P. 340, 354, 379
Newman, S. 83, 84

Index of Names

Newton, B. 52
Noonan, M. 136, 157
Noske, R.G. 257, 265

O'Connor, J.D. 380
Odden, D. 252
Ohala, M. 144
Okello, B. 157
Orešnik, J. 6

Palacas, A. 8
Peterson, G. 353
Pétursson, M. 6, 60-62, 64
Pike, E.V. 342, 352, 279-80
Pike, K. 338-340, 342, 343, 346, 352, 354, 379-81
Pillinger, O.S. 275
Poser, W. 127, 144, 156-7, 214, 252, 322, 324, 326, 329, 450
Prince, A. 4, 27, 74-5, 116, 157, 159, 160, 172, 278, 295, 298, 342-3, 380
Pulgram, E. 354
Pyle, C. 254

Raphael, L.J. 381
Redhouse, Sir J.W. 352
Rischel, J. 381
Rivas, A. 144, 157, 322
Robins, R.H. 333-4
Rosetti, A. 382

Safir, K. 311
Saib, J. 380
St Clair, R. 35
Sapir, E. 8
de Saussure, F. 260, 265
Schein, B. 123
Selkirk, E.O. 28-9, 73-4, 115-6, 258-60, 267, 269, 276-8, 295-304, 311-2, 317, 341, 350, 352, 360, 381
Sezer, E. 121, 128-9, 156, 250, 252, 311, 319, 322, 324
Shibatani, M. 215
Sigurd, B. 47
Smalley, W. 379
Smith, H.L., Jnr. 354
Smith, N.S.H. 159, 214, 252, 257

Sohn, H.-M. 5, 146, 158
Sommerstein, A.H. 51-2
Spa, J.J. 257, 263, 292-3, 305, 308
Sportiche, D. 140, 142-3, 322, 385
Stanley, R. 74, 215
Steriade, D. 140, 146, 158, 431, 451
Stevens, K. 61
Stowell, T. 210
Strauch, R. 27
Suárez, J.A. 142, 157-8, 322, 325, 327, 329
Swadesh, M. 381

Ternes, E. 318
Thomas, L. 119
Thráinsson, H. 59-61, 63-65
Tobin, C. 381
Topping, D. 135
Trager, G.L. 354, 381
Travis, L. 419, 451
Trim, J.L.M. 380
Trubetzkoy, N.S. 262

Vago, R.M. 451
Venneman, T. 259, 306, 354
Vergnaud, J.-R. 2, 4, 7-8, 10-11, 15, 18-20, 24, 121, 127-8, 138-43, 156-7, 159-60, 165, 168, 180, 200, 209-10, 251, 260, 277-8, 287, 295, 301-4, 312, 316-7, 322, 330-2, 335, 341-2, 385-6, 437, 440, 451
Vogel, I.B. 257, 259-60, 267, 306, 382
Vogt, H. 47

Walter, H. 303
Waterson, N. 242, 254
Welmers, W. 156
Wheeler, D. 257
Whorf, B.L. 380
Wilkins, W. 8
Woock, E. 136, 157

Yavash, M. 226-7, 254-5
Yip, M. 157, 311

Zimmer, K. 224-5, 227
Zubizarreta, M.-L. 145, 157-8, 209-10, 311

Language Index

African languages 122
W. African languages 386
Aguatec 210
Akan 127, 214, 216, 25 , 387, 392
Altaic languages 218, 255
Apinayé 39, 46
Arabic 3, 241, 253, 312, 315-7, 321, 342
Arabic (Egyptian/Cairo) 265, 380

Bantu languages 123
Baoulé 387, 392
Berber 342, 380
Burmese 62

Capanahua 15, 311, 312, 330, 332-5
Chamorro 135, 137
E. Cheremis 105, 167, 210, 211, 311
Chinese 311
Chinese (Mandarin) 138, 154, 155, 157
Chukchee 216
Chumash (Ineseño) 131, 139, 140, 152, 153
Chumash (Ventureño) 158
Czech 168, 210

Danish 276, 282
Dida 401
Diola-Fogny 216
Dioula 392
Dutch 30

English 4, 5, 13-15, 18, 28, 29, 35, 36, 46-52, 55-57, 66, 165, 200, 209, 276, 282, 295, 305, 337-9, 342-352, 357-359, 363-79, 381, 392
English, Old 259
Estonian 380

Finnish 216
Finno-Ugric languages 165

French 10, 15, 230, 257-310, 342, 373-74, 392, 394

Gaelic 58
Gaelic (Applecross) 59, 312, 317-24, 326, 328-32
Gaelic (Lewis) 58, 59
Gaelic (Ross) 59
Garawa 19
Gbeya 35
German 52, 56, 265-66
Germanic 46
Germanic, North 58
Germanic, West 56
Gothic 48
Greek 75, 76, 117
Greek (Ancient) 306
Greek (Attic) 306
Greek (Byzantine) 230
Greek (Lesbian) 117
Greek (Rhodes) 52, 54, 55
Greek (Thessalian) 117
Guaraní 37, 127, 129-31, 142-4, 156-7, 252, 312, 321-332
Hindi 144
Hungarian 216

Icelandic 6, 58-60, 62-4, 66
Italian 230
Italian (Venetian) 230

Japanese 101, 120, 210
Japanese (Hirosaki) 175-9, 181, 190, 205
Japanese (Izumi) 170, 172-3, 201
Japanese (Kagoshima) 170, 173-5, 205
Japanese (Kameyama) 211-2
Japanese (Kôshi) 190-193, 200, 201, 205, 212
Japanese (Old Kyoto) 209
Japanese (Marugame) 187-190, 200, 204-5

Japanese (Miyakonozyô) 170-3, 205
Japanese (Osaka) 101, 179-88, 190, 200, 206, 208, 211-2
Japanese (Shimogawa) 170-1, 201
Japanese (Tôkyô) 193-8

Kabardian 37
Kaingáng 46
Kalenjin 216
Kikuyu 150
Klamath 73, 75, 76, 82, 92, 115, 117, 119, 259
Komi (E. Permyak) 165, 167
Kru languages 386, 401

land Dayak 45
Lango 136-7, 157
Latin 48, 75, 76, 275-6
Luganda 40

Manchu 216
Mandé 392
Mazateco 340
Mongolian 216, 251, 335
Mongolian (Khalkha) 4

Navajo 9
Nez Perce 216, 251
Nilotic 252
Norwegian 47
Nyanga 38

Ojibwa, West 401

Panoan 15
Parintintin 314
Passamaquoddy 210
Persian 241
Polish 36, 52, 55, 119

Russian 3

Sanskrit 9
Semitic languages 123-4
Seneca 210
Shipibo 149
Shona 252
Sinhalese / Sinhala 40, 41, 43, 46, 108, 119, 306
Somali 216, 252
Spanish (Andalusian) 158, 210, 311
Sundanese 321, 330, 333-4
Swedish 47

Telegu 158
Tiv 38, 42. 51
Turkish 12, 67, 125-6, 128-31, 146, 149-50, 156, 213, 215-6, 218, 220-251
Turkish (Istanbul) 236, 249

Urdu 143
Uralic languages 218

Vata 385-452
Vata (Gosobro) 395
Vata (Zaroko) 395
Vietnamese 374

Welsh 58
Woleaian 5, 146, 149, 158

Yawalmani 73, 75, 76, 82-92, 115, 117-18
Yiddish 259
Yokuts 83
Yuk 209

Subject Index

Accent-glide 196-8
Accessible element 182
Adjacency 8
Adjacency constraint 9, 11
Adjunction 29
Adjunction transformation 361
Advanced tongue root (ATR) 136-7, 386-395
Affix 360, 388
    see also *Infix*
Affricate 35-6, 51-58
Allophone 363-6
Ambisyllabicity 354-5, 360, 364-5, 370-2, 376-9
Archiphoneme 214
    see also *Underspecification*
Aspiration 363-5, 368
    see also *Postaspiration, Preaspiration*
Assimilation 2, 9, 148
Assimilation, unbounded 153-5
Association 1, 321, 323, 326
    see also *Reassociation*
Association Conventions 124-5, 218-9, 330, 332
Association lines 11, 320
Associative construction 390-1
Autosegment, bound/lexically bound/attached/associated 313, 323-4, 327-8, 335, 387, 393, 417-9, 449
    see also *lexical association*
Autosegment, floating/free 320, 323-4, 326-8, 330-2, 381, 422, 432-3
    see also *P-segment*, floating
Autosegmental formalism 2, 18
Autosegmental phonology 311
Autosegmental theory 1, 122-6, 155, 214, 386, 392, 399-400, 402-4
Autosegmental theory of the syllable 355-6

Basic syllable composition 356-9, 361-3
Bidirectionality of vowel harmony 216-7, 249, 251
Bijectivity 150
Bijectivity Constraint 122-4
Blocker 139, 221, 241, 335
Blocking 332-3
Boundaries 149, 264, 288, 297, 353-4, 356, 388, 427
Boundary weakening 411, 415-6
Branching 139, 163-4, 318
Branching binary 336, 342
Branching, n-ary 336
Branching, uniform 145-7, 164
Branching node 181, 301-2
Branching sensitivity parameter 165

C_0 /
Cairns-Feinstein (C-F) metric 75, 98, 100, 110, 114
Categorical gesture 32
Cluster, consonant 6, 340
Cluster, sC- 46-51, 248
Cluster, stop +liquid 274-277, 285, 306
Coarticulation 143-5, 219
Coda 30, 161, 261, 265, 280, 284, 303-4, 338, 341, 343, 348-52, 400
    see also *Margin*
Collocational restriction 345-6, 348, 350, 352, 357-8
Compensatory lengthening 75, 78
Complement convention 306
Complex segment 35-8, 215
Composite markedness value (CMV) 75, 98, 100, 110, 114
Compounds 390-2, 396-406, 426-7, 437 9
Conditions on syllable template 261
Consonant-conditioned vowel harmony 238-43

Constituent integrity principle 165, 169
Constituent structure 340-1
Constraint on crossing association lines 11, 219
Contiguous autosegments 403-4
Conventions 445-50
Co-occurrence restriction 339
   see also *Phonotactic constraint*
Core grammar 200-9
Coronal Consonants 9
Cycle application 79, 134-5, 326, 334-5, 423
   see also *Transfermational cycle in phonology*

Degemination 275
Deleted vowel 80, 83
Deletion 69, 150
   see also *Rule deletion*
Deletion, schwa 257, 277-90, 296-7, 299-304, 309
Deletion, vowel 86-90, 96, 112-3
Delinking 150-55
   see also *Dissociation*
Dependency arc 29
Dependency Reversal 55
Dependency Structure 29
Dependency phonology 29
Depressor consonants 214
Depth of embedding (metrical tree) 141-45
Designated element 14, 181-2, 193
   see also *Designated terminal element*
Designated element, lexically 176
Designated terminal element 14, 139-43, 147-9, 157-8
Designated terminal position 139, 145
Determinant 8, 11, 13, 14, 21
Devoicing 5
Diacritic treatment 243
Diphthong 351, 441-2
Diphthong, falling 343
Diphthongs, monophonematic 261-3, 292
Diphthong, rising 343
Directionality 19, 20, 141
Dis(as)sociation 240, 361
   see also *Delinking*
Discontinuous dependency 11
Disharmonic epenthetic vowels 243-9
Disharmonic stems 394-5, 439-41

Disharmonic suffixes 231-2
Disharmonic word 390
Disharmony 213, 221-251
Disharmony, consonant 233, 236-7
Disharmony, vowel 221-32
Dissimilation 5, 138, 148
Dissimilation, unbounded 128, 154-5
Domain of association/spreading 311, 315-22, 325
   see also *Domain*, autosegmental
Domain, autosegmental 313-4, 404-5
   see also *Domain* of association
Domain, binary 148-9
Domain, foot 317-22, 327-9
Domain, grammatical 312
Domain, harmony/harmonic 148-9, 211, 217, 252, 387
Domain, phonological 311-2
Domain, prosodic 312-335
Domain of rule 138
Domain, segmental 1
Domain, stress-group 322, 329
Domain, syllable 315-17, 334, 342, 364
Domain, unbounded 21, 148-9
Domain, word 334-5
Double open syllable constraint (DOS) 87, 89-90, 117-8
Dual representation 79, 80

Elsewhere condition 332
Emphasis 315-7, 342
   see also *Independent emphatic*
Enchaînement 265
Epenthesis 69, 101-3, 129, 243-9
   see also *Rule*, epenthesis
Epenthesis, universal 108-10, 112-5
Exception 213, 226
Explanatory power 3
Extrametricality 172-3, 194-6, 327
Extrasyllabicity 246, 254

Fast speech 362
Feature, harmonizing 11
Feature, laryngeal 61
Feature, morphological 320, 324
Feature, percolating 170, 196
Feature, rule 213
Feature percolation condition 260
Feature specification, complete 214
Filter 345
Floating P-segment deletion 240

Subject Index 473

Floating tone 19, 183, 211, 215
Focus 8, 11, 13, 14
Foot 1, 13, 18, 28, 90, 161-3, 295-9, 302-3, 311, 318, 327
Foot, accent 181
Foot, bounded 168
Foot, degenerate 169
Foot, derived 295
Foot, harmony 180, 200
Foot, polarized 162, 181
Foot assignment 327
Foot formation 295, 299, 300
Foot tree 162
Functional conspiracy 91-2

Gemination 400-1
Generality 4
Generality, level of 5
Geometrical properties of metrical tree 163-4, 200
Geometric interpretation of metrical tree 141-7
Glottal opening 61-67
Glottalization 365, 372-3, 375-8
Governor 29

Harmony, ATR 136-7, 251, 386-95, 430-45
Harmony, backness 12, 213, 216, 218, 222-3, 251
Harmony, bidirectional 331
Harmony, consonant 213, 233-8, 253
Harmony, directional, 2, 20, 128, 131-6, 385, 430-45
Harmony, dominant 2, 19, 20, 136, 385-90
Harmony, Feature-changing 127, 131-5, 151-3
Harmony, height 419-27, 438-42
Harmony, laxing 311
Harmony, local 127, 135-7
Harmony, nasal 129-31, 317-29
Harmony, rounding/roundness 10-12, 125-6, 128, 213, 216, 218, 223-6, 335, 436
Harmony, sibilant 9, 131-5, 139-40, 152-3
Harmony, undirectional 331
Harmony, vowel 2, 4, 22, 24, 125, 213, 215-21
Head 29

Idiosyncratic specification 16-7
Immediate constituent principle 339, 346, 352
Independent emphatic 315
  see also *Emphasis*
Infix 334-5
Injectivity 123, 156
Integrity Constraint 122-4
Interlude 354
  see also *Ambisyllabicity*
Intonational phrase 28

Juncture 353-4

Labelling conventions/conditions 169-4, 209
Labelling of nodes 341, 342
Language-learning 169-70, 176, 179, 182, 189, 191, 194
  see also *Learnability*
Law of codes 306
Learnability 169-70
  see also *Language-learning*
Length, peak 353
Length, rhyme 353
Length, vowel 6, 9, 75-6, 101-12, 145-7, 158, 160
Lexical association 17, 214
  see also *autosegment*, bound
Lexical classification 315, 319
Linearity 214-5
Loan words 394
Local action of phonological rule 13

Mapping 171
Mapping conditions (metrical structure) 163, 165-6
Margin 93, 338
  see also *Onset, coda*
Margin Core 75
Markedness 24, 169, 176, 183, 196, 201, 321
Markedness condition 258, 278, 281-7, 289-92
Markedness convention 306
Markedness evaluation system 75
Maximal cluster approach (MCA) 267-270
  see also *Maximal onset principle*
Maximal onset principle (syllable) 359-63

see also *Maximal cluster approach*
Markedness metric 269-70
Maximality principle 165-6, 182
Markedness, syllabic 257, 269-74, 276, 284-5, 287-8
Medionasalized stop 46
Metrical formalism 2, 18, 140-9
Metrical locality constraint 10
Metrical phonology 311
Metrical structure 2
Metrical structure assignment, cyclic 327
Metrical theory 27, 29, 128, 138-40, 147-9, 155, 159-60
Modifier 29
Morphological conditioning 5
Morpheme Structure Condition 74, 85
Morphological Structure 73-4
Morphologically restricted phonological rule 81
Multilinearity 215

Nasality 15, 16
Nasalization 142, 266, 304, 317-29, 332-5
Nasalization, regressive 15
Nasal Span 142, 322, 329
Neutral segment 311, 315, 323
    see also *Neutral vowel, Transparent segment*
Neutral vowel 218, 252, 392
    see also *Neutral segment, Transparent segment*
Nonnative word 226
    see also *Loan word*
Non-overlap constraint 13
Nonundergoer 221, 241
Nuclear integrity constraint (NIC) 305
Nucleus 161, 298, 338, 340, 400
    see also *Peak*
Nuclear branching 145
Nucleus, universally possible 76-8
Numerical stress values, algorithm for 157

Obligatory character of vowel harmony 216-7
OBLICONS (output constraint) 307
OLICONS (output condition) 280-1, 307
Onset 1, 90, 160, 258-60, 270-1, 288, 338, 341, 343, 346, 359, 400
    see also *Margin*
Opaque elements/segments 139, 145-7, 151-3, 181-2, 193, 196, 214, 217-8, 220-1, 228, 231-2, 238-9, 241, 245, 255, 311-12, 314, 320, 324, 329-31, 336, 386, 392, 440, 449
    see also *Blocker, Autosegment, bound*
Opaque segment, lexical 196, 319, 322, 323, 331, 335
    see also *Autosegment, bound*
Open syllable schwa constraint 97, 99, 102, 105, 109
Oral span 322
Ordering paradox 249

Parameters (autosegmental) 138, 198, 217, 311, 316, 320, 323
Parenthesis-star notation 148
Parsability 358
Parsing 357
P-bearing unit/segment 131, 136, 137, 151, 154-5, 217-9, 311, 314, 330-1
Peak 338, 340-1, 343, 349-52
    see also *Nucleus*
Percolation 14, 139, 140, 314, 423
Pharyngealization 342
Phonetic gradation 142-3
Phonetic motivatedness of vowel harmony 216-7
Phonological phrase 21
Phonotactic constraint 339, 344, 354
    see also *Co-occurrence restriction*
Pitch-accent language 170
Polarization 176, 199, 211
Position slot 339
Postaspiration 59-61, 64
    see also *Aspiration*
Post-nasalized stops 36, 39, 45
Postoralization 323
Preaspiration 58-67
    see also *aspiration*
Precedence convention 32,1, 324, 328-30
    see also *Precedence of association*
Precedence of association 312
    see also *Precedence convention*
Prenasalized consonants 36-46, 323
Preservation of ancillary structure 14-16
Principle of inertia 232

Subject Index

Principle of syllabification to lowest possible markedness 273
Principle of syllabic structure preservation 368
Projection 7-10, 21, 139, 148
Projection, rhyme 160, 173
Projection, lexical category 138
Projection, segment 173
Projection vowel 6-10
Prominence 13, 14
Prominence, relative 31
Pronunciation savante 305
Proper domination 448
Prosodic Category 28
Prosodic levels 314-5
Prosodic unit 338
Pruning (tree) 10, 11
P-segment 217-9, 311, 330
    see also *Autosegment*
P-segment, Floating 240, 245-6, 320
    see also *Autosegment*, floating
Pseudo-disharmonic stems 392

Q 7

Reanalysis 212
Reassociation 5, 14-6, 151-4
Reduplication 229-30
Reduplicative prefix 95
Release 365, 373-6, 378
Residue of the autosegmental theory (RES(AS)) 127, 140-1, 147, 149
Resyllabification 78-9, 266, 269, 272, 274, 276, 282-3, 287, 356-7, 361-7, 369-72, 376-7
Resyllabification persistent 274, 276
Retroflexion 9
Reversed dependency 42-3, 45-7, 49, 50, 54
Rhyme (Rime) 1, 9, 20, 160-1, 258-9, 270-1, 301, 338, 341, 350, 352, 400
Rhyme, branching 145, 161, 165, 340
Root 350, 360
Rule, amalgamation 53
Rule, assimilation 23
    see also *Assimilation*
Rule, Autosegmental 7
Rule, bidirectional 20
Rule, directional 20
Rule, deletion 16

see also *Deletion, Process*, deletion
Rule, environmentless 277-8, 290
    see also *Rule*, maximally simple
Rule, epenthesis 86
    see also *Epenthesis*
Rule, garden variety 54, 147
Rule, harmony 180-1
Rule, iterative 17, 18, 21
Rule, language-specific association 331-3, 335
Rule, linear 147
Rule, linking 24
Rule, local feature-changing 153
Rule, low-level phonetic 6
Rule, maximally simple 445, 450
    see also *Rule*, environmentless
Rule, metrical 7
Rule, mirror-image 20
Rule, readjustment (syllabic) 268
Rule, resyllabification 2, 13, 276-7
Rule, spell-out 324, 326-7
Rule, stress-shifting 12
Rule, syllabification 267-74
    see also *Rule*, resyllabification
Rules, syllable formation (SF) 74-9, 93-4
Rule, syllable sensitive 71, 73-4, 263-4
Rule, tone 171-3, 175, 178, 187, 190, 192, 196
Rule, universal core 34
Rule ordering 293, 309, 335, 362, 428

Schwa 101-7, 113
Schwa-syncope 296-7
$[+seg]_o$ 7
Segmental core 12
Segmental formalism 2
Segmental integrity 214
Segmental position deletion 15, 16
Segmental slot 15
Semivocalization 257-8, 277, 290-3
Sequence reversal 55
Skeleton 399-402, 404
    see also *X-tier*
Sonority Hierarchy 27-8, 34, 46, 75, 284, 343, 380
Specivicity 4
Spreader 221, 241
Spreading 14, 143-145, 214, 219, 232, 313, 322-6, 329-32, 334-6, 387, 420

Spreading, bidirectional 332
Spreading, leftward 332
Spreading, parasitic 422-3, 426-7, 438-9
Spreading, rightward 333-4
Spreading unidirectional 330
Star 176, 183
Starless tone pattern 176, 178, 198-9
Starred element 14, 181, 193, 196
Starred tone pattern 176, 178, 199
Stray-rhyme adjunction 174
Stray syllable 329
Strength hierarchy/scale 260, 343
Stress 24
Stress, alternating 168
Stress assignment 362
Stress group 329, 331
Stress systems, typology of 4
Strong-weak (S-W) relation 342-3, 354
Structure conservation 16
Structure of segments 32-34
Structure preservation 198, 361-2, 367
Subjunction 29
Sub-onset 49
Supersyllable 298
Surjectivity 123, 156
Syllabic markedness of the prosodic unit 273
Syllabification 257-77, 287-8, 356-79
see also *resyllabification*
Syllabification, persistent 269, 279
Syllabification condition 258, 278-81, 287, 289, 290, 293, 310
Syllable 1, 18, 28, 337-83
Syllable, closed 2, 6, 10
Syllable, heavy 100, 354
Syllable, light 160
Syllable, open 2, 6
Syllable, possible 259-62, 265, 293, 306-7
Syllable (structure) assignment 69, 71, 258-77
Syllable assignment algorithm 78-83, 87-92, 97-100, 102-15, 119-20
Syllable-marginal C-deletion 108-9
Syllable/morphology interaction 78-81
Syllable onset, see onset
Syllable rhyme, see *Rhyme*
Syllable structure 2, 27, 69, 74-80, 83-4, 93-4
Syllable structure, lexically specified 265, 269

Syllable structure constraints 84
Syllable structure preservation condition 71
Syllable weight 9

Tapping 365, 372-3, 376, 378
Template, auxiliary 260, 268, 347, 357
Template, overgenerating 345
Template, syllable 27, 34, 259-60, 274, 284, 344-51, 357, 361, 367
t-flapping 13
Tier, autosegmental 1, 10, 12-14, 16, 387, 402-3
Tier, nasality 12
Tier, segmental 400
Tier, syllabic 400
Tier, tonal 14
Tonal representation 12
Tone preservation 14
Tone group 30
Transderivational constraint 245
Transformational cycle in phonology 4
see also *cyclic application*
Transparent segments 217-8, 333
see also *Neutral segment, vowel*
Tree, autosegmental 403-4
Tree, binary 435
Tree, bounded 140, 163
Tree, metrical 10, 420, 432
Tree, parasitic metrical 422
Tree, unbounded 163
Tree, well-formed 163
Tree, word, see *Word tree*
Tree construction 139, 432
Trigger 8, 139, 180, 331, 386, 431, 437, 440
Trubetzkoy's rule IV for monophonematic evaluation 262
Truncation, consonant 263-265
Truncation (vowel) 402, 409-16, 442-5

Umlaut 8
Unboundedness of vowel harmony 216-7
Undergoer 139, 149
Underspecification (lexical) 136
see also *archiphoneme*
Unfilled node 15
Uni-directionality of trees 164
Unified formalization 3

Subject Index

Universal constraint on syllable structure assignment 71
Universal grammar 169
Universal syllable assignment algorithm 72
Universal theory of stress 160
Utterance 28

Variable 7, 8
Variable interpretation convention 8
V-copy 95
Vowel 9
Vowel, full 114, 165
Vowel, high 417-429, 437
Vowel, inserted 80, 83
Vowel, long see Length, vowel
Vowel, reduced 114, 165
  see also *Vowel reduction*
Vowel/glide alternations 100-1
Vowel harmony system, asymmetrical 215-6
Vowel harmony system, symmetrical 215-6

Vowel quality 4
Vowel reduction 14, 15, 96, 97
Vowel sequences 395-417, 428-9
Vowel shortening 90-91

Well-formedness condition 124, 151, 156, 218, 404
Well-formedness constraint 10-3
Word 311, 350, 352, 360
Word (metrical) 161
Word, prosodic 28
Word tree 162-3
Word tree, degenerate 167
Word tree, polarized 176

X^0-level 74, 78, 92, 97, 104, 115, 117, 119
X-tier 313
  see also *skeleton*
$(X)^*$ 24